AQA A2
BUSINESS STUDIES

ANDREW ASHWIN

DENRY MACHIN

STUART MERRILLS

RICHARD THOMPSON

William Collins's dream of knowledge for all began with the publication of his first book in 1819. A self-educated mill worker, he not only enriched millions of lives, but also founded a flourishing publishing house. Today, staying true to this spirit, Collins books are packed with inspiration, innovation and practical expertise. They place you at the centre of a world of possibility and give you exactly what you need to explore it.

Collins. Freedom to teach.

Published by Collins

An imprint of HarperCollins*Publishers*

77–85 Fulham Palace Road
Hammersmith
London
W6 8JB

Browse the complete Collins catalogue at
www.collinseducation.com

© HarperCollins*Publishers* Limited 2009

10 9 8 7 6 5 4 3 2 1

ISBN-13 978-0-00-727038-5

Andrew Ashwin, Richard Thompson, Denry Machin and Stuart Merrills assert their moral rights to be identified as the authors of this work.

British Library Cataloguing in Publication Data.
A Catalogue record for this publication is available from the British Library.

Commissioned by Mike Upchurch
Project management by Jenny Draine
Edited by Jenny Draine
Original concept design by Newgen imaging
Page layout and cover design by Angela English
Illustrations by Jerry Fowler
Production by Simon Moore

Printed and bound by Butler Tanner and Dennis Ltd

Acknowledgements
Every effort has been made to contact copyright holders, but if any have been inadvertently overlooked, the publishers will be pleased to make the necessary arrangements at the first opportunity.

Photographs
The publishers would like to thanks the following for permission to reproduce pictures on these pages.
t=top, b=bottom, l=left, r=right, c=centre
The Automobile Association 165; Alamy 5c, 5b, 14, 24, 25, 38, 39, 54, 57, 64, 71, 75, 76, 100, 113, 141, 149, 157 l, 164 tr, 164 b, 170, 173b, 178, 183 b, 188 t, 196, 206, 209, 223, 224, 247, 279 t, 280 b, 325, 359, 363, 374c, 374b, 381, 393, 414b; amazon.co.uk 131; Apple Computer, Inc. 108 r, 164 tl; Asda Corporation 84; B & Q plc 243; Bank of England 292; Beatport 167; Biz/ed 103, 133; Blouzar Ltd. 353; British Gas 244; BT Group 261, 262; Cadbury 159; Christians Against Poverty, www.capuk.org, image reproduced with permission 267; Colin Cuthbert/Science Photo Library 375; Corbis 2, 342 t, 446; The Cotswold School 456; Cottam Brush 201 t & b; Dell Inc. 290 t, 379; Earl Scott/Science Photo Library 108 l; eBay.co.uk 26; genesis-music.com/UltraStar Entertainment 143; Getty Images 23 t, 166, 176, 191, 194 b, 215, 217, 330, 341, 352, 387 t, 389, 390, 405, 434; Google Inc. 147, 216; HEAT Ltd. 236 t & b; Holiday Rooms Direct 240; Hewlett-Packard Development Company 199; Innocent Drinks 92 l & r; istock photo 134, 156, 157 r, 177, 180, 188 b, 192 b, 208, 221, 260, 332 t, 338, 340, 342 b, 356, 364, 377, 439; John Lewis plc 16; Johnson Matthey, reproduced with permission 276; Kellogg Company 12 t, c & b; LEGO and the LEGO logo are trademarks of the LEGO Group, here used with special permission, © 2008 The LEGO Group 183 t; Lewis Windpower 445; Marks and Spencer plc 73; Manchester United Merchandising Limited 152; Mark Thomas/Science Photo Library 259; Newscast 5 t, 371; Molson Coors Brewing Company 234; Nokia UK Limited 350 b, 424; OFGEM 374 t; PA Photos 4 t & b, 63 t & r, 83, 106, 110, 214, 225, 273, 275, 279 b, 288, 298, 322, 350 t, 351, 376, 378, 396, 403, 415, 418, 420, 451, 462, 449; Photolibrary 347; Procter & Gamble 380 l & r; Rex Features 23 b, 33, 102, 109, 129, 193, 194 t, 204, 207, 212, 229, 230, 270 l & r, 321, 332 b, 372, 382 t & b, 409, 410, 414 t, 430; Sainsbury's Supermarkets Ltd. 55, 61, 391, 429; shoemoney.com 447; Sundance Spas, Inc 343 t; Tesco plc 94, 185, 448; Travelodge 77, Weetabix Limited 142.

Illustrations
Jerry Fowler 410, 425.

CONTENTS

The first half of your A2 Business Studies course examines 'Strategies for success' – the plans for action that will turn a business's goals into reality. In order to draw up these plans and put them into action, a business must consider three key questions:

1 **Where do we want to be?** Being clear as to the long-term **aims** of the business and the specific objectives that will enable these aims to be achieved.
2 **Where are we now?** Analysing the current position of the business to understand its strengths and weaknesses, and the external opportunities and threats that face it.
3 **How are we going to get where we want to be?** Generating the options for how aims might be achieved, deciding on the best **strategy** and planning how to monitor and evaluate it.

For many large businesses this will be a formal and ongoing process, while for many smaller businesses it may be no more than ideas in the mind of the entrepreneur. All organisations, though, need to have clear and realistic aims and objectives if they are to know how to succeed and when they have succeeded.

This first section – 'Functional objectives and strategies' – focuses on how businesses develop a range of specific objectives and plans for each department, or function, within the organisation. Each is designed to enable the overall corporate aims and objectives to be achieved.

Stelios, the 'serial entrepreneur' and chairman of easyGroup, came up with the original idea of low-cost, no-frills cruising for the masses

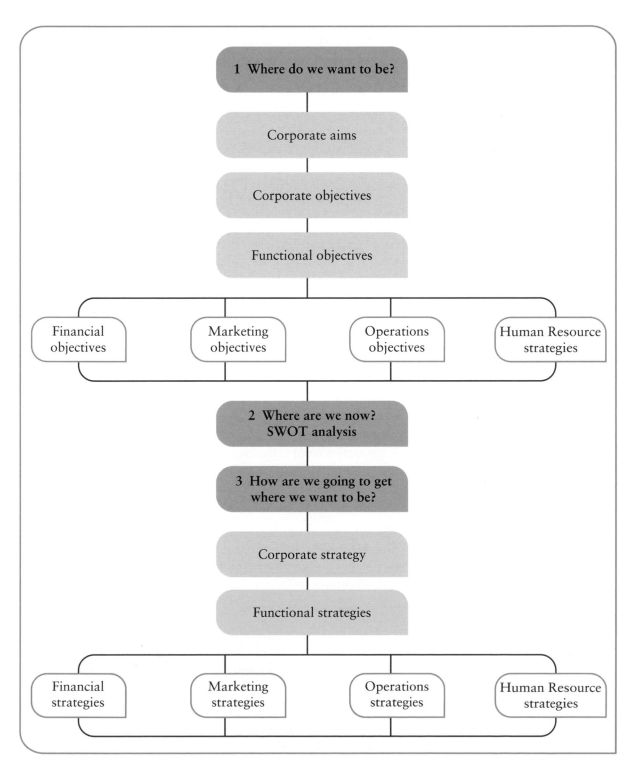

1 Where do we want to be?

Corporate aims

Corporate objectives

Functional objectives

| Financial objectives | Marketing objectives | Operations objectives | Human Resource strategies |

2 Where are we now?
SWOT analysis

3 How are we going to get where we want to be?

Corporate strategy

Functional strategies

| Financial strategies | Marketing strategies | Operations strategies | Human Resource strategies |

Chapter 1   Using objectives and strategies

Key terms

Corporate aims What a whole business is seeking to achieve in the long term.

Corporate objectives Measurable targets that focus a business on its long-term aims and enable it to be clear on whether progress is being made towards achieving them.

Functional objectives The specific targets set for each department, such as Marketing or Operations, within the business.

SWOT analysis An audit of a business's existing internal strengths and weaknesses, and the external opportunities and threats from its environment.

Functional objectives and their relationship with corporate objectives

This chapter sets functional objectives and strategies – the plans of Finance, Marketing, Operations and Human Resources – within the bigger picture of a business's overall corporate strategy. Only if each part, or function, of the business is pulling towards the same overall goal and only if there is effective coordination between the parts, will an organisation be able to achieve the success it strives for.

1 Where do we want to be? Aims and objectives

CORPORATE AIMS

An aim is a long-term goal or purpose. Setting **corporate aims** means to define what a whole business is seeking to achieve in the long term.

The panel below provides some examples of such corporate aims from a selection of large business organisations.

These five businesses are amongst some of the biggest corporations on the planet. Most have a wide range of business operations covering many different markets and including many different brands. Ultimately, all these organisations have to generate a profit in the long term to survive, but maximising profit

Shell plc:

'To engage safely, responsibly, efficiently and profitably in oil, gas, oil products, chemicals and other selected businesses and to participate in the search for and development of other sources of energy to meet evolving customer needs and the world's growing demand for energy.'

Source: http://www.shell.com/home/content/aboutshell-en/who_we_are/ our_purpose/our_purpose_31032008.html

Amazon:

'To be Earth's most customer-centric company, where customers can find and discover anything they might want to buy online, and endeavour to offer customers the lowest possible prices.'

Source: http://media.corporate-ir.net/media_files/irol/97/97664/2006AnnualReport.pdf

HSBC:

'HSBC's strategy is focused on delivering superior growth and earnings over time.'

Source: http://www.hsbc.com/1/2/investor-relations/strategy

Nestlé:

'To manufacture and market the Company's products in such a way as to create value that can be sustained over the long term for shareholders, employees, consumers and business partners. Nestlé does not favour short-term profit at the expense of successful long-term business development.'

Source: www.nestle.co.uk/OurResponsibility/BusinessPrinciples/

Unilever:

'To add Vitality to life. We meet everyday needs for nutrition, hygiene and personal care with brands that help people look good, feel good and get more out of life.'

Source:/www.unilever.com/ourcompany/aboutunilever/unilevervitality.asp

may not be the main aim. You will notice from the selection above that the word 'profit' is hardly mentioned at all. Without doubt, however, generating an appropriate level of profit will be a key aim of each of these businesses.

Corporate aims might include:

- **Maximising the profitability of the business** – moving from survival and break even in the short run to maximising revenues (by adding value) and minimising costs (through efficiency) in the long term.
- **Growing the size of the business** – expanding the size of the business through growing sales or by integrating with another business (for example, through a merger or takeover). Maximising sales or market share may itself become the main aim for a business.
- **Maximising shareholder value** – rewarding shareholders for their investment in the business by returning healthy dividends (a share in the profit of a business) or through an increase in the value of the shares owned by the shareholders, such as when the price of shares rises on the stock market.
- **Maximising the benefits of other stakeholders** – alongside the aims above, a business may also seek to benefit its other stakeholders, such as employees, the local community and customers.

These corporate aims are considered in more detail in Chapter 20.

CORPORATE OBJECTIVES

Having set out the corporate **aims** of the business, managers need to set out the specific and practical **objectives** that will contribute to the achievement of the overall goals.

These **corporate objectives** will focus the business on measurable targets, allowing it to be clear on whether progress is being made towards its long-term aims. For example, if the

Skills watch!

AO3 / AO4

What factors will influence a business's corporate aims? How important will each of these be?

long-term goal is to grow the size of the business, the corporate objectives for the year ahead may be to increase current sales by 10%.

These objectives are valuable because they:

- focus managers and employees on what the business needs to achieve
- set a time period for their achievement
- provide a measure of business performance
- can motivate managers and employees
- coordinate the actions of different parts of a business.

To be effective, objectives should be **SMART**: **s**pecific, **m**easurable, **a**greed, **r**ealistic and **t**ime-related.

SMART objectives

Specific	Sets out precisely what needs to be achieved.
Measurable	Evidence can be used to judge the outcomes and determine success or failure to meet the objective.
Agreed	All those involved understand and share a commitment to achieving the objective.
Realistic	Possible to achieve in the business's current situation and resources.
Time-related	Puts the target within a set timescale for completion or for results to be seen.

Activity

For *each* of the corporate aims explained on page 5, make up two possible corporate objectives that will help to achieve the aim and which all meet the SMART criteria.

FUNCTIONAL OBJECTIVES

Functional objectives are the specific targets set for each department, or **function**, within the business.

The starting point for deciding on functional objectives will be the business's corporate objectives. If functional objectives are achieved they will enable the business to achieve its corporate objectives, and so in turn move successfully towards its overall long-term aims.

Functional objectives should meet the SMART criteria and in this way will help each aspect of the business to focus on what it needs to achieve.

Functional objectives will focus on specific targets as related to areas such as Finance, Marketing, Operations and Human Resources.

Skills watch!

AO3 / AO4

Why is it important to make sure that objectives adhere to these SMART criteria? To what extent do SMART objectives help a business in meeting its objectives?

Financial objectives

These include:

- **cash flow targets** – ensuring the business has sufficient working capital to sustain and grow its operations
- **cost minimisation** – keeping both the overheads and the direct costs of production to a minimum so that the business can maximise its profit

- **Return on Capital Employed (ROCE)** – aiming for a specific level of profitability in relation to the size of the business
- **shareholders' returns** – seeking to ensure that shareholders are rewarded with a targeted level of dividends or share price growth.

Such financial objectives will be crucial in achieving corporate objectives relating to business profitability or maximising shareholder value. For example, in order to achieve a corporate objective of increasing profitability by 20% in the year ahead, a financial objective could be set of reducing overheads by at least 10%. Combined with success in other areas, such as increasing sales, this reduction in overheads could enable the business to achieve its profit target.

Financial objectives are explored in more detail in Chapter 2.

Marketing objectives

These include:

- **maintaining or increasing market share** – growing the business's sales as a proportion of the total market sales
- **breaking into a new market** – successfully launching into a new geographical or product market, or targeting a different market segment (such as a certain age group)
- **building a loyal customer base** – securing a base of repeat custom and ensuring that customers stay loyal rather than switching to rival products
- **establishing a unique selling point (USP)** – creating a perception in the minds of potential customers that the business's product has benefits or features that rival products cannot offer, and so providing a competitive advantage.

Marketing objectives are likely to be essential if the business is to achieve its overall corporate objectives. They will target aspects of business performance that can lead directly to increases in sales revenues and so profitability. Marketing objectives will, for example, provide the focus for a corporate objective of growing the size of the business.

Chapter 7 focuses on understanding marketing objectives.

Operational objectives

These include:

- **quality targets** – ensuring the product meets the required quality standards, with rejected products or customer returns kept below a target level
- **cost targets** – aiming to keep the **cost per unit** down by reducing the direct costs of production or increasing productivity
- **volume targets** – seeking to achieve a specified level of production within a period of time
- **innovation** – identifying new products, methods or technologies that will enable the production process to be improved
- **efficiency (including time)** – reducing waste in the production process – whether that be waste of materials, labour, time or capital
- **environmental targets** – reducing the environmental impact of the business's operations, such as reducing pollution, minimising energy usage or increasing the recycling of waste.

Achieving operational objectives will help a business to meet a range of its corporate aims and objectives. Innovation and quality can be crucial to marketing and in turn to boosting sales, market share and profitability. Cost, volume and efficiency targets will all serve to minimise business outgoings and so maximise profit and shareholder value. Environmental targets may be key in being socially responsible and meeting the needs of a business's wider stakeholders.

Chapter 11 develops operational objectives further.

Human Resource (HR) objectives

These include:

- **matching workforce skills, size and location to business needs** – ensuring that the business has the right number and type of employees in the right places at the right time
- **minimising labour cost** – keeping the costs of the workforce down, whilst still attracting and retaining the best employees
- **making full use of the workforce's potential** – seeking to boost the productivity of employees, developing and using their talents and ideas effectively
- **maintaining good employer/employee relations** – aiming to manage effectively communications and relationships between managers and workers.

People are a business's most valuable asset and are essential in giving a competitive edge over its rivals, whether this is in terms of customer service, product quality, productivity or cost efficiency. In any of these respects, Human Resource objectives will be crucial to achieving corporate aims of profit, growth or social responsibility.

Human Resource objectives are examined in detail in Chapter 16.

Skills watch!

AO3 / AO4

Explain *why* and *how* each set of functional objectives contribute to the achievement of corporate aims and objectives. How important is it for a business to set functional objectives if it wishes to achieve its corporate objectives?

The relationship between functional objectives and strategies

2 Where are we now? SWOT analysis

Once a business has clarified where it wants to be in the future – by setting corporate aims and objectives, which in turn inform functional objectives – it needs to fully understand its current position and performance.

By using a SWOT analysis, a business can 'audit' its existing internal **s**trengths and **w**eaknesses, and the external **o**pportunities and **t**hreats from its environment. The business can then identify where current performance differs from desired performance (that is, where it is not meeting its objectives) and can formulate future strategy.

Strengths and weaknesses lie in the reputation and resources of an organisation. To identify these strengths and weaknesses, a business will need to carry out an internal audit – an analysis of the business itself undertaken by a business's own managers and employees, or by management consultants.

An external audit analyses opportunities that are likely to benefit a business in the future, and threats that could limit success which lay outside the business. This 'external environment' includes:

- the competition, trends and conditions in the market
- the wider political, economic, social and technological conditions in the country as a whole.

A SWOT analysis may include consideration of the aspects shown in the diagram on page 9.

STRENGTHS
of the organisation – to be
built upon in the future.

WEAKNESSES
of the organisation – to be
addressed and turned into
strengths to achieve greater
success.

INTERNAL AUDIT

Analysing areas of the organisation such as:

- Finance – what is the profit margin on each sale and are we selling in sufficient volume to generate a healthy return?
- Marketing – how are our products perceived by customers?
- Operations – how efficient is our production process and is it assuring quality?
- Human Resources – are our staff sufficiently skilled, trained and motivated to deliver?

SWOT ANALYSIS

EXTERNAL AUDIT

Analysing the external environment including:

- The market – will the total market size be growing in value and volume?
- The competition – will new or existing competitors be threatening our market share?
- Political/legal – will changes to taxes or laws affect our business situation?
- Economic – how might future trends in the economy – boom or recession – affect sales?
- Social – will the lifestyles and habits of consumers change in a way that will impact on our business?
- Technological – will innovations change our production or our market?

OPPORTUNITIES –
new possibilities for achieving
objectives.

THREATS –
challenges from outside the
business that will need to be
overcome.

The value of SWOT analysis in enabling a business to turn objectives into strategy depends upon a number of factors:

- Has the internal audit been carried out honestly and objectively, drawing on the expertise and insight of the employees?
- Has the business been compared against the best in the industry?
- Has the external audit drawn on sufficient evidence about the future environment, not just the present?
- Have the results of the SWOT analysis been fully communicated to the employees and used to develop future strategy?

This final point is crucial – if the SWOT analysis is not used throughout the business as a starting point for meaningful strategic planning, it will have been a wasted exercise.

3 How are we going to get where we want to be? Business strategy

Having decided where it wants to go (objectives), a business needs to decide how it is going to get there (strategy). These **strategies** for success, the plans for action that will turn goals into reality, will be set at several levels, mirroring the objectives described above.

CORPORATE STRATEGY

This is the overall approach to be taken by the business in order to achieve its corporate aims and objectives. Corporate strategies will identify how the business will achieve or sustain an advantage over its rivals in a way that enables its objectives to be achieved. They will be developed by senior management and will plan ahead for a three to five-year timescale.

In deciding which strategy will best achieve this, a business will need to decide upon:

- **the scope and scale of its operations** – for example, whether it will seek to compete in the whole market ('mass marketing') or within just one small segment of it ('niche marketing')
- **the type of competitive advantage it seeks over rivals** – for example, whether it aims to establish a unique selling point that differentiates the product from its competitors or whether it seeks to compete through a low-cost, low-price advantage.

Corporate strategies are discussed in more detail in Chapter 20.

FUNCTIONAL STRATEGIES

These are the specific departmental plans set out to achieve the functional objectives, given the business's current strengths and weaknesses and the impact of the external environment. These functional strategies will all be closely linked to the corporate strategy to ensure it is being implemented in a clear and coherent way.

Set out in departmental plans, functional strategies are likely to be detailed and short-term, (such as 12-month) plans closely linked to SMART objectives that can be easily monitored and evaluated. Functional strategies may include the strategies listed below.

Financial strategies

These might include:

- **raising finance** – to fund expansion or solve cash-flow problems
- **implementing profit centres** – to monitor and evaluate costs and revenues more precisely
- **cost minimisation** – reducing overheads or direct costs in order to reduce total costs and so increase profitability
- **allocating capital expenditure** – choosing how and where to invest funds in order to achieve corporate objectives.

These financial strategies are considered fully in Chapter 5.

Marketing strategies

These might include:

- **low cost versus differentiation** – choosing whether to compete on the basis of low cost, low price or a uniquely different product
- **market penetration** – seeking to increase sales and market share with existing products in an existing market
- **product development and market development** – basing marketing strategies either on selling new products into existing markets or on selling existing products into new markets

- **diversification** – a riskier approach of selling new products into new markets.

These strategies are explained in detail in Chapter 9.

Operational strategies

These might include:

- **scale of production** – finding the best ('optimal') size for the business to gain from the efficiencies of size ('economies of scale') without suffering the problems of being too big ('diseconomies of scale')
- **resource mix** – identifying and moving towards the optimal mix of labour and capital, given the business's current strengths and weaknesses
- **innovation** – using research and development to identify and put into practice new products, approaches and processes
- **location** – seeking to locate the business in optimal sites, balancing a desire to maximise the benefits of a location with minimising the costs
- **lean production** – using a variety of strategies to minimise the waste of time and resources in order to increase productive efficiency.

Operational strategies are developed in Chapters 12–15.

Human Resource strategies

These might include:

- **workforce planning** – so-called 'hard' HR strategies to ensure the right number and type of staff are available at the right time and in the right place
- **effective communication and employee relations** – so-called 'soft' HR strategies that focus on the importance of communication and managing staff in a way that will motivate and avoid disputes.

These strategies are explored in Chapters 16–19.

Evaluating objectives and strategy

Every organisation will have aims, objectives and a strategy. In some, however, it may not be carefully thought through, precisely stated or written down. What matters is that a business's management knows what success will look like for that business, knows what the business's strengths and weaknesses are, and are adapting to meet a changing set of opportunities and threats.

The benefits of strategic planning rest in the clarity and focus it can provide for managers and employees, the way that objectives and strategies for each function within the business can be coordinated to achieve corporate aims, and the way it enables managers to build upon business strengths in responding to a changing external environment.

These theoretical benefits, however, may not always become a reality. The success of setting corporate and functional objectives depends in part upon the design of realistic and relevant targets, but also crucially on the effectiveness with which they are communicated. Every part of the business needs to know and understand what they are expected to achieve and why their role is crucial in achieving the business's overall goals. In this way, objectives can provide both a coherence and a coordination to a business's actions, but also a powerful focus and motivation for employees. On the other hand, a strategy that is not shared or understood is no more than a bureaucratic irrelevance.

In addition, businesses in rapidly-changing and complex markets may find that it is virtually impossible to anticipate future trends and developments. Strategic planning for three to five years in the future may in these circumstances prove less valuable.

For example...

BREAKFAST AND BEYOND

Kellogg's is the market leader in the UK cereals market, with a 42% share of the £1.1 billion per year sales. It has developed a range of 39 brands of breakfast cereal, targeted at a range of segments within the market. As part of its overall aim to demonstrate Corporate Responsibility and to be responsive to the needs of consumers, in 2006 Kellogg's chose to focus on a corporate aim that would enable everybody inside and outside the organisation to understand its beliefs and principles: 'to reinforce the importance of a balanced lifestyle so that consumers understand how a balanced diet and exercise can improve their lives'.

From this aim, Kellogg's developed a number of SMART corporate objectives that together would contribute to achieving the aim. These included:

- encouraging physical activity among all sectors of the population
- increase the association between Kellogg's and physical activity
- use the cereal packs to communicate the 'balance' message to consumers.

Each was communicated to all staff in a specific and measurable way, with a three-year time period set. Each departmental area within the business had its own functional objectives designed to help achieve these corporate objectives.

Having analysed its current position and identified what needed to be done to achieve these objectives, Kellogg's developed an overall strategy and a series of actions to implement it. These included:

- becoming the main sponsor of swimming in Britain
- running promotions that offer free cyclometers and pedometers with packs of breakfast cereal
- improving the labelling on cereal packets by clearer identification of Guideline Daily Amounts (GDAs), showing how Kellogg's cereals contribute to recommended daily levels of nutrients.

Kellogg's realised that the key to the success of its strategy lay in how well its objectives were communicated to consumers to convey the message 'eat to be fit'. External communication with customers used cartoon characters on cereal packets, as well as using TV advertising, leaflets and its website. Internal communication with employees used an in-house magazine for all staff and supplied staff with a free pedometer to help them understand the message.

Source: www.thetimes100.co.uk

Skills watch!

AO1

Choose any one **corporate aim** and draw a flowchart to show how it could lead to a specific **corporate objective**, then a **functional objective** and finally a **functional strategy**.

An important examination skill is being able to link together your knowledge to show understanding. A level is not just about remembering facts!

Summary and exam guidance

Summary

- All organisations need to have clear and realistic aims and objectives if they are to know how to succeed and when they have succeeded.

- **Corporate aims** define what a whole business is seeking to achieve in the long term – these may focus on profitability, growth, returns to shareholders or responsibilities to other stakeholders.

- **Corporate objectives** are the specific, measurable targets for the whole business that will contribute to the achievement of its overall goals.

- **Functional objectives** are the specific targets for individual departments within the business, such as Finance, Marketing, Operations and Human Resources.

- Internal and external **audits**, such as a SWOT analysis, help a business to understand its current strengths and weaknesses, together with the external opportunities and threats that will affect its success.

- **Business strategies** are the plans for action that will help move the business from its current position to achieve its overall goals.

Exam practice

Read the article on the following page and then answer the questions that follow.

Article A

HMV's next generation of stores aims to meet threat from Internet

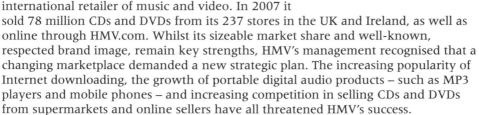

For some, the CD may as well be displayed in a glass cabinet in an ancient history museum. Internet downloading is undoubtedly the biggest challenge to the sale of CDs that high-street retailers have had to cope with. The sales of CD singles in the UK, for example, have slumped from 55.7 million in 2000 to only 8.6 million in 2007. The upsurge in downloading has caused some retailers, such as HMV, to rethink their strategies and create stores aimed at a new generation of music fans.

HMV's corporate aim is to be the most successful international retailer of music and video. In 2007 it sold 78 million CDs and DVDs from its 237 stores in the UK and Ireland, as well as online through HMV.com. Whilst its sizeable market share and well-known, respected brand image, remain key strengths, HMV's management recognised that a changing marketplace demanded a new strategic plan. The increasing popularity of Internet downloading, the growth of portable digital audio products – such as MP3 players and mobile phones – and increasing competition in selling CDs and DVDs from supermarkets and online sellers have all threatened HMV's success.

Its response was to set out three key corporate objectives to be achieved over a three-year period up to 2010:

- 'to protect and revitalise our core retail business'
- 'to grow revenue from new channels (e.g. online selling)'
- 'to drive cost efficiency'.

Each was accompanied by specific and measurable targets by which the success of its strategy could be evaluated – for example, to grow the sales of HMV.com to become 20% of the company's total sales. Functional objectives for each aspect of HMV's operations were also identified. To help revitalise the retail business, marketing would seek to improve the company's understanding of consumer behaviour and encourage the loyalty of high-spending customers. To drive cost efficiency, operational objectives would be to streamline supply chains and to increase administrative efficiency.

HMV's strategy for revitalising its retail business has been to transform a visit to its high-street stores into a social experience, with the launch of 5000 sq ft 'next generation stores'. The store will feature downloading kiosks and offer free Internet access. Expanding its range of digital audio products, MP3/4 players and accessories will help tap into a faster growing market, whilst a partnership with 3 Network – the UK's leading retailer of music-enabled mobile phone handsets – will allow in-store tie-ins to be offered and reduce HMV's dependence on the declining physical music category.

The industry and the way people purchase music is still changing and despite their strategic planning, it is unlikely that HMV know if their decisions are the right ones. With Internet retailers such as Amazon and Play.com having significantly lower outgoings than high-street retailers, and supermarkets able to sell loss leaders, the future of the high-street music retailer remains uncertain.

Sources: 'HMV's next generation of stores aims to meet threat from Internet', *The Times*, 29 May 2008 and www.hmvgroup.com.

(a) Analyse the process by which HMV is likely to have developed its strategic plan. (18 marks)

(b) To what extent might HMV's success in the future depend upon the effectiveness of its strategic planning? (22 marks)

Total: 40 marks

Breakdown of assessment objectives

AO1 – Knowledge and understanding – 8/40

AO2 – Apply knowledge and understanding – 12/40

AO3 – Analyse problems, issues and situations – 8/40

AO4 – Evaluate, distinguish between fact and opinion, assess and judge information from a variety of sources – 12/40

Suggested structure

You will need to:

- Demonstrate an understanding of how strategies are developed:

  - Explain the stage of setting aims and objectives, linking a corporate aim to SMART corporate objectives and in turn to functional objectives.
  - Explain the importance of internal and external auditing in identifying the business's current position.
  - Explain how strategies enable the gap from the current to the desired position to be filled, given the circumstances and resources of the business.

- Apply this understanding throughout your answer to the situation of HMV, using examples to illustrate HMV's aims, objectives, circumstances and strategies.

- Analyse how and why HMV has responded in the way it has, showing how its strategies link to its objectives, its strengths and weaknesses, and its opportunities and threats.

- Evaluate the benefits that HMV will experience through corporate planning, showing how the planning may help them to succeed. Consider why planning may not be sufficient to ensure success and what factors might influence the effectiveness of its planning.

- Arrive at a reasoned, evaluative judgment as to how crucial effective planning is to the success of a business.

This section examines the financial objectives of larger businesses which are key to achieving good business performance levels, and how a business's financial performance is analysed and judged.

It is important for large business organisations to be able to assess their financial position accurately so they can determine their strengths and weaknesses and make decisions on what strategies they can or need to employ to ensure the continued financial success of the business.

For large business organisations, which have many interested stakeholders, financial performance is not just about how much profit the business has made or how stable its cash flow position is; financial performance considers the current position in terms of what has been achieved, but also what the future potential of the business might be.

For example, this entails looking at not only how much profit was made, but *how* it was made and then how it was used. How any profit made was then distributed and utilised is going to have a major impact on the future potential of the organisation and its strategies for continued success. Shareholders, managers, employees, lenders/creditors and even external stakeholder groups such as customers, communities and pressure groups, all have an interest in how businesses have performed financially. In particular, these groups may focus on examining:

- what the business has achieved
- how the business has achieved this
- what the business is likely to achieve in the future.

For these reasons the examination of a business's financial accounts – its objectives and the strategies available and employed – is the key foundation in measuring and determining a business's current and future potential success.

Activity

Ideally in pairs or small groups, choose a large business organisation which is currently in the news for its financial performance. For example, there may well be stories about businesses who have recently declared their end-of-year profits, perhaps won an important new contract or who have just faced major downturns or problems in their marketplace.

Make a list of the key stakeholders who are interested in the financial performance of a business, and considering the business and news story you have selected, identify how each of the stakeholder groups could be affected.

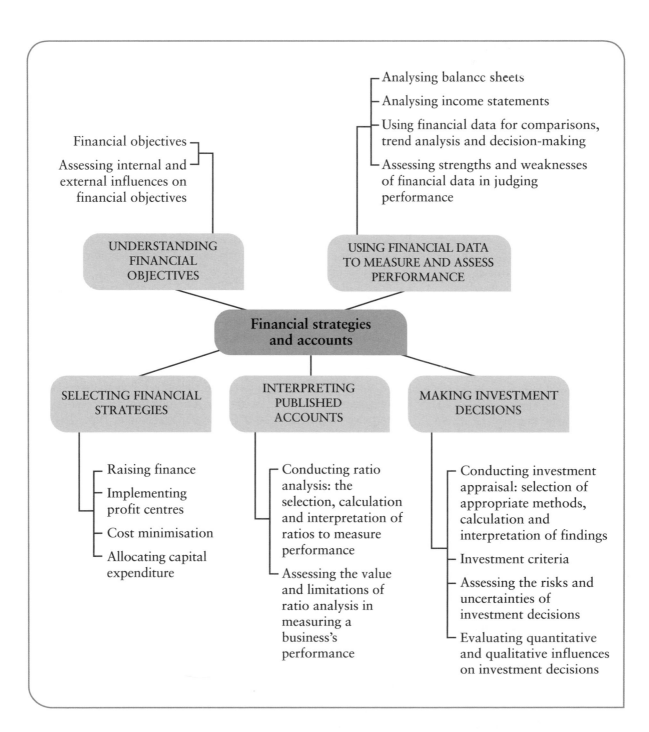

Financial objectives

Assessing internal and external influences on financial objectives

UNDERSTANDING FINANCIAL OBJECTIVES

Analysing balance sheets

Analysing income statements

Using financial data for comparisons, trend analysis and decision-making

Assessing strengths and weaknesses of financial data in judging performance

USING FINANCIAL DATA TO MEASURE AND ASSESS PERFORMANCE

Financial strategies and accounts

SELECTING FINANCIAL STRATEGIES

Raising finance

Implementing profit centres

Cost minimisation

Allocating capital expenditure

INTERPRETING PUBLISHED ACCOUNTS

Conducting ratio analysis: the selection, calculation and interpretation of ratios to measure performance

Assessing the value and limitations of ratio analysis in measuring a business's performance

MAKING INVESTMENT DECISIONS

Conducting investment appraisal: selection of appropriate methods, calculation and interpretation of findings

Investment criteria

Assessing the risks and uncertainties of investment decisions

Evaluating quantitative and qualitative influences on investment decisions

Chapter 2   Understanding financial objectives

Key terms

Benchmark The setting of performance standards by comparison with the most efficient producers in a given market/industry.

Debtors Customers who have bought goods on credit terms and have an agreed period of time before they are due to make payment, normally 30, 60 or 90 days.

Dividend The share in the profits of a company that is distributed to shareholders each year, in return for their investment.

Ethics The moral principles held by a business that influence its decision-making processes.

Hire purchase A method of purchasing expensive items of equipment whereby the purchaser pays a deposit and then buys the rest of the item using monthly payments. In total this is likely to cost more than buying the item outright straight away, but avoids large cash outflows.

Leasing A method of obtaining an asset for use by paying monthly rental/hire charges – however, you do not own the asset.

ROCE The return on capital employed.

Social responsibility The duty of care a business has towards its stakeholders.

Financial objectives

In the AS Unit 1, 'Planning and financing a business', you will have considered some of the financial objectives of business start-ups. These included:

- breaking even
- making an acceptable level of profit
- maximising profits
- providing a steady income
- providing a return for investors.

Whilst some of the above objectives will still hold true, for example, making a return for investors is an objective any business will have at any stage of its development, new or established, larger businesses may well have more in-depth and directed financial objectives and targets to achieve.

Consider in more complex business terms the idea of making an acceptable level of profit. For a sole trader, making a net profit level of say £500,000 may well be seen by the owner of the business as quite a considerable and acceptable result. However, would businesses like Manchester United, Tesco or BP make the same assessment?

Larger business organisations are likely not only to have key objectives like the ones above, but also more explicit objectives targeted to specific areas of financial management. These areas would normally focus on the areas of:

- cash flow
- cost minimisation
- the return on capital employed
- shareholders' returns.

Cash flow targets

From your AS studies you should have gained an insight into how important cash flow is to a business: to both its survival and its ability to achieve its targets and objectives successfully. Having cash available to fund day-to-day operations is vital to any business, as without sufficient cash flow, a business will start to suffer from liquidity and working capital problems. However, cash flow is important for much more than just funding these day-to-day costs. To be able to undertake specific projects or activities, businesses must also make sure they have the finance available to do so and as such, specific targets for cash flow management become essential. For example, a business wishing to launch a new product or marketing campaign needs to have the finances in place to do

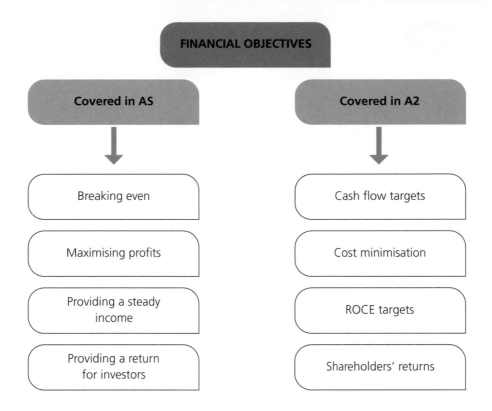

FINANCIAL OBJECTIVES

Covered in AS

- Breaking even
- Maximising profits
- Providing a steady income
- Providing a return for investors

Covered in A2

- Cash flow targets
- Cost minimisation
- ROCE targets
- Shareholders' returns

so; it is of no use to the business to plan a major marketing offensive only to discover it does not have the cash available to pay for it.

Cash flow targets may include:

- **Ensuring finance is available for specific projects** This could be, as outlined above, for a particular marketing campaign, but could also revolve around the purchase of large or expensive items of equipment, for example, new or replacement machinery. Rather than taking out loans, hire purchase or leasing agreements, a business can plan a precise target of when it would need to purchase new fixed assets or fund a planned activity, and set an objective to ensure it has the required finance available at the precise time it is needed.
- **Minimising interest payments and charges** Obviously the more interest a business pays on borrowed funds, loans or overdrafts, the less cash it has available for other areas, and the lower its reported profits will be. A simple objective for any business then is to examine the timing of its receipts and payments so as to minimise the length of time any interest is paid for, that is, to pay overdrafts and loans off as quickly as possible or structure the timing of payments to avoid going overdrawn.
- **Improving credit control** This area involves the collection of monies owed by debtors – customers who have bought items on credit. If customers do not pay on time, this restricts the cash inflow and money available for the business to use. Businesses will frequently set objectives to try to ensure that money owed to them is paid on time, or within a specified period.
- **Paying all suppliers within a set period** Here a business may set the objective of paying all suppliers within, for example, 10 days of receiving an invoice. This may at first seem a strange objective to set, but can bring the business very definite benefits. First, it enhances the business's reputation and supplier relations and makes suppliers much more willing to work in partnership with them. Second, many suppliers offer discounts to customers who pay their invoices faster than their actual

Synoptic search

As part of your AS studies, you will have considered the process and benefits of cash flow forecasting and cash flow management in some depth. It is important to realise from your previous studies that objectives of cash flow would involve *avoiding* cash flow problems, as well as methods of *improving* cash flow.

credit terms would allow, for example, the supplier offers 30 days credit but will deduct 5% of the total invoice if you pay them earlier than the 30 days you are allowed. The business paying the invoice thus gets a discount which would result in lower costs and increased profit margins.

Cost minimisation

The objective of cost minimisation is a fairly straightforward concept. However, it is important to realise that this does not necessarily mean just buying the cheapest option. Cost minimisation refers to keeping costs as low as possible whilst maintaining the quality and service standards the business needs. Obviously every cost incurred by the business reduces the profits the business makes – every cost will also at some point involve some cash flowing out of the business – so keeping costs down is an important objective in maximising financial performance.

Cost minimisation includes looking at and setting targets for areas such as:

- reducing waste
- avoiding duplication of tasks by employees
- reducing the times when employees or productive resources are idle
- minimising interest payments (as above)
- using efficient logistical and distribution channels
- enhancing communications to prevent errors and mistakes
- using effective marketing, that is, techniques that bring maximum return compared to cost
- controlling stock. For example, by bulk-buying a company can achieve purchasing economies of scale, that is, each unit becomes cheaper and fewer deliveries are needed which reduces costs. However, this stock then needs to be warehoused and stored which incurs increased costs. To minimise costs, most businesses need to assess their economic order quantity which attempts to calculate the optimum stock order quantity compared to the cost of holding stock.

Synoptic search

In Chapter 23 of the AS, you will have considered factors such as capacity utilisation, rationalisation, workforce management and managing stocks effectively. These are all key factors in the area of cost minimisation and need to be reconsidered by you at this point.

Whilst cost minimisation can be seen as a financial objective from the above points, it should also be apparent that such an objective has far-reaching implications for all the functional areas of a business. A final point to note is that cost minimisation does not just mean cost-cutting. For example, for employees, cost-cutting would perhaps involve removing training opportunities, whereas cost minimisation means using the most efficient and cost-effective training methods to achieve the desired results.

ROCE targets

This again is a topic covered in AS Chapter 18, 'Measuring and increasing profit'. To recap, the return on capital employed measures how well a business has performed by comparing the profit made in one year to the size of the business as shown by the total value of the funds invested in it.

The ROCE is sometimes referred to as the primary efficiency ratio and will be covered in more detail in Chapter 4, but at this stage the ROCE measures how good a business is at using the money invested in it to generate profits. The ROCE result shows the commercial viability of any business. ROCE targets should as a minimum reflect the amount of return investors could receive if the funds tied up in the business were instead to be invested in interest-bearing accounts at banks and building societies. Thus if an investor could receive 8% interest from a bank, then the ROCE target for a business should be over and above this level to make the risk of investing worthwhile.

ROCE targets should also be set by looking at how well competitors in the same industry have performed, or perhaps using an industry average. An increasing percentage result for the calculation of ROCE shows a business becoming more and more efficient at using its funds and assets in generating returns (profits). Hence the ROCE objective is a key one as it shows overall how worthwhile and successful the business is as a commercial opportunity.

Shareholders' returns

For any large limited liability company, private or public, the returns to shareholders are of paramount importance. It is the incentive of receiving a return on their investment that convinces people to buy shares and invest their money in companies in the first place. Thus companies must set realistic and acceptable objectives for the provision of returns to these investors as their reward for risking their money in the business.

If companies do not provide sufficient returns to shareholders they may well find it difficult to attract new investors in the future, hindering corporate growth opportunities. Current shareholders may well become disillusioned and sell the shares they hold, increasing the risk of takeover by competitors, or as the legal owners of the company, they could vote to dismiss the directors of the company and appoint a new board to run the company on their behalf.

To avoid the above circumstances a business must therefore set an objective to provide the shareholders with a level of return on their investment that they will find acceptable in comparison to the level of risk their investment represents. The return a shareholder receives on the shares they have bought in a company is termed a **dividend**.

An important point to note here is that any dividend paid to shareholders, although calculated on profits, must be paid out of the company's cash flow and so another cash flow objective would be to have sufficient funds to meet dividend payments to shareholders.

An investor in a company can also make a financial gain from holding shares in a company through capital growth. What this refers to is the fact that if a company itself grows and becomes more valuable then so do the shares in that company, that is, if an investor purchased some shares in Sainsbury's PLC, for example, at £5.40 each and Sainsbury's produce good profits, increase their market share position or grow in other ways such as opening new stores, the shares themselves may rise in value as well reflecting the increase in the success of the company, so they might now be worth £6.50 each. Thus the shareholder has made a financial gain which could be realised if or when they were to sell their shares. An important point to note here is that if the value of the company falls then so could the value of shares in that company and it is quite possible that shareholders could lose money on their investment.

Assessing internal and external influences on financial objectives

No business organisation operates in isolation; there are always going to be factors that will impact on the operations of a business influencing the objectives it is able to set and achieve. These influences can either be internal to the company or external.

Internal influences

As we have seen previously in this chapter, the financial objectives of the company have far-reaching influences on the other functional areas of a business, and in turn the objectives of the other areas have a reciprocating influence on the financial objectives of the firm.

Often the objectives of other areas, such as Marketing, Operations or Human Resources, will go hand in hand or compliment the financial objectives, for example, an objective of improving productive efficiency or reducing waste would go alongside the idea of cost minimisation.

However, objectives may also frequently conflict. Each area may well have projects that it wishes to undertake and needs the finance to be able to do so, but it may well be that the business does not have the cash flow to be able to support and fund all the projects proposed or even fund several simultaneously, hence choices between functional area objectives must be made.

Similarly, objectives can often conflict through timescale considerations, that is, the long-term versus short-term perspective. For example, in the short term the company needs to provide a return for its shareholders, a dividend, and it is under pressure to do so. However, short-term profits or its ability to pay dividends from cash flow could well be reduced if the business invested n new machinery, production techniques and training. Hopefully though, investment in these areas would bring increased profits and returns in the long term. Thus the short-term financial objectives are influenced by the longer-term business goals and aims.

External influences

External factors – factors outside the business's control – can have a huge impact on the financial objectives of a company. These external factors fall into three main areas:

- competitors
- economic
- social and political.

However, there can also be other factors that influence the financial outcomes and objectives of a business.

COMPETITOR INFLUENCES

In very simple terms, the financial performance of competitors affects the degree to which one company would view their financial performance as being a success or not. What may have been a totally acceptable ROCE target and result, or dividend payment one year, can easily be rendered as unacceptable if competitors all turn in better results. As a result, companies that are setting objectives by benchmarking against industry standards will obviously be affected if those standards improve or decline.

Alongside this, the actions of competitors will also influence the current use of available finance by a business despite what internal objectives or plans they have. If competitors launch a marketing offensive or invest in new production techniques in order to remain competitive and retain customers, many businesses may well have to suspend their own objectives to be able to respond to the current threat posed. Cash flow earmarked for one project or payment of suppliers may well have to be diverted to counteract competitor actions.

ECONOMIC INFLUENCES

This is a very complex area, especially for businesses that operate on an international scale, hence facing economic influences from more than one economy. However, the main influences here revolve around the key economic influences listed below.

Interest rates

The level of interest rates has several major influences. First, it makes the cost of borrowing or using overdrafts more expensive and so impacts on how willing businesses are to borrow money and thus in turn affects the amount of finance a business may have available to undertake specific projects or actions. Higher interest rates also raise costs and lower profits and so could influence the targets set for ROCE or dividend payments. Conversely, investors can now get higher rates of return on bank deposits.

For example...

Virgin Media executives face drop in pay as target is missed

Virgin Media's top executives saw their pay packets slashed last year after bonuses were cancelled.

A messy legal battle with BSkyB over Virgin Media's bid for ITV and a fall in customer numbers in 2007 contributed to the broadband giant missing a £1.3 billion cash flow target for Virgin.

Virgin Media blamed the failure to reach its target operating cash flow on intense competition from BskyB and falling product prices in the UK. The company has struggled in the past couple of years. Virgin Media cut Sky channels from its service, resulting in an influx of customers demanding reductions on

the price of their subscriptions. Virgin's results for 2007 showed that it had lost more than 70,000 customers.

Source: adapted from http://business.timesonline.co.uk/tol/business/industry_sectors/media/article3716366

For example...

BMW set to miss 2008 targets

BMW bosses have warned that deteriorating business conditions and the effect of the credit crunch will cause it to miss its targets for 2008.

The German car manufacturer reported a 44% drop in quarterly pre-tax profits to the end of June and predicted that trading conditions would remain tough.

BMW blamed the fall in profits on the rises in the price of oil and raw materials, caused by the ongoing economic downturn and weakness of the US dollar exchange rates.

Exchange rates

Exchange rate fluctuations can have a major impact on a business's finances. For businesses that trade internationally in any way, the costs of importing and exporting goods and hence profit margins and cash received/paid also fluctuate as exchange rates change. For example, any business importing anything from the EU would find their costs increasing and hence cash outflows also, any time the pound was to fall in strength against the euro. Changes in exchange rates can therefore easily impact upon a company's expected profits and thus influence ROCE targets and dividend payments made, as well as effecting cash inflows and outflows.

The effects of a recession may be positive for some companies like Aldi

The trade cycle

This is the way an economy moves through the stages of boom, recession, slump and recovery at different times. Obviously, where an economy is in the trade cycle affects business and investor expectations, and the level of financial performance that would be deemed successful for differing markets/industries. As a result, the whole range of financial objectives set will vary dependent on the current or forecasted market conditions.

Exactly how economic factors will affect any business is entirely dependent on that individual business's circumstances, for example, does it import or export, or both? What type of product does the business sell? For example, sales of new cars like Ford, BMW or Citroën will be far harder hit by increases in UK interest rates than a business such as McDonald's, although all four are global companies.

Similarly you may consider that the effects of recession may well be positive for some companies such as Lidl, Aldi or Netto, for example.

SOCIAL AND POLITICAL INFLUENCES

In the last decade, businesses, especially large PLCs in the public eye, have faced increasing pressure from society and governments to act in more socially responsible and ethical ways, for example, fair trade goods or environmental protection schemes such as sustainable resources. These social movements and pressures have influenced many businesses' financial objectives, particularly in areas such as cost minimisation. For example, clothing companies like Nike, Gap and Primark have all been in the news for sourcing their supplies from countries using poorly-paid or sometimes child labour. Similarly, major companies like BP and Shell have been criticised for excessive profits and large payouts to shareholders at the expense of environmental damage.

OTHER EXTERNAL INFLUENCES

Other external influences impacting on financial objectives could be:

- seasonal factors and weather
- the needs and expectations of creditors to receive payments
- technological change and the need to update investment to remain competitive.

For example...

Wet weather hits Sports Direct

Wet summer weather has hit profits at sportswear retailer Sports Direct. Sports Direct is controlled by UK billionaire businessman Mike Ashley, current owner of Newcastle United.

In 2007 the firm, which owns the Dunlop and Kangol brands, said that profit before tax was down 70% to £21.2m for the 26 weeks to 28 October in what was its 'most difficult trading period' to date.

'It has been an exceptionally challenging trading environment for the UK sports retail sector, with the wettest May to July since records were first kept in 1776, and the worst flooding in the UK for 60 years,' the firm said.

Revenues look set to continue to slide with England's failure to qualify for Euro 2008 likely to hurt sales of football-related items, the firm said. The firm said revenue next year would be between £30m to £70m lower because of England's failure to qualify for Euro 2008.

Umbro will now only manufacture one million new replica England Away shirts rather than the three million it had planned, the firm said and Sports Direct owns 30% of Umbro shares.

Source: adapted from http://news.bbc.co.uk/1/hi/business/7151245.stm

Summary and exam guidance

Summary

- Large business organisations will set specific short-term financial objectives mainly relating to cash flow, cost minimisation, ROCE targets and shareholders' returns.

- Cash flow targets can help to make sure the business has the liquidity it requires in place to finance its operations at the right time and helps to prevent cash flow problems occurring.

- By minimising costs the business helps to increase its overall profits and reduces cash outflows.

- ROCE targets are set to try to ensure the business remains an attractive and commercially-viable proposition to investors.

- Shareholders will want to see a return, dividend payment, on their investment. Businesses will therefore set profit and cash flow targets to ensure an acceptable level of return can be paid.

- Financial objectives have an impact across all the functional areas of a business. To achieve financial targets requires a coordinated and synchronised approach by all of the business.

- Financial objectives cannot operate in isolation, however, much as they influence the actions of other functional areas, so in turn the needs of these other areas will influence the financial objectives that are set.

- Similarly, a business does not operate in isolation when setting objectives. The business must also take into account the state of the economy and their marketplace, as well as considering competitor actions and results.

- Finally, a business needs to take into account its social responsibility and the perception of varying stakeholder groups when setting its financial objectives.

Exam practice

Read the article below and then answer the questions that follow.

Article A

In times of global economic slowdown you might think that online auction site eBay would benefit as consumers look for bargains and access to cheaper products rather than buying new from traditional retail outlets. However, that does not appear to be the case. The company's most recent financial statement gives a relatively conservative forecast for sales in the months ahead.

The success of eBay has been widely documented; the company was founded in 1995 by Pierre Omidyar. Since that time it has grown into a global business with expected sales for 2008 in the region of $9 billion. eBay said that its second quarter sales rose 22% from $1.8 billion to $2.2 billion; its earnings rose from $376 million to $460 million. The company, however, disappointed investors by saying that it expected third quarter sales would be lower than expected.

Given the range of products traded on eBay it might not be that surprising that as the economic slowdown begins to take hold people decide that shopping for items on eBay can take a back seat in their spending plans. Such an explanation would be very simple and one that perhaps might not cause too many longer-term worries for the company. However, there may be a possibility that other things are happening with the business that may be a little more worrying and which it might need to consider. Every product or service has a life cycle. At what stage is eBay in the life cycle? The novelty of the business has largely worn off and whilst it is still the case that there are plenty of reasons to use eBay as a means of purchasing goods, the nature of the business has changed. Many people use eBay as the conduit for their own individual businesses. Trading via eBay can reduce costs but many of the larger sellers that make a living through eBay are perhaps not as cheap as buyers expect. Real bargains are becoming rarer and many sellers have minimum starting bids or put items on that are 'Buy it now' or 'Best offer'.

eBay has also had to manage some adverse publicity in recent months as it defends itself in court against claims from luxury goods business LVMH, which owns the Louis Vuitton and Christian Dior brands, that it allows online auctions of fake goods bearing its brand names. In recent months the company also revamped its feedback system, one of the key reasons for its success. As with any market, sellers and buyers have to rely on trust but there will always be some who abuse this trust and the feedback system is seen by sellers and buyers as an important guide to the extent to which a transaction can be safely entered into.

In the revamp, eBay introduced a new rule which forbade sellers from leaving negative feedback about buyers. A large number of sellers felt this was wrong although the company claimed that systems were in place to help sellers who did not receive payment or who experienced other problems. It seems that sellers were waiting to receive feedback from buyers before posting the return feedback. If the buyer feedback was negative then the seller would retaliate even if such an action was unjustified.

In its financial statement the company said that listings had increased by 19% on the same quarter last year but that the number of new active users had risen by only 1%. Maybe there are more fundamental factors slowing down the business than simply the state of the economy?

Source: http://www.bized.co.uk/cgi-bin/chron/chron.pl?id=3136 (18 July 2008)

(a) Analyse the main reasons why a business such as eBay would benefit from setting financial objectives. (18 marks)

(b) With reference to the article, consider how the state of the economy and other external influences may have an impact on eBay's financial objectives. (22 marks)

Total: 40 marks

Breakdown of assessment objectives

AO1 – Knowledge and understanding – 8/40
AO2 – Apply knowledge and understanding – 8/40
AO3 – Analyse problems, issues and situations – 12/40
AO4 – Evaluate, distinguish between fact and opinion, assess and judge information from a variety of sources – 12/40

Suggested structure

For part (a) you will need to:

- Identify at least two reasons how eBay could benefit from the setting of financial objectives.
- Break down your reasons into clear paragraphs that apply to circumstances of a business such as eBay.
- Make sure your answer fully relates to and gives details why your identified reasons would lead to clear benefits for the company.

For part (b) you will need to:

- Identify the external factors that could potentially influence eBay's financial objectives.
- Offer a detailed examination of how and which financial objectives could be affected by each external influence.
- Relate your responses clearly to the circumstances of eBay and demonstrate how your answers relate to the company.
- Comment on the significance, level and degree of each of the factors you have discussed, coming to a clear conclusion/judgement. A good strategy here is to try to weigh up the relative importance of each factor.

Chapter 3   Using financial data to measure and assess performance

Key terms

Balance sheet key terms

Assets The resources owned by an organisation that have a monetary value.

Balance sheet A statement that shows an organisation's **assets** and **liabilities** on a particular day. In effect, it shows what a business owns and where it got the money from.

Liabilities Debts owed by the organisation to other parties. Liabilities are sources of finance and provide the means by which some of the company's **assets** have been bought.

Liquidity An assessment of a business's ability to be able to pay its short-term debts. It is a measure of whether or not the business has enough cash available to pay bills and invoices as they come due for payment. It is assessed via the **balance sheet.**

Reserves and retained earnings Funds that have been accumulated by the business over the years it has been operating. Any prudent owner will not take out all the profits their business makes each year but will keep some in the business. These reserves and retained earnings actually belong to the shareholders, but they are reinvested to help the business grow and become stronger, so hopefully, the shareholders will gain bigger dividends in future years.

Share capital The money that has been invested by the owners into the business. This is used by the business to purchase **assets** and to help finance operations. It is called share capital as the owners invest money via buying shares. Having purchased shares, the company never has to give shareholders their money back, so the business has a certain amount of money for its own permanent use. Shareholders are rewarded for investment via dividends.

Income statement key terms

Depreciation The method by which the cost of a fixed asset is allocated across the financial periods in which the cost of the asset will be incurred, that is, it is the process of matching the cost of the asset to the periods in which it is used.

Distribution costs and administration expenses The costs that are incurred by a business in its day-to-day running, that is, items that are bought by the business to be used in its operations, for example, stationery, utility bills or employees' labour.

Gross profit The difference between **revenue** generated by sales and the cost of the products which have been sold. It measures profit made on buying and selling activities.

Income statement A formal financial document that shows a business's revenue generated over a trading period and all the relevant costs (expenses) experienced in earning that revenue.

Loss This occurs when **revenue** is *less* than the total cost of the goods sold and distribution costs and administration expenses added together.

Profit from operations The actual amount left after all other costs (distribution and administration) associated with running that business are taken into account, for example, expenses like marketing costs or electricity.

Revenue The total value of income made from selling goods and services over a given period of time.

Assessing performance

- Owners/Shareholders
- Managers
- Employees
- Lenders
- Suppliers
- Potential investors

Income statements
- Revenue
- Gross profit
- Profit from operations
- Dividends
- Retained profits

ANALYSE

Balance sheets
- Assets
- Liabilities
- Depreciation
- Working capital
- Investment
- Retained profits

TO ESTABLISH

- Trends
- Comparisons
- Strengths and weaknesses
- Financial stability
- Profit utilisation
- Profit quality
- Retained profits

The financial performance of a business is an area of key interest for many stakeholder groups ranging from owners (shareholders) to managers and employees within the company, to banks, lenders and creditors outside the business. The assessment of a business's financial position can tell an interested party a great deal of information regarding how that business may perform in future, whether or not it is a good investment opportunity, or even if that company is one which you would like to work for or do business with.

Assessing the financial strengths and weaknesses of any organisation falls into two main categories:

1 How have they performed in recent times (that is, over the last trading year)?
2 How have they performed over all the years the business has been trading?

To undertake a good financial assessment of a business's position, we examine two different documents: the balance sheet and the income statement, and this section examines each document in turn, looking at the main areas covered by each and the type of information they contain.

Analysing balance sheets

A balance sheet is a formal document that states in detail the asset, liability and capital structure of a business. The balance sheet shows us what the business has managed to achieve over its entire existence. It shows us all the assets that have been built up over time, that is, what the company actually *owns*, and where all the money has come from to purchase these assets, whether invested by the owners or borrowed from an external source, like a loan from a bank. A balance sheet can be regarded as telling you how strong a business is. One of the areas that informs us of business strength is **liquidity**.

Alongside this, by studying how much an individual company actually owns and comparing that with how much it owes, you can also establish a fair idea of what that business is worth. Many stakeholders will make important decisions based on the information contained within the balance sheet: from a supplier deciding whether or not to supply goods on credit, to a bank assessing whether or not to lend money to a business who may want a loan to build a new factory, for example.

Figure 3.1 shows an example balance sheet. From this example, you can see that a balance sheet is split into five main parts. These will be examined in detail on the following pages.

Assets

NON-CURRENT ASSETS

This is a list showing the value of those items owned by the business that have a long-term function and can be used repeatedly, such as property, vehicles or machinery. These are assets the business plans to keep and use for more than one year, and are sometimes known as **fixed assets**. This shows anybody looking at the accounts what the business actually possesses and intends to keep.

Businesses may have various other non-current or fixed assets that are termed **intangible assets**. These are items that the business owns that also have a value, but not a physical presence. A good example of this would be items like brand names, goodwill, copyrights and patents held. In the example balance sheet of Meredith shown in Figure 3.1, you can see that the total value of non-current assets held total £237,400,000. This gives a key indication of the strength of the business in terms of the assets that it possesses and has at its disposal to use.

Depreciation

Fixed assets such as machinery, vehicles and even premises do not last for ever. They have a limited useful life to the business that has bought and used them. Consider if a business

MEREDITH PLC BALANCE SHEET AT 31 DECEMBER 2008

ASSETS	£000s	£000s
Non-current assets		
Property, plant and equipment	237,000	
Intangible assets	400	237,400
Current assets		
Inventories	4,000	
Trade and other receivables	500	
Cash and cash equivalents	20	4,520
Total assets		**241,920**
EQUITY AND LIABILITIES		
Equity		
Share capital	160,000	
Other reserves	518	
Retained earnings	1,000	161,518
Non-current liabilities		
Long-term borrowings		77,000
Current liabilities		
Trade and other payables	2,600	
Short-term borrowings	160	
Current tax payable	300	
Short-term provisions	342	3,402
Total equity and liabilities		**241,920**

Figure 3.1   An example balance sheet for Meredith plc

purchases a new van for £20,000 and four years later sells it for £5,000. The value of the van can be regarded as having fallen by £15,000 in the four years that the company owned it. This is depreciation, representing the drop in value of an asset over time. Non-current assets on a balance sheet are shown at their original cost minus any accumulated depreciation, that is, they are shown at the value that represents the asset's remaining economic value to the firm. This allows anyone reading the accounts to make a fair assessment of the fixed assets' strength of the business.

Depreciation is not an actual cost that the business has to pay out on a regular basis, but a method of spreading the cost of the asset across the years in which the asset will be used. For example, using the figures for the new van earlier, the business will have actually paid out £20,000 at the time it purchased the van, but for accounting purposes it would be unfair to charge all this cost to that one year in which it was bought if the company intends to keep and then use the van for the next four years. To truly reflect the cost and usage of the van, the business uses depreciation to spread the cost across the years. In this case in a simple form the business would write £3,750 per year off the value of the asset.

This is important as the costs charged each year are not actually 'real', that is, there is no equivalent cash payment being made each year the van is owned. All the cash went out right at the beginning when the van was purchased.

As a final point, the depreciation each year is actually deducted as a cost from the amount of profit the business has made that year, thus reducing the level of any profit declared by the business on its income statement as well. Depreciation is therefore one of the key areas why cash and profit are not the same.

CURRENT ASSETS

The next section shows the value of items the company owns that are likely to be turned into cash before the next balance sheet is drawn up. These are short-term assets whose value will change during the course of one year. The business does not intend to keep these for repeated use year after year, but intends to use them every day to help run the business. These are cash or near-cash equivalents that the business has or will have available in the next few months in order to pay bills and invoices received. They are listed in order of **liquidity**: this is a measure of how soon or easy it is to turn the items into cash, with the most **illiquid** been listed first. Using Figure 3.1 we can see that this section consists of three main areas:

- **Inventories** These represent the stocks of goods or items that the business possesses.
- **Trade and other receivables** These are made up of short-term debts that are owed to the business (for example, customers who owe them money (debtors) or a tenant who owes the business rent).
- **Cash and cash equivalents** This shows how much money the business has in physical cash and bank deposits.

This section therefore tells us how much money the business currently has in its possession or will have soon. Again using the example balance sheet of Meredith, you can see that the business has £4,520,000 in current assets, although this is not all in usable cash form at the moment. For example, £4,000,000 of that value is stock which will need to be sold before it becomes cash in reality.

TOTAL ASSETS

Total assets is simply the sum of all the assets the business possesses, that is:

Total assets = Non-current assets + Current assets

The top half of a balance sheet finishes with this figure. In Figure 3.1, this would be £241,920,000.

Equity and liabilities

The second part of a balance sheet starts here. The idea of this section is to show how the business has financed the purchase of all total assets it possesses. Businesses can raise money to purchase assets in three main ways:

- raising money from investors, that is, selling shares
- using its own profits generated through trading
- borrowing it from a third party, for example, a bank loan.

EQUITY

The equity section shows the capital invested by the owners and the funds retained in the company in the form of reserves and retained profits (retained earnings). This part is therefore telling us how much of the company's resources or asset strength have actually been financed by investment rather than borrowing. This looks at how much money the owners have invested and how much the company has grown from making profits.

NON-CURRENT LIABILITIES

For this area the company is now going to provide information regarding any debts, loans or mortgages it has borrowed from external agencies – like a bank – in order to help them purchase their non-current or fixed assets, and finance their operations.

Here we can make an assessment of the company's financial strength by comparing the value of the assets owned (from the non-current assets section) to the amount borrowed. Obviously it is better if the company has not borrowed too much money, but has bought a lot of assets. Looking at the balance sheet of Meredith plc in Figure 3.1 you can see that their non-current assets total £237,400,000, whereas their non-current liabilities were £77,000 in the form of long-term borrowings, that is, loans.

This therefore allows us to see how much money the company actually owes to other parties, and by comparing these figures we can determine how much of the company's fixed assets are actually owned by them.

Non-current liabilities might be loans from banks or other external agencies

CURRENT LIABILITIES

Current liabilities represent debts that are due or need to be paid within one year; in other words, these are short-term debts that will need to be paid back quickly. In this segment the company lists all the debts, bills and invoices it has to pay within the next 12 months, that is, the ones that they will need to pay with their cash or near-cash equivalents (current assets) soon. For example:

- **Trade and other payables** These show the amounts that the business owes to short-term creditors, such as suppliers or utility companies.
- **Short-term borrowings** These would represent any loans that have less than one year to run before they need to be repaid, or if the business had gone into an overdraft position with its bank account.
- **Current tax payable** This is fairly self-explanatory: any limited company needs to pay corporation tax on the profits it has made. This amount details the current amount of tax the business has to pay, but has not yet paid.
- **Short-term provisions** This is a section that covers any other type of debt that the company may have to pay out in the near future. A good example of this is dividends. At the end of a financial year after a company has calculated and declared its profits, the investors/owners will want their share, but also the company will want to keep some profit for reinvestment (retained earnings). The directors will therefore **propose** a dividend to shareholders. If accepted, this proposed dividend becomes a short-term debt, that is, the company has to give its shareholders their part of the profits but again it just has not done so at the moment, but it will do within the next 12 months.

This section is therefore telling us how much money the business has currently got to pay out or will have to pay soon.

Working capital or net current assets

This is a key measure of the financial strength of the company. Here we determine the **liquidity** of the business. We do this by examining its ability to be able to pay its short-term debts (current liabilities). This is found by comparing the value of its current assets with the value of its current liabilities. An alternative explanation is that we are looking at how much cash the business has currently got or will have soon, as against how much cash the business has currently got to pay out or will have to pay soon. It is found by removing current liabilities from current assets. For example, Figure 3.2 compares the figures for current assets and current liabilities for Meredith plc.

Current assets		
Inventories	4,000	
Trade and other receivables	500	
Cash and cash equivalents	20	4,520
Current liabilities		
Trade and other payables	2,600	
Short-term borrowings	160	
Current tax payable	300	
Short-term provisions	342	3,402
Working capital		1,118

Figure 3.2 Calculating working capital for Meredith plc

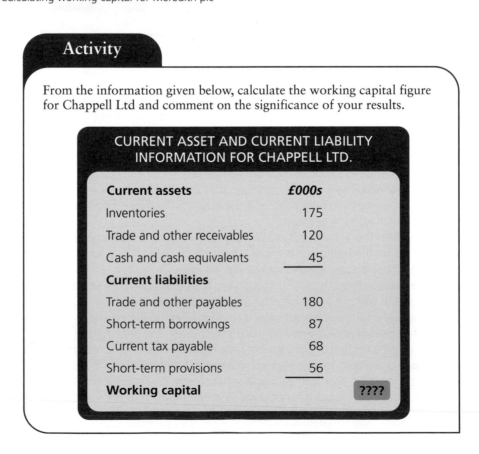

Activity

From the information given below, calculate the working capital figure for Chappell Ltd and comment on the significance of your results.

CURRENT ASSET AND CURRENT LIABILITY INFORMATION FOR CHAPPELL LTD.

Current assets	£000s
Inventories	175
Trade and other receivables	120
Cash and cash equivalents	45
Current liabilities	
Trade and other payables	180
Short-term borrowings	87
Current tax payable	68
Short-term provisions	56
Working capital	????

The resulting figure of *current assets* minus *current liabilities* is often called **working capital** as it shows how much finance the company has available for day-to-day operations even after all its short-term debts have been paid, that is, how much it has available to work with.

So Figure 3.2 clearly shows that Meredith plc have sufficient working capital to be able to pay all its short-term debts. However, for many businesses this may not be the case; a negative result for working capital would indicate a business that has insufficient current assets to meet its current liabilities. In this case, the business would be termed **illiquid** and could be a strong indicator of financial weakness in that business.

Analysing income statements

An income statement is the method by which an organisation determines the level of profits they have made. As profit is so important to so many different stakeholder groups, it is vital that it is calculated accurately; therefore guidelines have been laid down as to how profit should be calculated. The idea is that it should not matter *who* prepares the profit and loss account: they should arrive at the same answer. Profit is also such an important measure of a business's performance, that it is measured in several different ways. Figure 3.3 shows an example income statement for Meredith plc which we shall examine in detail.

Before you can start to appreciate, analyse and interpret a company's income statement, you need to have a thorough understanding of all the main terms and sections that the income statement is describing. The next section covers each key area in detail:

MEREDITH PLC INCOME STATEMENT FOR THE YEAR ENDED 31 DECEMBER 2008

	£000s
Revenue	1,800
Cost of sales	(800)
Gross profit	**1,000**
Distribution costs	(150)
Administration expenses	(260)
Profit from operations	**590**
Investment income	16
Finance cost	(26)
Profit before tax	**580**
Tax expense	(150)
Profit after tax	**430**

Figure 3.3   An example income statement for Meredith plc

- **Revenue** This is the total income received by the business in its normal trading activities. In its simplest form it represents the number of goods sold times the quantity of goods sold. However, for many large businesses this is too simple an explanation. Large businesses may well receive income from a range of activities such as:

  - selling goods
  - selling services, expertise or information
  - renting out some of their premises or other non-current assets to other firms
  - commissions on selling goods, that is, acting as an agent for another company's products.

- **Cost of sales** This is how much it cost to make or buy the products that have been sold in the current financial period. This is taken off the revenue generated to see how much gross profit was made.
- **Gross profit** This is the first measure of profit. This shows how much profit the business has made on buying and selling activities, that is, how good they are at trading. This is an important figure as it can be used by businesses to assess this key area of performance, that is, trading. Companies can look at their gross profit and

then compare it to previous years or with competitors' figures to determine if their business is in a strong or weak position, or if the trading operations are improving or declining.

- **Distribution costs and administration expenses** There is more to running a business than just buying and selling; these other aspects (costs) need to be considered so the final amount of profit can be found. These additional costs are the expenses. Expenses are overheads or indirect costs that a company incurs that are not directly involved in production, buying or selling activities. Typically expenses are characterised as being items which the business has paid for and 'used up' in conducting its activities, and consist of items like:

  - wages and salaries
  - rent and rates
  - advertising/marketing expenses
  - utility bills
  - motor expenses
  - warehouse costs
  - **depreciation**.

- **Profit from operations** This form of profit represents the amount made after all the earnings from regular trading activities have been accounted for, less all the costs associated with generating that revenue. However, this form of profit does not include any income and costs from the business's activities that are unlikely to repeated in future, that is, they are not part of the business's normal activities.
- **Investment income** This represents interest or any form of payment received from any investments the company may have, such as shares in other companies or long-term deposits.
- **Finance cost** This shows the amount the company has paid in interest on loans, overdrafts and other borrowings.
- **Profit before tax** This shows the amount of profit the business has made on which they have to pay corporation tax. This is also a key figure for businesses as this represents the main measure of how well they have actually performed. This figure can be used to measure the efficiency of the business, that is, how well is it being run, as it indicates how much of the **gross profit** was used up in the other costs of running the company. Profit before tax is often used when undertaking **ratio analysis** to investigate and interpret company account results. This topic is covered in detail in the next chapter of this book.
- **Tax expense** This displays the amount of tax charged on the profits the company has made and now has to pay.
- **Profit after tax** This then represents the amount of profit from all the business's activities for that year that is left over and available for the business to distribute or utilise (see section on profit utilisation below).

Profit utilisation

After any company has calculated its **profit after tax** figure, it has to decide what to do with it. In other words, this is the total profit remaining to the company after all costs and tax deductions have been made, so the directors of the company now have to decide how to best use this money. Directors have to decide:

- How much of the profit after tax should be given to shareholders as dividends. This is the return they receive as the reward for their investment in the company.
- How much of the profit after tax should be transferred to reserves or kept as retained earnings for reinvestment in the company, for example, financing growth.

This is a very important factor when assessing a business's income statement, but viewpoints may differ from different stakeholder groups. For example, managers and directors will want to see profits being retained as this is a very cheap source of finance for investment, and reinvesting profits in the company enhances future opportunities for growth, performance, competitiveness and financial stability.

However, shareholders may not want to wait for future growth to see a return on their investment. Current shareholders and potential investors may well assess the company's performance on how much is paid out in dividends now. But would shareholders want to see a business that did not retain any profits for its own growth and security?

It is frequently normal then for the **profit after tax** to be split between dividends and retained earning or reserves.

Skills watch!

A02 / A03

Download the annual report and accounts of any large plc in which you have an interest. From the income statement, identify the key figures outlined above and make an assessment of how well you think the business has performed and how it has utilised its profit after tax.

For this task, to be able to make an informed assessment you have to think specifically about the business you have researched and consider factors such as how well competitors performed, what the market conditions were like in that industry and what proportion of profit after tax has been retained.

Profit quality

When analysing and assessing a business's income statement it is not sufficient just to look at how much profit a company made; it is also important to look at *how* that profit was made. The amount of profit and the quality of profits made is not equal.

Profits that come about through normal trading and that are likely to be repeated year after year are known as high-quality profits. These are high quality as the business can assume that they can rely on these in future; this type of profit is likely to come about from loyal customers who make repeated purchases.

Low-quality profits may be regarded as being profits that are not repeatable or sustainable in the future, that is, they are profits from one-off sources or events. These are known as:

- **Extraordinary items** These are financial transactions that have taken place during that financial period that are not part of the business's normal trading operations, for example, in one particular year the business may report an extraordinary profit (or cost) as it has sold off some of its property or other assets.
- **Exceptional items** These items do arise from normal trading activities but were of such a significant scale that they have provided a distortion to the accounts. For example, a business that suddenly made huge and unexpected returns on one of its investments, that it would not expect to be repeated in future, would include this as an exceptional item. By doing this, the business clearly shows the profit that has been made, but also indicates to shareholders and other interested parties that this part of the profit is unlikely to be repeated in future. Similarly, if the company has encountered items that have been large one-off costs that have caused profits to decrease, these too would also be shown as exceptional items, that is, exceptional costs.

For example...

Exceptional business

The following extract is taken from the annual report and accounts of Virgin for the year 2004. This extract clearly shows Virgin reporting additional exceptional turnover of £17.2 million. It also shows Virgin reporting exceptional costs of £23.5 million.

In their annual report Virgin explain that these exceptional profits and costs have arisen mainly from an issue of shares, reorganisation of the company structure and introducing an employee share option scheme.

	To 31 Mar 2004 £ million
Turnover before exceptional items	470.4
Exceptional turnover	17.2
Turnover	**487.6**
Cost of sales	(255.8)
Gross profit	**231.8**
Total administrative expenses before exceptional items	(132.5)
Exceptional operating costs	(23.5)
Administrative expenses	(156.0)
Operating profit before exceptional items	82.1
Exceptional items (net)	(6.3)
Operating profit	**75.8**
Finance charges (net)	(9.6)
Profit on ordinary activities before taxation	**66.2**
Tax on profit on ordinary activities	27.1
Profit for the financial year	**93.3**

Using financial data for comparisons, trend analysis and decision-making

The function of financial information is to provide data on how a particular organisation has performed over a period of time. The analysis of the financial accounts represents one way business performance can be assessed.

For example...

Morrison's income statement

The following information is taken from Morrison's annual accounts for 2008. This extract quite clearly shows the company's income statement for 2008 side by side with the corresponding income statement for 2007. This is so that any interested party can undertake a horizontal analysis of the figures immediately.

CONSOLIDATED INCOME STATEMENT
52 weeks ended 3 February 2008

	2008 £m	2007 £m
Turnover	**12,969**	12,462
Cost of sales	**(12,151)**	(11,826)
Gross profit	**818**	636
Other operating income	**30**	21
Administrative expenses	**(268)**	(272)
Profits arising on property transactions	**32**	38
Operating profit	**612**	423
Finance costs	**(60)**	(82)
Finance income	**60**	28
Profit before taxation	**612**	369
Taxation	**(58)**	(121)
Profit for the financial period attributable to equity holders of the parent	**554**	248

Final accounts, such as the income statement and the balance sheet, are used for three main purposes:

- financial control
- planning
- accountability.

Thorough analysis can help in interpreting financial information and assist managers and owners in making decisions to achieve the above objectives.

Methods of financial analysis

For managers to gain the information they need, the analysis of final accounts is not a random operation. A well-ordered and structured process needs to be followed.

- **Initial reading** This is used to gain a broad understanding of the company's financial position: the type of industry/market in which it is operating and a rough idea of its recent financial performance.
- **Vertical analysis** This considers the interdependence of one figure to another. For example, gross profit is not only affected by the level of sales, but also by the cost of sales.
- **Horizontal analysis** This compares current financial statements with statements from previous years. This is done on an item-by-item basis, to determine whether there have been any particular areas of change, for example, whether sales have risen or fallen compared to last year (see the example on page 39).

For example...

For example, we could use horizontal analysis to see if there had been any consistent change in the level of sales over three or four years. We could then also use vertical analysis to see if there had been a secondary effect on the level of gross profit reported. The following extract, again from Morrison's annual report, allows interested parties to perform just that sort of investigation.

SEVEN YEAR SUMMARY OF RESULTS
52 weeks ended January

Consolidated income statement

| | New format | | | Previous format | | | | | |
| | IFRS GAAP | | | IFRS GAAP | | UK GAAP | | | |
	2008 £m	2007 £m	2006 £m	2006 £m	2005 £m	2005 £m	2004 £m	2003 £m	2002 £m
Turnover	12,969	12,462	12,115	12,115	12,104	12,116	4,944	4,290	3,915
Cost of sales	(12,151)	(11,826)	(11,793)						
Other operating income					19	18	6	1	2	1
Raw materials and consumables				(9,156)	(9,110)	(9,110)	(3,682)	(3,186)	(2,944)
Gross profit	818	636	322	2,978	3,012	3,012	1,263	1,106	972

- **Trend analysis** The current figures are compared with those from several consecutive previous years in an attempt to determine the presence of any significant trends. This can be done on a horizontal or a vertical basis, or both (see the example on page 40).
- **Ratio analysis** This uses financial ratios to compare and interpret financial statements. This method allows for in-depth monitoring of financial performance from one period to another, comparisons over time, comparisons with other companies and analysis of current financial performance. Ratio analysis is covered in depth in the next chapter.

Assessing strengths and weaknesses of financial data in judging performance

Strengths

Balance sheets and income statements offer valuable information to a wide range of stakeholders. The final accounts provide information ranging from the level of revenue made and profits, to the asset base and strength, as well as the likely long- and short-term financial stability of the business.

They also provide details of the costs incurred in running the company, so assessments of efficiency can be made, and how any final profits were utilised, providing guidance on how successful the business may be in the future. They also allow managers, owners and other interested parties to make a judgement about the type of profit generated, that is, its quality and the likelihood of it being achieved in future years, alongside an analysis of trends and comparisons with previous years or competitors' results.

Weaknesses

Whilst a business's accounts are used and assessed by many stakeholder groups, their actual value can be limited for the following reasons:

- They are based on historical information and the figures may not reflect the current market conditions, the economic situation or recent actions and developments by competitors. The final income statement and balance sheet for a company can take a long time to be produced, several months in some cases, and as soon as they are published can already be out of date.
- Many figures on the accounts are summarised, such as cost of sales, distribution costs and admin expenses. Summarised figures hide much of the detail about what has taken place exactly, such as precisely how much was spent on advertising or on staff wages. This means that any external stakeholders will find it hard to perform any in-depth assessments of the business's performance.
- Window-dressing occurs which is legal, but means that a certain amount of massaging of figures may take place which presents the company in the best possible light. For example, a revaluation of premises may have recently taken place to boost the non-current assets on the balance sheet.
- The human aspect such as labour turnover, levels of workforce morale and absenteeism rates are not included, which can tell the user a lot about the qualities and characteristics of the workforce, such as qualifications and experience, which cannot be seen by the published accounts alone.

Summary and exam guidance

Summary

- A balance sheet is a statement that shows a company's assets, equity and liabilities. It shows what a business owns and where the money came from. It can be used to assess a business's long-term financial strength.

- Working capital is calculated from a balance sheet by comparing a company's current assets and current liabilities. This is a key indicator of a business's ability to pay its short-term debts and is an important indicator of short-term financial stability.

- An income statement details a business's profit performance over the last financial year. It also shows how this profit was distributed or retained (used) by the company.

- Assessing the level of profit made is not enough; a thorough judgement would involve looking at the profit quality as well, that is, can the profits declared be repeated in future or are they just a 'one off'?

- Analysing financial statements can be done in various ways to ascertain vital information regarding a company's current and future prospects. This can involve comparisons with its own previous years, comparison with competitors, in-depth ratio analysis and the identification of any key trends likely to have a future impact.

- Although containing lots and lots of information that can be used by different stakeholder groups to inform their decision-making, balance sheets and income statements have several limitations. These include a lack of information in areas that cannot be assessed by financial means, for example, morale, experience and motivation levels.

- The financial statements published by businesses may well be window-dressed, that is, the accounts have been manipulated to show the company concerned in the best possible light, potentially misleading any assessment made.

Exam practice

Read the text below and then answer the questions that follow.

Text A

Thomas Cook plc – creating millions of travel dreams for 167 years

Everyone knows Thomas Cook. It's the oldest, most respected name in the travel business (according to their own publicity). Study the following financial information.

THOMAS COOK GROUP PLC INCOME STATEMENT 2008	
	€ m
Revenue	**9,439.3**
Cost of providing tourism services	(7,191.4)
Gross profit	**2,247.9**
Other operating income	55.7
Personnel expenses	(988.0)
Depreciation and amortisation	(152.5)
Amortisation of business combination intangibles	
Other operating expenses	(707.7)
Profit on disposal of businesses and property, plant and equipment	–
Profit on disposal of non-current assets held for sale	–
Profit from operations	**455.4**

THOMAS COOK GROUP BALANCE SHEET 2008

	2008 £m
ASSETS	
Non-current assets	
Property, plant and equipment	6,205
Lease prepayments	239
Investment property	239
Financial assets	43
	6,726
Current assets	
Stocks	442
Debtors	199
Financial assets	74
Cash and cash equivalents	191
	906
Non-current assets classified as held for sale	4
	910
LIABILITIES	
Current liabilities	
Creditors	(1,679)
Other financial liabilities	(77)
Current tax liabilities	(97)
	(1,853)
Non-current liabilities	
Other financial liabilities	(774)
Deferred tax liabilities	(424)
Net pension liabilities	(68)
Provisions	(139)
	(1,405)
Net assets	4,378

(a) Discuss whether the level of profit earned by Thomas Cook as shown by its income statement is a good measure of the business's level of success. (15 marks)

(b) Analyse how the information from Thomas Cook's balance sheet could be of use to their stakeholder groups. (10 marks)

(c) Assess the value of Thomas Cook's financial accounts to a potential investor's decision-making. (15 marks)

Total: 40 marks

Breakdown of assessment objectives

AO1 – Knowledge and understanding – 8/40
AO2 – Apply knowledge and understanding – 10/40
AO3 – Analyse problems, issues and situations – 10/40
AO4 – Evaluate, distinguish between fact and opinion, assess and judge information from a variety of sources – 12/40

Suggested structure

For part (a) you will need to:

- Discuss the differences between the types of profit reported.
- Consider how reported profit could be considered a measure of success.
- Discuss factors such as the quality of reported profit and business aims when reaching a judgement.

For part (b) you will need to:

- Consider how different stakeholder groups might use and benefit from the information contained in the financial statements and how.
- Consider which stakeholder groups may not gain so much benefit from an examination of a company's balance sheet.

For part (c) you will need to:

- Explain with relevant examples how the financial accounts could be help in making investment decisions.
- Analyse the strengths and limitations of financial information.
- Make a fully justified conclusion as to the usefulness of the information provided in the scenario given.

Chapter 4   Interpreting published accounts

Key terms

Liquidity ratios

Current ratio = Current assets : Current liabilities expressed as ?:1

Acid test = Current assets − Stock : Current liabilities expressed as ?:1

Profitability ratios

$$\text{ROCE} = \frac{\text{Operating profit}}{\text{Total capital employed}} \times 100 = \text{?} \%$$

Financial efficiency ratios

$$\text{Stock turnover} = \frac{\text{Cost of goods sold}}{\text{Average stock}} = \text{? number of times per year}$$

$$\text{Debtor collection period} = \frac{\text{Debtors}}{\text{Credit sales}} \times 365 = \text{? number of days}$$

$$\text{Creditor payment period} = \frac{\text{Creditors}}{\text{Credit purchases}} \times 365 = \text{? number of days}$$

$$\text{Asset turnover} = \frac{\text{Turnover}}{\text{Net assets}} = \text{? times per year}$$

Gearing

$$\text{Gearing} = \frac{\text{Long-term liabilities} + \text{Preference shares}}{\text{Total capital employed}} \times 100 = \text{?} \%$$

Shareholder ratios

$$\text{Dividend per share} = \frac{\text{Total dividend}}{\text{Number of issued shares}} = \text{? number of pence}$$

$$\text{Dividend yield} = \frac{\text{Dividend per share}}{\text{Share's market price}} \times 100 = \text{?} \%$$

Synoptic search

In your AS studies Unit 2, Section A, you will have looked at measuring and increasing profits as well as how to calculate and improve ROCE for a newly-formed business. Although companies are much larger in scale, many of the methods and techniques outlined in this area of your studies are still relevant.

It may also be worthwhile reminding yourself at this point of the difference between cash and profit, as this distinction has an impact on the interpretation of liquidity and financial efficiency ratios.

POSSIBLE ROUTES FOR ANALYSIS

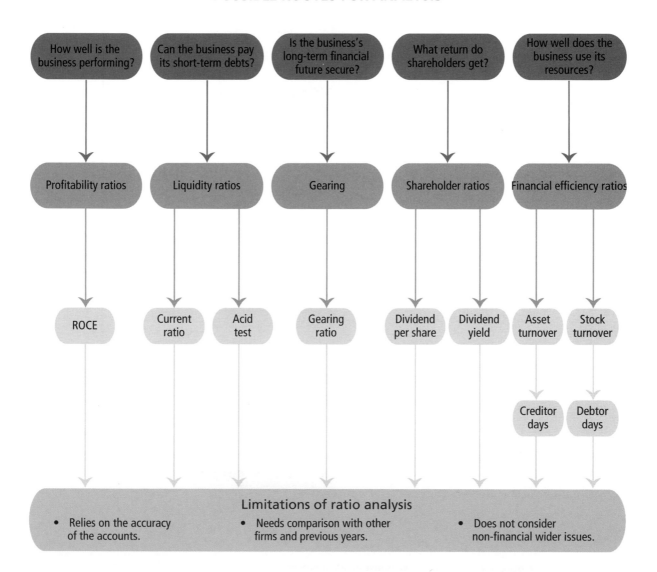

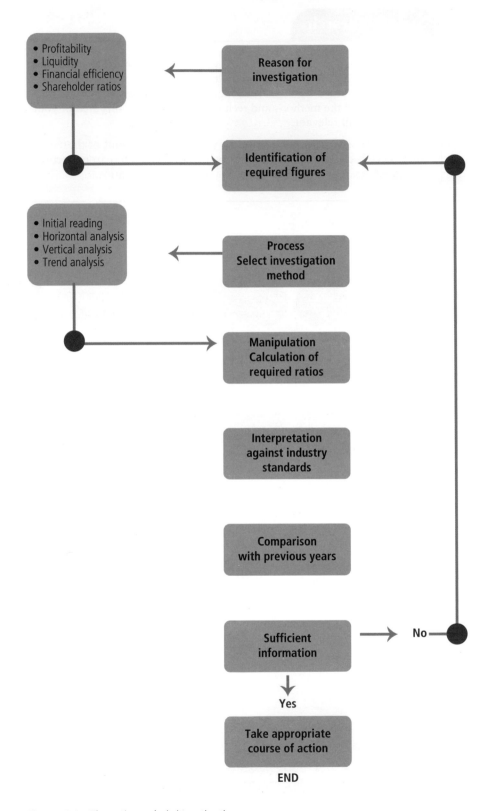

Figure 4.1   The ratio analysis investigation process

Conducting ratio analysis: the selection of ratios

Financial information is vital in planning and controlling the activities of a business. Managers need to know whether the business is making a profit or a loss, how much money is available for equipment, whether they need to alter the way the organisation operates, and so on. Only if accurate and up-to-date financial information is available can they make important decisions about the business or plan for the future. One of the main ways in which a business monitors its performance is through the use of **ratio analysis**.

Monitoring business performance allows informed decisions to be made by owners and managers. Better decisions are made when people are well informed. Information is required both to understand all the possible outcomes that could arise and also to measure the value of these outcomes.

There are a number of important issues that the interpretation of financial information can identify or address. These include:

- **Profitability ratio** This examines the relationship between profit and capital employed. It is sometimes referred to as being the **primary efficiency ratio**.
- **Liquidity ratios** These investigate the short-term financial stability of a business by examining the relationships between current assets and liabilities.
- **Financial efficiency ratios** These are used to assess the all-round performance of a business and tell a business how frequently a business is moving its stock, how hard its assets are working and how good its credit control is.
- **Shareholder ratios** These examine the relationship between the number of shares issued, dividends paid, value of the shares and company profits. For obvious reasons these are quite often categorised as **investment ratios**. They are of primary interest to existing and potential shareholders.
- **Gearing** This looks at the long-term financial stability of a business by comparing how much of the business has been financed by borrowed money and how much by investment.

Thus it can be seen that different ratios assess differing areas of the business's financial performance. It is important that when conducting an investigation into the finances of a given organisation, the appropriate ratios are selected to measure and assess the correct required information. The ratio analysis investigation process is shown in Figure 4.1 (see opposite).

In the next section we will examine each category in greater detail, using Figure 4.2 as an example in each case (see next page).

Conducting ratio analysis: the calculation and interpretation of ratios to measure financial performance

Profitability

This area of ratio analysis is used to provide an essential assessment of the overall success of the business. It is predominantly used by managers, shareholders, competitors and creditors to judge how well a given company has performed that year.

RETURN ON CAPITAL EMPLOYED (ROCE)

This is sometimes referred to as being the primary ratio and is considered to be one of the most important ratios available. This ratio measures the efficiency of funds invested in the business at generating profits.

LOMAX PLC BALANCE SHEETS AT 31 DECEMBER 2008				
	2007		**2008**	
ASSETS	£000s	£000s	£000s	£000s
Non-current assets				
Property, plant and equipment	921		957	
Intangible assets	140	1,061	138	1095
Current assets				
Inventories	50		100	
Trade and other receivables	175		130	
Cash and cash equivalents	27	252	15	245
Total assets		**1,313**		**1,340**
EQUITY AND LIABILITIES				
Equity				
Share capital £1.00 ordinary shares	750		750	
Other reserves	100		120	
Retained earnings	120	970	157	1,027
Non-current liabilities				
Long-term borrowings		207		137
Current liabilities				
Trade and other payables	90		127	
Short-term borrowings	16		2	
Current tax payable	28		44	
Short-term provisions	2	136	3	176
Total equity and liabilities		**1,313**		**1,340**

cont...

Figure 4.2   An example balance sheet for Lomax plc

LOMAX PLC INCOME STATEMENT FOR THE YEAR ENDED 31 DECEMBER 2008

	2007	2008
	£000s	£000s
Revenue	600	670
Cost of sales	(350)	(405)
Gross profit	**250**	**265**
Distribution costs	(50)	(54)
Administration expenses	(60)	(67)
Profit from operations	**140**	**144**
Investment income	16	14
Finance cost	(18)	(11)
Profit before tax	**138**	**147**
Tax expense	(28)	(30)
Profit after tax	**110**	**117**
Dividends paid and proposed	50	60
Transferred to reserves	30	20
Retained profits	30	37
Notes		
Market share price	160 pence	185 pence
Opening stock (inventory)	£30,000	£50,000
Credit sales percentage of turnover	60%	65%
Credit purchases percentage of cost of goods sold	80%	80%

Calculating the ROCE

$$\text{ROCE} = \frac{\text{Operating profit}}{\text{Total capital employed}} \times 100$$

This is expressed as a percentage where:

Total capital = Ordinary share capital + Preference share capital + Reserves + Debentures + Long-term loans

Or = Total assets employed

For each type of company the idea is to try to determine how much profit has been made for distribution from the total amount of assets employed by that business. For example, to make £100,000 profit when you have a £million to invest is somewhat easier than making the same £100,000 profit when you've only got £50,000 of total capital employed by your business.

This is why we use profit before tax and interest charges when calculating ROCE for a limited company. The cost of these items will fluctuate due to factors outside the business's control, for instance, taxation rates are set by the government and the interest rates by the Bank of England. Therefore if we were to measure profit after tax and interest, we would get significant variations in our results year by year. These would not reflect changes in the performance of the business, but external factors.

Interpreting the ROCE

As with the other ratios examined so far, the higher the value of the ratio, the better. A higher percentage can provide owners with a greater return. Inevitably this figure needs to be compared with previous years and other companies to determine whether this year's result is satisfactory or not.

Alongside this the percentage result arrived at for ROCE for a given organisation needs to be compared with the percentage return offered by interest-bearing accounts at banks and building societies. Ideally, the ROCE should be higher than any return that could be gained from interest-earning accounts.

The return on capital employed can be improved by:

- increasing the level of profit generated by the same level of capital invested
- maintaining the level of profits generated but decreasing the amount of capital it takes to do so.

Activity

Now calculate the **ROCE** for Lomax for the year 2008 and comment upon your result and the company's financial position. (See the worked example below.)

Worked example using the accounts of Lomax plc for 2007 in Figure 4.2*

$$\text{ROCE} = \frac{\text{Operating profit}}{\text{Total capital employed}} \times 100$$

$$= \frac{138{,}000}{1{,}313{,}000} \times 100 = 10.51\%$$

Liquidity

These ratios are concerned with the examination of the short-term financial stability of the organisation. They are mainly concerned with the organisation's working capital and whether or not it is being managed effectively. Working capital is needed by all organisations in order for them to be able to finance their day-to-day activities: too little and the company may not be able to pay all its debts; too much and they may not be making most efficient use of their resources.

Although profitability is important for a firm, it is often short-term lack of cash (liquidity) that causes businesses to fold (liquidate). An unprofitable company can survive in the short term so long as it still has sufficient financial resources to pay debts as they become due. These ratios would mainly be used by managers, suppliers and other forms of creditors in assessing the financial strength of the business.

---

* All results shown for worked examples will be shown to two decimal places where appropriate.

THE CURRENT RATIO

This looks at the relationship between current assets and current liabilities; it is often referred to as the **working capital ratio** and examines the liquidity position of the firm. This is what is called a pure ratio where everything is expressed to the lowest form, that is, whatever it is = to one.

Calculating the current ratio

This is calculated by comparing the total current assets held by the business to its total current liabilities using the formula:

Current ratio = Current assets **:** Current liabilities

Worked example

Current assets = £25,000
Current liabilities = £10,000
Current ratio = Current assets : Current liabilities
= £25,000 : £10,000

By dividing the value of current assets by the value of current liabilities, and current liabilities by itself, we are able to find the answer to the ratio expressed as a proper ratio, for example, 2:1 or 3:1. So:

$$= \frac{£25,000}{£10,000} : \frac{£10,000}{£10,000}$$
$$= 2.5 : 1$$

Answer current ratio = 2.5:1

Interpreting the current ratio

Using the above example, the result shows that there are two and a half times as many current assets as current liabilities. This means that they have £2.50 of short-term assets available to pay for every £1 of short-term debts. This company is therefore in a comfortable position to pay its debts.

Accepted knowledge is that an ideal current ratio should be approximately somewhere around the values of 1.7 to 2:1, that is, £2 of current assets for every £1 of current liability. Any higher and the organisation has too many resources tied up in unproductive assets, such as holding too much stock, which could be invested more profitably. A low result, something like 0.7:1, means a business may not be able to pay its debts as they fall due. This shows the firm only has 70p of current assets available to pay every £1 it owes and is not actually able to cover its short-term debts should all of them need to be paid at the same time.

If the business is holding far too many resources in either stocks, cash or bank accounts, or has too many debtors, the current ratio will be too high, for example, 4:1. This can easily be solved by converting some of these assets to cash and investing it back in the business, such as buying better machinery or training for employees, that is, the money being held in current assets could be used more effectively by the business in increasing efficiency of operations, or perhaps researching or promoting products.

If the ratio is too low the company may well be faced with the situation whereby they have to sell off some of their fixed assets or sell and lease back to obtain a more liquid position, or obtain additional long-term sources of finance from somewhere, such as selling more shares or obtaining a long-term loan. This would enable them to inject cash into the business so that they are then able to pay debts when required.

Worked example using the accounts of Lomax plc for 2007 in Figure 4.2*

$$\text{Current ratio} = \text{Current assets : Current liabilities}$$
$$= 252{,}000 : 136{,}000$$
$$= 1.85 : 1$$

Activity

Now calculate the **current ratio** for Lomax for the year 2008 and comment upon your result and the company's financial position. (See the worked example above.)

Stock (or inventories), such as Audis in a car showroom, are removed when calculating the acid test, to give a more accurate picture

THE ACID TEST

This is also sometimes called the **quick** or **liquid ratio**. It too examines liquidity by comparing current assets and liabilities, but it removes stock ('inventories' on the balance sheet) from the total of current assets. This is done, as stock is the most illiquid current asset, that is, it is the hardest to turn into cash without a loss in its value. In many cases, in order to convert stock into cash or bank deposits quickly it is sold off cheaply. To achieve its full value it can take a long time to convert stock into cash. Consider, for example, how long it would take a car showroom selling Audis to clear every car off its forecourt.

Furthermore, stock held in warehouses and so on may be old or obsolete and thus unsellable. With the removal of stock we are able to directly relate cash and near-cash equivalents (cash, bank and debtors) to short-term debts. This therefore provides a much more accurate measure of the firm's liquidity than the previous current ratio.

Calculating the acid test

This is calculated by comparing the total current assets less stock to its total liabilities using the formula:

$$\text{Acid test} = \text{Current assets} - \text{Inventories : Current liabilities}$$

And again this is expressed in the proper ratio form, for example, 1.6:1.

Worked example

Total current assets = £25,000
Inventories = £12,000
Current liabilities = £10,000

$$\text{Acid test} = \text{Current Assets} - \text{Stock : Current liabilities}$$
$$= £25{,}000 - £12{,}000 : £10{,}000$$
$$= £13{,}000 : £10{,}000$$
$$= 1.3 : 1$$

Answer acid test = 1.3:1

* All results shown for worked examples will be shown to two decimal places where appropriate.

Interpreting the acid test

An ideal result for this ratio should be approximately 1.1:1 showing that the firm had £1.10 to pay every £1.00 of debt. Here the business could pay all its debts and has a 10% safety margin as well. A result below this, for example, 0.7:1, indicates that the firm may well have difficulties meeting short-term payments. However, some businesses are able to operate with a very low level of liquidity. Supermarkets like Asda or Tesco, for example, who have the majority of their current assets tied up in stock, will always appear to have a very low acid test result.

Companies may wish to convert current assets to productive investment if the result is considered too high, or alternatively seek methods of injecting cash resources into the firm if the result is considered too low.

Supermarkets such as Asda will always seem to have a very low acid test result, as most of their current assets are tied up in stock

Skills watch!

A02 / A03

Learning and understanding any type of mathematical calculation can really be enhanced with practice. Completing example calculations will help you to be able to apply your knowledge to other business situations.

Calculate the current ratio and the acid test results from the following information. Comment on your results, explaining whether or not they would be considered a strength or a weakness.

Current assets	Current liabilities
Stock £82,000	Creditors £27,000
Debtors £15,000	
Bank £13,000	

Worked example using the accounts of Lomax plc for 2007 in Figure 4.2*

Acid test = Current assets – Inventories : Current liabilities
= 252,000 – 50,000 : 136,000
= 202,000 : 136,000
= 1.49 : 1

* All results shown for worked examples will be shown to two decimal places where appropriate.

Activity

Now calculate the **acid test** for Lomax for the year 2008 and comment upon your result and the company's financial position. (See the worked example on page 55.)

Financial efficiency ratios

These are also sometimes called **activity ratios** or **asset utilisation ratios** and are concerned with how well an organisation manages and uses its resources. Mainly they investigate how well the management controls the *current* situation of the firm. They consider stock, debtors and creditors, and the use of its assets. These ratios are primarily used by managers, shareholders and competitors.

ASSET TURNOVER

The **asset turnover ratio** shows how effective assets have been in generating sales, and how effectively a business's sales staff has used its assets to generate sales.

Calculating asset turnover

$$\text{Asset turnover} = \frac{\text{Turnover (or sales revenue)}}{\text{Net assets (or assets employed)}}$$

This is expressed as a number of times per year where:

$$\text{Net assets} = \text{Total assets} - \text{Total liabilities}$$

Interpreting asset turnover

This ratio is difficult to interpret, as different industries will expect to see very different results. An asset-intensive industry, that is, one that uses a lot of machinery, for example, will have a relatively low figure, whereas an industry with low asset costs and high sales volume should have a greater asset turnover. In general terms though, the higher the result, the better, as this shows the company is generating more sales compared to the value of assets it possesses.

Activity

Now calculate the **asset turnover** for Lomax for the year 2008 and comment upon your result and the company's financial position. (See the worked example below.)

Worked example using the accounts of Lomax plc for 2007 in Figure 4.2*

$$\text{Asset turnover} = \frac{\text{Turnover (or sales revenue)}}{\text{Net assets (or assets employed)}}$$

$$= \frac{600,000}{1,313,000 - (136,000 + 207,000)} \times 100 = 61.86\%$$

---

* All results shown for worked examples will be shown to two decimal places where appropriate.

STOCK TURNOVER

This ratio measures the number of times in one year that a business turns over its stock of goods for sale. From this figure we can also establish the average length of time (in days) that stock is held by the company.

Calculating stock turnover

$$\text{Stock turnover} = \frac{\text{Cost of sales}}{\text{Average stock}}$$

This is expressed as a number of times per year where:

$$\text{Average stock} = \frac{(\text{Opening stock} + \text{Closing stock})}{2}$$

Interpreting stock turnover

This ratio needs to be interpreted with knowledge of the industry/market in which the firm operates. For example, remember the Audi car sales from earlier in this chapter? If we were examining the accounts of a car sales business, we would not expect them to turn over their entire stock of cars and replace with new ones every day – maybe about once a month or every five to six weeks – therefore we would see a result round about nine or ten times a year.

We can also compare this year's result with previous years or other similar-sized firms in the same market. As a general rule, the quicker a business is selling its stock, the quicker they are going to realise the profit on it so, the higher the rate of stock turnover, the better. A falling stock turnover figure can indicate falling sales or that the company is holding a large amount of obsolete or slow-selling items. It could also result from an inefficient purchasing system that is not effectively matching purchasing to selling. A note of caution though: the rate of stock turnover can be increased by firms selling off stock cheaply (below the normal market price). In many circumstances this could be undesirable, so stock turnover results should be closely compared with profitability.

The rate of stock turnover required depends on the nature of the business. A sports retailer would need to turn stock over much faster than a car sales business in order to remain profitable.

The stock turnover ratio can be improved by:

- reducing the average level of stocks held, without losing sales
- increasing the rate of sales without raising the level of stocks.

Important note: the stock turnover ratio cannot be used for service industries as they do not buy or sell stocks of goods.

> ### Worked example using the accounts of Lomax plc for 2007 in Figure 4.2*
>
> $$\text{Stock turnover} = \frac{\text{Cost of sales}}{\text{Average stock}}$$
>
> $$= \frac{350,000}{(30,000 + 50,000)/2} = 8.75 \text{ times}$$

* All results shown for worked examples will be shown to two decimal places where appropriate.

Activity

Now calculate the **stock turnover** for Lomax for the year 2008 and comment upon your result and the company's financial position. (See the worked example on page 57.)

DEBTOR DAYS

The **debtor days ratio**, also known as the **debt collection period ratio**, is designed to show how long, on average, it takes the company to collect debts owed by customers who have bought goods on credit terms. This shows how good the business is at actually collecting the money owed to it and is an important ratio in assessing financial efficiency, as failing to collect monies owed as they fall due for collection can have a major impact on a business's liquidity and cash flow situation.

Calculating debtor days

$$\text{Debtor days} = \frac{\text{Total value of debtors}}{\text{Credit sales}} \times 365$$

This is expressed as a number of days where:

Debtors = The value for trade and other receivables on the balance sheet

Often the figure for credit sales is not actually provided on a business's income statement. In this case the total sales/turnover figure should be substituted and used instead.

Interpreting debtor days

Different industries allow different amounts of time for debtors to settle invoices. Standard credit terms are usually for 30, 60, 90 and 120 days, although some companies like furniture retailers, for example, allow buy now, pay in ten months or one year deals. The debt collection period figure should therefore be compared against the *official* number of days the business allows for debts to be settled. This has important implications for cash flow as it shows how effective the organisation's credit control system is at collecting monies owing to them. For this ratio, the nearer the result to the actual period allowed, the better. Results over the period show that whilst the company may be good at selling goods, they are not so good at collecting the money owed.

The debtor collection period can be improved by:

- reducing the amount of time credit is offered for, for example, from 90 to 60 days
- by offering incentives for clients to pay on time, for example, cash discounts
- stepping up the efficiency of the credit control department. If there is a real problem in this area, some companies may consider **debt factoring**. Debt factoring is the process of raising finance by selling some of your debts. When goods and services are sold on credit, businesses have to wait to receive their money. However, if they want to raise finance and receive the money quicker, then they can sell this debt to a specialist debt factoring company. They will receive the bulk of the money owed to them immediately from the debt factoring firm, and the debt factoring business will then collect the debt from the customer when it is due and take a percentage of the money as their fee.

Worked example using the accounts of Lomax plc for 2007 in Figure 4.2*

$$\text{Debtor days} = \frac{\text{Total value of debtors}}{\text{Credit sales}} \times 365$$

$$= \frac{175,000}{(600,000 \times 60\%)} \times 365 = 177.43 \text{ days}$$

* All results shown for worked examples will be shown to two decimal places where appropriate.

Now calculate the **debtor days** for Lomax for the year 2008 and comment upon your result and the company's financial position. (See the worked example on page 58.)

CREDITOR DAYS

This is also called the **creditor payment period** and shows how long, on average, it takes the company to pay debts owed to suppliers.

Calculating creditor days

$$\text{Credit payment period} = \frac{\text{Total creditors}}{\text{Credit purchases}} \times 365$$

This is expressed as a number of days where:

$$\text{Creditors} = \text{The figure for trade and other payables from the balance sheet}$$

Again, the exact figure for credit purchases is often not actually provided. In this case, the figure for total purchases should be substituted and used instead.

Interpreting creditor days

This ratio shows how good a company is at actually paying its suppliers. So if a supplier offers 30 days' credit, they can use this ratio to forecast whether or not they are likely to be paid on time by the business that is asking for the credit terms.

Companies with poor credit payment periods may therefore find it hard to negotiate and receive new credit agreements in the future.

A key area for analysis here is the comparison between debtor and creditor periods; obviously it would be better for most businesses if debtors pay them sooner than creditors fall due for payment. Thus they ensure cash flow is present to enable payments to suppliers to be made.

The credit payment period can be improved by:

- ensuring invoices from suppliers are paid on time
- improving cash flow and working capital management to ensure funds are available to meet payments as they fall due.

Activity

Now calculate the **creditor payment period** for Lomax for the year 2008 and comment upon your result and the company's financial position. (See the worked example below.)

Worked example using the accounts of Lomax plc for 2007 in Figure 4.2*

$$\text{Credit payment period} = \frac{\text{Total creditors}}{\text{Credit purchases}} \times 365$$

$$= \frac{90,000}{(350,000 \times 80\%)} \times 365 = 117.32 \text{ days}$$

Gearing

Gearing is given its own section in ratio analysis as this ratio focuses on long-term financial stability rather than short-term, like liquidity ratios. It measures how much of the total capital employed by the business has been borrowed in the form of long-term debts.

Calculating gearing

$$\text{Gearing} = \frac{\text{Long term liabilities}}{\text{Total capital employed}} \times 100 = ?\%$$

* All results shown for worked examples will be shown to two decimal places where appropriate.

Where:

Total Capital employed = Ordinary share capital + Preference share capital +
Reserves + Debentures + Long-term loans + Mortgages
Long-term liabilities = Long-term loans + Mortgages + Debentures +
Preference shares

Interpreting gearing

The **gearing ratio** shows how risky an investment a company is. If loans represent more than 50% of capital employed, the company is said to be **highly geared**. A highly-geared firm has to pay interest on its borrowings before it can pay dividends to ordinary shareholders or retain profits for reinvestment. The higher the resulting figure for gearing, therefore the higher the degree of risk, as ordinary shareholders should enjoy a greater rate of return from lower-geared companies. Low-geared companies, that is, those under 50%, should provide a lower-risk investment opportunity. Lower-geared companies should also be able to negotiate new loans much more easily than a highly-geared company, as they are not already financed by a high proportion of debt.

The gearing ratio can be altered in several ways depending on whether the organisation wishes to raise or lower its gearing figure.

Raising gearing	**Reducing gearing**
• Buy back ordinary shares.	• Issue more ordinary shares.
• Issue more preference shares.	• Buy back debentures (redeeming).
• Issue more debentures.	• Retain more profits (increase reserves).
• Obtain more loans.	• Repay loans.

Many students often think that raising finance by increasing gearing (taking more loans) is bad, however, the advantage to raising gearing as a method of increasing capital employed rather than, for instance, issuing more shares, is that loans will eventually be paid back, whereas new shareholders will receive dividends for as long as the company is in existence, and that by taking out loans there is no further dilution of the ownership of the business.

Activity

Now calculate the **gearing ratio** for Lomax for the year 2008 and comment upon your result and the company's financial position. (See the worked example below.)

Worked example using the accounts of Lomax plc for 2007 in Figure 4.2*

$$\text{Gearing} = \frac{\text{Long-term liabilities}}{\text{Total capital employed}} \times 100 = ?\%$$

$$= \frac{207,000}{1,313,000} \times 100 = 15.76\%$$

* All results shown for worked examples will be shown to two decimal places where appropriate.

Shareholder ratios

Shareholders and potential shareholders are primarily concerned with assessing the level of return they might gain from an investment in a particular company. These ratios are necessary as the value of shares can vary quite considerably, therefore some mechanism is required in order for accurate comparisons to be made. This area concentrates in the main on the relationship between profits available for distribution (dividends), to shareholders and the value of their shares. They do, however, have the effect of causing companies to suffer pressure from shareholders to achieve short-term profits as against long-term investment sometimes. In other words, shareholders want the maximum amount of profits possible distributed to them, whereas the company may well prefer to retain a greater share. These ratios are obviously principally used by current and potential shareholders, however, managers of a business will also take an interest in how the profits of the company are being used.

DIVIDEND PER SHARE

This is a key ratio for shareholders or potential investors to examine as it simply shows how much money (in pence) each share receives as its dividend (share of profits) payment for the year. This provides shareholders with a guide to how much money they are receiving from the company as it can easily be multiplied up by the number of shares each individual shareholder owns. Alternatively, potential shareholders can use it as a good comparison when deciding where to invest their funds.

Calculating dividend per share

This is found by using the formula:

$$\text{Dividend per share} = \frac{\text{Total ordinary dividend}}{\text{Number of issued ordinary shares}}$$

It is expressed as pence per share.

Note that many companies will pay out dividends in two stages: an interim dividend paid part-way through the year and a final dividend based on year-end profits. This helps to keep shareholder confidence in the business and also eases pressures on cash flow, as dividend payments can be made in two smaller sections rather than one large outflow. When calculating dividend per share it is the total dividend (interim + final) paid over the year that is used.

For example...

Sainsbury's annual profits up 28%

Supermarket Sainsbury's has reported strong growth in profits. Underlying profits reached £488m in the year to 22 March 2008, showing a 28% rise on the year before. Following an interim dividend payment of 3p, the board is recommending a final dividend of 9p per share, bringing the full-year dividend to 12p – an increase of 23%.

Interpreting dividend per share

The interpretation of this is really quite straightforward: the greater the value of dividend per share, the more money shareholders are receiving on their investment. However, it must be recognised that high dividends per share may come at the expense of retaining profits for company growth, so a more long-term view may see lower dividend per share results as being more favourable. However, in reality, the result here needs to be compared with the dividends payments being offered by alternative companies and how much the shares cost to buy.

For example, companies A and B may both declare a dividend per share of 25p, but if it costs £2.00 to buy one share in company A and £3.50 to buy one share in company B, then obviously company A's shares are making a far higher return to their owner. This comparative information can be found by using the dividend yield ratio.

Activity

Now calculate the **dividend per share** for Lomax for the year 2008 and comment upon your result and the company's financial position. (See the worked example below.)

Worked example using the accounts of Lomax plc for 2007 in Figure 4.2*

$$\text{Dividend per share} = \frac{\text{Total ordinary dividend}}{\text{Number of issued ordinary shares}}$$

$$= \frac{50{,}000}{750{,}000} = 6.67\text{p per share}$$

DIVIDEND YIELD

Dividend yield is therefore a continuation on from dividend per share, and compares the return in pence per share with the market cost of buying the share. This provides shareholders and potential shareholders with a far more accurate view of how one share compares against another.

Calculating dividend yield

$$\text{Dividend yield} = \frac{\text{Dividend per share (in pence)}}{\text{Market price (in pence)}} \times 100$$

This is expressed as a percentage.

Interpreting dividend yield

Quite simply: the higher the result, the better, although again, a consideration of retaining profits for long-term use by the business needs to take place. But for shareholders wanting a quick return on their investment, the higher the level of dividend yield, the more money they are making. However, it would definitely need to be compared against previous years and competitor results, as the market value of shares can fluctuate widely across financial periods.

Activity

Now calculate the **dividend yield** for Lomax for the year 2008 and comment upon your result and the company's financial position. (See the worked example on page 63.)

* All results shown for worked examples will be shown to two decimal places where appropriate.

Worked example using the accounts of Lomax plc for 2007 in Figure 4.2*

$$\text{Dividend yield} = \frac{\text{Dividend per share (in pence)}}{\text{Market price (in pence)}} \times 100$$

$$= \frac{6.67}{160} \times 100 = 4.17\%$$

Assessing the value and limitations of ratio analysis in measuring a business's performance

The value of ratio analysis

Financial data can provide vital information about the liquidity, profitability and performance of a business. Accurate financial data and interpretation gives owners, managers and other stakeholder groups an opportunity to make informed decisions to avoid liquidity problems, maximise profits and improve financial efficiency.

Interpretation of the data also allows comparisons to be made between accounting periods of the same firm or to compare the performance of two separate firms in the same type of business. Accurate data are also essential to secure and maintain finance from external sources and to plan the future direction of a business.

Ratio analysis also allows comparisons to be made easily with similar businesses

The limitations of ratio analysis

Although so far in this section we have discussed at length the uses, users and information to be gained from using ratio analysis to examine a business's financial performance, it must be remembered that ratio analysis does not possess the answer to every question or problem a business may face. Using ratios to interpret financial statements has some major drawbacks:

- Accounts cover financial and numerical information only. They make no consideration of workforce morale, management style or developments in market technology. Thus a company whose accounts perform exceptionally well under

* All results shown for worked examples will be shown to two decimal places where appropriate.

analysis could in actuality be facing a workforce that is about to strike, an experienced managing director who is about to retire and a product that is about to become obsolete due to a technological advancement by a competitor.

How much is a brand name such as Heinz worth?

- All the information contained in a set of accounts is historical, that is, it shows what *has* happened, and not what *will* happen. They therefore do not reflect anticipated changes in the economy. In some industries, for example, changes in the rate of exchange can have dramatic effects on their profitability, both good and bad. Thus an awareness of economic policy and political change is also a useful tool when trying to assess the future performance of a business.

- The figures actually presented in the accounts may not necessarily be an accurate representation. For example, assets such as buildings are listed at cost; though this may well be what they cost several years ago it may not be a true reflection of what they are worth now. Similarly, the value of depreciated assets shown is only their book value that may have no bearing whatsoever on their 'true' market value. However, remember that value is subjective, whereas cost can be proven.

- For major businesses like PLCs the picture can become even more muddied. PLCs tend to own intangible assets such as brand names or copyrights. However, how do you accurately determine what a brand name like Virgin or Heinz is actually worth? The difficulty of obtaining a 'true and fair' valuation for these intangible assets makes it entirely possible that businesses can drastically overstate or understate their value in the balance sheet. Only purchased brand names are allowed to be included as intangible assets.

- Although ratio analysis is used as a tool for making inter-firm comparisons, it is actually rather difficult to find two or more companies that make and sell exactly the same product. Taking our two companies mentioned earlier, who else would you compare with Heinz and the range of different products they sell? Similarly, who could you compare with Virgin?

- Finally, there is the issue of 'window dressing' accounts. This is the practice adopted by some companies of massaging their profit figures and balance sheet valuations to make the company look as if it has performed better than it has in reality. One of the main problems that arises here is that a balance sheet shows information for one day only, that being the financial year end date. Businesses may well try to window dress the accounts for this day, thus if the accounts are being examined three months later, the balance sheet being analysed may have no relation whatsoever to the current circumstances of the business.

Summary and exam guidance

Summary

- Financial information and analysis are key elements in business decision-making. Ratio analysis provides an accurate and consistent method for measuring a business's performance.

- **Profitability ratios** measure the performance of a business by looking at how high a return the business makes on the capital invested in it.

- **Liquidity ratios** are concerned with assessing the short-term financial stability of a business.

- **Financial efficiency ratios** are used to measure how effective the business is in its day-to-day operations, such as selling stock or collecting payments for debtors.

- Shareholders and potential shareholders will want to be able to measure how well any money invested in a company performs, that is, what return on investment is made. This is done by calculating the **dividend per share** and **dividend yield ratios**.

- **Gearing** is a particular ratio that is used to compare the level of debt a business has to the total amount of capital employed. It is used to gauge the longer-term financial stability of a business.

- Although beneficial to owners, managers, creditors and many other stakeholder groups when making business decisions, ratio analysis is only an assessment tool of what has happened; it is no guarantee of future performance.

- Ratio analysis only considers the financial performance of a business. It does not take into account any non-monetary factors, such as the morale of employees, state of the market or economy, for example.

Exam practice

Read the article below and then answer the questions that follow.

Article A

Farnworth Foods Ltd is a small chain of frozen food wholesalers operating in the North West of England. In recent years Farnworth Foods have found it increasingly hard to deal with the growing size and price competiveness of the major supermarkets and other frozen good retailers such as Iceland. Farnworth's Managing Director, Bakhtab Patel, is sure the only way to gain back his business's competitive position is to expand and gain from the benefits that being a larger business operation can bring.

At the moment he is considering the possibility of buying one of two potential businesses that are currently on the market. Both are in the same market as Farnworth Foods and as such both businesses have also been suffering. However, Bakhtab is unsure which of the two businesses would present the best investment opportunity.

cont...

	Company A	Company B
	£	£
Net profit	180,000	240,000
Capital employed	500,000	1,200,000
Sales	5,000,000	2,000,000
Mortgage	120,000	150,000
Cost of sales	2,100,000	450,000
Opening stock	200,000	50,000
Closing stock	150,000	30,000
Debtors	300,000	20,500
Long-term loan	Nil	40,000
Creditors	150,000	70,000
Bank/Cash	120,000	(5,000) overdrawn
Dividend paid	80,000	150,000
Number of shares issued	500,000 at £1.00 each	1,200,000 at £1.00 each
Market price	160 pence	125 pence

(a) Calculate the following. (12 marks)

	Company A	Company B
The return on capital employed by each company.		
The net profit margin for each company.		
The rate of stock turnover for each company.		
The dividend yield for each company.		
What is the debtor collection period for each company?		
The level of gearing for each company.		

cont...

(b) Using appropriate ratios, analyse the liquidity position of each company. Why is liquidity an important factor for Bakhtab to consider? (12 marks)

(c) To what extent is ratio analysis a useful tool to Bakhtab in making the decision on which business to purchase? (16 marks)

Total: 40 marks

Breakdown of assessment objectives

AO1 – Knowledge and understanding – 12/40
AO2 – Apply knowledge and understanding – 12/40
AO3 – Analyse problems, issues and situations – 10/40
AO4 – Evaluate, distinguish between fact and opinion, assess and judge information from a variety of sources – 6/40

Suggested structure

For part (a) you will need to:

- Identify the correct formula to use and apply it to the data given for each company.
- State your results using appropriate expressions.

For part (b) you will need to:

- Identify suitable ratios to assess each business's liquidity position.
- Comment on the strengths and weaknesses of each of the business's liquidity position.
- Comment on the significance of your results given the potential purchase of each business.

For part (c) you will need to:

- Consider the ways in which ratio analysis provides useful information to aid decision-making.
- Compare and contrast the usefulness of ratio analysis with its potential limitations.
- Make a fully justified recommendation whether or not ratio analysis is a useful tool to use in this situation. Note that the question is *not* asking you to recommend which business he should purchase.

Chapter 5 Selecting financial strategies

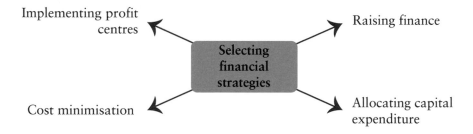

Raising finance

As a business continues to grow and develop, or faces changing market conditions and new challenges, it will often need to be able access new sources of funds to finance its activities and objectives. In Chapter 2 of this section we looked at the potential financial objectives of a business namely:

- cash flow targets
- cost minimisation
- the level of return on capital employed
- shareholders' returns.

In an ideal world it would be great if a business could generate all the finance it needs from its own internal sources, that is, profits, and indeed this is a potential source of finance for many projects and plans undertaken. However, it must be realised that even for very profitable businesses, profits are generated over time and to accumulate substantial funds for investment purposes may well take too long; opportunities could be missed or competitiveness lost as the business tries to 'save up' its profits over time. Therefore businesses must be able to access alternative sources of funding available to them. Alongside this, it must be considered that the use of profits for reinvestment has an impact and knock-on effect to the financial objectives of the business. For example, reinvesting profits in new, more efficient machinery may well help to achieve cost minimisation targets, but would be detrimental to the level of return (dividends) shareholders receive.

The method by which a company chooses to raise additional funding for the business can have a key influence on how the business functions. Students should consider each potential method of raising finance and consider:

- How does this affect the ownership of the business?
- How does this affect the capital structure of the business, in particular, gearing?
- How does this affect the profitability of the business, in both the short and long term?
- How would each method of raising finance affect or impact upon the functional objectives of the company?

We will start with examining retained profits as a method of raising finance, and then look at the alternatives.

Synoptic search

In your AS studies Unit 1, 'Planning and financing a business', you will have covered potential sources of business finance for financing a business start-up. Many of these sources are still applicable for your A2 studies, so it would be worthwhile to refresh yourself of the AS details before starting this section. This section is also connected to the legal structure of the business concerned.

Retaining profits

Retained profits are that proportion of profit that is kept by the business after all costs and expenses have been paid and all taxes and dividends have been accounted for. This is an important source of long-term finance for any business, as it does not have to be paid back at any point to a third party or incur extra costs such as interest charges.

However, it is important for you to realise that often retained profit does not actually represent a big bag full of cash that the business can spend; remember again from AS that profit and cash are not the same thing. So whilst retained profit adds to the financial strength of a company and provides some finance for reinvestment, it must be understood that this profit is built up in small amounts across a financial year and therefore may not actually be matched by cash availability in the business's bank account.

As well as not having to be paid back and no interest charges, retaining profits has the further advantage that there is no dilution in the ownership and control of the business, that is, the current owner(s) do(es) not have to give away a partial stake in the business to someone else who will then want a share of future profits. But the more a business chooses to retain, the less that is distributed to the owners/shareholders themselves. Retaining high levels of profit, whilst a good source for investment, can cause conflict as it means the investors in the business receive a lower short-term return on their investment (lower dividend payments). This therefore frequently causes pressure on organisations not to retain as much profit as they may perhaps like.

Selling shares

Private limited and public limited companies can raise finance by selling shares; sole traders and partnerships can also do this by converting to limited company status, but you need to recall the limitations on private limited companies of selling shares such as:

- the restriction of share capital to £50,000
- the inability of selling shares to the public.

These areas were again covered at AS.

For the purpose of this section we will be concentrating on the larger forms of company structure in the UK, namely PLCs who are quoted on the stock market, have a minimum level of capital of £50,000 and who can sell shares to the general public. Public limited companies can raise finance by selling shares in two ways:

- a public issue of shares
- a rights issue of shares.

A PUBLIC ISSUE OF SHARES

A business can sell shares for the very first time, when it is turning into a PLC, called a flotation, or after it has been an established PLC for a number of years and the business has grown and increased its value. When a business raises money through the selling of shares, it is actually selling off part of the business. The ownership of the business passes to shareholders in the proportion of the amount of shares they have bought. Once a company is listed on the stock exchange, members of the general public, other businesses, investment fund managers or pension fund managers can buy and sell shares in the company. This gives a very wide range of prospective buyers if shares in the business are put up for sale.

Selling shares or additional shares in a public issue has some definite advantages:

- The huge potential target audience of buyers means that for a successful and popular business this can be an easy way to raise very large sums of money relatively quickly – a public issue of new shares can be completed within a three- or four-month time period.
- The capital (money) raised from a public issue of shares never has to be paid back to shareholders. Once sold, the money raised is the company's to keep; if a shareholder wants their investment back, they must find another buyer for their shares.
- The capital raised from the sale of shares carries no interest charges or other costs.

However, selling shares in a public issue also has some disadvantages too:

- New shareholders become part owners and thus will want a share of the profits made by the business (dividend) year after year, for every year that they remain a shareholder. This could potentially be for the life of the business and in the very long term massively outweigh any interest charges the company might have paid.
- As now part-owners, new shareholders will get a say in how the company is run, influencing key decisions and even the company's overall direction and aims. The original owners therefore lose some control of their business even to the potential extent of a possible takeover. This will then have a knock-on effect to the objectives set and direction taken by the individual functional areas within the business itself.
- A public issue can be very expensive; shares need to be advertised and potential buyers attracted. Where and how often would you advertise shares in a major PLC for sale? How much do you think this would cost? It is usual for companies undertaking a public issue of shares to produce a company prospectus – a glossy and attractive brochure advertising the business's success and potential. Alongside this are legal, accounting and administration costs to be met.
- A financial effect will also be felt on dividends, as profits will be more thinly spread because more shares will exist. However, the company could find itself in a stronger position and earn higher profits in future years.

This means that a public issue of shares is only suitable if the business is trying to raise a very substantial sum of money, otherwise the costs make it prohibitively expensive to do. However, if it is a very substantial sum of money the business needs, then this is a very effective method.

For example...

HBOS rights issue

In 2008 HBOS announced plans to raise £4bn of extra funding from existing shareholders through a rights issue. HBOS has about two million shareholders and is the most widely-owned share in a UK company.

HBOS is the second UK bank to announce such a move in response to the impact of the worsening global economy. Companies issue extra shares to raise money. They are offered to existing shareholders, usually at a discount to the current share price.

Existing shareholders will be offered two ordinary shares for every five existing shares they hold for 275 pence per share. HBOS said it was offering the shares at a price that was 45% less than the closing price of 495.75p on 28 April 2008 – the day before the announcement was made.

It says the extra funding would allow it to grow internationally and invest in its residential mortgage and savings business.

This follows from the previous week, when the Royal Bank of Scotland (RBS) announced it was planning a £12bn rights issue – one of the largest seen in UK corporate history.

A RIGHTS ISSUE OF SHARES

A rights issue of shares is similar to a public issue in that the company concerned is offering new shares in the company for sale. However, in this instance the company is not offering them to the general public, but giving existing shareholders the right to buy more shares in the company alongside the ones they already own. This has several key advantages:

- Advertising costs are reduced or removed as the company just needs to write to the shareholders concerned and make the offer.
- If shareholders take up the offer there is no change in the current ownership. Shares are offered to shareholders in proportion to the amount they already own, so there is no further dilution of ownership or control.
- Existing shareholders have demonstrated they already have an interest in the business by purchasing shares previously. This implies they may well be interested in buying more. And due to the substantially lower cost of a rights issue, the shares for sale are often offered at a discount (less than their market value) to convince shareholders to buy them.
- Rights issues can therefore again be used to raise substantial sums of money and at less cost than a public issue.

The drawback though is that the list of potential buyers is limited to existing shareholders and if the rights issue fails to attract enough buyers, the company may well not be able to raise the amount of money it wants/needs and may then face the problems of either not been able to implement their plans or having to seek alternative sources as well.

Debentures

Debentures are an alternative to selling shares as a method of raising long-term finance. However, a debenture is not a share; it is a form of long-term loan. Selling debentures does not dilute the ownership and control of a business – the debenture holder gains no rights to have a say in how the company is run.

DEBENTURES

Advantages

For the company
- They do not dilute the current ownership and control of the business.
- They do not have to be paid back in full until the date they mature.
- They have a fixed lifetime and once paid back they are finished (unlike issuing shares).

For the debenture holder
- They are secured against assets so are fairly low-risk investments.
- They pay a fixed rate of interest which is not dependent on profits (unlike dividends).

Disadvantages

For the company
- Interest must be paid every year of the debenture's life, reducing overall company profits and profit for distribution.
- At the end of its lifetime a debenture must be repaid in full (redeemed).
- Issuing debentures instead of shares raises the gearing level of the business.

A debenture is a form of bond or long-term security, with underlying collateral on which it is secured that records a long-term loan arrangement to the company that carries a fixed rate of interest for a fixed period of time.

For example, an 8% debenture dated until 31 December 2015 would pay the holder an interest rate of 8% of the value of the debenture until 2015, when it would have to be repaid in full. Debentures are usually issued with security against specific assets that belong to the company, so if the company fails to pay the interest or goes into liquidation, the debenture holder has the right to claim and sell the asset their loan was secured on.

Borrowing versus equity

Securing any form of outside funding will inevitably place pressure on owners of a business. Loans will need to be repaid and shareholders demand high returns. Financing a growth strategy therefore needs to be carefully planned and managed. Bank finance in the form of a loan or overdraft is usually cheaper than selling shares/equity in your business – those shares could be worth a lot of money one day. However, unlike shareholders, banks can force a business into liquidation if it does not repay the debt to agreed terms, so taking out bank loans carries increased risk. This can be seen by calculating the gearing ratio of any business.

Excessive debt financing through loans and debentures may also lower the company's credit rating and its ability to raise more money in the future. If a business has too much debt, it may be considered an over-extended, risky and unsafe investment. In addition, it places itself at greater risk of not being able to survive unanticipated economic downturns, credit shortages or interest rate increases.

Synoptic search

Methods of raising finance covered at AS included:

- loans
- overdrafts
- venture capital
- business angels.

It is often the case that when a business needs to raise finance it will use a combination of sources to achieve the level of funding it needs. A business may well be reluctant to rely entirely on loans or a new share issue, and prefer a mixture of sources to be used. You need to be aware of the possible alternative sources of finance covered at AS, as a business may well consider some of these options in a raising finance package.

Conversely, too much equity financing (selling shares) can indicate that you are not making the most productive use of your capital as any increases in shares issued will, in the short term, cause the result for the return on capital employed ratio to decline. This is because even though the business has more capital invested in it, this new capital will take time to generate increased profits.

In reality, for many businesses, raising funds is not an either/or decision and may involve several sources.

Implementing profit centres

A profit centre is a part of a business for which it is possible to identify the costs that it incurs and the revenue that it generates. A common way of describing profit centres is that they are a 'business within a business', that is, each part can set its own budgets and generate its own income statement against which its performance can be measured. Here then it is possible to establish the individual profit of this part of the business, hence the term 'profit centre'.

A profit centre may be:

- a functional department or branch – for example, many department stores like Marks and Spencer will make each department within that store a profit centre, as well as each individual branch;
- a geographical area – such as a sales region or factory location; a business like BMW would consider each different European country as a separate profit centre;
- a brand or product type – a large company, like Unilever, will want to distinguish between the costs of each of its main product types, such as Bird's Eye frozen foods and Wall's ice cream;
- a type of equipment or individual machine – a business may wish to study the cost of running a machine, such as a 'slush' drinks machine in a children's play centre with the revenue it generates;
- an individual – such as a salesperson or manager, whose costs and revenues can be identified to evaluate their benefit to the business.

Any area of a business can be made a profit centre if both the costs incurred by the area and the revenues it brings into the business can be identified. A separate profit and loss account can be drawn up for each centre, allowing the business to make decisions on the basis of what are its most profitable or loss-making centres. Some parts of a business cannot be made full profit centres, because identifying the revenues that they bring in is not possible. The administration element of a business is an example, as this has no revenue-generating aspect of its operations.

You need to consider that although profit centres bring some very definite benefits, they also take considerable time, training, reorganisation and expense to implement. Nor are profit centres suitable for every type of business organisation. For example, a

Each department within stores like Marks and Spencer will have its own profit centre

PROFIT CENTRES

Advantages

- **Accounting** The use of cost and profit centres enables firms to identify specific areas of the business that are inefficient or making a loss. British Airways, for example, identified its London–Belfast route as a loss maker, once it had made each of its routes a separate profit centre. By cutting this route, BA increased its profitability.

- **Organisational** Creating cost and profit centres enables budgetary control to be exercised at a lower level and for smaller units. As discussed in your earlier studies, doing this can provide more easily-identifiable and measurable objectives, clear lines of responsibility and improved coordination.

- **Motivational** Allowing managers and workers to take responsibility for meeting costs and revenue targets within their own profit centre could act as a valuable motivator. It provides opportunities for achievement in meeting targets to be recognised and for involvement in the financial planning, monitoring and review process.

- **Comparison** By comparing similar profit centres, managers can identify efficient and inefficient areas. Managers can then focus their activities on attempting to improve less efficient areas by employing strategies used by more efficient profit centres, thereby making a more profitable business overall.

- **Flexibility** Using profit centres allows geographically diverse businesses to make decisions on a more local level, that is, the market conditions and competition levels for a branch of Starbucks in Paris may not be the same as for a branch located in Glasgow. Thus a large business is able to be more flexible in responding to differing local conditions and consumer wants and needs, for example, carrying different stock levels or varying prices in each branch to reflect what local consumers are willing to pay. This should again lead to lower costs and higher profits for the overall business.

Disadvantages

- **Accounting** Allocating costs to an individual cost or profit centre is not always straightforward. Whereas direct costs, such as raw materials, can easily be attributed to a cost centre, indirect costs – overheads, such as a national marketing campaign – are much more difficult to allocate to individual profit centres. Different methods of allocating overheads to an individual profit centre may create very different impressions about its efficiency.

- **Organisational** Establishing separate profit centres may lead to conflict rather than coordination! Managers and subordinates may not wish to take on additional responsibilities and stress, and employees may struggle to cope. Creating profit centres will involve substantial training for employees, as well as the need to create a new organisational structure and channels for communication throughout.

- **Motivational** Additional responsibility to achieve budget targets for sales or costs may prove demotivating. Managers may feel excessive stress, while feelings of job insecurity may undermine the morale of workers who fear the closure of a loss-making profit centre. Furthermore, decisions to close loss-making profit centres may have a negative impact on the business as a whole. Marks and Spencers' decision to close loss-making European stores had a disastrous public relations effect on the company in the UK.

- **Comparison** Creating profit centres can create rivalry between centres, and managers become unwilling to help each other as they concentrate on making their area 'the best'. Inevitably, comparing centres will lead to a winners and losers situation for some.

- **Flexibility** Allowing each profit centre a certain level of autonomy to respond to local conditions may lead to the profit centre pursuing its own interests, rather than those of the whole business, and competing for funds, financial rewards or even for customers with other centres. Managers may lose focus of the overall business aims and functional objectives, and concentrate solely on their own targets and goals.

For example...

Reorganising a traditional business

In 2007 business turnaround specialist Cameron Gunn and his partners Craig Morgan and Mark Supperstone set up together.

The three put their own money into buying the South Wales bakery *Ferrari's* out of administration. They saved 580 jobs and are now dedicated to making sure the 95 year-old, £12 million turnover company, started by an Italian immigrant, will continue and grow into the future.

In the two years before they bought the company, sales were plummeting by ten per cent each year. That's now been reduced to zero. They took on the entire work force (no redundancies were made) and, discovering that one person had previously been expected to oversee what to them were clearly two separate businesses, separated the bakery business and the retail outlets to create two divisions. Each division had its own manager promoted from within the company.

The bakery factory, at Hirwaun in the Cynon Valley, has been renamed Best Bakeries. The shops will continue to trade as *Ferrari's* (apart from 20 Sweetman's shops acquired last year before the Sweetman's company went into administration). Each division will have to run as a profit centre so the bakery will have to become more competitive and the shops will have to improve their processes and wastage levels to improve the business's profits overall.

Source: heavily adapted from: http://www.execdigital.co.uk/Re-engineering-a-traditional-business_642.aspx

business with a highly-autocratic management may well be unwilling to delegate responsibility and decision-making down the hierarchy. Similarly, a business that employs a lot of unskilled staff may not have the level of employee required to take on the required skills needed.

A business must consider how the move toward profit centres would affect the objectives it has set in each of its functional areas and if the benefits to be gained would outweigh the costs of structural reorganisation and training.

Cost minimisation

For many students the idea of cost minimisation as a financial strategy would seem to be one that is self-evident, that is, surely every organisation would be aiming to achieve this. However, this is not the case; you must remember that any financial strategy adopted will have a far-reaching impact on the functional objectives of each area of the business.

The strategy of cost minimisation implies that the business organisation under consideration is attempting to provide a certain level of service or product at its lowest cost, not the lowest possible cost. For example, a business like Heinz may employ a strategy of cost minimisation in the production of its baked beans by employing strategies of bulk-buying ingredients, minimising waste and reducing times when employees may be standing around idle. This does not mean they are producing a lower-quality, lowest-cost product like other tins of beans available.

Cost minimisation can impact across the functional areas of the business in a range of ways.

THE IMPACT OF COST MINIMISATION

Financial objectives

- Minimising interest payments on loans and overdrafts.
- Improving credit control so that payments from debtors are received on time and the number of bad debts (non-payments) is reduced.

Marketing objectives

- Using the most cost-effective forms of advertising, promotion or research techniques suitable for that company.
- Looking for joint cost promotion opportunities, for example, a washing machine manufacturer and washing powder manufacturer sharing advertising costs and endorsing each other.

Human resource objectives

- Using the most effective forms of training or recruitment and selection processes for different levels and types of employees.
- Employing strategies and techniques to reduce labour turnover and retain the workforce.
- Implementing more flexible working practices and contracts.

Operations management objectives

- Reducing waste.
- Minimising employee idle time.
- Reducing machine/production line non-operating time.
- Lowering stock holding costs.

Joint cost promotion is quite often used between washing machine manufacturers and washing powder manufacturers

Activity

Swiftcover was founded in 2005. It was a unique proposition offering good value car insurance online only. Swiftcover was also the first UK insurance company to offer its customers the convenience of printing their own car insurance certificate.

Unlike most of its competitors who rely on both the telephone and the Internet to sell car insurance, Swiftcover's sole source of business is the Internet. As a result of being an online-only company, customers can do everything they need online using the Swift Space customer area.

Swiftcover advertise themselves with the line:

'100% online car insurance means a faster service – instant, no hassle, car insurance cover, at much lower premiums.'

Using the article above, examine two ways Swiftcover have introduced the strategy of cost minimisation to their business.

Cost minimisation therefore seeks the most cost-effective way of providing the level of quality the company requires. Taken to its extreme, cost minimisation strategies can most effectively be found at what is often referred to as the 'no-frills' end of the market. 'No frills' is a term used to describe any service or product for which the non-essential features have been removed. In business terms, extra services offered to customers for no additional charge may be called a 'frill' – for example, free meals and drinks on short-hop airline journeys. No-frills businesses operate on the principle that by removing luxurious additions, it lowers their costs and customers may then be offered lower prices in return.

Good examples of no-frills cost minimisation organisations may include businesses such as:

- Supermarkets like Lidl and Aldi, where carrier bags are charged for, the businesses have not spent large sums on expensive product displays and fixtures, and they do not provide fresh bakery, deli and butchery options.
- No-frills airlines, who will typically cut overheads by flying from more remote airports (with lower access charges) and by using a standard type of aircraft. Cabin interiors may be fitted out with minimum comforts, dispensing with luxuries such as cushions, video screens, in-flight radio, reclining seats and blinds; whilst not cost minimisation as such, some airlines even sell advertising space inside the aircraft passenger cabin to increase revenue.
- Holidays where customers are expected to make their own arrangements for transfers between airports and accommodation, or there is no travel representative from the company available in the area and in many cases the accommodation provided would be regarded as being at the more basic end of the scale.

However, cost minimisation and especially the 'no frills' strategy can come with some limitations. A strategy of cost minimisation may mean that the business does not have any spare capacity or stocks to deal with unexpected surges in demand or it may well be alienating the market of those customers who prefer a higher or more luxurious product, place or level or service. Alongside this, it must be recognised that by implementing a no-frills approach you may well minimise costs, but it also minimises the price companies can charge.

Skills watch!

AO2

The strategy of cost minimisation is one that can be followed by many business organisations. The key to applying this strategy is to consider how far a particular business can take it. For example, hotel chain Travelodge provides basic no-frills accommodation; guests will not find hairdryers or little bottles of shampoo, conditioner and bubble bath in their rooms. Travelodge try to apply the concept of cost minimisation in every area, but this total approach would not necessarily be suitable to another business organisation in the same industry, for example, one targeting a different consumer segment, such as the Hilton group of hotels.

Travelodge is a good example of cost minimisation – no-frills accommodation at a sensible price

Allocating capital expenditure

Capital expenditure is expenditure by the business on items that are to be used in the business over a long period of time, that is, more than one year. A capital expenditure is incurred when a business spends money either to buy non-current assets (fixed assets) or to add to the value of an existing fixed asset with a useful life that extends beyond one financial year. Capital expenditure is used by a company to acquire or upgrade physical assets such as equipment, machinery or property. In accounting, a capital expenditure is added to the assets on a company's balance sheet, thus increasing the business's assets base.

Included in capital expenditures are amounts spent on:

- buying fixed assets
- delivery, installation and any cost associated with preparing an asset to be used in business
- restoring property or adapting or enhancing it to a new or different use
- improving the capabilities of machinery and equipment.

Capital expenditure as such does not, therefore, have any direct impact on the income statement of a company, but could have a direct effect on profitability, as the purchase, improvement or updating of fixed assets should hopefully lead to the business being more efficient in its operations. In this way the larger the capital expenditure for any given functional area, the more economical and cost-efficient it should become, and with more resources at its disposal, the easier its objectives should be to achieve.

However, any business only has a certain amount of funding available for capital expenditure across the whole business, which needs to be shared out (allocated) to each function. As each function in a business is as important as each other, capital expenditure needs to be allocated on a basis that is seen as been fair and sufficient for each area's needs.

Capital expenditure could be shared out in a variety of ways:

- **Simple method of allocation** – simply dividing the amount of funds available by the number of functional areas so that each area receives an equal share. This is quick and easy, but takes no account of the size and complexity of each function. For example, the Human Resources department is unlikely to require the same amount of capital expenditure on machinery and equipment as Production and Operations would.
- **Allocating using an agreed base** – allocating capital expenditure depending on value, size or number of employees, that is, the larger the area, department or profit centre on the basis selected, the greater the allocation of capital expenditure. This is slightly more equitable than the previous method, but could still be allocating funds to areas that do not at the present require it and underfunding others. Managers will also argue over the basis to be used.
- **Allocation on a rotating basis** – allocating expenditure on a rotational basis, so that each area receives a basic allocation and then once every few years receives an enhanced amount to enable them to upgrade their equipment, IT systems or premises, for example. This system works reasonably well, as each area receives a minimum level of funding and knows it will get the chance to improve when its allocation is enhanced. But this system, and the others above, takes no account of the business's current market, operating conditions, aims and objectives.
- **Zero allocation** – the best but also most complicated system is to use a zero allocation approach, that is, each functional area initially receives no allocation but, based on their objectives and plans for the next financial year, each area must demonstrate and justify what capital expenditure they need and what benefits it will bring. A production manager, for example, would be required to bid for funds to finance specific new machinery for his department, or a branch manager bid for

new fixtures and fittings. This system allows the costs and benefits of each desired capital expenditure to be assessed and allocated to the areas where the company as a whole feels it will bring the most benefit. It also brings the additional benefit of potentially reducing costs for the whole company, as no capital expenditure is undertaken on the basis of spending the area budget for the year – each item of expenditure must be necessary, justified and bring a definite agreed benefit. As with any system in Business Studies though, this is again not without its drawbacks:

- First managers will need to be trained in using the system, making presentations and forecasting/budgeting their needs.
- Putting together bids and presentations is a time-consuming process for managers who could be using their time more effectively.
- Managers who do not get their 'bids' accepted may well feel unappreciated and demotivated by the process.
- There also exists the danger that capital expenditure is allocated on the basis of which manager is the most persuasive, not where it is most needed.

Summary and exam guidance

Summary

- Businesses will often face times when they need to raise finance to provide funds for investment, growth or particular activities. There are various sources of finance available to a firm, but each may have an impact on the ownership, gearing and long- and short-term profitability of a firm.

- Businesses need to match the level of finance they need to an appropriate source, or combination of sources, and assess the impact and knock-on effect of any methods chosen to the operations of the functional areas of the firm.

- Profit centres are a method of splitting a business into smaller parts so that they can more easily be monitored, compared and assessed. This should in turn improve management decision-making, efficiency and profitability. However, this process can be costly and time-consuming and may not be suited to every type of organisation.

- Some businesses may follow a strategy of cost minimisation, that is, providing an agreed level of quality for the lowest cost possible. Cost minimisation can be applied across the functional areas in an effort to achieve greater efficiencies and improve profits. At its extreme, cost minimisation can be seen most clearly at the no-frills end of any market.

- The performance of any functional area will be affected by the level and modernity of assets available for its use. Capital expenditure is vital for many areas in remaining up to date and competitive. Functional areas thus compete for capital expenditure allocations to improve their potential performance. Although varying methods of allocating capital expenditure exist, any allocation made should be done with a focus on the functional objectives to be achieved.

Exam practice

Read the article below and then answer the questions that follow.

Article A

Double Express plc

Starting in 2002 after a holiday to Japan, Naeem Patel decided it was time to open his own business based upon his Japanese holiday experience, and he has now built his success up, owning 54 outlets across the UK and a turnover of £16 million. His idea was a success from the start and growth in his segment was rapid, despite competition from established high-end operators like Starbucks, Caffè Nero and Costa Coffee. Double Express's success had been built on targeting the no-frills end of the market.

Naeem developed a simple but effective business model and identity. Double Express was built on the foundation of those customers who want a coffee and snack on the go and who don't want to pay over-the-top prices. Double Express outlets are, as far as possible, identically laid out with identical products available at each. Each outlet consists of a range of vending machines selling hot drinks and snacks with basic seating areas. The outlets do not offer customers toilet facilities or any staff service at all. Each outlet is open 24/7 and placed in busy city centre locations, mainline train stations or airports and has one member of staff, working 8.00am until 5.00pm, whose job it is to stock machines, call out maintenance if required and remove and bank cash taken at the end of the day.

Naeem has had a deliberate policy of spending as little as possible on marketing, training and finance costs. The expansion of Double Express was rapid following its flotation in 2005, and growth has been financed mainly through the increased investment by shareholders and some retained profits. But Naeem wants the business to expand and grow further before rivals set up and start to compete for his customers. He has suggested another public issue of shares to raise finance.

However, some of the other directors wish to assess their current situation before further expansion. In particular, some are concerned that although the overall business is doing well, they currently do not know how successful each individual outlet is and what locations are the most profitable. A suggestion has been put forward to the board to examine the possibility of each outlet being its own profit centre.

(a) Examine two disadvantages to Naeem and Double Express plc of using a public issue of shares to raise finance. (10 marks)

(b) Double Express has deliberately employed a strategy of cost minimisation; examine the advantages and disadvantages of this approach. (12 marks)

(c) To what extent do you agree with the proposal for each Double Express outlet to become a profit centre? (18 marks)

Total: 40 marks

Breakdown of assessment objectives

AO1 – Knowledge and understanding – 8/40
AO2 – Apply knowledge and understanding – 10/40
AO3 – Analyse problems, issues and situations – 10/40
AO4 – Evaluate, distinguish between fact and opinion, assess and judge information from a variety of sources – 12/40

Suggested structure

For part (a) you will need to:

- Identify and explain at least two factors that may have a negative impact on Naeem, the company and other shareholders.
- Break down your reasons why these are disadvantages into clear paragraphs that apply to circumstances of a business that has grown and developed in the way Double Express has.

For part (b) you will need to:

- Consider the benefits to be gained from such an approach contrasted with limitations and disadvantages that may occur as well.
- Apply your arguments to the situation and context of the business and target market of Double Express.
- Reach a conclusion that is fully justified as to whether this approach is suitable in the context of this market.

For part (c) you will need to:

- Discuss the advantages and disadvantages to a business like Double Express of introducing profit centres.
- Include a detailed analysis of factors that would impact on the decision being made and the extent to which they have an influence.
- Make a fully justified recommendation whether or not Double Express should implement this strategy.

Chapter 6 Making investment decisions

Key terms

Average rate of return (ARR) A method of investment appraisal that measures the average profitability of an investment per annum as a percentage of the original outlay.

Discount factor The amount used to reduce the value of future cash inflows such that they represent the value of money at its actual value in current terms.

Discounting The process of reducing future cash inflows to account for the time value of money (this is the fact that the value of money decreases over time, that is, you cannot buy the same amount of goods with £100 now as you could have bought 10 years ago).

Interest rate The cost of borrowing money or the return on money deposited in a bank. This is the factor that is used as the basis of the cost of capital for an investment project and for calculating the discount factor.

Investment appraisal The term given to the application of a set of quantitative methods used to judge the viability of individual investment opportunities.

Net present value (NPV) The total return of an investment expressed in current monetary value terms (total **discounted** cash inflow less initial investment).

Payback A method of investment appraisal that measures how long an investment takes to recover its own cost.

Qualitative factors Issues surrounding an investment decision that are not based on financial information but are based on subjective data (opinions, feelings, qualities, hunches, and so on); they often involve consideration of factors such as environmental concerns or impact on employee morale.

Quantitative factors Those that are measurable and can be calculated to give comparable results on potential investments.

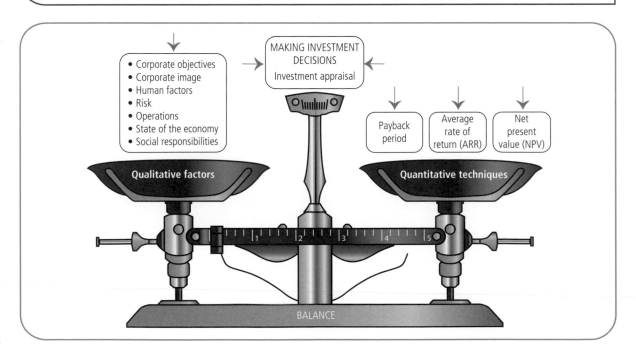

Conducting investment appraisal: selection of appropriate methods, calculation and interpretation of findings

Why do businesses invest?

Businesses frequently have to make capital investments, either to replace old, worn-out assets, to buy new ones for expansion or to update machinery and products to remain competitive. However, because finance is limited, they often have to choose between different investments. For instance, a business may have to choose:

- between two alternative production locations
- to launch one product rather than another
- to purchase one machine rather than another
- between different types of training for staff
- what type of vehicle to purchase and then which make and model.

Football clubs, for example, may even conduct investment appraisal between which players to potentially buy.

Businesses must make these choices all the time. Equipment, machinery, vehicles and even premises will all need replacing at some point, or expanding if the business is growing.

Businesses will also need to undertake investment decisions in order to remain competitive in their marketplace. Again, this could be the choice between launching different products, the purchase of new technology to keep up to date or the purchase of a new location, for example.

Businesses will also invest to help achieve the objectives of functional areas of the business. For example, achieving 10% growth in market share will require investment in marketing campaigns and operations. To launch new products requires investment in research and development, as well as possibly new machinery and staff training to produce the new product. Similarly, improvements in production techniques, productivity, output, cost and efficiency may again require investment in new machinery and training. A very simple example of this in operation is if a company wants to see an improvement in customer service quality levels, it would have to invest in a training programme for staff.

The example at the top of the next page outlines one interesting area of business investment.

Football clubs may conduct investment appraisal between which players to buy

Quantitative methods, selection, calculation and interpretation of findings

To help businesses make these choices, there are a range of quantitative techniques (methods that use numerical data) that allow investment opportunities to be compared. This is known as investment appraisal. The three main methods used are:

- payback
- average rate of return (ARR)
- net present value (NPV).

Each method compares the expected level of cash inflows or return each project is likely to make over the course of its lifetime, but each method examines a slightly different set of criteria

Keeping a tag on them

Employees in warehouses across Britain are being 'electronically tagged' by being asked to wear small computers to cut costs and increase the efficient delivery of goods and food to supermarkets.

The change in working practices comes as companies invest in new US satellite- and radio-based computer technology. The technology is spreading rapidly, with up to 10,000 employees using it and investment in the product by household names such as Tesco, Sainsbury's, Asda, Boots and Marks and Spencer.

Employees wear computers on their wrists, arms and fingers that tell them where to go to collect goods from warehouse shelves. The system also allows supermarkets direct access to the individual's computer so orders can be beamed straight from the store. The computer can also check on whether workers are taking unauthorised breaks and work out the shortest time a worker needs to complete a job.

The companies say the system makes the delivery of food more efficient, cuts out waste, lowers costs, reduces theft and can reorder goods more quickly. This helps the business to achieve a whole range of functional objectives.

Other monitoring devices are being developed in the US, including ones that can check on the productivity of secretaries by measuring the number of key strokes they make on their word processors; satellite technology is also being developed to monitor productivity in manufacturing jobs.

Two London firms are considering investing in satellite technology to direct sandwich board holders, making sure they are not shirking, and moving them to areas with more people to make their advertising message more effective.

Source: adapted from http://www.guardian.co.uk/technology/2005/jun/07/supermarkets.workandcareers

so there is no one method that is better than the others. Businesses will typically use several methods alongside a consideration of qualitative factors when making investment decisions.

Payback

The simplest form of investment appraisal is the payback method. This method measures how long an investment takes to pay back its original investment (its initial cost). A business comparing investments is likely to choose the project with the shortest payback period; this is because the shorter the payback period, the quicker the project covers its own cost and starts to generate money for the business. In calculating payback periods it is normal for businesses to work to the nearest month.

The payback period for an investment project is found by calculating the net yearly cash inflows the project is expected to achieve over its estimated life and then deducting the cost of the project to find out how long it takes before the project has effectively paid for itself.

This is found by using the formula:

Payback period = number of full years + ((amount left to pay/cash inflow in the following year) × 12)

This gives an answer of X number of years and Y months.

Initial cost of investment = £1,000,000

	Expected net cash inflows	Has it paid for itself?	Amount left to pay
Year 1	£240,000	No	£760,000
Year 2	£240,000	No	£520,000
Year 3	£240,000	No	£280,000
Year 4	£240,000	No	£40,000
Year 5	£240,000	Yes	

Figure 6.1   Calculating payback: example 1

So in the example in Figure 6.1, the number of full years = 4
The amount left to pay after 4 years = £40,000
The cash inflow in the following year (year 5) = £240,000
Therefore, applying the formula:

Payback period = 4 + ((40,000/240,000) × 12) = 4 years and 2 months
to the nearest month

However, things aren't always this simple. In the example in Figure 6.1, the project made constant returns each year; this is rarely the case. In some cases returns will be initially low as employees get used to using new equipment or a new product takes time to gain a foothold in the market. Similarly, with many investment projects returns may start to decline in later years as machinery becomes less efficient or products start to reach maturity and decline stages.

Initial cost of investment = £300,000

	Expected net cash inflows	Has it paid for itself?	Amount left to pay
Year 1	£100,000	No	£200,000
Year 2	£100,000	No	£100,000
Year 3	£150,000	Yes	
Year 4	£240,000		

Figure 6.2   Calculating payback: example 2

In Figure 6.2, the investment clearly pays back the initial cost of investment in the third year, but by the end of the third year £50,000 more has been generated than is needed.
Again, to calculate the payback period, the same formula is used:

Payback period = number of full years + ((amount left to pay/cash inflow in the following year) × 12)
Payback period = 2 + ((100,000/150,000) × 12) = 2 years and 8 months

It is important to note that what happens to cash inflows after an investment has repaid its original outlay is ignored. Payback is used solely to calculate how long a project takes to cover

PAYBACK METHOD

Advantages

- Easy to calculate.
- Takes into account cost of investment.
- Focuses on short-term cash flow (a business might want to know how quickly new IT equipment will pay for itself, as it is likely to have a very short, useful life).
- Useful for businesses with poor cash flow that need projects to start generating returns on their investments quickly.

Disadvantages

- Ignores the overall return on a project.
- Ignores the time value of money.
- Encourages a short-term approach (an investment with a longer payback period may actually be more profitable for the business).

its own cost, that is, to pay for itself. Payback does not consider which project would make the most money/profit overall. For this reason, the payback method is often used alongside other methods of investment appraisal.

Skills watch!

A02

Learning and understanding any type of mathematical calculation can really be enhanced with practice. Completing example calculations will help you to be able to apply your knowledge to other business situations.

Use the following information to calculate the payback period for two potential investments. Which option would you recommend?

OPTION 1 Initial cost = £500,000	OPTION 2 Initial cost = £550,000
Expected returns	Expected returns
Year 1 – £100,000	Year 1 – £80,000
Year 2 – £100,00	Year 2 – £200,000
Year 3 – £150,000	Year 3 – £220,000
Year 4 – £240,000	Year 4 – £240,000

Average rate of return

The average rate of return (ARR) method measures the average annual profit generated by a project, expressed as a percentage of the total investment cost. This allows businesses to compare the average profit from different projects and to see which gives the best percentage return on its initial outlay (the cost of the project). Remember this was something payback did *not* do.

The formula used is:

$$\text{Average rate of return (ARR)} = \frac{\text{Average annual profit}}{\text{Initial cost of investment}} \times 100 = ?\%$$

STEPS TO CALCULATING ARR

Step 1

Calculate the **total profit** the project would make over its estimated life, that is, add up cash inflows made each year and deduct the project's initial cost:

Total profit = Total net cash inflows − Initial cost of investment

Step 2

Work out the **average annual profit** made by dividing the total profit from Step 1 by the estimated lifetime of the project:

$$\text{Average annual profit} = \frac{\text{Total profit}}{\text{Project lifetime}}$$

Step 3

Calculate the **ARR** by applying the formula:

$$\text{Average rate of return (ARR)} = \frac{\text{Average annual profit}}{\text{Initial cost of investment}} \times 100 = ?\%$$

Example – calculating ARR

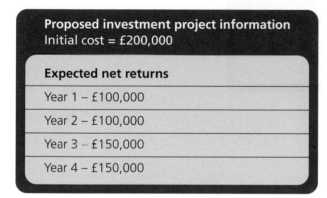

Proposed investment project information
Initial cost = £200,000

Expected net returns
Year 1 – £100,000
Year 2 – £100,000
Year 3 – £150,000
Year 4 – £150,000

Calculation Average rate of return is calculated by dividing the total profit from an investment by the number of years over which that profit is earned.

- **Step 1:**

    Total profit = Total income − Initial cost

    Total income = £100,000 + £100,000 + £150,000 + £150,000 = £500,000
    Initial cost = £200,000
    So total profit = £500,000 − £200,000 = **£300,000**

- **Step 2:**

    $$\text{Average annual profit} = \frac{\text{Total profit}}{\text{Project lifetime}} = \frac{£300,000}{4 \text{ years}}$$
    $$= \textbf{£75,000} \text{ per year}$$

- **Step 3:**

    $$\text{Average rate of return (ARR)} = \frac{\text{Average annual profit}}{\text{Initial cost of investment}} \times 100 = ?\%$$

    $$\text{So ARR} = \frac{£75,000}{£200,000} \times 100 = \textbf{37.5\%}$$

Once calculated, the percentage return of one investment can be compared with the percentage return of other investments. Investment with higher values of ARR will be preferred. However, where the ARR is very low, for example, less than 7%, the investment might be rejected in favour of an alternative investment, such as a high-interest bank account. ARR can therefore be used to compare investments and to set a lower limit on expected returns below which a business would reject all investments.

ARR focuses on the key decision-making factor for investment decisions, that is, the overall profitability of an investment, as it takes into account all the cash inflows generated over the project's entire life. However, ARR ignores the timing of cash flows. The quicker a project pays back its initial outlay, the lower the risk. ARR does not take this into account. A project with a high ARR but a long payback period is likely to be favoured over a quick payback period and a lower ARR. However, there are some circumstances when a quick payback period will be favoured, such as by a business with a poor current cash flow position.

Consider the following example shown in Figure 6.3. Using this information, Project 2 would be chosen as it has a higher average rate of return, that is, it is more profitable. But Project 1 is less risky as it pays for itself quicker and although it has a lower ARR, it would start generating profits sooner.

However, based solely on the ARR method, Project 2 would be chosen.

	Payback result	ARR result
Project 1	2 years 8 months	22%
Project 2	3 years 7 months	26%

Figure 6.3 Comparing ARR and payback results

Skills watch!

A02

Although the key skill is in calculating the required figures, an important aspect is to also understand what the results mean. In this example, try to develop an extended answer that demonstrates the reason behind your choice for part (b).

(a) Use the following information to calculate the ARR for two potential investments.

(b) Which option would you recommend?

OPTION 1 Initial cost = £500,000	OPTION 2 Initial cost = £600,000
Expected returns	**Expected returns**
Year 1 – £120,000	Year 1 – £180,000
Year 2 – £140,00	Year 2 – £220,000
Year 3 – £170,000	Year 3 – £240,000
Year 4 – £240,000	Year 4 – £260,000

AVERAGE RATE OF RETURN (ARR) METHOD

Advantages

- Measures profitability.
- Easy to compare percentage returns against other investments.
- Considers the total profit made over the whole of the project's life.

Disadvantages

- Ignores the timing of cash flows.
- Ignores the time value of money.
- Ignores the risk factor of having a long payback period.

Net present value

The payback period and ARR methods of investment appraisal do not consider the impact of time and its effect on the value of money. The length of time over which investment returns are made affects the true value of those returns.

For a start, inflation erodes the value of money. A pound (£1) today is worth more than it will be in five, 10 or 15 years' time. What you can buy today with a pound may well cost two pounds in five years' time. From an investment point of view £100,000 received today is worth more than £100,000 received in five years' time.

Added to this is the opportunity cost of investing. If interest rates are 5%, then £50,000 left in a bank would increase to £63,814 over five years. As shown with ARR, any investment must better the potential return from merely investing money in the bank. It can also be seen that £50,000 kept 'under a mattress' will effectively decrease in value over that period. No interest will be earned over that period and inflation will erode its purchasing power – its relative value has therefore fallen.

Added to these is the 'risk factor': any income from investment projects is estimated – it is forecasted or projected income, and there can be no guarantee that the promise or estimation of cash inflows from a project five years into the future is accurate. For example, investment in new machinery can be quickly nullified by technological advances; a new product launch can quickly flop if a competitor responds by launching something better. In accordance with this, therefore, it always better to have real money now than promises of money in the future.

For a business this means that the money it receives from an investment in future years will not have the same value as it does today. Receiving £1,000,000 from an investment in five years' time might sound good, but how much will £1,000,000 really be worth then, relative to its value today? A business must consider whether to risk investing the money now or whether it will be better just to put the money into a bank account.

At a simple level, to determine the true value of investment returns over their life, interest rates are used to calculate a **discount factor**. Future returns from an investment are discounted (reduced) according to predicted interest rates for the years ahead, that is, it is like working interest out but backwards. In practice, firms often use discounting factors over and above the rate of interest. This is done to take account of the level of risk involved and the potential returns of other, perhaps safer, investments.

By discounting the future value of money down, the business achieves what is known as the 'present value' of money, that is, what money in the future is really worth in today's terms. Appropriate discount factors are based on what the business believes the average rate of interest will be over the life of the project. Don't worry: you don't have to calculate these; tables of discount factors for varying rates of interest were worked out long ago. All you have to do is discount down future cash inflows to their present value using the discount factors that will be given to you.

For example...

Assume a business wishes to undertake an investment project and estimates the normal rate of interest will be 6% over the project's life. Using discount factor tables, the discounts to be applied each year would be:

Discount factor
Year 1 – 0.94
Year 2 – 0.89
Year 3 – 0.84
Year 4 – 0.79

Project information Initial cost = £250,000

Expected net returns
Year 1 – £100,000
Year 2 – £100,000
Year 3 – £125,000
Year 4 – £150,000

Calculating present values

	Expected returns		Discount factor		Present value
Year 1	£100,000	×	0.94	=	£94,000
Year 2	£100,000	×	0.89	=	£89,000
Year 3	£125,000	×	0.84	=	£105,000
Year 4	£150,000	×	0.79	=	£118,500
Total discounted returns					**£406,500**

Once the discounted returns are known, a business can calculate the net present value (NPV) of an investment. This compares the discounted income against the cost of the project:

Total income at present value = **£406,500**
Less initial cost = (£250,000)
Net present value = £156,500

At today's values, the project would return £156,500 more than it cost. When comparing investments, the project with the highest NPV will be chosen.

If the final result for the NPV calculation is a negative figure (a minus number), then the project will be rejected. This is because the cost of the project is therefore higher than the total income it is expected to generate at present values. Investment projects are only worth carrying out if the NPV value is positive.

NET PRESENT VALUE METHOD

Advantages

- Takes the discounted time value of money into account.
- Considers the total returns made over the project's life.

Disadvantages

- More complex to calculate.
- More difficult to communicate results to non-financial managers.
- Difficult to compare projects with different initial investment costs.

Skills watch!

Use the following information to calculate the NPV for two potential investments. Which option would you recommend? The business estimates the normal rate of interest will be 10% over the project's life. Using discount factor tables, the discounts to be applied each year would be:

Discount factor
Year 1 – 0.91
Year 2 – 0.83
Year 3 – 0.75
Year 4 – 0.68

OPTION 1 Initial cost = £500,000	OPTION 2 Initial cost = £500,000
Expected returns	**Expected returns**
Year 1 – £110,000	Year 1 – £240,000
Year 2 – £150,00	Year 2 – £150,000
Year 3 – £150,000	Year 3 – £150,000
Year 4 – £240,000	Year 4 – £100,000
Total = £650,000	**Total = £650,000**

Investment criteria

Quantitative factors

For each of the quantitative techniques outlined it is likely that a business will set predetermined minimum criteria that any potential investment project must pass before it is accepted. This is because the three methods outlined above can give conflicting results. As we have seen when comparing two projects, a project with the highest ARR does not have to have the fastest payback time. Similarly, having now introduced discount factors, the total NPV of a project is determined not only by the total returns (inflows) made, but also by the timing of those returns. The further away in years the cash inflow is, the lower its present value is, for example. Under this scenario, it is quite possible for a project with the highest ARR value to also possess the lowest NPV result. Thus preset criteria are used so that a potential project must pass all quantitative tests before investment takes place. The exact criteria will vary from business to business depending on their size, marketplace and resources available to them. However, businesses may set a range of criteria such as:

- payback must be sooner than three years
- ARR must be higher than 20%
- NPV must be positive and exceed £100,000.

These processes help businesses to rate and rank investment proposals and select the overall best option available, or even reject all projects put forward if none meet the prescribed criteria. However, the business may also take into account qualitative factors as set criterion when making investment decisions.

Qualitative factors

When conducting investment appraisal, a business will take into account qualitative data as well as quantitative data. Profitable investments may be rejected in favour of less profitable ones for a variety of qualitative reasons:

- **Corporate objectives** Which investment most closely suits corporate objectives? Are profit objectives long term or short term? A firm with long-term profit horizons

For example...

Innocent drinks

innocent drinks produce a range of fruit smoothies. In their own words: 'We call them *innocent* because our drinks are always completely pure, fresh and unadulterated. Anything you ever find in an *innocent* bottle will always be 100% natural and delicious.'

If you visit the *innocent* drinks website and look at the section entitled 'Our ethics'/ 'Sustainable packaging' you will find the following information:

sustainable packaging

We want our packaging to have the lowest possible impact on the world around us.

We aim for 4 main sustainability characteristics in our packaging:

- To use 100% recycled or 100% renewable material in our packaging. All our bottled smoothies are now cradled in **100% recycled plastic bottles.**

- To use the least possible amount of material per pack.
- To use materials with a low carbon footprint.
- To use materials for which there is a widely available sustainable waste management option.

Due to their brand and corporate image it is very unlikely that a company such as *innocent* drinks would invest in projects that would spoil, ruin or damage their reputation with consumers.

Source: http://www.innocentdrinks.co.uk/us/ethics/ sustainable_packaging/

may consider investments with long payback periods, whereas a business facing a cash flow crisis may prefer shorter payback periods.

- **Corporate image** A business will consider how an investment project will affect its overall image and brand (for example, it would be unwise for Ferrari to invest in speed camera manufacture!), and many businesses now promote themselves on their ethical stance and so would not undertake investment projects that would tarnish their image and brand.
- **Human factors** A business may reject an investment simply because it is not favoured by management. The opinions of staff, the need for staff training, potential redundancies and the effect on workplace culture may all be taken into account.
- **Risk** The degree of risk a business is willing to take might affect investment decisions. Virgin is willing to take risks, whereas Marks and Spencer has traditionally avoided risk.
- **Operations** Which investment most suits current production capacity? What effect will the investment have on current production? Will quality standards be maintained? A business may have close links with its currents suppliers and be reluctant to trade with new suppliers.
- **State of the economy** The current state of the economy and economic forecasts will have a big effect on investments. If economic conditions are difficult (such as those faced in 2008), a business is unlikely to invest heavily.

- **Social responsibilities** Many businesses will also take into account their social responsibilities when making investment decisions, particularly in areas like environmental concerns, pollution, use of sustainable resources and impact on stakeholder groups, for example, noise or traffic impacts on local communities.

Assessing risks and uncertainties of investment decisions

Investment decisions are, by their very nature, risky. It is usually expensive, meaning that potential losses are high. It is often long term, making forecasting difficult, and it is usually at least semi-permanent. Take, for example, building new production facilities. This will almost certainly be expensive, it may take a year or more to complete and, by the time it is complete, market conditions may have changed – hence it is risky. Once complete, the building may not be easy for the business to sell if the facility is no longer required. Therefore the decision is, to some extent, permanent.

Forecasting future revenues could prove to be inaccurate for various reasons and each business would need to make an individual assessment of the following when determining the level of risk of any investment:

- The length of time of the project – the further into the future a business forecasts, the less accurate and more risky a proposal becomes.
- The source of any information on which forecasts are based – small businesses are unlikely to be able to afford in-depth research. Businesses should question where forecast data comes from, how it was gathered and how reliable it is.
- The type of market they operate in – the faster the market moves, for example, fashion or high-technology goods, the more uncertain any future projections become.
- The size of the investment compared to the size of the total company – that is, how much they are risking compared to their overall financial strength. For example, £20 million may sound a lot but many football teams would pay considerably more than this just for one player.
- Future economic prospects and whether the economy is heading toward boom or slump conditions at any point over the project's estimated life.
- The type of investment project they are undertaking – there is a large variation in risk factors associated with launching a new product to existing customers compared to diversification into new products and markets, perhaps in a new emerging market overseas.

Businesses may also need to borrow money in order to finance any investment project. This in itself involves a risk as the business puts itself into debt to a third party such as a bank, and guarantees to make payments to repay the money borrowed. A business that fails to uphold any loan agreement can find itself facing legal action from lenders and ultimately, in extreme cases, liquidation. Thus businesses also face this potential risk if any investment project undertaken does not make cash returns or profits as expected.

Evaluating quantitative and qualitative influences on investment decisions

The quantitative results obtained by using any of the three methods outlined in this chapter are only as accurate as the data upon which they are based and calculated and as such, could prove to be highly inaccurate, especially in times of changing market environment or periods of uncertainty about future economic conditions.

However, the alternative, therefore, is to use no quantifiable methods at all and base all investment decision-making on the basis of experience, hunches/gut feeling and/or guesswork; potentially this is an even more inexact method than the quantitative methods outlined.

By using pre-set criteria as a basis for investment decision-making, risk factors can be accounted for by making the criteria more **sufficient**, that is, harder to pass, and so managers can introduce a degree of safety margin and certainty into their decision-making processes. Alongside this, market research, forecasting techniques and computer software packages allowing businesses to model 'what if' situations are all continuously improving, allowing businesses to more accurately simulate potential situations and scenarios to aid decision-making.

Finally, recent years have seen more and more businesses accept the ideas of social responsibility and ethical decision-making, and it is the more qualitative factors that are having a key influence on investment decisions.

For example...

Ethics or profits?

Tesco.com is the first company in the UK to run a fleet of battery-powered zero-emission home delivery vans. 'The carbon neutral vans we have ordered for the dotcom business are both quiet and pollution free – a double benefit for urban environments.'

The vans, supplied by Coventry-based company Modec, have the same carrying capacity as a standard Tesco.com van, cover a range of over 100 miles before they need recharging and are governed at a maximum speed of 50 m.p.h.

Modec benefits from considerable savings relating to operating costs. Paying zero road tax, zero operator licence and, where applicable, zero congestion charge are just some of the financial incentives associated with this vehicle. Minimal servicing costs are incurred and the threat of rising fuel prices means the Modec makes economic sense in the long run.

When Tesco bought new Modec zero emission electric delivery vans for its online shopping deliveries, it was definitely being socially responsible.

Summary and exam guidance

Summary

- Businesses will undertake investment projects for a variety of reasons. These include replacement of assets, expansion and maintaining a competitive position.

- Payback is the simplest method of investment appraisal and measures how long a project takes to cover its initial cost. It does not consider overall profits made.

- Average rate of return (ARR) does consider the overall average level of profits, but does not calculate the payback period.

- Net present value (NPV) uses discounting techniques to take into account the time value of money – something neither payback nor ARR do. NPV does consider the overall returns made but does not consider payback period.

- Each method focuses on different criteria for appraisal, so businesses should never use just one method. By using pre-set criteria to judge the viability of projects, businesses can reduce the risk of investment decision-making.

- Qualitative factors also need to be considered when making investment decisions, such as the affect on corporate image or the workforce required.

- All investment decisions carry a degree of risk as they are usually long-term projects. Businesses need to make an assessment of the level of risk associated with any proposal before deciding to proceed or not.

- In recent years the assessment of qualitative factors, such as social responsibility and business ethics, have had an increasing influence on business investment decisions, especially since nowadays many large corporations undertake and publish social audit information.

Exam practice

Read the article below and then answer the questions that follow.

Article A

Magazine makeover

Mint is an established, popular, fortnightly magazine aimed at 'tweenage girls' (10–13-year olds). The magazine features news, fashion, interviews, a problem page and all the other usual features of such a genre, and has achieved great success in the market at times. However recently, competition in its marketplace has increased with the launch of a rival magazine, and sales of *Mint* have started to decline.

By interviewing a small focus group of 'tweenagers', the publishers of *Mint* have come to the conclusion that their current publication is now becoming somewhat dated in its appearance and content, and that their target market is looking for a magazine product that is seen as being a bit more cutting edge.

The publishers of *Mint* are therefore considering two options:

- **Option 1** A complete relaunch, with the magazine renamed, redesigned and rebranded. The content would remain broadly similar, but would be upgraded to appeal to a wider age range and have a supporting website featuring protected chat room facilities, games and updates on celebrity gossip, fashion and follow-ups to the magazine stories. The new hook is that access codes to different website areas will change each fortnight and girls must purchase the magazines to gain the new codes.

- **Option 2** The magazine undergoes a makeover. It would keep its established title and content would remain virtually unchanged, but the style and appearance of the magazine would be changed to reflect a more modern design and audience.

The following investment information has been drawn up.

Option	1 Relaunch	2 Makeover
Initial cost	£150,000	£50,000
	Projected returns	
Year 1	£45,500	£27,300
Year 2	£41,500	£20,750
Year 3	£37,500	£12,750
Year 4	£34,000	£8,840

The company estimate that the average cost of capital across the project's life will be 10% and gained the following discount table:

Year	8%	10%	15%
1	0.93	0.91	0.87
2	0.86	0.83	0.76
3	0.79	0.75	0.66
4	0.74	0.68	0.57
5	0.68	0.62	0.50

(a) Examine two qualitative factors that *Mint* may wish to consider when making their investment appraisal decision. (10 marks)

(b) Using appropriate financial techniques, assess the relative merits of the two options. (12 marks)

(c) Using your findings from part (b) and any other relevant information, discuss which option the publisher should choose. Justify your decision. (18 marks)

Total: 40 marks

Breakdown of assessment objectives

AO1 – Knowledge and understanding – 8/40
AO2 – Apply knowledge and understanding – 13/40
AO3 – Analyse problems, issues and situations – 10/40
AO4 – Evaluate, distinguish between fact and opinion, assess and judge information from a variety of sources – 9/40

Suggested structure

For part (a) you will need to:

- Identify and explain at least two qualitative factors that may have an impact on this decision.
- Break down your reasons into clear paragraphs that apply to the circumstances of a business producing a magazine focused at 'tweenagers'.
- Provide a considered response that details how the qualitative factors may have an influence on any decision made.

For part (b) you will need to:

- Apply suitable techniques to assess the relative strengths/viability of each option.
- Offer a detailed explanation of your findings.
- Comment on the significance of your results.

For part (c) you will need to:

- Use your findings from part (b) to make an assessment about which option is the most financially viable.
- Include a detailed analysis of any other factors that would impact on the decision being made and the extent to which they have an influence.
- Make a fully justified recommendation on which option *Mint* should choose to follow.

In the AS book, marketing was dealt with at an introductory level with the focus on marketing in small businesses and for business start-ups. In the A2 book, marketing will be looked at from the perspective of a larger business, from a corporate level. Many of the basic principles about marketing in the AS book need to be remembered and used in this section. Larger businesses, however, have the funds to be able to carry out more sophisticated marketing activities and will also adopt a scientific approach to decision-making on marketing. This involves analysis of existing and new markets, building up evidence for marketing activities and using evidence to inform decision-making.

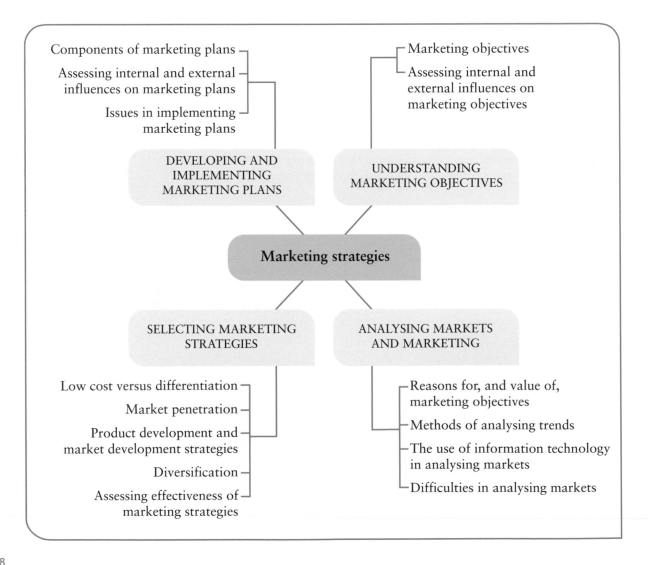

Components of marketing plans

Assessing internal and external influences on marketing plans

Issues in implementing marketing plans

Marketing objectives

Assessing internal and external influences on marketing objectives

DEVELOPING AND IMPLEMENTING MARKETING PLANS

UNDERSTANDING MARKETING OBJECTIVES

Marketing strategies

SELECTING MARKETING STRATEGIES

ANALYSING MARKETS AND MARKETING

Low cost versus differentiation

Market penetration

Product development and market development strategies

Diversification

Assessing effectiveness of marketing strategies

Reasons for, and value of, marketing objectives

Methods of analysing trends

The use of information technology in analysing markets

Difficulties in analysing markets

Chapter 7 Understanding marketing objectives

At the outset of this chapter it is important to remember, and to keep in mind, the meaning of marketing. Marketing is the process whereby customer needs are researched, anticipated and identified and satisfied at a price that allows a business to generate a profit. Marketing, however, is also used by non-profit organisations; in their case, the aim is still to satisfy customer needs but this might have to be done to cover costs or to generate a surplus that might be used to reinvest in the organisation or its aims.

Marketing objectives

Marketing is one of the key functions of a business but it is important to remember that it does not function in isolation of the other business functions. All business functions have to work together to achieve the aims set by the organisation. These aims are long-term goals that the business has set. To enable the business to meet these long-term aims, the marketing function has to reflect and support those long-term aims.

Marketing objectives are closely linked to the overall corporate objectives of a business which were outlined in Chapter 1. These overall corporate objectives drive the business. Most large businesses have a wide range of operations covering many different markets and including many different brands. Ultimately, all these organisations have to generate a profit in the long term to survive, but maximising profit may not be the main aim. Without doubt, however, generating an **appropriate** level of profit (however the business defines it) will be a key aim of each of these businesses.

For businesses that do not have profit as a major aim, such as social enterprises, the aim of the business may have a different focus. If profits are made, they are likely to be used in different ways compared to private sector corporations such as Shell. One example is the Baywind Energy Cooperative. This is an organisation which has community ownership of a wind farm generating electricity in Cumbria in north-west England. The cooperative was set up in 1996. It does make a profit and this is shared out amongst the members of the cooperative. Its aims, however, go far beyond just generating profits with a concern for cutting energy use, conservation and education.

> ## Key terms
>
> **Competitive advantage** The ways in which a firm appeals to its consumers through adding value which makes the firm unique in some way. This uniqueness can be both defended and is distinctive, and means that it is difficult for its rivals to be able to imitate or replicate these features.
>
> **Marketing objectives** The set of targets or statements that a business intends to achieve in the short term to support corporate objectives.
>
> **Market share** The proportion of total sales accounted for by any one business.
>
> **Social enterprise** A business run as a non-profit-making organisation, with the main aim of using business to promote or support a social, environmental or cultural purpose or value.

The complexity of business and the widespread concern over the effect of business operations on the environment means that larger corporations cannot ignore the necessity of building in concerns over the impact of its operations in its aims.

Marketing objectives might include lessening the impact of the business on the environment

These longer-term aims must be supported by the work of the marketing function. If market research tells the corporation that its customers are increasingly concerned about the impact of its operations on the environment, then the corporation has to respond to these concerns and investigate how it can meet these concerns. Corporate objectives relate to where the business is heading and what it wants to achieve in the long term. These are the objectives that are encapsulated in the value and mission statements that firms establish.

Marketing objectives need to be carefully thought through; simply coming up with generalised statements is of little value. To remind everyone in the organisation about the importance of the marketing objectives, they are set, like other objectives, according to the **SMART** criteria. The SMART criteria were outlined in Chapter 1.

Having got to this stage, specific marketing objectives can be developed. Remember that the objectives have to relate to the SMART criteria and can be summarised under the four key headings outlined in Chapter 1. Examples of these objectives can be found opposite.

You can see from the list on page 101 that marketing objectives can be quite wide-ranging and often very specific. It is important that the marketing objectives can be linked to the overall corporate objectives. These objectives can be classified according to different marketing areas – sales, profits, revenue, price, product, promotion, place, market research, new product development, corporate social responsibility objectives, and so on.

Synoptic search

In the AS course you learned about product portfolio analysis and the Boston Matrix. In determining marketing objectives, these two methods might be part of the decision-making process. Larger corporations with many different products serving different markets will have to manage products at different stages of the life cycle and who exhibit different characteristics in terms of market growth and market share. Decisions about what to do with these products and how best to market them (for which marketing objectives will be required) will necessitate using such tools to help formulate the plan and take into account changing market circumstances.

'Our marketing strategy is designed to increase customer traffic to our websites, drive awareness of products and services we offer, promote repeat purchases, develop incremental product and service revenue opportunities, and strengthen and broaden the Amazon.com brand name.'

Source: http://media.corporate-ir.net/media_files/irol/97/97664/2006AnnualReport.pdf

The following is an extract from the annual report of Amazon.

These are part of Amazon's overall corporate objectives. In order to realise these objectives, more specific marketing objectives will be set that will specify how much the customer traffic is to be increased and by when, targets for the number of repeat purchases, what service revenue opportunities are to be established and by when, and in what ways the Amazon.com brand name can be strengthened and broadened.

Note that in each case we have not said *how* these are to be achieved. This would be covered by the marketing strategy; the marketing objectives specify *what* and *when*.

EXAMPLES OF MARKETING OBJECTIVES

Maintaining or increasing market share

- Increase monthly sales by 5% compared to the previous year.
- Each of the sales team to make contact with 10 new potential clients each month for the next three months.
- Convert five enquiries into confirmed sales each month.
- Increase market share by 1% over the next year.
- Set up feedback and discussion session at annual sales conference to review product X performance (product X may not be doing as well as expected!).
- Increase consumer purchase of product X by 5% over the next six months.
- Increase footfall into stores by 2% a week for the next quarter.
- Attend five sales exhibitions across Europe in the next year.
- Increase number of customer visits by 3% over the next six months.

Breaking into a new market

- Achieve penetration into 80% of all distribution outlets for product X.
- Conduct five focus groups on planned launch of new product.
- Achieve 20,000 user trials of product X over the next three months.
- Increase website traffic by 10% over the next year.

- Expand number of dealers/agents for the product by 5% over the next year.

Building a loyal customer base

- Ensure customer queries/complaints are followed up within 24 hours.
- Gain 25% brand recognition by target customers within six months.
- Increase the database of customer details by 1,000 per month for the next six months.
- See through launch of two new products a year for the next three years.

Establishing competitive advantage

- Identify two prototype products to meet perceived changing market conditions, over the next 12 months.
- Research the market needs of a newly-identified market segment.
- Reduce carbon dioxide emissions from the business's operations by 0.25% over the next year.
- Research outsourcing possibilities to help reduce costs and facilitate price reductions for consumers.
- Have an average price comparison lower than main rivals for the next year.
- Target a maximum of five minutes per customer call for the sales team.
- Reduce order processing time by 50%.

Skills watch!

AO2

Go through the list of marketing objectives at the end of page 100 and try to classify them according to the list of generic corporate objectives in the box above. Write a short sentence explaining how the marketing objective would help to contribute to the corporate objective.

Assessing internal and external influences on marketing objectives

Having an objective is one thing but with any business, large and small, there are going to be a number of factors that will influence the extent to which the business is able to set these objectives in the first place and whether they can be achieved.

This section will look at some of these influences. However, the crucial thing that you must do is to look at these influences and consider the extent to which they will influence marketing objectives in different business scenarios. This is what 'assessing internal and external influences on marketing objectives' means. You will have to make a judgement about whether the influences you are looking at will affect marketing objectives in a major way, quite a lot, to a small extent or hardly at all!

In examinations, you will be expected to make such judgements at A2 level and this will be an important skill to demonstrate if you want to achieve the higher grades. It is important to remember that there are rarely right answers to the questions that you will face. The answer will depend on the context you are given and your ability to apply your knowledge of the influences on marketing objectives and the context in making your judgement.

We can classify the influences on marketing objectives as internal and external. Internal marketing objectives are likely to be something that the business has some control over, whereas the external influences might be largely outside the control of the business. Remember as we discuss the next section that marketing objectives are about where the business wants to be in the *future*, not how it gets there – the latter will be included in the marketing plan.

Internal influences on marketing

The main internal influences include the following:

- finance
- human resources
- operational issues
- corporate objectives.

We will deal with each one in turn.

FINANCE

A major influence on marketing objectives is finance. Take the following two objectives we identified in the list above:

Amazon.co.uk's warehouse in Bedford – a big investment which will have required significant finance

- Reduce order processing time by 50%.
- Reduce carbon dioxide emissions from the business's operations by 0.25% over the next year.

Both of these objectives will have positive benefits on customers and the business's ability to achieve relevant corporate objectives. However, in setting these objectives the business will have been mindful of the SMART criteria. To make these objectives realistic and achievable, the business has to have the funds available to put what is necessary into practice to achieve the objectives.

Reducing order processing time, for example, may require investment in new technology. Such technology might be more powerful and sophisticated allowing a greater number of orders to be processed in a shorter space of time; it might require time to be invested by the firm's IT teams to install and test the software, and there might also be training needs for staff to familiarise themselves with the new technology. All of these things, not to mention the acquisition of the software in the first place, will need to be financed.

There would be little point in setting such an objective if the business knew that it only had a limited budget. If the whole objective had been budgeted at costing £350,000 but the firm only had £200,000 available, there would be serious consequences if it chose to set the objective knowing the finance was not fully in place. What it might mean is that corners are cut to meet the budget constraints; staff might become frustrated at the lack of preparation and familiarisation with the technology. The IT team might find that it simply cannot get the correct systems set up and tested in time for its launch.

Of course, many businesses do go ahead with setting objectives within tight budget constraints. The outcome of the process will depend on the extent to which the finance meets the requirements of the objectives. If the budget is only marginally under the amount needed, it might be possible to still set the objective and get appropriate outcomes; if the budget is way under then the outcomes may be unrealistic and not achievable in the time frame set by the objective.

In the example quoted above, if there was a £150,000 shortfall in finance but the firm decided to go ahead and set the objective anyway, what might be the consequences? It could be that the staff pull together and find ways to implement the objective. It is quite possible, however, that once the system is up and running, cracks begin to show. Customers may find that the experience they have is less than satisfactory; staff may not know how to deal with certain queries, the software could have various bugs and technical problems, staff may feel demotivated and overwhelmed. Ultimately, order processing time may not be reduced by anything like 50% and in fact might even increase.

Skills watch!

AO3 / AO4

e-on is the second largest energy-generating company in the UK. Its power stations generate around 10% of the UK's electricity. It does this through a combination of gas, wind, coal, oil and hydro.

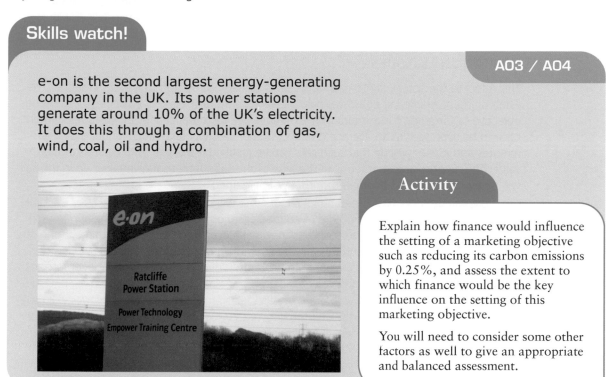

Activity

Explain how finance would influence the setting of a marketing objective such as reducing its carbon emissions by 0.25%, and assess the extent to which finance would be the key influence on the setting of this marketing objective.

You will need to consider some other factors as well to give an appropriate and balanced assessment.

HUMAN RESOURCES

Many larger businesses have a considerable number of employees. Many of these larger businesses will have a human resources department who, as part of its work, will liaise with other functions in the business to match the skill and ability profile of the staff with the objectives of the business. In setting marketing objectives it is highly likely that humans will be the ones that will be at the heart of the work to realise the objectives.

It is important, therefore, to consider human resources factors in setting objectives. Key questions will be:

- Does the organisation have enough staff to carry out the objective?
- Do the staff have the necessary skills and qualifications to carry out particular tasks and projects within the objective?
- What communication approaches are necessary to introduce and explain the objective to staff?
- What role will motivation play in the successful setting and execution of the objective?
- What will be the professional development and training implications of setting the objective?
- Will outside expertise need to be brought in if the objective is set?
- What costs will be incurred in implementing the human resources actions implied by the objective?

- Will the objective set be capable of being met by those tasked with its implementation – part of the SMART criteria?
- Will the objective have any implications for recruitment or reorganisation of human resources within the business?
- Are there systems in place for staff to communicate their thoughts on the objectives they are likely to be affected by?
- Are there systems in place to enable staff to contribute to the formulation of objectives?

For large firms, these questions are crucial. There may be plenty of staff in the organisation, but they may not be in the right place in terms of the match between their skills and the objectives that are being set that involve them.

OPERATIONAL ISSUES

This refers to the actual day-to-day work that is carried out by staff in the organisation. The establishing of marketing objectives has to take account of these. For example, a marketing objective of targeting a maximum of five minutes per customer call for the sales team might have to be expressed as an average. Some customer calls will take much longer than five minutes and it may well be that such calls can be justified if the sale that results is of high value. The additional cost in terms of the time of the sales representative taken up in the call will be more than offset by the return that will be gained.

There will be other basic operational factors that will have to be considered, for example, geography. Some sales reps might be given marketing objectives related to the number of clients they see or the number of contacts they make over a certain period of time. If the rep is working in south-east England this may be entirely possible; if their patch is Sweden or Scotland then getting to clients might be much more difficult because of the geographical spread and the transport limitations that exist.

Some businesses have many different product lines and so marketing objectives will have to take account of this and might limit the degree to which specific objectives can be set. In the publishing industry, a business like HarperCollins and Cengage Learning (who own Biz/ed) might have hundreds of different titles in their product list. These titles might range from academic textbooks aimed at higher education through to introductory books for students in primary schools, to novels, cookery books and non-fiction titles. In such cases marketing objectives such as 'Increase market share by 1% over the next year' and 'Gain 25% brand recognition by target customers within six months' might have little meaning in practice. What is the definition of market share in this industry – the proportion of the market for A2 level Business Studies textbooks? The proportion of the market for romantic novels? What would brand recognition look like? Is it the name of the author of a textbook – usually far more readily associated with students than the name of the publisher?

Other operational issues might include the supply of raw materials for the product or production delays. These have to be considered when setting marketing objectives as they will have an influence on the SMART criteria. In many cases they cannot be anticipated or controlled, but most business leaders and managers know these things do happen and so have to think about how marketing objectives could be affected. This, in turn, can affect the way in which the objectives are set in the first place to ensure that they do meet the SMART criteria.

Some other broader operational issues are listed below.

Product fit

This refers to the number of possible customers in a market who have needs that the business's product meets at the existing price, in proportion to the total market. If this fit is relatively low, that is, your product only meets the needs of 10% of the current market, then marketing objectives can be set to try and improve that product fit. This could involve a change to the product but in so doing there might be an implication for cost in relation to possible market research, product innovation and new production facilities, which must be taken into consideration.

Market presence

When a customer goes to buy a product, there will invariably be a range of competing products on offer. Market presence looks at the degree to which consumers consider a particular company's product in making that decision. Market research may be a useful way of establishing market presence and the outcome of that research might influence the marketing objectives that are set.

Close rate improvement

If a customer is considering a business's product in relation to competitors, how often do they settle on your product compared with those of your rivals? This is what close rate improvement looks at. The aim is to get consumers to choose the business's product over its rivals. The more they do this, the higher the closing rate. Market research may help a business to identify marketing objectives that help to increase the closing rate.

CORPORATE OBJECTIVES

Marketing objectives have to reflect corporate aims and provide the means by which the organisation is able to measure the progress it is making to achieve those aims; they provide a benchmark to achieving these overall aims. Marketing objectives can be very specific or broader in their scope. They help to put the company on the road to where it wants to be at some point in the future. They specify what is to be achieved and when results can be expected to be seen to measure the progress to that achievement.

To see the relationship between corporate objectives and marketing objectives, below is a generic outline of some possible corporate objectives (a generalised list that can be applied to many different types of business).

Examples of corporate objectives

- Increase sales.
- Increase sales revenue.
- Increase profits.
- Increase shareholder value.
- Become the first choice for consumers in the market.
- Become recognised for environmental and ethical responsibility.
- Improve operating efficiency.
- Raise awareness of the company and its products.

For non-profit-making organisations, the objectives might be different.

Examples of corporate objectives for non-profit-making organisations

- Maximise operating surplus.
- Maximise the number of users.
- Ensure break even is reached – referred to as 'full-cost recovery'.
- Reduce the reliance on subsidy – referred to as 'partial-cost recovery'.
- Make the best use of the funds or the budget that the organisation has.
- Satisfy the needs of staff who work for the organisation.
- Increase the range of people who can access the organisation's products/services.

Whatever the corporate objective, if you look at the lists on page 105, at the heart of them all are the two essential principles that underpin any business – costs and revenues. These two things drive all other aspects of the business's operations and objectives. For example, if a business wishes to improve its environmental and ethical credentials, it will have to accept a changed way of working. This changed way of working is likely to incur additional costs, but these costs might (or might not) help the business to generate additional revenue by attracting more customers. The business will have to think through the implications of these objectives and make judgements about whether the benefits they will receive will outweigh the costs of putting them into operation.

Most of the corporate objectives listed above are very generalised and in some respects 'woolly'. It is all very well having an objective of raising awareness of the business in the market, but how is this to be achieved in practice? There will be a number of stages that a business will go through to define its marketing objectives. It will need to have an understanding of its market – who its customers are, and what their needs are and might be in the future. This information is likely to have been gathered through the experience the business has of its operations and its ongoing market research.

Having analysed its customers, the business will then have some idea of the extent to which its products match consumer needs. If they do not, then the business will have to think of ways that it can better achieve this match. This might involve developing new products, amending existing products or finding new markets. This is where the marketing plan will begin to take shape. The marketing plan will encompass the strategy and the marketing mix. For many larger businesses, the marketing mix is not just the four Ps of price, product, promotion and place, but also includes people, process and physical environment. Many of the top 50 European companies are service providers: companies like HSBC, Vodafone, Credit Suisse, AXA, ING, Allianz and Banco Santander.

Part of the plan will require the need to set clear marketing objectives. The marketing objectives will in turn determine the marketing strategy that the business will follow. In large

Skills watch!

A03 / A04

In late March 2007, British Airways (BA) opened up the new Terminal 5 (T5) at Heathrow. The terminal was touted as being the answer to many of the problems the airline had been facing, and an end to queues and baggage problems was one of the major hopes that BA had for the £4.3 billion

building; the marketing objectives appeared to be clear. However, the first week of its operations from T5 proved to be a disaster. Willie Walsh, the chief executive of BA, admitted that it was not one of the company's finest hours. Over 20,000 items of baggage were not handled and hundreds of flights had to be cancelled. Staff said that they had not been given sufficient training, and the opportunity to familiarise themselves with the building and the equipment they had to work with. Some could not even find their way to where they were supposed to be working on the first day T5 opened!

Unhappy passengers faced delay and disruption at T5 – exactly what the new building was not meant to do!

Activity

Discuss the internal factors that might have influenced the marketing objectives of BA in the light of the story above.

corporations there is a likelihood that there will be a product portfolio, possibly covering different regions and markets. The overall strategy of the corporation may be clearly stated but each product will have to contribute to that strategy. However, the way it does so will vary depending on the circumstances.

External factors influencing marketing objectives

The main external influences include the following:

- competitors' actions
- market factors
- technological change.

External factors influencing marketing objectives might be out of the direct control of the business, unlike internal influences. However, this does not mean that the business can ignore them. It may be that the business has to adapt its marketing objectives in the light of these external influences.

COMPETITORS' ACTIONS

Competitors' actions might include the launching of a new product, a change in pricing strategy, a change in promotion tactics, changes in distribution methods – indeed any action designed to seek to gain some form of competitive advantage. Such actions will impact on existing objectives and might necessitate changes to those objectives to meet the new circumstances.

For example, if an objective exists to achieve penetration into 80% of all distribution outlets for product X and a competitor introduces a new distribution channel, then this objective may have to be changed or amended.

MARKET FACTORS

Markets are subject to constant changes. These changes could be immediate short-term changes such as those that occur when there is a food scare, or can be longer-lasting changes where a trend develops and becomes more obvious over time. Market changes can themselves be triggered by the actions of competitors, for example, if a new product is launched that means that consumer needs are being met more appropriately. The downloading of music has meant that the market for music has changed considerably. It may have started off as a relatively small phenomenon confined to those who were confident in the use of PCs and file-sharing programmes, but has become a trend that reflects a changed attitude to the way we access and listen to music.

Many businesses are now very conscious of the impact of their operations on the environment and of their ethical responsibilities. There are an increasing number of people who have changed their behaviour to take into consideration corporate social responsibility (CSR); they may actively look to buy from companies who they feel they can trust and who they believe take their CSR seriously. There is nothing to suggest that this trend will diminish, and so it will make sense for businesses to look at their operations and to amend and change their marketing objectives in the light of this. By doing so, the business will be hoping to anticipate and identify consumer needs more effectively and to amend their operations to meet those changed needs.

TECHNOLOGICAL CHANGE

In many ways the changes in technology are linked closely to the other two influences in this section. Technology does not always change as quickly as we might imagine but the consequences of changes in technology can sweep a market relatively quickly. The development of the Internet had its origins in the late 1950s but it did not reach a mass audience until the 1990s. Since that time, however, its application to business has been exponential as companies have looked to exploit the potential it offers. This has opened up new markets but has also had significant impacts on others.

The UNIVAC (1962) and the MacBook Air (2009): computer technology has come a very long way over the past 50 years!

The music industry is one such example. The traditional industry was undergoing change following the development of the compact disc and digital technology. The development of the Internet has, more than likely, changed the industry for ever. Powerful companies in the industry have been relatively slow to adapt to those changes and to see the changed customer needs that now exist. This has opened up the opportunities for new business models and new products to help meet those changing needs.

The changes in technology mean that marketing objectives have to be constantly reviewed to take into consideration these changes and how they affect customer needs. It could be argued that the music industry was slow to recognise changing customer needs and that their marketing objectives did not reflect these needs. Objectives relating to market share, increasing sales and improving footfall into stores for a company like HMV, for example, might be wide of the mark in relation to the changes in the way that the market wants to buy and access its music.

Technology also influences the setting of marketing objectives in terms of the extent to which the objectives can meet the SMART criteria. For example, the development of customer-tracking technology through cookies on the Web or through loyalty card schemes have enabled businesses to understand who their customers are, to develop a profile about their behaviour and to understand their needs more effectively. This, in turn, means that marketing objectives can be set that can be achieved and which are realistic.

Skills watch!

A03 / A04

Sainsbury's, one of the big four supermarkets, invested £1.8 billion in a new IT system in 2000 to improve its supply chain systems. The investment was meant to improve the efficiency of its ordering and distribution functions. However, it soon became clear that things were not working. Stores had bare shelves and customers found that they could not access the goods they wanted when they wanted them. The company's profits fell and in 2004 it announced a loss – the first ever! In addition, market share also fell.

Activity

Consider the possible corporate and marketing objectives that might be put in place in the light of this problem.

Assess the factors that might influence the setting of the marketing objectives that you identify.

Summary and exam guidance

Summary

- Marketing objectives are closely linked to overall corporate objectives.

- Marketing objectives should adhere to the SMART criteria.

- Internal influences on marketing objectives include:
  - finance
  - human resources
  - operational issues
  - corporate objectives.

- External influences include:
  - competitors' actions
  - market factors
  - technological change.

Exam practice

Read the two articles below and then answer the questions that follow.

Article A

Ticket sales at Glastonbury

In April 2008, tickets for that summer's Glastonbury Festival went on sale. In recent years the demand has been staggering and tickets have sold out within two hours of going on sale. In 2008, however, the story seemed to be a little different. The initial sales offering generated interest but the 137,500 tickets did not sell out and as a result the organisers took out an advert to remind people that tickets were still available.

The reasons for the failure to sell out as on previous occasions have been put down to a variety of factors. Some people complained that the price of tickets  was too high and that they were being priced out of the market. There were similar claims in 2007 and the preponderance of middle-class, middle-aged people at the festival was put down to the fact that they were more likely to be able to afford to attend. Other factors include the weather and the line-up. For the first time a rap artist

cont…

headlined the festival; Jay-Z topped the bill and some saw it as a cynical and not very sophisticated ploy to encourage a younger audience and a departure from the traditional Glastonbury headlining act.

Source: Biz/ed In the News: http://www.bized.co.uk/cgi-bin/chron/chron.pl?id=3069

Article B

Tesco Fresh & Easy

Tesco has opened a range of convenience stores on the west coast of the US called Fresh & Easy. Tesco's plans were to open up to 1,000 of the stores and to have 200 of these up and running by 2009. The initial store openings were in California, Nevada and Arizona. The business model is based around small convenience stores serving the needs of local communities.

Tesco spent many years researching the market to try and understand the shopping habits and needs of customers in the US. It has been well reported that the US grocery market is highly competitive and attempts by UK-based retailers to break into the market have not been very successful. Tesco faces challenges in setting up the stores because they will also need distribution networks for the stores and will also need to be able to build relationships with local suppliers; they are trying to source 60% of

the products that will be sold locally. The company has also set up a mock store in a warehouse in Los Angeles to test the layout and the systems – nothing it seems, has been left to chance.

Understanding the US market is essential to the success of the project but even so market research will not guarantee that the stores will be successful.

Source: Biz/ed In the News: http://www.bized.co.uk/cgi-bin/chron/chron.pl?id=3059

(a) Identify possible corporate and marketing objectives that Glastonbury Festivals (the organisers) and Tesco in the US might have in relation to the two articles. (18 marks)

(b) Discuss the key factors that are likely to influence the marketing objectives for both Glastonbury Festivals and Tesco. (22 marks)

Total: 40 marks

Breakdown of assessment objectives

AO1 – Knowledge and understanding – 8/40
A02 – Apply knowledge and understanding – 12/40
A03 – Analyse problems, issues and situations – 8/40
A04 – Evaluate, distinguish between fact and opinion, assess and judge
   information from a variety of sources – 12/40

Suggested structure

You will need to:

- Make clear the distinction between corporate and marketing objectives.
- Identify at least two corporate objectives for each.
- Identify at least three marketing objectives for each.
- Relate these to the SMART criteria.
- Demonstrate an understanding of the context of the two businesses in relation to these objectives.
- Identify and comment on at least two internal and two external factors affecting marketing objectives for both businesses.
- Make judgements about how important these will be in influencing marketing objectives for both – will they influence the objectives by a very large amount, a medium amount or hardly at all?

Chapter 8   Analysing markets and marketing

Key terms

Average The measure of central tendency in a set of data.

Correlation The extent of the relationship between two or more pieces of data.

CRM Customer relations management – the use of IT systems to analyse and monitor the market, and communicate with customers.

Dispersion The extent to which data varies around the mean.

Extrapolation A technique of forecasting based on analysis of previous data history.

Growth rate The increase in data from one time period to another, expressed as a percentage.

Market analysis The process whereby a business seeks to find out and understand the market it operates in.

Moving average A forecasting technique that smoothes out short-term fluctuations in data to highlight longer-term trends and patterns.

Neuromarketing The use of brain-scanning technology to identify and explain patterns of behaviour, and the role of the brain in that behaviour.

NS-SEC National Statistics Socio-economic Classification.

Test market Simulating the launch of a product or service in a small market to assess the likely success of that product or service prior to national (or international) launch.

Time-series analysis The analysis of data over a period of time – days, weeks, months, hours, years, and so on.

Reasons for, and the value of, market analysis

Whatever the size of a business, its market is essential for the business's success. Knowing what the market is and how it is changing is an important part of the marketing process. There are a number of techniques that businesses use to analyse markets and a number of reasons for doing so. This chapter will explore these reasons and methods.

What is market analysis?

Market analysis involves developing an understanding of the market that a business is currently operating in or is planning to operate in at some point in the future. If the business is able to understand its market, it will be in a better position to understand the needs of that market, how it is made up and thus be able to develop products that meet consumer needs.

In carrying out market analysis the business will look to find out some or all of the following things:

- The market size – how big is the market? What is the potential number of sales that could be made over a period of time? Does it run into hundreds, thousands, millions or billions?
- The extent of market growth – is the market growing and if so, how fast is it growing? Has this growth been going on for some time or is it a relatively new market?

- The types of consumers in the market – what characteristics do they have? Do they have common characteristics that can be identified? What sort of income do they have?
- The behaviour of these consumers – how do they buy products, when do they buy them and how often do they make purchases? How do they make purchasing decisions?
- The structure of the market – the number and extent of the competition that exists within it.
- Market position – is the product a challenger in an existing market? Is it likely that the product will have to compete in an established market with an existing market leader (market follower), will it be a market nicher or does the product hold the position of market leader? In developing market positioning the following generic factors might be used:

  - What part of the market is the product serving – is it top of the range or aimed at more affordable markets?
  - The level of service offered – is service level vital?
  - Value for money offered – could be subject to different interpretation!
  - The reliability of the product – in some products reliability is essential.
  - Its attractiveness – again, could be subjective.
  - Whether it is a well-known brand name or not.
  - The country of origin – can make a difference – for example, Swedish design, German engineering, etc.
  - Selectivity – the ability to be able to recognise small differences in a product offering compared to rivals.

- Market trends – are there particular social, economic, political or legal drivers in establishing market trends?

It is crucial for any business to look at current market trends, and to find out the needs and wants of its customers

A typical approach to the process of market analysis can be summarised below:

1 Define the market – find out what the market is, how big it is, what the main features of the market are.
2 Understand the purchasing process of customers – find out the needs and wants of customers in the market and what benefits they expect from the business's offerings.
3 Define the market in more detail – identify key market segments and investigate the structure of the market.
4 Describe the market – establish as accurate a picture of the market as possible – requires an objective analysis.
5 Analyse competitor positions – what is the competitor offering? How does the business establish brand loyalty and what is its current market share?

Reasons for market analysis

There are two main reasons why a business might want to conduct market analysis. These are:

- Gathering evidence to devise a new strategy.
- Identifying a significant pattern in sales.

GATHERING EVIDENCE TO DEVISE A NEW STRATEGY

When devising a new marketing strategy, many larger corporations are concerned with finding ways in which they can

Synoptic search

Remember competitive advantage? It is a vitally important concept that you will have covered in AS. It is essential that you bear this concept in mind at all times with regard to marketing and especially the key characteristics of competitive advantage – its defensibility and distinctiveness.

gain competitive advantage. If the strategy does lead to some form of competitive advantage, then the chances of the organisation being able to survive and grow in what are likely to be highly competitive market conditions, will be increased. The strategy itself might be based on very simple principles: to reach the consumer, to motivate them to buy your product or service and, importantly, to use it and then to repeat purchase.

When settling on a new marketing strategy, information about the market is vital. High-quality, accurate information will enable the organisation to be able to better devise its strategy to target the right consumers, find ways of motivating them to purchase and then to repurchase. If the organisation knows detail about its market, it is in a better position to offer products and services which meet the needs of consumers and which can be differentiated appropriately from rivals in the market. A key element of any marketing strategy will be finding customers and then keeping them!

This evidence may be based on a number of basic principles that you will have covered in your studies at AS.

There are a number of standard ways that can be used to segment a market. Two such ways are outlined below and on the next page. These are based mainly on occupation but each have a slightly different emphasis.

Synoptic search

Part of your AS content in marketing looked at market segmentation – the splitting up of consumers into groups which have related buying characteristics. These characteristics might include consumers who have particular needs and/or who exhibit similar buying habits and behaviour. Segmenting a market allows a business to be able to split what can be very large numbers of people in the market as a whole into smaller groups with different needs, and as a result be in a position to be able to provide products and services that better meet their different needs.

You will need to remember and be able to use the knowledge you gained of different ways of segmenting the market in your understanding in this section.

Institute of Practitioners in Advertising (IPA) grouping

A – Higher managerial, professional and administrative

B – Middle management, professional and administrative

C1 – Supervisory, clerical and junior management

C2 – Skilled manual workers

D – Semi and unskilled manual workers

E – Pensioners, casual workers, unemployed

The IPA is an industry group and professional body whose members are involved in the advertising media and marketing communications industry.

The National Statistics Socio-economic Classification Analytic Classes (NS-SEC)

1 Higher managerial and professional occupations:

1.1 Large employers and higher managerial occupations (these are people such as company directors, those in senior management positions in corporations, those in senior positions in the police, armed forces and other public sector occupations, and senior civil servants.

1.2 Higher professional occupations – this includes people in occupations such as surveying, accountancy, law, the clergy and teachers.

2 Lower managerial and professional occupations – including members of the police force and armed services in less than senior ranks, nurses, prison officers, journalists, and so on.

3 Intermediate occupations – for example, office workers and secretaries.

4 Small employers and own account workers – those who are self-employed or who employ others in small businesses such as taxi drivers, decorators, publicans and farmers.

5 Lower supervisory and technical occupations – plumbers, satellite engineers.

6 Semi-routine occupations – shop assistants, bus drivers, childcare workers, dairy herdspeople.

7 Routine occupations – such as construction workers, labourers, refuse collectors, production line workers, etc.

8 Never worked and long-term unemployed – this might include students.

You might think that the NS-SEC is a little hierarchical and possibly elitist! It is not meant to be. It has been constructed using sophisticated research and statistical techniques. The basis of the NS-SEC is not about individuals but about positions and the social relationships that exist in the workplace. The information is derived from census data which is collected every 10 years; the last being in 2001.

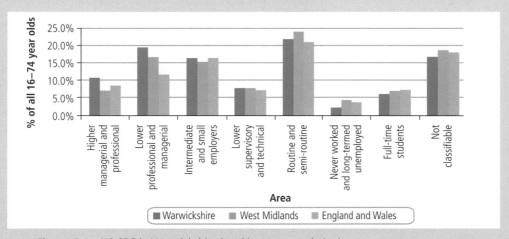

Figure 8.1 NS-SEC in Warwickshire (working age population)

Source: 2001 Census Key Statistics: Crown Copyright (http://www.warwickshire.gov.uk/Web/corporate/pages.nsf/Links/8C7DFE62359BCB2E80256E7800465902/$file/NS_SEC.pdf)

The diagram above shows the classification in Warwickshire. Such information can be extremely useful to a business in analysing its market and building its understanding of its customers. Such information can be useful in identifying appropriate test markets (see the examples on page 129).

The classification of the working population in this way is very useful to businesses trying to develop information about their market. It helps them to piece together a picture about the behaviour of individuals in their market. Organisations will use the full range of tools of market research to gather relevant information. The data will help to develop the marketing plan that will help deliver the key aims of the strategy.

Marketing strategies are generally focused on particular aspects of the market. The three main ones are described below.

The single-market strategy

This is also referred to as niche marketing. In this case the organisation will focus on a specific part of a market where it believes consumer needs are not being met. Some larger organisations have the resources to be able to target these specialised markets – provided they are deemed to be financially viable.

Multi-market segment

In this case a business might seek to provide a generic product but modify the product in some way to meet the needs of different markets. For example, a manufacturer of cartons might provide products to meet the needs of businesses making long-life milk, instant custard, soft drinks and fruit juices, and so on. Each of these businesses is likely to have different needs and specifications for the carton and as such these needs will have to be identified and understood.

Total-market strategy

In this case a business will be looking to serve as many of the market segments that exist in their market as possible. Some brewing firms, for example, will have a range of products that they offer, from stout right through to the latest range of alcopops, in an attempt to cover all the market; vehicle manufacturers will have products that range from larger vehicles such as lorries and vans through to small passenger cars and luxury vehicles; some publishers have a wide range of books that they publish which include fiction and non-fiction titles, children's books and academic books.

IDENTIFYING SIGNIFICANT PATTERNS IN SALES

Because markets are constantly changing, businesses must gather information to identify trends in the market over time. Some of these trends can start to happen quickly whilst others might develop over a longer period of time. There are problems in identifying trends – some changes might be seen as a blip and it might be that sales patterns settle down soon after; in other cases, sales can be affected by seasonal variations or through other normal routines that exist in customer behaviours.

One of the key skills in marketing is to identify and, to a large extent, anticipate sales trends. To do this, marketers will look to identify patterns in data that has been collected from market research. This research will, of course, be both primary and secondary. It is important to notice the word 'significant' in the sub-heading for this section – minor trends in data can signal more significant changes ahead but not necessarily! A number of large firms are able to make use of specialist market research companies to carry out market analysis on their behalf. Such secondary research is often highly detailed and complex. For these large corporations, such information is essential.

One of the main difficulties facing any business is knowing when a pattern is emerging and the extent to which events that they observe are correlated. Just because two things are changing together – whether positively or negatively – does not mean that there is necessarily any causal relationship between the two, however intuitive that the correlation might appear to be.

One example that can be put forward to highlight such a problem is in the case of babies and storks. Assume that a region of the UK records an increase in the stork population, whilst at the same time there is an increase in the birth rate. We have all been told at some point in our lives that storks bring babies. Apparently the story goes back to pagan times. Does the fact that the two pieces of data occur together mean that it is in fact true that storks bring babies and the rise in births in the area can be attributed to the storks?

Such an example highlights the potential dangers that exist in analysing data to find patterns and trends. There are a number of techniques that are commonly used to analyse trends. These are dealt with in more detail below.

Methods of analysing trends

There are a range of methods used to analyse data. The most common ones in use include:

- growth rates (nominal and real)
- averages:
  - mean
  - median
  - mode
- measures of dispersion:
  - range
  - standard deviation
- correlation
- time-series analysis.

GROWTH RATES

It is often not enough to know that sales growth is occurring; the rate at which growth is occurring can give valuable information about trends. Calculating the rate of growth makes it easier to compare similar products and is often more meaningful to the observer than numbers alone.

For example, take the two products in Figure 8.2.

	Sales 2007 (million)	Sales 2008 (million)
Product A	240	300
Product B	15	25

Figure 8.2 Product sales for two businesses, 2007 and 2008

In terms of sales growth, Product A has seen sales increase by 60 million over the year – an impressive figure surely? Product B has only seen sales rise by 10 million in comparison. It might be concluded that Product A is performing far better than Product B. However, if we look at the rate of growth of both products (Figure 8.3), we find the following:

	Sales 2007 (million)	Sales 2008 (million)	Sales growth rate (%)
Product A	240	300	25
Product B	15	25	66.6

Figure 8.3 Product sales and sales growth rates, 2007–2008

Sales of Product B are rising much faster than those of Product A. If such a trend were to continue into subsequent years then it might suggest that this was a product with a bright future. However, two years' worth of figures does not tell us a great deal and it is only over a period of time that a picture can emerge about the overall growth trend of a product.

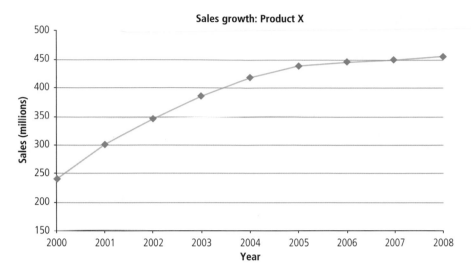

Figure 8.4 Sales growth

The chart in Figure 8.4 shows sales growth over a period of time for product X. When presented as a chart it is easier to see that sales begin to slow down markedly after 2004 and are almost flat between 2006 and 2008. Analysis of the growth rate for this product might help the business to make decisions about the marketing it needs to do for this product.

It is important to place the growth in context – is growth occurring in a new market, a mature market or a declining market? If the sales figures for Product X in Figure 8.4 above was in a declining market, then it may be a sign to the business that there might be hard decisions to make in the near future about the longer-term prospects for this product, and whether it would be economically viable to spend further money on supporting or promoting this product.

Synoptic search

This type of information may be used in conjunction with the variety of techniques you have covered in product portfolio analysis, including product life cycle and the Boston Matrix.

Real and nominal figures; comparing like-with-like

When looking at growth figures it is important to compare like-with-like. You might often see sales figures reported in the press for well-known firms expressed as 'like-for-like' sales. What this does is to remove any distortions to the data. For example, assume the electrical retail store Curry's reports a rise in sales of 7% over the last year. Does this data include sales from new stores that might have opened in the last year? If it does, then it is not comparing like-with-like. The sales of 250 stores are likely to be lower than the sales of 260 stores! Like-for-like sales figures removes the effects of new store openings or closures, or where there might be differences in the types of products offered. For example, the major supermarkets often report sales figures excluding sales of petrol, as not all their stores have petrol stations attached to them.

In the same way, we also need to ensure that our data is expressed in the same values. Inflation can affect the prices of products, and given that sales data is often calculated by multiplying number sold by price, we can see that inflation can distort the accuracy of data over time. If the effects of inflation have been taken into consideration in the data calculation, then it is expressed as 'real' data as opposed to nominal data.

AVERAGES

The average is a measure of central tendency – the most likely or common item in a data series. Averages are calculated through three measures:

- mean
- median
- mode.

The mean

The mean is found by taking the sum of items in the series and dividing it by the number of items in the series.

For example, assume we were given the following sales figures for a business for the first seven months, as shown in Figure 8.5.

	January	February	March	April	May	June	July
Sales (000s)	600	340	560	460	520	460	530

Figure 8.5   7-month sales figures for a business

The average monthly sales would be found by taking the sum of the seven sales figures (the series) and dividing by the number of items in the series – seven in this case.

The mean would be: 3,470/7 = 495.7 or a mean sales level of 495,714 per month.

The median

The median is the middle number of the series. To find the median, arrange the data in numerical order and find the middle item. In the table above the median would be 520. If there is an even number of items in the series then take the two values in the middle and divide them by 2 (this is, of course, finding the mean of the two values).

The mode

The mode is the most frequently-occurring value in a data series. In the example above, the number 460 occurs twice and so is the mode. For example, a business might want to get a picture of the age distribution of its customers and when arranging the data finds that the most common age of its customers is 43.

The fact that we have three different measures of average in the data above highlights one of the limitations of using averages. In more complex data, the average can hide a number of statistical quirks and there are sophisticated techniques available to try to take account of these quirks and make the data more accurate.

The average is essentially a measure of how representative the figure is of the data set being worked on. In some cases that figure can be relatively accurate and in others not so, because of the nature of the data set being used. Some items in the series might be wildly out of character with the rest of the items in that series and so will skew the data. For example, if we were trying to find the average profits of a group of companies but one of the companies had exceptional profits, the inclusion of that company would skew the average.

As with any statistical data, therefore, care must be taken in its use and interpretation. Placing reliance solely on statistics is rarely done in business decision-making without some recourse to qualitative data – even down to gut instinct!

MEASURES OF DISPERSION

To help make interpretation of averages more accurate, measures of dispersion are used.

The **range** is used to show the difference between the highest and the lowest items in the data series. This is important to get some idea of the number of items in the series and helps to show the breadth of data in the sample.

The **standard deviation** is used to measure the variance of the data set from the mean and can help highlight how reliable the mean is as being representative of the data set.

It is highly unlikely that you will have to use the standard deviation in an examination question; however, you should be aware that there are ways of using statistical techniques like this to help improve the accuracy of interpreting data.

Looking for patterns in data collections

One of the keys to successful market analysis is identifying patterns in data. Take a look at the diagram below in Figure 8.6.

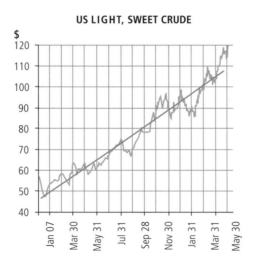

Figure 8.6   Oil prices, January 2007–May 2008
Source: Bloomberg (http://news.bbc.co.uk/1/hi/business/7387203.stm)

If you look at this chart carefully you can see that it has lots of jagged parts to the yellow line showing periods where the oil price rose and other times when the oil price fell. Between July and August 2007, the oil price fell from around $75 a barrel to around $65 a barrel. Similarly, prices fell back between December 2007 and January 2008. However, it is fairly clear to see that in this data there is a very obvious pattern to oil prices – they are rising! A green trend line has been added to highlight this pattern.

Much of the data that will be observed by those in business is what is called 'time-series' data (see page 122); this simply means information or variables that change over a period of time. Such data might include economic growth, sales data, stock levels, share prices, and so on. When looking at such data, analysts might be interested in developing hypotheses about the behaviour of the variables being analysed and any patterns that might exist. Such hypotheses can then be used to assess relationships between variables and contribute to strategic planning and decision-making.

Unfortunately, not all data exhibit such clear patterns or trends. In such cases it is important that certain factors are taken into consideration in attempting to identify a trend.

Ultimately a trend is going to be one of three things – a rising trend, a falling one or a stable trend. In each case the degree of rise, fall or stability may be the important thing to try and identify.

To help identify patterns in data, we might try to look for the frequency and reliability of trends. How often does the trend occur? Does it occur with any sort of regularity? Is the trend repeating itself over time? These might be some of the things to ask when observing patterns in data. The analyst might also need to be aware of the impact of external factors, for example, seasonal variations, random events and cyclical trends. Many larger businesses will make use of sophisticated statistical techniques in analysing data. These advanced statistical techniques will take into account the fact that in some cases, patterns of volatility are difficult to identify. This is called heteroskedasticity. Again, you will be relieved to know, no doubt, that you will not have to learn about this technique but again, it is important to be aware that even advanced statistical analysis of data does not mean that patterns can easily be identified.

CORRELATION

Correlation refers to the degree to which there is a relationship between two or more random variables. We have seen from the stork and babies example above that, as with other statistical techniques, correlation has to be viewed with caution despite the techniques that are available to test the significance of the correlation.

If a relationship can be identified, then the closer the relationship, the higher the degree of correlation. The letter 'r' is used to denote the correlation; a perfect correlation would be where $r = 1$.

Let us take an example to show how correlation might be used.

For example...

A small business in a town sells fruit and vegetables. Two years ago a new supermarket was opened on the outskirts of the town. The owner has noticed a steady decline in sales since the opening of the supermarket. The owner puts the decline in sales down to the fact that his former customers are shopping at the supermarket rather than his shop. He is not happy with the opening of the supermarket.

On the face of it in the example above, the link between the decline in sales and the opening of the supermarket seems overwhelming; it is logical and entirely intuitive to see a direct causal relationship between the two. However, there might be other factors that could have caused the drop in sales. There might be other competition that exists, the quality of the service he offers might have been poor, the quality of the product might have been poor – all of which could have led to a decline in sales even if the supermarket had not have opened.

Whilst cause and effect relationships appear to be strong, it must always be asked whether there are other factors that need to be considered and how strong these factors may be in any cause and effect relationship.

TIME-SERIES ANALYSIS

Time-series analysis is used to analyse movements of a variable over a time period – usually years, quarters, months, and so on. Such analysis helps to assess the importance of trends, the effect of seasonality, key moments in any change in trend (sometimes referred to as 'tipping points') and the magnitude of changes. The use of time-series data has a number of advantages:

- Data from several years can sometimes give an accurate guide to future performance and is therefore useful in forecasting.
- Statistical techniques can make the data informative and useful as well as relatively accurate.

However, the accuracy and reliability of the analysis of such data depends on the quality of the data and the accuracy of the techniques used to analyse it. Data may not always be reliable or accurate. Analysts often have to work with historical data – variables or events that have already happened. Depending on the source of the data, it might be several months before accurate data can be gathered that can be used; by this time it might be out of date. Such data is sometimes referred to as a 'lagging indicator'. It must also be remembered that what happened in the past is not always a reliable indicator of what might happen in the future.

Some businesses appreciate the limitations that statistical analysis can present. Some have made use of astrologers to help them in business forecasting. There is even an International Society of Business Astrologers. In one instance, an astrologer was asked to pit her skills against a group of leading fund managers in predicting the level of the FTSE Index of leading shares. She ended up being far more accurate than the fund managers in her prediction because it was said she was able to take in to account the effects on the global economy of the Kobe earthquake in Japan in the mid-1990s; the fund managers did not see this major disaster occurring!

As with statistics, however, we must take the results of such 'experiments' with a pinch of salt. Ultimately, if statisticians or astrologers could really see into the future, through whatever means, then the world of market analysis would be much simpler!

Sales forecasting

There are a number of tools to help a business measure and forecast sales. These include:

- extrapolation of existing sales data
- the use of moving averages
- using test markets.

EXTRAPOLATION

If a set of data is being used to analyse past trends, then the data might be capable of being subject to **extrapolation**. This is a technique that enables the user to construct new data outside the existing data set. The new data is based on prior knowledge. There are, again, statistical techniques to get relatively accurate extrapolated data but at its simplest, extrapolation involves extending an existing trend.

Extrapolation can be effective as a means of analysing possible future trends in markets and in sales forecasting, but relies on the prior knowledge used being reliable and showing a stable trend over a period of time.

COMPANY X	
Year	Sales (£000s)
2004	3,000
2005	3,600
2006	4,200
2007	4,800
2008	5,400
2009	

Figure 8.7   Company X sales figures, 2004–2008

To show the basic idea behind this technique – not using any sophisticated maths here – look at the data in Figure 8.7.

If we present the data in Figure 8.7 as a graph, we get the following (see Figure 8.8).

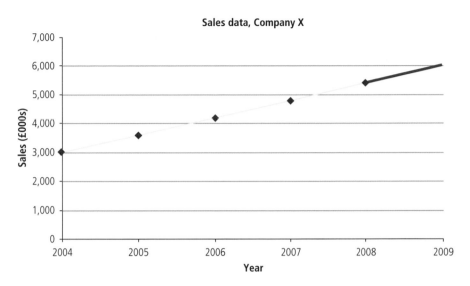

Sales data, Company X

Figure 8.8   Company X sales data, 2004–2008

We can see from the graph that sales are rising at a constant rate between 2004 and 2008. Given this history it would be reasonable to assume that we could extrapolate the projected sales figures for 2009 by extending the line shown in red on the graph above. This would be a simple example of extrapolation.

Of course, for many businesses, sales data is rarely this neat and tidy, but the principle still holds – we can use historical data as a guide to future trends. Take the example in Figure 8.9. A graph of this data is shown in Figure 8.10 on the next page.

The more volatile nature of sales in Company Y makes it harder to be able to extrapolate with any degree of certainty. We could extrapolate based on the data from the last year (2007–2008) as shown in red, but this ignores the data from previous years and may not be representative. In this example, a trend line has been added (in blue) and it may be more accurate to follow this line in extrapolating the sales data for the coming year (as shown by the red dashed line).

To some extent, how such data is extrapolated will depend on the purpose of the data. A more optimistic extrapolation might be relevant if the data is being used to make a pitch either to senior managers within the company or to other businesses which the company is dealing with. It will be for the intended audience to decide, and often question, the reason why the extrapolation has been made and on what evidence the forecast is based upon.

COMPANY Y	
Year	Sales (£000s)
2004	2,000
2005	2,200
2006	3,000
2007	2,600
2008	5,600
2009	
2010	

Figure 8.9   Company Y sales data, 2004–2008

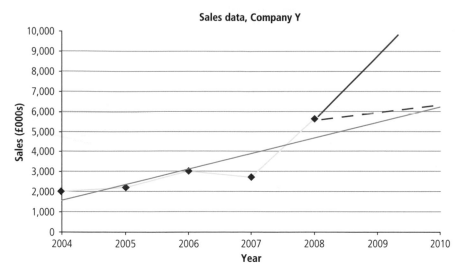

Figure 8.10   Company Y sales data, 2004–2008

MOVING AVERAGES

Moving averages is a technique of analysing time-series data. The technique allows the analyst to smooth out short-term fluctuations and in so doing, highlighting longer-term trends and patterns. Again there are fairly sophisticated techniques available to do this, but the following example will highlight the basic principles to calculate moving averages. We will walk you through the process in a series of steps.

The aim is to use the data in Figure 8.11 to predict the level of sales for 2009.

Step 1: Graph this data (Figures 8.11 and 8.12).

We can see from the graph in Figure 8.12 that the path of sales is not smooth – there are peaks and troughs in the data. However, despite these peaks and troughs there is a recognisable trend in the data – sales are gradually improving over the time period shown.

Step 2: Add a trend line (Figure 8.13).

The data is from a reasonably lengthy period of time (12 years) and the explanation for the changes in the data could be due to a variety of factors, but might be something to do with the normal changes in the economic cycle – the fluctuations in economic activity over a period of time.

Year	Actual sales (£m)
1996	150
1997	153
1998	157
1999	151
2000	149
2001	156
2002	163
2003	159
2004	154
2005	153
2006	159
2007	165
2008	162

Figure 8.11   Company Z sales data, 1996–2008

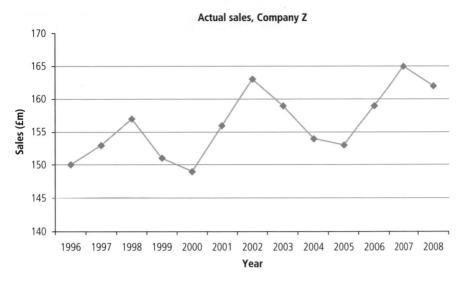

Figure 8.12   Company Z sales data, 1996–2008

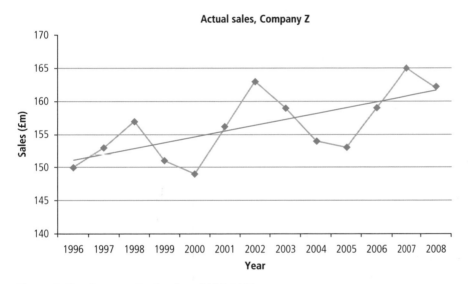

Figure 8.13   Company Z sales data, 1996–2008

Step 3: Decide what 'points' are to be used.

Depending on the data being used, different 'points' can be used – 3, 4, 5, 10 and so on, but in so doing the principle remains the same. If the data was highlighting quarterly sales figures, then a 4-point moving average might be used.

We are going to calculate a 5-point moving average. If you were to use a 3-point moving average, you would do the same process but use only three years, and the same with other points figures.

Step 4: Calculate the moving total (Figure 8.14).

- To start the process, add the first five years data (1996–2000) – the resulting sum appears in the column next to the fifth year.
- The next calculation starts with the data for 1997 adding the total of the next five years, and so on.

Step 5: Calculate the moving average (Figure 8.15).

- Calculate the 5-point moving average by dividing the 5-point moving total by 5 (that is, 760/5 = 152).
- The result should be placed in the middle box of the first series of five points (1998 would be the slot in this example).

Year	Actual sales (£m)	5-point moving total
1996	150	
1997	153	
1998	157	
1999	151	
2000	149	760
2001	156	766
2002	163	776
2003	159	778
2004	154	781
2005	153	785
2006	159	788
2007	165	790
2008	162	793

Figure 8.14   5-point moving total, Company Z

Year	Actual sales (£m)	5-point moving average
1996	150	
1997	153	
1998	157	152
1999	151	153.2
2000	149	155.2
2001	156	155.6
2002	163	156.2
2003	159	157
2004	154	157.6
2005	153	158
2006	159	158.6
2007	165	
2008	162	

Figure 8.15   5-point moving average, Company Z

Step 6: Graph the data (Figure 8.16).

If we now plot the 5-point moving average data on a graph, the result is shown opposite.

Step 7: Calculate the cyclical variation (Figure 8.17).

- The cyclical variation = the actual data minus the trend data (the 5-point moving average).
- The table on page 127 has the point in the cycle added in.
- This is simply done by starting with the first year and assigning that as point 1 and then counting down.
- This allows us to identify which year in the cycle our prediction year is. In our example, 2009 is point 4 in the cycle.

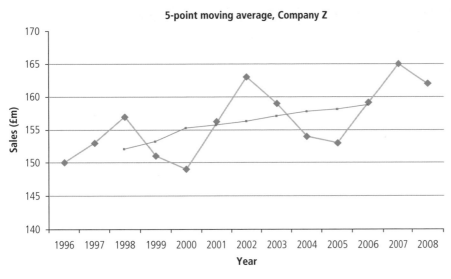

Figure 8.16   5-point moving average, Company Z

Year	Actual sales (£m)	5-point moving average	Cyclical variation	Point in the cycle
1996	150			1
1997	153			2
1998	157	152	5	3
1999	151	153.2	−2.2	4
2000	149	155.2	−6.2	5
2001	156	155.6	0.4	1
2002	163	156.2	6.8	2
2003	159	157	2	3
2004	154	157.6	−3.6	4
2005	153	158	−5	5
2006	159	158.6	0.4	1
2007	165			2
2008	162			3
2009				4

Figure 8.17   Cyclical variation

Step 8: Calculate the average cyclical variation.

- To calculate the average cyclical variation for point 4 in the cycle, find the sum of the cyclical variations for that point in the cycle.
- In our example, the sum of the cyclical variations for the two point 4s in the cycle is −2.2 + −3.6 = −5.8.
- Divide this figure by the number of points identified (in this case it there are two point 4s in the cycle) but could be more depending on the amount of data used and the number of points, chosen, i.e. whether it is 3 point, 4 point, and so on).
- The answer will be −2.9.

Step 9: Predict sales forecast (Figure 8.18).

- The last moving average data we have is for 2006.
- To make an assumption about what the moving average would be for 2007 and 2008, we can expect the data in this example to change by using the following method:
  - Calculate the interval between the years 1997 and 2006 (9).
  - Subtract the moving average figure for 2006 (158.6) from that of 1998 (152) and divide by the number of intervals.
  - The answer comes to −0.73.
  - This figure can be added onto the moving average of 2006 to give you the likely trend for 2007 and 2008.

Year	Actual sales (£m)	5-point moving average	Cyclical variation	Point in the cycle
1996	150			1
1997	153			2
1998	157	152	5	3
1999	151	153.2	−2.2	4
2000	149	155.2	−6.2	5
2001	156	155.6	0.4	1
2002	163	156.2	6.8	2
2003	159	157	2	3
2004	154	157.6	−3.6	4
2005	153	158	−5	5
2006	159	158.6	0.4	1
2007	165	157.87		2
2008	162	157.14		3
2009				4

Figure 8.18   Trend sales, Company Z

Step 10: Forecast the expected range.

- We can take the –0.73 figure we have calculated earlier and use this to do a + and – calculation to the 2008 figure we have just calculated.
- This will produce a range within which the forecast might be reasonably being expected to sit.
- In this example we might expect forecast sales to be within the range 156.41 and 157.87.

Obviously this process seems long-winded and rather involved. Many larger businesses will have software that can carry out the technique for them. However, it is important to have some idea of how the process works and to have a basic idea of how cyclical variations in data such as seasonality or economic cycles can be smoothed out. There are a number of statistical formulas that can be applied to such data to improve the accuracy and reliability of the resulting data.

TEST MARKETS

In the process of developing new products and services, a business will have carried out, often, extensive market research. Despite this, it is never certain that a product will succeed in a market. If the product is aimed at a national market, the cost of rolling out the product nationally only to see it fail can be prohibitively expensive. To reduce the risk involved in such a launch, businesses might use test markets to replicate the launch but on a much smaller scale.

If the product is a success in a test market then it could be assumed that it will equally be successful on a national scale. Obviously this assumption is based on a number of factors, most notably that the test market is representative of the national market that the product will eventually be launched to. A test market might be a particular region of the country, a particular town or a specific outlet. The crucial thing is that the test market has characteristics that can be generalised to the wider market the product is aimed at.

In the United States, for example, the retail supermarket store, Safeway, has around 270 petrol stations located within its stores. In February 2007, it carried out some test marketing of biodiesel. It chose one of its stores in Seattle as the basis for its test marketing. The north-west of the US, in which Seattle is located, is seen as being particularly environmentally-friendly and if the product sold well in this market then it was reasonable to assume that it could be rolled out to other stores in the north-west area and possibly across other parts of the US where Safeway has gas stations.

If the test market is successful the product may be withdrawn from sale temporarily whilst production facilities are geared up to cope with the estimated capacity. The test market might be used to test the whole range of the marketing mix or just one element of it.

In the 1980s Cadbury launched its new chocolate bar *Wispa* in a test market in the north-east of England. The product promised to be a huge success and Cadbury used the results of the test market to build new production facilities to cope with the volumes that the test market suggested it would sell. When the product was withdrawn from the test market customers missed it and were asking what happened to it. Word of mouth spread and the launch of the product nationwide was much anticipated. The product went on to be very successful for Cadbury. However, in a highly competitive market where many new products fail, the use of a test market was very beneficial and cost-effective.

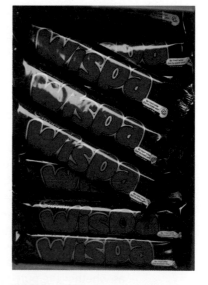

Wispa – when it was originally launched, a test market helped Cadbury to assess the likely success of the product

Qualitative data

Market analysis does not just rely on quantitative data. Businesses will also make use of a range of qualitative data to help inform decision-making. Qualitative data will tell a business more than just how many items will (or will not) be bought; it tells them why customers would buy a product, how many times, how frequently, what they like or dislike about a product, and so on. Qualitative data can be gathered by the following methods:

- Focus groups – a group of individuals selected and assembled by researchers to discuss and comment on, from personal experience, a topic, issue or product.
- User groups – similar to focus groups but consisting of those who have experience in the use of a product, system, service, etc.
- Panel surveys – repeated measurements from the same sample of people over a period of time.
- Delphi method – a technique which calls upon the expertise and insights of a panel of experts to help with forecasting. Experts answer a series of questionnaires – at least two – and the results of the questionnaires from each round are then summarised anonymously by a so-called facilitator. The process leads to a consensus of views and opinions which can make the resulting analysis being more reliable than data analysis only. Participants to this process could be drawn together from around the world as there is no need to have people together at the same time.
- In-house judgements – this makes use of the expertise and judgements of those involved in the business itself in aiding and making judgements.

The use of information technology in analysing markets

The ever-increasing sophistication of market analysis requires ever greater use of technology to help with the building, sorting and analysing of such data. We have already mentioned how software packages help with detailed statistical analysis, but the use of IT is increasingly used in other ways.

Customer relationship management (CRM)

The development of digital technology has enabled businesses, especially large that can afford to build and monitor IT systems, to access and to build large databases of customer information. CRM relates to the methods used by a business to organise its activities around specifically-defined market segments. CRM will utilise technology to identify and profile customers through their interaction with the business. This interaction may be through a website or through the use of data-tracking devices such as loyalty cards or guarantee registrations. The use of loyalty cards, for example, enables a business to capture details about when a customer uses its products and services, how often, what they buy, when they buy it, how much they spend and when. This all helps to build a profile of the customer and provides the business with valuable customer information.

Such profiles mean that a business is able to market products more specifically to target markets that are interested, and who are likely to make use of those products.

Businesses will enter into partnerships and also register with agencies that specialise in matching possible customer profiles with particular products. If a customer, for example, buys a dishwasher, the guarantee registration card also asks for a variety of other information such as whether the purchaser has a car, when the insurance is due, whether they are a homeowner, what their hobbies and interests are, and so on. This information can, within the confines of the Data Protection Act 1998, be shared with other businesses that are then able to target promotion and advertising at those customers. Around the time that a car owner's insurance comes up for renewal, they can expect to get a number of pieces of mail from motor insurance companies offering details of their products!

All this information needs to be managed, handled, stored and sorted, and IT is used extensively for such purposes. In addition to this, businesses that have a Web presence are increasingly making use of ways to mine information about those who visit the business's website, and if they have an e-commerce facility, what their spending habits have been. Cookies are used to track customer purchases. Cookies are bits of information that are sent from a Web browser to a server each time an individual uses that server. In future visits, the server is able to recognise the individual and tracks information about that individual.

Amazon, the online retailer, uses this technology very successfully. It enables Amazon to send information to the customer based on their buying history and what the customer has viewed on the site. If an individual likes and has bought music by Amy Winehouse, for example, then the technology at Amazon is able to recognise this and send information to the customer about other artists and music similar to Amy Winehouse. This information might be based on what other customers who have bought music by Amy Winehouse have also bought, and this can be sent to the customer.

Note in the image below that Amazon also provides a list of other items that might be of interest to a customer looking for products from Amy Winehouse – how many people can resist, at least, looking for other items when they are displayed?

Such targeted information is sometimes referred to as one-to-one marketing. The use of the Internet as well as the other means of tracking customer information has made this process more achievable. The use of e-mail and cookies means that consumers can be sent specific information that is relevant to their tastes and needs, and reduces the potential waste of delivering messages that the customer is not interested in and which does not meet their needs. One of the central elements of a CRM system is analysing which market segments are profitable and which are not.

Amy Winehouse products available on Amazon

Research has shown that a relatively small number of customers generally account for the bulk of a business's revenues. The 80/20 principle states that 20% of the customers of a business account for around 80% of demand. Of course, this does not hold in every case, but as a general principle it has been found to have some validity. It makes sense, therefore, for any business to know who these 20% are and what their characteristics and behaviours are.

The diagram below highlights the main elements of a CRM system.

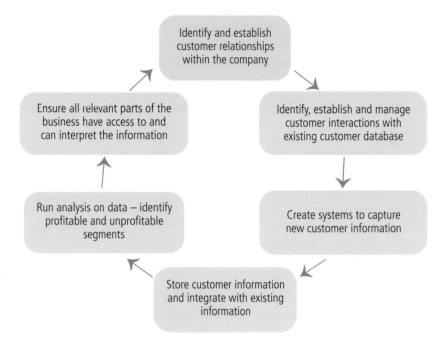

Figure 8.19   Main elements of a CRM system
Source: Diagram after Hair, Bush and Ortinau, 2002

Skills watch!

A02 / A03

If you or members of your family have used a website to purchase products (for example, Amazon, supermarket home deliveries, etc.) look at your home page on the site and check out the 'recommendations' section. How relevant are the products that have been recommended to your needs or the needs of your family? Write a short commentary on the accuracy of the data and how it could be used by the business concerned to improve its sales.

Affiliate marketing

Another aspect of Internet marketing that makes use of IT is affiliate marketing. If you have used the Web at all then it is highly likely that you will have been exposed to affiliate marketing. The way it works is simple. A customer accesses a website, for example, Biz/ed. If you access Biz/ed then it is likely that you are interested in information about business education. Key words on the site will be used to trigger adverts and links to other sites that might be offering goods and services that would be of interest to the user.

The image below is taken from a Biz/ed page featuring one of the 'In the News' articles. At the top of the image you can see a banner advert for office supplies company Viking. If the user selected this link it represents a 'click-through' and Biz/ed will be paid a small sum of money per number of click-throughs – for example, 10p per 1,000. For a company like Viking, the benefit of having exposure on popular sites that generate large volumes of traffic is important – the more traffic, the more likely it will be that Viking will receive sales. What is important is that the page on which the banner advert is appearing has some relevance and some relationship to the affiliate business. As a business education website Viking might benefit from teachers and lecturers using the site and who may require office supplies and stationery.

On the left- and right-hand side of the page you can see links to different organisations – the Coca Cola Education site, a site for help with A level coursework, DVDs and videos for Business Studies, and so on. These ads are delivered by Google Adsense and IT is used to link key words related to Biz/ed to make sure that the links are relevant to the user. If the user selects any of these links, a small fee is paid to Biz/ed by Google.

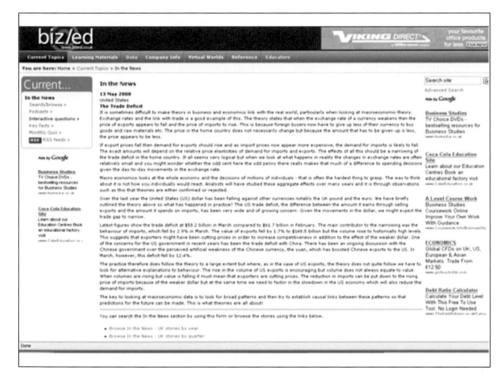

Banner advert on Biz/ed

Affiliate programmes rely on large volumes of users; to generate large revenues it is necessary to have millions of users selecting the links. The use of affiliate programmes is increasing and a number of businesses see the benefits of such programmes and believe that the market for this stream of income is likely to increase as technology becomes even more sophisticated.

Neuromarketing

Technology is also having an impact in other ways to help understand how consumers behave. The advances in understanding how the brain works have taken major strides in the last ten years. The development of magnetic resonance imaging (MRI) techniques allows researchers to monitor brain activity and to identify how humans react to certain stimuli.

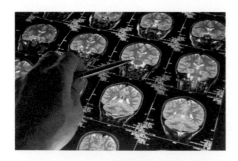

Still in its early stages, neuromarketing allows researchers to study brain activity in order find out what might influence consumers in their purchasing decisions!

Businesses will be interested in why people make decisions on purchases, because it gives them more information on which to base their marketing and pricing decisions, and to better understand the market.

Everything we do as human beings has something to do with the brain. The most involuntary reflex through to the carefully-calculated decision is all channelled through our brain. Its power and capacity puts the most sophisticated computers to shame. Whilst our understanding of the brain has risen exponentially, we still only understand a fraction about how it works. The complex chemical and electrical processes that go into any action are at a very early stage in our understanding.

There is evidence, however, that brain activity around purchasing decisions and the response to brands and adverts might trigger behavioural or affective (to do with emotions) responses which might influence what we eventually end up buying and our behaviour.

Neuromarketing is at an early stage in its development, but larger firms are becoming increasingly interested in the findings that are being published by researchers on this area. It is likely that, for larger businesses, investment into a better understanding of consumers through neuromarketing will become an increasingly important element of market analysis.

Difficulties in analysing marketing data

Human beings!

Despite the range of techniques we have covered in this chapter, it must be recognised that ultimately, markets consist of human beings and humans are not always predictable and reliable in their behaviour. In most cases, market analysis has to rely on the 'law of large numbers' – it must identify patterns and trends, and these can be difficult to identify. In hindsight, trends are relatively easy to spot, but the key to successful market analysis is often to identify trends and patterns before they happen. For example, is the move to buying music on vinyl a sign of a change in consumer tastes or just a temporary fashion associated with a relatively small market segment?

The limitations of statistical analysis

The use of forecasting and the plethora of statistical techniques all have limitations. The quality of the data used, the accuracy of the statistical techniques being used, the way statistical data is reported and interpreted will all have an effect on their value in market analysis. Simple human error can make any amount of analysis worthless. Market research data can be useful in informing forecasting, but where the information has come from, its accuracy and reliability as well as its validity, is equally important if market research is to really aid decision-making about market analysis. Validity and reliability refer to the extent to which a device actually measures what it is supposed to measure. If the device was used again and again, would it yield similar results? The statistical analysis of primary market research data might be severely compromised if people have not responded honestly to a customer survey.

We have touched on the difficulties of identifying patterns in data. The work of economists, particularly econometricians, has increased our understanding of how complex statistical data can be and also how unreliable pattern identification can be, especially over longer periods of time.

Corporate buy-in

Even if the data that drives market analysis is reliable and accurate, there are problems facing the business in getting corporate buy-in. To be successful, the data has to be understood by all in the business and used appropriately. In large organisations in particular, the gap between those setting the strategy and the 'ordinary' workers who are tasked with implementing these strategies and using the data in the process, is often wide. 'Ordinary' workers may feel alienated from the organisation and its aims. Such problems are part of the diseconomies of scale that can arise and can make the business less efficient in meeting customer needs effectively. Some research by a consultancy firm, Badenoch and Clark in 2007, suggested that a quarter of UK office staff were unhappy in their work – not a situation where workers are likely to embrace corporate objectives with enthusiasm!

Skills watch!

A03

John Lewis Partnership

Despite the limitations of market analysis data, it can be extremely useful in informing business decision-making. John Lewis, the retail department store, has become very successful in identifying consumer needs. It uses a wide range of techniques to analyse its market and adjust its offerings to meet consumer needs.

Its employees are not called workers or employees; they are partners in the business. The profits generated by the business are shared between the 60,000 partners. To what extent is the success of the business due to this relationship rather than an understanding of its market?

Summary and exam guidance

Summary

- Businesses increasingly use sophisticated methods of analysing markets to understand changing customer needs and wants, and to be able to anticipate those customer needs and wants.

- Businesses will use a range of data – both primary and secondary – to segment the market into customers who have similar buying habits and behaviours.

- Businesses will use a variety of statistical (quantitative) techniques and qualitative techniques to analyse a market.

- Information technology is playing an increasing part in the way in which businesses gather, measure and analyse its customers' behaviours and buying patterns.

- As with any statistical device, a business has to treat any data with a degree of caution – the output is only as good as the quality of the inputs.

Exam practice

Read the article below and then answer the questions that follow.

Article A

Junk mail is normally very obvious, and the myriad offers of better deals on car and home insurance, along with offers to re-pebbledash the exterior of the house, invariably find their way unopened into the nation's waste bins. Marketing is about anticipating, identifying and satisfying customer needs profitably. In order to do this those needs must be identified. Good marketing targets customers who are likely to buy the product from the business concerned. The following identifies two ways that are used to target customers who might buy products from the business.

Royal Mail runs a mail redirection service for people moving home. It works in association with other businesses to make information available to them. These companies can use this information to target customers who are more likely to want to buy products. One example is the do-it-yourself group Homebase. They will send vouchers offering discounts off items to households who have just moved house. Homebase will know that one of the first things many people do when moving into a new home is to start decorating and doing other projects round the house – new shower enclosure, furniture, lighting, tiles, sheds, and so on. The company can target its market more effectively through analysing the market using such techniques.

The second example relates to the Tesco Clubcard which can be used to collect points that can be redeemed for goods, hotel breaks, flights and leisure activities and many other things! When a homeowner moves house, especially if they move to a new area, Tesco needs to amend its database details. It will send through a new Clubcard (and key fob holder) to the householder. The key fob, so Tesco says, means that if the customer loses their keys, the bar code can be scanned and the owner contacted to have their keys returned. The Clubcard allows the householder to purchase an 'exciting range of products and gifts'. The literature with the Clubcard is designed to sound very appealing and to encourage the customer to visit their nearest Tesco and start building up their points score.

What the literature does not say is that by having the Clubcard, Tesco is in a position to build a profile of the customer and their shopping behaviour. There is no large print telling the customer 'We know where you shop, when you shop and what you buy. We know how frequently you buy certain things, what your favourites are, what you might consider luxuries – things you only buy infrequently – whether you buy own brand or branded items', and so on.

(a) Analyse the main reasons why businesses conduct market analysis. (18 marks)

(b) With reference to the article, assess the importance of information technology to effective market analysis. (22 marks)

Total: 40 marks

Breakdown of assessment objectives

AO1 – Knowledge and understanding – 8/40
A02 – Apply knowledge and understanding – 8/40
A03 – Analyse problems, issues and situations – 12/40
A04 – Evaluate, distinguish between fact and opinion, assess and judge
information from a variety of sources – 12/40

Suggested structure

For part (a) you will need to:

- Identify at least two reasons why a business conducts market analysis.
- Break down the reasons into paragraphs to offer a clear explanation of the purpose of market analysis.
- Use examples, where relevant, to highlight the points you are trying to make and show awareness of the link between theory and practice.

For part (b) you will need to:

- Offer a clear definition of what effective (key word) market analysis is – briefly!
- Offer an explanation of the role of information technology in market analysis. State the main ways in which IT is used in market analysis.
- Relate your explanation above to the article to show how both examples cited in the article are of relevance.
- Think about and comment on other factors that go towards creating effective market analysis.
- Draw your analysis together with a concluding paragraph where you arrive at a judgement about the importance of IT in *effective* market analysis. Is IT the most important component of effective market analysis or are there other factors that you would consider to be more important? Justify your conclusion. You might do this by considering what *effective* market analysis might depend upon.

Chapter 9   Selecting marketing strategies

Key terms

Ansoff's Matrix A tool which models the risks inherent in different market strategies.

Differentiation A strategy to somehow make the product/service or offering of a business appear to be different to that of competitors.

Diversification A strategy of offering new products in new markets.

Low cost A strategy that involves keeping the price low in order to attract sales and generate revenue.

Market development A strategy aimed at attracting new business away from competitors.

Market penetration The strategy of attempting to expand sales in an existing market.

Product development The strategy of offering a new product to existing customers.

In Chapter 1 we outlined the meaning of the term 'strategy'. An effective strategy is one that plans how to reach the goals and specific objectives from the current position of the business. Selecting the most appropriate strategy relies on ensuring that there is a clear definition and understanding of what strategy means. There has been much written about marketing strategies; some analysts believe that strategy needs to be loosely defined in terms of future goals, whereas others prefer the strategic plan to be more tightly defined. We must remember that a detailed strategic marketing plan is likely to be out of date before it is ready to be circulated amongst the team, and as such it must be borne in mind that it must be flexible enough to respond to changes in the market. When working through this chapter you should make sure that you bear in mind that the appropriate marketing strategy will be dependent to a large extent on the marketing objectives that have been set (see Chapter 7).

Marketing tools

In order to decide which marketing strategies are most suitable and least risky, businesses can use marketing models to consider and analyse strategies.

One of the leading gurus in strategy, Igor Ansoff (1918–2002), defined strategy as: 'the positioning and relating of the firm/organisation to its environment in a way which will assure its continued success and make it secure from surprises'*.

There are a number of key ways in which a business can seek to position itself in such a way. The remainder of this chapter will look at some of these ways, and will be based on the so-called Ansoff's

Synoptic search

The heart of marketing strategy is to gain success in the marketplace at the expense of rivals. To do this, organisations look to build competitive advantage. The idea of competitive advantage was covered in more detail in the AS course so you will need to make sure you go back and ensure you understand this important concept.

Competitive advantage, in terms of cost, may allow a firm to charge lower prices. This might be achieved through lower labour costs or through more efficient production methods. A superior brand, a high-quality product, excellent customer service or superior distribution, among many other things, are all examples of other types of competitive advantage that can be exploited through marketing.

* Ansoff, H., 1984. *Implementing strategic management*. Harlow: Prentice Hall

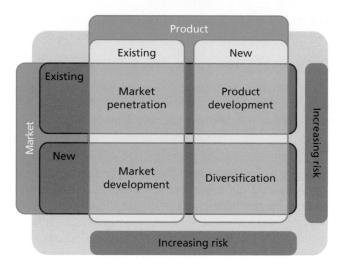

Figure 9.1 Ansoff's Matrix

Matrix. Ansoff represented the risks inherent in different marketing strategies in the form of a matrix as shown in the diagram (see Figure 9.1). This considers whether a business is entering a new market and/or developing new products, and shows the degree of risk involved.

Low cost versus differentiation

Low-cost strategies

The term 'low cost' can be a little misleading. In business there is a distinction between 'cost' and 'price', but in everyday use we use the words 'cost' and 'price' interchangeably. This is not always helpful!

Price refers to the amount of money that a consumer is willing and able to exchange to acquire a good or service. Cost refers to the amount that a business has to pay out to make the product or service available to a consumer. However, we rarely use such formal language when referring to purchases; we tend to tell our friends that a good 'cost me £5' when what we really mean is that we had to give up what £5 could have bought in order to acquire that good. However, whilst it is important to bare this distinction in mind, in this section we will continue to refer to 'low cost'.

'Low cost' refers to a strategy where the price paid by the consumer will be kept at a competitively low level to try and capture market share. It is also referred to as penetration pricing. Low-cost pricing is a strategy aiming to position the business in a mass market. The aim is to set the price at a level where penetration into the market can be made to capture a relatively large market share. If, therefore, a business's marketing objective is to increase market share, low-cost pricing may be part of a strategy employed to achieve that aim.

There are a number of implications of implementing a low-cost strategy.

LOW MARGINS

The firm will have to be confident it can operate on low margins. Low-cost pricing means that the difference between the cost of production and the price charged is often narrow – in some cases it can be pennies – and in such cases it is important that the firm makes sure that it sells sufficient volumes to be able to generate the profit levels it requires. For example, if easyJet are selling seats on flights with a margin of only £2 per seat, then to make a profit of £20,000,000 a year it will need to sell 10 million seats over the course of the year.

PRICE ELASTICITY OF DEMAND

In markets where the price elasticity of demand is relatively high, low-cost pricing can result in a larger proportionate rise in sales. If there are a number of relatively close substitutes and the market is competitive, customers may be more sensitive to price.

COST STRUCTURE

Some businesses have a very high proportion of their costs tied up as fixed costs, with the variable costs being relatively small. Of relevance here is the concept of marginal cost: the cost of producing one more (or one fewer) units of output. Again with the airline industry, the cost structure is heavily weighted towards fixed costs. If a flight is scheduled to operate from London to Chicago, whether the plane leaves with a full load of 300 passengers or whether there is only one passenger on the flight, the bulk of the costs will have been incurred. This helps explain why some airlines are able to offer very low prices for seats because the revenue generated can make a contribution to the fixed costs. If the seat was empty it makes a zero contribution, but by selling the seat the price charged is likely to be higher than the marginal cost of having that passenger on board.

IMPACT ON IMAGE

Operating in a low-cost market brings with it an inevitable image of the firm being at the cheap end of market positioning. Some firms have no problem with such a position and cheerfully exploit this. Ryanair, for example, makes no bones about its 'cheap' image, but firmly believes that customers are looking for value for money and they believe they provide exactly what customers want in that respect. For established firms, entering into a new market using this strategy can affect its other markets, and so it has to be aware of how its image in other markets might be affected if it does choose to operate as a low-cost provider in a particular market.

ENTRY INTO THE MARKET

Any business has to be aware that they face the prospect of new entrants to the market seeking to exploit the profits that may exist. Operating in a low-cost market, however, may not be as easy as in other premium markets; new entrants would have to have the capacity to operate on a large scale to satisfy a mass market and be competitive. The cost of entering a mass market might be prohibitive for new entrants, and the returns on the investment needed are likely to be relatively low. This may discourage potential new entrants and be of benefit to existing firms in the market.

Differentiation

Low-cost leadership in a market is difficult to achieve and can result in low profitability, so many businesses differentiate their products – that is, they offer customers something different or superior to that offered by the competition.

The aim of differentiation is to compete through making customers aware of the differences between the firm's product offering and that of its rivals. If a firm is able to make customers sufficiently aware of the difference, they may then be in a position to be able to charge a higher (premium) price for the product. It is essential to this strategy that the customer actually believes that the premium they are paying represents value for money, that is, that there is added value.

A firm can differentiate its products in a variety of ways, but the source of the differentiation comes from having a good or service that may be physically different in some way. In some respects this difference might be very obvious; for example, some mobile phones will have significantly more features than others, first or business class travel on an airline provides a different level of service and comfort, and some cars equally offer different specification levels for which a manufacturer can charge.

The other main source of differentiation comes through the promotion of the product or service. Often, over a period of time, a firm is able to convince customers that the product is sufficiently different from its rivals in the market. This can be an intangible difference, especially if the firm is operating in a market that is highly competitive and where there are a wide range of similar products. In the carbonated drinks market, for example, Coca-Cola has been successful in presenting its brand as a market leader. The quality and image associated with Coca-Cola comes from its longevity, the consistency of the product, its availability worldwide and even down to the logo and the shape of the bottles it uses. All these things combined go to create a brand image for the product that consumers are able to identify with and which they associate with quality.

If the firm can differentiate successfully then in some cases it is able to charge a higher price than its rivals even if the market is a volume one and where there are low-cost alternatives. Heinz *Baked Beanz*, for example, was able to withstand an onslaught from a highly-competitive promotion from supermarkets who were offering own-brand beans at very low, sometimes even negative prices. Despite the promotion, Heinz was able to hold on to its market share of around 75%, even though its 290g tins were priced around 30p more than the own brand tins.

It is possible to differentiate most products even if they appear, to all intents and purposes, homogenous (identical). Milk is differentiated by subjecting it to a variety of treatments – pasteurised, filtered, semi-skimmed, and so on – which helps milk producers to compete. Potatoes are now being differentiated according to variety, with some being sold as being more suited to roasting or mashing, chipping or baking.

Heinz are able to charge more for their *Baked Beanz* due to product differentiation

There are good business reasons, apart from generating profits, which a business can give for justifying charging a higher price for a differentiated product. The process of differentiating the product involves extra cost and may reduce the revenue-generating opportunities afforded by selling higher volumes. For example, on airlines, the very fact that the quality of food available, the range of drinks, the larger seat sizes, the staff to passenger ratios and the in-flight entertainment and service costs more to provide helps airlines like British Airways to justify the additional price they charge for passengers using business or first-class travel.

Perfume manufacturers have tried to defend the prices they charge in department stores, and to resist their products being sold in cut-price stores like Superdrug, because they argue that the service they provide through trained staff at specialist concessions in department stores is a service that is important in customer service and that forms part of the whole product offering.

The nature of the differentiation can also be very minimal – it does not have to involve major redesigning or shifts in production techniques and facilities. In such cases, the promotion of the product is designed to build customer perception and might be important in influencing how the differentiation is perceived rather than actual tangible (physical) differences. For example, a branded shirt may be identical to an unbranded one in quality (it may even have been made in the same factory!), but the presence of a well-known logo and brand name helps to differentiate the branded shirt and justify a higher price. Equally, Nike and Adidas know that they can sell trainers and other sports footwear at premium prices because there is a perception that their products are of better quality. These trainers are often produced by the same manufacturer in south-east Asian countries like Thailand and

Indonesia, but the existence of a Nike 'swoosh' or the three stripes of Adidas enables both firms to charge premium prices. It is unlikely that a pair Nike trainers priced at £80 is four times the quality of a pair of unbranded trainers priced at £20!

Market penetration

As the name suggests, this is a strategy designed to try and expand sales in an existing market. It may take several forms. Earlier in this section we spoke of the 80/20 principle – the observation that 20% of customers account for 80% of the profits generated by a business. Of the remaining 80% of the customers that a business has, some will be what are described as irregular or incidental customers. These customers may use the business infrequently. One of the challenges of market penetration strategies is to turn these incidental customers into regular ones. To help in this process, the analysis of the existing market and an understanding of the range of customers that the business has may be of great help in being able to develop the right approach and marketing plan to achieve this aim.

In their 'Weetabix Week', Weetabix tried to persuade customers that Weetabix can be enjoyed at different times of the day and in a variety of ways

In addition to this, market penetration might involve finding ways of selling more to existing customers; of exploiting the brand loyalty that exists and encouraging greater use and consumption, and as a consequence gaining a rise in sales. For example, Weetabix sought to persuade customers to try eating the product at breakfast in different ways with its 'Weetabix Week' campaign, and in addition, to not just eat the product at breakfast but to see it as a product that could be enjoyed in a variety of ways at different times of the day.

The marketing plan to achieve market penetration might involve promoting the product, repositioning the brand or encouraging increased usage. Pricing strategies can be used to achieve greater market share at competitors' expense, but such strategies are often seen as being potentially self-destructive as they involve operating at very low margins.

Implementation of such a strategy would be dependent on how strong a market position the business believes it has. Other methods such as promotion might be deemed less risky.

Examples of cases where businesses have tried to boost market share through market penetration include Kellogg's, who advertised *Corn Flakes* as 'good to eat at any time of the day'; BT who offer a range of incentives to encourage customers to use their phones and associated services more regularly; eBay who often have 'listing free' events and The Mortgage Business who put on a series of roadshows in 2006 to try and boost its penetration into the market. This latter example is one where the strategy was focused on the B2B market.

Product development and market development strategies

Product development

Product development strategies involve offering new products to existing customers. New product offerings are developed to replace existing ones. For example, mobile phone companies constantly develop new phones and then attempt to get existing customers to upgrade. Once again, having a detailed knowledge of the market and the needs of customers in the market is of great importance.

The example below highlights one way that this might occur. In 2006, the band Genesis decided to reunite for a world tour, the first for 15 years. The band were formed in the late 1960s and sold over 130 million albums worldwide in a varied career that saw them build up a devoted fan base. The tour took in a large part of 2007 and the band played to 1.4 million fans in Europe alone before travelling to the United States to play 25 other dates.

Genesis has been able to take advantage of their popularity by selling a whole range of products on the back of their main business

Genesis is big business. Their core business is playing music which is either bought via CD or via tickets to tours such as the one in 2007. The opportunities for expanding the business to more than music is considerable. The business is able to provide a range of new products that are associated with the business, but which are not part of the core business. Mugs, T-shirts, key rings, books, posters and even babywear have all been developed to take advantage of the market opportunities that exist.

Similarly, companies like Nike have used their existing markets to develop new products that complement those markets. Such products include high-specification sports watches and heart monitors.

Apple attempted to exploit its brand loyalty and customer base by launching the *iPhone*. The product has been a reasonable success in the US, but at the time of writing has been reported to have seen sales in Europe, where it was launched in mid-2007, less than anticipated.

Product development strategies are considered to be medium risk.

Market development strategies

Market development involves attracting new business from competitors. This will normally be through selling existing products into new markets. The manufacturer of the *Wii* games console, Nintendo, has been very successful in targeting and moving into new markets that were not traditionally associated with gaming. The *Wii* has been heavily marketed at males and females in the 40+ age group – not a group that would traditionally have been a market of such a product.

Market development may also involve companies expanding their operations to new regions or countries. Many firms are looking at the opportunities that exist to expand into markets in China, Russia and the new members of the European Union, particularly eastern European countries.

Universities are an example of non-profit-making organisations that have been looking to utilise these new market sources. Tesco has been expanding to eastern European countries and a number of travel operators have been looking at the possibilities of exploiting new markets in countries like Bulgaria, Romania, Hungary, the Czech Republic and the Baltic states of Latvia, Lithuania and Estonia.

Market development is not just restricted to expansion overseas, however. Many firms will follow aggressive strategies to try and capture market share from rivals, and such strategies have been seen in the UK between the four major supermarkets, and in Canada, fast-food restaurant chain Tim Hortons has been capturing market share from McDonalds.

Market development strategies are considered to be medium risk primarily because the business is operating with known products, but will be seeking to enter new markets which it might not have experience of and therefore might lack complete understanding of the market.

Diversification

Diversification refers to cases where a business develops new products and launches these products into new markets. Diversification is a high-risk strategy. One of the main reasons is that the business is moving out of its comfort zone into markets in which it has not had experience of before. In planning such a move, the business is likely to have carried out extensive market research, but it is always going to be a market that will be new, and therefore potentially vulnerable. Sony is one company that now has a wide product portfolio and covers a range of markets, including gaming, music, movies, technology and electronic goods.

There are plenty of examples where companies have attempted to diversify and where the strategy has failed: Harley Davidson attempted to extend its brand presence into perfume; Heinz tried to move into the household cleaner market with a natural cleaning vinegar; Bic, the manufacturer of pens, attempted to launch a range of underwear; the women's magazine *Cosmopolitan* attempted to launch a range of yoghurts. All these failed.

However, there are other firms that have been successful in pursuing this high-risk strategy. Virgin is perhaps one of the most well known and best examples of such an approach. The business has an extensive portfolio of products in different markets including airlines, music, condoms, financial services and products, rail travel, space travel, mobile phones and TV. However, it has had some failures, for example, Virgin Cola, which was unable to make an impression.

One of the key reasons why a business might choose to diversify is to take advantage of profits that it believes are possible in a new market. It might also believe that its brand strength is such that consumers will be willing to trust it with new products in different markets. Few rail travellers will not have heard of Virgin when the company announced that it was attempting to buy a franchise in the newly-privatised rail network, but it was still a high-risk entry. In addition, firms may believe that there are markets to be exploited that currently have few competitors, and thus where market share is likely to be relatively easy to capture and sales high.

There are four main types of diversification. These are:

- horizontal diversification – a new product in an existing market;
- vertical diversification – seeking to expand into a supplier's or customers' market;
- concentric diversification – developing a new product for a new market but where the new product is closely related to the existing core business;
- conglomerate diversification – the development of a new product in an entirely new market.

DIVERSIFICATION

Benefits

- Spreads risk across different markets.
- Opportunity of accessing profits in growth markets.
- Increase in brand loyalty and awareness.
- Can be a relatively easy source of expansion – if the market is right!

Risks

- Unknown markets.
- Possibility of requiring new technologies and skills.
- Likely to require significant investment.
- Cost of entry into new markets can be high.
- Detracts from core business.

Entering international markets

The global nature of business means that many organisations, both large and small, will be attempting to sell their products in international markets. This brings with it specific problems and issues that have to be dealt with. The main considerations are listed below.

RESTRICTIONS TO WORLD TRADE

Getting access to markets is not always easy because of the various barriers to trade erected by countries or trading blocs. The North American Free Trade Agreement (NAFTA), for example, makes it harder for firms from Europe to get access to certain markets. In addition, there will be other trade barriers, such as tariffs and quotas, and non-tariff barriers, such as regulations and licensing, that make penetration of international markets harder.

EXCHANGE RATE MOVEMENTS

The changes in the value of currencies affect the degree of competitiveness of businesses trading overseas. If the domestic currency rises in value, for example, exporters find it harder to compete as it appears that the price of their products is now more expensive to foreign buyers.

DIFFERENT CULTURES

Cultural norms in different countries can present significant challenges to some businesses. Understanding the culture of the country you are dealing with is an important part of building relationships and establishing a market overseas. For example, the view of interest payments on loans by Muslim societies is different to that in some western societies; etiquette and manners in some Asian countries are viewed differently to those in Europe. Companies like HSBC have made its understanding of the needs of its international markets a key feature of its marketing in recent years.

POLITICAL

Some international markets may be potentially lucrative but volatile. In Nigeria, for example, rebels have disrupted oil supplies; in Iraq, the dangers of operating in that country have increased since the invasion by coalition forces; in Zimbabwe, the regime of Robert Mugabe has created additional uncertainties that put off potential foreign investors. The more politically unstable a country, the more challenging the marketing task.

ACCESSING INFORMATION

In the UK, access to official data is widespread. The Office for National Statistics (ONS) is a well-respected organisation. However, access to data is not always easy or reliable in many countries. This may be because of political reasons or simply that there is not the infrastructure to be able to generate such information. For companies looking to move into some international markets, the cost of accessing reliable data can be a significant factor to take into account.

FINANCE AND REGULATORY SYSTEMS

Different countries have different regulatory systems that govern the way business operates. There will be different rules on health and safety, employment practices, employee rights and responsibilities, product standards, and so on. The greater the variety of regulatory bodies that a business has to deal with, the more complex and costly the administration. In addition, the cost of changing production lines to meet different specifications and regulations can, in some cases, reduce the viability of operating in a particular market and make it harder to compete with local businesses. In financial markets, both regulations and accounting standards vary from country to country. The UK's financial regulatory system differs from that of the US and there have been lengthy debates between accounting bodies about bringing into line accounting standards – whilst there has been some movement on this front, there is still much work to do.

Assessing effectiveness of marketing strategies

To assess the effectiveness of marketing strategies, Ansoff's Matrix provides a useful framework. The effectiveness of the strategy will depend on what the aim is. How far the strategy meets the aim is a benchmark to its effectiveness. The use of Ansoff's Matrix allows the business to assess the risk involved in pursuing a particular strategy. The higher the risk, the greater the rewards, but the greater the chance that the strategic aim of the marketing might fail.

The low-risk options for a business involve utilising existing products in existing markets. Such firms will know their market and will be able to make decisions that have a high chance of success in relation to the strategic aim. Launching a new product in an existing market carries with it a greater degree of risk, however. Despite the fact that the business might know its market, it can never be entirely sure that a new product will be a success – despite the results of the market research that will have been carried out.

Coca-Cola has introduced a variety of new products into the carbonated drinks market – apart from regular *Coke* there is *Cherry Coke*, *Diet Coke*, *Vanilla Coke*, *Caffeine-free Coke* and *Coke Zero*. Such products are designed to try and extend the market penetration of the business. These drinks have all been reasonably successful ways in which Coca-Cola has been able to extend its market penetration, but having a name and a reputation does not always guarantee success.

Coca-Cola may have learned from the launch of *New Coke* in 1985. The company decided to launch its main drink with a new formula. It did so in response to the changing nature of the competition it was facing. What Coca-Cola misinterpreted was the strength of the attachment that its customers had to its original brand. It had carried out extensive market research and had conducted blind taste-tests which all indicated its new product would be a success. It did not, however, test out the attachment of customers to the brand. It quickly did a U-turn and reintroduced the original formula.

Working through Ansoff's Matrix, businesses can make some judgements on the risk in relation to the strategic aim. The greatest risk involves entering new markets, and if entering new markets with new products, the risks increase further. Diversification, therefore, provides the greatest risk. If a business is considering entering a new market with existing products, it has to provide something which consumers see as being added value. Google is a good example in this respect. The business is no longer simply a search engine. It has grown to encompass a range of products that seek to enter new markets but where the business has some experience.

Google – a software company at heart, but selling different products to different markets

Google now has G-mail, Google Desktop, Froogle, Skype, Google Chrome, Google Earth, as well as an extensive advertising business and the provision of metrics for online businesses. What the business is selling is essentially software, but software targeted at new markets thus allowing it to not only develop its market, but also to enter into product development. In such cases there are blurred edges between what is the business's existing market and what constitutes a new market and existing/new products.

Ansoff's Matrix is a useful tool in assessing the success of a marketing strategy. In addition, it is also important to consider some of the following factors which will contribute in some way to an effective marketing strategy.

THE DEGREE OF CONFLICT WITHIN THE ORGANISATION

When a decision-making process is underway in any organisation there are always going to be conflicts that arise. Sometimes these conflicts can be positive and on other occasions, negative. The extent to which these conflicts can be positive will depend on the way the organisation is structured and designed, the extent to which departments are connected, the strength of the barriers to communication, the extent to which team spirit is fostered and the degree of centralisation in the organisation. If there is a high level of team spirit and low barriers to communication, for example, then the conflict can drive improvement and help make the strategy more successful.

THE COST OF ENTERING MARKETS

The higher-risk strategy involved in entering new markets, whether through market development or diversification, can be compounded by a number of factors in relation to entering those markets. The existing market strength of the business, whether it can access low-cost resources, its experience, financial stability and reputation can all have an important contribution to the success of the strategy.

The organisation will have to consider existing industry standards, the existence of regulation and quality control issues. If it enters a new market it will have to consider how its rivals are going to retaliate, and have plans in place to counter those retaliatory actions. It may be that the business has to think of ways in which it can erect barriers to entry to make it harder for potential rivals to enter the industry to take advantage of profits that may exist, and it will have to consider how big the market is and what the medium- and long-term growth potential of the market will be.

THE QUALITY OF MARKET ANALYSIS

In Chapter 8 we looked at market analysis. The development of a marketing strategy is made in response to the marketing objectives, which in turn are informed by the market analysis. If the market analysis is flawed then the strategies that are designed to deliver these objectives may well not work.

INTERNAL COMMUNICATIONS

A key factor in the success of any marketing strategy will be the extent to which the business is able to communicate all aspects of the marketing plan to employees in the organisation – Chapter 10 covers this aspect in a little more detail. Suffice to say that if the employees do not fully understand the objectives and the strategy, then its effectiveness will be compromised.

EXOGENOUS FACTORS

The word 'exogenous' refers to forces that act on a business over which it has no control – external forces. Such exogenous forces can include the behaviour of the economy, changes in government, new government regulation and legislation, the weather, changes in interest rates, the response of competitors, and so on.

Summary and exam guidance

Summary

- Different market strategies carry with them different elements of risk.

- Businesses can use a tool such as Ansoff's Matrix to help them analyse the risk involved in adopting different market strategies.

- Two key market strategies involve using price and differentiation.

- The four main strategic methods outlined by Ansoff include:
  - market penetration
  - product development
  - market development
  - diversification.

- Each carries a different degree of risk depending on the familiarity of the business with the market and the products it is offering in that market.

- Many businesses face additional challenges if they are seeking to enter international markets.

- International markets present issues such as culture, language and regulatory framework which the business has to embrace and overcome.

- The success of marketing strategies will be influenced by internal and external factors which include the extent to which the people in an organisation understand and embrace the strategy.

Exam practice

Read the article below and then answer the questions that follow.

Article A

Tim Hortons eats into McDonald's share

An ice-hockey legend and a cup of reasonably good, cheap coffee have provided the ingredients for one of Canada's hottest public share offerings.

Tim Hortons, which operates about 2,600 coffee shops across Canada and another 300 in 10 northern US states, was listed on the Toronto and New York stock exchanges in 2006.

Tim Hortons has been wholly owned for the past 11 years by Wendy's International, the Ohio-based hamburger chain. Wendy's will retain an 85 per cent stake for the time being. In spite of its present US parentage, Tims, as many customers call it, is a Canadian icon.

It is named after its founder, a member of the Toronto Maple Leafs ice hockey team for two decades. The chain started in 1964 as Tim Horton Donuts. The 'Donuts' was dropped in the late 1980s as the chain, then heavily dependent on breakfast traffic, broadened its menu to attract more customers later in the day.

The menu now includes such items as chicken noodle soup, a turkey and bacon sandwich and yogurt and berries. Stores are required to brew fresh coffee at least every 20 minutes, and a cup of Tim Hortons coffee costs about 50 cents less than at Starbucks. Industry analysts give Tim Hortons high marks for speedy service, especially at the drive-through windows attached to many outlets.

Tim Hortons claims to have garnered 22.6 per cent of fast-food restaurant sales, almost a quarter more than its biggest rival. Its market penetration in Canada far exceeds that of McDonald's in the US. The business is planning on expanding south of the border; the chain aimed to have 500 outlets in the US by the end of 2008.

But the risks are high. The share prospectus notes: 'Many of the US markets into which we intend to expand will have competitive conditions, consumer tastes and discretionary spending patterns that differ from our existing markets.'

For instance, while coffee makes up 46 per cent of the chain's revenues in Canada, it accounts for only 32 per cent at its US outlets. Americans also eat fewer doughnuts than Canadians.

Source: http://find.galegroup.com/ips/infomark.do?contentSet=IAC-Documents&docType=IAC&
type=retrieve&tabID=T004&prodId=IPS&docId=CJ143604435&userGroupName=bized&version=1.0&
searchType=BasicSearchForm&source=gale

(a) Use Ansoff's Matrix to analyse the marketing strategy that Tim Hortons is carrying out. (18 marks)

(b) Evaluate the factors that could affect the success of Tim Hortons marketing strategy. (22 marks)

Total: 40 marks

Breakdown of assessment objectives

AO1 – Knowledge and understanding – 8/40
AO2 – Apply knowledge and understanding – 8/40
AO3 – Analyse problems, issues and situations – 12/40
AO4 – Evaluate, distinguish between fact and opinion, assess and judge information from a variety of sources – 12/40

Suggested structure

For part (a) you will need to:

- Make it clear that you understand the main elements of Ansoff's Matrix.
- Make it clear what you have gleaned from the article are the main features of Tim Hortons' marketing strategy.
- Consider the risks involved to Tim Hortons of the strategy, and ensure that you clarify which elements of the Matrix you think the plans of Tim Hortons relate to.

For part (b) you will need to:

- Offer a clear explanation of what you think success would mean in this instance.
- Identify and explain at least three factors that could affect the success of the strategy.
- Throughout your analysis of the above, ensure that you offer some balance to the points you are making in each.
- Draw your analysis together to arrive at a judgement about the relative importance of the factors that you have analysed. Which of the factors will have the most influence on the success, and which the least and why? Make sure you support your judgements by appropriate reference to your previous analysis.

Chapter 10 Developing and implementing marketing plans

In previous chapters we have covered detail about marketing objectives and strategies. These do not sit in isolation but instead have to be drawn together in a plan that is capable of being communicated to all in the organisation so that objectives can be realised. In many larger corporations, the marketing function is an important and dominant part of the business; it can also be highly complex in that it needs to link together a range of other functions in the organisation. To make the marketing strategy clear, a marketing plan will invariably be constructed to clarify the marketing proposal.

> **Key terms**
>
> **Marketing plan** A document that sets out the strategies to tackle changes in the market.
>
> **Situation analysis** A means of trying to understand the internal and external constraints acting on a business, often carried out through a SWOT analysis.

What is a marketing plan?

A marketing plan will look to explore and anticipate future changes in the market and set out clear strategies for tackling these changes. In addition, the plan will set out the organisation's strategies for achieving the stated marketing objectives. The plan will clarify exactly what the product offering to the customer is (sometimes referred to as the product lines), the distribution channels that will be used, the pricing and the means of communicating with the market.

In summary therefore, we can state that the marketing plan will clarify what the business is selling, who it is aiming to sell it to, and when and how it will sell. This forms an important part of the sales proposition – what the business has to offer its potential customers to meet their needs.

Components of marketing plans

Marketing plans are individual to each project and each organisation. However, they do contain a number of common features which include:

- The mission statement for the project.
- A clear outline of the marketing objectives.
- An overview of the target market and possibly a 'situation analysis'. This might be in the form of a SWOT analysis.
- An overview of the key budgets.
- Sales forecasts.
- Market strategies – details of the ways in which the objectives are going to be achieved.
- Implementation and time lines.

Constructing a marketing plan

The construction of the marketing plan is a valuable tool for all in the organisation. In specifying the objectives and making it clear how these objectives will be achieved, it provides a means of communicating a common message to all in the organisation. This helps everyone to work towards common shared goals. In addition, it helps those who are working directly in

the market with customers, especially the sales teams, to be aware of the possibilities and problems that they might expect to come up against so that they can be prepared.

We will look in turn at each main component of the marketing plan in a little more detail.

MISSION STATEMENT

The mission statement makes it very clear what the business is. Mission statements in marketing plans are often brief and concise, but give a clear guide to all of the business and its values. The mission statement for the production of this book, for example, might be:

'Collins/Biz/ed is in the business of providing high-quality educational resources for the A2 Business Studies market and facilitating the improvement in teaching and learning of the subject.'

Such a statement helps all involved in the production of the book to understand the aim of the overall intention of the project.

> To work with the best people and create the best products and services, for the best football club in the world.
> MUML mission statement

The mission statement of Manchester United Merchandising Limited, proudly displayed in the entrance hall to its offices opposite Old Trafford

Source: Biz/ed images

MARKETING OBJECTIVES

Chapter 7 covered marketing objectives in some detail. In the marketing plan these objectives will be clearly stated and be the result of the discussions that will have taken place as the objectives and strategy were being formulated. As stated in the section on marketing objectives, it is important that the objectives meet the SMART criteria so that they can be measurable and achievable. Using the example of this textbook, a possible marketing objective might be to achieve 500 pre-publication enquiries and requests for evaluation copies in the three months prior to publication.

The writing of objectives that are both challenging and achievable is a skill that should not be underestimated. Business leaders not only have to have the 'bottom line' (the profit generated) at the foremost of their thinking, but they also have to know their staff, what motivates them, what the reality of the market they are working in is and a knowledge and understanding of the product/service itself. The construction of marketing objectives can help to improve the clarity of thinking over the project and injects a sense of reality into the whole thing.

SITUATION ANALYSIS

A situation analysis will help all in the project to understand the internal and external constraints acting on the business. The use of a SWOT analysis is often of value in this respect. By clearly thinking through and collating information on the strengths, weaknesses, opportunities and threats facing the business, a greater degree of clarity and understanding of the scope of the strategies that need to be employed can be developed. For example, it is possible for the organisation to identify production and capacity constraints, resource limitations, employee capabilities, employee strengths, and so on, all of which are essentially internal to the business. The opportunities and threats represent the external environment that the business operates in and is crucial in establishing appropriate marketing strategies.

A well-constructed situation analysis will help a business to recognise and thus seek to exploit any potential competitive advantage that they might have over their rivals in the market concerned. The market strategy might then be focused on ways of highlighting and defending the source of the competitive advantage.

Again, using the example of this textbook, the publishers will know what their strengths and capabilities are; a strong presence in the schools market and a well-respected back catalogue of other textbooks in the field might be an important source of brand loyalty which can be exploited by the sales team, in addition to enabling them to be able to get access to key markets. The publishers will have also carried out some analysis of the rivals in the market – what other publishers are offering – and this can help in formulating clear messages to potential customers about the benefits of purchasing this textbook rather than others on offer.

Key sources of competitive advantage might come from the recruitment of experienced authors, who are not only teachers of the subject concerned but also experienced senior examiners. These people will be in a position where they are able to take advantage of the experience they have gained in developing examination courses, writing and marking exam papers and advising schools in training events. They can bring this experience to bear on the book and the supporting resources. The tie-up between Collins and Biz/ed gives customers access to a well-known website and updatable resources at a price that is very competitive compared to static support material available on a CD-ROM, for example. It may be that the cost of setting up a rival website to mirror the service that Biz/ed/Collins can provide would be too expensive for rival publishers and thus is a distinctive and defensible source of competitive advantage.

THE KEY BUDGETS

The incorporation of budgets is a key element of the marketing plan. Budgets are used to provide a discipline to all in the organisation. Such budgets might include an overall marketing budget and comprise a sales budget, a promotion budget and advertising budget. This makes it very clear to all what funds are being made available to support the project.

The setting of a budget helps to define the strategies used; for example, the decision on whether to use a prime-time TV advertising campaign with twenty 30-second slots costing £20,000 each might be easier to make when a budget is clearly set. Decisions over how best to get messages across to consumers can be taken in the light of this. If the overall advertising budget is set at £450,000, then this particular route, which would eat up nearly the entire budget, might not be the best use of the available funds. With such a discipline to guide those involved, decisions on how to best reach the target market can be made more effectively with less effective methods being discarded.

SALES FORECASTS

In Chapter 8, we looked in detail at forecasting methods. Having a clear guide to the potential sales in the market will help, particularly the sales team, to establish a benchmark against which they can monitor the success of their strategies. The use of time-series data can provide important milestones for all to check on progress towards achieving the marketing objectives. If these milestones are being missed, then remedial action may need to be taken to get sales back on track; if they are being exceeded then plans may still need to be adjusted. More detailed sales forecasts will allow region-by-region analysis to be conducted to help identify trends and patterns in sales in relation to the plan and once again, remedial action taken to solve possible problems that arise.

MARKETING STRATEGIES

The marketing strategies that will be set are designed to achieve the marketing objectives. The objectives will define *what* is to be achieved; the strategies will define *how* they are to be achieved. Marketing strategies have to ensure that the target market, the market segment, is clearly identified. The strategies will typically revolve around the elements of the marketing mix. Chapter 9 looked at a range of marketing strategies in the context of Ansoff's Matrix.

Factors that might influence the choice of marketing strategy might include some or all of the following:

- Brand name.
- After-sales service.
- Packaging.
- Customer-perceived value.
- Reputation and image.
- The ways of getting the product/service to the consumer.
- How the product/service can be accessed by the consumer – will the product be available through a retail outlet, wholesaler, online, by post, through an agent, etc.?
- Methods of promoting the product – point of sales promotion, advertising, leaflets, user tests, free gifts, etc.

It is important to note that the appropriate marketing strategy will be informed by many of the other features of the marketing plan including the budgets set and sales forecasts.

Synoptic search

Knowledge of the marketing mix is a crucial part of understanding the formulation of marketing strategies to achieve the marketing objectives. You will need to make sure you are fully aware of each element of the mix and how this can inform the development of a marketing strategy.

Skills watch!

AO1 / AO2

Throughout this section we have used the production of this textbook as an example to highlight some of the key points in marketing plans. Write a short 500-word report suggesting what strategies Collins/Biz/ed might use to achieve a marketing objective of capturing market share from other A2 textbooks being produced for Business Studies. Use your knowledge of the main elements of the marketing mix on which to base your strategies.

Implementation

The plan will, of course, need to be implemented and a timescale will need to be set for its implication. Such a timescale might be incorporated within the actual plan itself. Implementation might involve producing specific job descriptions or assignments which will be given to the various individuals and teams that are part of the project. The extent to which the plan is implemented will be heavily dependent on the degree of understanding of those involved in its implementation. This is where communication of all the elements of the plan is essential in making sure that this understanding is clear and what each individual and team's role is in the project.

Assessing internal and external influences on marketing plans

Having a plan is one thing; making sure it is successfully implemented so that it meets the marketing objectives is quite another. Detailed plans can often get created with a great deal of care and attention, only to be put on a shelf where they never again see the light of day. There are some management and leadership gurus, for example, Henry Mintzberg, who cast doubt on the value of the time and energy expended in producing strategic plans, and who suggest that the thicker and more detailed the plan, the less useful it is.

To avoid the potential problem of a marketing plan becoming burdensome and not fulfilling its function, a balance has to be met between detail and practicality. Even if this balance is successfully struck, there is no guarantee that the plan will lead to stated marketing objectives being met.

Issues in implementing marketing plans

There are a number of influences on the development and implementation of a successful marketing plan.

Internal influences

AVAILABLE FINANCE

Despite the fact that many large corporations will have extensive financial resources, the amounts set aside for producing appropriate marketing plans may not be high. The available finance will have an impact on the scope of the objectives being set and also the type of strategies that can be identified in the plan. Finance will be needed for a range of aspects of the planning process. For example, will there be sufficient funds available for extensive (or any) market research to be carried out?

The plan is only going to be as good as the information that goes into it and so the amount of finance available to produce the plan will to a large extent determine its usefulness.

OPERATIONAL ISSUES

These could include a wide range of factors that are peculiar to particular organisations. The extent to which the business encourages cross-functional cooperation may influence the degree of information-sharing and identification of shared goals. Some organisations may have inadvertently created isolated departments or functions that may be highly competitive with other departments to the detriment of the overall goals and aims of the business. This might be particularly relevant to organisations with different regional offices located either within a country or across national boundaries.

The culture of an organisation can have a significant effect on the extent to which the marketing plan is taken seriously. If the business's leaders are from a marketing background it may be that it is taken more seriously than if the leaders are from (say) a production background. There is a perception by some in the corporate world that the marketing function is a little out of touch with the real world and that it is too 'woolly' and lacking in hard evidence to justify its existence. Whilst it is often difficult to draw a correlation between marketing activities and changes in sales, the very fact that many large organisations spend so much money on the marketing function would suggest that it is considered an important aspect to the success of a business project. Such a view is not always shared by everyone in an organisation, however.

It must also be remembered that management inertia might be a factor that constrains the success of a marketing plan. Some senior managers may not be involved in shaping the marketing plan and if there is a less than positive view from the top about the value of the plan, it is likely to be taken less seriously by those at other levels in the organisation.

Within any business, especially larger business organisations, there will be systems in place to deal with communication, change and decision-making. These systems will have to be flexible enough to cope with the elements of the marketing plan, and the changes that might need to be made when it is being implemented and information is flowing back to the business. A plan that is too detailed might be more difficult to implement and to change because of the complexities that are caused as a result of any change in the plan. If systems are inflexible then this will, in turn, both limit the design of the plan and the implementation of it.

To create a vibrant plan, the employees in the business will need to be motivated and dynamic. There is evidence that many larger organisations have a rump of employees who are loyal, dedicated and hard-working but who are burnt out and lack motivation. The characteristics of such a group have been called 'middlescence'. In addition, some organisations may have reward systems in place that conflict with the objectives and strategies being laid out in the plan. Staff are hardly likely to be enthusiastic about developing or implementing a plan which has an impact on their bonuses in the short term.

Bored and demotivated staff will not help when trying to develop a successful marketing plan

External influences

COMPETITOR ACTIONS

No business operates in isolation. Once a decision has been made and is either in the planning stage or being implemented, it will be looked at by competitors. They, in turn, will take into account the information they receive and use it to help formulate and amend their own marketing plans. It is effectively a continuous process designed to protect competitive advantage or to steal it if possible.

It is likely, therefore, that a marketing plan might be drawn up in the first place in response to an action by a competitor. For example, the development of *iTunes* by Apple has necessitated a rethink by more traditional firms in the music industry about the way they market CDs and music in general. The existing business model upon which the marketing was based has changed with the development of computer technology. Illegal file-sharing and downloading was a problem to the industry. Apple responded by providing customers with a way of legally accessing music the way they wanted to – and crucially, accessing the music at a price that they were prepared to pay to remain legal. The changed emphasis on the different elements of the marketing mix has presented a challenge to firms like BMG, Sony, Warner Bros, and so on, in the way they market the music of the performers on their books. Equally, it has presented a significant challenge to retailers of music such as HMV who have had to reformulate their marketing objectives and strategies to compete in a changed market.

ECONOMIC AND ENVIRONMENTAL INFLUENCES

Longer-term planning might be affected by short-term changes in economic conditions – for example, changes in interest rates, exchange rates, government policy, and so on. The credit crunch of late 2007 through 2008 will have had an adverse impact on the likely success of marketing plans that may have been devised during more stable economic times during 2006 and early 2007. Those involved in selling financial products such as mortgages, and those involved in the housing market such as removal firms and estate agents, will have had to adjust to considerable changes in their business as a result of the credit crunch. For mortgage providers, the emphasis changed relatively quickly from a marketing plan that was focused on battling for customers in a highly-competitive market set against a background of low interest rates and easy access to funds, to one where inter-bank borrowing dried up, interest rates were rising and the demand for mortgages fell sharply.

Many estate agents in 2006 were operating in a buoyant market with both a strong demand and supply of property. From early 2007, demand started to fall and the rate of growth of house prices started to slow down. By mid-2008, house prices were actually falling and many estate agents were facing their most challenging market conditions since the recession of the early 1990s.

Most firms operating in the 21st century cannot fail to have to take into consideration the impact of their activities on the environment and the concern being expressed about the effects that human action is having on the environment. In any marketing plan,

13 billion plastic bags are given out to customers each year, causing major problems both to wild animals as well as with the vast quantity sent to landfill sites

therefore, it is highly likely that some of the marketing objectives and strategies will have to take into consideration how the business is going to meet its corporate social responsibilities. Such objectives might entail reducing waste, limiting the use of packaging and reducing carbon emissions. It may be that the whole marketing plan is based on an attempt to present the business in a new light to its customers in response to concerns about the impact of its operations.

Each year in the UK 13,000,000,000 (that's 13 billion) plastic shopping bags are handed out to customers in supermarkets and other retail outlets. There has been growing concern at the environmental effects of these bags. Tabloid newspapers present pictures of rare species of animals dying as a result of the fact that these bags are being dumped inappropriately. Turtles are apparently eating them, sea birds are being strangled or suffocated by them and the images are distressing and not good marketing for the businesses that provide the bags.

As a result of the concern, a number of the major supermarkets, who are responsible for the bulk of carrier bags dispensed, are battling amongst themselves to demonstrate to customers their environmental credentials. To change consumer behaviour will require a major marketing exercise and the supermarkets will have been putting together plans to find ways of reducing the use of plastic bags.

Marks and Spencer (M&S), for example, trialled charging 5p for plastic bags at some of its stores and found that demand for them fell by over 70%. The trial is being rolled out across all of its stores. The money raised from the charge will be going to an environmental charity. In this example, the marketing objectives will relate back to a wider strategic aim of the business to reduce waste sent to landfill sites to zero by 2012. If one of the marketing objectives was to reduce the use of bags at its stores by customers, there will have been a variety of strategies that it could have used to achieve this. Presumably, M&S felt that using price was likely to be the most effective strategy to achieve its objective.

Summary and exam guidance

Summary

- A marketing plan pulls together the different parts of the marketing function and will include marketing objectives, budgets, sales forecasts and marketing strategies.

- Implementation of a marketing plan is critical. Some business gurus are not convinced that detailed plans necessarily lead to success, because the market changes too quickly and they need to be more flexible.

- There are internal and external influences that affect the success of a marketing plan. These include: finance, operational issues, competitors' action, the economy and environmental issues.

Exam practice

Read the article below and then answer the questions that follow.

Article A

Wispa on the web

In 2007 Cadbury announced the relaunch of the *Wispa* bar. It seemed that the demand for the return of the popular '80s chocolate bar was overwhelming and had persuaded Cadbury to make it available once again – albeit for a relatively limited period of time. Most people will have cherished memories of favourite sweets from their childhood. Sadly, for many of these people, these products run their life-cycle and eventually are withdrawn from the market when sales start to decline significantly. What this does not seem to do is to dampen the enthusiasm and nostalgia for these long-gone products by those who enjoyed them at the time – even if they did not support the product by continuing to purchase them!

Manufacturers of chocolate bars know that they are in a highly competitive market. The introduction of new products is highly risky and many do not survive. The market continues to be dominated by products that have been around for many years and which seemingly belie the product life-cycle model. *Mars* bars, *KitKat* and *Polo* mints were all originally launched in the 1930s; Cadbury's *Dairy Milk* made its first appearance in 1905 and Fry's *Chocolate Cream* can claim its origins in the 1860s. What can be done to chocolate and sugar to make a product that will tempt customers has pretty much been exhausted and it seems that customers will continue to go back to the products that have stood the test of time – the likes of *KitKat*, *Mars*, *Flake*, *Galaxy* and *Dairy Milk*.

However, as with the case of *Wispa*, if companies believe that there is a market for resurrecting an old favourite then they will more than likely relaunch it. Other products that have been withdrawn include the *Texan* bar, *Aztec*, the *Prize* bar, *Junglies* and *Spangles*. Each will have failed for a particular reason. *Junglies*, for example, were a jelly sweet which had a relatively high price and were well liked by customers but was not a product that consumers bought over and over again. They tended to be bought for special occasions and that was insufficient in a mass market where volume counts.

Apart from the odd special occasion (for example, the *Aztec* bar made a brief reappearance at the turn of the Millennium) manufacturers will be very wary of bowing to perceived public pressure to bring back 'old faves'. It might be that there is a website set up to champion the return of a childhood favourite but to justify the investment in relaunching a product into this sort of market there has to be solid research and a definable and measurable market in existence.

Source: Biz/ed 'In the News', http://www.bized.co.uk/cgi-bin/chron/chron.pl?id=3100

(a) Discuss the main features in the design of a marketing plan for the relaunch of a confectionary product such as *Wispa*. (18 marks)

(b) To what extent might the success of the relaunch of a confectionary product depend upon the preparation of an effective marketing plan? (22 marks)

Total: 40 marks

Breakdown of assessment objectives

AO1 – Knowledge and understanding – 8/40
AO2 – Apply knowledge and understanding – 8/40
AO3 – Analyse problems, issues and situations – 12/40
AO4 – Evaluate, distinguish between fact and opinion, assess and judge information from a variety of sources – 12/40

Suggested structure

For part (a) you will need to:

- Demonstrate an understanding of the main components of a marketing plan.
- Demonstrate an understanding of some of the key influences on the design of a marketing plan in the context of a confectionary bar.
- Ensure that you take into account the possible difference that a 'relaunch' might have on the marketing plan (as opposed to a plan for a completely new product).
- Make some judgements on the relative importance and significance of the different components of the plan that you outline.

For part (b) you will need to:

- Consider the role of a marketing plan in the successful relaunch of a confectionary product like *Wispa*.
- Offer a clear definition of the meaning of 'success' in this context.
- Take note of the importance and relevance of the word 'effective' in the question.
- Consider, and analyse, some other factors that might contribute to the success of a relaunch.
- Balance out the role of the marketing plan with the other factors that you identify.
- Draw your answer to a conclusion with a judgement which relates directly back to the question.

AS level introduced the concept of operations management decision-making and explored effective operations with respect to:

- **Capacity utilisation** – understanding the importance of capacity utilisation and strategies for managing capacity usage, including dealing with under-utilisation and expanding capacity.
- **Quality** – defining quality, understanding its importance and analysing strategies for achieving quality.
- **Customer service** – the significance of good customer service and methods for achieving this.
- **Working with suppliers** – issues involved with choosing effective suppliers and evaluating the value that successful relationships with suppliers can add.
- **The impact of technology** – the impact of technology on operations, the benefits to be gained from exploiting technology and the possible drawbacks.

At A2 the focus is on the strategic implications of operations management, building on knowledge gained at AS and evaluating the contribution *operations strategy* makes to achieving corporate vision.

This section will consider:

- **Operational objectives** Building on material in Chapter 1, Chapter 11 analyses the relationship between corporate vision, corporate objectives and operational objectives. The chapter explores the nature of operational objectives, such as objectives related to first-mover advantage (that is, speed) and considers factors that influence the successful implementation of such objectives (for example, the impact of competitors).

- **Scale and resource mix** Achieving an appropriate scale (size) relevant to context can add significantly to a firm's competitiveness and profitability. Chapter 12 evaluates issues related to business scale, the advantages and disadvantages of size, alongside a consideration of the appropriate mix of labour and/or capital used in relation to business scale and overall aims.

- **Innovation** Few markets are free from the impact of technology and thus developing innovative new ways to exploit technology – whether the result is a new product or new process – can be a key source of competitive advantage. Chapter 13 looks at the nature of innovation, its purpose and the costs, and the benefits and risks associated with innovation-driven operational strategies.

- **Location** It is both a cliché and a truism that location is, perhaps, the single most important factor in business success. Whilst communications technology has reduced somewhat the significance of location, it remains central to operational strategy. Chapter 14 evaluates location as a strategic choice, considering the competitive advantage to be gained from optimal location (including issues related to international location).

- **Lean production** Alongside Human Resources, operations contributes significantly to costs incurred by a business. Managing these costs has a direct impact on competitiveness and profitability. Chapter 15 considers ways in which lean production seeks to minimise waste (in all of its forms) and supports competitive advantage through both cost efficiency and speed of operations.

Every business function could make claim to being the most important; operations is no exception. Operations management deals with producing quality products, in sufficient quantities, getting these products to customers in a timely fashion and doing so in a cost-efficient way. Operational strategies deal with *how* these things are achieved, underpinned by operational objectives that determine *which* strategies, for a given business, are the most significant. Successful operational strategy for one firm may involve a pursuit of quality, with other factors being largely secondary to this. For another firm, competitive advantage may be gained through a low-cost approach. The nature of such operational objectives and the factors that influence their relevance to different firms and potential for successful implementation are explored throughout this section.

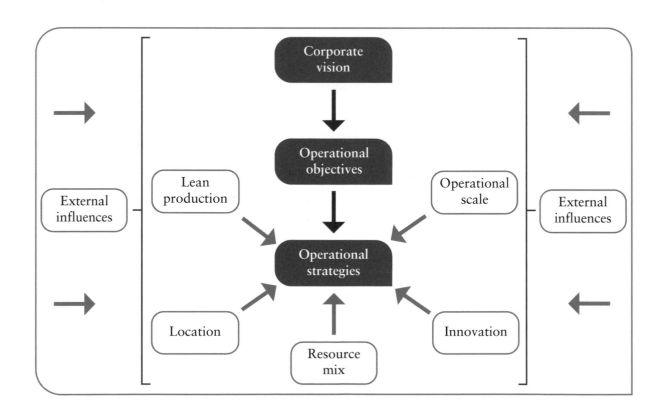

Chapter 11 Operational strategies: understanding operational objectives

This chapter will analyse the nature of operational objectives, such as improving efficiency, and will consider the internal and external factors that influence successful implementation of these objectives.

Operational objectives

Types of operational objective

Operations management is often associated with day-to-day rather than strategic business issues. Operations management might be seen to be concerned with issues such as:

- meeting a daily production target
- making sure enough delivery vans/drivers are available to get goods to customers
- solving daily quality problems.

The role of operations is, however, much more significant than just day-to-day issues. Operations management, no matter what the product or service, has a core role in any organisation. Significant strategic advantage can be gained by improving operations, perhaps, for instance, by getting goods to customers faster than competitors.

Hence, operations is concerned not just with the day-to-day, but also with the longer-term implications of the strengths and weaknesses a business has, and the opportunities and threats it faces. Analysis of such factors, alongside consideration of the long-term direction of the business, will yield a series of specific, functional operations objectives (such as improving quality), and thus operational strategy (how quality will be improved) that allow a firm to *better* meet the needs of customers and gain competitive advantage.

> ## Key terms
>
> **Capital intensity** Processes based mainly on the use of capital (such as machinery).
>
> **Diseconomies of scale** The disadvantages of increasing size that cause unit costs to rise.
>
> **Economies of scale** Factors, such as bulk-buying, that cause the average cost per unit to fall as output increases.
>
> **Efficiency** A measure of how well a business uses its resources, achieving a given output whilst minimising input.
>
> **Labour intensity** Processes where the main input is labour.

> ## Guru's views
>
> 'I was once asked if a big business man ever reached his objective. I replied that if a man ever reached his objective he was not a big business man.'
>
> *Charles M. Schwab*

QUALITY OBJECTIVES

Achieving quality is about meeting customers' expectations. These expectations will differ according to the nature of the business, but in simple terms quality is about 'getting things right' – delivering a product or service to customers that they see as representing fair value for money. Examples of quality objectives might include:

- manufacturing a component within specific tolerance levels
- manufacturing a durable product with a long, useful life
- ensuring that stores are clean and tidy
- ensuring rejected products or customer returns are kept below a target level.

For example...

For examples of the value operations can add, consider, for instance, the achievements of Apple over recent years: its success is based largely on its ability to deliver high-quality, innovative products. Or consider McDonald's: it has built a brand based on its ability to duplicate operations practices globally, allowing it to produce a consistent product and service experience in all of its locations – a key feature of its corporate objectives.

Guru's views

'Your most unhappy customers are your greatest source of learning.'

Bill Gates

Ultimately, achieving quality reduces costs; if the amount of rework, customer complaints and time associated with poor quality can be reduced, so too will costs. Indeed, so high the possible benefits of achieving quality that Crosby, a business guru, states that 'quality costs nothing', suggesting the savings made outweigh the costs of achieving quality.

Quality is a major influence on customer satisfaction and thus quality objectives, whether achieving high quality or expected quality, are a key part of corporate aims and thus operational objectives.

SPEED OBJECTIVES

Lead time, or speed of service, can be a major source of competitive advantage. Objectives related to speed might include:

- a hospital minimising the time a patient waits to be seen by a doctor
- ensuring that every customer is served within three minutes of entering a restaurant
- reducing the time it takes from ordering a good to receipt (lead time)
- speeding up the time to complete a particular service (i.e. dry cleaning).

Speedy service: a possible USP

Not only can speed itself be a USP (offering, for instance, a one-hour dry cleaning service) it also reduces stockholding and other risks. If goods are delivered to customers in a timely manner, the potential for damage (or perishing), theft or obsolescence to occur is reduced (helping to keep wastage and thus costs down).

In the case of fashion retailers, for instance, speed to market reduces the risk of missing a trend. Zara, for example, gets clothes from the design stage to shops in less than six weeks, maximising sales as it hits a trend at its peak and minimising stock left unsold that is no longer fashionable.

Operational objectives related to time are considered in more detail in Chapter 15 (Lean production).

For example...

Roadside races

A key factor in the competition between breakdown companies such as the AA and the RAC is speed of response. Reducing the time it takes for a motorist to contact a call centre, for that information to reach a technician and for that technician to reach the customer, is a key operational challenge. Improvements in this process, such as more efficient call centre operations and GPS locaters showing the nearest technician, have seen average response time, from call to arrival of a technician, fall to below 40 minutes.

FLEXIBILITY OBJECTIVES

Flexibility refers to a business's ability to change what it is doing to meet customers' needs. Objectives might include:

- to implement production methods that allow for unique customisation or mass customisation
- to implement systems able to react swiftly to changing levels of demand (ensuring, perhaps, in a supermarket that all staff are trained to operate tills)
- to implement systems that allow customers to determine delivery date/time.

Flexibility increases the likelihood that a customer's needs can be met and thus sales secured. Customers faced with long checkout queues may prefer to shop at a store flexible enough to open new tills as required by demand.

COST OBJECTIVES

Managing costs will be a key objective for all businesses. Such an objective will not be limited to operations, but given the costs associated with operations, savings here can be significant. Possible objectives might include:

- increasing labour productivity to reduce **labour cost per unit**
- improving the efficiency of a process, reducing time taken and thus labour cost
- designing products for simple, low-cost manufacture
- establishing just-in-time relationships with suppliers to reduce stockholding costs.

Where a company competes on price, achieving cost savings might give competitive edge (enabling it to be the lowest cost player in a market). Where a company does not compete on price, every penny saved is added to profit or creates funds that can be used elsewhere in the business (enabling, for instance, a firm to increase its spending on marketing).

For example...

Manchester U'flighted

AirAsia, an official sponsor of Manchester United, is Asia's leading low-fare, no frills, airline. Started in December 2001 with only two aircraft, AirAsia now operates with more than 30 aircraft with hubs in Malaysia, Thailand and Indonesia.

Like all low-cost airlines Air Asia's success is based on tight management of operations practices. In addition to no-frills flying (no onboard snacks for instance), costs are saved through ticketless check-in and efficient turnaround of airplanes (the more they fly, the more revenue generated). Volume is achieved by doing away with business/first class and putting the maximum numbers of seats on planes possible.

The flexibility of unknown demand faced by many airlines is addressed by offering deeply discounted tickets for early booking, with limited, if any, ability to change (airlines then know what demand is months in advance and can plan capacity accordingly). Added to this, no-frills carriers faced with low demand will cancel flights and bump passengers to the next flight, thus saving costs. Additional restrictions on baggage keep the weight of planes and thus fuel costs down.

The model of no-frills flying is based on stripping the operations of running an airline to the bare minimum, saving cost wherever possible in an effort to offer the lowest possible prices.

VOLUME OBJECTIVES

Meeting volume targets requires achieving specified levels of production within a given period of time. Volume targets might include:

- producing sufficient products to meet daily sales targets
- achieving set production levels to benefit from economies of scale (see Chapter 12)
- building up surplus stock ahead of peak demand.

Volume itself can be a further source of competitive advantage; the ability to satisfy customer orders 100% of the time may be significant in securing customer loyalty (see box on page 167).

INNOVATION OBJECTIVES

Innovation is the introduction of a new product or process. For business, innovation is the successful exploitation of new ideas. Success might be defined as a more efficient process, or a profitable new product. An operational objective to increase innovation might, for example, be seeking to:

- secure first-mover advantage
- create a new market
- establish a product USP and/or develop brand image
- improve process efficiency.

The significance of innovation as an operational objective can be witnessed in the BBC's recent successes in the highly-competitive and saturated media market. It offers a range of innovative programmes (both radio and TV), through a variety of mediums (including a

BIG Beats

In the world of digital downloads, choice and price are key. MP3 download sites generally compete on the number of tracks available for download and on the price of each track. Volume enables download sites to benefit from economies of scale offered by record labels (lower royalties per track depending on the volume of sales) and reduces the unit costs of storing tracks to very low levels.

However, some download sites, seeking to differentiate themselves, use excess capacity (surplus hard disk storage space) generated by this volume approach to offer higher-quality tracks. Both Beatport and iTunes offer higher bitrate downloads for customers not happy with basic MP3/AAC quality. Volume strategies have allowed both companies to be creative with the excess capacity created (and to generate higher revenues on this excess capacity through sales of the premium-priced higher-quality tracks).

considerable presence online) and has been a leader in offering innovative concert formats and promotional events, enhancing its reputation as a cutting-edge media company.

Operational objectives related to innovation are considered in more detail in Chapter 13.

EFFICIENCY OBJECTIVES

Operational objectives that relate to efficiency may include:

- reducing the **time** a process takes to complete
- increasing **output** to meet sales targets
- reducing waste (and thus **cost**) in the production process.

Primarily, as the above objectives demonstrate, efficiency is about speed, volume and cost; achieving desired outcomes with the best combination of inputs. A volume target, for example, may be easy to reach if enough money is spent on staff or machinery, however, if the same output could be achieved through improvements in production processes or better staff training, that is, through more efficient operations, not only are costs lowered, but needless investment also saved.

Efficiency is considered in more detail in Chapter 12.

ENVIRONMENTAL OBJECTIVES

As consumers and society in general becomes more aware of and more concerned with environmental issues, having objectives that relate to the environment is increasingly essential. It is in areas related to operations that, often, the environmental 'footprint' of firms is highest, thus operational objectives in this area are critical. Examples might include:

- reducing pollution caused by the production process
- increasing the efficiency of production processes to reduce raw material requirements
- increasing the proportion of firm's vehicles that run on lower-emission fuels
- positively contributing to environmental regeneration by, for example, using byproducts as alternative energy sources or fertiliser.

There is much debate as to the motivation of firms for pursuing such objectives. Do firms pursue environmental objectives because it is morally right, or because doing so helps to lower costs (through, for example, increased recycling) and improves a firm's reputation (and thus sales)?

Business impact on the environment, associated issues and objectives are considered in more detail in Chapter 23.

Turning objectives into strategy

As discussed in Chapter 1, objectives such as those suggested above need to be developed in terms that are SMART (**S**pecific, **M**easurable, **A**greed, **R**ealistic and **T**ime-related). These objectives will then be taken on by functional teams and turned into strategies that will detail the processes by which each objective will be reached.

Figure 11.1 gives examples of how corporate aims may relate to operations aims and thus subsequent operational strategy.

Activity

In relation to a business of your choice, take a relevant operational objective, rewrite it in SMART terms and develop a broad strategy as to how the business might work towards achieving this objective.

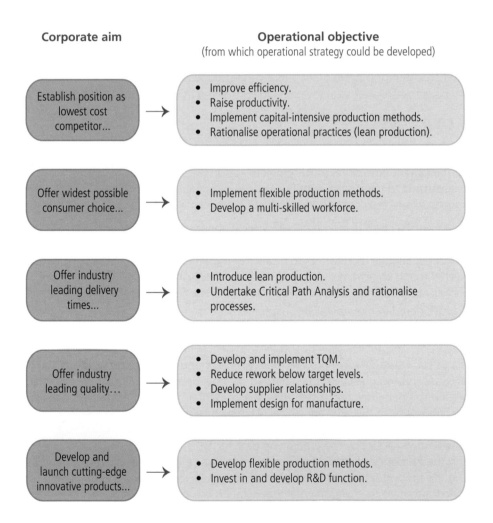

Corporate aim

Operational objective
(from which operational strategy could be developed)

Establish position as lowest cost competitor… →
- Improve efficiency.
- Raise productivity.
- Implement capital-intensive production methods.
- Rationalise operational practices (lean production).

Offer widest possible consumer choice… →
- Implement flexible production methods.
- Develop a multi-skilled workforce.

Offer industry leading delivery times… →
- Introduce lean production.
- Undertake Critical Path Analysis and rationalise processes.

Offer industry leading quality… →
- Develop and implement TQM.
- Reduce rework below target levels.
- Develop supplier relationships.
- Implement design for manufacture.

Develop and launch cutting-edge innovative products… →
- Develop flexible production methods.
- Invest in and develop R&D function.

Figure 11.1 Strategic influences on operational objectives

Conflicting objectives

Considering the possible range of operational objectives it is clear that often they will be in conflict. Designing manufacturing systems for flexibility may conflict with the needs of design for volume or low cost. Other possible conflicts can be seen in Figure 11.2.

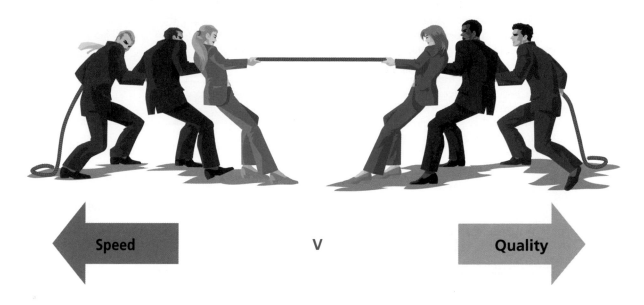

Objective		Objective
Speed	vs	Quality
Low cost	vs	Reliability
Innovation	vs	Low cost
Volume	vs	Quality
Environmental concerns	vs	Speed

Figure 11.2 Example of possible conflicts between operational objectives

The challenge for operations managers is to balance these conflicts, determining which objectives are more significant given market position, customer needs, competitive pressures and overall corporate strategy.

Skills watch!

Stack them high

Aldi and Lidl, the discount food retailers, typically offer a very limited range of products compared to the vast choice at conventional supermarkets. Stocking such a small range of products enables them to benefit from significant economies of scale and offer very low prices. The trade-off is choice; customers often find that they have to shop at one of the discounters and another supermarket. For many retailers, deliberately restricting choice in the full knowledge that customers will need to visit a competitor could spell disaster. For Aldi and Lidl this is no issue, offering the lowest prices is the primary concern – they believe, with recent performance supporting the strategy, that if prices are low enough customers will keep coming back.

Lidl - low prices, limited choice

Activity

Consider the competitive position of Aldi and Lidl in relation to other supermarkets and the current state of the economy. To what extent do you believe a strategy based solely on cost is likely to be successful?

The challenge of evaluation, a key skill in examinations, is weighing up which of the arguments presented might, given the context of a business, be the most significant. In the case of Aldi and Lidl, operational strategy is based on price; for another retailer a strategy based on choice may be more significant.

Assessing internal and external influences on operational objectives

Management is not free to determine operational objectives in isolation; internal and external factors will have a bearing on how realistic and relevant different objectives might be.

Internal influences

In addition to corporate vision, a variety of other internal factors will affect operational objectives.

NATURE OF PRODUCT

The type of product sold will influence operational objectives:

- A firm selling a relatively generic product (such as milk), may need to focus on volume and efficiency to keep costs (and therefore price) down.
- A printing company may need to focus on speed.
- Games console manufacturers need to focus on innovation.

The stage a product is at in its product life cycle may also influence operational objectives as illustrated in Figure 11.3.

HUMAN RESOURCE ISSUES

A strategy based on quality and flexibility may require highly motivated and skilled staff; the availability of such staff may influence the extent to which a firm is able to pursue this strategy.

The influence of trade unions may also affect objectives. A volume strategy may be best achieved through a greater degree of automation; the extent to which trade unions are able to influence a firm's decisions may influence how much automation occurs.

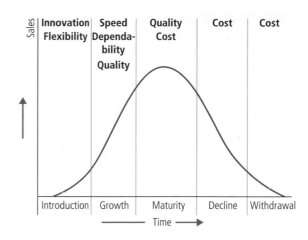

Figure 11.3 Product life cycle and possible operational objectives

FINANCE AVAILABLE

The amount of capital available to a firm may determine the scope and scale of operations. A corporate aim to capture market share might be achieved through a capital-intensive, volume-based approach or through focusing on differentiation (perhaps through speed of delivery). The amount of finance available might influence which strategy is chosen.

External influences

THE MARKET

The level and consistency of demand in a market affects operational objectives. A firm facing highly seasonal demand will need flexible operations practices; a firm facing steady demand may be able to focus on reliability and consistency.

COMPETITORS' ACTIONS

The actions of competitors have a significant and varied impact on operations. The presence of a dominant competitor may influence a smaller firm to focus its operations on quality, or in the absence of competition suggest a volume strategy to capture market share.

In the mobile phone industry, competitive pressure demands constant innovation. Motorola has struggled over recent years to keep pace with this innovation (in both function and design) and sales have slumped as a result.

It is important to note that the type of competitive advantage a firm seeks over its rivals, for example, whether it aims to establish a unique selling point that differentiates its product from the competition or whether it seeks to compete through a low-cost, low-price strategy, will be determined as much by the external actions of competitors as by internal aims.

CONSUMER PRESSURE

Companies face increasing pressure by consumers to reduce their environmental impact. The greater the environmental 'footprint' of a firm and/or the greater the pressure from consumers, the more significant environmental objectives may be.

Skills watch!

Business in practice

Ultimately, it is likely that the distinction between factors that are internal or external will, in practice, be blurred – a decision to compete in a niche market (thus perhaps suggesting an operational focus on quality) may be determined as much by external competitive pressure, as by a firm's internal strength with regard to quality.

A further question to consider is to what extent operational objectives are determined *by* these factors or rather emerge *from* them. Management may be merely reacting to these various influences and not considering them in a strategic way. Operational objectives may then emerge from day-to-day issues (customers are reporting quality problems – how do we solve them?) rather than being determined by longer-term corporate aims.

The existence of text book theory does not automatically mean that this is followed by business. Dealing with day-to-day issues takes up the vast majority of most managers' time; in practice, strategy, rather than being proactive, may simply be a reaction to daily issues.

Activity

Investigate how much time a manager known to you spends dealing with day-to-day problems versus longer-term strategic issues.

Summary and exam guidance

Summary

- Operations management has a key role to play in the success of any organisation. Whether product- or service-based, firms need to have operational practices in place that meet the needs of customers. Developing operational practices that *better* meet the needs of customers can add significant value and be a key source of competitive advantage.

- Linked to overall corporate aims and influenced by internal and external factors, operational objectives determine the main areas in which operations can support and drive business improvement.

- Operational objectives include things such as a focus on quality, volume targets, speed, reliability, efficiency, and increasingly, environmental targets.

- Operations objectives (what are we going to do?) determine operational strategy (how are we going to do it?).

- Internal factors, such as the type of product being sold and human resource issues, determine, in part, the nature of operational objectives.

- External influences, such as the actions of competitors, also have a significant effect on operational objectives.

- Operational objectives may emerge from day-to-day issues as well as from longer-term strategic thinking.

Exam practice

Read the articles below and then answer the questions that follow.

Thirsty business

On the outskirts of Chandler, a small city in the US, where the few remaining farms fade into the scrub, stand three huge Intel computer chip manufacturing plants: Fab 12, Fab 22 and the gleaming new Fab 32.

Chip fabrication is a thirsty business. Every day the Intel plants use 2 million gallons of water. Much of this is recycled; water used to wash chips is then used in the plants' cooling system and 'grey' water (water too dirty to be recycled) is used to irrigate the landscaped gardens.

Intel isn't simply trying to be a good corporate citizen; nor is it merely out to save money. Sustainable operations help to smooth regulatory processes. Because Intel was well within the US

The gleaming interior of an Intel microchip plant

government's environmental impact regulations, when Fab 32 was built it did not require an (expensive and time-consuming) water use permit.

Amazon.everything

Inside one of Amazon's huge distribution warehouses it's a Donkey Kong world of overhead conveyer belts, automated chutes and robotic tilt trays. Such complex automation allows Amazon to deal with 1000s of daily transactions getting the right products to customers quickly and reliably.

Amazon has not, however, always got it right. When, faced with competitive pressure from eBay, Amazon attempted to move into online auctions; its operations were, at the time, not built to cope. Problems with speed, reliability and capacity forced Amazon to radically alter its operations strategy, massively increasing the volume its computer servers and warehouses could cope with.

Much of Amazon's transformation from simple online book retailer to massive online storefront for everything from DVDs to lawnmowers has, in many ways, happened by evolution rather than design. Back in the dark days of dial-up (i.e. slow) internet access Amazon needed a cheap and easy way to expand their reach; at the time the

technology to realise Amazon's vision of stocking every book, CD and DVD ever produced did not exist. Amazon tweaked its operations model, allowing others to sell products through its site in the 'Amazon Marketplace', taking the retailer a step closer to its aim.

A stock control nightmare?

Source: adapted from *Wired* Magazine, 16 May 2008

(a) With reference to the two case studies, evaluate the factors that may motivate a firm to set and pursue environmental objectives. (15 marks)

(b) To what extent are a firm's operational objectives determined solely by corporate vision? (25 marks)

Total: 40 marks7

Breakdown of assessment objectives

AO1 – Knowledge and understanding –6/40
AO2 – Apply knowledge and understanding –11/40
AO3 – Analyse problems, issues and situations –10/40
AO4 – Evaluate, distinguish between fact and opinion, assess and judge information from a variety of sources –13/40

Suggested structure

For part (a) you will need to:

- Show clear understanding of environmental objectives.
- Analyse arguments supporting why businesses pursue environmental objectives.
- Support this analysis with examples from the case studies.
- Evaluate to what extent pursuing such objectives may be driven by internal or external factors.

For part (b) you will need to:

- Show a clear understanding of operational objectives and corporate vision.
- Discuss operational objectives that may be linked to corporate vision.
- Analyse corporate objectives that may be driven by factors other than corporate vision.
- Support this analysis with references to the case studies.
- Discuss possible issues related to the relevance of vision to dynamic competitive environments.
- Conclude with a reasoned evaluation in relation to the question, identifying significant drivers of operational objectives and factors that will influence the extent to which a firm is free to pursue a corporate vision.

Chapter 12 Operational strategies: scale and resource mix

A major strategic issue facing businesses is that of scale – what is the optimal size (scale) at which to operate? This chapter will focus on the strategic issues of **efficient** operations for small, large and growing businesses, with reference to the advantages and disadvantages of increasing scale. Additionally, consideration will be given to the appropriate balance of labour or capital usage given a firm's scale, context and strategic direction.

Efficiency

The concept of efficiency refers to how well a business is using its resources. Consider the following example in Figure 12.1.

Despite making the same amount of profit, it is clear that business B is more efficient – to achieve the same level of profit it has used fewer staff and less capital.

Efficiency then, is not just about output, it is also about how well inputs are used to create outputs. If the same output can be achieved with fewer inputs, efficiency has improved.

Business	Profit	Number of staff	Capital employed
Business A	£5m	500	£75m
Business B	£5m	200	£50m

Figure 12.1 Basic comparison of business performance

A key measure of efficiency is how well costs are being managed. This could, for example, be the cost of stock or the cost of transportation. Often the main cost a business faces is labour costs (for a school, labour costs – mainly the employment of teachers – can be as high as 80% of total costs). Thus a key measure of efficiency might be how well a business is using its labour (**labour productivity**):

$$\text{Labour productivity} = \frac{\text{Output (per period)}}{\text{Number of employees (per period)}}$$

The higher the result, in simple terms, the more efficiently labour is being used.

Efficiency might also be measured by considering how well capital (buildings, machinery, etc.) is being used:

$$\text{Capital productivity} = \frac{\text{Output (per period)}}{\text{Capital employed (per period)}}$$

Again, the higher the result, the more efficiently capital is being used.

Efficiency is important because better-managed costs can lead to greater price competitiveness and/or improved profitability.

Inefficiency, on the other hand, can be demotivating for staff, frustrating for customers and damaging to the environment. Where a business operates efficiently, staff may enjoy a greater level of job satisfaction (there are fewer barriers to them doing a good job); equally, customers may enjoy faster service and shorter lead times (improving sales). Efficient businesses may produce less waste, recycle more and consume less power, all reducing impact on the environment (and enhancing reputation).

A productive workspace or just a messy one?

However, businesses do not always pursue maximum efficiency; lack of motivation, knowledge and management skills often mean that organisations never achieve, nor aim to achieve, optimal efficiency. Indeed, it is possible for an organisation to survive and profit despite not being as efficient as it could be. A firm in a monopoly position (such as Microsoft) may enjoy such high profits that there is little perceived need for managers to worry about efficiency.

For a business aiming to improve profitability, ensuring the knowledge, skill and motivation exist to maximise efficiency is a key strategic challenge. Part of this challenge lies in ensuring that the business operates, to the extent possible, at its most efficient scale (size).

Skills watch!

AO2

Remember that efficiency and productivity are concerned with output *and* how well **inputs** are used; output may remain the same but inputs fall and thus efficiency improves.

Equally, it is possible for output to rise, but efficiency to fall if, for instance, 10% more labour only resulted in a 5% increase in output.

Being wary of such subtle differences, having secure knowledge of key topics and being mindful of the language being used in answers (for example, profit versus profitability) is an important skill at A2.

Choosing the right scale of production: economies and diseconomies of scale

Economies of scale

Economies of scale cause the **average cost per unit** to fall as output increases. In simple terms, economies of scale can be seen as the main advantage of increasing business scale (size). Consider the following example in Figure 12.2.

As Figure 12.2 shows, when more T-shirts are made, the average cost of producing **each** T-shirt falls; total costs rise, but the **cost per unit** falls.

Graphically this can be seen in Figure 12.3.

Output	Average cost per unit	Total cost
10	£4 per unit	£40
100	£3 per unit	£300

Figure 12.2 T-shirt manufacturer

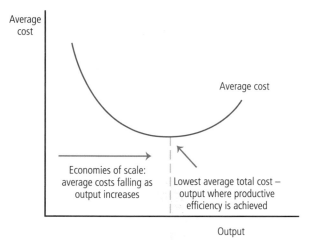

Figure 12.3 Economies of scale

It is through economies of scale that, for instance, large supermarkets such as Tesco are able to offer much lower prices than smaller competitors and make such high profits (£2.85bn for the year end April 2008).

For example, if the average unit cost of producing a pizza for Tesco is £1 but for its competitors is £1.50, if the competitor prices at £2.99, Tesco can undercut this at £2.79 *and* still enjoy a higher profit margin (Tesco receives £1.79 per item, whilst the competition only receive £1.49).

There are two types of economies of scale: **internal** and **external**.

INTERNAL ECONOMIES OF SCALE

Bulk-buying economies

If you purchased 100 T-shirts from a store you would expect to pay less **per T-shirt** than if you bought only one. The larger an order, the greater the customers' bargaining power and thus the lower cost per unit.

For example...

Peeeeerfect

Vets, evidence suggests, are one of the most profitable business categories in Britain, squeezing a 37% return on capital from their pooch-loving customers.

Wealthy pet-owners, who once visited the vet only for simple things such worming tablets, neutering or due to pet illness, now demand heart surgery, chemotherapy and costly alternative medicines. The number of procedures being completed has seen economies of scale drive costs down.

Pet owners have, however, complained that these economies are not being passed on in the form of lower prices. For instance, the average charge for simple feline dental work is £232, similar treatments on a human cost half that!

No wonder then that vets enjoy such a high return on capital, they are able to charge high prices for a premium product, whilst economies of scale drive costs down – a puuuurfect situation!

Source: adapted from http://business.timesonline.co.uk/tol/business/industry_sectors/support_services/article4144160.ece (June 16th 2008) and http://www.tescofinance.com/personal/finance/insurance/petins/elh/vet-fees.html

---

Technical economies

As a business grows, the viability of using machinery also increases. A small firm may have little use for a machine capable of efficiently producing 10,000 units per week, whereas a larger firm may be able to use the machine and benefit from lower labour and lower unit costs as a result. Even if both firms (small and large) used the same machine, the large firm may use it more fully (better **capacity utilisation**) and thus fixed costs are spread over more units of production (the average fixed cost per unit produced would be higher for the smaller firm).

Additionally, as a firm grows it may be more feasible for a firm to undertake R&D (maybe coming up with new, more efficient methods of production) and, for example, to use computer systems to increase efficiency.

Financial economies

Larger firms often enjoy better access to finance than smaller ones. The terms of loans are often better for larger firms (lower interest rates and longer repayment periods) and finance easier to get (banks are more willing to loan to 'safer', larger businesses with proven track records). Better finance terms thus contribute to lower average costs.

Marketing economies

The more units sold, the lower the cost of marketing **per unit**. For instance, in Tesco's case, the cost of a multi-million dollar marketing campaign is spread over many thousands of products sold; for small firms a similar campaign may add significantly to the average cost per unit and may not be feasible. Figure 12.4 illustrates this concept further.

Figure 12.4 Marketing economies

Managerial economies

Larger firms are able to employ staff and managers to perform specialist functions (e.g. accounting). Specialised staff are likely to be more efficient at performing tasks leading to lower overall costs. In smaller firms numerous decisions will be made by a relatively small group (possibly just the owner) and may not be completed as efficiently.

For example...

Tesco TV

In addition to lowering costs through economies of scale, larger firms also enjoy the benefits of being able to spread risk. For example, Tesco's profits are not dependent on any one line of products. A recession might cause sales of luxury goods (such as TVs and DVD players) to fall, but for Tesco sales lost here may be more than made up for by sales of other (lower-priced, so-called 'inferior') goods. A small firm, selling only TVs and DVDs, may be dependent on these products and thus severely exposed in times of recession.

EXTERNAL ECONOMIES OF SCALE

Where a whole industry grows in size (think of the mobile phone industry over the last decade) individual firms can benefit from lower unit costs as a result. These benefits are outside of the firm's direct control and thus are known as external economies of scale.

Infrastructure

As an industry grows, systems needed to support it also grow; for instance, better communication links (roads built to a particular area) or better access to ICT (faster broadband connections). For example, Silicon Glen in Scotland has benefited from improved air and road links, lowering transport costs for firms located there.

Supply of labour

For firms operating in larger industries, the greater availability of skilled labour can reduce recruitment and training costs (as the mobile phone industry has grown, so too has the pool of skilled labour). Smaller industries may find recruitment of suitable staff more difficult and may face much higher training costs (if, for instance, new staff need to be retrained).

Supplier networks

As an industry grows, so too will the number of suppliers. A larger number of suppliers can, through increased competition, help to keep raw materials' costs down. There may also be an increase in firms providing support services (for example, mobile phone repair) again, through competition, helping to lower costs.

These external economies are enjoyed by firms that operate in large, national markets but might equally be enjoyed where firms in a particular industry locate together (known as **concentration**). For example, many of the above examples would apply to firms located in the Cambridge Science Park (an area of Cambridge with a high concentration of high-tech, research firms).

Skills watch!

A02 / A04

Survival of the smallest?

The existence of economies of scale begs the question: how do small firms survive? If large businesses enjoy such advantages, why do small businesses make up the majority of the economy?

The answer is that small businesses are able to exploit some of the disadvantages of size suffered by large firms (known as diseconomies of scale – see next page). Some examples are found below.

Personal service

Smaller firms are able to give more individual service; many people are happy to pay for better service and better product knowledge (consider buying an expensive plasma TV from Tesco versus from a small specialist store!).

Flexibility

Small firms may be able to react faster to customer needs and secure sales as a result. Small firms may be willing to 'do deals' whereas a large firm may not (imagine asking for a discount in Tesco when buying a TV and DVD; in a specialist store such discounts might be the norm).

Specialisation

Small firms often produce highly-specialised, possibly unique products in niche markets. Such firms do not compete on price and thus economies of scale become less relevant.

In some industries it is simply the case that there are few economies of scale to be exploited. For instance, childcare for toddlers is usually offered by small firms as it would be difficult for a large firm to exploit any economies and thus achieve competitive advantage. Large firms are thus 'discouraged' from entering these markets.

Remember, high marks come from being able to present a balanced picture. It is not simply the case that larger is better; business size needs to be appropriate to context.

Guru's views

'What counts is not necessarily the size of the dog in the fight; it's the size of the fight in the dog.'

Dwight David Eisenhower

Diseconomies of scale

Diseconomies of scale occur when a business grows so large that costs per unit increase. Figure 12.5 illustrates diseconomies of scale graphically; beyond the **minimum efficient scale**, average costs rise as output (scale) increases.

Diseconomies of scale occur mainly as a result of human resource issues:

Average cost

Average cost

Diseconomies of scale

Average costs rise as output increases

Output

Figure 12.5 Graphical representation of diseconomies of scale

- **Motivation** In large businesses staff often feel very distant from management. Workers may feel isolated from decision-making, undervalued by management and may not feel that they 'belong' to the organisation. This can lower motivation, cause productivity to fall and thus increase average labour costs per unit. Additionally, lower motivation might see absenteeism and labour turnover rise (further adding to costs).

- **Poor communication** The larger the business, the more difficult effective communication becomes. Getting messages to all staff in a timely manner and ensuring that they are understood can be very challenging for large firms (to combat this some firms, for instance, Richer Sounds, send weekly videos from the CEO to all staff). Poor communication not only slows a business down and allows mistakes to be made, it also contributes to declining motivation (staff may be unsure what to do, who to talk to and what to do if something goes wrong).

- **Alignment to the vision** A challenge for large firms is to ensure that all staff work towards the same strategic goal. Ensuring everybody is doing the right thing, in the right way, becomes much more difficult as a firm grows. To combat this, layers of supervision may be added (increasing cost) and rigid procedures introduced (increasing bureaucracy, slowing a business down and adding to costs).

Skills watch!

A02

Earn and learn

Students are, potentially, in an ideal position to witness diseconomies of scale in action. Many jobs undertaken by students involve working part time for large firms. Part-time workers are often the first to feel the effects of diseconomies of scale. The very nature of part-time work makes communication and motivation difficult

(management may not even be working when part-time staff are). As a result, part-time staff may not be as efficient/productive as full-time workers – systems in place (see opposite) to ensure efficiency may not 'stretch' to all part-time staff.

Business Studies does not just happen in the classroom; relating theory to the real world can add significantly to understanding and, ultimately, to grades!

MANAGING DISECONOMIES OF SCALE

Such are the potential costs of diseconomies of scale that firms spend considerable energy in managing them. In fact, many of the strategies discussed in this book are borne of managements' desire to handle potential diseconomies of scale more effectively.

Such possible strategies include (for more detail refer to relevant chapters in this and the AS level text):

- **Matrix management** – an attempt to manage large firms in the same, team-based manner as small firms.
- **Empowerment** – attempting to motivate staff (and speed business processes up) by delegating decision-making power throughout an organisation.
- **Job enrichment** – adding variety and challenge to jobs to enhance motivation.
- **Decentralisation** – decision-making is delegated to individual business units (for instance, a branch of a high-street chain). The individual unit then operates more like a small firm, but under the broad direction of a head office.
- **Profit/Cost centres** – individual units are made responsible for controlling costs, or generating profits in much the same way as a single, small business would be.

Ultimately, as size increases, diseconomies of scale are inevitable. However, the existence of diseconomies is not a reason to suggest that all firms should remain small; indeed the success of Tesco has been based on is ability to exploit economies of scale whilst minimising the impact of diseconomies of scale. It is perfectly possible that a firm, such as Tesco, facing significant diseconomies of scale, makes more profit than it would at a smaller scale (**profitability** may be lower, due to higher costs, but overall profit may actually be higher).

Choosing the optimal mix of resources: capital and labour intensity

Choosing the optimal mix of resources refers to how much of one factor of production (such as labour) is used in relation to other factors (such as capital, i.e. machinery). Achieving the optimal mix of resources is important as it can determine profitability and the extent to which economies of scale can be exploited.

Capital intensity vs labour intensity

A **capital-intensive** firm will use a greater proportion of capital than labour. Capital-intensive firms should, in theory, enjoy higher productivity than labour-intensive firms. Capital-intensive firms often sell products aimed at the mass market.

A **labour-intensive** firm will use a greater proportion of labour than capital. Labour-intensive firms may enjoy higher profit margins than capital-intensive firms as they can charge price premiums for products (the labour-intensive nature perhaps being a USP). Labour-intensive firms often sell products aimed at niche markets.

Figure 12.6 on page 182 gives a comparison of the two strategies.

Key

= Possible benefit

= Possible drawback

Factor	Capital intensive	Labour intensive
Economies of scale	Potentially able to benefit from significant economies of scale and thus lower unit costs.	Less able to exploit economies of scale.
Pricing	Likely to be competing, at least to a degree, on price and thus needs to exploit the lower unit costs of capital-intensive production methods.	Less likely to be competing on price, potentially premium-priced products utilising labour-driven production as a USP.
Flexibility I	Potentially able to react to increases in demand at relatively short notice. Customer orders can usually be fulfilled.	Availability of skilled labour may restrict a firm's ability to react quickly to changes in demand (it may take a long time to train staff). Long waiting lists for products may be the norm.
Flexibility II	Limited ability to alter production to suit individual needs.	Labour-driven approach may allow a firm to alter products to suit customer needs.
Break even	Due to significant cost of installing machinery (high fixed costs), break even may be very high (many units need to be sold for capital-intensive processes to pay for themselves).	Low investment in capital means break even is low. The main component of cost is that of labour (variable).
		However, margins of safety may be low – a small reduction in output may push a firm below break even as each unit sold is making a significant **contribution**.

Figure 12.6   Comparison of labour vs. capital intensity

GETTING THE MIX RIGHT

Choosing the right mix of capital versus labour intensity will depend on the following factors.

Internal factors

A business needs to consider its internal strengths, weaknesses and areas of competitive advantage. For example, a firm with well-motivated, highly-skilled staff may be able to exploit this as a USP and thus a labour-intensive process may be most relevant.

Additionally, capital intensity usually requires the building of expensive production lines or the purchase of expensive machinery. If such large sums of finance are not available, a firm may be limited to a more labour-intensive approach.

Size and nature of market

Larger markets may be better exploited by capital-intensive approaches (enabling a firm to price for the mass market). For example, LEGO, a global product with a staggering 400 billion pieces in circulation, manufactures 19 billion pieces a year through a very capital-intensive manufacturing process.

On the other hand, niche markets may be better exploited by labour-intensive approaches, where customers prefer 'hand-crafted' products or require flexibility. An Aston Martin car, for instance, has the name of the worker who built the engine stamped on it and Aston will go to great lengths to meet a customer's specific needs (customising interiors, for example).

Some industries, however, require human input, making it impossible to move to more capital-intensive processes (consider the role of a plumber – the job production nature of their work gives little scope for automation).

LEGO – 400 billion pieces in circulation

Availability of labour

Labour-intensive processes obviously require the availability of suitably-skilled labour. If such staff are in short supply, it may be more cost-effective to switch to a capital-intensive process. Equally, a firm may be labour-intensive because it is able to exploit the availability of cheap, low-skilled labour.

For example...

Traditional techniques, cheap labour

The process of clothing manufacture is, to an extent, relatively easy to automate. Machines could do much of the work. Despite this, most clothing is predominantly handmade. Clothing manufacturers exploit the low labour costs in countries such as China, Vietnam and Cambodia. Despite using relatively old-fashioned and, in modern terms, inefficient manufacturing processes, labour is so cheap that costs remain low.

External factors

A significant increase in wage costs (perhaps due to a rise in the minimum wage) may drive a business towards capital intensity. Rising costs (such as the rising price of oil) may squeeze a firm's profit margins. In an effort to lower costs a firm may move towards more capital-intensive production methods (this has, in fact, been the case with Aston Martin, in a shrinking sports car market it has needed to move towards a *more* capital-intensive process to lower costs).

For example, a mass-market product requiring high volumes with limited product variety and a simple production process lends itself to a capital-intensive production method.

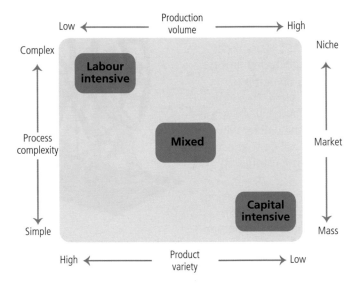

Skills watch!

AO4

The significance of size

Whilst growth is not the aim of every business, given the advantages inherent in increasing scale, it is a significant aim for many. Importantly, this does not mean that all businesses want to be the next Microsoft. Bigger is not always better; absolute size does not matter. Most significant is how a business manages its size, balancing economies and diseconomies of scale, and seeking competitiveness and profitability through efficient operations.

Figure 12.7 Getting the mix right: diagrammatic representation of capital versus labour intensity process choice, showing relationship between volume, complexity, variety and market strategy

Summary and exam guidance

Summary

- Efficiency, making the best use of resources, is important to all businesses. Managing efficiency becomes more difficult as firms grow.

- Economies of scale are the advantages a business gains as it grows. Larger firms benefit from lower costs per unit and thus a greater ability to compete on price.

- Diseconomies of scale, such as poor communication, are the disadvantages firms suffer as they grow.

- Small firms are able to exploit the diseconomies suffered by large firms, for instance, providing a more personal service, and thus surviving and prospering.

- The optimal mix of capital versus labour intensity is achieved by balancing a firm's internal strengths (such as skilled labour) and weaknesses against the context in which it operates (for instance, niche or mass market).

Exam practice

Read the article below and then answer the questions that follow.

Is big beautiful?

So-called 'big box', out-of-town stores such as Tesco have traditionally been considered a significant threat to small, local retail operations; the recent trend for larger retailers to open small-format city centre stores is, however, painting a different picture.

In urban areas, rather than driving out small competing businesses, evidence suggests that small-format stores, such as Tesco *Metro*, can actually increase customer traffic in an area; something that benefits all businesses.

Stores such as Tesco *Metro*, with their discounted prices, are in effect creating external economies of scale for all firms in an area. Rather than driving to out-of-town superstores to benefit from low prices, customers can now get the same prices (albeit with less choice due to smaller store size) in the new urban stores. The spillover effect, benefiting small firms, is that customers headed for the new stores might also pay them a visit.

One small retailer noted, 'People come in here looking for service; they go to the big stores and no one can or will help them. I offer service and flexible choice... They only have price.' She added, '...if I have not got something in stock, I will pick up the phone and get it; if a customer has special needs I will do what I can to meet them.' Notably, she also claimed that the big stores often look to her for market guidance: 'I tend to stock lunchtime snacks for the office crowds. Over the years I have got to

Small, local stores can attract customers to shop locally

know what people like; at first they (the big stores) didn't stock these things, but they do now. Never mind, I change my line-up faster than they can and people still buy from me – who wants to eat the same type of lunch all of the time?'

Research suggests that if a business can distinguish itself sufficiently and play to strengths – such as service – in areas where bigger stores are weak, it is possible to compete even with the likes of Tesco's massive economies of scale.

Even the successful small firms do, however, strike a note of caution – firms such as Tesco offer such deep discounts with which small firms simply cannot compete generally. The minor successes of a few small retailers located near to new *Metro* style stores is little consolation to the many thousands of smaller stores put out of business by the might of the 'big boxes'.

(a) 'Bigger is better – small businesses will always struggle to compete against larger ones.' With reference to the case study, to what extent do you agree with this statement? (25 marks)

(b) If diseconomies of scale are inevitable, why do businesses choose to grow to a point where they exist? (15 marks)

Total: 40 marks

Breakdown of assessment objectives

AO1 – Knowledge and understanding – 6/40
AO2 – Apply knowledge and understanding – 10/40
AO3 – Analyse problems, issues and situations – 10/40
AO4 – Evaluate, distinguish between fact and opinion, assess and judge information from a variety of sources – 14/40

Suggested structure

For part (a) you will need to:

- Show clear understanding of economies/diseconomies of scale.
- Present an analysis of arguments supporting larger businesses.
- Present an analysis of arguments showing how small businesses might compete.
- Show application of knowledge with regard to how small firms compete within the context of the case.
- Evaluate the extent to which your arguments may or may not apply to all small businesses.
- Draw a conclusion, indicating the significant factors in relation to the statement 'Bigger is better…'.

For part (b) you will need to:

- Show clear understanding of the causes of and possible solutions to diseconomies of scale.
- Analyse the issues surrounding solutions to diseconomies, including lack of knowledge.
- Demonstrate an understanding of the benefits of growth and evaluate these benefits against the diseconomies associated with growth.
- Assess the validity of the statement 'diseconomies of scale are inevitable'.
- Draw an evaluative conclusion, indicating the significant factors in relation to pursuing growth and the associated diseconomies of scale.

Chapter 13   Operational strategies: innovation

In this chapter you will learn about the role of innovation in business strategy. You will learn that innovation can be present in products and processes, and that innovation is not just about the use of technology. You will be encouraged to reflect on how strategic innovation can create USPs, be a driver for reduced costs and be motivating for staff. You will learn that, generally, innovation is routed in R&D (research and development), that it can be costly and risky, but potentially a significant source of competitive advantage.

Innovation, research and development

What is innovation?

Innovation is simply the introduction of something new. This might be a new product, an adaption/update of an old product, a new use for an 'old' product or the implementation of a new or refined process.

Innovation is often driven by new technology, but does not have to be. Simply doing something in a new or different way can be considered innovative. Take, for example, Formula 1 motorsport; one of the most innovative changes to F1 in recent times was the introduction of a new night race in Singapore (a process innovation – doing something in a different way).

Innovation is a fundamental part of human life. Our development as a species has been driven by innovation (fire was once innovative, as was the wheel).

In business terms, innovation is the successful exploitation of new ideas. Success might be defined as a more efficient process, or a profitable new product. Most companies innovate in some way; those that do not may struggle to remain competitive. Even a company selling a 'traditional' product (perhaps a hotel, well

For example...

LIGHT YEARS AHEAD?

Nike's strategic approach to the competitive football boot market is based on constant innovation – providing ever more innovative football boots through the use of increasingly lighter materials and new features. The successful introduction of the Nike *Total 90 Laser II* football boot (lighter and more accurate than previous boots) is an example of Nike's strategy of innovation driving sales, enabling Nike to secure a 56% share of the football boot market in the Premiership.

Source: www.nike.com

Skills watch!

A01

You're too young to smoke!

Some cigarette vending machines in Japan now require customers to provide ID for purchase. The legal smoking age in Japan is 20 and vending machines are capable of scanning ID cards to confirm age. The technology for mobile phones to be embedded with ID cards is also being developed allowing m-payment, as is the ability of the vending machines to compare an image of the purchaser with the image on the ID (prohibiting the use of somebody else's ID!).

Activity

Is this the process of product innovation? Why do you believe this to be the case?

known for its traditions) needs to innovate (the way a guest experiences the hotel may feel 'traditional', but it is likely that, behind the scenes, processes are radically different from even ten years ago).

Innovation is usually based on research and development, though there are many examples where an innovative product was simply 'discovered'. A classic example of this is *Post-it* notes; the glue on *Post-its* was a product being developed for a different purpose. It was pure chance that a member of 3M's staff saw an alternative use for the glue.

As you will learn, innovation has implications for all aspects of a business – notably marketing, finance and human resources.

Post-it notes: a classic example of innovation

Skills watch!

A02

Can you think of any businesses that have survived without being innovative? Why have they survived?

Consider the English Premiership; the product (football) has fundamentally changed very little. What have clubs done to differentiate themselves? How have they moved themselves forward? Why is the Premiership considered to be one of the best leagues in the world? What role has innovation had in this?

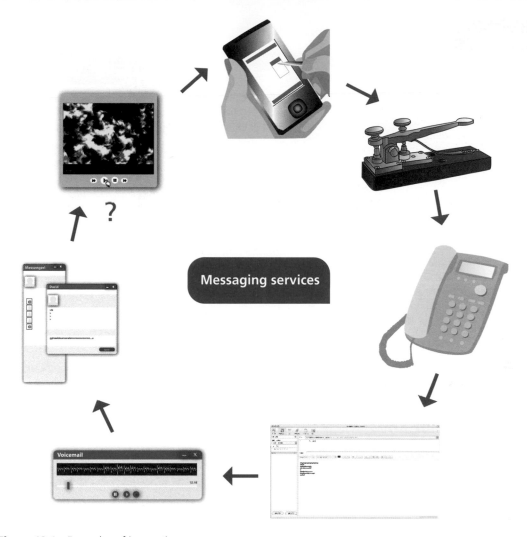

Figure 13.1 Examples of innovations

Purpose, costs, benefits and risks of innovation

Why innovate?

The reason for innovating is simple – to survive, to make profit and to grow. More specific reasons to innovate are listed below.

FIRST-MOVER ADVANTAGE

Getting to market first (with a new product/idea) can capture significant market share (for example, the online retailer, Amazon) and higher margins (the Apple *iPhone*, for instance).

CREATING NEW MARKETS

Companies that move first into truly new market segments (with very new, innovative products) have, for a time at least, the whole market to themselves and can reap the rewards of the high prices early adopters are willing to pay, and secure

Guru's views

'It's kind of fun to do the impossible.'
Walt Disney

Skills watch!

A04

Fast followers

First movers do not always benefit from being first. **Second-mover advantage** occurs when a business enters a market after the first mover, but is able to gain greater *market share*, despite having entered late.

First movers often face significant R&D and marketing costs necessary to launch a new product. A second mover can learn from the experiences of the first mover and may not face such high R&D costs. A second mover also does not face the marketing challenge of educating consumers about the new product

(the first mover has already done so). As a result, the second mover can focus on making better products or on better marketing.

For example, Nintendo entered the games console market before Sony, but through both a superior product and superior marketing, Sony, with its *Playstation*, has dominated the market for a number of years. Notably, Nintendo chose to face the challenge posed by Sony not by being technologically superior, but by being more innovative (the *Wii* control system).

Remember, being first is not *always* better.

long-term brand loyalty. Facebook may fast be catching MySpace up in terms of members, but MySpace (the site largely credited with introducing online social networking) still commands significant loyalty and higher rates for ads placed on the site.

COMPETITIVE ADVANTAGE

Consider the overall success of Apple. Its products are considered highly innovative and even though it is not always first to market (believe it or not, personal music players existed before the *iPod* – remember the *Walkman*?), Apple is highly successful (the *iPod* holds 70% of the MP3 player market (*Wired Magazine,* April 2008)). Apple's USPs are often based on innovative features (such as its touch-screen technology).

SHORTER PRODUCT LIFE CYCLES

Constant innovation means that many products have very short life cycles. In the case of electronic products, new innovations can mean that products are 'old' within a year of introduction. The more innovative products and markets become, the greater the need for companies to innovate in order to stay ahead.

EFFICIENCY

Process innovation, new/better/faster machinery and new technology can all contribute to a lowering of costs; this in turn can lead to increased profitability or improved competitiveness. Consider, for example, the role of robotics in the production of cars, a technology that, for mass market brands, has significantly increased productivity and lowered costs of production.

MOTIVATION

Google has been noted for a number of years to be amongst the best companies in the world to work for. Alongside the many perks, staff cite working for such an innovative company as a motivating factor – it is exciting to work for a company at the cutting edge of new technology, in an environment where staff are encouraged to be creative. Virgin and Apple have similar reputations. Recruitment, retention, productivity and even innovation itself (creativity breeds creativity) benefit as a result.

The Computer v2.0

Microsoft *Surface* is a tabletop computer that's controlled by physical touch instead of a mouse or keyboard.

Since unveiling the Microsoft *Surface* in late 2007, Microsoft has gotten plenty of feedback from businesses and enthusiasts who want to get their hands on the technology. Microsoft feels confident that the touch-based computer could be affordable enough for consumers within a few years.

Surface is a computer built into a table (or flat surface), and its screen is controlled by touch rather than by a mouse/keyboard. *Surface* can be used to track objects, as well as hand gestures. For example, in one Microsoft demonstration, special coasters are used on the *Surface* table to show how it might identify a drink in a bar, and allow a customer to re-order digitally.

While the possibilities for gaming, retail and hospitality are pretty obvious, it's not clear where

Surface would go beyond that. The technology is so new that nobody has yet thought of how it might be used beyond the immediately obvious. Though, if techno-history teaches us anything, it is that the technology will likely be spun off and used in all sorts of new innovations and we will wonder how we ever lived without it (SMS messaging was similarly thought off in the early days of mobile phones).

But such questions of use are for later – for Microsoft and *Surface* fans it's about the thrill of innovation and for them, the sooner *Surface* surfaces the better.

Source: adapted from CNN Money.com, 26 March 2008 (http://money.cnn.com/http://bigtech.blogs.fortune.cnn.com/2008/3/26/microsoft-surface-consumer-version-in-2011/)

Microsoft *Surface* – will we soon wonder how we lived without it?

Activity

1 Why might a company such as Microsoft invest so heavily in unproven technologies such as *Surface*?

2 To what extent does the example above suggest that Microsoft is product or market orientated? Evaluate the likely success of such a strategy.

3 Evaluate Microsoft's strategy of announcing the *Surface* technology a number of years before its commercial launch.

EXTERNAL INFLUENCES

All companies face increasing pressure by governments and consumers to reduce their environmental impact and to conduct business in socially responsible ways. Over recent years this has been a key driver of innovation (for example, the introduction of new bio-diesel and LPG car engines, and the development of less harmful/wasteful methods of production).

How to innovate

Being innovative is not easy. For every *iPod*, *Wii* or Facebook, there are dozens of failed innovations. Coming up with ideas is the first challenge; good ideas then need further development, and finally need to be marketed successfully.

R&D deals with the first of these two stages (idea generation and development); marketing the latter. That said, in the most innovative of companies, innovation is treated in a similar way as quality is treated in organisations following TQM, the philosophy that quality is the concern of everybody within an organisation – innovation is part of the culture and is seen as part of everybody's job.

Once generated, ideas are then reviewed and analysed for development potential. Several ideas may then be taken forward, prototypes made, and market potential and financial viability analysed. From many dozens of ideas, only a few may make it to this stage, and only one or two to eventual production.

Implications of innovation

Innovation is an important component of success for many businesses. It can create USPs and can be a key component of competitive advantage. It can be highly motivating for staff and can contribute to a positive public image for companies (even amongst non-customers, for example, the launch of the *iPhone* generated $400m worth of free PR for Apple).

For companies such as Microsoft, Google and even more traditional companies such as Mercedes, innovation is at the heart of their corporate strategies – bringing a new feature to market first (such as Mercedes *Telematics* – a system through which cars avoid collisions by electronically 'talking' to each other) can impact significantly on sales and, through the ability to charge premium prices, profitability.

For example...

An innovation in the art of DJing

Serato *Scratch Live* is a software programme used by DJs. The product itself is very innovative, allowing DJs to play MP3 files from laptops controlled by special vinyl records or CDs. The product is not unique though; several competing products do a similar thing. What is unique, though, is Serato's quality, customer service and attitude to innovation:

Innovation
Upgrades to the software are free, for life. The company updates and improves the product regularly (adding new, innovative features every few months). Customers are invited to submit ideas for new features to the Serato website; developers discuss these ideas (online) with users and, if possible, incorporate them in new updates. A very innovative approach to product development.

Quality
The Serato product is rock solid. It has to be; a DJ playing to 1000s of people cannot afford for the product to malfunction. Serato has built a reputation for reliability, so much so that it will not introduce innovations (no

matter what the level of demand) if reliability might be compromised.

Customer service
The Serato developers are also working DJs, meaning they understand customer needs. They are all active on the website and answer many customer queries directly. Developers often give out their direct work phone numbers so customers can call for more specific help.

In response to customer demand, Serato has recently introduced a video version of its software allowing DJs to manipulate audio and video simultaneously – a technology that is set to innovate the whole experience of clubbing.

A focus on innovation suggests long-term thinking. A company focused on short-term profit maximisation is unlikely to invest heavily in R&D or tolerate losses due to 'failed' innovations. Payback periods may be long, or perhaps, financial rewards impossible to measure (a particular innovation may yield little direct return, but significantly enhance a company's brand and thus yield long-term benefit).

Though innovation is important, it may form only part of a company's strategy – innovation alone is not enough. Even the very best ideas will fail if the other aspects of good business (as discussed throughout this book) are not present. As in the case of Serato (see opposite), innovation needs to be supported by other strategies and must be backed up by other business functions, such as marketing, finance and human resources.

A company pursuing innovation as part of its strategy needs to consider the following factors.

RISK

Innovation naturally carries with it risk. As we have seen, for every successful product there are many failed products. In early 2008, Toshiba gave up the HD/Blu-ray battle with Sony. Toshiba reported its losses on the 'failed' technology to be $1.1bn. Toshiba's HD technology was sound, but Sony was able to market Blu-ray better and gain better support from suppliers (in this case, movie companies and other DVD manufacturers).

Risk can be managed through extensive market testing, research and reactive development processes, but there is a balance to be struck here between speed to market and research. Sometimes it might be better to risk less research and market testing in order to secure first-mover advantage. The extent to which a company balances research against speed will depend upon its attitude to risk.

FINANCE

A company's willingness to face possible losses is an important component in innovation. Companies spend large sums of money on R&D ($700m in the case of some pharmaceutical drugs). Such sums might be 'wasted' on products that do not even make it to market.

This might suggest that innovation is only possible in large firms able to spend/risk such large sums of capital. It is often the case, however, that it is smaller firms that are the most innovative.

Skills watch!

A03 / A04

Investigate, analyse and evaluate why smaller firms *might* be more innovative than larger firms.

MARKETING

There are many examples of products that have created a 'new' market and fulfil needs that we did not know we had. Touch-screen MP3 players (*iTouch*), toasters with countdown LEDs (the Breville *Smart Toaster*), bagless vacuum cleaners and satellite navigation are all examples of products that we now take for granted, but for which there was no perceived need until their invention. Through careful marketing, companies have 'created' a need for such innovations, encouraged consumers that they cannot live without them and have convinced us that such innovations are worth paying significant price premiums for.

However, there are examples of good ideas that are not marketable (Internet-enabled toilets?) or in some cases, at least, were not marketable at the time. A classic example of this is the *Sinclair C5*, launched in 1985; its concept was similar to that of the modern-day *Segway*. The *Segway* has met with some success, yet back in 1985, the *C5* was a flop. Perhaps the *Segway* was marketed more effectively (the *C5* was promoted as a mass-market

The *Sinclair C5*: a 1980s' flop

product; the *Segway* as more of a niche product), or perhaps the *C5* was simply ahead of its time. No doubt, if launched today, with environmental concerns at the fore, the *C5* would certainly stand a much greater chance of success.

It is clear then that marketing has an important part to play in innovation. Marketing informs the innovation process (through market research), establishing which innovations are commercially viable, and turns clever ideas into marketable products – Apple has good products, but equally (and perhaps more importantly), it has a strong marketing.

The *Segway*: a recent innovation

Skills watch!

A04

APPLE: the anti-example?

It is a credit to its CEO (Steve Jobs) that Apple, which fifteen years ago seemed doomed, is considered to be at the forefront of innovation. Steve Jobs always had a talent for turning silicon and software into sales, but who knew he could build sales of $24 billion from a portable jukebox and a computer (the *Mac*) with a single-digit market share?

The strategy is very simple: Apple products work, and if you buy more than one (*iPod-iTunes-iMac*), they work better – it helps that they look cool.

Yet the culture at Apple is very different to that of most innovative companies. Steve Jobs retains very close control over every detail of product development, staff are given very little autonomy – the exact opposite of companies such as Google. Products are developed in secret within the company, cross-fertilization of ideas (where different departments share developments – a key source of innovation in many companies) is not allowed in Apple. Suggestions from customers are ignored (a website run by an Apple fan was closed down and the author sued). Staff are motivated through fear; Steve Jobs is famous for making staff cry. Despite the immense PR, the press are ignored and poked fun at. Steve Jobs refuses most interviews and at a MacWorld conference in 2004 sarcastically dismissed the idea of a video *iPod*, adding 'we want it to make toast instead' – less than a year later the video *iPod* was launched.

Yet, despite this culture, Apple commands over 70% of the MP3 player market and its market share of the operating system market (its main rival being Microsoft **Windows**) has more than doubled over the last few years. It is also one of the most innovative companies in the electronics/software industry.

Source: *Wired Magazine*, April 2008

Steve Jobs, CEO at Apple: using fear to motivate?

Activity

Why, despite its culture, do you think Apple is so successful? Investigate the company a little further and analyse the reasons for its success. Evaluate the role of culture in innovation. To what extent does a strong leader (such as Steve Jobs) contribute to corporate success?

CULTURE

Innovation requires risk, and with risk comes the potential for mistakes. For innovation to succeed, corporate culture needs to be such that creativity is allowed to flourish and mistakes tolerated. For many innovative companies this means flexible working practices, a playful culture (Google employees are well known for skateboarding around the offices!) and a 'can do' attitude. At Google, staff choose which projects they would like to work on and with whom. Google's culture also encourages staff to spend time on their own projects. This approach is relatively risk-free for Google and has generated some of the company's most well-known products, for instance, Gmail.

HUMAN RESOURCES

As discussed, innovation requires the right culture. It also requires training. Innovative cultures require staff that are flexible, knowledgeable, responsive to customer needs and are able to work with the autonomy that most innovative cultures give. Training and maintaining staff with such skills all add to the cost of being innovative. Recruiting staff that can contribute to innovation is also a challenge – consider the salaries and perks given by companies such as Google, Microsoft and Intel to attract the very best software programmers.

OPERATIONAL PRACTICES

Process innovation is likely to mean changes to the way that business is done, products are produced and the way staff undertake their jobs. All of these require careful management. Process innovation relies on effective operational implementation. Staff will require training, the new process will need to fit smoothly alongside current processes (requiring planning) and operational logistics may need to adjust to incorporate the new innovation.

CHANGE MANAGEMENT

In such dynamic cultures, change management (the process of anticipating, planning for and managing the impact of change) becomes ever more important. Where constant innovation drives change, management needs to consider the impact of such change on staff and processes:

- Does the organisational capacity exist to cope with continual innovation and change?
- Are staff aware of and able (do they have the right skills and the right attitude) to assimilate the change?

In some cases, such as Google, the culture of change and innovation, as noted, can be motivating, but without the right systems in place to support such rapid change, morale, motivation and productivity may suffer (the result of being burdened with too much change).

PROTECTING INNOVATION

Given the importance innovation can have in corporate strategy, protecting such innovations is vital. Companies do this through the use of patents, trademarks and copyright. Pfizer, the developer of *Viagra* (and the owner of its patent), spends large sums of money protecting the money they invested in developing *Viagra*. They employ lawyers in countries where patent infringements are common (such as China) to investigate and, if necessary, sue companies breaking Pfizer's patent. Both the cost of protecting patents and the cost of not protecting a patent need to be factored into a strategy of innovation.

Summary and exam guidance

Summary

- Innovation is the introduction of something new. This might be a new product/feature or a new process.

- Innovation, especially in markets linked to technology, can be a major factor in corporate strategy.

- In all markets, management needs to consider the future – what innovation might be around the corner that could fundamentally change a market?

- Innovation might lead to first-mover advantage. However, is it always better to be first? Management needs to consider the disadvantages of being first and balance this against the advantages of a later market entry.

- Human resources, marketing and finance are all closely linked to innovation. A strategy of innovation will have a much greater chance of success when supported by these other functions.

Exam practice

Read the article below and then answer the question that follows.

Article A

Gaming: the return of Nintendo

Game over or is the new game just beginning? As electronic gaming moves from niche to mass market, the big players, Sony, Microsoft and Electronic Arts, are fast seeing their high scores slip down the leader board.

In a market worth $18m annually in the US alone, the big story is that the games industry's growth over the last few years has been driven by its smaller players. Nintendo's popular *Wii* is a prime example, though it is joined by games such as *Guitar Hero, Rock Band and Singster*. Companies that are making games accessible are seeing sales soar, whilst those continuing to focus on the old (single male) market are seeing sales stagnate.

A key feature of this growth has been an innovative approach to the way games are promoted. Traditionally, game advertisements have focused on showing the game. Nintendo's ads are now shot showing families and friends having fun together – the actual game may not even feature. Nintendo realised that emphasising the communal experience would captivate a larger audience (female and older players) and generate more sales.

Wii: top of the leaderboard?

cont...

The *Wii*'s USP is its control system – the point being that the games are much more fun when played by groups. The traditional features that differentiate games (graphics sound and detail) are not relevant; such features are, in the world of *Wii*, secondary to the fun factor.

The likes of Sony and Microsoft are only just catching up to this new approach. In fact, the outgoing President of Sony's gaming section, commented on the Japanese companies' reluctance to embrace the new model of gaming, believing the culture of the company to be routed in the single-player gaming experience.

For Nintendo, the game continues. They are making 1.8 million *Wii* units per month and are struggling to keep up with demand. Yet, as any savvy gamer does, they keep looking over their shoulder – Nintendo may have got there first, but Sony and Microsoft are chasing hard and they are carrying some big (virtual) guns.

Source: adapted from Database, Bangkok Post, 5 March 2008

Discuss the extent to which technological superiority alone will guarantee the success of a strategy based on innovation. (40 marks)

Total: 40 marks

Breakdown of assessment objectives

AO1 – Knowledge and understanding   8/40
AO2 – Apply knowledge and understanding – 8/40
AO3 – Analyse problems, issues and situations – 10/40
AO4 – Evaluate, distinguish between fact and opinion, assess and judge information from a variety of sources – 14/40

Suggested structure

You will need to:

- Demonstrate an understanding of the role and importance of technology in innovation, and of the nature of innovation.
- Clarify assumptions about 'success' and evaluate the extent to which success can be guaranteed.
- Use knowledge, understanding and evidence from the case to discuss other factors (such as marketing) that may contribute to success.
- Evaluate external factors that may affect the success of innovation and analyse the significance of these factors in different contexts.
- Conclude your analysis and arrive at a reasoned, evaluative judgement in relation to the question. Is technological superiority alone a guarantee of success in innovation:
  - to a large extent (it is quite an important factor)?
  - to some extent (other factors are just as important)?
  - to a minor extent (other factors are more important)?

Chapter 14   Operational strategies: location

At AS level, location is concerned, primarily, with factors that influence start-ups: the quantitative and qualitative factors a business may consider when choosing its initial location(s). The challenge at A2 is to consider location as part of corporate strategy. The basic principles of AS remain, but at A2 the focus is on location issues that affect larger, particularly multi-national, businesses.

Methods of making location decisions

Many businesses depend on their location for success (for instance, a newsagent's is dependent on passing foot/vehicle traffic; few people would travel significantly out of their way to reach one). As a business grows, the need to expand capacity might require expansion of current premises or a complete relocation. For some businesses, the need to remain competitive and thus a need to keep costs down may lead to certain functions being located overseas. In other cases, a business may be 'pushed' from its current location due to rising costs, falling demand or increased competition.

With particular reference to relocation and expansion decisions, the following factors are important considerations.

Quantitative factors

MARKET FACTORS

Does the nature of a business require a location close to customers (a retail chain), or is it possible to locate anywhere (an online bank)? A business that can locate more or less anywhere (known as **footloose** – they are not tied to a particular location) has relatively open relocation options. A business tied to its market may have restricted options for expansion/relocation.

TYPE OF PRODUCT/PRODUCTION METHOD

Where a business sells a product that is bulk-increasing (products gain in bulk as they move through the production chain – such as washing machines), the cost of transporting the bulkier finished good may well be higher than the cost of transporting the components, thus a location closer to the market will be chosen.

Alternatively, where bulk reduces throughout the production chain (bulk-reducing), it may be cheaper to remain located near to the source of raw materials. The cost of transporting the finished product may be cheaper than transporting the raw materials (such as a paper mill).

The bigger picture

Hewlett Packard recently invested 15 million Shekels (£2.3 million) to build a new printer factory in Israel.

Yariv Avishar, vice president at HP Israel, claimed, 'The purpose of the new factory is to meet growing demand and to allow for diversification into new, large-format print technologies.' He claimed the industrial area in Israel was chosen for its 'green factor' and also because the land reserves in the area allow for future expansion.

HP currently employs 4,000 people in Israel and has also, to date, invested $5.7 billion in the country. HP gives its reasons for such significant investment in Israel as the low cost of labour, its

geographic location with regard to Asian and European markets and the skill/productivity of Israeli workers.

Source: adapted from - http://www.theinquirer.net/gb/inquirer/news/2008/03/03/hp-goes-bigger-picture-israel

LAND

The availability and cost of suitable land (including land available for future expansion) may be an important factor. Many companies have relocated from expensive inner city locations to out-of-town locations where more land is available at lower prices (the Qualification and Curriculums Authority recently relocated from its London offices to Coventry, as did the Office for National Statistics, moving to South Wales).

INFRASTRUCTURE/FACILITIES

Transport links for staff, customers and suppliers are important. Access to good ICT connections, suitable/reliable power supplies and waste disposal facilities may all also be important.

HUMAN RESOURCES

Whereas one business may require highly-skilled, specialised staff, another may need a source of plentiful, cheap labour (for example, for this reason, Nissan switched production of the *Micra* to India). Both will need to consider whether suitable labour exists to support expansion and the availability/suitability of labour in any new location.

GOVERNMENT POLICY

Governments often offer incentives for businesses to locate/relocate in particular areas. These incentives might be in the form of tax benefits, subsidised buildings, rent or grants (for instance, the UK government recently gave a £6m grant to Nissan to expand its Sunderland plant; this grant was a significant factor in Nissan's decision to build a new SUV in the UK rather than overseas).

The overriding factor in much of the above is cost. The benefits of the new or expanded location need to be weighed up against the cost of the expansion/move. Businesses will usually undertake extensive research into the decision and will consider questions such as:

- Is expansion of our current location cheaper than relocation?
- Can our current location be adapted/expanded to suit?

- Does expansion offer sufficient long-term benefit? Is it cost-effective over the long term (for how long will the new capacity be sufficient)?
- Do we keep our current location and open in additional locations? Or, is it better to relocate entirely?
- Do the advantages of relocating outweigh the (usually significant) costs (loss of existing skilled workers, redundancy payments, and so on)?
- These questions (and many more!) will be factored into an investment appraisal. The payback period of each location may well be calculated, the cost considered against other possible investments (through internal rate of return) and the long-term implications considered in an average rate of return calculation. These methods of investment appraisal are considered in more detail in Chapter 6.

These quantitative factors will then be weighed against qualitative considerations such as those listed below.

Qualitative factors

IMPACT ON STAFF

If relocating, will current staff move? How do they feel about the move/expansion? In considering the impact of any relocation on staff, management may need to think about issues such as social facilities in the new area(s), quality of schooling, availability of suitable housing, crime rates, and so on. Ultimately, the business will need to factor in the impact of a relocation on morale and goodwill.

RELATIONSHIPS WITH SUPPLIERS

A business may be able to replicate financial terms with a new supplier in a new location, but the relationships, trust and understanding that have potentially been developed with current suppliers may be much harder to replicate. The intangible value a business adds to its customers because it enjoys good relationships with suppliers may be lost.

PUBLIC RELATIONS

Will the decision generate positive or negative PR? If relocation leads to redundancies, the impact of negative PR (and impact on sales) may outweigh any cost advantage.

ENVIRONMENTAL CONCERNS

Increasingly, businesses are factoring environmental impact into their decisions, and location is no exception. A site, despite being the cheapest, may be rejected because of environmental concerns, or another more expensive site favoured, as it offers, for example, recycling options. The extent to which this is significant will depend upon management attitudes to environmental concerns.

AESTHETICS

Management is becoming aware of the impact that positive working environments have on staff morale, productivity and creativity. A site may be preferred because it offers a more rural environment for staff, or offers modern/fashionable office space.

MANAGEMENT PREFERENCE

Ultimately, a decision may simply come down to the preference of management. Management may themselves prefer to live in one location rather than another, or for intangible reasons simply favour one location over another.

For example...

Relocation

Boosts **r**ush **u**siness

Cottam Brush expected annual turnover to rise from £2.6m to £2.9m after the 150-year-old firm transferred from a site near the Stadium of Light, Sunderland to South Tyneside.

Established in 1858, the company is now run by the sixth generation of the family, led by managing director Ben Cottam.

Mr Cottam said: 'Our 35 loyal staff have gone from occupying seven different buildings in Sunderland, to all being under the same roof in Tyneside.

'We do have a history, but with our new facilities we are now a much more modern operation, and are looking towards improving our product development and design skills.'

As part of the move, Cottam Brush has forged educational ties with nearby South Tyneside College, which is providing sales personnel with technical training.

Source: http://www.shieldsgazette.com/news/Relocation-boost-famous-firm39s-profits.3807304.jp

Activity

1 Using the case above, outline the key benefits of the move for Cottam Brush.

2 Given its context, what factors might Cottam Brush have considered significant when planning its move?

Skills watch!

AO4

To what extent are the qualitative factors likely to be less, equally or even more important that the quantitative ones? What factors might your answer to this depend upon? Consider things like aims of the business, size/type of business, financial situation, type of staff and style of management.

Benefits of optimal location

Achieving the best balance of the factors above and securing an ideal location can lead to significant benefit for a business. These benefits might include the following.

FINANCE

Location decisions are often one of the most expensive decisions business face (the new BMW factory in South Carolina cost BMW $750 million; in 2007, Intel spent $3bn on a new factory in Arizona). A cost-effective location may contribute significantly to profitability. Remember though, depending on a business's aims, cost may not be *the* most important factor.

CAPACITY

An expansion or relocation may give a business increased capacity in order to meet demand. This might not only be important for profit, but also for reputation. For instance, AMD (the computer chip manufacturer) recently added 13,400sqm of production space in Germany as part of their aim to produce 100 million processors a year: part of a strategy to capture 30% of the microchip market.

HUMAN RESOURCES

Locating near to cheap labour will benefit in terms of cost-effectiveness and may improve a business's ability to compete on price (or its profitability). Locating near to skilled staff may give a firm an advantage over competition as a result of the value added by these staff.

Additionally, if a relocation results in an improved working environment for staff, this may have long term benefit for recruitment and retention.

LEAD TIME

Relocating close to suppliers or customers, or to an area with improved infrastructure, may allow a business to cut its lead time and to use this as a source of competitive advantage.

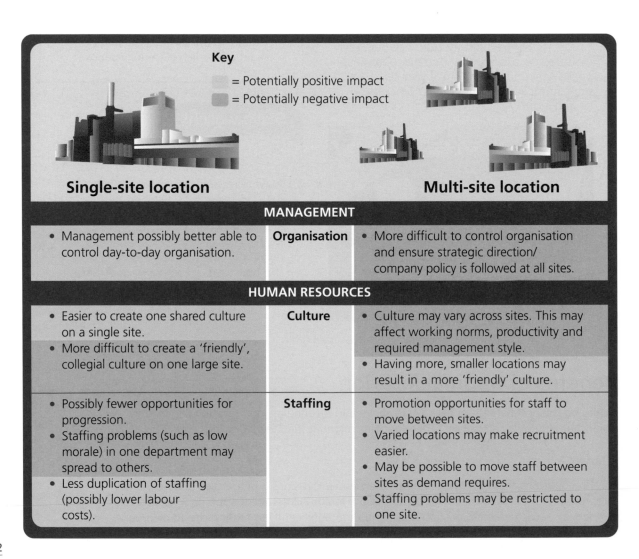

Key
= Potentially positive impact
= Potentially negative impact

Single-site location   **Multi-site location**

MANAGEMENT		
• Management possibly better able to control day-to-day organisation.	**Organisation**	• More difficult to control organisation and ensure strategic direction/ company policy is followed at all sites.

HUMAN RESOURCES		
• Easier to create one shared culture on a single site. • More difficult to create a 'friendly', collegial culture on one large site.	**Culture**	• Culture may vary across sites. This may affect working norms, productivity and required management style. • Having more, smaller locations may result in a more 'friendly' culture.
• Possibly fewer opportunities for progression. • Staffing problems (such as low morale) in one department may spread to others. • Less duplication of staffing (possibly lower labour costs).	**Staffing**	• Promotion opportunities for staff to move between sites. • Varied locations may make recruitment easier. • May be possible to move staff between sites as demand requires. • Staffing problems may be restricted to one site.

Single-site location		Multi-site location
FINANCE		
Able to gain from economies of scale. Greater potential for sharing of resources across site.	**Economies of scale**	• Running costs may be higher as less able to benefit from economies of scale. May be duplication of some resources.
OPERATIONS		
• Potentially difficult to manage changes to capacity (due to scale and number of staff involved).	**Capacity**	• May be easier (from a logistical and human resource point of view) to add/reduce a small amount of capacity at each site.
• The economies of one site may lead to the potential for greater efficiency; less duplication of processes; sharing of best practice.	**Efficiency**	• Duplication may lead to inefficiency; systems working at one site may not (due to local factors or culture) work at another (possibly leading to lower overall efficiency).
EXTERNAL INFLUENCES		
• Unforeseen events (fire, flood, etc.) may close the entire site and cause operations to cease.	**Unforeseen events**	• Even if one site closes due to an unforeseen event, others may remain in operation (e.g. Toyota was forced to temporarily close a plant in China after the 2008 earthquake, but was able to increase production at other plants).

Figure 14.1 Diagrammatic representation of advantages and disadvantages of multi-site locations

The advantages and disadvantages of multi-site locations

A consideration for growing firms is whether to restrict their location to one site or to open up new sites in addition to current ones. Clearly, the ability to expand on one site requires that sufficient land and labour is available. Both options rely on enough capital being available to fund the expansion/new location.

Multi-site location decisions concern many types of businesses. For example:

• A computer manufacturer may need to decide between one large production facility or many smaller ones spread around a country.
• An online bank may need to decide if it is beneficial to have head offices, call centres and IT centres located together or separately.

Some of the advantages and disadvantages of multi-site versus single-site locations are represented in Figure 14.1.

Often, in multi-site decisions, qualitative factors will be given at least as much weighting as quantitative ones. In essence, management may have accepted the costs of multiple sites, but will need to ensure, to the extent possible, that qualitative factors will not constrain the success of the investment.

It is important to remember that factors beyond the firm's control may restrict choice of strategy. Suitable land may not exist to expand a current site or open new sites, government regulations may prevent expansion, or adequate labour may not be

Skills watch!

Location decision

JazzBah, a medium-sized business specialising in design and fittings for bars, due to growing demand needs to expand capacity. Currently located in Manchester city centre, room for expansion is limited. Jazzbah intends to open a new site (whilst retaining the Manchester site). After extensive research it has collected the following information:

AO3

Activity

1 Consider what more you would need to know about JazzBah before being able to suggest a suitable site.

2 What factors might their decision depend upon?

3 Based on the data you have, what site might they choose?

| | Finance concerns | | | Size details | | Local area | | | | | | |
	Cost (£)	Payback period	IRR	Size	Labour	Infrastructure	Environmental concerns	Housing	Social facilities	Schooling		
Site A	5.1m	8 years	7%	S	High-skilled, but limited availability.	Excellent.	*Rural location.* Good/cheap recycling/waste options.	Excellent, but expensive.	Excellent.	Good, but limited other than expensive private schools.
Site B	6.4m	5 years	12%	M	Skilled, but expensive.	Good.	*Edge of city business park.* Options for recycling/waste management, but costly.	Good value housing available.	Excellent.	Good (private and state options).
Site C	7.7m	10 years	14%	L	Cheap and plentiful.	Good, but congested.	*Brownfield site.* Limited options for recycling/waste.	Cheap.	Average.	Large local school and college, but average quality.

available. It may also be considered that expansion within the company's home country is too expensive and that a location overseas may be preferable.

Issues relating to international location

Improvements in global communications, transportation, the prevalence of the English language and the removal of barriers to trading in certain countries, have all contributed to a significant increase in the number of businesses operating in overseas locations. These operations may take several forms:

- Opening branches/outlets outside of home markets (Starbucks now operates 15,700 branches, in 43 countries).
- Moving all/some production facilities overseas (Mazda operates 16 production facilities throughout the world).
- Moving some key functions to overseas locations (BT operates a number of customer service call centres in India). This is known as **offshoring**.

Reasons for operating overseas

There are a number of reasons why companies may choose to operate in overseas markets.

ACCESS TO GLOBAL MARKETS

The Internet and the impact of global media have contributed to a convergence of markets (for example, a teenager in the UK is not so different to a teenager in China, or India – they listen to similar music, watch the same films and buy similar products). This has created opportunities for companies, as in the example of Starbucks above, to successfully sell their products in many countries (18% of Starbucks' revenue in 2007 came from overseas (non-US) markets).

For production companies, having locations overseas can shorten lead time for delivery to important markets, and allows products to be made with a degree of localisation (for example, Toshiba produces home entertainment products in Plymouth for the European market).

COST REDUCTION

One of the primary reasons for operating in overseas locations is cost. Skilled labour may be available at significantly lower cost.

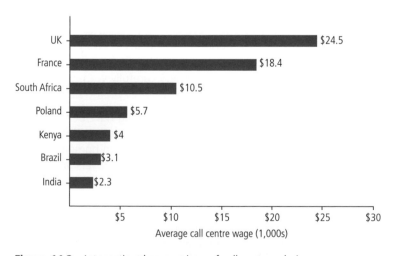

Figure 14.2 International comparison of call centre salaries

Source: (2007 Data) http://www.swivel.com/graphs/show/25504184

For instance, as Figure 14.2 shows, average call centre salaries in the UK are about $24,500 (£12,500 a year), compared with $2,300 (£1,200) in India. Indian call centre workers are generally highly-educated, English-speaking university graduates.

There may also be cost savings and output gains associated with employment regulations. In many overseas locations, employment regulations are not as strict as in the UK, allowing firms to give fewer benefits (thus lowering costs).

Land may also be cheaper in other countries (consider the average price of office space in

London; £666 in 2007, compared to £175 in Morocco – measured per workstation per month*).

It is often simply the case that the overall cost of doing business is cheaper overseas. Largely this is due to cheaper labour costs, but also includes lower transport costs, lower catering costs, lower supply costs, and so on.

TRADE RESTRICTIONS

Countries often put laws in place to protect home industries (for example, restricting or taxing the import of overseas products). By operating production facilities in different countries, businesses are able to avoid these trade restrictions.

For example...

How much?!

The import tax on cars shipped into Thailand is as high as 300%! A Mini *Cooper* produced in the UK (and sold for £16,000) is sold in Thailand for 2.6m Baht (£42,000). The Thai government sets such high taxes, in part, to protect Thai industry, but the import taxes also encourage companies to set up production facilities in Thailand, creating jobs and adding to growth of the Thai economy.

Both BMW and Mercedes, popular brands in Thailand, have production facilities there, helping them to avoid the high import taxes.

Guru's views

'Clients do not expect the infrastructure to be any less reliable just because the service is being delivered from an offshore location.'

Sanjay Kumar

Skills watch!

AO4

Investigate the Fair Trade policies of companies such as Gap, Starbucks or Nike. How do they attempt to ensure that their overseas operations operate within an ethical framework? Why do they have such policies?

The pros and cons of offshoring

Deciding to operate overseas requires careful consideration of the following factors:

- A business will need to be certain that quality standards (whether production or service) can be maintained.
- Many companies have aims that relate to community, support of the local economy and ethical business practices. Such firms would need to consider offshoring very carefully with respect to these aims.

The ethics of practices such as offshoring have been widely debated in the media. Companies have been criticised for making large numbers of staff redundant in home markets, whilst employing staff in cheaper countries overseas. The working conditions of staff in many overseas locations are also called into question. Are companies operating ethically if they exploit the opportunity to use staff in a way that, whilst legal overseas, would not be allowable in their home markets? What impact might such practices have on a firm's reputation?

* Source: http://www.choregus.co.uk

PUBLIC RELATIONS

What will be the impact if redundancies are made at facilities in home markets? What affect might this have on a firm's reputation and thus sales? For example, BT has suffered negative publicity as a result of moving much of its call centre operations overseas.

SUPPLY ISSUES

Does the overseas location have adequate/suitable suppliers? If not, will transportation of components add to lead times? How might this affect stock management decisions?

DELIVERY ISSUES

On the one hand, having multiple locations might speed global delivery; however, transport links in many countries where labour costs are low are often poor. A business will need to consider the impact this may have on getting goods to customers.

Another issue might be maintaining quality throughout the delivery chain. Due to poor transport links, a product that leaves the factory in perfect condition may not arrive with the customer in the same condition.

INTELLECTUAL PROPERTY

Companies operating in countries with limited intellectual property laws (laws such as patents that protect ideas/processes) need to consider the possibility that knowledge of products/processes may actually create competition. For example, China has exploited the know-how gained from producing western products, and is now producing vast quantities of cheaper imitations and selling them back to western consumers.

Skills watch!

A04

Reverse offshoring

The rising cost of paying engineers in Bangalore has prompted some companies to save money by closing Indian operations and moving the jobs back to home countries.

While this 'reverse offshoring' remains unusual, it points to a broader belief that the savings that drove jobs to India's technology capital are quickly eroding.

Remember, there are often two sides to every argument. What is true for one business may not be true for another. In this case, engineering firms are finding it increasingly expensive to locate in India; this is not true for other types of businesses (the number of call centres in India continues to grow, albeit more slowly than in the past).

Source: adapted from FT.com, 1 July 2007 (http://www.ft.com/cms/s/0/4eeded70-27fb-11dc-80da-000b5df10621.html?nclick_check=1)

It is likely, as technology continues to develop, that companies will increasingly face the need to embrace globalisation, and thus, offshoring and international location decisions. As China and India mature as economies, their impact on global markets will increase. To compete, firms will need to see not just their own country as a base for operations, but also countries worldwide. The same may also be true for labour. As business spreads itself across the globe, consistently seeking the most cost-effective location, labour needs to be flexible enough to follow. It is highly likely that university graduates today will enjoy careers spent working in a number of different countries.

Summary and exam guidance

Summary

- The location of a business is a critical decision.

- Location can have a significant impact on costs (primarily land and labour costs) and on sales.

- Detailed investment appraisal, in addition to a consideration of qualitative factors, will usually be conducted when considering a relocation/expansion or multi-site location options.

- Increasingly, businesses are considering international location options, such as offshoring (due to the lower cost of labour and land).

- The extent to which a location is right for a business (including overseas locations) depends very much on the nature of that business.

Exam practice

Read the articles below and then answer the questions that follow.

Article A

All white goods

The New Zealand domestic white goods manufacturer F&P Appliances, facing stiff competition, recently closed three factories: its dishwasher plant in New Zealand; its refrigerator factory in Australia; and its cooking appliance factory in California, shedding more than 1,000 jobs, in favour of production facilities in Thailand, Italy and a recently purchased factory in Mexico.

On completion of the move, F&P Appliances had nearly halved its New Zealand workforce from around 3,000 to just 1,600. Chief executive John Bongard justified the decision by pointing to cost savings of around $NZ50 million (£19m) a year. The company made an after-tax profit last year of $61 million (£24m).

Bongard cited 'the access to global markets and lowering of labour costs' as the main reasons for the relocations. Bongard also blamed recent free trade agreements with Thailand and China for creating an influx of cheaper products from Thailand and China, making it hard to compete.

The company's strategy had been to concentrate on producing 'innovative and high-end' appliances aimed at the premium European and US markets. But now, according to Bongard, 'unless we can bring our costs down, particularly the cost of labour, we will not be able to provide an adequate return to our shareholders'. Mexican workers will be paid on average $NZ4.50 (£1.76) an hour, a sixth of the wage F&P paid to its New Zealand workers.

Source: John Braddock, 30 April 2008, World Socialist website. Copyright 1998–2008.

Article B

A bad call

Before becoming a call centre agent, working late into the night to answer queries from customers, Vinita Rawat was a post-graduate student in English Literature. Rawat, 26, sees herself as a professional, and has a managerial position as a 'team coordinator'. She is a prime example of a, so-called, Indian 'cyber coolie' – an expensively-educated, highly-intelligent graduate, performing exhausting, repetitive tasks for the call centre industry.

Over the past decade, India's success at winning contracts from the West has been cited as a positive face of globalisation – providing good salaries and new career opportunities in the developing world.

However, there is criticism that the emerging industry has developed a system for hiring 'productive but docile workers', with few labour rights and little job security.

Critics argue that staff are employed under constant surveillance, and claim that quotas for calls or emails successfully attended to are often fixed at such a high level, that staff have to burn themselves out. With employees working through the night to cater for clients in different time zones, the work takes a heavy toll on staff health.

But more broadly, critics claim, call centre work leads to a wastage of human resources and deskilling of workers, which will have a high impact on Indian industry in the long term. As a result of such claims and raising costs in countries such as India, a number of companies have closed offshoring operations and reopened sites in the UK.

Source: adapted from http://www.buzzle.com/editorials/10-29-2005-80166.asp, May 2008 and *The Observer*, 30 October 2005

(a) With reference to the two articles above, discuss the key factors that are likely to influence a business considering offshoring its production facilities. (22 marks)

(b) To what extent might it be more challenging to operate production, rather than service facilities, overseas? (18 marks)

Total: 40 marks

Breakdown of assessment objectives

AO1 – Knowledge and understanding – 8/40
AO2 – Apply knowledge and understanding – 12/40
AO3 – Analyse problems, issues and situations – 8/40
AO4 – Evaluate, distinguish between fact and opinion, assess and judge information from a variety of sources – 12/40

Suggested structure

You will need to:

- Demonstrate an understanding of factors affecting, in particular, international and multi-site location decisions.

  - Identify and analyse at least **two** factors for locating production overseas.
  - Identify and analyse at least **two** challenges in locating production overseas.

- Demonstrate an understanding of the context as described in the two examples and relate this to your analysis of the factors affecting location decisions.
- Identify relevant and significant material from both cases.
- Demonstrate an ability to analyse and evaluate the challenges facing both production and service businesses in operating overseas.
- Conclude your analysis and arrive at a reasoned, evaluative judgment in relation to the questions.

Chapter 15   Operational strategies: lean production

Key terms

Critical Path Analysis (CPA) A management tool for indentifying tasks and timescales associated with a project, enabling resources to be used most efficiently to ensure the project completes on time.

Just-in-time production (JIT) Ensuring supplies are delivered just as they are required, rather than 'just-in-case'; reduces the cost of stockholding.

Kaizen (改善) Japanese for 'continuous improvement'; continually looking to improve in all aspects of business.

Lead time The time taken between order of a good and delivery.

Lean production A Japanese management philosophy focusing on eliminating waste, better management of time and efficient use of resources.

Management by exception Management focus their energies only on tasks/staff where performance is different to established standards or aims.

Network diagram The diagrammatic representation of CPA.

Simultaneous Engineering Organising business processes such that, where possible, tasks are carried out together (simultaneously) rather than sequentially one after another.

To survive and succeed in today's dynamic marketplaces businesses need to be able to react swiftly and be flexible enough to keep pace with (or even drive) change. These pressures have seen, over the last few decades, lean production techniques become central to operations management. This chapter will evaluate lean approaches to business and the value of time-based management in ensuring that businesses can survive and succeed in ever-more challenging marketplaces.

The effective management of resources through methods of lean production

Lean production

Lean production is a Japanese management approach that focuses on reducing waste, better management of time and resources, eliminating duplicated or redundant processes and ensuring quality.

Lean production aims to remove processes that do not add value to operations, such as reworking faulty products, stockholding, and unnecessary movement of resources (if people and products spend less time moving, higher productivity can be achieved).

The main advantages of lean production are:

Guru's views

'One thing you can't recycle is wasted time.'

Anon

- Lead times are cut; products get to customers faster.
- A greater focus on customer needs; if customers don't want it, why make it? (This approach can both lower costs and increase sales.)
- Damage, waste and loss of stocks/equipment are lowered.

- Through kaizen (see page 215) and quality circles, product quality is improved.
- Lower costs may contribute to improved profits.
- Staff are more involved in processes and thus potentially more motivated.
- Working environments are safer and cleaner (the lean approach encourages cleanliness and a clutter-free environment).

Lean production is a philosophical approach that encompasses operational strategies such as just-in-time production, kaizen, cell production quality circles and Simultaneous Engineering.

For example...

Lean facts... the Toyota way

On the assembly line at one of Toyota's plants, Laura is not happy. There is something wrong with a seatbelt on the Camry she is working on. Laura pulls a cord, stopping the production line – prompting fellow workers to crowd round. They soon find and fix the problem. 'I don't like to let something like that go,' Laura says. 'That's really important for people who buy our cars.'

- Workers at Toyota plants pull the cord as often as 2,000 times a week – and their care is what makes Toyota one of the most reliable, and most desired, car brands. In contrast, workers at Ford, pull the cord sometimes only twice a week – the legacy of generations of mistrust between shop-floor workers and managers.
- In 2006, Toyota could build a car with just 29 hours' labour, while it took General Motors 33 hours.
- More than 400 trucks a day, from over 300 suppliers, come in and out of Toyota's

plants. Ensuring good-quality parts, delivered on time, is one of the keys to lean production. A missing or faulty component can bring the assembly line to a halt.

- Toyota can develop a new model in 18 months; its rivals can take up to 3 years.

Source: http://news.bbc.co.uk/2/hi/business/6346315.stm (February 2007)

Just-in-time production (ジャストインタイム)

Just-in-time production (JIT) is concerned with ensuring that supplies are delivered just as they are required, reducing the need to hold large amounts of raw materials, work in progress or finished goods. Rather than stocks being held 'just in case' (buffer stock), stocks are 'pulled' through the production process determined by customer orders.

The example in Figure 15.1 shows that as a customer orders a new computer, this triggers an order for the relevant components (they are not held in stock). The relevant monitor and software is not delivered to the manufacturer until just before final assembly and the boxes/manuals are not delivered until just before delivery.

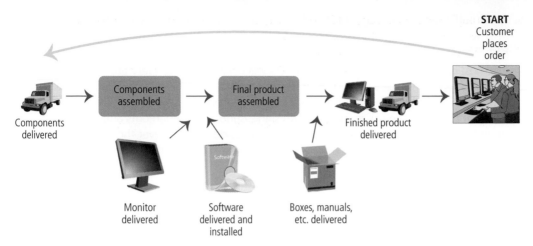

Figure 15.1 Example of JIT for computer manufacturer

GRAPHICAL ILLUSTRATION OF TRADITIONAL VS JIT STOCKHOLDING METHODS

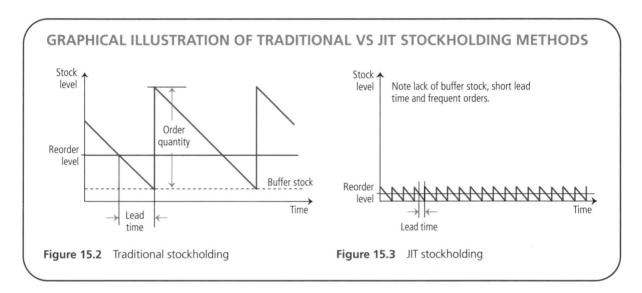

Figure 15.2 Traditional stockholding   **Figure 15.3** JIT stockholding

THE ADVANTAGES OF JUST-IN-TIME PRODUCTION

The main advantage of JIT is reduced stockholding. This has several benefits:

- **Warehouse space** Less space is required to hold stock (more space can be given to production, storage space does not need to be built and unused space can be sold off).
- **Storage costs** Other costs associated with storing stock include insurance, the cost of heat, light or refrigeration, the cost of securing the stock from theft, and wage costs for warehouse staff. With JIT these costs can be significantly reduced if not eliminated.
- **Opportunity cost** Money that would otherwise be tied up in stocks can be used elsewhere (a firm might invest in fixed assets, such as delivery vehicles).
- **Spoilage** Reducing stockholding minimises exposure to the cost of goods that perish and become unsaleable. Restaurants need to operate JIT to ensure that the food they sell is fresh and wastage is minimised. Similarly, the possibility of goods being damaged or becoming obsolete and thus unsaleable is reduced (would you buy an older model *iPod* for the same price as a new model?).

Successful JIT relies on a number of factors.

Suppliers

A firm must have total confidence that suppliers will deliver on time, every time. Suppliers must be flexible enough to cope with changing levels of demand and must be willing to make multiple deliveries, often daily. In many cases companies may use several suppliers for the same component to reduce the risk associated with single-supplier arrangements and, through competition between suppliers, keep component prices down. Whatever the number of suppliers, close, open and communicative relationships are essential if JIT is to succeed.

Production systems

If customer demand is to be met effectively, production systems must be fast and flexible. Any benefit of JIT may be lost if stock is held up in lengthy, slow production processes. Production systems also need to be able to cope with variable demand – being able to switch from production of one product to another as demand dictates.

Quality

With limited, if any, buffer stock, JIT is reliant on zero defects. A customer cannot be offered another item from stock if none is held; production may be delayed if faulty components are delivered. All stages of the production process (including suppliers) need to work towards zero defects.

Staffing

JIT requires a greater level of involvement from staff than traditional just-in-case approaches. Staff will need to take more responsibility for quality, will need to manage JIT ordering systems (usually through kanban (看板) – a card-based system used to trigger frequent orders) and will need to work flexibly to cope with changing levels of demand (daily production targets may well vary depending on demand). This requires that staff are both trained to operate within a JIT environment and equally importantly, motivated to work with JIT.

Design rationalisation (design for manufacture)

JIT works most efficiently where fewer components are involved. For example, Ford reduced the number of petrol caps it uses on vehicles from over 100 different variations to just two. This has allowed Ford to develop strong links with a smaller number of suppliers, to better ensure quality and to allow staff to become familiar with a smaller number of designs (contributing to raised productivity).

THE DISADVANTAGES OF JUST-IN-TIME PRODUCTION

So, why don't all firms use JIT? As ever, the reality of business practice is much more complex than textbook theory. For JIT to be successful a business must manage all of the factors above (easier said than done!) and must be mindful of the disadvantages of JIT.

Stockouts

If a supplier is unable to deliver components or required quantities are not ordered correctly, a business may not have enough stock to meet demand (a **stockout**). This may cost a business in terms of lost orders and, perhaps more importantly, lost customers and damage to reputation.

Delivery costs

There is a balance to be struck between the cost of frequent, small deliveries versus lower delivery costs achieved through less frequent, larger deliveries. It may be that the cost benefits of JIT with regard to stockholding are offset by higher delivery charges.

Suppliers

Developing and maintaining relationships with suppliers takes time and will incur costs. The time and money spent on supplier relationships need to be considered against the benefits of JIT.

Staff

As mentioned, staff need to be trained and willing to engage in JIT. The cost (both monetary and time) of achieving this may be high. Do the benefits of JIT make it worthwhile?

Administration

The cost of frequent orders (paperwork, managing delivery schedules, and so on) soon mount; these additional costs will offset to some degree the benefits of JIT.

Risk

The more suppliers, the more components, the more difficult (and riskier) JIT will be to implement. A business will need to balance the possible benefits of JIT against these risks; for example, the cost of a stockout. A business's attitude to risk may determine the extent to which it embraces JIT.

Skills watch!

A04

As can be seen, JIT is more than just a stock management system. JIT requires trained and motivated staff, close relationships with suppliers, an efficient production process and product design rationalisation. JIT should be seen as an operational strategy, encompassing a wide range of operational issues alongside important links to human resources, finance and even marketing.

Any question about JIT will require you to consider the wider strategic implications, not just those related to stock management.

Kaizen (改善)

Kaizen is Japanese for 'continuous improvement'. Put simply, kaizen means continually looking to improve in all aspects of business. Kaizen, like lean production, is a philosophical way of doing business. It encourages staff at all levels to consider how things could be done better.

Kaizen can be seen as an evolutionary process; small and continual change becomes part of normal practice (for example, production processes are frequently tweaked). As Figure 15.4 shows, this is very different to Business Process Reengineering (BPR). In BPR change happens only occasionally, but when it does it is significant (for example, the introduction of a completely new production process).

Kaizen requires that staff are empowered to drive change, and uses things such as quality circles and focus groups to ensure that staff are involved in the change process.

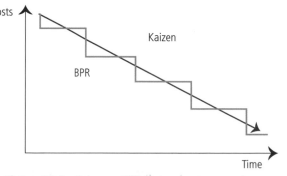

Figure 15.4 Kaizen vs BPR (for an improvement that lowers cost)

THE ADVANTAGES OF KAIZEN PRODUCTION

The main advantages of kaizen are listed below:

- Focuses staff on improvement.
- Motivating for staff.
- Discourages staff from resting on past successes.
- Encourages an outward/forward-looking approach.
- Empowers staff to contribute to decision-making.
- Makes improvement part of everybody's job description.
- Linked to and contributes to the achievement of both TQM and zero defects.

For example...

Google's gains

Consider these extracts from Google's business philosophy:

- **'It's best to do one thing really, really well'** The name Google is solidly linked to Internet searching, yet despite their success Google are constantly looking for ways to improve search functions.

- **'Fast is better than slow'** Google may be the only company in the world whose stated goal is to have users leave its website as quickly as possible. By fanatically obsessing on improving every process, Google has broken its own search speed records time and again.

- **'Being great isn't good enough'** Google does not accept being the best as an endpoint, but a starting point.

It is evident that, even though it is successful, Google follows the principles of kaizen – always looking to improve.

Source: http://www.google.co.uk/intl/en/corporate/tenthings.html

THE DISADVANTAGES OF KAIZEN PRODUCTION

However, continual change (albeit, hopefully, for the better) has disadvantages.

Impact on staff

The pressure on staff to always improve can be stressful and wearing. Staff may feel denied the opportunity to celebrate success (having to always consider 'what we could do better', rather than 'what went well' might lower morale).

Impact on customers

Customers may be frustrated if change is too frequent. (Ever tried to find something in a supermarket only to be told it has moved? Supermarkets change sales floor layout frequently, always seeking the best way to maximise sales.)

Uncertainty

If systems, procedures and policies are constantly changing, staff may face uncertainty. Are they doing things the right way? Have things changed? This can have an impact on morale and productivity.

It can be argued that under BPR staff have time to get used to new systems and to reach peak efficiency before further change is introduced. Under kaizen this may not be possible.

For example...

iRebate

Both Apple and Microsoft have, over the last few years, had to give rebates to customers who have purchased a product to find that only weeks later it was replaced by an upgraded model. Similar rebates were given by companies (such as Amazon.com) selling HD-DVD players, once it became clear that Blu-Ray was to be the dominant format.

Not only do companies have to consider the cost of writing off obsolete stock, they also need to factor in, as in the examples above, the cost of retaining customer goodwill.

Skills watch!

AO3

Should it not be a case of 'let the buyer beware'? Why do companies feel the need to give such rebates? Assumedly, the companies value the loss of goodwill (and future sales) more highly than the cost of rebates.

At A2 level, higher grades come from looking beyond the 'facts', considering why companies take certain actions and evaluating the possible significance of such actions.

Risk aversion

Whilst kaizen suggests that risks should be taken to drive improvement, often, the drive to always be better and to achieve zero defects actually reduces staff's willingness to take risks (and thus, to improve). The extent to which this is significant will depend on management's tolerance of mistakes and the extent to which improvement is demanded rather than encouraged.

The effective management of time

Simultaneous Engineering

Simultaneous Engineering involves organising business processes such that, where possible, tasks are carried out together rather than one after another. Simultaneous Engineering is a time-based, project (matrix) management approach, where specialists from various functions (operations, marketing, R&D, and so on) work together to cut lead times in getting products to market.

The approach can be seen as part of lean production as it aims to reduce duplicated/ wasteful processes and focuses on productive allocation of resources.

Skills watch!

AO4

The concept of kaizen is a relatively simple one to understand. Remember though, the need to evaluate the pros and cons and to consider context. Kaizen may well be successful for one business, but unsuccessful in another.

Guru's views

'For every minute spent in organizing, an hour is earned.'

Anon

In practice, Simultaneous Engineering is often achieved through time-based management approaches that require tasks and processes to be measured and defined so that the best way of ordering the various tasks can be analysed – this is known as **Critical Path Analysis**.

Assessing the value of Critical Path Analysis

Critical Path Analysis (CPA) is a time-based project management tool that:

- details the activities in a project
- indicates the order in which activities should be completed
- shows which activities are linked (that is, activity X cannot start until Y is completed)
- indicates where activities can be completed simultaneously
- gives an indication of the minimum amount of time it will take to complete a project
- anticipates any (critical) activities that may delay a project.

CPA is often used in the construction industry (though it is widely used in others) where projects are lengthy and require careful planning. For example, a constructor will need to coordinate the fitting of windows, roofing, electrics and plumbing, and so on, seeking to avoid wasted time while staff wait for other jobs to be completed (painting may need to wait until plumbing and electrics have been completed).

CPA diagrams (known as network diagrams) are based on nodes and lines (see Figure 15.5).

For example, consider the process of getting ready for school/college/work. A breakdown of the activities might look like the table in Figure 15.6.

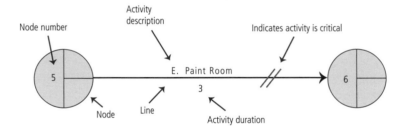

Figure 15.5 An example network diagram

Task	Activity	Order	Duration
A	Alarm sounds, press snooze, get up...	Starts activity	10 minutes
B	Shower and get dry	Start when A is complete	10 minutes
C	Get dressed	Start when B is complete(!)	15 minutes
D	Prepare and eat breakfast	Start when C is complete	10 minutes
E	Watch TV/Listen to radio	Start when C is complete	8 minutes
F	Clean teeth, do hair, make-up, etc.	Start when D and E are complete	15 minutes
G	Pack bag	Start when F is complete	2 minutes
H	Lock door, turn off lights... Leave for school/college/work	Start when G is complete	2 minutes

Figure 15.6 Activity breakdown

Laid out in sequence this process would be:

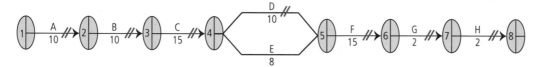

Figure 15.7 Activities converted to network diagram

We can now calculate the earliest time that each activity can start (that is, what time to tell our parents/housemate to put the kettle on for breakfast!) and the latest time each task must finish without delaying the next (what time bag-packing *must* start to ensure leaving is not delayed).

First we calculate the earliest start time (EST) for each activity.

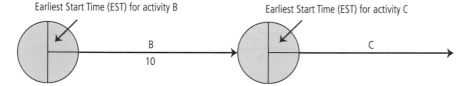

Figure 15.8 Identifying location of ESTs

To determine ESTs, we calculate left to right on the diagram. The EST for B is 10 minutes (10 minutes to wake up/get up). To calculate the EST for activity C we add the 10 minutes it takes to shower, so the EST for C (getting dressed) is 20 minutes:

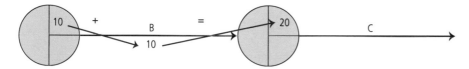

Figure 15.9 Calculating ESTs

Next, we calculate the latest finish time (LFT) for each activity:

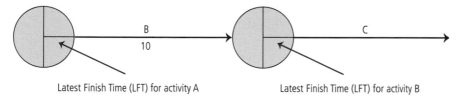

Figure 15.10 Identifying location of LFTs

LFTs show the latest time a preceding activity can finish without delaying the next activity (waking up/getting up must not take longer than 10 minutes, otherwise activity B is delayed). LFTs are calculated from right to left on the diagram:

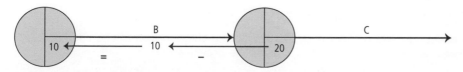

Figure 15.11 Calculating LFTs

Where 'junctions' are concerned when calculating ESTs, the higher number is taken; when calculating LFTs, the lower number is taken. For example:

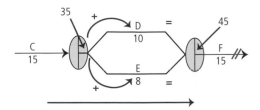

Figure 15.12 ESTs – direction of calculation (larger number taken)

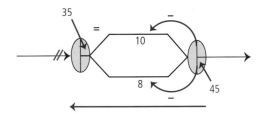

Figure 15.13 LSTs – direction of calculation (smaller number taken)

The final network diagram would look like this:

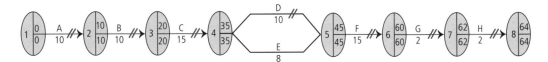

Figure 15.14 Completed network diagram

This shows that in order to avoid being late for school/college/work, the alarm clock must be set 64 minutes before the time to leave. All activities, except for E, are critical (//).

Relating this to how a business might use CPA, we would now examine the network to see if any time could be saved (10 minutes in the shower!) or where more tasks might be undertaken simultaneously (pack bag whilst cleaning teeth?). The benefit to us might be more time in bed(!); for a business it might mean time saved can be used elsewhere, costs lowered (staff needed for less time) or customer orders met faster.

Skills watch!

AO1

CPA — things to remember...

- CPA always begins and ends on one node.
- Each node must be numbered; each line must have a label.
- Lines represent the passing of time; nodes are summaries.
- Lines must not cross.
- Blank lines (dummy nodes), for exam purposes, are not required.

- The critical path is usually marked with '//'.
- ESTs are calculated, left to right, by adding the duration of a task to the previous EST.
- LFTs are calculated, right to left, by subtracting the duration of the task from the previous LFT.

For example...

A hot time for *Cooler*

Cooler are anticipating a warm summer and high demand for their range of iced drinks. In order to meet demand, a new delivery vehicle is needed. To accommodate this extra vehicle, modifications to the loading bay are required.

It is important that the van and bay are ready ahead of the summer season. *Cooler* identifies that the following activities will be required:

Task	Description	Order	Duration
A	Order and delivery of van	Completed first	8 days
B	Fitting of refrigeration unit	Start when A is complete	10 days
C	Signwriting for van	Start when A and B are complete	10 days
D	Fitting of internal van storage units	Start when A and B are complete	4 days
E	Recruitment and training of new driver	Can start with A	24 days
F	Modifications of loading bay	Start when A is complete	7 days
G	Testing	Start when E, D and F are complete	4 days

The network diagram would look like this:

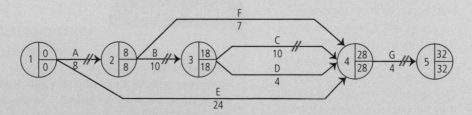

Figure 15.15 Completed network diagram for *Cooler*

The diagram shows that *Cooler* needs to order the van 32 days before it anticipates an increase in demand. Having identified the critical activities, *Cooler* could, if required, move staff between tasks to ensure completion in time (for example, staff being used on the loading bay modifications could be used to assist with signwriting up to day 21; the loading modifications can start as late as day 22 without delaying the whole project).

THE ADVANTAGES OF CPA

The main **advantages** of CPA are:

- Drawing up a CPA diagram ensures that a project has been carefully thought through and planned – improving the chances of success.
- As seen in the example on page 221, it allows a business to identify where some tasks have 'slack' (known as **float**) and thus, if needed, resources could be drawn from these to activities on the critical path (**management by exception**). This helps management to ensure that a project completes on time.
- CPA can identify inefficiencies in a process, allowing management to see where tasks might be removed or run simultaneously.
- Accurate CPA also facilitates the achievement of JIT; in the example on page 221, *Cooler* knows not to order signwriting materials until day 18. As resources are not ordered until required, this helps with cash flow management. A business can plan when cash is required for purchases and can ensure that cash is not tied up in supplies not yet required.

EVALUATING THE USE OF CPA

As with many business tools, CPA should be used with a few notes of caution:

- Having a network diagram does not, on its own, ensure the success of a project. Much management skill will be required to keep the project on time, to move resources around accordingly and to manage costs.
- Usefulness may depend on how accurate/realistic estimates of time taken are and on how easily staff and resources can actually be moved between activities if delay occurs (for example, are other staff skilled enough to help *Cooler* with signwriting?).
- The use of CPA as a tool may be limited as the scale of a project increases. A project such as the building of Wembley Stadium would require many 1000s of unique activities. Not only might it be extremely difficult to estimate length of activities and to foresee all of the tasks required, the resulting diagram may be so complex as to be of limited practical use.

However, whilst it is certainly true that, the more unique a project, the more difficult accurate preparation of a CPA diagram is, with modern computer software very complex projects can easily be broken down into manageable chunks. Projects such as the building of Heathrow's Terminal 5 rely heavily on IT in managing projects, allowing managers to change the models 'on-the-fly' (they can change the models as delays occur, or investigate 'what if' scenarios).

Ultimately, CPA is merely a tool for ensuring the successful and timely completion of a project. The launch of a new product may complete on time, but the product may fail because it was marketed poorly, ill-conceived or simply bettered by the competition. Successful CPA needs to be supported by successful HRM; marketing and the strategy itself needs to be correct ('doing the wrong thing right' versus 'doing the right thing right').

Skills watch!

AO4

Many factors *contribute* to business success; very few factors **on their own** will determine success or failure. If a project fails because it was beaten to market by competitors, CPA *may* be significant; if it was launched on time, but poorly supported by marketing, CPA may not be significant.

An important skill in the examination is determining to what extent any given factor is significant

Summary and exam guidance

Summary

- Lean production is a management philosophy that focuses on reducing waste, better management of time and resources, eliminating duplicated or redundant processes and ensuring quality.

- Just-in-time production (JIT) is concerned with ensuring that supplies are delivered just as they are required, reducing stockholding and associated costs.

- Kaizen, like lean production, is a philosophical way of doing business. It encourages staff at all levels to consider how business can be improved.

- Critical Path Analysis and Simultaneous Engineering are concerned with ensuring projects are completed as effectively and efficiently as possible.

- Lean production is only one possible element of business success. The cost and time savings associated with lean production need to be supported by successful marketing, effective HRM and, ultimately, successful corporate strategy.

Exam practice

Read the articles below and then answer the questions that follow.

Article A

Zesty Zara

In a highly competitive market Zara, the high street clothes retailer, has achieved phenomenal success.

Zara has managed, over its 33 year history, to establish itself globally (it now has 1421 stores worldwide) and to frequently record double-digit sales growth.

A key to Zara's success has been getting fashionable clothes into its shops – fast. Seen something you like on a catwalk model? It will be in Zara shops within a matter of weeks; rival products might take twice as long. Zara quickly copies catwalk designs and sends small quantities to its shops; feedback on the sales of these 'test' runs is then fed back to the production process; the more popular colours and styles are then produced on a larger scale. In true kaizen style, this feedback loop is continual, ensuring that Zara always has the most popular, most fashionable lines in its stores. The fast-fashion approach also helps Zara reduce its exposure to fashion faux pas. The company produces batches of clothing in such small quantities that even if it brings out a design that no one will buy it can cut its losses quickly and move on to another trend.

This lean (and thus low cost), fast approach, has seen Zara develop strong brand awareness for 'disposable fashion' and become a high street leader.

Source: http://www.businessweek.com/globalbiz/content/apr2006/gb20060404_167078.htm?chan=search;%20www.inditex.com/en/who_we_are/our_group#

Zara: fast fashion

Article B

Big delays

When was the last time you read about a major project that completed on time? Wembley Stadium – late. Terminal 5 – late. London underground extensions – late.

Despite major planning, detailed network diagrams and highly paid managers, such projects invariably run into difficulties and are completed late. Testament to the level of planning, managers are able to give exact details of how late ('84% and forecast to be 187 days late'), but, ironically, are unable to get projects finished on time.

The late completion of Wembley Stadium saw losses rise to over £100m and damage to its reputation that remains to this day.

Wembley: woefully late completed

The reasons for delays are as varied as the projects. Bad weather, industrial disputes and unforeseen difficulties (especially as projects of such nature are invariably unique). Often, the estimated completion times were unrealistic in the first place, set to win construction contracts and to please stakeholders.

(a) With reference to the two cases, discuss the value of Critical Path Analysis. (20 marks)

(b) To what extent will successful lean production guarantee the success of a business? (20 marks)

Total: 40 marks

Breakdown of assessment objectives

AO1 – Knowledge and understanding – 8/40

AO2 – Apply knowledge and understanding – 12/40

AO3 – Analyse problems, issues and situations – 8/40

AO4 – Evaluate, distinguish between fact and opinion, assess and judge information from a variety of sources – 12/40

Suggested structure

You will need to:

- Demonstrate an understanding of CPA and analyse, in relation to the cases, at least two factors for and against its value.
- Evaluate the importance of CPA in relation to other business factors, as relevant within the context of the case studies.
- Demonstrate an understanding of lean production, JIT, kaizen and time-based management strategies.
- Apply your knowledge of lean production to the case studies and analyse how such strategies may (or may not) contribute to success.
- Demonstrate the ability to evaluate the potential significance of lean production techniques to success and discuss the relative importance of other factors (such as marketing).

Whether it is Sir Alan Sugar on *The Apprentice* or the Dragons on *Dragon's Den*, there is agreement on one crucial aspect of business success – that people matter. More than that, business success depends above all on its people: on their skills, attitudes, ideas, motivation and relationships. It is entrepreneurs, business leaders, managers and employees throughout the organisation who between them have the capacity to raise a firm above its competitors and provide a sustainable competitive advantage.

The term 'Human Resources' (HR), though it may not sound very caring or personal, is intended to reflect that **people** are a vital *asset* in achieving business success. Managing HR effectively has become one of the principal ways in which an organisation seeks to achieve its overall goals and objectives.

This section explores the strategies by which this is achieved. Chapter 16 provides the overview of how human resource objectives are shaped and the types of strategy that can be used to achieve this. Chapter 17 focuses on the so-called 'hard' HR strategy of workforce planning – ensuring the right numbers of people with the right skills are employed at the right time and in the right place. Chapter 18 examines how organisational structures can be adapted to remain flexible and competitive. The importance of effective employer–employee relations and the means by which this can be achieved are considered in Chapter 19.

Sir Alan Sugar with winning apprentice Lee McQueen

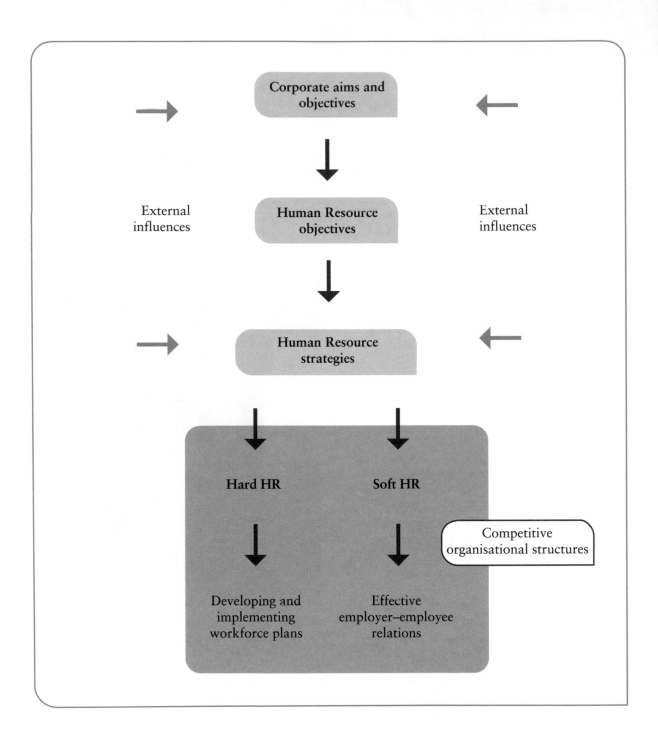

Chapter 16 Understanding HR objectives and strategies

This chapter examines how HR fits into the strategic plan of a business, what objectives may be set for HR and how these are shaped, before examining the types of HR strategies that can be used to achieve these objectives.

What is Human Resource Management?

Human Resource Management (HRM) is a *strategic* approach to managing people that emphasises the importance of planning and developing the workforce to achieve the overall aims of the business. This means that the purpose of HRM is to ensure that the organisation achieves success through its people.

The tools that HR managers use include:

- workforce planning (see Chapter 17)
- developing competitive organisational structures (see Chapter 18)
- building effective relations between employers and employees (see Chapter 19)
- recruitment, selection and training (covered in AS Business Studies)
- appraisal, motivation and reward of employees (also covered at AS level).

The distinguishing feature of HRM is that these tools are not used in isolation from each other and from the other functions of the business. Rather they are part of an integrated corporate strategy – that is, working in cooperation with all other parts of the business to enable the business to achieve its overall objectives.

The objectives for HR will be determined by the business's corporate vision and HRM will seek to ensure the resulting corporate aims are achieved. Internal strengths and weaknesses alongside external opportunities and threats will, as for the whole business, shape the HR strategies used to achieve its objectives.

The diagram below illustrates how the HRM process mirrors the process of corporate strategy and is closely tied to it:

> ### Key terms
>
> **'Hard' HR strategies** Focusing on detailed workforce planning to ensure that the right number of people with the right skills are in the right place at the right time.
>
> **Human Resource Management (HRM)** A strategic approach to managing people that emphasises the importance of planning and developing the workforce to achieve the overall aims of the business.
>
> **'Soft' HRM strategies** Developing and motivating the organisation's people to meet the business's present and future needs.

Corporate aims and objectives — Where do we want to be?	→	Human Resource objectives
Internal and external influences — Where are we now?	→	Internal and external influences on HR
Corporate strategy — How are we going to get there?	→	Human Resource strategy

Human Resource objectives

The overall goal for the Human Resources function of a business is to enable the organisation to deliver its business goals. HRM will help to achieve these through making the most efficient use of the organisation's people and focusing them on its priorities. Thus the specific objectives at any given time for managing HR may include those discussed below.

Matching workforce skills, size and location to business needs

Perhaps the most fundamental objective of HR is to ensure that the organisation has the right number of people, with the right skills, in the right place at the right time, to enable a business to achieve its overall goals.

If the business is seeking to grow to meet increased demand or to diversify into new markets, the size of the workforce may need to expand to enable this to happen. This is an example of what is known as 'strategic resourcing' and will involve *recruiting* and *selecting* the right number and type of workers to meet the organisation's corporate objective. Of course the opposite may also be true – falling demand or a need for cost savings may require *redundancies* to be made and the total size of the workforce to be reduced.

This workforce planning needs to go beyond mere numbers of workers to consider the skills and experience required to meet business needs. An expansion of sales into emerging markets in Asia, for example, will require people with language skills and a knowledge of local culture. *Training* and *development* of staff may be vital to ensuring the required skills base across the organisation's workforce.

Finally, a business needs to ensure people are available in the right location at the right time. This may mean ensuring sufficient staff are employed at each branch, with larger and busier branches employing the staff they need to maintain customer service. It may involve ensuring each department or function within the business has sufficient staff and may need staff to be multi-skilled so that they can be *redeployed* from one function to another. The business may also need to look at the location of its people in terms of cost efficiency, seeking to reduce overheads such as premises or to reduce labour costs – by recruiting workers in lower-wage economies such as India.

To achieve this crucial objective of matching the workforce to business needs, HR managers will need to plan ahead, assessing the organisation's future demand for workers and predicting the available supply of people from within and outside of the business. This so-called 'hard HRM' is considered in more detail below and the processes of this 'workforce planning' are explained in Chapter 17.

Minimising labour costs

If an organisation is seeking to maximise profits or returns to shareholders as its corporate goal, one of its key objectives will be to make efficiency savings and so reduce costs. Minimising labour costs – whilst still meeting the business's needs for the right number and type of workers – can therefore be a crucial HR objective.

Staffing costs will often make up a major proportion of the overall costs of the business – usually between 25% and 50% of total costs – and so it is vital to keep these costs down by making the most efficient use of labour. If a business can keep labour costs down, prices can be low and thus, possibly, a crucial competitive advantage gained (and/or profitability improved).

There are a number of ways in which a business might seek to minimise labour costs:

- Reducing the total size of the workforce – and so cutting the total wage bill. However, the business still needs to have sufficient staff to produce a quality product and maximise the quality of customer service.

For example...

EMI confirms thousands of job losses

Thousands of staff at troubled music group EMI will lose their jobs in a wide-ranging cull by the company's new private owners. EMI's worldwide headcount will be cut by between 1,500 and 2,000 as it slashes costs. Confirming EMI insiders' worst fears, the company said ahead of staff briefings this morning that it was launching 'a series of wide-ranging initiatives within its recorded music division to enable the group to become the world's most innovative, artist friendly and consumer-focused music company'. The comments follow a year of dire news for EMI which issued a series of profit

EMI artist Lily Allen

warnings, reshuffled management and failed to get the sales it had hoped for from various big albums. By merging divisions, weeding out duplication and slashing jobs, EMI's owners hope to be able to shrink costs by up to £200m a year. Functions such as sales, marketing, manufacturing and distribution will be brought together in a single division. At the same time EMI will reposition itself to better find and develop new artists.

Source: *The Guardian*, 15 January 2008

Activity

Consider what the main HR objectives for EMI may be. How are these being shaped by the company's corporate goals?

- Reducing workers' wages and salaries – this too needs to be used with care, otherwise it may provoke dissatisfaction and industrial disputes. Some businesses may achieve this reduction in wages by relocating production or other key processes to lower-wage economies elsewhere in the world.
- Increase **labour productivity** – higher labour productivity means that each worker is producing more units of output, on average, in the same amount of time as before. By achieving this, a business can increase its output without employing any more workers. This will reduce the **'labour cost per unit'** of production – that is, the average cost of the labour needed to produce one unit of output. The lower this is, the greater the profit margin on sales. A business may seek to increase labour productivity by improving skill levels through training, by investing in improved technology to enable workers to be more efficient, or by seeking to motivate or incentivise workers to work more effectively.

Making full use of the workforce's potential

An organisation's workforce is not just pairs of hands and feet to get a job done, but a valuable resource of ideas, skills and qualities. These will be essential if a business is to succeed and sustain a competitive advantage. Product innovation, quality and high standards of customer service will all depend upon how effectively a business can make full use of the workforce's potential.

Getting the best out of the workforce is the aim of so-called 'soft' HRM strategies – developing and motivating the organisation's people to meet the business's present and future needs. This is considered in further detail below.

Maintaining good employer/employee relations

Good relations between business owners, managers and workers are crucial in achieving corporate goals and so is a central HR objective. A positive relationship between employer and employee is a key factor in motivation. Effective communication throughout the business will help to increase its efficiency and responsiveness. Finding ways to involve workers in decision-making will not only help to make them feel valued, and so in turn help to motivate, but may also generate more innovative ideas that will enable a business to keep on improving. By seeking the cooperation and consensus of employees in key decisions, damaging disputes can be avoided. These issues are discussed in more detail in Chapter 19.

Assessing internal and external influences on HR objectives

The specific objectives that a business sets for its Human Resource function will depend upon a range of internal and external influences. The common theme to all these influences is that they are shaping what HR needs to do to enable the business to move from its current position to where it wants to be, helping it to successfully achieve its corporate aims.

Internal influences

CORPORATE OBJECTIVES

The most significant influence on an organisation's HR objectives will be the wider corporate objectives the business has set itself. All the elements of HR – workforce planning, recruitment and selection, training and development and so on – must all be focused on enabling the business to achieve success.

OTHER BUSINESS FUNCTIONS

HR plays a crucial role in enabling other functional areas – such as marketing or operations – to achieve their objectives. If the marketing department is seeking to develop and launch a new product, HR may have the specific objectives of recruiting and selecting the new staff that will make it a success. It may be that different types of employees need to be selected to

For example...

HR objectives at Boots

Boots, the pharmaceutical, health and beauty retailer, decided in 2005 that the fall in sales and profits in the previous three years needed to be reversed and that HR would be central to achieving this. The focus would be on engaging and motivating staff in every store, using their ideas and recognising improved performance. HR objectives to lower staff turnover, reduce absence and improve staff attitudes enabled Boots to boost customer service and increase sales. The result was 1.4 million additional customers and an increase in profit of £5.8 million.

Activity

With reference to this and other chapters, consider what strategies (that is, how) Boots might have sought to address these issues.

manage products at different stages in their life cycles – innovative and competitive risk-takers for products in the introductory or growth stages; shrewd and experienced efficiency-seekers to manage products in maturity or decline phases. Operations managers may be seeking to improve quality or cost efficiency through the use of new technology; HR's objective may be to ensure sufficient training and development to make the new technology a success.

CORE STRENGTHS AND WEAKNESSES

Analysis of the organisation's existing strengths and weaknesses will shape what HR needs to achieve if the business is to succeed. It may be that the business has a very positive reputation for customer service and an image as a caring and loyal employer. HR's objective may be to build on this reputation in order to attract a high calibre of new recruits in a competitive labour market. On the other hand, a key weakness of the business may be a demotivated staff and poor relationships between managers and workers, harming both efficiency and customer service.

South West Trains had faced just these problems up to 2002 when HR was set the objective of engaging staff in becoming more customer-focused. By involving staff in making improvements, recognising their achievements and responding to their views, the business succeeded in rebuilding trust with its employees and in so doing dramatically increased customer satisfaction.

RESOURCE CONSTRAINTS

HR objectives will also be influenced by the constraints of existing business resources, such as the current workforce or the availability of finance. If a high proportion of the current workforce is planning to leave, perhaps due to retirement or dissatisfaction with the company, a key objective of HR planning will be to ensure that suitable recruitment and selection plans are in place; reducing labour turnover in the future may also be a priority. Financial constraints may have a major impact on the levels of staffing, the pay packages staff can be offered and the amount that can be spent on training and development. The overall profitability of the business, together with liquidity and cash flow issues, will all be important in determining financial resources available for HR management.

External influences

CUSTOMERS

Ensuring that the business is focused on the needs of the customer is an important objective for HR. As customer needs change, so HR will need to ensure these changing needs are effectively communicated and that employees are skilled and trained to meet them. The future level of demand from customers will also define HR objectives, with an expansion of the workforce potentially needed to meet increasing demand or a reduction in staffing if demand is predicted to fall. Many primary industries such as coal mining, or secondary industries such as steel-making or ship-building, have seen dramatic declines in numbers employed in the UK as demand has fallen or cheaper supply become available elsewhere. If customers are especially price-sensitive in making purchasing decisions, increasing labour productivity and so reducing labour costs will be a vital objective.

COMPETITORS

Competitors will influence HR objectives in several ways. A need to respond to increased competition, increased marketing by competitors, new product developments or improved customer service will all have implications for HR.

In addition, competitors in the customer marketplace are also competitors in the employee marketplace. HR needs to ensure it has a strategy to attract and retain the best staff in order to gain a competitive advantage through its people over rivals. This may involve paying higher wages or bigger incentive payments.

LOCAL, NATIONAL AND GLOBAL LABOUR MARKETS

The availability of labour in the local, national and global labour markets will shape what HR is able to achieve and its future planning. If the local area does not offer sufficient workers with the right skills, HR may either need to seek to recruit labour from further afield or develop its own training to bring workers up to the right skill levels. Population growth, for example, through immigration, can have major effects on the availability of labour. Employment in the hotel and restaurant industry in the UK, for example, has been dramatically changed by the arrival of migrant workers from Eastern Europe. Wage levels in different labour markets will also shape what HR is able to achieve – minimising labour costs may best be achieved by relocating operations to elsewhere in the world where wages are lower.

ECONOMIC FACTORS

The state of the national and global economy can have a major impact on HR objectives. If the economy is in a period of recession or low growth, demand may be falling and this will affect future workforce planning. On the other hand, increasing unemployment and lower wage deals may also provide an opportunity for HR to target increased cost efficiencies.

LEGISLATION

UK and EU laws may force significant changes on the HR function. The introduction of the National Minimum Wage in the UK in 1997 forced many businesses to increase their wages for their lowest paid workers. This in turn caused businesses to reflect on the levels of staffing and the relative benefits of being based in the UK or elsewhere in the world. Legislation in a wider range of employment areas, such as discrimination, unfair dismissal and industrial relations, has increasingly constrained the actions of HR managers.

TECHNOLOGY

The availability of new technology in production, sales and communications continually changes HR objectives. Ensuring a workforce is sufficiently flexible and skilled to adapt to new technology is vital if efficiency and quality are to be maintained. Technology can also reduce the demand for labour and so threaten the job security of workers – for example, with the rise of Internet banking the numbers employed by banks has fallen considerably. A key HR objective could be to prevent technology undermining staff motivation in this way.

Human Resource strategies

HR strategies are the overall plans by which the business seeks to achieve its HR objectives in order to help the business achieve its corporate goals. These plans cover a broad range of areas as explained above and can be categorised under the headings of 'hard' and 'soft' HR management.

'Hard' HR strategies

The hard side of HR strategies focuses on the workforce as a *resource*. It focuses on the specific and detailed **workforce planning** that is essential if the business is to have the right number of people with the right skills in the right place at the right time.

Workforce planning involves:

- predicting the likely future level of demand for workers;
- assessing the current supply of workers from within the business, their skills and experience;
- predicting the future supply of these workers, by estimating likely labour turnover;
- planning how any gap between future supply and demand will be met, by expanding, reducing, redeploying or relocating the workforce.

The process of workforce planning is covered in more detail in Chapter 17.

Hard HR strategies will be devised out of this workforce plan and will include:

- **recruitment and selection strategies** that set out how the right numbers and types of workers will be attracted, the qualities and experience that will be sought and the selection methods that will be used to choose the ideal candidates;
- **remuneration strategies** that set out how each type of worker will be rewarded through a combination of wages, salaries, financial incentives and other benefits;
- **performance appraisal and training strategies** that set out how the performance of each type of worker will be measured and appraised, and what training is needed to equip the workforce with the required skills.

The importance of hard HR strategy lies in its crucial contribution to business planning. Without it, the business would be unable to deliver on its objectives, lacking the right number or types of workers to compete effectively. A planned and skilled workforce could provide a competitive advantage over rivals, demonstrated in product quality, customer service or cost efficiency.

The problems facing hard HR strategies stem from the difficulties and dangers of such forward planning. Predicting future demand and supply rests on uncertain internal and external events – the proportion of staff who decide to leave, the actions of competitors and the state of the economy are all unknowns that will have a significant impact on the HR strategies required. The workforce plan will need to be constantly monitored, assumptions updated and strategies will need to remain flexible if hard HR is not to become a rigid and bureaucratic exercise.

A further weakness of hard HR strategies will become apparent if they are the only approach that the business takes to managing its people. Whilst this level of statistical planning can be very important to medium and large businesses, employees are people, not numbers. Getting the best out of the workforce requires an approach to HR management that focuses on motivation, culture and development – so-called 'soft' HR strategies; without these in place, a business may find it has the right number and types of workers but also that they are demotivated and unproductive.

'Soft' HR strategies

Where 'hard' HR focused on the workforce as a resource, the 'soft' HR approach emphasises the *human* element. Soft HR starts from the assumption that workers will respond better when the business recognises their needs as individuals. Getting the best out of the workforce will therefore involve:

- rewarding and motivating workers
- developing a positive and productive business culture
- supporting, training and developing employees
- building positive relations between managers and workers.

Soft HR uses a 'human relations' framework to the leadership and motivation of staff, that is, that a happier and more fulfilled workforce will also be a more productive and loyal workforce. By meeting

Synoptic search

Using theories, such as Maslow's hierarchy of needs which you learnt at AS level, will help you to analyse why soft HR may have a positive impact on the motivation of staff. You should be continually revising AS content such as this and be able to use it, on a range of issues and questions, to deepen and broaden the explanation you give.

Activity

Use Maslow's hierarchy of needs to explain why soft HR strategies might motivate staff.

each of the levels of need set out, for example, in Maslow's hierarchy of needs, the business will be able to 'connect' with workers as individuals. The motivation this creates will help businesses that need workers who are flexible, creative and innovative.

The benefits of soft HR are that workers will not just be recruited, selected and set objectives, but that they will feel valued and respond by being more effective. In this way soft HR strategies are more likely to create the competitive advantage through people that many businesses seek. They may have very specific and measurable benefits in terms of:

- increased labour productivity and so reduced unit labour costs
- reduced absenteeism
- reduced labour turnover
- fewer industrial disputes
- improved product quality or customer service.

For example...

Fermenting careers

Although its products are made for pure enjoyment, Coors Brewing Company takes some things very seriously. As the world's seventh largest brewer they have a reputation to keep up and with well known names such as Carling, Grolsch and Worthington in their stable they have high standards to maintain. They believe one way to do this is to have highly motivated staff.

All of their 700 employees are invited to take part in 'The Coors Experience'. The idea is to instill in everyone involved in every stage of the production process the same vision and values. This means people from all over the plant get to come together to hear more about the company, share their experiences and find out how they can go further in their career. Everyone from actual brewers and telesales people to new graduates and even senior management gets involved.

Coors believe giving career development opportunities is vital to running a successful business.

The company employs around 3,000 people across the UK. It takes on about 4% of these each year as it loses about the same amount. Coors believe the career development opportunities they offer help them achieve this good record in staff retention. They claim most companies have a turnover of around one eighth of staff every year.

Opportunities at Coors are varied. Many jobs are similar to those available at many large companies, for instance, sales, marketing and finance. So the brewery has to think carefully about how to attract the right staff that will fit into their mindset. They also have to highlight what would be different about working for them. It is vital that peoples' skills are matched with their position. One of the more unusual jobs at Coors is being on the taste panel. Specially recruited people come in three mornings a week. Over the years Coors have found that, despite men drinking more of it, women often make better beer tasters.

The company says this is because by drinking less beer women can recognise individual brands more easily. Women also tend to have better descriptive skills and can communicate their findings better. 'We also have sessions with cheese, chocolate and snacks to develop our sense of taste,' says Jo Morris, a member of the panel. It's a hard life for some!

Source: http://news.bbc.co.uk/1/hi/ programmes/working_lunch/4007219.stm

Activity

Consider in what ways Coors is using both hard and soft HRM strategies. Evaluate the impact these strategies are likely to have.

Whether these benefits occur in practice will depend upon several factors. Soft HR strategies assume that the workforce will respond in the way set out by the 'human relations' motivation theorists. McGregor's Theory Y suggests that workers seek the development and empowerment opportunities offered by soft HR and will respond through engagement, creativity and motivation. If, however, workers are more like the Theory X model, soft HR is unlikely to have any impact or even be counter-productive – workers simply seek to earn a fair day's wage for a fair day's work.

The history of relations between managers and workers, the existing culture in the business and the personalities of leaders will all impact on the extent to which soft HR is seen as desirable or is successful in practice. It is often seen as vague and woolly by business leaders wishing to see the 'bottom line' impact of HR; strategies such as personal development and training are therefore often the first to be cut when a business needs to reduce expenditure.

Summary and exam guidance

Summary

- Human Resource Management (HRM) is a *strategic* approach to managing people that emphasises the importance of planning and developing the workforce to achieve the overall aims of the business.

- The HR function needs to work in cooperation with all other parts of the business to enable the business to achieve its corporate objectives.

- HR objectives might include:
  - matching workforce skills, size and location to business needs
  - minimising labour costs
  - making full use of the workforce's potential
  - maintaining good employer/employee relations.

- The HR objectives an organisation has will be shaped by both internal and external influences.

- Internal influences will include corporate objectives, other business functions, resource constraints and the organisation's existing core strengths and weaknesses.

- External influences, beyond the organisation itself, will include the needs of customers, the actions of competitors, the nature of local, national and global labour markets, the state of the economy, legislation and technology.

- 'Hard' HR strategies focus on the detailed *workforce planning* that is essential if the business is to have the right number of people with the right skills in the right place at the right time.

- The 'soft' HR approach emphasises the *human* element and focuses on getting the best out of the workforce through communication, employee development and effective motivation.

Exam practice

Read the article below and then answer the questions that follow.

Article A

Turning the heat up on the opposition pays off

Strong training and communication, managers who are excellent role models and a real sense that work is to be enjoyed all add up to HEAT Ltd being one of the UK's favourite places to work, according to a 2008 survey by *The Sunday Times*. HEAT (Heat, Energy and Associated Technology) specialises in the design, installation and maintenance of central heating for social housing within the UK, Northern Ireland and the Republic of Ireland.

Work is enjoyable at HEAT Ltd

HEAT 's triumph in this survey over its predominantly white-collar rivals is founded on one key quality, according to its founder and managing director Bill McCandless: communication. 'We work hard to make it simple,' he says. 'People confuse simple with easy. But simple is actually very hard. If you make it simple, everybody understands and that makes it more likely to last.

'We like to think we have a degree of professionalism and the culture of a large company in terms of training and investment, with the tight-knit element of a small company.'

HEAT has been successful in filling skills gap for its European recruitment policy and its apprentice training programme (ATP). Communications Officer with HEAT, Julie Brien, said: 'The skills gap is the major challenge facing the construction industry today. In the heating industry, there have been far-reaching changes with the use of high efficiency boilers and renewable energy technologies. The traditional approach of training a young person in just one discipline is no longer relevant, as the market requires apprentices to have knowledge of electricity, gas and plumbing.'

To meet its immediate requirement, for suitably skilled staff, to counteract the impact the skills shortage was having on the delivery of its core services, HEAT devised a strategy to recruit skilled labour from EU countries and particularly the Czech Republic. It also developed an apprentice training programme to produce central heating engineers skilled in plumbing, electrics and gas.

The company has an ongoing programme of training opportunities to assist its staff in developing their knowledge and skills base.

HEAT Ltd: winner of *The Sunday Times* '100 Best Companies to Work For' award in 2008

cont...

To assist workers to fulfil their potential, Personal Development Plan (PDP) sessions are conducted annually between each member of staff and their respective line manager to identify and discuss training needs. By keeping in close touch with personal development, the aim is to ensure that the individuals that make up the HEAT team are engaged and satisfied by what they do in the workplace. Julie continued: 'The overall benefit to HEAT is the development of a cohort of committed technical experts who will be sufficiently motivated to make long-term contributions to the company.'

Source: www.heat.co.uk

(a) Analyse the influences on HEAT's HR objectives. (15 marks)

(b) Evaluate the relative importance of hard HR compared to soft HR strategies in HEAT's success. (25 marks)

Total: 40 marks

Breakdown of assessment objectives

AO1 – Knowledge and understanding – 6/40
AO2 – Apply knowledge and understanding – 10/40
AO3 – Analyse problems, issues and situations – 10/40
AO4 – Evaluate, distinguish between fact and opinion, assess and judge information from a variety of sources – 14/40

Suggested structure

For part (a) you will need to:

- Demonstrate a knowledge and understanding of potential HR objectives and influences.
- Apply your understanding to the case study, identifying what the main HR objectives have been and explaining how both internal and external influences will have shaped these objectives.

For part (b) you will need to:

- Show a sound understanding of the difference between hard HR and soft HR strategies.
- Link to the case study and provide examples of each type of strategy in practice.
- Consider the benefits and importance of each type of strategy, weighing up the extent to which they can enable the business to achieve success.
- Arrive at a reasoned, evaluative judgment as to whether one set of strategies is any more important than the other.

Chapter 17 Developing and implementing workforce plans

As introduced in Chapter 16, central to achieving corporate vision is a Human Resource strategy that enables a firm's workforce to become a source of competitive advantage. Hard HR strategies help to achieve this by ensuring the right numbers of people with the right skills are in the right place at the right time to enable the business to compete effectively. For this to be achieved, **workforce planning** is essential.

This chapter will explain what workforce planning is and what it involves; what internal and external factors influence workforce planning; and what issues will affect the implementation of these workforce plans. We will also evaluate how valuable a workforce plan might be to an organisation.

What is a workforce plan?

A workforce plan is a forward plan that matches what human resources will be needed by the organisation in the future (its *demand* for labour) with what labour is available both inside and outside the organisation (the *supply* of labour). This involves assessing not just the number of employees that will be needed, but the types of worker, their skills and their location. The purpose of the workforce plan is to ensure the business is able to achieve its corporate objectives, such as growing market share or minimising costs. In this way, the workforce plan is a central feature of putting the overall business strategy into action and must be closely integrated with other functional strategies.

Workforce planning will need to be carried out on a short-term and long-term basis. Short-term planning will involve meeting staffing needs over the following weeks and months – for example, to ensure there is sufficient cover scheduled for staff on holiday. Longer-term planning will be based on delivering the future plans of the business, such as expansion into new markets, adapting its brand image or increasing operational efficiency.

The diagram on the next page summarises this process.

Components of workforce plans

The starting points for a workforce plan are the corporate objectives and strategies that define where the business wants to be in the future and how it is going to get there. The outcome of the workforce plan will be a continually monitored and evaluated set of practical plans and actions that show how the workforce will be able to deliver success. So what are the components, or stages, of this planning process?

Assessing future HR needs – the demand for labour

Using the corporate objectives and strategies as the starting point, workforce planning will seek to estimate the size, type and skills of workers that will be needed in the future

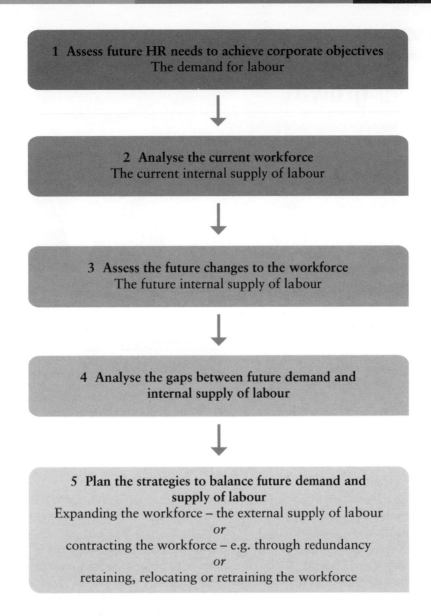

1 **Assess future HR needs to achieve corporate objectives**
The demand for labour

2 **Analyse the current workforce**
The current internal supply of labour

3 **Assess the future changes to the workforce**
The future internal supply of labour

4 **Analyse the gaps between future demand and internal supply of labour**

5 **Plan the strategies to balance future demand and supply of labour**
Expanding the workforce – the external supply of labour
or
contracting the workforce – e.g. through redundancy
or
retaining, relocating or retraining the workforce

to put the business's strategies into action. This is known as the organisation's 'demand for labour'.

This process of forecasting future demand for employees is not easy. Past data about the size of the workforce, its productivity and how effectively it met the demand for the product will be crucial information. However, this will need to be amended to reflect:

- **Changing business goals** – such as expansion into new markets or a need to 'delayer' (see Chapter 18) to improve efficiency.
- **Future demand for the product** – based on sales forecasting techniques.
- **Changing productivity levels** – that is the output per worker, which may be affected by changing working practices or new technology.
- **Changing business environment** – an increase in competition, the development of new products or new employment laws could all influence the number or type of workers needed.

As well as how many workers are needed, this stage of the planning process will need to identify what type and level of workers are needed. For example, whether it is an expansion of

For example...

Planning for **growth**

In its first 4 years since being established, Holiday Rooms Direct grew from nothing to an annual turnover of £7 million, making it the fastest-growing private technology business in 2007. With 40,000 properties listed on its website, the online travel agency offers a full range of accommodation, from budget apartments to luxury five star spa hotels. Based in Doncaster, the company is led by Chief Executive, David Henry, together with founder and managing director, Jennifer Davis. Henry claims that a commitment to the highest levels of customer service and heavy investment in search engine marketing resulted in phenomenal sales of growth of 516% from 2004 to 2006. Henry and Davis now plan to tap into the European market by opening a call centre in Ukraine in the near future. Other new initiatives include the development of city break products, which will be launched on the website later in the year.

Source:
http://www.fasttrack.co.uk/fasttrack2002/migrati on/dbDetails.asp?siteID=3&compID=2164&yr=2007

Holiday Rooms Direct: a success story for Chief Executive David Henry and founder and managing director Jennifer Davis

Activity

Is planning future demand for labour likely to be important to a firm like Holiday Rooms Direct? What constraints may there be on its ability to produce such a plan?

IT experts, marketing managers or sales assistants that will be needed in the years ahead; or whether it is shop-floor workers or middle management that should be cut to reduce the overall size of a workforce.

The skills, experience and training required by those employed in the future also need to be assessed and planned. A move into Internet selling may require an expansion of IT expertise, whilst a move into new markets abroad may require staff to possess specific language skills.

Finally, the location of its demand for employees will also be relevant to multi-site organisations. Whilst the overall size of the workforce may remain largely unchanged in the future, dramatic changes may be planned for where that workforce is to be employed – for example, in relocating a call centre from the UK to India.

Analyse the current workforce – the current internal supply of labour

The next stage of the workforce plan is to analyse the organisation's current workforce. An audit of current employees will examine all of the business's personnel records to identify:

- the number of employees working in each part of the business
- the job roles that they are carrying out
- the characteristics of employees in terms of their age, length of service, full or part time, and so on
- the skills, training and experience within the workforce.

This information will be vital in allowing the business to estimate the likely size and skills of the workforce in the future.

Assess the future changes to the workforce – the future internal supply of labour

A business cannot assume that its current workforce will remain unchanged in the years ahead. It must forecast likely changes in the number, type and skills of workers – the *future* internal supply of labour. This is likely to be different from the *current* internal supply for a number of reasons.

Firstly, a proportion of the current staff is likely to leave the firm. This may be to move to other organisations or to leave employment altogether, for example, at retirement. Labour turnover is the measure of that rate of change of personnel within a company's workforce over time. It is calculated as:

$$\frac{\text{Number of staff leaving per period of time}}{\text{Average number of staff per period of time}} \times 100 = \% \text{ labour turnover}$$

Past labour turnover figures will be a useful piece of information in estimating future labour turnover, but other factors will also need to be considered. The current age profile of the staff, for example, will indicate what proportion of staff – and of what types and skills – are approaching retirement age. Dissatisfaction amongst staff or very competitive labour markets are other factors that can cause higher labour turnover, and an organisation will need to assess how this will impact on its own future supply of labour.

The future supply of labour will also be affected by potential changing working practices, such as the length of the working day, flexible hours or the multi-skilling of workers (see below). It is important to remember also that the future supply of workers also means their skills, experience and training. So a business that has a range of training and development opportunities in place for staff will hope to benefit from an increased supply of skilled workers in the future – assuming it can retain them!

Analyse the gaps between future demand and internal supply of labour

The outcome of these first three stages in workforce planning will be the ability to analyse the gap between the forecast future demand for workers and the expected future internal supply. This analysis may indicate a gap in terms of numbers, skills, attitudes or desired locations of workers. In considering the strategies to address these gaps, a business may be constrained by finance, time, legislation or other factors. These will shape what the business decides and how it is implemented in practice.

Plan the strategies to balance future demand and supply of labour

The gap analysis explained above may indicate a need to:

- **Expand the workforce** If the workforce plan indicates that future demand for workers is likely to exceed the internal supply, the business will need to plan to use external recruitment to meet the gap. This will involve attracting suitable workers from local, national or global labour markets. The organisation's ability to do so effectively will depend upon a range of external influences, explained below.
- **Contract the workforce** The workforce plan may indicate the need to reduce, or 'downsize', the total number of workers if future demand for labour is less than predicted future supply. This could be achieved through 'natural wastage' (not replacing workers when they choose to leave the business), through redundancy or through flexible working practices, such as job-sharing.

- **Retain, relocate or retrain the workforce** Strategies may instead focus on the existing workforce and how they can be retained, adapted or developed to meet the organisation's future needs. This may include pay and reward structures, relocating workers to new areas, or use of training and development programmes to 'up skill' workers.

Assessing internal and external influences on workforce plans

Forecasting future demand for labour, estimating the future internal supply of labour and planning how the external labour market may be needed for recruitment are all challenging and uncertain processes. In seeking to reduce some of the unpredictability of workforce planning, organisations must try to understand the *internal* and *external* factors that will shape its workforce of the future.

Internal influences

CORPORATE OBJECTIVES AND STRATEGIES

The purpose of the workforce plan is to enable a business to achieve its overall objectives by successfully putting its corporate strategies into action. So it is these whole-business objectives and strategies that are the starting point for assessing the number and type of skills of workers that will be needed in the future. Where growth is the objective, the business may be planning to increase sales by targeting new markets or launching new products. The workforce plan will need to set out how the people required to make this happen will be recruited, retained, developed or relocated. If cost minimisation is the goal and workforce efficiency is one of the strategies, plans will need to be in place to boost productivity, cut wage bills or delayer the organisational structure.

FUNCTIONAL OBJECTIVES, STRATEGIES AND CONSTRAINTS

Other business functions may have specific objectives that are required to implement the corporate strategies discussed above. These functions need to work closely with Human Resources to ensure the right number and types of people are in place to make these happen. For example, the marketing function may be seeking to diversify the product range and may need staff with expertise in the new product areas; or the operations team may be seeking to innovate in product design or the production process and may require a greater diversity of worker skills and experience to achieve this. These other functional areas may also place constraints on the workforce plan. A planned expansion of the workforce to meet an increased future demand may be constrained by a lack of financial resources or liquidity problems in putting the plan into practice.

THE NATURE OF THE CURRENT WORKFORCE

The characteristics of the existing labour force will shape much of the planning of both labour demand and supply in the future. Current labour productivity will help to forecast how many workers are needed to meet product demand in the future. The skills, experience and attitudes of workers, together with current training and development programmes, will be the baseline from which the future internal supply of labour is forecast. The level of labour turnover in recent years will help to predict how many staff may then leave; this will need to be adjusted to take into account the age profile and known future plans of staff to help predict how many and what type of staff need to be recruited externally. An ageing staff may suggest high rates of retirement approaching and this could either be an opportunity to 'downsize' the workforce without having to use redundancy or it may signal the need for a major recruitment drive if the workforce size needs to be maintained.

External influences

DEMAND FOR EXISTING AND NEW PRODUCTS

Future consumer demand for the organisation's products will be a crucial influence in shaping the future demand for labour in the workforce plan. Working closely with the sales forecasting or the marketing department, HR planners will need to identify not just the numbers of workers needed to make, sell or manage products, but also the skills, attitudes and experience they will need to have. The workforce plan will then detail the recruitment, training and location plans for the future workforce that will be able to meet this product demand successfully.

LABOUR MARKET TRENDS

Labour markets on a local, national and global level can have a major effect on the future supply of labour. Wage levels, the rate of unemployment and competition from other businesses will all affect how easy or difficult it is to retain staff, as well as to recruit new staff. The ability to recruit suitable staff in any particular area will depend upon the availability of workers with the right skills. Businesses such as hi-tech engineering firms, for example, may require workers with specialist skills and could depend upon local colleges and training providers to help build the necessary skills base; other firms may seek to provide their own training schemes to meet this same need.

DIY chain B&Q are well known for employing more mature staff

The nature of the local workforce will also be shaped by demographic trends – that is, by the size and characteristics of the working population. An ageing population with a longer life expectancy in the UK is providing a growing number of older people willing and able to carry on working. Some businesses, such as the DIY chain B&Q, have taken advantage of this demographic trend to employ older staff who bring greater experience and knowledge which can improve the quality of customer service.

Migration (the movement of people from one region or country to another) can also have a significant effect on labour markets and so workforce planning. Since 2004, over 700,000 migrant workers have come into the UK from the new Eastern European member states of the European Union (the vast majority from Poland). 80% of migrants have been under the age of 34, most seeking the higher wages of the UK compared to their home country. This has meant a dramatic increase in the external supply of workers to agriculture, manufacturing and service industries, such as catering and hospitality. This has enabled many businesses, especially in London and the South East, to fill gaps in their workforce at the lower end of the pay scale, which without migrant labour may have been very difficult to fill.

LEGISLATION

UK and EU employment legislation and regulations can influence both the future demand for and supply of labour. Any legal changes which affect demand for the final product will in turn affect the demand for labour by producers – for example, tobacco companies saw a 7% drop in sales in England and Wales in the first month after a ban on smoking in public places was introduced in 2007.

Legal regulations on workers' pay and conditions will also influence the number of workers needed by an organisation. For example, the EU Working Time directive restricts the number of hours employees are allowed to work during a week, as well as the length of holidays and rest breaks. When first introduced this had a significant effect on some businesses in that employees may have been able to work substantially fewer total hours than previously, effectively reducing internal labour supply.

TECHNOLOGY

Technology can influence workforce plans in a number of ways. New technology may open up opportunities to expand an organisation's product range, move into new markets or sell in new ways. This would then influence the demand for workers and the skills they would need to have to make these plans a success. Technology could also reduce the demand for labour, however, if it involves replacing workers with automated technology in the production process. The rise of Internet banking has reduced significantly the number of staff employed in the banking industry; car manufacture is now far less labour-intensive than it was in previous decades as a result of computer-aided design and manufacture.

For example...

British Gas Services (BGS)

Managers at BGS conduct a programme of forecasting to predict how much the UK market for domestic gas engineering services will grow. This helps the company decide how many additional engineers it will need in the future. BGS makes detailed forecasts of its demand for engineering personnel for one year in advance and makes more general estimates for a further two years into the future.

In BGS, workforce requirements are driven by two different demands. First, there are contract customers that have service agreements with the company. Second, there are customers who call for one-off assistance if they have a specific problem. Demand for both these services has grown. In the last three or four years, BGS's need for engineers has expanded accordingly. This has meant that it has had to recruit more staff.

There are several other factors that influence workforce planning for BGS. Engineering skills, such as those related to health and safety issues or new technologies, need to be constantly updated. Workforce planning then needs to manage not just numbers, but also the skills balance of BGS's engineers.

Engineers can work all their careers in the field until they retire. Qualified engineers may spend up to 10 years gaining their skills, qualifications and experience. They have valued practical skills that are needed to deal with equipment and customers. However, BGS also needs suitable people for promotion to higher roles, such as management jobs. It needs managers to plan, organise and coordinate the teams of engineers. It therefore needs to attract and recruit a wide range of people into the organisation.

Source: http://www.thetimes100.co.uk/case-study-workforce-planning-at-british-gas-services-137-330-5.php

Activity

Evaluate the most significant influences on workforce planning for British Gas Services.

Issues in implementing workforce plans

The workforce planning process can be a difficult one, resting as it does on the forecasting of future trends and the uncertain external environment. Equally, putting a workforce plan successfully into practice can be just as problematic.

Employer/employee relations

Effective relations between business owners, managers and workers are vitally important to the success of a business (see Chapter 19). The issues raised by a workforce plan can have a major effect on these relationships because they impact directly on both business objectives and on peoples' needs in employment, such as job security, pay, location, promotion prospects and personal development.

For business owners and managers, the workforce plan sets out how corporate goals of growth or cost efficiency are going to be achieved through its people. This may involve relocating operations, delayering the organisation or reducing the size of the workforce through redundancies. Employees may view these same plans as undermining their jobs or undervaluing their skills. The result may be worsening employer/employee relations and even industrial disputes. It is essential that in implementing the workforce plan these issues are fully thought through and ways of avoiding conflict with the workforce considered. This may be through consultation with trade unions or directly with employees, through using 'natural wastage' rather than redundancy or through supporting workers with change such as a new location or new ways of working. The success of the workforce plan may depend upon the effectiveness with which these implementation issues are dealt with in practice.

Cost

Efficient implementation of a workforce plan will mean enabling HR objectives to be achieved at minimum cost. Ineffective workforce planning would mean the wrong number or types of people are employed, preventing the business from achieving its overall goals.

However, even if the plan is successful in getting the balance of labour right, this needs to be done at the lowest possible cost if it is to be considered efficient. Excessive staffing levels, for example, could meet production and quality targets but with a higher wage bill than was necessary.

Implementing a workforce plan can incur a diverse range of costs on a business. Any expansion in the demand for labour could require a process of recruitment, selection and training, all of which can be expensive and time-consuming. The business will need to plan its cash flow carefully to ensure it has sufficient liquidity to fund such an expansion of the workforce. Similarly, a reduction in the future internal supply of labour – for example, as a result of a high labour turnover – will impose the same kinds of costs if the business is to use external labour supply to fill the gap.

Whilst a workforce plan may seek to reduce costs by downsizing the workforce, even this is not without its costs in the short term. For example, if redundancy is to be used to shed jobs, the cost of redundancy payments can be considerable. Very often, firms go beyond the minimum required in order to look after their staff – higher payments, advice, even retraining are often offered to redundant workers. The inefficiency of expanding and contracting the workforce in response to short-term factors has led many organisations to adopt a more flexible business model in which temporary contract workers or outsourcing firms are used to meet increases in the demand for labour. This enables the firm to contract their workforce back to its core, quickly and cheaply, if their demand for labour falls again.

Corporate image

Organisations need to consider the impact that implementing a workforce plan can have on their image and reputation with employees and customers alike. A business that is perceived as being uncaring and mercenary because of its decision to contract staffing levels, for example, could face subsequent problems resulting from its negative image. Within the workforce this could be lost trust and loyalty, lower motivation and higher labour turnover. Where the company's decisions are high profile, customers too may feel that the business is behaving poorly towards its workforce. In a market where ethics and trust are important to customers (for example, banking and financial services), this could prove damaging to the company's reputation and ultimately level of custom and profitability. On the other hand, companies that have gained a reputation as caring employers – such as John Lewis or Marks and Spencer – can benefit from the positive image that customers gain of the organisation.

Training

The need for a coherent training and development programme for staff will be a key element of many workforce plans. This needs to be a rigorous and systematic process focused on enabling staff to meet corporate, functional and individual objectives. Such a process can be resource-intensive and expensive for an organisation. Where the external labour force has insufficient skills to meet the company's needs, training will be crucial to ensure new recruits are able to meet the standards in their work required by the business.

The cost of training can be one of the main reasons why workforce plans are not successfully implemented. When a business is seeking to minimise costs, training is often one of the first types of expenditure to be cut as, in the short term, there may be no obvious benefit in terms of revenue and profitability. Expenditure on training can also prove wasted if trained staff leave their job before the organisation has gained a return on the time and money invested in their training.

Skills watch!

AO4

Business theory is often equally relevant to small and large businesses but in different ways – workforce planning is no exception. It will happen in very different ways, from formal and systematic, to informal and ad hoc, but remains important to all types of business. Given the unique context of each different organisation, there is no single, right or wrong approach. Examination answers must take this into account using balanced language to discuss possibilities, not certainties. For example:

*Given the huge impact that losing just one member of staff **could** have on a small business, this informal process **may be** just as crucial as the more formal equivalent **might be** for bigger businesses.*

The value of using workforce plans

For most small organisations, there is no need for a formal workforce planning process or documented actions. Their need for labour and the types of skills required for business success, however, will be daily considerations, and informal workforce planning will be happening all the time. The small business, however, will still need to look ahead to assess its customers' demands in the coming months and years, and will need to have an informal plan as to how the workforce needs to adapt and change over time to meet these demands.

Intense competition, now global as well as local and national in many markets, has made effective workforce planning more crucial today than in the past. For the business to succeed, the right people, in the right place at the right time with the right skills, is essential. More frequently-changing consumer tastes and fashions, shorter product life cycles, rapid advancements in technology and a focus on speed of delivery in business have all meant that a business must be equipped to adapt swiftly and constantly. Workforce planning is the key to this as it seeks to anticipate how such changes will impact on the skills and attitudes required in employees; flexibility has become the new buzzword.

Fluctuating economic conditions demand a swift response from businesses. A surge in demand presents opportunities for profit but unless there are sufficient staff in production and sales to meet the demand, these opportunities will be missed. Conversely, the impact on many businesses – especially UK housebuilding firms – of the 'credit crunch' in 2008, was to significantly cut demand for the end product. A swift and

McDegrees

McDonald's, Network Rail and Flybe are to be allowed to award nationally recognised qualifications through their training programmes. The government is set to announce that the three employers will accredit their own training programmes equivalent to GCSEs, A Levels and degrees. McDonalds's will train staff for a certificate in basic shift management, which includes modules on human resources, finance and hygiene. Government Skills Secretary, John Denham, has only recently come round to the idea of allowing employers to award their own qualifications, seeing it as a way of boosting workplace skills. John Cridland, deputy director-general of the CBI said 'Companies currently invest £33bn every year in training their staff, but only one third of employer training leads to qualifications because not enough official courses offer the competencies that employers require. Firms have instead run their own bespoke training programmes and formally recognising this employer training will lead to more relevant qualifications and give a greater recognition to business and employee investment in skills'.

Source: www.personneltoday.com, 28 January 2008

Activity

What will be the benefits of allowing firms to award their own qualifications for the training they offer? To what extent might the £33bn a year spent on training by business be considered to be money well spent?

dramatic reduction in the workforce was needed to minimise costs and losses. The need for workforce planning is not reserved solely for the private sector. Public sector organisations, such as hospitals and schools, need to plan ahead to ensure their objectives of customer care and service delivery are met. The changing demands of government policy and fluctuations in budgets for these public sector services require exactly the same kinds of forward-planning and flexibility as the private sector.

As well as delivering the hard HR strategies required to deliver specific corporate objectives, workforce plans can also provide a valuable framework for the soft HR strategies of individual development and motivation. By setting out the corporate objectives that the workforce needs to deliver, individual employees can better understand their own roles and focus on the common goals that can provide a sense of direction and purpose. Training and development opportunities that are built into the workforce plan can enable workers to advance their own skills and careers, as well as offering motivational benefits and helping people to adapt to change.

Workforce planning is not an easy process, nor does it provide a crystal ball that enables the business to predict future events and needs. HR planners will need to be skilled and experienced, understanding the market within which the business operates. They must also understand the practical realities (such as cost, time, resistance to change, unforeseen disruption) that can prevent plans from being successfully implemented. If plans are overly ambitious or overly rigid – not building in the ability to adapt to changing events – they may well fail. A workforce plan is a long-term framework within which business needs to be flexible enough to adapt to short-term factors. If the organisation understands both the importance and the limitations of workforce planning, it will be well placed to gains the benefits such a plan can bring.

Summary and exam guidance

Summary

- Workforce plans match what human resources will be needed by the organisation in the future (its *demand* for labour) with what labour is available both inside and outside the organisation (the *supply* of labour).

- The starting points for a workforce plan are the corporate objectives and strategies that define where the business wants to be in the future and how it is going to get there.

- If additional labour is required, recruitment from local, national and global labour markets may be required; if different skills or attitudes are necessary, training and development need to be planned.

- If the future demand for labour is less than existing supply, the business will need to find ways to downsize its total workforce, potentially through redundancy.

- Workforce planning is shaped by a range of internal and external influences; these provide a direction but also uncertainties for the planning process.

- The workforce planning process is essential to both small and large organisations, private and public sector, though the degree of complexity and formality in the planning process will vary.

Exam practice

Read the articles below and then answer the questions that follow.

Article A

Tomorrow's people

Councils could face a skills shortage in vital areas such as adult care, environmental health and planning unless more council chiefs take a long-term view of workforce planning, a report by the Audit Commission has warned. The 'Tomorrow's People: Building a local government workforce for the future' report claimed that only one in four English councils had adequate or effective workforce strategies.

Top performing councils were more likely to be those with forward-looking plans for staff recruitment and retention, the report said. These councils had fewer vacancies and falling hiring costs. But a third of council employees across the country were now aged over 50 and councils were having difficulty recruiting young people and some key professionals. This demographic time bomb would have serious repercussions for services and those who rely on them, with the number needing social care support rising in the coming years.

Source: www.personneltoday.com, 27 June 2008

Article B

Boom and bust in the NHS

The Health Select Committee of MPs said NHS workforce planning had been a disastrous failure with too few people with the ability and skills to do the task. It urged 'more time, effort and resources' to be devoted to the challenge. The committee's report, entitled 'Boom and Bust in the NHS', said little thought was given to long-term planning as managers strived to hit 'demanding' government targets.

Between 1999 and 2004, nursing numbers increased by more than 67,000, 340% in excess of original targets. GP numbers rose by more than 4000, double the original target over the same period. These huge rises in workforce numbers have since been followed by redundancies, cuts to training and recruitment freezes. 'The planning system remains poorly integrated, and there is an appalling lack of coordination between workforce and financial planning', the report concluded.

Source: www.personneltoday.com, 2 April 2007

(a) Analyse the factors that will influence workforce planning in organisations such as these. (15 marks)

(b) Evaluate the relative importance of workforce planning to public sector organisations compared to private sector businesses. (25 marks)

Total: 40 marks

Breakdown of assessment objectives

AO1 – Knowledge and understanding – 6/40
AO2 – Apply knowledge and understanding – 10/40
AO3 – Analyse problems, issues and situations – 10/40
AO4 – Evaluate, distinguish between fact and opinion, assess and judge information from a variety of sources – 14/40

Suggested structure

For part (a) you will need to:

- Demonstrate knowledge and understanding of workforce planning and the factors that influence it – both internal and external.
- Explain why these factors shape the process of balancing demand and supply of labour.
- Apply your understanding to the two case study organisations and seek to explain which influences are most important in these examples.

For part (b) you will need to:

- Explain why workforce planning is important to achieving an organisation's corporate objectives, whether it is in the private or the public sector.
- Use examples from the case studies to show how a lack of workforce planning will have a major impact on the objectives of public sector organisations such as councils and hospitals.
- Consider why it might be that public sector organisations place a lesser importance on workforce planning or may be less successful at it.
- Arrive at a reasoned, evaluative judgment as to whether workforce planning is equally important and beneficial in both public and private sectors or whether there is a significant distinction to be made between the two.

Chapter 18 Competitive organisational structures

For an organisation's people to be successful in achieving the corporate goals and objectives, the way in which they are organised to work together is vitally important. This **organisational structure** – how people are arranged in order to help carry out the business activity – will affect many aspects of the competitiveness of the business: the quality of production or customer service, the ability to respond to a changing marketplace, cost efficiency and ultimately profitability will all be impacted by organisational structure. This chapter will examine the factors that determine the choice of organisational structure before considering how businesses can adapt their organisational structures in order to improve competitiveness.

What types of organisational structures can a business use?

An organisation's structure refers to the way in which its people are organised to work with each other. It shows:

- The structure of *authority* within the business – who is in charge of and responsible for whom.
- The roles and titles of individuals within the business – that is, who is *responsible* for different areas.
- The person to whom individual employees are *accountable* – known as a 'line manager'.
- The routes by which *communication* passes through and around the business.

The types of organisational structure a business can use represent different ways of grouping people together, which then shape issues such as authority, responsibility, accountability and communication. Unit 2 of AS Business Studies examined the main types of organisational structure in detail (a summary is given in Figure 18.1 opposite).

Factors determining choice of organisational structures

Organisational structure needs to enable corporate aims to be achieved. The structure best suited to achieve this will be determined by a range of factors.

Internal influences

MANAGEMENT STYLE AND PERSONAL VIEWS

Some managers will prefer to retain direct control over an organisation, using a tall pyramid or an entrepreneurial structure, whereas others may be more willing to empower others, using a flatter pyramid and wider spans of control. One of the reasons why Marks and

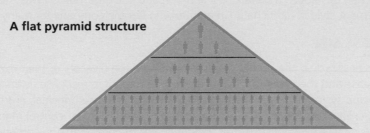

A flat pyramid structure

- Few levels of hierarchy mean short chains of command.
- Wide spans of control lead to broader, more independent job roles.

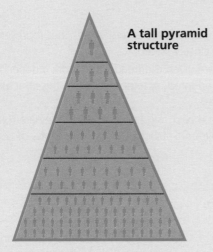

A tall pyramid structure

- Many levels of hierarchy produce a much longer chain of command.
- Narrow spans of control mean that managers each have fewer employees to control.

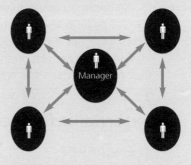

An entrepreneurial structure

- Key central figure (usually business owner or entrepreneur) issues power and instructions to a few key employees.
- Often adopted by small businesses or organisations where speed of decision-making and communications are vital to succeed.

A matrix structure

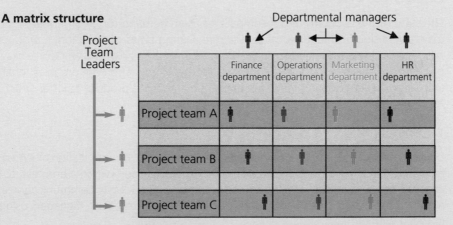

- Project teams bring together individual employees from different functional departments.
- Less formal and more task-focused than traditional pyramid structures.

Figure 18.1 Types of organisational structure

Spencer had developed a hierarchical and bureaucratic organisation was the autocratic management style of Sir Richard Greenbury who led the company for many years.

BUSINESS SIZE

As a business grows, the number of employees and the diversity of their roles and locations will increase and the organisational structure must adapt in response. More formal control systems and systematic lines of communication often replace informal, entrepreneurial structures. Layers of hierarchy are often added to keep spans of control manageable. The outcome is taller pyramid structures, longer chains of command and sometimes problems with the speed of communication and decision-making. The alternative is to shift to a matrix structure that avoids this kind of hierarchy through the use of project teams.

CULTURE

The structure of organisation and its culture, the attitudes and values that represent how things are done within an organisation, are closely linked.

An informal culture in which individuals are given the freedom to work independently will need to be reflected in the type of structure adopted. Attempts to make this structure more hierarchical may then be resented and resisted.

Other cultures rest on the assumption that each worker does what they are told to do by their line manager – this will require a tall pyramid structure of narrow spans of control and many levels of hierarchy.

External influences

THE MARKET

A business that operates in a market where change is frequent, such as IT companies, will need a structure that promotes speed of communications, quick decision-making and allows flexibility. Empowering employees through wider spans of control in a flatter pyramid may help to achieve this; the flexible teams of matrix structures can provide similar benefits in this situation.

ECONOMIC FACTORS

The state of the economy and the impact it has on demand for an organisation's products may have a significant influence on structure. During times of recession, if product demand is falling, a business may need to cut costs – reducing the size of the workforce may be one way of doing so. These workforce changes will inevitably impact on the organisational structure. One option is 'delayering', removing levels of hierarchy to produce a flatter structure (see later for more detail).

TECHNOLOGY

Developments in technology, especially Information and Communications Technology (ICT), have had a massive impact on the way people are organised within a business. ICT has enabled remote working (away from the workplace) and mobile communications. These have made it possible for much wider spans of control to be used, with managers using ICT to stay in touch with workers.

No one type of structure can be held up as the ideal model for all organisations in all situations. Rather the type of structure used needs to be responsive and adaptable to achieve changing business objectives in a dynamic marketplace. Getting the balance of control versus independence, manageable spans of control versus effective chains of command, and clear lines of authority versus flexible teamwork, requires leadership skill and an understanding of the important implications of business structure.

Adapting organisational structures to improve competitiveness

Improving competitiveness may mean:

- cutting overheads to improve cost efficiency
- sharpening a brand image to become truly distinctive from competitors
- becoming more innovative
- improving product quality.

How organisational structures need to adapt to help achieve greater competitiveness will therefore depend upon what the specific challenge facing the business is. The key is that the structure must be adaptable; that neither an established leadership style nor employee resistance should prevent a flexible and responsive approach to the type of structure being used.

Three important methods of adapting organisational structures to improve competitiveness will be considered here:

- centralisation and decentralisation
- delayering
- flexible workforces.

Centralisation and decentralisation

Whatever type of structure is adopted, one of the main variables is the extent to which decision-making power is kept by senior managers or whether workers are empowered to make decisions for themselves. When most business decisions are made by senior management, this is known as **centralisation**, as authority is being kept at the centre (or top!) of the business.

As shown in the diagram below, in a traditional high-street retail chain this might mean that all decisions are made at head office. All stocking, staffing and operational decisions will be taken centrally. Local managers would merely implement head office instructions. McDonald's uses a very centralised strategy to control more than 25,000 restaurants.

Decentralisation involves delegating decision-making power down the hierarchy. An individual store, for instance, might be given the authority to decide what goods it stocks and whom it employs. Guidance and feedback pass between head office and stores, but not the direct instructions and control typified by centralisation (see Figure 18.2 below).

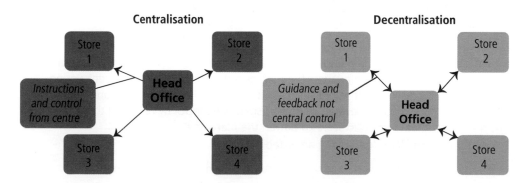

Figure 18.2 Centralisation versus decentralisation

Centralisation may, for some businesses, be seen as important to remaining competitive. With tight control over the organisation by senior management, it will be possible for products, processes, quality and image to be kept consistent and to a high standard.

Decisions can be made swiftly, without the need to involve a wide variety of staff in the decision-making process. A tighter focus on the corporate aims and objectives can also be maintained rather than allowing individual branches or staff to pursue their own objectives. Centralisation may also bring greater cost efficiency from the economies of scale that can be generated by centralised purchasing, marketing or distribution.

On the other hand, centralisation may for some businesses become an obstacle to remaining competitive. The communication of central decisions may become an issue – slow, inaccurate or resented by those who have no say in the decision-making process. Junior staff may become demotivated without the authority to make decisions for themselves. Their experience and expertise may be ignored, whilst their knowledge of local conditions and differences will be lost.

In these circumstances, a move towards decentralisation (passing the authority to make decisions down the hierarchy) may help to improve competitiveness in a number of ways. The opportunity to take decisions for themselves may motivate staff by meeting their esteem needs and providing the potential for self-actualisation. This positive impact on motivation may help to boost labour productivity or reduce labour turnover, both of which could boost cost efficiency. The quality of decisions, of communication and of product quality could all be improved by using more fully the experience and knowledge of staff who are closer to the customer and may understand their needs better. This can enable the business to adapt more swiftly to new competition or changes in consumer tastes. At the same time, the workload of senior managers can be reduced enabling them to focus on key strategic roles, rather than the detail of operational matters.

Delayering

Since the 1990s, the concept of **delayering** has become central to business thinking about how to make organisational structures more competitive. Delayering means the removal of layers of hierarchy – typically junior and middle management – in order to create a flatter pyramid structure.

The starting point for the use of delayering is the view that tall pyramid structures – with many levels of hierarchy, narrow spans of control and long chains of command – can make a business uncompetitive. The many levels of hierarchy are made up of numerous management and supervisory positions creating high salary overheads. The narrow spans of control can prevent more junior employees from taking responsibility or showing creativity, potentially reducing motivation and innovation. The long chains of command can produce a slow, unresponsive bureaucracy that is more focused on carrying out very specific job roles than on meeting the needs of the customer. The desire to delayer could be for any one or combination of these reasons.

Delayering in practice could involve one of several approaches. A layer of the management hierarchy could literally be removed by eliminating (or automating) the tasks they carry out and making the managers themselves redundant. Alternatively, delayering could simply involve reallocating responsibility and accountability for tasks to one manager instead of being spread across several. Widening spans of control by reducing the number of job types and pay grades will also serve to flatten the hierarchy.

The potential benefits of delayering are listed below:

- A reduction in salary overheads should result through redundancies and fewer middle management pay grades.
- The shorter chains of command in the new flatter structure improve communication by making it quicker and enabling more effective feedback from junior to senior staff.
- The organisation becomes more responsive to the needs of consumers because senior managers are now less distant from them in the business hierarchy.

Delayering at Marks and Spencer

Marks and Spencer reacted to their own need to become more competitive in the high-street retail market by creating a flatter organisational structure through delayering. This occurred both at Head Office in London where around 3,000 people are employed and throughout the retail store network of more than 60,000 employees.

M&S's explanation of the need for delayering was that it provided employees throughout the business with more responsibility and enabled them to make quick decisions when required. It also made employees more accountable than before, meaning they must be prepared to explain and justify the decisions that they take. M&S saw real benefits in the motivation of staff, the response to customer needs and in creating a task-focused culture.

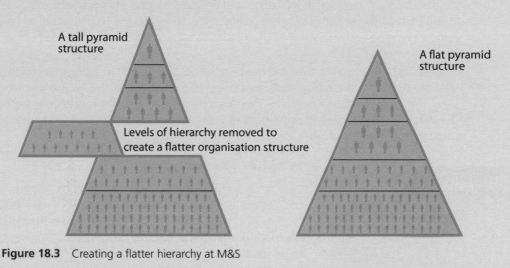

Figure 18.3 Creating a flatter hierarchy at M&S

- Junior employees feel more motivated because, with wider spans of control, they are given more independence and responsibility.
- The quality of decision-making may improve if the experience and expertise of shop-floor workers are now used more effectively to generate innovative new ideas.

The reality of implementing delayering is less clear cut. All sorts of issues are raised by the use of delayering, many of which can cause different types of problems for a business. These potential problems include:

- The impact of redundancy on the organisation. Not only can this be expensive in the short term, due to redundancy payments and reorganisation, there can be longer-term impacts on motivation and industrial relations. Those left working in the organisation after delayering may experience so-called 'survivor syndrome' – anxious and insecure about their own jobs, and resentful, even guilty, that their previous colleagues have been made redundant. The impact can be demotivation, loss of productivity, higher labour turnover and possible industrial conflict between employees and senior management.
- The increased workload placed on senior managers who now have wider spans of control and so a greater number of employees for whom they are accountable. Together with the uncertainty of reorganisation, this could cause serious disruption to the leadership and management of the business.

- Retraining for workers with new job roles may prove expensive and time-consuming.
- The loss of employees may impact negatively on the experience and expertise available to the business, weakening the quality of decision-making.

A number of practical issues in the implementation of delayering will determine how effective it is in producing a more competitive business structure.

First, the change needs to be well planned and thought through. The business needs to have defined goals for the delayering, based on an evaluation of why the existing structure is a source of problems. This should not be based on a general theory that tall pyramid structures are inefficient, but rather on a practical assessment of their current structure and what kind of structure is needed to deliver their corporate goals. Planning should include clear performance indicators to measure the success of the change and the use of feedback from trials or pilots of the new structure.

Second, a move to a flatter structure needs to be implemented if possible with the agreement and involvement of the workforce. Consulting workers about how they wish to see their own job roles, communication and decision-making changing in the future will help to win their commitment to delayering should this be necessary. This commitment may in turn help to minimise any demotivation from redundancy and disruption from the reorganisation that delayering brings.

Third, delayering on its own will not bring about the desired increase in competitiveness. Training, support and development for workers and managers with new job roles and new ways of workings will be essential if they are to be able to respond successfully to the change. The HR function will need to encourage and support a cultural shift that values accountability, empowerment and teamwork.

Skills watch!

AO4

AO4 requires that business theory such as delayering is, as in the text above, evaluated. Possible benefits must be balanced against potential problems and, in the pursuit of a top grade, the significance of each argument considered.

EVALUATING DELAYERING

Delayering is not a simple or universal solution to becoming more competitive. The evidence as to its impact is mixed. There has, in recent years, been a reaction against the rather simplistic approach of the 1990s that saw delayering as a guarantee of a leaner and more cost-efficient organisation. The problems of its implementation can often undermine the potential benefits delayering offers, and as with so many aspects of business, it is not just what is done but the way it is done that determines its success or failure. Delayering on its own will certainly not be sufficient. It needs to be part of a wider and more radical change to how people work and what their priorities are; it also needs to be part of a whole strategy that equips the workforce to be more flexible and competitive.

Flexible workforces

A flexible organisation means adapting quickly to changing markets, taking advantage of new technology, meeting changing customer needs and being able to change the scale of operations swiftly and cost-effectively. A flexible workforce is one that has the skills, the capacity and the willingness to adapt what they do and how they do it in order to remain competitive.

Flexible working can involve varying hours, patterns and ways of working as well as the location that work is done. Flexitime, for example, is when an employee can choose when their allocation of hours is worked – for example, coming in and leaving at different times from other workers.

Supermarket smiles

Supermarket giant Asda has launched a new flexible working scheme for its employees to improve their work–life balance. 'Asda Flex' contains six flexible working programmes to encourage all 165,000 staff (whether hourly paid or salaried, or working in stores or depots) to work flexible hours according to what suits them. The scheme, which enables people to take up to 3 years' unpaid career break, also includes an option to take time off to donate blood and up to 12 weeks paid leave for organ donation. Chris Stone, Asda colleague relations manager, said 'Creating a flexible approach to supporting colleagues with their individual needs underpins our core values. Working with our colleagues to ensure they can balance their work and home commitments makes for a very happy workforce'.

Source: www.personneltoday.com, 19 May 2008

Barriers to flexible workforces may be:

- **The impact of specialisation and the division of labour** – training and equipping workers to perform one task and carry it out repetitively; whilst this may produce productivity gains, it limits what each worker is able to do and so prevents them from switching to complete other tasks.
- **A full-time, permanent workforce organised into a rigid, hierarchical organisational structure** – where a business is tied by employment contracts to a sizeable and permanent workforce, it will have difficulties in adjusting the number of employees it wishes to employ swiftly and cheaply.
- **Trade unions and employee attitudes** – where flexibility is seen as meaning undermining job security or demanding that workers change their job roles, there may be considerable resistance to change from employees and their representatives.

Three different aspects of flexible workforces will be considered here:

- core and peripheral workers
- outsourcing
- homeworking.

CORE AND PERIPHERAL WORKERS

A flexible business needs to be able to adapt the total size of its workforce according to its need for labour at any one time. Growing product demand and a corporate objective of expanding sales and market share are likely to necessitate an expansion of the workforce. On the other hand, economic recession, increasing competition or a need to make cost efficiencies, may require the size of the workforce to be cut back.

If a business has a workforce solely made up of permanent, full-time workers, it will prove expensive and wasteful to expand and contract the workforce to meet current circumstances. Costs of recruiting, inducting and training new employees when expanding will be considerable; if the business then 'downsizes' when times are tough, not only will there be redundancy costs, but also the expenditure on training and developing those staff over time will have been wasted.

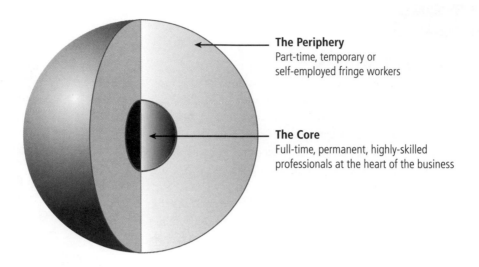

The Periphery
Part-time, temporary or
self-employed fringe workers

The Core
Full-time, permanent, highly-skilled
professionals at the heart of the business

Figure 18.4   The core and periphery model

In order to be flexible with the number of staff employed, many businesses have developed a so-called 'core and periphery' structure to the workforce. 'Core' workers are full-time and permanent employees performing the roles that are central to the business's core functions. The business is likely to invest heavily in these core workers – the pay and conditions that will retain them, the training and development that will equip them to succeed in their roles and the job security and opportunities needed to motivate them. The workers who make up the 'periphery', on the other hand, are on the edge of the organisation in many ways. They are likely to be part-time, temporary or self-employed workers who are brought into the organisation when there is a need for them, but then released or removed from the organisation when that need has gone (see Figure 18.4).

Professor Charles Handy's model of the flexible firm is that of a 'shamrock organisation': the three leaves of the shamrock being the core, a flexible peripheral workforce and a contractual fringe who actually lie outside the organisation but to which functions can be 'outsourced' as needed (see below).

Whilst the core and periphery model gives business the ability to be flexible in the numbers and types of workers employed, it brings with it a number of dangers. Workers who find themselves in the periphery could feel undervalued, demotivated and lacking in loyalty to the organisation. Productivity and quality could suffer, with typical personnel problems emerging – high labour turnover, high absence rates, and so on. The disruption and expense caused by frequent hiring and firing of workers will also threaten to undermine the intended efficiency gains of flexible working.

OUTSOURCING

Outsourcing is when a firm 'contracts out' a particular job or business function to another organisation. This organisation is paid to take on the responsibility of completing that task to the standards and deadlines set down by the client organisation. Examples of business functions that are often outsourced include IT, accountancy and HR functions such as payroll administration or recruitment. Within the marketing function, market research, product design and advertising are often contracted out to expert organisations. Manufacturing companies regularly outsource significant elements of their production process to other firms: car production, for example, is often more about the assembly of outsourced components than it is about production.

For example...

Nurse Needs

Use of agency nurses in the NHS has led to lower efficiency after changes to shift patterns, personnel directors and unions have claimed. Agency nurses are brought into hospitals on a temporary basis when the permanent workforce is unable to cope with the level of patient demand. Trusts are now reverting to traditional shift patterns and more family-friendly policies.

John Adsett, head of personnel at Basildon and Thurrock General Hospitals Trust, commented 'At one time we were all being preached at that you have to have a core workforce and a peripheral workforce. It was at a time when we were told that what was good for industry was good for the NHS. Part of the problem was that you had staff to whom the organisation was not particularly loyal because we only asked them in when there was a crisis. Consequently you do not get the loyalty in return.'

Many nurses had left permanent employment in hospitals to join agencies because they wanted the flexibility of working shifts that fitted their own circumstances. To get nurses back into hospitals as permanent employees, hospitals are having to realise they must offer good career development and the opportunities for flexible working that many employees want.

Source: www.personneltoday.com, 25 January 2000

Activity

In reference to the case, analyse the value of using a core/periphery model to achieve a flexible workforce.

Outsourcing brings a number of benefits in enabling a firm to be more flexible. Fewer core workers are needed, reducing wage overheads. Those that remain are undertaking the core tasks specific and unique to that organisation – its strategy, innovation and creativity, for example. Functions such as IT, finance and payroll are largely standardised activities – not unique to any one organisation. Outsourcing firms offer expertise and economies of scale, which enable functions to be carried out more cost-effectively than if each firm employed their own staff and processes directly.

Handing over responsibility for a business function to another organisation inevitably brings risks. The loss of control could lead to a reduction in quality with the dangers this brings for customer satisfaction. The ethics of the outsourcing company need to be in line with that of the client organisation if its image and corporate reputation are to be maintained. Given that the outsourcing provider needs to make a profit margin, it is possible that the hoped for cost savings may not be delivered. Finally, if a company switches from directly employing workers to perform a function to outsourcing, the reduction in staff numbers that results could bring with it conflict with the workforce and the threat of industrial action (see Chapter 19).

HOMEWORKING

Allowing a flexible working location enables employees to choose more convenient places to work from – such as at home ('homeworking') or on the move ('remote working'). Advances in ICT and the widespread availability of broadband have all made it possible for many jobs to be carried out away from the traditional office environment. Over 3.4 million workers, around 12% of the total UK workforce, now work mainly from home. Many others work at home on one day per week – with Friday proving the most popular! The highest proportion of homeworkers is in the South East (excluding London) at around 15% of the workforce.

The benefits to employee and to the business are potentially considerable. The employee can gain from:

Working from home can be beneficial to both employee and employer

- reduced travel and commuting time. British workers currently spend longer travelling – equivalent to 47 working days per year – than in any other European country;
- a better work–life balance as a result of increased productivity and more leisure time;
- reduced costs of having to travel and of being away from home – food, drink, parking, as well as petrol;
- a reduction in stress from being in a familiar and personal environment;
- being able to live in remote locations without being disadvantaged by distance from the business.

A business that encourages homeworking gains a range of benefits from this flexibility:

- Fewer workers needing a base to work from will help reduce the size and cost of the accommodation the business has to provide.
- The reduction in time wasted travelling will benefit the business in terms of increased employee productivity. It has been estimated that by 2025, road congestion will be costing UK businesses £22billion per year in wasted time – the scope for homeworking to cut business costs is therefore considerable; the benefits to the environment are also obvious.
- Benefits to employee work–life balance and stress levels will help to improve motivation, employee loyalty, retention, and potentially product quality and customer service. It could also enable the business to attract a wide range of quality applicants when it is recruiting.

Of course there is a wide range of job roles that simply aren't suitable for homeworking, ranging across primary sector, manufacturing and retail businesses. Even where it is suitable, there are a number of challenges to be overcome if the potential benefits discussed above are to be realised. Employers need to ensure the systems and culture are in place to monitor and support the effectiveness of homeworking. Employees still need to be effectively managed, appraised, developed and motivated. The logistics of having employees in different locations at different times will need careful planning to ensure that the scheduling and efficiency of the organisations do not suffer. By law the business must be consistent and fair in its dealings with those who work at home rather than in the office; health and safety issues also need to be addressed to ensure that the employee has the right environment to work in at home.

The employee also needs to meet a variety of challenges if homeworking is to work for them. The danger of working from home is that work and leisure can become blurred and work can end up taking over. This could have the opposite effect on stress levels to that intended! Having the right place to work at home with the right technologies to get the job done are essential prerequisites of homeworking.

There is evidence that many employees are not taking up opportunities for homeworking because they fear that being away from the workplace will lead to them being overlooked for promotion, or that managers will perceive them as slacking. Those who do work at home need to find ways of maintaining their visibility and staying in the information loop.

As with other types of flexible working, homeworking presents valuable opportunities for both business and its employees, but needs careful planning and monitoring to avoid causing a different set of problems.

Summary and exam guidance

Summary

- Being able to adapt the organisational structure is key to maintaining business competitiveness as it can affect all aspects of efficiency and effectiveness.

- The type of organisational structure a business chooses will need to enable corporate aims to be achieved and will be influenced by a range of other internal and external factors.

- The extent to which decision-making and authority is kept at the centre of the business is known as the degree of centralisation; there are many benefits, as well as pitfalls, to decentralising decisions lower down the hierarchy or to individual branches.

- Many businesses have used delayering – removing layers of middle management – to make their organisational structures flatter and more cost-efficient.

- Flexible workforces are those that can adapt in size, skills and attitudes to the changing demands of the marketplace; methods for achieving such flexibility include use of a core/periphery approach, outsourcing and homeworking.

Exam practice

Read the article below and then answer the questions that follow.

Article A

Flexible Working at BT

BT, the telecommunications and internet company, has undergone a massive change over the last decade. The workforce has reduced from a quarter of a million down to 98,000 employees and a key component of this change has been the introduction of flexible working – known as the BT Workstyle Project. Ten years ago it had just 400 teleworkers and it now has 63,000 people on some form of flexible working and over 12,000 employees working at home.

BT has harnessed communications technology to transform the way the company runs, moving from a more static, site-based workforce to an 'e-BT' of employees who work flexibly and/or from home. One of the main drivers of this change has been the reduction of office space. £350 million has been saved in the last 10 years from reduced accommodation costs. The company's flagship headquarters building in London has been

cont...

recreated with a modest 1,600 workstations to cater for 8,000-plus BT people who choose to visit the building every day to work when they are in the centre of London.

BT estimates that every home worker employed saves the company around £6,000 per annum on overheads. Travel costs have been reduced by £9.7 million per annum and 1,800 person years of travel time is saved each year. Another benefit has been the retention of key skills and the ability to attract talent, reducing employee turnover. Productivity has increased by 20% and the company reports an absenteeism rate 20% lower than the national average.

BT believed that flexible working required a fully inclusive programme of cultural change, asking its managers and employees to behave in very different ways. Clear leadership on the issue from the top down was vital. But the firm's group strategy director, Clive Ansell, has admitted that it was not easy to bring in these changes. 'There were teething problems. It was a training of managers issue,' he said. 'You have to go up several levels of management, and there is a trust issue: "If I can't see you, I don't know you are working".'

Source: http://www.employersforwork-lifebalance.org.uk/case_studies/bt.htm and http://www.btglobalservices.com/business/global/en/docs/case_studies/BT_Practitioner_Flexible_Working_Case_Study_EN.pdf

(a) Analyse the factors that are likely to have influenced BT's decision to introduce flexible working. (15 marks)

(b) To what extent will flexible working ensure business competitiveness? (25 marks)

Total: 40 marks

Breakdown of assessment objectives

AO1 – Knowledge and understanding – 6/40
AO2 – Apply knowledge and understanding – 10/40
AO3 – Analyse problems, issues and situations – 10/40
AO4 – Evaluate, distinguish between fact and opinion, assess and judge information from a variety of sources – 14/40

Suggested structure

For part (a) you will need to:

- Demonstrate a knowledge and understanding of the different aspects of flexible working.
- Explain the types of internal and external factors that can influence a business to adapt its working practices and structures.
- Apply your understanding to the case study and examine why flexible working was especially relevant to a company such as BT.

For part (b) you will need to:

- Show a sound understanding of the benefits that flexible working can bring to a business such as BT.
- Explain the link from these benefits to the achievement of increased competitiveness and business success, using examples from the case study.
- Consider some of the potential problems of flexible working and the reasons why the potential benefits are not always realised.
- Arrive at a reasoned, evaluative judgment as to whether flexible working can ensure business competitiveness.

Chapter 19 Effective employer/ employee relations

Key terms

ACAS The Advisory, Conciliation and Arbitration Service – an independent organisation, funded by government, to promote effective employer/employee relations and help resolve disputes.

Arbitration Resolving disputes through an independent arbitrator who, having heard opposing cases, reaches a decision on the solution that can be binding.

Channels of communication The main routes, formal or informal, by which information or ideas can be exchanged within an organisation.

Collective bargaining The process by which employers negotiate with representatives of employees on matters of pay and conditions of work.

Conciliation Helping to settle disputes by bringing two sides together to help them resolve the dispute themselves.

Methods of communication The specific ways and media by which information can be exchanged, such as using ICT, written or verbal methods.

Trade union An organisation established to represent the collective views and interests of workers.

Works council A permanent body through which employers will listen to, and take account of, the views of employee representatives on a range of issues.

Modern human resource management recognises the importance of good relations between employers and employees as central to business success. Effective employer/employee relations are likely to be characterised by:

- *cooperation* rather than conflict, with potential disputes being resolved;
- a culture of *teamwork* rather than a 'them and us' attitude;
- good *two-way communication* between employees and business owners/managers;
- high levels of *motivation* and *productivity*, enabling *quality* and *cost efficiency* to be achieved;
- employees showing *pride* in their work and *loyalty* to the organisation, with low levels of staff turnover and absence;
- *involvement* of staff at all levels in generating ideas, leading to greater *creativity* and *innovation*.

This chapter will examine three key aspects of achieving effective employer/employee relations: managing communications with employees, methods of employee representation, and methods of avoiding and resolving industrial disputes.

Managing communications with employees

Any good team relies on good communication. For the crew of a yacht, good communication can mean the difference between life and death; for a football team, it might well be the difference between winning and losing. The same is true in the business world.

Effective communication is essential to business success. Without it, a business would not be able to function effectively. For instance, if communication with suppliers is poor, raw materials may arrive at the wrong time or not at all; sales may suffer if communication with customers fails to inform and persuade them.

What is good communication?

Good communication means that information – be it an instruction, a fact or an opinion – is sent, received by the intended recipient and understood clearly by them. Unless a message is received and understood by the right person, at the right time, in the right way, the sender has failed to communicate effectively.

An effective communication process will involve:

- **Sender and receiver** – the sender of the message is the person wishing to communicate information or a point of view – for example, a manager speaking to her team about their duties for the day. The sender needs the skills to get across the message effectively and also needs to consider carefully who the intended audience or *receiver* is, ensuring that the message arrives correctly.
- **Message** – a clear message, communicated in a way that can be understood – for example, by avoiding technical 'jargon' which only some people will understand.
- **Channel and method of communication** – the sender choosing an appropriate channel and method of communication:

  - *Channels of communications* are the main routes by which information can be passed – formally, following lines of authority or across departments within a hierarchy, or informally, through workplace chat or rumour. Enormous problems can be caused by choosing the wrong channel – for example, using rumour as a way of informing staff of forthcoming redundancies.
  - *Methods of communication* are the specific ways and media by which information can be exchanged. These can include written, visual, verbal and electronic methods. Media can include e-mail, fax, SMS, video-conferencing, presentation software, company newsletters letters or posters.

- **Feedback** – the opportunity for the receiver of a message to confirm it has been understood and to offer their response is essential. Only if this happens can the sender be sure the communication has been effective.

How can good communication be achieved?

All sorts of barriers can get in the way of good communication, disrupting the process of a message being sent, received and understood. These barriers include:

- Problems with the message – a message can be distorted as it moves through a communications channel (just like in the game 'Chinese whispers'). A message may not have been expressed in terms that the receiver can understand, or the message may simply have been wrong in the first place. Both the sender and the receiver need the skill to complete the communications process effectively (a secretary may not understand the technical language in a letter and might send a message containing errors).
- Problems with the media – if the medium breaks down, or the recipient does not have the necessary equipment, a message may fail to be delivered.
- Noise – 'noise' might refer to the effects of actual noise (a shouted instruction on a factory floor being misunderstood), the distortion of a message in transit (a blurred fax) or information overload (so many e-mails are received that some are missed amid the 'noise' of all the others).

For example...

Accident Insurance Group

The Accident Insurance Group was a company specialising in the pursuit of compensation claims for victims of accidents either at work or elsewhere. Following a fall in the success rates for personal injury claims and the withdrawal of a key financial backer, the company ceased trading in 2003. Approximately 2500 staff lost their jobs. Before the closure, rumours about the future of the company began to circulate amongst staff when some received text messages saying there were problems paying salaries. There were then stories of the company actually notifying staff of their dismissal by text message. The Chairman of the company, Mark Langford, claimed the decision to tell workers they had been made redundant through text message was not his and blamed the administrators, Price Waterhouse Coopers.

Source: www.bized.co.uk

- Wrong receiver – a message may be sent to the wrong person, causing confusion, delay or dissatisfaction.
- Culture/language problems – a message may be altered in translation from one language to another, with slight differences having a significant effect on the overall meaning of the message. Cultural differences may mean that the ways things are said or done are interpreted differently by different people.

Achieving good communication is about removing these barriers. Dr Heinz Goldmann, a business communications guru, believes that poor communication is commonplace in business, and that managers may know the importance of communication, but are nevertheless notoriously bad at it.

Dr Goldmann's view is that the skill of communication is one that can be learned and that managers should invest time in training, practice and coaching to develop their ability to communicate. His advice to business managers on communicating well includes:

- Communication is a *dialogue*, not a monologue – it is not about talking and telling others what you want them to know, but about actively involving others in a conversation and listening carefully to their views.
- Good communication begins with *preparation* – knowing clearly what message needs to be communicated and understanding the attitudes and expectations of the audience.
- What matters is not what is said, but what people hear and *perceive* – this will be shaped by their mentality and existing attitudes. The communicator needs to shape the message and choose the medium and style of communication bearing this in mind.
- Managers must *empathise* with those they are communicating with – that is, be able to put themselves in the other person's shoes and understand the implications of what they are saying for those people. They must also find common ground to build a *shared bond* with employees.
- Communication depends upon a *strong projection* of the message, carefully selecting the best method of communication; face-to-face communication is 90% more effective than written messages.

For example...

Dream team

Christians Against Poverty: staff
and employer have shared values

The strong bond between employer and employee has helped to lift the Bradford-based debt-counselling charity, Christians Against Poverty (CAP), to the top spot in *The Sunday Times* 'Best Small Company to Work For' competition. The positive responses of its 123-strong workforce show that staff feel they share a strong set of shared values with their employer and that together they are making a difference to the world they live in. Matt Barlow, the charity's chief executive, who won the special award for leadership, heavily influences the culture of the organisation and is seen by staff as a leader who both listens to and cares about staff. Employees believe they have the dream job and are proud to work for the charity.

There wasn't a single aspect of employer–employee relations on which small companies performed worse than larger companies, indicating that employees in smaller companies are generally happier than their corporate colleagues.

Source: *The Sunday Times*, 2 March 2008

Activity

1   What are the likely (a) causes and (b) effects of effective employer/employee relations at Christians Against Poverty?

2   Why do you think employer/employee relations in smaller companies appear to be more positive than in larger companies?

Why is good communication so important to effective employer/employee relations?

Good communication is vital to helping the organisation achieve its corporate objectives successfully. For employees to do their jobs efficiently and to a high standard, they need to understand what their job is about and how they can best fulfil their own responsibilities. They need to understand what the business is seeking to achieve and how they can contribute to its success. By communicating well, roles and responsibilities are clarified and the actions of each part of the business can be more effectively coordinated.

Two-way communication enables employees to share their views and ideas with managers. This participation in the communication process helps employees to feel valued and involved in the decisions of the business. By meeting 'higher order' needs of esteem and self-actualisation, good two-way communication can motivate employees. The commitment and loyalty that should flow from this motivation can in turn bring a range of benefits to employer/employee relations.

Guru's views

'It is one thing identifying all the processes which make up a business's activities; quite another to inform, inspire or communicate with the people who have to bring the process to fruition.'

Dr Heinz Goldmann

Methods of employee representation

Employees are involved to a greater or lesser extent by managers and employers in every organisation, large or small. Whenever employees are more formally involved in the decision-making process, this is known as **employee representation** or **participation**. This representation can range from trade union involvement to small informal groups contributing ideas. There are legal obligations on organisations to consult and involve employees on certain issues; many organisations, however, go beyond what is required by law, believing that employee representation will bring real benefits to the business.

Employees' views may be represented to employers for a number of reasons:

- **Personal issues** In disciplinary or grievance matters, such as when an employee is accused of misconduct or in cases of workplace bullying/discrimination, the worker has a legal right to have their view heard and to be represented, if they wish, by a trade union or other representative.
- **Negotiating pay and conditions** *Collective bargaining* (see below) involves the organisation seeking agreement on matters of pay/conditions of work with a trade union or other employee representatives.
- **Formal consultation** Employers are required by law to consult on issues such as planned redundancies and health and safety. Consultation is more than just informing – it is to jointly discuss and consider an issue before making a decision. Larger organisations – with more than 250 employees – must show in their annual report what they have done to consult and involve employees in business decisions.
- **Partnership working** Managers may want to involve workers in discussion and decision-making about how to improve working processes and relationships. Workers may be able to contribute innovative ideas that will enable the business to improve its quality and efficiency. This may happen through continual, routine conversations but can also be formalised through quality circle (see below) or team meetings.

There are many different ways in which employees can be listened to or involved in decision-making. The scope and depth of the representation employees are given will vary enormously, from simply being informed at one end of the spectrum, to being fully empowered to take decisions at the other (see box below).

HOW MUCH DO YOU INVOLVE YOUR EMPLOYEES?

If you say:	It's called:
'This is what I've done.'	Briefing
'This is what I've done/want to do – what do you think?'	Communication
'What are the options and which one do you think we should take?'	Consultation
'Let's get together to discuss the problem and see if we can agree what we ought to do.'	Joint problem-solving
'Can we reach a deal on what to do?'	Negotiation
'This is the problem – you decide what to do.'	Empowerment

Training can help managers and employee representatives understand when and how to use each form of employee involvement.

Source: ACAS booklet 'Managing Conflict at Work', 2007

The different types of employee representation are discussed below.

WORKS COUNCILS

Works councils are the most common method of consulting employees on a wide range of issues within an organisation. These are permanent bodies through which employers will listen to, and take account of, the views of employees. Regular works council meetings will discuss issues such as:

- company vision and objectives
- business prospects, job security and staffing levels
- staff health, safety and welfare
- use of new technology or processes
- staff training and development
- equal opportunities.

Works councils do not usually discuss specific issues of pay and conditions, as the process of collective bargaining is carried out separately, very often through trade unions (see below).

European Union regulations now state that any medium or large-sized organisation operating in more than one EU country should operate a company-wide **European Works Council.** This guarantees the right of employees to be informed and consulted at a European level on issues affecting employees' jobs and conditions of work.

EMPLOYEE GROUPS

Employees and managers come together in a variety of groups to consider and solve business problems. Joint working groups will identify issues of quality, efficiency and production processes, pooling ideas as to how these can best be improved.

One type of employee group is the **quality circle**. This is a voluntary group of workers meeting regularly together to solve the immediate problems that affect their working processes – the flow of work, the layout of the production process, the systems for dealing with customer complaints, and so on. They emerged from the Japanese 'kaizen' approach to management, empowering workers to find ways to continuously improve quality and efficiency (see Chapter 15).

Another type of employee group is an **autonomous work group**, where responsibility is given to teams to organise production or service in the way they think best. Whilst this limits employee representation to decisions affecting only their immediate working environment, it provides more control and ownership than other forms of consultation. This ownership is likely to ensure the commitment of workers to the success of decisions.

TRADE UNIONS

Trade unions are organisations of workers whose aim is to represent the interests of their members. They do this by negotiating, bargaining and campaigning to maintain and improve the working conditions of the workers they represent. This can include a wide range of areas including:

- maintaining and increasing rates of pay
- improving the hours of work, breaks or length of holidays
- seeking to secure greater job security for its members
- improving facilities for workers or conditions of health and welfare
- agreeing contracts of employment or arrangements for redundancy.

Trade unions have been carrying out this job of representation for over 200 years. Membership of a trade union is voluntary and, although trade union membership has declined in recent decades, around 30% of all workers – over seven million in the UK – are currently trade union members. Over half of all workplaces have at least some members who belong to a trade union.

There are many different types of trade unions, many of them representing workers in a specific industry or trade – such as the National Union of Mineworkers (NUM) or the Musicians Union (MU). Others are general unions, made up of workers with various skills and employed across a range of industries. Examples include the UK's largest unions: UNITE (whose two million members cover every industrial, occupational and professional sector of the economy) and UNISON (representing workers across local government, health and other industries).

Trade unions represent workers' views and interests on both a collective and individual level.

Collective bargaining is the process of union representatives negotiating on behalf of all their members on issues of pay and conditions. The bargaining power of workers is increased by grouping together in this way; the threat of industrial action by all the union's members may be sufficient to persuade employers to offer improvements to pay rates that would not have been offered if they were negotiating with individuals or small groups. At the same time, collective bargaining can help employers to reach a deal more swiftly than negotiating separately with individuals and to ensure that all workers sign up to the deal once it is agreed.

UNITE and UNISON are two of the UK's largest unions

Evidence suggests that trade unions are successful in representing the voice of workers on issues such as working conditions, job security and redundancy more powerfully and persuasively than if workers were left to negotiate for themselves. In terms of pay, the hourly earnings of union members are nearly 20% higher than the average for non-union employees.

At an **individual** level, trade unions represent their members in a range of situations that an employee may face. These range from disciplinary actions against the employee to redundancy and discrimination. Trade union representatives can accompany employees to meetings, provide legal advice or information, or deal directly with management on an employee's behalf. In recent years, trade unions have extended the range of personal services and advice they offer to individual employees, to include areas such as training on health and safety, or financial help and discounts.

Trade unions today

The role and power of trade unions has changed dramatically over recent decades. The peak of trade union power and influence was the 1970s when big industrial unions were able to use industrial action, such as strikes, to force big employers, including the government, to agree with their demands for pay or job security. The Conservative governments of the 1980s and early 1990s passed a number of laws that significantly reduced the power of trade unions, in particular, limiting how and when strikes could be called. The decline of many traditional UK manufacturing industries at this time and the accompanying mass unemployment reduced the membership of trade unions from 13 million workers in 1979 to only seven million by 2002.

Over the last 10 years, however, trade unions have found a changed, but important role once again. Globalisation, flexible working and new technology have all challenged employees' job security and working conditions, providing an important role for trade union representation. Legislation passed by the Labour government since 1997 has reinforced trade unions' role of representation. The Employment Relations Act 1999, for instance, established a legal right to trade union recognition wherever 50% or more of the workforce belong to a union. Union recognition means that employers must accept a trade union's right to bargain on behalf of its members over pay and conditions. At the same time, a new approach to industrial relations has, in many industries, placed partnership working and collaboration rather than conflict at the heart of trade union dealings with employers. With an increased emphasis on supporting and advising individual employees, trade unions continue to provide a vital method of representation for employees.

Evaluating employee representation

Employee representation covers all sorts of ways in which employees' views and ideas are heard on a diverse range of issues. The depth of representation will vary from one business to another, ranging from simply being informed at one extreme, through formal consultation and bargaining, to empowered employees taking decisions for themselves at the other extreme.

The extent of representation will depend in part upon the culture and tradition of the business; whether workers and managers both wish to see a dialogue and joint decision-making. Leadership styles, the strength of trade union power and external factors, such as legislation, will also have an influence.

THE ADVANTAGES OF EMPLOYEE REPRESENTATION

Employee representation can bring a number of significant benefits to a business:

- By involving employees in decision-making they are likely to feel listened to, valued, even empowered. Many motivation theorists, including Mayo, Maslow and Herzberg, would all make a link between this involvement and a positive impact on motivation. This in turn can boost productivity, reduce labour turnover, increase cost efficiency and improve quality.
- Enabling employees to share their expertise and ideas on working processes may help to improve the decisions that are taken; the business may become more innovative, flexible and responsive to change.
- Employees who have been consulted and involved in making decisions are likely to feel a greater commitment to those decisions and to the business; this in turn should help the business to achieve its corporate objectives more successfully.
- Workers themselves are likely to become better informed about the wider business issues and see that long-term business success depends upon their commitment and cooperation.
- Effective representation and consultation with employees is likely to lead to compromise and trade-offs on both sides rather than conflict; in this way, damaging industrial disputes (see next page) can be avoided.

THE DISADVANTAGES OF EMPLOYEE REPRESENTATION

Employee representation is not, however, without its problems. Consulting workers can prove time-consuming, slowing up decision-making and preventing a business from adapting swiftly to new circumstances. For example, a fall in demand may require a swift cut in staffing levels in order to maintain cost efficiency, but a legal requirement to consult employees on planned redundancies makes this a slow and expensive process.

Equally, employees' interests will often be different from those of employers and so representation can provide obstacles to change. The introduction of new technology, for example, may increase productivity and cut costs, but if it threatens job security it is likely to be opposed by workers. For this reason, it is not always possible for conflict to be avoided and when employees have a powerful role in decision-making this could frustrate management in seeking to achieve business objectives.

Skills watch!

AO4

Employee representation is certainly a valuable element of effective Human Relations management but, as with so much in this area of business, it is not as simple as setting up methods and processes. Its success will rest on when, where, why and, crucially, *how* it is done. In Human Resources, successful management of people is often more important than management of systems. Managing people is often the most significant challenge businesses face.

Top answers will avoid over-simplification and will acknowledge the inevitable complexity of human issues and human decision-making.

Where a culture of partnership and cooperation is not established, neither employers nor employees may be satisfied with the processes of employee representation. Managers may feel that their authority to manage and make decisions is being undermined by workers (whose expertise and understanding they doubt). Employees may feel that managers are merely paying lip service to consultation and that their ideas are rarely listened to. They may respond to this by showing no desire to share their ideas or get involved in decision-making – becoming the classic 'Theory X' employee outlined by McGregor.

Methods of avoiding and resolving disputes

Industrial disputes occur when employers and employees find themselves in conflict. Such conflicts can arise from a variety of issues, as shown in the diagram below, whenever the two groups have opposing objectives.

Disputes can lead to industrial action by employers or employees, each side seeking to use their respective power to ensure their own objectives are achieved.

Industrial action by employers can involve taking sanctions against individuals or groups of workers, including tighter discipline and supervision, demotion or even dismissal. If these are used, careful consideration needs to be given to ensure they are fair and legal, as all these areas are regulated by employment law. Other actions can be taken against all workers in the

CONFLICT

Employees want:

- higher rates of pay
- better terms and conditions of employment, e.g. holidays
- improved facilities at work
- job security
- fair and equal treatment at work.

Employers want:

- increased productivity
- cost efficiency
- profit maximisation
- improved quality and customer service
- a flexible and responsive workforce
- use of technology to improve production.

business. These may be removal of overtime or bonus payments, or even closure and relocation to an alternative site.

Employees' industrial action is usually organised through representative groups, such as trade unions. Types of action include:

- **Strikes** – workers refuse to work and so seek to stop the business from operating.
- **Work to rule** – employees carry on working but only doing the minimum required of them by their contracts.
- **Go slow** – similar to working to rule, but working at a slower pace to reduce productivity and output.
- **Sit-ins** – occupying or refusing to leave a work premises, for example, when it is threatened with closure.

Industrial action causes problems for both sides in the dispute. The disruption to the business will lead to lost output, sales and profitability. A negative impact on customer service may result and with it a loss of reputation and customer loyalty. Workers will lose earnings if they refuse to work and ultimately they too will lose from the harm done to a business's prospects.

For these reasons, both employers and employees seek to avoid disputes or to resolve them swiftly when they occur. Most organisations and workforces will successfully avoid disputes most of the time, by addressing and solving areas of conflict as they occur.

Skills watch!

AO2

Chaos looms over council strike

Schools' gates could stay shut and rubbish remain in the street uncollected if council workers walk out in a planned two-day strike over pay. Unions say 600,000 staff across England, Wales and Northern Ireland are prepared to walk out after rejecting a 2.45% wage offer. Unison and Unite are asking for a rise of 6%, or 50p an hour. But council bosses said the strikes were an exercise in futility as the 2.45% pay deal was 'their last and final offer' and industrial action would not change that. Jan Parkinson, managing director of the local government employers, said, 'The settlement on the table is affordable for the council taxpayer. If it is any higher, then councils will be forced to make the unpalatable choice between cutting frontline services and laying off staff. Neither unions nor employers want to see this happen.'

Source: http://news.bbc.co.uk/1/hi/uk/7507304.stm, 15 July 2008

Activity

Review a recent news item, identifying the key terms it includes and the links to business theory in this and other chapters.

The study of business should not be restricted just to the classroom. Top grades come from being able to apply textbook theory to real world issues.

The methods by which this is achieved include all those already discussed in this chapter:

- **Communication** – effective two-way communication is the most powerful way of avoiding disputes. Where employers and employees are each able to communicate clearly their views, where each is listening to the other and considering their needs (empathising) and where each is able to give feedback to what they have heard, there is a strong likelihood that potential conflicts can be dealt with swiftly.
- **Employee representation** – where employees are being routinely consulted and involved in making decisions it is more likely that conflict can be avoided. The sense of ownership employees have, together with a wider understanding of the business's aims and circumstances, should lead to a commitment to help the business succeed. Similarly employers will value the role of workers in sharing ideas and improving the business. All of these gains depend upon there being a culture of partnership, not just the existence of a joint committee which could potentially just become a forum for confrontation.
- **Collective bargaining** – an organised and agreed set of procedures for representatives of both employers and employees to negotiate pay and conditions is extremely valuable in reaching agreement. Where these collective bargaining agreements exist, employers cannot ignore the view of the workforce; at the same time, once a deal is agreed, workers agree to be bound by the decisions of their representatives. The outcome should be a much more efficient system of sorting out pay issues – the single biggest cause of disputes.

Where these processes do not succeed in avoiding disputes, **negotiation** between the two sides is needed to resolve the particular issue of conflict. Depending on the type of dispute and the nature and circumstances of the organisation, this negotiation could be at an *individual* level, a *local* level (specific to just one or two locations), *regional*, *national* or even *international* level. Where negotiation fails, industrial action by employees or employers may result, as discussed earlier in the chapter. Further negotiation may lead to a resolution or the employer may end up imposing a solution that the workforce is unhappy with.

THE ADVISORY, CONCILIATION AND ARBITRATION SERVICE (ACAS)

Where the employer and the workforce are unable to resolve a conflict on their own, the help of an independent organisation can sometimes enable a solution to be found. The Advisory, Conciliation and Arbitration Service, known as Acas, is an independent organisation funded by the government. The job of Acas is to promote effective employer–employee relations (see box opposite) and one aspect of their work is dispute resolution.

The emphasis of Acas' work is that prevention is better than cure. This means that Acas works with employers and employees to establish procedures and the skills to prevent disputes happening in the first place. This is done through advice, guidance and training.

Acas also offers a variety of services to help resolve disputes if they do occur.

Individual conciliation

This is a free and voluntary service offered to individual employees who are making a claim to an employment tribunal that their employer has treated them unfairly (such as discrimination). Acas will talk to both the employee and the employer to seek a compromise solution, acting entirely independently and impartially. It cannot force a solution on either side; if the conciliation does not work, the case will go on to be heard by an employment tribunal. Only one in four of cases dealt with by Acas have to go on to a tribunal.

Collective conciliation ('mediation')

Where employers and groups of employees (such as trade unions) are in dispute, Acas can seek to bring them together to resolve the issues using a process of collective conciliation, often now known as mediation. A neutral Acas mediator will talk to both sides separately and later on together, suggesting possible approaches or ways of reaching a solution but at no stage telling either side what they should do. No solution will be imposed by Acas and any agreements reached are not legally binding. The value of such mediation is that it can help to remove the barriers that have stopped the two sides listening to each other or seeking compromise.

Arbitration

The limitation conciliation is that, in the end, the two sides still need to reach their own solution and stick to it. Sometimes employers and trade unions can be so far apart in the negotiating positions that compromise is almost impossible. If both sides agree, they can ask for Acas to solve the dispute by arbitration. This involves an independent person from Acas – an arbitrator – examining the opposing points of view and reaching their own judgement as to the solution – for example, on what level of pay rise should be awarded. If both sides agree in advance, this recommendation can be made legally binding so that everyone has to go along with the Acas solution.

ACAS

Our vision

- Acas's vision is to be Britain's champion for successful workplaces and a motivated workforce.

Our aim

- To improve organisations and working life through better employment relations. Our belief is that prevention is better than cure.

What we do

- We promote best practice in the workplace through easily accessible advice and services.
- Our experienced national and regional advisers help organisations improve their employment practice, as well as solve problems when things go wrong.
- We offer an independent and trusted service for dealing with disputes (collective conciliation) between groups of workers and their employers (collective disputes).
- We also deal with disputes where individuals claim their employer has denied them a legal right.
- We also provide authoritative advice and guidance on employment and work policies to the Government and social partners (trade unions and employers).

Fact file

- First established by Government in 1896.
- 1974/75 – made independent of Government and renamed as Acas.
- Advice and guidance given to 800,000 callers a year via telephone helpline.
- Much of Acas' conciliation work is now focused on individual complaints to employment tribunals. These complaints are passed to Acas and at present 75% are settled or withdrawn without ever reaching a tribunal hearing.
- An independent study has revealed that Acas saves the UK economy £800 million a year.

Source: www.acas.gov.uk

Summary and exam guidance

Summary

- Effective employer/employee relations are essential to business success. They can have a direct impact on productivity, cost efficiency, quality, customer service and so ultimately, on profitability.

- Central to these effective relations is good two-way communication – both employers and employees able to get across their ideas and views in a way that is received and understood.

- Poor communication can lead to misunderstanding of roles and responsibilities, a lack of direction and of personal motivation.

- Opportunities for employee representation can range from basic communication to empowered decision-making; typical methods of representation include works councils, various employee groups and trade unions.

- Conflicts can arise between employers and employees because they have some conflicting aims, as well as some that are shared; processes of collective bargaining can help to resolve such conflict before they become disputes.

- Where disputes do occur, the independent organisation Acas can provide services of conciliation or arbitration to help reach a resolution.

Exam practice

Read the article below and then answer the questions that follow.

Article A

Building partnership at Johnson Matthey

Johnson Matthey plc is a speciality chemicals company with seventeen sites around the UK, including one in Clitheroe, Lancashire employing around 200 full-time staff. Around 80% of this workforce belongs to a trade union.

A joint consultative committee (a type of Works Council) had long been used at the Clitheroe site as a way for employees' views to be represented. However, the monthly meetings of the committee tended to be adversarial and focused on trivial issues. Communication was poor and an ethos of confrontation rather than cooperation was the norm. There was also no framework in place for collective bargaining, meaning that neither employers nor employees at the site had any experience of negotiating pay and conditions.

Both management and unions decided to approach Acas to help them develop a new relationship based on effective partnership. Acas provided conferences, training and visits to other organisations for both management and union representatives. These focused on building trust amongst the whole workforce and understanding the benefits of joint working. Wider initiatives within the company occurred at the same time – changes in recruitment and selection procedures, new

cont...

shift patterns and manufacturing improvement teams. Greater use of informal communication enabled employees to discuss ideas more regularly and easily.

A gradual and ongoing process of change in the relations between management and unions became apparent. Trust began to be rebuilt and confrontation gave way to communication. Issues such as changes to the employees' grading system continued to cause conflict but these were more easily addressed within a spirit of partnership. Union representatives felt they were listened to and their opinions more valued; in turn they understood better how the business operated. The impact of the change process was clear – substantially improved onsite efficiency, higher output and profitability. Both management and unions recognised the crucial role that Acas' neutrality, skills and experience had contributed to this success.

Source: www.acas.gov.uk

(a) Analyse the benefits to a business of using works councils. (15 marks)

(b) To what extent is good communication sufficient to prevent industrial disputes? (25 marks)

Total: 40 marks

Breakdown of assessment objectives

AO1 – Knowledge and understanding – 6/40
AO2 – Apply knowledge and understanding – 10/40
AO3 – Analyse problems, issues and situations – 10/40
AO4 – Evaluate, distinguish between fact and opinion, assess and judge information from a variety of sources – 14/40

Suggested structure

For part (a) you will need to:

* Demonstrate a knowledge and understanding of works councils as a method of employee representation.
* Explain what benefits can in theory arise from consulting and involving employees in this way and why – make links to theories, such as motivation, and concepts, such as productivity and labour turnover.
* Apply your understanding to the case study and question whether these benefits were realised and if not, why not – what else was needed?

For part (b) you will need to:

* Show a sound understanding of what good communication means and explain what is needed for it to be achieved.
* Explain the link between good communication and the prevention of industrial disputes.
* Link to the case study and provide examples of how communication was central to the problems and the subsequent improvement.
* Consider why good communication may not be enough to prevent industrial disputes – what else might be needed? Why? Can disputes ever be wholly prevented? Arrive at a reasoned, evaluative judgment on this issue.

Chapter 20 Understanding mission, aims and objectives

Chapter 1 of this book covered aims, objectives and corporate strategies. You are advised to revisit Chapter 1 to refresh your memory about the key differences between these terms. This section will look at how corporate strategies are linked to a business's aims and objectives, how stakeholders have different interests in a business, and how these (often) conflicting interests can affect both strategy and decision-making in a business.

Mission statements

Many businesses have adopted mission statements in recent years. Whether they are large or small businesses, or profit or non-profit organisations, a mission statement is often a prominent part of the communication between the organisation and those who deal with the business. It is important to distinguish between a mission statement and a vision statement, although the distinction is not often as clear in the mission statements of businesses.

A **mission statement** helps to clarify the question 'Why does the company exist and what is the purpose of its existence?' The statement will try to articulate in just a few words or a short sentence or two the purpose of the company to its stakeholders. The mission is a statement of the current position of the organisation: where it is now. Whilst mission statements do vary in length and content, the main features that you would expect to see clarified are the organisation's capabilities – what it can do, its responsibilities to its customers, what it does, its philosophy, its activities and how the business is made up. In many respects the mission statement helps stakeholders to see the bigger picture. For example, SonyBMG do not simply produce music CDs; they provide entertainment, an opportunity to allow people to feel emotion, excitement, creativity, be moved by the music, and be lost in another world when they are listening to their favourite band/artist. Somehow the mission statement has to communicate that bigger picture.

A **vision statement** articulates where the organisation would like to be in the future.

A mission statement serves to make clear to all the people who have an interest in the business – its stakeholders – the purpose of the business. For employees, for example, it helps to provide a focus and a purpose for their work, and for customers it helps them to understand what they can expect from the organisation. Whatever the statement, for profit-making organisations, the interests of the shareholders/owners is generally seen as being paramount, but the complexity comes in the way in which that interest is articulated. It could be, for example, that high levels of corporate social responsibility is very much in the long-term interests of the shareholders even if it may not appear so in the short term.

The following are some examples of mission statements of well-known business organisations.

STARBUCKS

To Starbucks, 'The Starbucks' mission statement is more than words on a piece of paper – it's the philosophy that guides how we do business every day'.

Its mission statement is:

Establish Starbucks as the premier purveyor of the finest coffee in the world while maintaining our uncompromising principles while we grow.

The company follows up this statement with the following:

The following six guiding principles will help us measure the appropriateness of our decisions:

- *Provide a great work environment and treat each other with respect and dignity.*
- *Embrace diversity as an essential component in the way we do business.*
- *Apply the highest standards of excellence to the purchasing, roasting and fresh delivery of our coffee.*
- *Develop enthusiastically satisfied customers all of the time.*
- *Contribute positively to our communities and our environment.*
- *Recognise that profitability is essential to our future success.*

Source: http://www.starbucks.co.uk

THE BBC

Our mission
To enrich people's lives with programmes and services that inform, educate and entertain.

Our vision
To be the most creative organisation in the world.

Source: http://www.bbc.co.uk/info/purpose/

THE DELL CORPORATION

The Dell Corporation's mission statement is:

The products that we produce shall meet all customer requirements.
Our response time to our customers' inquiries and
requirements shall meet our customers' needs.
We shall maintain sufficient profits.

Dell also has a vision statement – compare the
difference between the vision statements below and
its mission statement:

Customer satisfaction
We are an established company
striving to satisfy customers by
meeting their demands of quality,
responsiveness, and competitive
pricing. Each customer is #1.

Team satisfaction
Management and employees are committed to cooperating as a team for the purpose of
profitability and gratification of a job well done.

Community satisfaction
We will provide jobs in a clean, safe, environmentally sound atmosphere and be an active
participant in community affairs.

Source: http://www.dellmfg.com/mission.htm

INTEL

- **Our mission**
  Delight our customers, employees, and shareholders by
  relentlessly delivering the platform and technology
  advancements that become essential to the way we work
  and live.

- **Our values**
  Customer orientation
  Results orientation
  Risk taking
  Great place to work
  Quality
  Discipline

- **Our objectives**
  Extend our silicon technology and manufacturing leadership
  Deliver unrivalled microprocessors and platforms
  Grow profitability worldwide
  Excel in customer orientation

Source: http://www.intel.com/

These four are typical examples of mission statements where the organisation states its purpose but also provides some amplification to clarify its values and in some cases makes links with its vision statement.

When thinking about writing a mission statement, a number of key principles need to be considered.

- What are the mission statements of your competitors and how can your mission appear distinctive in comparison?
- Make sure that the statement is reflective of what the business actually is and not what you would like it to be – stakeholders will quickly see through a lie!
- The statement should be flexible enough to cater for changes in the market and the business over time – it is not advisable to keep changing the mission on a frequent basis.
- Do not make the statement too long.
- Make sure that the statement has some substance rather than a series of business catchphrases or waffly sentiment.
- Many organisations will seek to involve their employees in the development of their mission statements to create a sense of ownership and involvement.

Having a mission statement is one thing; living up to it is quite another. Laying bare the beliefs and values of the business, and making claims about what you think the organisation does and represents, can be seen as a constraint on the organisation or it can be seen as something that the organisation is striving to live up to. If the mission statement is effective then it can help to shape and clarify how the business relates to its stakeholders. This can include the way the business views and treats its employees, its suppliers, the attitude and beliefs of the leadership of the organisation, the role of people within the organisation – whether they have open-plan offices, whether the senior managers/leaders have their own offices or work amongst their colleagues, and how it intends to respond to change.

Skills watch!

AO2 / AO3

To work with the best people and create the best products and services, for the best football club in the world.

This statement appears in the entrance to the offices of Manchester United

Merchandising Limited outside the main Old Trafford ground (see also page 152). Discuss the value of this mission statement to the business's stakeholders.

The mission statement can be used to help a business establish its aims and objectives. In theory these should all be aligned to reflect the mission and vision of the organisation. In addition, the mission statement can help to shape the culture of an organisation, one of the most difficult things to change and to maintain. This means getting the message through to every employee, so that when they deal with customers and suppliers and any other external stakeholder of the organisation, that mission is projected. It is not always possible to do this or to monitor it. Take the Dell mission statement, for example. It states that 'Each customer is #1'. The question is: does every experience customers have with Dell reflect this; does each customer feel like they are really number 1?

Corporate aims and objectives

Corporate aims and objectives were dealt with in detail in Chapter 1. However, it is useful to revise the meaning and key differences between these two terms.

Aims refer to the long-term goals of an organisation – where it wants to be in the future. Objectives state how the business intends to achieve its long-term aims.

Corporate strategies

As explained in Chapter 1, corporate strategy refers to the overall approach to be taken by the business in order to achieve its corporate aims and objectives. Corporate strategies will identify how the business will achieve or sustain an advantage over its rivals in a way that enables its objectives to be achieved. They will be developed by senior management and will plan ahead for a three- to five-year timescale.

The main corporate strategies are discussed below.

Maximising the profitability of the business

Profit is the driving force behind many businesses. Ultimately if a business does not make a profit it will fail. However, the amount of profit a business makes can and does vary considerably. It used to be assumed that the main aim of a business was to 'maximise profits' which implies squeezing every last drop of profit out of the business. More subtle definitions of profit-maximising now exist and reflect a different perspective on the approach to the 'bottom line'.

Profitability is the ability of an organisation to generate net income on a consistent basis over a period of time. For many larger businesses, often operating in mature markets, generating this new income year after year is challenging because the market is relatively static. For other businesses in growing markets, they may be wary of the drive to maximise profits simply because this might alert potential new entrants and competitors into the industry which may not be something that the business wishes to advertise! In such circumstances, the idea of 'profit satisficing' may be appropriate. This means that a satisfactory level of profit is identified but that it does not represent the maximum amount of profit that a business might seek to generate.

A business's profitability is an important measure of its success, particularly to potential investors. With this in mind, investors will take note of the price earnings ratio, a key measure of profitability. The price earnings ratio is given by the market price of the share divided by the earnings per share (EPS) where the EPS is the net income of a business divided by the number of shares in the business.

Skills watch!

A01 / A02

Is making a profit and profitability the same thing? Explain with reference to a business with which you are familiar.

Growing the size of the business

For many businesses, expansion through either internal or external growth is a key aim. Internal growth is generated through the use of profits to expand the business. External growth occurs through acquisition – merger or takeover. The latter is often a quicker form of growth but carries with it a greater degree of risk especially if the takeover is of a business in a new market. Chapter 9 covers the risks associated with various growth strategies in relation to Ansoff's Matrix.

The reasons for the growth of the business may be to try to capture market share or to increase sales in a market. In some cases, these can become an aim in themselves and acquisition would be one way in which the business would be able to achieve these aims.

Maximising shareholder value

The amount of profit and the potential for profits in the future made by larger businesses is a significant factor in determining the demand for shares for a business. Public limited companies exist to serve the interests of their owners – the shareholders. These organisations have a responsibility therefore to ensure that the returns that shareholders get from their investment are maximised. These returns are a mix of the dividends that a shareholder receives (the share of the profits returned to shareholders) and the share price of the business. A rising share price indicates that the business is valued higher because it is a sign that expectations of the future success of the business are present in the market.

If share prices rise it gives shareholders the opportunity of selling shares and, assuming they bought the shares for a lower price than they sold, of realising some return on their investment.

However, shareholders are the last to be paid out of the income that a business generates. Creditors have first call. What is left after all the creditors have been paid from income is referred to as 'free cash flow'. Shareholder value can be defined, therefore, as the value of a business after the future claims on the business have been subtracted. These future claims are essentially the debts of the business. For many shareholders, the income streams that they expect to gain from their ownership is likely to be over a period of time, so net present values (NPV) are used to discount these future income streams. The debts are then subtracted to give a more accurate interpretation of shareholder value. NPV is a means of recognising that income received at some point in the future is not worth as much to the receiver as it is today.

Maximising the benefits of other stakeholders

There are also a number of other stakeholders in a business whose needs and interests must be considered. In recent years the view that a business exists simply to satisfy the needs of its stakeholders is being questioned. The complex web of responsibilities that a business has to employees, customers, the local community, and so on, plays an increasingly important part of the corporate view of its operations. It is recognised that there will be times when shareholder interests and shareholder value will be improved if greater consideration is given to the needs of these other stakeholders. There may well be short-term costs involved in so doing, but business leaders are increasingly presenting compelling arguments to shareholders about the need to balance the needs of different stakeholders for the greater good of the business and the improvement in shareholder value over the medium and long term. Finding ways to manage the conflicting stakeholder interests is covered in more detail later in this chapter.

There are other corporate strategies that businesses might have. These include:

- Developing competitive advantage – something which gives the organisation some advantage over its rivals and which makes its offering both distinctive and defensible.
- Cost advantage – a strategy to seek out and secure a cost advantage of some kind: lower average costs, lower labour costs, and so on.
- Price leadership – gaining a position in the market which allows the business to exercise some dominance over the industry. This puts the business in a position to be able to take the lead in pricing decisions which others follow. This can put the business in a powerful position in managing its market and its revenues.
- Global strategies – seeking to expand global operations.
- Reengineering – thinking outside the box – looking at new ways of doing things to leverage the organisation's performance. This might often be focused on utilising the business's existing strengths (its core competencies) and finding ways to use these in different, possibly, unrelated ways to secure new markets or develop new products.

The above tend to be external strategies but there may be internal strategies that a business will also have. External strategies are those that tend to affect the wider competitive environment in which the business operates, whereas internal strategies refer to the ways in which businesses change their own structure and way of operating to achieve their aims.

Internal strategies include:

- Downsizing – selling off unwanted parts of the business – similar to contraction.
- Delayering – flattening the management structure with the intention of removing bureaucracy and speeding up decision-making.
- Restructuring – complete rethink of the way the business is organised. This can be very disruptive but also necessary in response to changing competitive pressures, changing markets and technology, and possible changes in ownership.

The relationship between corporate strategy, aims, objectives and stakeholders

The aims and objectives of a business are captured in its corporate strategies. These strategies to a large extent determine the setting of aims and objectives in the broader corporate strategy. In setting these aims and objectives, decisions will have to be taken to implement the actions that will allow the business to achieve its aims. In taking these decisions, the business will have to understand that these decisions will impinge on those who interact with the business. Not every stakeholder will be enthusiastic for a decision and as a result conflicts arise because of the different stakeholder perspectives that exist.

Differing stakeholder perspectives

In the course of its operations, an organisation will interact with a large amount of people. These people will be affected by the actions of the business in a huge variety of ways. Given this interaction, it has been increasingly realised by many businesses that the organisation has a responsibility to these people and groups. The theory to explain this interaction and responsibility is called 'the stakeholder model'.

Stakeholders are groups of people or organisations who have an interest in a business. This interest may be direct in that they are employed by the business as managers or employees, or it may be that individuals or groups interact with the business in some other

Figure 20.1   A stakeholder model

way. For example, business operations impact on the communities in which they are located and in many cases far beyond these immediate communities.

Stakeholders can be seen as being either **external** or **internal** to the organisation.

Owners, shareholders, managers and staff or employees are considered to be internal stakeholders, whilst customers, suppliers, intermediaries (such as retailers, wholesalers and agents), community and government (in its widest sense) are external stakeholders. Internal stakeholders are those who are 'members' of the business organisation. External stakeholders are not part of the business.

Some business theorists include competitors as stakeholders in a business whilst others do not. A business does interact with its competitors in that it seeks to access information from competitors to enable it to develop competitive advantage; some businesses will look to try and discredit competitors in various (often very subtle) ways and may even collude with competitors. Each of these might have wider effects on the other stakeholders in the business.

The responsibility of an organisation to its stakeholders lies in the relationship between the individual or group with the organisation. Employees, for example, are employed to add value to the business, but in return they expect a fair level of reward for the work they do and to be able to work in conditions that provide a level of safety and welfare. In addition they might expect to benefit from certain rights that they have under law which the business is obliged to provide them.

The relationships between the organisation and its stakeholders

The main relationships between the organisation and its stakeholders are listed below.

OWNERS

The type and number of owners and the roles they carry out differ according to the size of the firm. In small businesses there may be only one owner (sole trader) or perhaps a small number of partners (partnership). In large firms there are often thousands of shareholders, who each own a small part of the business. Some of these shareholders may be individuals who own shares in a business. During the 1980s, many of the large natural monopolies that were nationalised (state-owned) had their ownership transferred to the private sector (referred to as privatisation). Organisations such as British Gas and British Telecom (BT) were obliged to offer their employees the opportunity to buy shares and the privatisation process created millions of small shareholders. However, the dominant shareholders in large corporations tend to be institutional investors who make a living out of buying and selling shares. These institutions include insurance companies, pension funds, banks and other leading financial institutions. Institutional shareholders can wield significant power in the direction and actions of a business.

MANAGERS

Managers organise, make decisions, plan, control and are accountable to the owner(s). Managers can be present at all levels of a business, and in many cases businesses who realise that management is needed at all levels (not just in the boardroom) may see major benefits from the empowerment that these people are given.

EMPLOYEES OR STAFF

A business needs staff or employees to carry out its activities. Employees agree to work a certain number of hours in return for a wage or salary. Pay levels vary with skills, qualifications, age, location, types of work and industry, and other factors. In addition to pay, employees expect a range of other benefits that may be seen as being linked with motivation, but which might also be expected through legislation. Such legislation might cover redundancy, unfair dismissal, maternity and paternity rights, access for the disabled, and so on.

CUSTOMERS

Customers buy the goods or services produced by firms. They may be individuals or other businesses (B2C and B2B). Firms must understand and meet the needs of their customers otherwise they will fail to make a profit or, indeed, survive in the long term. In response, customers expect to receive goods that meet legal requirements, be expected to be treated under the basic requirements of the law and in many cases far beyond the basic requirements of legislation. Customers expect honesty, fair prices, quality, and increasingly an ethical and socially-responsible approach by the business to its activities.

SUPPLIERS

Firms get the resources they need to produce goods and services from suppliers. Businesses should have effective relationships with their suppliers in order to get quality resources at reasonable prices. This is a two-way process, as suppliers depend on the firms they supply. In recent years, many more businesses have come to regard the relationships with their suppliers as increasingly important parts of the whole business operation. This can not only lead to an improvement in efficiency and a reduction in costs, but can also help the business in times of difficulty. For example, if a business was hit by a natural disaster or by some other external shock, including terrorism, the help of its suppliers to minimise disruption might be vital to get the business back up and running again and thus minimise the impact on customers.

COMMUNITY

Firms and the communities they exist in are also in a two-way relationship. The local community may often provide many of the firm's staff and customers, and in return the business often supplies goods and services vital to the local area as well as investing in other aspects of the community, including social opportunities, education and training, sponsorship, improvements in infrastructure, and so on. At times the community can feel aggrieved by some aspects of what a firm does: tensions can grow when a business might decide to move to another location, build plant in sensitive areas, dispose of waste, increase congestion and other forms of pollution including noise.

GOVERNMENT

Government economic policies affect firms' costs (through taxation and interest rates), whilst legislation regulates what business can and cannot do in areas such as the environment and occupational safety and health. Successful firms are good for governments as they create wealth and employment, and also contribute to tax revenues.

Resolving stakeholder conflict

The outline of the rights and responsibilities of stakeholder groups and the organisation above highlight where conflicts can arise as a result of an organisation's behaviour and its decision-making. It is now widely agreed that business operations have to consider the differing stakeholder perspectives that exist. The problem for the business is that resolving these conflicts is not easy and can present significant challenges to the business.

Corporate strategies, aims and objectives can seek to address these conflicts and establish protocols for the way in which they are dealt with and how stakeholder interests are addressed. The mission statement and the values outlined by the firm is one way in which a benchmark is established in relation to these differing perspectives. Having a mission statement and effective strategies does not mean that these conflicts are avoided, but they might provide the basis for dealing and coping with them.

STAKEHOLDER CONFLICTS

Below are some examples of where decision-making in an organisation can lead to stakeholder conflicts.

1 A business has decided to find a way of reducing its costs and boosting profits by moving its production facilities to China. The move would save £200 million over five years, but the closure of a plant in north-east England would result in the loss of 400 jobs, and impact on the local community as well as suppliers who rely on the business for their work.

2 A business has decided to increase the length of time that it takes to pay its bills by 30 days, thus improving its cash flow position. Suppliers are very upset at this, especially the small ones who rely on fast payment to maintain their cash flow position. The decision, however, helps cut costs and allows the firm to offer more competitive prices to its customers.

3 A business has an excellent reputation for its environmental policy but this means prices are generally 10% higher than its competitors.

4 A business operates in a competitive environment and is resisting attempts by trade unions to increase wages by 2% above the rate of inflation. Workers claim pay rises over the last five years have been below inflation and that their standard of living has been eroded. Meanwhile the company has boosted profits by 30% and directors have been reported to have received bonuses that boost their salaries by 60%.

5 Employees have expressed concern that health and safety measures at a business have been weakened in an attempt to cut costs. Managers are saying that workers are obstructing the introduction of new technology which would improve productivity and help improve the competitive position of the business. This is essential to maintain the current size of the workforce.

Each of the above are typical situations that face businesses every day. The decisions taken in each case have effects on one or more stakeholders and each stakeholder group may have different perspectives about the decision. The task for the business in each case is how to resolve the conflicts that arise and help the business to progress.

For example...

Primark and ethical responsibility

In June 2008, an investigation by the BBC found that suppliers contracted by the clothing retailer Primark had subcontracted work to children. The BBC informed Primark prior to the investigation being aired on its *Panorama* programme. Primark acted immediately to distance itself from the problem. It cancelled contracts with three suppliers in India and announced that it had launched an investigation into the report as well as setting up an independent body to audit its suppliers to ensure that its ethical standards were being maintained.

In this example, the differing stakeholder perspectives can clearly be seen. Customers value Primark because it provides good-quality clothing but at very low prices. This strategy has led to the growth of the business in recent years. It employs over 23,000 people and is one of the top five clothing retailers in the UK. The growth of the business has led to a growth in profits for its parent company, Associated British Foods (ABF). In 2006–2007, sales rose by 36% to £721 million and it opened 23 new stores in that period, bringing more jobs to local communities across the UK.

The story by the BBC is one of a number that have been published in recent years about the relationship that Primark has with its suppliers. Primark has vigorously defended its position and insists it maintains the highest ethical standards in its operations with its suppliers. The company released a statement in response to the BBC investigation which included the following comment:

> 'Primark's prices are low because we don't overcharge our customers. Most of our clothes are bought from the same factories as other fashion retailers and people producing them are paid exactly the same whatever the label and whatever the price in the shop. We are able to offer good value and good quality because of low mark-ups and big volumes. We use simple designs, our overhead costs are extremely low and we don't run expensive advertising campaigns.'*

This example serves to illustrate the difficult balancing act that companies have to maintain. Customers like Primark because it offers good quality at very reasonable prices; equally, customers may be concerned when they hear about possible exploitation of labour in the supply of goods to Primark. Local communities benefit from the growth of the business in that new stores are opened, jobs are created and income to the government is generated through tax revenues. The owners of Primark have to understand the differing perspectives of its stakeholders and balance that against the desire to generate profits. Short-term decision-making can lead to long-term problems that damage the profitability of the business and thus their interests. The problem is making sure that these different interests and perspectives are balanced and reflected in the strategies and objectives set by the business.

* Source of quote: www.ethicalprimark.co.uk

Summary and exam guidance

Summary

- Firms create mission statements to give stakeholders a clear understanding of the purpose and values of the business.

- This may also be accompanied by a vision statement which clarifies where the business aims to be in the future.

- These help to lay the foundations and tie in the strategic aims and objectives of a business.

- Aims are the long-term goals of a business and objectives are the means by which a business intends to achieve those aims.

- The main corporate strategies can be summed up as:
  - maximising profitability
  - pursuing growth
  - maximising shareholder value
  - maximising benefits to stakeholders.

- Other strategic aims might include internal restructuring which in turn may involve such tasks as downsizing and reengineering.

- Stakeholders represent individuals and groups who have an interest in the business and who interact with the business.

- Businesses have to recognise the responsibilities they have to different stakeholder groups and the different perspectives stakeholders have of the business's operations.

- Stakeholder conflicts arise in response to the decisions that a business makes in relation to the way it pursues its strategic aims and objectives. One of the key challenges facing businesses is to try and find ways to resolve these stakeholder conflicts.

Exam practice

Read the articles on the next page and then answer the questions that follow.

Article A

Cadbury and Salmonella

In June 2006, chocolate manufacturer Cadbury had to withdraw around a million bars of chocolate from sale after it was discovered that there were traces of salmonella found in some of the bars. Around 40 people were affected by the bug, three of whom had to be treated in hospital.

Cadbury apparently knew about the problem some time before but did not do anything about it. The hearing over nine counts of breaching food and hygiene regulations was held at Birmingham Crown Court. The problem arose after Cadbury changed its quality testing systems, in an effort to improve efficiency and cut costs. A leaking pipe had allowed salmonella to be introduced into the product at the company's Marlbrook plant in Herefordshire. This happened between January and March 2006 but Cadbury had allowed the contaminated products to be put out for sale.

The court found Cadbury guilty of serious negligence and imposed fines totaling £1 million on the company. Cadbury admitted that it was at fault and has offered its sincere apologies, saying that it regretted the incident. The judge in the case pointed out that the severity of the fine was a signal to other similar firms that the law exists to protect the public, and that companies such as Cadbury could not abrogate their responsibilities which the law places on them.

Source: Biz/ed In the News: http://www.bized.co.uk/cgi-bin/chron/chron.pl?id=2891

Article B

All gas and profits

Energy supplier British Gas caused anger and outrage after it announced profits for 2007 that were six times higher than those in 2006. The profit of £571 million for 2007 was up from £95 million in 2006. The announcement of its profit was made a short time after the company announced that retail prices for domestic gas users would rise by 15%. The rise in energy prices was of concern because of the number of people who would have to set aside more of their income to pay for gas and electricity supplies. The concept of 'fuel poverty', where consumers spend more than 10% of their income on gas and electricity, has been developed to highlight the problem. It has been estimated that more than 4.5 million UK households are in fuel poverty.

The company argued that they had to absorb rising wholesale costs and that they needed to pass on some of these costs to consumers. Profit, they argued, is important to enable them to satisfy their shareholders and also to be able to invest in new technology to secure energy supplies in the future. British Gas also pointed out that they reduced prices by around 20%% in the first half of 2007.

Source: Biz/ed In the News: http://www.bized.co.uk/cgi-bin/chron/chron.pl?id=3032

(a) Analyse the different stakeholder perspectives in the two articles. (16 marks)

(b) Make a justified recommendation on ways in which both British Gas and Cadbury could resolve the stakeholder conflicts that exist in the two stories. (34 marks)

Total: 50 marks

Breakdown of assessment objectives

AO1 – Knowledge and understanding – 8/50
AO2 – Apply knowledge and understanding – 12/50
AO3 – Analyse problems, issues and situations – 15/50
AO4 – Evaluate, distinguish between fact and opinion, assess and judge information from a variety of sources – 15/50

Suggested structure

For part (a) you will need to:

- Identify and explain the different stakeholders that are highlighted in the two articles.
- Explain what their different perspectives might be in relation to the main point of the story.
- Apply your knowledge of stakeholder theory to the specific context of the articles – not just any business, but these two specific businesses.
- Demonstrate an understanding of the main issues that arise for the business as a result of these different perspectives.

For part (b) you will need to:

- Identify the key stakeholder conflicts that exist in both stories.
- Consider the various ways in which both companies could react to the conflicts that arise as a result of the story.
- Offer an explanation of the costs and benefits to the business in relation to their possible corporate strategies.
- Make judgements on the costs and benefits to the businesses concerned of the ways in which they could resolve the conflicts.
- Arrive at a justified conclusion about the most appropriate resolution and why you think this would be appropriate.

This section of the book deals with the external environment with which businesses have to cope with. Most businesses can exercise a degree of control over their own internal affairs, such as their production facilities and their human resources, and can direct their operations accordingly. However, there are a wide range of things that happen outside businesses that they cannot control but which they have to cope with and adapt to. For example, the Bank of England may announce changes in interest rates, governments pass new laws and announce new policies, and over time the changing structure of the population will all have an effect on the way businesses operate. One of the key factors that any business has to consider is the extent to which it has adequate and accurate information about what is happening in the external environment and how this information can be used in decision-making to further the aims and strategic plans of the organisation.

Interest rates set by the Bank of England are one of the external factors that will affect how businesses operate

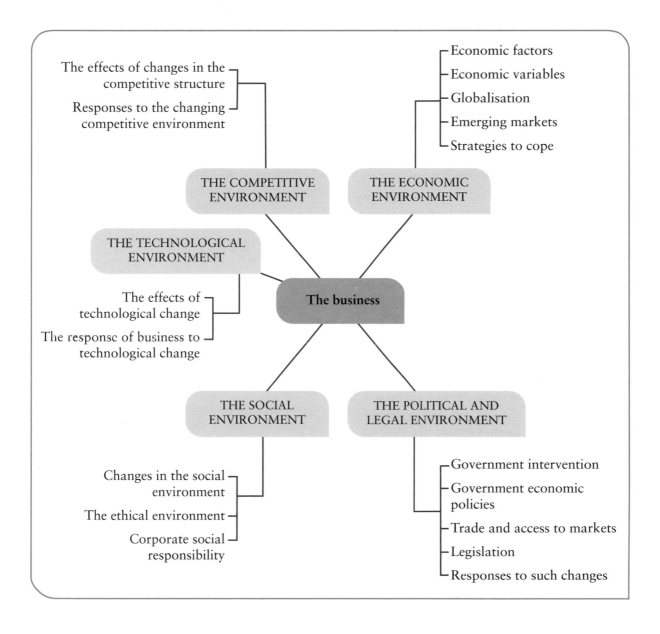

The effects of changes in the competitive structure

Responses to the changing competitive environment

THE COMPETITIVE ENVIRONMENT

Economic factors

Economic variables

Globalisation

Emerging markets

Strategies to cope

THE ECONOMIC ENVIRONMENT

THE TECHNOLOGICAL ENVIRONMENT

The effects of technological change

The response of business to technological change

The business

THE SOCIAL ENVIRONMENT

Changes in the social environment

The ethical environment

Corporate social responsibility

THE POLITICAL AND LEGAL ENVIRONMENT

Government intervention

Government economic policies

Trade and access to markets

Legislation

Responses to such changes

Chapter 21   The relationship between businesses and the economic environment

Key terms

Discretionary spending The amount of income that consumers have available to spend after covering essential items. The amount they choose to spend on 'luxuries'.

Economic activity The amount of buying and selling that takes place over a period of time.

Economic growth An increase in an economy's ability to produce goods and services.

Emerging markets Countries that are in the process of making a transition between developing and developed economy status.

Exchange rate The price which has to be paid to buy a currency, expressed in terms of the amount of another currency that has to be given up.

Globalisation The movement towards the expansion of economic and social ties between countries, through the spread of corporate institutions and the capitalist philosophy that leads to the shrinking of the world in economic terms.

Gross domestic product (GDP) The value of output produced in a country over a period of time, usually a year.

Hedging A means of insuring against future changes in prices of currencies or commodities through securing contracts to buy or sell at agreed prices.

Income elasticity of demand The responsiveness of demand to changes in incomes. A high income elasticity of demand implies that demand is very responsive to changes in incomes and vice versa.

Inflation A rise in the general price level over a period of time.

Interest rates The price of acquiring capital.

Standard of living A measure of welfare that looks at the amount and quality of goods and services households are able to buy with their incomes. This implies that the higher the amount of goods and services that can be acquired, the higher the standard of living.

The economy The term used to refer to the sum of economic activity that takes place usually within a country, for example, the UK economy, the US economy, and so on.

Assessing the effects of key economic factors on business organisations

There are a number of key economic factors that businesses have to take notice of. Changes in these factors affect different businesses in different ways. Part of this section is assessing the extent to which organisations will be affected by changes in these factors. The key factors we will look at will be:

- economic growth
- the business cycle
- interest rates
- exchange rates
- inflation
- unemployment.

At the heart of all of these things is the concept of economic activity. We often loosely use the terms 'the economy' and 'economic activity' without really thinking too carefully about what they mean. Economic activity refers to all the millions of transactions that take place every day. These transactions, at the simplest level, involve a buyer and a seller agreeing to exchange a good or service for some monetary return. The simple act of buying a chocolate bar from a corner store is one of billions of such transactions that take place every day. The greater the number of transactions, the greater the level of economic activity.

The economy and economic growth

The economy is simply the sum of all this economic activity. If the economy is growing then economic activity is rising, but if economic activity slows down then the economy may also be slowing down. It is vital to remember in the following discussion that we are always referring to the amount of transactions that take place over a period of time.

Economic growth is defined as an increase in an economy's ability to produce goods and services over a period of time. If we experience economic growth then the economy produces more goods and services in one year compared to the last. If, for example, we simply measured economic activity as the amount of steel produced in a year, then if in 2008 the UK produced 25 million tonnes of steel and in 2009 it produced 28 millions of tonnes then we would have experienced economic growth. If in 2009 the UK produced 24 million tonnes of steel then we would have experienced negative economic growth compared to 2008. Economic growth is given as a percentage which indicates the rate of growth over a period.

Economic growth is usually expressed as the percentage increase in gross domestic product (GDP) over a period of time. GDP measures the value of output of goods and services over a period of time. In simple terms this is found by multiplying the number of goods and services produced by their price to get the value of output. Real GDP takes into account changes in inflation over a period of time and gives a more accurate picture of economic activity.

The business cycle

Economists have studied levels of economic activity and have found that there are discernable patterns in these levels over time. There will be periods of time when economic activity is rising and other times when the level of economic activity slows down. Nobel Prize winning economists Finn E. Kydland and Edward C. Prescott spent many years studying these patterns. They looked at the trend rate of growth in an economy. This trend growth is the increase in economic activity over a period that one would expect if no external shocks affected the economy. They observed that economic activity varied around the expected trend in the growth of economic activity over a period, sometimes higher and sometimes lower than this trend. They viewed business cycles as periodic changes from trend growth in an economy. They based their analysis on observations of historical behaviour of economies over long periods of time.

These deviations from the trend can occur for a variety of reasons. In recent years there have been terrorist activity, wars, natural disasters, droughts, floods, and so on that have caused major changes in global markets. Oil prices have risen rapidly, commodity prices have risen as a result of drought or flood but also because of changes in demand patterns. Emerging economies such as China and India are experiencing rapid economic growth and the demand for raw materials such as steel and oil has further driven up commodity prices.

These changes can affect not just the local economy but the global one. Few businesses are immune to such changes in some form or another. For example, in 2007, news that there had been a rise in the number of people defaulting on mortgage payments in the United States led to a global contraction in financial markets. The effects filtered down to even small businesses such as restaurants, who began to see a fall in demand for their product as consumers 'tightened their belts' as a direct result of the impact of the so-called 'credit crunch'.

When these major shocks occur, the long-term trend in an economy can be disrupted, and as a result economic activity can rise or fall, and this affects many businesses in different ways. If businesses could rely on the economy growing at a steady 2% over the next twenty years, planning would be much easier. Such a steady trend, however, is unlikely. There will be periods when economic activity rises quickly and businesses will have to be in a position to take advantage of that growth. Equally, in times when the economy slows down, businesses will need to have strategies in place to cope in order to survive and prosper when things do eventually improve.

Many textbooks will look at business cycles in terms of four main phases – boom, slowdown, recession, growth. However, such a simplistic view is not really appropriate for the 21st century. The danger is that we see such a view as being inevitable; that if we are in a boom period (where economic activity is rising rapidly) that it must *inevitably* be followed by a slowdown which in turn will *inevitably* be followed by recession, and so on. The work of Kydland and Prescott suggested that this is not the case.

Since the early 1990s, changes in the way the economy works and changing approaches to economic policy have led to a far more stable pattern of economic growth in the UK. There have been times when economic activity has slowed, but between 1997 and 2008 the UK enjoyed consistent economic growth. In early 2008, the signs were that growth would slow markedly.

What is important to remember is what we mean by 'slowdown' and 'recession'. If economic growth is 3.0% this means that the amount of output produced by the UK economy is 3.0% higher than the equivalent period last year. If next year economic growth is 2.4% then growth has slowed *but* it is still positive; the country has produced 2.4% more output than it did the previous year. The term 'recession' has a particular definition. It is a period of two consecutive quarters of negative economic growth. Negative economic growth means that the country has produced less output than in the previous period. If growth in one period changed from 2.4% to -1.3% then this would represent negative growth. The distinction is important.

For many businesses, therefore, the challenge facing them in dealing with the external economic environment is to manage the business in the face of these changing levels of economic activity. When economic activity slows down, some businesses are affected more than others; likewise, when economic activity increases, some firms benefit more than others.

The basic relationship works as follows. If economic activity slows down then there are not as many transactions taking place. Some businesses might see demand for their goods and services slowing down. In turn this means that their revenue might be less than expected but they may well have incurred costs of stock and so will have to adjust to the changing economic conditions. Some businesses will, in turn, be affected by the response to stock levels. Suppliers may also start to see demand slow down and they in turn will adjust orders of raw materials from their suppliers, and so on.

On the other hand, in times of rising economic activity, businesses may see demand for their products rising. They may not have anticipated this increase and so have to order in more stock to cope with the rise in demand. Suppliers then see an upturn in their business and so the process continues. The key is how far demand changes. For food retailers such as the large supermarkets the effect of changes in economic activity tends to be relatively minor; there might be a shift to buying different types of product at different points in the business cycle but the general level of demand stays relatively stable. After all, we all need to eat!

This does not mean that the likes of Sainsbury's and Asda are immune from changes in economic activity. In 2008 the UK experienced a slowdown in economic activity. There were reports that discount supermarkets like Aldi and Lidl were seeing a rise in the number of customers visiting their stores. The explanation was that shoppers were turning to Aldi and Lidl because they were cheaper than the other large supermarkets and that the main reason was because rising food prices and the downturn in the economy was making people more careful about what they buy and how much they were paying for food.

Other businesses see far more varied swings in the level of demand for their products. In particular, products with a relatively high income elasticity of demand are likely to be affected more substantially by changes in economic activity. The following two examples highlight how different businesses can be affected by changes in the business cycle.

For example...

The knock-on effects of the housing market

SP Carpets and Furniture is a medium-sized business trading primarily within a regional market in the north east of England. They provide a carpet delivery and fitting service and sell a range of furniture including beds, lounge suites, dining room furniture, cupboards, and so on. They tend to carry relatively large amounts of stock in order to demonstrate the range of products that they have available but will then order in the actual goods for delivery when customers have placed an order. Such orders generally have a six-week lead time (that is, the time between order and delivery).

One of the key factors for this business is the housing market. In times of rising economic activity the housing market tends to be active with people buying and selling houses. When people are moving house they tend to want to impose their own identity on their homes and this includes purchases of carpets and furniture. When economic growth is rising fast, demand at SP Carpets and Furniture tends to be buoyant also. This can lead to problems with consumers who want the goods quickly but the capacity of the suppliers may well be limited. SP Carpets may well benefit from having close relationships with its suppliers to try and maintain flexibility in the light of the uncertainties in demand.

However, when the economy slows down they tend to be one of the first businesses affected. If the housing market slows down then this affects sales at a firm like SP Carpets. However, there are sometimes some hidden benefits. People may not be moving house in quite such numbers but some households may consider decorating or extending their existing homes rather than moving and this can lead to unexpected increases in demand for SP's products.

For example...

Holidays and income elasticity of demand

First Choice is a holiday company. Each year, First Choice will book flights, hotels and villas for package holidays that it sells to consumers. In the summer these holidays are likely to be in places where the sun shines and in winter it may be ski packages. Forecasting demand for holidays is notoriously difficult, but First Choice will have to make decisions about how many hotel rooms and flights to book months in advance of the season. A holiday is one of the most expensive single items of spending that most consumers will have to consider in a year. The income elasticity of demand tends to be relatively high.

If the economy is experiencing a slowdown in activity, households may look at their financial position and make decisions in the light of the slowdown. Some people might have lost their jobs as a result of slowdown and others may fear the possibility in the near future. In times of slowdown wage rises tend to be more modest and so people may not feel confident about major spending decisions like holidays.

A proportion of households may decide to defer a holiday in this type of economic

climate – possibly deciding to take a few day trips or a few weekend breaks rather than a two-week holiday in the summer. For First Choice such decisions will start to become more obvious in the key booking periods of January to March. If they experience a slowdown in bookings compared to last year they may find that they have a larger number of hotel rooms, flight spaces and so on available than they anticipated. In such circumstances, First Choice will have to make decisions about what to do with the surplus holidays they have. They might decide to try and offload the holidays by offering reduced prices to try and encourage holidaymakers to take up the surplus, but they might also work out that by discounting they are actually losing more money on the holiday than if they simply accepted the loss.

Skills watch!

A03 / A04

The two examples above highlight different effects of changes in economic activity on different businesses. What is vital to remember is that a slowdown does not mean that all businesses will 'have to close down' or 'go bankrupt' because 'no one is buying their goods'. This is often the response of students in exam questions on this topic. To provide considered answers at A2 you need to make some judgements about the extent to which different businesses are affected by changes in economic activity.

Some might be affected so badly that they have to close down, but many businesses will, whilst experiencing difficulties, find ways to get through the changes in demand and to meet customer needs. Be wary, therefore, of making judgements that are extreme and think about the likely size of the effect of changes in the business cycle on businesses. The extent to which the change in economic activity alters is also going to be a key consideration. If economic growth slows from 2.6% to 2.4%, many businesses will hardly notice any difference at all in sales!

Interest rates

Most businesses will be affected by changes in interest rates. The interest rate is the price of borrowing. Most businesses will have loans that attract interest and will also have overdraft facilities with their bank which they use as a short-term means of financing cash flow.

Since 1997, the Bank of England has been given operational responsibility for controlling inflation. The main way that inflation is controlled in the UK is through monetary policy – changing the cost of borrowing to influence economic activity. The Bank of England sets Bank Rate – the rate at which it lends money to the financial system – and this in turn influences the structure of interest rates in the economy as a whole.

In simple terms, the Bank is likely to raise Bank Rate if it believes that there are inflationary pressures that will push inflation above the target rate set by the government (at the time of writing this is 2.0%). In times of economic slowdown when inflationary pressures are less, the Bank will reduce Bank Rate.

If the Bank does change rates then this spills down through the financial system and interest rates on loans, overdrafts, savings, and so on will all change roughly in line with the change in Bank Rate. This means that firms who have loans will find that the amount they pay in interest payments each month or whatever agreed time period will also change. The amount that a business pays in interest is referred to as debt servicing. If interest rates rise, then the amount that a business has to set aside to service its debt will also rise, and if interest rates fall, this can reduce its debt servicing costs. Equally, changing interest rates will affect the cost of overdrafts in a similar way. Businesses that are highly geared, that is, they have a large proportion of loan capital in relation to share capital, are likely to be hardest hit by changes in interest rates.

The extent to which businesses are affected depends on the amount of debt they have and on the size of the business and its perceived risk. Smaller businesses tend to be seen as riskier investments by banks and so interest rates can often be several points above Base Rate. If Base Rate was 5.25%, for example, some small firms may only be able to get loans at 10% and above. The interest rate charged on overdrafts may also be higher for smaller firms than larger ones.

THE EFFECT OF CHANGES IN INTEREST RATES ON BUSINESS

An increase in interest rates

- An increase in costs – interest on loans will rise.
- Businesses with investments might find returns increasing.
- As the cost of servicing debt rises, businesses have to consider whether to pass on rises to consumers in the form of higher prices.
- Some businesses may cut costs in other areas to compensate.
- Consumer spending will tend to slow down and may affect sales.
- The exchange rate may strengthen – importers benefit from lower import prices; exporters find that they are less competitive.

A fall in interest rates

- A fall in costs – interest on loans will decrease.
- There is an incentive to borrow for investment as interest rates are lower.
- Lower interest rates may encourage increased consumer spending.
- Businesses have to be prepared for possible increases in demand.
- The exchange rate may weaken – importers find that the cost of imported raw materials, etc. will increase; exporters find they are more competitive.

A large business with a loan of £350,000 with an interest rate of 8% is likely to have to pay around £28,000 a year in interest or £2,333 per month. A rise in interest rates of a quarter of a percent would add around £875 a year to interest payments. If the trend is towards rising interest rates then the additional interest rate burden faced by firms can be significant. If interest rates on the loan rose to 10% it would add around £7,000 a year to interest payments. For large and small firms this money has to be found from somewhere.

Interest rates do not just affect the cost of servicing debt. The level of interest rates has an effect on the level of economic activity. The Bank may increase interest rates to slowdown economic activity and if this happens, then consumer spending can also slow down. Many adult people in the UK are house owners with mortgages. When interest rates change, the cost of servicing their mortgages also rises and this can have a major impact on spending decisions. It can cut what is called discretionary spending – the amount of income available for spending on what the individual chooses rather than things they have to pay out, such as their mortgage. If discretionary spending contracts, then businesses who sell products and services that tend to be responsive to changes in income (that is, income elastic) tend to be affected most by such decisions.

Exchange rates

The exchange rate is the amount of one currency that has to be given up to acquire another. An exchange rate of £1 = $2 means that to acquire (say) $5,000 dollars, a UK citizen has to give up £2,500. For a US citizen seeking to buy pounds, buying £5,000 means they have to give up $10,000.

The exchange rate is determined by the demand and supply of different currencies on the foreign exchange markets which specialise in dealing in foreign currency transactions. One of the factors that influence the demand for a currency on the market is changes in interest rates. If the foreign exchange markets anticipate a rise in UK interest rates it tends to have the effect of increasing the value of the pound. This is because investors will look to buy UK assets since they now command a higher return. As the demand for sterling rises it pushes up the exchange rate.

When the exchange rate alters it affects the degree to which firms are competitive in foreign markets, and also affects the cost of imports of raw materials, components and semi-finished products as well as foodstuffs. If the pound rises in value compared to the euro or the dollar, for example, it means that exporters will find that they are less competitive since foreign buyers now have to give up more euro or dollars to buy the same amount of pounds. To those foreign buyers it seems like the goods and services have risen in price and this can affect demand for UK exports. At the same time, UK buyers of foreign goods

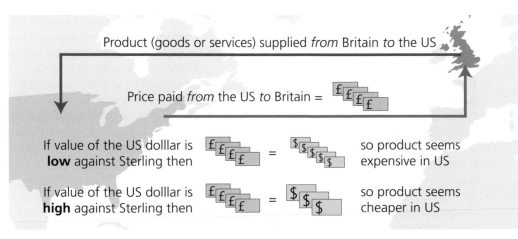

Figure 21.1   The effect of changes in exchange rates on the price of imports and exports

(imports) will get more dollars or euro for their pound and it will feel to them like import prices have fallen. The reverse applies if the exchange rate falls in value and the pound is worth less against other currencies.

The precise effect on a business will depend on the extent to which it trades abroad. Some firms sell the majority of their output in overseas markets and they can be particularly vulnerable to changes in exchange rates. The picture can be especially complex if the firm buys goods from abroad and also sells in foreign markets. For many large firms this is very much the case, but they may have the size and expertise to be able to manage changes in interest and exchange rates more effectively through having dedicated departments that buy currency on the futures markets as a hedge against the volatility in the foreign exchange markets and unanticipated changes in interest rates.

Inflation

Inflation is a general rise in the price level over a period of time. It is calculated by the Office for National Statistics who regularly take a record of thousands of prices of around 650 goods and services from many different outlets. The monthly inflation figures are published using the government's preferred measure called the Consumer Price Index (CPI).

The CPI is a measure of the rate at which prices on average are rising. The sophistication of the collection and measurement techniques are beyond the scope of this book but the ONS website has more details on how the statistics are collected and calculated.

Inflation is seen as being a central economic factor. Changes in the rate of inflation have significant effects on businesses and individuals. Inflation is important for the following main reasons:

- Changes in prices make it more difficult for businesses to plan ahead – especially in terms of calculating input prices – but also in planning future prices for their goods and services.
- Inflation affects the return on investments over a period of time. £1,000 today is worth more in terms of the goods and services it can buy than £1,000 in 10 years' time. Firms have to take this into account when investing in projects where the return on their investment might not be realised until a number of years in the future.
- Inflation affects the value of money. The value of money refers to the amount of goods and services that a given sum of money can buy at a particular point in time. If prices rise faster than the incomes of individuals then that can effectively mean that those individuals are worse off. This might influence their spending decisions.
- Because inflation can erode standards of living, employees may demand wage increases to at least match the rise in inflation (and possibly more) to maintain expected rises in their standard of living. Such wage demands can put pressure on firms' costs and this in turn can lead to inflationary pressure. Wage increases may be granted on the basis of the inflation figures without any corresponding increases in efficiency or productivity, thus increasing a business's costs.
- For some in society, their income does not rise in line with inflation and when this happens they effectively are worse off as they can now afford to buy fewer goods and services. For those at lower income levels this can be particularly significant and in turn affects their spending. Some businesses can, therefore, suffer the consequences of this effect on their sales.
- Inflation which is running at a higher level than in competitor countries can reduce the competitiveness of UK businesses. If prices are rising faster in the UK than, say the US, then firms selling to US markets might find that they are less competitive compared to other prospective sellers as well as domestic US competitors.
- If inflation is volatile then this can create an uncertain business climate and in such a climate the willingness to invest is less. Business people will be uncertain of the return on their investment and this can affect productivity in the short term.

```
┌─────────────────────────────────────────────────────┐
│  SUMMARY – THE EFFECTS OF INFLATION                   │
│                                                        │
│   • Creates uncertainty – difficult to plan ahead.    │
│   • Affects return on investments.                    │
│   • Affects the value of money.                       │
│   • Erodes standards of living.                       │
│   • Increases pressure on wage costs.                 │
│   • Affects those on fixed incomes.                   │
│   • Affects competitiveness abroad.                   │
│   • May deter investment.                             │
└─────────────────────────────────────────────────────┘
```

In the period since 1995, the UK has enjoyed a period of relatively low inflation. Inflation around the target level of 2.0% is considered to be important for a thriving economy. If prices are rising then there are incentives for firms to invest and to produce goods and services to satisfy growing demand. The trick is to try and balance the level of demand in the economy and the corresponding level of supply. That is part of the Bank of England's job although it does not control the economy per se.

Inflation above 2.0% can create too many uncertainties, but inflation under this target rate can equally be damaging. In the first five years of the 21st century, Japan experienced deflation – a period of generally falling prices. In this situation there is little incentive to invest and the country experienced a prolonged recession. Most advanced western economies would want to see inflation rates at or around 2.0% and would consider this a sustainable level of price increases.

Unemployment

Unemployment is the number of people available for work and actively seeking employment (the definition used by the International Labour Organisation – ILO). The unemployment *rate* is the percentage of the labour force actively seeking employment.

The number of people out of work at any one time may be related to the level of economic activity. In times of economic slowdown the level of unemployment might rise and vice versa.

Unemployment affects businesses in a variety of ways, mainly linked to the way in which businesses interact with the labour market. The labour market is represented by the demand for labour by employers and the number of people willing and able to offer their services in that market (the supply of labour).

If unemployment is high and rising it implies that there is a pool of labour willing and able to work. This has implications for the ease with which businesses might be able to recruit workers and also the price that they have to pay to acquire this labour (the wage rate). The existence of a pool of unemployed labour does not necessarily mean that they will have the skills or experience to be able to do the job required, so whilst recruiting them might be cheaper and easier (subject to the law relating to the National Minimum Wage of course and other employment legislation) there might be additional associated costs of recruitment in terms of training. The productivity of workers who do not have the right skills and experience tends to add to wage costs for businesses.

In times of rising economic activity the problems facing businesses might be quite different. Unemployment may be low and falling and this implies that the pool of labour willing and able to work is less. The workers who tend to get jobs first are those who are flexible and who are able to demonstrate some skills. There will tend to be a shortage of highly-skilled workers in times of high economic activity. Firms looking to recruit such workers may find that the only way they can recruit is to offer better rewards packages and this tends to push up costs. In some cases acquiring the right sort of worker is very difficult and some businesses will find that they have to operate with key positions not filled. This can seriously affect productivity and acts as a constraint to growth for the business.

The majority of workers that are left tend to be those who have few skills and limited experience, and many are not suited to the requirements of businesses that do have labour shortages. So there may be unemployment and a high level of demand for workers but the two are not matched. This leaves businesses in a position where they have to consider ways of meeting their employment needs, possibly through restructuring and/or internal training regimes. A further problem of large scale unemployment is that some workers who may have recently been made redundant may be highly skilled in their job but the work that is available cannot make use of those skills. The longer these workers stay unemployed, the more likely it is that the skills they do have will become outdated and many long-term unemployed have difficulty finding new work because they forget the discipline and routines that are required in recruitment. The challenge for businesses in seeking to recruit these types of workers becomes even greater – and more expensive.

THE IMPACT OF UNEMPLOYMENT

High unemployment

- Available supply of labour.
- Wage rates likely to be competitive.
- Problems of deskilling.
- Available workers may not have the right skills.
- A sign of slowdown in economic activity.

Low unemployment

- Possible shortage of labour.
- Skilled labour likely to be in particularly short supply.
- Rising wage costs.
- Limits possibilities for expansion.
- Symptom of rising economic activity.

Trends in key economic variables

Business cannot be conducted in isolation and it is important that businesses keep abreast of trends in key economic variables. Historical data will provide some useful information, but it is the extent to which the business is able to anticipate future trends that is often a key competitive advantage. If inflation, for example, has been gradually creeping up over the past few years, then this might suggest that it will continue to rise in the near future – but not necessarily.

Businesses will have to consider what this trend means for them in terms of their costs, their prices, wage demands, competitiveness, and so on. They will also have to monitor what the policy response might be by the Bank of England, as this might also have an impact on their operations. If, for example, the statements from the Bank of England imply that inflation is rising too quickly, then it may well be highly likely that they will be considering increasing interest rates. If so, what will the rise be – a series of three, quarter point rises over the next year, a quarter point rise each month for the next four months, or some other combination? When will interest rates peak and how long will they be likely to stay at their peak for?

As with all of the chapters in this section, the crucial ingredient that might help the business cope with the changes in the external environment will be the quality and quantity of information that they have at their disposal and what use the business makes of this information. Businesses need to take notice of the trends in key economic variables and be aware of the interrelationships between these key variables and what they mean for both the business, government economic policy and the international economy.

SUMMARY OF KEY TRENDS

The graph in Figure 21.2 shows UK GDP over a five-year period from 2003 to 2008. It can be seen that there was a considerable degree of difference in the performance of the economy over that time. Around quarter 2 of 2004, the economy was experiencing strong growth but this growth slowed a year later, and whilst activity picked up in 2006 and 2007, the credit crunch of 2008 started to impact on activity, and forecasts for growth in 2008 as a whole were more in the region of 1.0%. Growth in 2009 was forecasted to be negative.

Businesses will have to adjust to the changes in economic activity over time; it may not be easy to predict and has a considerable impact on planning, stock levels, pricing tactics, and so on.

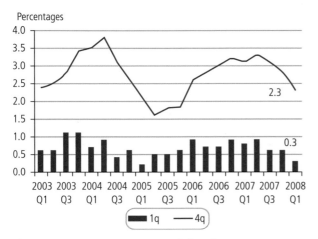

Figure 21.2 UK economic growth (GDP) 2003–2008

Source: http://www.statistics.gov.uk/cci/nugget.asp?id=192

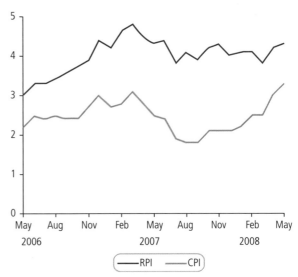

Figure 21.3 UK inflation as measured by the Consumer Price Index (CPI) and the Retail Price Index (RPI) 2006–2008

Source: http://www.statistics.gov.uk/cci/nugget.asp?id=192

The Retail Price Index was a measure of inflation used by the UK until 2003. It is still published and many businesses look at this as a guide to what wage demands might be from employee representatives. The CPI and the RPI differ in various technical ways. The RPI 'basket' is meant to represent the spending of a typical household. It excludes the richest 4% and the poorest pensioners. The CPI covers everyone, including foreign tourists and even prisoners. Housing costs are treated differently in the two indices.

From the graph in Figure 21.3 we can see that the trend for inflation between 2007 and 2008 as measured by the CPI has been upwards. This was largely a reflection of the rise in fuel and food prices. Such a rise reflects the difficulties that face businesses in planning ahead with such volatile prices. It also means that businesses face rising costs for things like fuel, and they have to decide whether to pass on those costs (which will contribute to inflationary pressures) or absorb them and face smaller profit margins. Given that the CPI was above the target rate of inflation in the early part of 2008, the implications might be that there would be little room for the Bank of England to cut interest rates and possibly there would be an incentive to increase rates. However, the dramatic slowdown in economic growth led to the Bank of England fearing inflation would fall way below the target rate, and as a result, it cut interest rates to below 1%.

The unemployment rate in the UK has remained relatively stable over the period shown in Figure 21.4 (see opposite) and has seemed to fall during 2007. However, there is a hint that there is an upturn in the rate of unemployment towards the middle of 2008. Unemployment is not always easy to interpret because the statistics tend to be out of step with the performance of the economy. The effects on employment do not show up for some time after economic shocks have occurred. For this reason, unemployment is referred to as a lagged indicator – it tends to hide the true picture of what may be happening to unemployment in the longer term. The slowdown in the UK economy as indicated by the GDP graph above might suggest that we could reasonably expect unemployment to also start to rise as 2009 progresses. Is this what has happened? You will be in a position to tell this as you read this book and the figures will have been updated.

The graph in Figure 21.5 shows the official Bank of England interest rate over the last 30 years. You can see that the last 15 years up to 2009 have been a great deal more stable than the previous 20 years! However, within that 15-year period there has been volatility in interest rates and the experience of the past might tell us that interest rates could reach historically high levels again at some point in the future. The implications for businesses of such high rates are significant if they ever were to reach such heights again. For businesses, stable interest rates provide a better environment for planning than times when interest rates are changing regularly.

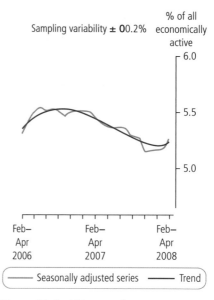

Figure 21.4 UK unemployment rate 2006–2008

Source: http://www.statistics.gov.uk/cci/nugget.asp?id=12

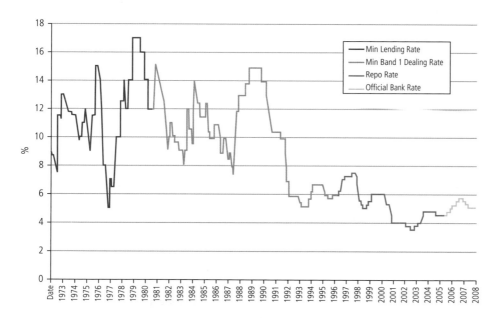

Figure 21.5 Interest rates in the UK 1970–2008

Source: http://www.bankofengland.co.uk/statistics/rates/baserate.pdf

Once again the charts in Figures 21.6 and 21.7 (see next page) show just how volatile key economic factors can be. In this case the changes in the value of the pound against the dollar and the euro are quite different and for businesses dealing in Europe and the US the implications are different and complex. The depreciation of the pound against the euro will have benefited UK exporters to Europe but increased the costs of imported goods from Europe (with the possible knock-on effects for inflation in the UK if the increase in costs gets passed on in the form of higher prices).

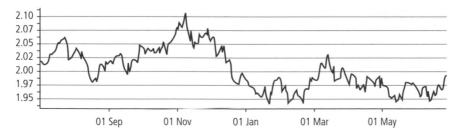

Figure 21.6   UK Pound vs US Dollar Exchange Rate 2007–2008

Source: http://newsvote.bbc.co.uk/1/shared/fds/hi/business/market_data/currency/11/12/twelve_
month.stm

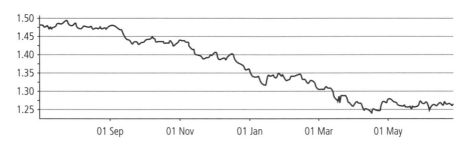

Figure 21.7   UK pound v Euro 2007–2008

Source: http://newsvote.bbc.co.uk/1/shared/fds/hi/business/market_data/currency/11/13/twelve_
month.stm

For businesses trading in the US the changing value of the pound against the dollar would have made planning much more difficult, both in terms of the effect on import prices and on export prices.

Skills watch!

A01 / A02 / A03 / A04

A UK manufacturing firm secures 90% of its raw materials from Europe and sells 90% of its output to the US. The business is highly geared and operates in a highly-competitive US market. It is currently operating at maximum capacity.

Use the data above to assess the effect on this business of changes in economic variables which you have covered in this section.

Globalisation of markets

The term 'globalisation' is one that has become more common in recent years, yet exactly what it means is perhaps more difficult to pin down. Is it an economic phenomenon, a social phenomenon or a cultural phenomenon? There are likely to be elements of all three in globalisation but we can define it as:

The movement towards the expansion of economic and social ties between countries as a result of the spread of business activity worldwide, leading to the shrinking of the world in economic terms.

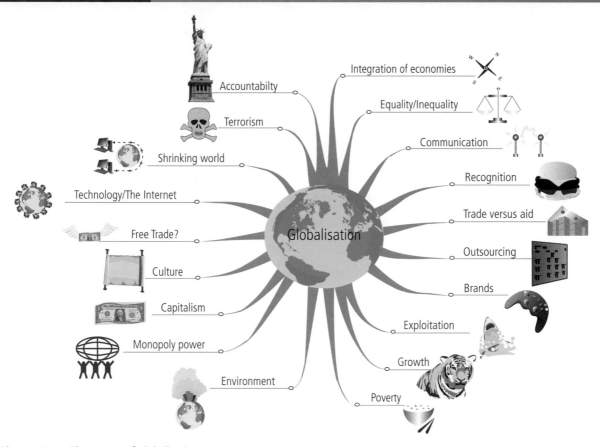

Figure 21.8   The extent of globalisation

Figure 21.8 above highlights the extent of globalisation – it covers a very wide range of areas and issues, and raises perhaps many more questions than it provides answers for.

Globalisation is characterised by the increasing reliance of economies on each other and the degree of interdependence of economies on one another. The events of 2007–2008 in the United States concerning the so-called sub-prime market (loans for house purchases for those who have low credit ratings) have spread across the globe and have affected many businesses, not only in the financial markets but in all sorts of other areas of economic activity.

The deregulation of markets, the increases in technology and the extent to which information is now widely shared means that there are opportunities to be able to buy and sell in any country in the world. In addition, the removal of barriers to entry means that both labour and capital are now more easily able to locate anywhere in the world. To a large extent this has been facilitated by the growth of global markets in finance.

These changes have been made possible as a result of the following:

- technology
- communication networks
- Internet access
- growth of economic cooperation – trading blocs (EU, NAFTA, etc.)
- collapse of 'communism'
- movement to free trade.

Such changes, however, are not without their costs despite the fact that there are massive advantages to businesses and their consumers of these changes. Wherever you go in the world it is highly likely that you will come across a McDonald's, a Ford motor vehicle, Coca Cola, and so on. These organisations have a presence in almost every country in the world, either through having production facilities in a diverse range of countries or a means to sell their products in these countries. Some have commented that such corporate domination brings with it its own costs, which include damage to the environment, the exploitation of labour, the growth of monopoly power, economic degradation, the damage to traditional cultures and the increased use of non-renewable resources.

Some of the consequences of these changes include issues of the degree to which business organisations are accountable in a global environment, the increased gap between rich and poor which fuels potential terrorist reaction, the extent to which businesses behave with ethical responsibility and the effect on rich and poor of the efforts to remove trade barriers.

SUMMARY OF THE EFFECTS OF GLOBALISATION

Costs of globalisation

- Interdependence can lead to problems in one country cascading to others.
- Negative impact on cultures.
- Lack of variety – too much standardisation?
- Possible exploitation of labour.
- Lack of accountability of large firms.
- Increased gap between rich and poor.
- Economic degradation:
  - effect on women and children
  - deforestation
  - desertification
  - pollution and externalities
  - increase in climate change.
- Terrorism stimulated by clash of cultures/beliefs.

Benefits of globalisation

- Interdependence can lead to economies of scale.
- Greater variety of goods and services available for all.
- Lower prices for goods and services.
- Increases in efficiency in use of resources.
- Sharing of knowledge and expertise.
- Increase in the availability of jobs.
- Increased standards of living.
- Investment can help to reduce poverty.
- Deregulation and removal of barriers to entry opens up markets to all.
- Freeing up trade helps less developed countries to expand.

Developments in emerging markets

Emerging markets or emerging economies are those countries that are in the process of making a transition between developing and developed economy status. Developing economies tend to have a limited industrial base, a greater reliance on primary production such as mining and agriculture, and have a number of economic problems that limit the standard of living of the population. Developed economies, on the other hand, have a high proportion of their total output in tertiary, quaternary and quinary production sectors – service industries, finance, trading, health, education, research, and leisure and recreation. The main countries that fall into the emerging economy category are Argentina, Brazil, China, Egypt, India, Mexico, Poland, Russia, South Africa, South Korea and Turkey. Wider definitions of emerging markets would also include countries like Israel, Hungary, Malaysia, Taiwan, Pakistan, Peru, Colombia and the Czech Republic.

These are countries that are experiencing rapid industrialisation and which have the potential to be major developed economies in the future. The International Monetary Fund has predicted that emerging economies will grow by an average of around 6.3 to 6.4% in 2008 and 2009. At the moment, however, many of them still have significant economic and social problems, and despite the rapid expansion in economic growth that they are experiencing, the benefits of this growth are not as yet spreading to all sectors of society. As a result there are imbalances of

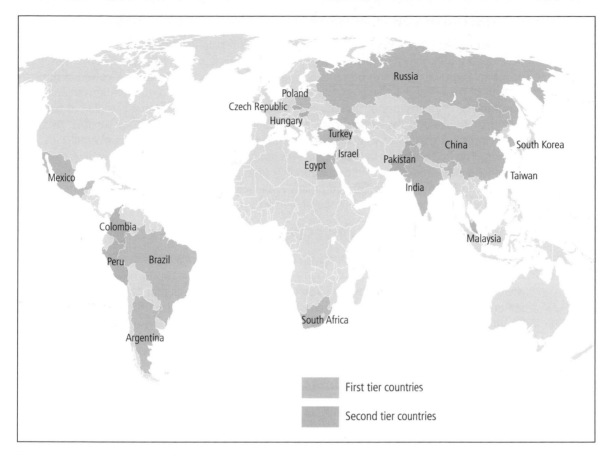

Figure 21.9   Emerging economies

income distribution and relatively large numbers of people who live in poverty or face extreme hardship.

For businesses in these countries, there are problems in accessing global markets. The existence of trade barriers is one of the most significant. These barriers can be obvious, such as tariffs and quotas, but equally can be non-tariff barriers such as regulations, rules, voluntary export restraints, legislation and exacting standards or specifications. At the same time, these countries also have some problems in exploiting their natural resources because they do not have the expertise or the infrastructure to make the best use of any natural competitive advantages they do have.

THREATS FROM EMERGING ECONOMIES

There are concerns amongst some established businesses in developed markets that the competitive threat from these countries is significant. The United States, for example, has developed a massive trade deficit with China and believes that the Chinese authorities have artificially kept the value of the Chinese currency, the Yuan, below its true value thus helping to stimulate exports from China to the US whilst restricting US exports into China. The existence of large numbers of low-cost yet highly-educated workers in many of the emerging economies does mean that the potential of these countries to produce high-quality products at low prices is a possible competitive threat which must be considered. In the long term, trade restrictions are not the way in which this threat can be dealt with. Globalisation will tend to start to eat into the restrictions that exist, in addition to the drive to try and free up the world economy to realise the benefits of trade to all.

OPPORTUNITIES THAT ARISE FROM EMERGING ECONOMIES

However, whilst emerging economies do present a threat to established businesses in the developed world, they also provide massive opportunities. Investment by the authorities in the economy is growing and this presents businesses with opportunities to be involved in the growth of the economy. Many established businesses have offices and operations in emerging economies; they make use of the expertise that is developing. For example, India has become a popular source of access to low-cost, high-quality information technology services. Asia, of which India is a part, now accounts for more than a quarter of the global market in IT services. The opportunities to investigate emerging economies for new markets as locations for outsourcing production and distribution facilities and exploiting opportunities for joint ventures and acquisitions is high, and many companies are heavily involved in ensuring that they have a presence in these countries in some form or another.

RISKS ASSOCIATED WITH INVESTMENT IN EMERGING ECONOMIES

There are, of course, risks associated with developing operations in some of these countries. Political instability is a key problem; countries like South Africa not only have their own political and social problems, but are also close to other countries that have fragile political structures. Cultural differences, different attitudes and approaches to financial dealings, views on interest in Muslim countries, for example, where Sharia law forbids charging interest on loans (also called 'usury'), language, and so on, all play a part in the decision-making on the extent of the benefits of investigating opportunities in emerging markets.

AO4

Evaluate three possible costs and benefits to a business, such as a major UK supermarket chain, of seeking to expand operations in an emerging economy like Russia, China or India. Use Ansoff's Matrix to help you with your evaluation.

SUMMARY – EMERGING MARKETS

Ultimately, companies have to consider the trade-off between the benefits that can arise from investing in emerging markets and the potential risks that arise. In addition to this, many companies have to consider at a strategic level where they believe their future priorities and opportunities lie. Many large companies in developed economies are operating in mature markets where the opportunities for market growth are limited and the challenges of growing the business get greater every year. Emerging markets provide the chance to enter into a phase of development that can provide significant market growth opportunities, but as discussed in Chapter 9 in relation to Ansoff's Matrix, companies do need to consider the extent of the risks they face and the type of marketing strategy they invoke in these economies.

Evaluating the strategies businesses might deploy in response to changes in the economic environment

The first thing to remember when assessing responses is that businesses often have little control over the external economic environment. That does not mean to say that when the economy changes they can simply do nothing in response. The following looks at some of these responses and offers a discussion to help assess the extent to which these strategies might cope with the changes faced.

Scenario planning

Many businesses will conduct some form of scenario planning in order to anticipate potential changes in the level of economic activity and to changes in interest rates, exchange rates, and so on. This will enable them to have in place the means of dealing with them if and when they arise. If a slowdown in the market is expected then a business might seek to analyse which of its markets is most likely to be hit, how much it will be affected and what methods it can put in place to limit the impact. The success of the planning process depends on the quality of the information and the forecasts that the business uses and the skills of the staff to implement these strategies when they are put into effect.

Pricing strategies

An obvious means of dealing with a slowdown would be to look at the pricing structures that the business has and identify where different pricing strategies can be adopted to respond to the changes. For example, a slowdown in the economy might imply that a business should look at reducing prices in response to encourage sales. In some cases this might work and the decision will have to be how far to cut prices to have the desired effect: 5%, 10%, 20%, 50%? If the firm has some understanding of the price elasticity of demand as well as the income elasticity of demand for its products, then it might be better able to adopt a pricing strategy that will maximise its revenue returns given the existing economic environment.

The effect will also be influenced by the market structure the firm operates in and the extent of the competition. If the business is a market leader then it may well be in a position of setting prices that it knows will remain competitive and provides it with appropriate margins, but if it is a market follower then it may have to respond to the price changes implemented by the market leader.

The impact of a pricing strategy will also depend on the type of market that the business operates in. In 2008, the economic slowdown saw a shift in consumer spending to supermarkets like Aldi and Lidl who have a reputation for low prices. There was some evidence that consumers were shifting from the more expensive big four supermarkets. Aldi and Lidl have lower overheads because of the relative sparseness of their stores in relation to supermarkets like Sainsbury's and Asda, and they focus specifically on providing low prices.

Exploiting technology and services

The developments in IT mean that many businesses have high-quality information about their businesses and the subtle changes that are occurring which they may have to respond to. This information can provide details of the market, what their buying habits are, how they are changing, and so on. Analysis of this technology can help a business formulate plans to counter the negative effects of such changes.

In some cases, particularly in the financial services industry, software can be developed to automatically respond to changing patterns of prices, sales and consumer behaviour. Firms who have extensive dealings in foreign trade or who use commodities in their production processes can use the futures market to attempt to hedge price changes. The futures market enables businesses to buy commodities or currencies at an agreed price for future delivery. For very large firms, the contracts on which these transactions are based can also be traded in what is called the derivatives market. As with any such market activity, the success of such a strategy will depend on the quality of the information available, the skills and experience of the staff who manage the transactions and their ability to be able to accurately forecast and analyse future market trends.

Stock control

In times of economic slowdown, firms can be left with large amounts of stock which might not be able to be sold or might have to be heavily discounted and could impose significant financial strains on the cash flow of the business. The developments in managing stock through so-called just-in-time (JIT) methods, and in managing supply chains effectively, have contributed to reducing the costs associated with such effects but at the same time maintain high degrees of flexibility to respond quickly if and when an upturn arises. The key strategy is building relationships with suppliers and treating them almost as part of the wider business rather than seeing them as being separate entities. Such strategies take many years to build and to implement, but when they are in place they can be highly beneficial in maintaining the ability to respond to changing economic conditions – whether it be a slowdown or an upturn.

Product changes

Changing economic circumstances might mean sales fall, costs are rising and profit margins are squeezed. A response that focuses on price has obvious risks and because of this, some businesses will look to maintain price but focus instead on the product offering. In 2008, a number of firms including Kellogg's and ice cream manufacturers like Breyers and Edy's, both of which operate primarily in the US, took decisions on their products. These companies decided to reduce the size of their product offering on some lines; Breyers in the US reduced the size of their ice cream tubs from 56 ounces to 48 ounces; Kellogg's reduced the size of boxes of some cereals by between two and four ounces. It was estimated that this was equivalent to a price rise of 5%.

Other manufacturers have also done this in the past. Mars made their iconic bar longer but slimmer at one time, for example. The success of such strategies depends very much on the extent of consumer reaction. Many consumers may not notice the changes but if news organisations and consumer forums get hold of the information there tends to be a negative reaction to the strategy and this could backfire on the business. The extent to which the business can rely on customer loyalty and how it presents the strategy will be a major influence on the longer-term success and outcome of the strategy.

Cost strategies

Focusing on cost is one method that business can use that they do have some control over. If an economy is slowing down, the focus on where costs can be cut may well be one of the first responses of a business. Cost-cutting could include making staff redundant, finding cheaper sources of raw materials or components, possibly through outsourcing, restructuring, rationalising the business and closing inefficient plant. Equally, a business might look at ways in which they can improve productivity as a means of reducing cost. Whatever method is chosen, the business will have to think long term about what their position will be in X years' time when the economic circumstances have changed. Will they still have the skills needed to be able to cope with an upturn? Is the short-term benefit counterbalanced by the longer-term costs that might have to be incurred in staff recruitment and training if human resources are cut?

Market distribution strategies

If customer buying habits are changing in response to changing economic circumstances, then it may be that a business will try and consider ways in which to make it easier for consumers to access the products that they have for sale. This could be as relevant to B2B as well as B2C organisations. Such strategies might look at ways of cutting out middle men, improving the speed of delivery and the ease of order, implementing technology to cut out waste and improve efficiency in distribution, and so on. All of these methods could provide a source of competitive advantage over rivals, and whether an economy is slowing down or expanding, the need to improve the ease and convenience with which customers can acquire products is important.

Diversification strategies

Diversifying activities helps spread the risk of vulnerability to economic changes both in a domestic economy and to global economic changes. Changes in demand or economic activity in one market might be balanced out by increases in demand elsewhere. Such a strategy helps smooth out fluctuations in demand.

Labour strategies

Businesses are increasingly aware of the opportunities for outsourcing and the need to build and retain flexibility in their workforce. Some core operations can be outsourced to countries where the labour costs are significantly lower, although a balance has to be struck between the cost benefits of doing this and the possible disadvantages that may arise. For example, some businesses that outsourced call centres are moving back to the UK because customers did not respond well to dealing with people several thousand miles away who may not understand local UK conditions and issues.

In addition, having a workforce that is trained to be able to handle a wide range of functions within the business means that they are better able to be moved from task to task as required and this helps a business to maintain flexibility in response to external economic changes.

Summary and exam guidance

Summary

- Businesses can control many aspects of their internal affairs but have limited control over external changes in the economy.

- The economy refers to all the buying and selling that takes place over a period of time – in any one day this will amount to billions of transactions ranging from small to very large!

- There is a tendency for economies to demonstrate patterns of growth and slowdown over a period of time, referred to as the business cycle.

- As the rate of economic activity changes, so businesses will be affected in different ways depending on the type of business and the market they operate in.

- Key influences on business include inflation, interest rates, unemployment, economic growth and exchange rates. These are all intertwined in many ways and present complex challenges to businesses in coping with changes in these variables.

- Analysis of historical trends in economic variables may give some guide to future trends, but external shocks such as terrorist attack or natural disaster can cause significant changes that are difficult to account for.

- Emerging markets present both threats and opportunities to established and new businesses.

- Changing economic circumstances have to be dealt with by businesses that may develop a range of strategies to cope.

Exam practice

Read the article below and then answer the question that follows.

Article A

External influences on business

In the period 2004–2008 Sir Stuart Rose presided over a transformation of Marks and Spencer. Profits in 2007 topped £1 billion. Sir Stuart's achievements were lauded by City analysts. However, he now faces a challenge that may not be something he is able to do a great deal about. The problems M&S faced in the early part of this decade were internal; they were factors that the company could change to win back customers. These included store refurbishments and crucially offering customers the sort of clothes and products that they wanted rather than relying on the traditional lines that had served M&S so well in previous years.

The problems now facing Sir Stuart are external. The slowdown in the economy is hitting the business and the executive chairman has warned that sales have been slower and that he expects further difficulties in the coming months. He suggested that the slowdown is likely to last at least two years and that his company would have to adapt to the changed circumstances. He commented that consumers are changing their behaviour in response to the economic pressures that they are experiencing. For example, he pointed out that consumers may not be travelling to out of town retail centres, where M&S has some larger stores, as often as they were – perhaps making one journey rather than two and choosing to walk to local shopping facilities rather than take the car and journey to larger outlets.

Sir Stuart reiterated the fact that M&S' market position was clear in that they were offering quality food products and that they would have to find ways of attracting customers into stores. He did, however, stress that the rump of customers who contribute most to the company's revenue, would still be loyal to M&S but that the company would have to find ways of convincing this 80% to continue putting their faith in the business and that they would have to 'stay close' to the 20% who may be looking at cheaper alternatives.

In the three months to June 2008, like for like sales fell 5.8% and research by Experian showed that footfall fell by the same amount in June 2008 compared to June 2007. The share price on the stock exchange was around the 240p mark in the middle of 2008.

Source: Adapted from Biz/ed In the News: http://www.bized.co.uk/cgi-bin/chron/chron.pl?id=3125

Make a justified recommendation on ways in which Marks and Spencer could respond to the challenges of a slowdown in the UK economy. Your answer should include some reference to the economic variables that exist in the economy at the time of writing and the effect of these on M&S' strategies. (50 marks)

Total: 50 marks

Breakdown of assessment objectives

AO1 – Knowledge and understanding – 10/50
AO2 – Apply knowledge and understanding – 10/50
AO3 – Analyse problems, issues and situations – 15/50
AO4 – Evaluate, distinguish between fact and opinion, assess and judge information from a variety of sources – 15/50

Suggested structure

You will need to:

* Identify and explain the main economic variables that might impact on M&S.
* Show an ability to be able to understand the type of market that M&S operates in and the competitive pressures it faces.
* Be able to explain the impact on M&S of the slowdown in economic activity and be able to relate the different impact that might be experienced on different parts of its business.
* Use appropriate terms and concepts to be able to analyse and explain the effects (for example, price and income elasticity of demand).
* Outline at least two strategies that M&S might adopt to cope with the slowdown. Make sure that these are outlined in the context of M&S rather than just applying to any business.
* Make supported judgements about the likely success of the strategies you have outlined.
* Arrive at a conclusion in direct response to the question about the recommendation that you consider would have the most effect in coping with the slowdown for M&S.

Chapter 22   The relationship between businesses and the political and legal environment

Key terms

Aggregate demand The sum of all consumption spending, investment spending and government spending, and the difference between the amount generated from selling exports and that spent on imports, in the economy.

Aggregate supply The productive capacity of the economy; the total amount that could be produced given the existing resources within an economy.

Discretionary spending The amount of spending from income that is optional rather than compulsory, for example, mortgage spending would be seen as compulsory whereas the decision to buy a new HD TV would be part of discretionary spending.

External costs The costs of business activity that are experienced by a third party.

Fiscal policy Influencing the level of economic activity through changing the level of government income and expenditure.

Flexible labour markets A situation where the demand and supply of labour can adjust to changes in market conditions relatively quickly, for example, where workers have the transferable skills to be able to move from one occupation to another with ease.

Monetary policy Influencing the level of economic activity through affecting the price of money (interest rates) and/or the supply of money in the economy as a whole.

Private sector That part of the economy where business activity is owned, controlled and financed by private individuals.

Public sector That part of the economy which is owned, controlled and financed by the government.

Regulation Rules designed to control business behaviour.

The political and legal environment is closely bound together. In the UK, laws are made by Parliament. The focus of politicians invariably depends on what are considered to be important issues of the day. Legislation both from the UK government and from the European Union has a significant effect on businesses and the way they operate. The effects might include the regulations which they have to abide by, the legal requirements they have to meet, the effect on them directly of government economic policies, and the indirect effects that attempts to change behaviour for a particular reason have on business operations and their wider stakeholders. This chapter will offer a broad overview of this environment, and look at ways in which businesses are affected and how they respond to the challenges presented by government and the legal system.

The impact on businesses of changes in the political and legal environment can be summarised as follows:

- coping with changes which affect cost
- coping with the impact on competitiveness
- coping with the need to change behaviour
- responding through changes to product development and innovation.

Government intervention in the economy

Governments are elected to represent the will of the people. The ruling political party will have put forward a number of manifesto commitments on key areas including health, education, the economy, and so on. Once elected, they seek to put into place laws and structures to try and achieve the aims they set out in their manifesto. In so doing, governments impact on businesses in many ways, and in addition have to uphold existing laws and regulations.

Governments have two main objectives:

- **Economic objectives** – associated with maintaining stability in the economy. This will include creating the right environment for economic growth to occur, keeping control of inflation, working towards full employment (where those who want work are able to get it), whilst at the same time reducing the less desirable effects of economic growth – pollution and other external costs such as congestion.
- **Non-economic objectives** – these are associated with particular policies such as the reduction of child poverty, improving transport infrastructure, improving the health and general welfare of UK residents, reducing crime, and so on.

These two broad objectives impact on the way businesses operate in a significant way. For example, decisions on limits to carbon emissions, tax decisions on fuel, road pricing, and policies to improve education and training will all have a direct impact on the way businesses operate and their costs of production. In addition to this, government is an active part of the economy. Governments collect tax revenue and borrow money to finance a wide range of activities. The provision of services by the government will involve private sector businesses either working for or with the government on the provision of these services. Many businesses as a result are dependent to a large extent on contracts they have with government, both local and national. Businesses will be affected by the thrust of government economic policies and will also have to take account of changes that occur in legislation that are designed to bring about change and improve welfare. For example, the ban on smoking in all of the UK has had a significant impact on the way businesses have to work, on the way they organise their activities, and for some businesses, on their revenues and costs.

We can classify government intervention in the economy under four broad headings:

- regulation
- taxes and subsidies
- legislation
- economic policies.

The latter two will be dealt with in more detail later in this chapter. In addition to this, the government also provides a wide range of products. These include:

- health services
- education and training
- justice and legal services
- security through the armed forces and the emergency services
- scientific advice and professional scientific services, such as forensic science
- advice and practical help for businesses in foreign export markets
- bodies set up to provide advice and support for small businesses
- housing
- transport services
- help and advice for agriculture, for example, the government veterinary service
- environmental services, for example, the Environment Agency which deals with a wide variety of aspects with regard to the rural economy
- provision of sporting and arts facilities, such as museums, art galleries, and so on.

Regulation

Regulation is the setting of rules and codes of practice which business has to abide by. Regulation is generally set up to achieve particular aims, such as ensuring competition or reducing the potential harm that business activity can have on peoples' lives. The regulatory authorities tend to be independent bodies that have been set up specifically to monitor the behaviour of businesses within their remit and to take action where it is shown that there has been a breach of the regulations. Regulation provides a discipline within which businesses must operate, but in so doing it can mean that opportunities cannot be taken to expand the business and increase profitability, and meeting regulations can increase costs of production for businesses.

Regulation can be put in place to:

1 Help maintain health and safety for workers and others who come into contact with the business through the Health and Safety Executive (HSE).

2 Maintain standards; for example, the Advertising Standards Authority (ASA) monitor adverts by businesses and make recommendations in cases where members of the public have voiced complaints about an advert, either because it is seen as being misleading, making false claims, is offensive or inappropriate in some way.

3 Ensure that businesses do not exploit any market power that they may have to limit competition. This can relate to such cases as price fixing, where a group of businesses agree to fix the level of prices above the normal competitive rate; sales agreements where firms may 'share out' sales in particular regions and agree not to 'interfere' in each others' sales patches; price maintenance – linking prices together in some way or recommending a particular price be charged; sharing market information or any other form of collusion with the intention of restricting competition.

   The two main bodies associated with regulating competition are the Office of Fair Trading (OFT) and the Competition Commission. The main role of each is best summed up by the bodies themselves (see boxes opposite).

4 Control former nationalised industries. Since the 1980s, many large industries have been privatised; the ownership of these industries has passed into the private sector. The intention was to create a more competitive environment and improve services to customers. The very fact that some of these industries were split into a small number of very large firms with considerable monopoly power meant that regulatory bodies were set up to ensure that they did not abuse this power. Examples include Ofwat, the Water Services Regulatory Authority, Ofgem which regulates the gas and electricity supply industries and the Office of Rail Regulation.

In addition to these bodies, there are a number of local government trading standards offices which monitor business behaviour in relation to legislation at a local authority level.

SELF-REGULATION

There are also a number of voluntary agreements between firms in an industry to regulate themselves. There is an incentive for such firms to do this properly because they know that if they do not, then they run the risk of statutory regulation which could be far more limiting and damaging to them. Examples of self-regulatory bodies include the Portman Group which represents those in the alcoholic drinks industry, and the Press Complaints Commission which handles complaints about the press and enforces a code of practice agreed by the newspaper industry.

The Office of Fair Trading

The OFT is the UK's consumer and competition authority. Our mission is to make markets work well for consumers.

We pursue this goal by:

- encouraging businesses to comply with competition and consumer law and to improve their trading practices through self-regulation
- acting decisively to stop hardcore or flagrant offenders
- studying markets and recommending action where required
- empowering consumers with the knowledge and skills to make informed choices and get the best value from markets, and helping them resolve problems with suppliers through Consumer Direct.

Source: http://www.oft.gov.uk/about/

The Competition Commission

The Competition Commission (CC) is one of the independent public bodies which help ensure healthy competition between companies in the UK for the benefit of companies, customers and the economy.

We investigate and address issues of concern in three areas:

- In mergers – when larger companies will gain more than 25% market share and where a merger appears likely to lead to a substantial lessening of competition in one or more markets in the UK.
- In markets – when it appears that competition may be being prevented, distorted or restricted in a particular market.
- In regulated sectors where aspects of the regulatory system may not be operating effectively or to address certain categories of dispute between regulators and regulated companies.

Source: http://www.competition-commission.org.uk/about_us/index.htm

Taxes and subsidies

TAXES

The government raises funds to pay for its activities in the form of taxes. There are two main forms of taxation:

- Direct taxes are levied on the individual who is responsible for their payment. Examples of direct taxes include income tax and stamp duty.
- Indirect taxes are levied on a business that may pass on some or all of the tax to the consumer in the form of higher prices. The business is responsible for paying the tax, however. Examples of indirect taxes are VAT and excise duties on alcohol, tobacco and fuel.

The amount the government raises in taxes is staggering – over £550 billion in 2007. Government spending accounts for around 40% of total UK spending. The chart in Figure 22.1 (see next page) shows the main sources of government income.

The funds raised in tax revenue go towards providing the massive range of services associated with government – and the business opportunities that go with this provision.

The chart in Figure 22.2 (see next page) highlights the main areas of government spending.

Whilst one of the main functions of taxes is to raise revenue, they do impact on businesses significantly. Many smaller businesses find that they have to devote a considerable amount of time to completing documentation and understanding the requirements to pay the right amount of tax. For small businesses, understanding VAT returns can be particularly time-consuming and it not only adds to cost but also takes time away from the main purpose of

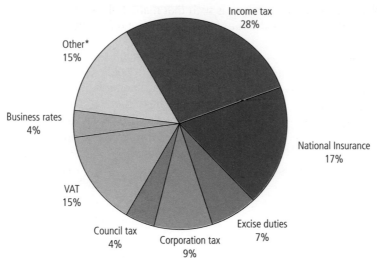

* Other receipts include capital taxes, stamp duties, vehicle excise duties, and some other tax and non-tax receipts, for example, interest and dividends.

Figure 22.1 C3: Government receipts by function 2008–09 (projections)

Source: http://www.hm-treasury.gov.uk/economic_data_and_tools/finance_spending_statistics/ pubsec_finance/psf_statistics.cfm

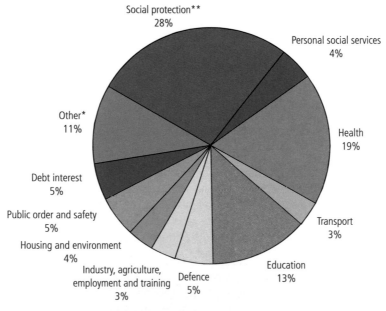

* Includes spending on general public services; recreation, culture and religion; international cooperation and development; public service pensions; plus spending yet to be allocated and some accounting adjustments.
** Includes tax credit payments in excess of an individual's tax liability, which are now counted in AME, in line with OECD guidelines.

Figure 22.2 B4: Government spending by function 2008–09 (projections)

Source: http://www.hm-treasury.gov.uk/economic_data_and_tools/finance_spending_statistics/ pubsec_finance/psf_statistics.cfm

the business. The complexity of tax for larger firms is such that many will employ tax specialists via their accountants to manage their tax responsibilities and find ways of reducing their tax liability.

Governments also use the tax system to change incentives and behaviour. This can relate to incentives to consumers to change behaviour and also incentives for businesses in the way that they operate. The tax system can be used to encourage businesses to invest, for example, to locate in particular areas, to invest in research and development, and so on. Taxes can also be used to discourage production and consumption of goods that are deemed inappropriate to the aims of a particular policy. In recent years, the duty on leaded petrol was higher than that on unleaded petrol. The incentive to both producers and consumers was to switch from leaded engines to unleaded, and within 10 years leaded petrol had become a thing of the past. In the same way, government has been increasing the tax on vehicles that emit higher levels of pollutants and which are less efficient in fuel use. The incentive for producers will be to search for more efficient engines and for consumers to also purchase vehicles that are subject to lower tax rates.

A tax on a product like a car has the effect of raising the price in some way. Either the tax is added directly to the product (as is the case with tobacco) or is levied on the producer who may in turn pass on some of the tax burden to the consumer in the form of a higher price. Basic knowledge of demand and supply tells us that when prices are higher, demand will fall.

One of the major social problems of the first part of the 21st century has been so-called 'binge drinking' – the consumption of five or more alcoholic drinks in any one session, often consumed quickly with the sole intention of getting drunk. Binge drinking imposes a number of social costs on society including increased vandalism, violence and anti-social behaviour, not to mention the cost of policing and the impact on the health service of treating those who are involved in accidents or violence.

One possible way of tackling the problem might be to discourage drinking by raising the tax on alcohol and thus increasing its price. The success of such a policy will depend on how large the tax increase is and who to levy it on. If levied on the producer, for example, they may choose to absorb the tax increase to maintain sales; if levied on the retailer they may also find ways of absorbing the tax, although smaller retailers like off-licences might not be able to do this and are affected more significantly. Either way, there is no guarantee of success as businesses are likely to find ways of minimising the impact of the tax change on their operations and sales. Consumers might not always react in the way that governments might expect or predict, which adds a further level of complexity to the government's plans or to the way that businesses react. The effect on consumption will also be dependent on the price elasticity of demand for alcohol. If price elasticity of demand is relatively elastic then a tax on alcohol will result in a larger proportionate change in demand, but if it is inelastic the increase in price might raise more revenue but have a limited effect on consumption.

Binge drinking has led to a number of social and health problems arising. There is a debate as to whether taxing alcohol more heavily would reduce consumption.

SUBSIDIES

A subsidy is the opposite of a tax. It is a sum of money given to a producer to help lower the cost of production or make a product more affordable to the consumer. Subsidies are used to encourage production or consumption of goods and services that the government believes are important or desirable. For example, whilst taxing tobacco might be one way of discouraging consumption of cigarettes, government has also provided subsidised access to nicotine patches as a way of helping people kick the habit.

The most high-profile use of subsidies has been in agriculture. The European Union (EU) has used them to promote the production of a wide range of commodities, including milk and beef, and internationally subsidies have been used to promote production of bananas, cotton, coffee and steel, amongst others. Subsidies can be very effective at increasing production, but by artificially reducing the cost of production they distort the market mechanism and the signals that price gives to both producers and consumers. In the EU there has been considerable over-production of some agricultural products and the existence of subsidies in the cotton industry has affected the livelihoods of cotton growers in less-developed countries in a negative way.

Similarly, subsidies to encourage the production of biofuels have had effects on other markets. Biofuels use agricultural crops such as wheat, sugar cane, oil seed rape, palm oil and corn. The rising price of oil-based fuels has driven the search for alternative fuels, and biofuels have been seen as one way of diversifying the consumption of energy. To encourage production of crops for biofuels, various subsidies were put in place. The effect has been significant according to some reports. The diversion of crops to biofuel production has contributed to shortages in supplies of some crops when demand is rising, and in addition the subsidies have encouraged more felling of trees to clear land in the rainforests to produce palm oil. Some are suggesting that the subsidy has helped to distort the market and in any event, the cost in terms of carbon emissions in the production of biofuels more than cancels out the benefits to the environment!

Subsidies have been used to encourage the production of crops for biofuels

Subsidies can, therefore, be of benefit in changing consumption and encouraging production, and businesses that can access subsidies can see major benefits. What has to be taken into account in the discussion on subsidies are the wider costs and benefits associated with their introduction, not least in this consideration is that tax payers effectively have to fund subsidies.

Legislation

There are very few laws passed or which exist that do not impact on businesses in some way. Many laws are passed to directly influence business behaviour and are designed to provide protection for consumers, employees, shareholders, and other stakeholders such as the wider community who may be affected by business behaviour and operations. Key legislation affecting business covers employment, consumer law, contract law, financial transactions and reporting, taxation, competition, acquisitions, company organisation, responsibilities of companies and their owners, minimum wage legislation, laws relating to health and safety matters, fraud and corruption and insolvency – to name but some.

The need to abide by legislation will add to businesses' costs. Small businesses can be affected disproportionately by some types of legislation. For most businesses they will have to adapt the way they operate to accommodate their legal responsibilities, and this can affect their competitive position not only domestically but in international markets. The situation becomes even more complex when businesses operate in different countries that may have different legal requirements and structures. A broad outline of key employment and consumer legislation is considered later in this chapter.

Government economic policies

One of government's most important functions is to preside over a stable and growing economy. Given that government spending accounts for around 40% of total spending, it can use this to influence the level of economic activity. There are three main ways in which the government (or its representatives) can affect the economy:

- monetary policy
- supply-side policy
- fiscal policy.

We will deal with each one in turn.

Monetary policy

Monetary policy attempts to influence the level of economic activity (the amount of buying and selling in the economy) through changes to the amount of money in circulation and the price of money – short-term interest rates. By altering interest rates, various effects ripple through the economy to bring about the desired changes in economic activity. These changes do not necessarily occur quickly and it has been estimated that the full impact of interest rate changes may not be seen for 18 months.

Since 1997, the responsibility for monetary policy has been with the Bank of England. It is given a target rate of inflation by the government (2% at the time of writing) which it is required to achieve over a period of time. The Monetary Policy Committee (MPC) of the Bank of England meets over two days each month to discuss the prospects for inflation and decide on the Bank Rate. This is the rate at which the Bank of England will lend to the banking system and it determines the whole structure of interest rates in the UK. In simple terms, if the Bank increases its lending rate, then other lending institutions throughout the banking system will be likely to increase theirs, and vice versa.

What this means is that whether you are an individual looking to borrow money to buy a car, a couple looking to buy a home, a business seeking lending for investment, a saver looking for a good return on your savings, a multi-national company with dealings on the foreign exchange markets, or an insurance company or pension fund looking to find the best return for clients, the interest rate will affect your decision and the outcome of those decisions in some way.

The three diagrams in Figures 22.3 to 22.5 (see next page) illustrate the way in which changes in interest rates work their way through the economy and affect the key elements of economic activity – consumption and investment.

The diagrams show just how pervasive and powerful changes in interest rates can be on business activity. Businesses, large and small, will not only have to cope with the direct effect of any change in the interest rate on their operations, such as a rise in the cost of loans if interest rates are increased, for example, but also the indirect effects which work through the way in which interest rates impact on discretionary spending and consumption, and investment decisions.

Skills watch!

A01/A03/A04

Assess the likely impact on a publisher of school textbooks, of a decision by the government to subsidise the purchase of textbooks, whilst at the same time imposing a tax on Internet use through a charge on broadband accounts.

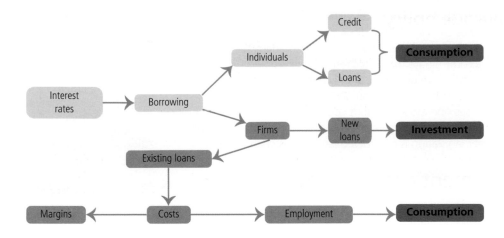

Figure 22.3 The effect of a change in interest rates on individuals and firms

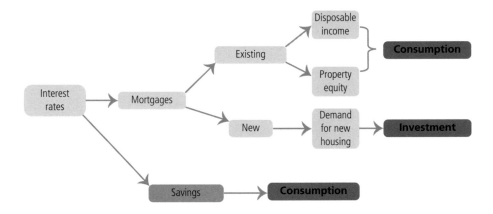

Figure 22.4 The effect of changes in interest rates through the housing market

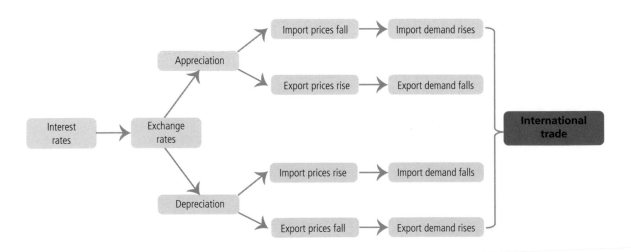

Figure 22.5 The effect of changes in interest rates on foreign trade

Supply-side policy

An important part of the economy is the level of **aggregate demand** which includes all the consumption decisions by households, investment by firms, government spending and the difference between the amount earned through selling exports and that spent on imports. The level of aggregate demand helps determine the level of economic activity. However, on the other side is the ability of the economy to produce goods and services, and this is referred to as **aggregate supply**.

A healthy economy should be capable of adapting to changes in aggregate demand, but there might be a number of structures that exist that might limit this capability. Governments now place great importance on pursuing policies to try and improve the flexibility of the economy to be able to respond to changes. The intention of supply-side policy is to increase the long-term productive capacity of the economy. If the supply side of the economy can be improved, then it will be possible to sustain economic growth in the long term without increases in demand causing pressure on prices – in other words, generating inflation.

These policies tend to be long-term policies and there are arguments about how effective they are. An example of a supply-side policy would be lowering personal and business taxes to increase incentives, with the aim of reducing welfare dependency, and increasing the ease and urge to find work. The extent to which such policies work is subject to considerable debate.

Supply-side policies also aim to influence the productivity and efficiency of the economy. A key feature of them are attempts to open up markets and deregulate to improve efficiency in the working of markets and the allocation of resources.

The main areas of policy are listed below.

THE LABOUR MARKET

This includes:

- Policies to reduce the difficulties the unemployed find in getting jobs and the ease with which businesses can create jobs, for example, reducing bureaucracy and 'red tape' with the intention of creating flexible labour markets.
- Monitoring the power of trade unions – legislation passed in the 1980s still has an impact on businesses in this respect.
- The availability of short-term contracts and flexible working arrangements.
- The ease with which firms can respond to changing demand through recruiting and shedding labour.
- Contracts, terms and conditions, pay.

Job centres aim to try to help those looking for work find information and get advice about job vacancies that exist, to help improve the efficiency with which people can find work

The main criticism of such policies is that they put the needs of employers above those of workers which can lead to exploitation and an infringement of workers' rights.

TAX AND WELFARE REFORM

This includes:

- More stringent benefit regimes which make it harder for individuals to claim benefits, or which encourage claimants to seek work rather than claim benefits (through making it worthwhile to have a job rather than claiming benefits).
- Tax reform to encourage people to find work. This might include ways of making it easier for single-parent families to access work by providing subsidised childcare.
- Improving access to training and education.

EDUCATION AND TRAINING

This includes:

- Improving access to training and education.
- Reform of 14–19 education.
- Encouraging the development and availability of modern apprenticeships.
- Expansions of vocational qualifications such as NVQs that tend to be competence-based, and assess the extent to which individuals can demonstrate key skills in the workplace rather than focusing on examinations that assess different skills.
- Expansion of university access – the aim of the Labour government after 1997 was to have 50% of school leavers going on to university education.

INCENTIVES AND TECHNOLOGY

This includes:

- Tax reform to encourage incentives and entrepreneurial spirit.
- Incentives to develop new technology to improve investment and innovation.
- A drive to embracing the 'knowledge-driven economy'.
- Regional policies to encourage enterprise, investment, location and expansion.

In theory, the benefits of supply-side policies in the longer term are huge. The problem is that because they often take many years to implement, it is hard to measure the precise effects. There is little doubt, however, that the business landscape has changed markedly over the last 30 years and that many businesses now understand and embrace the idea that flexibility is a key source of competitive advantage in a global economy that is changing at a rapid rate.

Fiscal policy

Fiscal policy refers to attempts to influence the level of economic activity though manipulation of government income and expenditure to achieve desired objectives. Because government spending is such a large part of total aggregate demand, the way it chooses to raise finance and what it decides to spend tax revenue on has a powerful effect on economic activity as a whole.

Fiscal policy was primarily associated with Keynesian demand management policies after the Second World War, where it seemed that government attempts to use its income and expenditure to maintain low levels of unemployment and encourage economic growth worked. Its role is now seen as being rather different, but there is still no doubt that government spending policies do have major influences on the level of economic activity as a whole.

One of the problems of fiscal policy is that spending decisions by government requires funds, and tax revenue is dependent on the level of economic activity. If economic activity slows down, then tax revenue is lower, and so government has to borrow money to fund its spending plans. Increased borrowing by the government has the effect of pushing up interest rates and will also build debt which future generations have to pay off. The reverse is also the case and would be a possible aim of government in times of greater economy activity.

Monetary policy has tended to take the primary role in overall influence on the economy, whereas fiscal policy can be used to change incentives and behaviour to create desired outcomes.

For example, if the government's aim is to reduce child poverty, then the tax system, the welfare benefits system and spending plans can all be mobilised to try to help bring about conditions to reduce the number of children in poverty. This might affect businesses in terms of policies to encourage them to take on employees, spending on refurbishment and building of infrastructure and housing, improving education and training to help people find work and legislation on the minimum wage. All these would affect businesses both directly and indirectly.

A decision to raise the minimum wage affects businesses – directly by raising wage costs and indirectly by workers seeking to maintain wage differentials.

When considering fiscal policy as a means of influencing economic activity, a number of important issues arise. It is rare that governments actually change the rate of income tax if they want to influence consumer spending; instead changes can be brought about through the adjustment of income tax allowances which change the amount that people earn before they are liable to income tax. VAT has been at 17.5% since the early 1990s when it was increased from 15% – but not on all goods. The government has used extensions and/or amendments to the range of goods covered by VAT as a means of changing incentives and behaviour. In 2008, there was a temporary reduction in VAT from 17.5% to 15% to try to stimulate demand in the face of the economic slowdown which was occurring.

Governments will also change the rules under which tax has to be paid – married persons' allowances, inheritance taxes, stamp duties, and so on, all of which have an impact on different businesses. The changes to stamp duty (the tax paid on capital gains from house sales) has affected the housing market significantly including estate agents, solicitors who handle conveyancing, house builders, and so on. Certain taxes have been abolished which affects people in different ways, for example – MIRAS (Mortgage Interest Relief At Source). Opposition parties will invariably accuse government of seeking to introduce 'stealth taxes' – taxes which affect people without them really knowing it! Much of this is a 'tinkering' with the tax system to achieve certain aims.

Political decisions affecting trade and access to markets

The UK is part of the European Union (EU). The EU contains 25 countries at the time of writing and has been enlarged considerably since 2000. Membership of the EU has implications for member states. Within the EU there are meant to be no barriers to the movement of goods, services, capital and labour. For firms outside the EU, the existence of a common external tariff has the effect of making it harder to sell their goods and services within the EU. Equally, for businesses from member states of the EU, trade with countries outside the EU may be subject to different trade barriers including tariffs, quotas and non-tariff barriers.

Removing barriers to trade is seen as a key driver for future global economic growth and an important method of helping poorer countries to gain access to markets in the EU and elsewhere. The political will to make this a reality is always tempered by recognition of the effects that such decisions will have on domestic businesses. Opening up markets in the EU to businesses from Africa, South America and parts of Asia opens up the possibility of large-scale structural changes in the economy, with many firms in the EU finding that they are

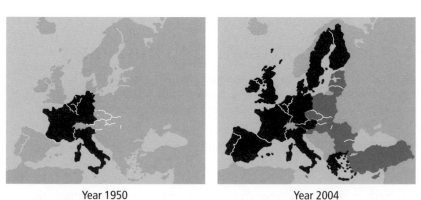

Year 1950   Year 2004

Member states

Applicant status

Figure 22.6 Growth in EU population

unable to compete with the low wages paid in many of these countries, and as a consequence the significant cost advantages that businesses in these countries might have.

For businesses in the UK and EU, the possibilities of a greater threat from competition as a result of the opening up of markets and freer trade, is counterbalanced by the opportunities that present themselves for investment and joint ventures in these markets, as well as the opening up of significant marketing opportunities. Many larger-scale businesses in Europe are operating in mature markets where the prospects for growth are very limited. If the movement to free trade accelerates in the coming years, then the opportunity to build market share in these emerging markets is significant.

The market for motor vehicles and tobacco are two such examples of where potential market growth exists. Car manufacturers are finding that sales in mature markets in the UK and the EU are fairly flat and, despite the development of new vehicles, the scope for significant expansion is limited. Tobacco producers have found that the legislation restricting smoking, the wealth of data concerning the danger to health of tobacco products and the high levels of duty on tobacco products have severely dented sales.

Both car and tobacco manufacturers are looking at markets in Africa and Asia as being opportunities to revive their fortunes and grow their markets. Of course, with a product like tobacco there are considerable ethical issues associated with expansion into these markets where education and training in relation to the dangers of tobacco are likely to be far less widespread than those in the UK or EU.

The enlargement of the EU

As new countries have joined the EU there have been major changes – both threats and opportunities – to businesses that have come about as a consequence. Many of the countries that have joined were former communist bloc states which operated under a very different political and economic system. These economies have undergone rapid structural change and as a result are now classed as emerging economies. The enlargement of the EU has increased the potential market for business by many millions.

The changes to these economies and their integration into the EU have led to many changes. Businesses have had the opportunity to be able to invest and expand their operations in these countries. There are opportunities covering a wide range of different businesses. For example, the accession of Bulgaria to the EU has opened up the chance for tourism with companies like First Choice offering both summer and winter holidays in the country. Nokia, the Finnish mobile phone manufacturer, had a plant in Germany making handsets. In 2008 it announced that it was closing the plant and moving operations to Romania. The reasons were simple – the cost of German workers was around 10 times that of their Romanian equivalents. The move created over 4,000 jobs in Romania but led to the loss of 2,300 jobs at the German plant along with a further 1,000 estimated in firms involved in the supply chain network to the plant in Germany.

The impact of legislation relating to businesses

The extent of the legislation relating to business has been outlined earlier in this chapter. At A2 you are not required to have any detailed knowledge or understanding of these laws but instead to have a broad understanding of the scope of the laws affecting business and how such laws affect a business.

We will now take an overview of these laws.

CONTRACT LAW

A contract is a legally binding agreement between two or more businesses or individuals. Each party to a contract has a legal right to redress if the other party breaks the contract in any way. Entering into a contact therefore places obligations and responsibilities on both

THE ADVANTAGES AND DISADVANTAGES OF EU ENLARGEMENT

Advantages

- **Economic growth** Enlargement will generate economic growth. UK business could find trade and investment opportunities increase with the new states.

- **Stability** Membership of the EU will bring with it political stability to the new democracies of Eastern Europe as they reform their legal and government institutions as part of the accession process. Such stability is important to UK businesses considering investing in these new economies.

- **Foreign Direct Investment (FDI)** Membership of the EU and the euro will increase the amount of Foreign Direct Investment in the New Member States. This could benefit the financial sector in the UK which is a major player in such markets.

- **Structural funds** The regional aid which attempts to redistribute funds from the wealthier regions of the EU to the poorer ones will be made available to the New Member States. This will help develop these countries and improve infrastructure. Improvements in infrastructure will again be a benefit to trade and investment by UK businesses. Many UK businesses might also benefit directly through being involved in such projects.

- **Migration** Enlargement could produce high levels of migration as workers move from the new member states to the old member states. UK businesses might find that it benefits from the skills that these people have.

Disadvantages

- **Common Agricultural Policy**
  The controversial Common Agricultural Policy will be extended to the new member states, many of which have predominantly rural economies. The CAP includes measures such as subsidies and income guarantee schemes for farmers, which could prove to be hugely expensive if extended and a drain on the economies of old member states. UK agricultural businesses could suffer as a result.

- **EU standards and systems** There are concerns that some New Member States will not have the necessary standards and systems in place, e.g. in meeting standards in food hygiene, and regulations on agricultural production. UK businesses might experience problems in adjusting to these standards and working with them when they are operating in and with the new member countries.

- **The legacy of the Soviet Economy**
  In some of the states of the former Soviet bloc, certain areas of industry may not have had time to catch up with those of the EU, but as a result they have considerable cost advantages, especially labour costs. This could lead to a tendency to look to relocate in low-cost labour countries such as Romania.

parties. Contracts form a fundamental part of any business operations. Contracts will be signed between firms relating to the carrying out of specific tasks and work, the provision of services, the obligations relating to the supply of goods, employment contracts, acquisitions, and so on.

A simple example of such a contract would be where one business enters into an agreement with another to supply a specified quantity of a component part with particular specifications over an agreed period of time. If there was a delay to the delivery which was deemed to be due to the negligence of the supplier, the business could sue for damages caused to the business. Such damages might include loss of earnings as a result of the delayed delivery.

If contracts are breached there are usually four main ways in which the courts can respond:

- Order the party guilty of breaching the contract to pay compensation, known as damages, to the injured party.
- Order a party to carry out and meet its obligations under the contract.
- Issue an injunction preventing one party from doing something.
- Issue a declaration which clarifies the position of the contract to which both sides must comply.

CONSUMER LAW

The interaction between the consumer and business is the subject of a wide variety of legislation. The key laws are listed below.

The Sale of Goods Act 1979

This law covers the basic relationship between the customer and the business. It states that goods must be as described, of appropriate quality and fit for purpose. If a good breaks these basic rules, the consumer has the right to a refund, a replacement or compensation. There are a number of rules that relate to the rights of both parties.

What would this have to do to qualify under the Trade Descriptions Act?

Trade Descriptions Act 1968

This aims to prevent businesses providing misleading information or claims to consumers. The Act will be affected by the adoption in the UK of the EU Unfair Commercial Practices Directive, which came into force in April 2008 and aims to try and harmonise laws on consumer protection in the EU.

The Supply of Goods and Services Act 1982

This covers work done by tradespeople, professionals such as dentists, solicitors and hairdressers, and so on. The Act covers the use of materials, the care and attention paid to the work, prices, completion dates and crucially, the fact that a supplier of services has a duty of care to the customer and the property if appropriate. This means that the supplier must take every care to reduce the potential for injury or damage resulting from their work.

The Weights and Measures Act 1985

This law and its various updates helps protect consumers in relation to the weights and volumes of goods they are sold. If a consumer pays for a litre of petrol at a filling station, they should expect to get a litre – not any more nor any less.

The Food Safety Act 1990

This law aims to protect consumers from danger from food production. The Act covers everyone who is involved in food production, food processing, storage, distribution and sale of food.

The Consumer Credit Act 2006

This requires any business that seeks to provide finance or loans to consumers to be licensed by the Office for Fair Trading, which provides guidelines and strict rules for the provision of consumer credit. It provides the right to the customer to cancel a credit agreement within certain time periods.

EMPLOYMENT LAW

There are a number of laws that establish the rights and responsibilities of employers and employees in the workplace. One of the underlying principles of such legislation is the equal treatment of workers regardless of their age, race, sex, disability, and so on. Employment law also establishes the rights and responsibilities of employers and employees with regard to the way that workers are recruited, how they are treated in the workplace, their health and safety and welfare, and their rights to paid holidays, time off work for pregnancy, for compassionate leave, and their rights in relation to redundancy or dismissal.

In addition, the introduction of minimum wage legislation in 1999 has had a significant impact on workers, but also many businesses, especially those that tend to employ relatively low-paid workers or who are in low value-added businesses. The following are the main employment laws affecting businesses:

- The Equal Pay Act 1970
- Employment Relations Bill 2004
- Sex Discrimination Act 1975
- Trade Union Reform and Employment Rights Act 1993
- Control of Substances Hazardous to Health Regulations 2002
- Disability Discrimination Act 1995
- Race Relations Act 1976
- Employment Act 2002
- Health and Safety at Work Act 1974
- Employment Equality (AGE) Regulations (2006) Act.

Laws such as the Disability Discrimination Act 1995 also have implications for businesses that have websites, for example. A website must provide the opportunity for anyone to access it fully regardless of their ability. For example, some users might not be able to operate a mouse, read text or may suffer from colour blindness. Web developers must take these factors into consideration when building websites.

There are also a number of EU directives which firms in the UK have to abide by. Many of these directives echo the laws already in existence in the UK, but some do have implications for some businesses outside UK law. For example, the Working Time Directive (WTD) seeks to lay down some basic ground rules regarding the number of hours individuals are expected to work. The WTD imposes a limit of an average of 48 hours' work for each seven days, specifies the amount of rest periods workers should get and the amount of statutory holiday periods they should be entitled to. It does not prevent people working over a certain number of hours at any particular time, but rather specifies the average number of hours per week that is deemed appropriate, on health and safety grounds, to work. It is possible, therefore, for a worker to have to put in 60 hours per week during a busy time, provided that at some point in the future that extra time is recognised and the **average** working week does not exceed 48 hours.

Other relevant EU directives include:

- Equal Pay Directive
- Equal Treatment Directive
- Part-time Workers Directive
- Parental Leave Directive
- Pregnant Workers Directive.

Skills watch!

AO3 / AO4

Discuss the likely impact of the main aspects of consumer and employer legislation on a business such as a fast food restaurant. Which of the range of legislation do you think will be the **most** important to such a business and why?

DATA PROTECTION ACT 1998

The other major law that has had a significant impact on business is the Data Protection Act 1998. The DPA covers the rules relating to the way that information on living persons is collected, stored and handled. The Act is very complex and the responsibility it places on businesses for the way it handles information about people is significant. It has a high degree of relevance given the massive amount of information that businesses are now able to generate and collect about customers as a result of developments in technology and the use of the Internet. The emphasis on the need to afford appropriate degrees of privacy in the way

Businesses have access to large amounts of information about customers/clients/patients, etc. The DPA has a significant effect on businesses.

that information is handled can provide customers with problems as well as businesses. For example, a business should not discuss financial matters with the husband if the account under discussion is in the name of his wife unless there has been express permission granted by both parties. This can be frustrating for both customers and businesses but is something that businesses have to adapt to.

ENVIRONMENTAL LEGISLATION

There is a wide range of laws covering protection of the environment, such as the Environmental Protection Act 1990, The Water Resources Act 1991, The Clean Air Act 1993, The Control of Substances Hazardous to Health Regulations 1994 and The Environment Act 1995. These laws, along with a host of other regulations, specify the responsibilities businesses have with regard to pollution, waste, dealing with contaminated land, dealing with asbestos, the transport and handling of dangerous and toxic substances, how emergencies are to be dealt with, the level and quality of emissions allowed, disposing of waste into water courses and rivers, and so on. In addition, the government also levied a tax on waste disposed in landfill sites (The Landfill Tax).

HEALTH AND SAFETY LEGISLATION

The main act relating to health and safety at work is the Health and Safety at Work Act 1974. The Act covers the responsibilities that businesses have in relation to occupational health and safety. The Act is wide-ranging and is enforced by the Health and Safety Executive (HSE). Its main provisions include:

- Ensuring the workplace is safe and without risks to health.
- Ensuring plant and machinery are safe and that adequate protection and safety devices are in place.
- Making sure that policies and procedures to maintain health and safety are implemented.
- Ensuring potentially dangerous substances and items are moved, stored and used safely.
- Provision of training and information to ensure that health and safety are maintained.
- Making sure that everyone is aware of first aid facilities and emergency procedures.
- Drawing up a health and safety policy in businesses which have more than five employees.
- Ensuring that equipment is maintained and that all precautions against defects are taken.
- Taking adequate precautions to protect employees from radiation, electrical shock, noise and danger from accidents.
- Providing adequate protective clothing and ensuring that the work environment meets minimum standards of hygiene, warmth and ventilation.
- Making sure that warning signs are maintained, clear and understood by employees.

Health and Safety laws place demands on businesses to meet certain responsibilities. Such laws help to protect but add to costs.

Evaluating responses of businesses to a changing political and legal environment

At the start of the chapter we identified the main ways in which businesses are affected by changes in the political and legal environment. Many of the changes outlined in this chapter have to be incorporated by businesses – if a new law is passed that directly impacts on a business, they have to find ways to accommodate that law. It is the success with which a business is able to adjust to the changes that is important and which will impact on its long-term future.

Coping with changes which affect cost

Changes in the regulatory framework, tax policies, economic policies such as interest rate changes, and legislation, will all tend to have a varying impact on costs. For example, legislation in the UK on disabilities meant that businesses had to ensure that their premises were accessible to everybody regardless of their situation. Many had to make changes to their premises to accommodate this legislation which might have included accessible entrances, lifts for wheelchairs, sound loops to help the hard of hearing, vocal announcements in lifts, information presented in large type or Braille for those who have sight defects, and so on.

For some small businesses, the cost of meeting the legislation might be prohibitive and in those cases they would have to show that they had taken all reasonable steps to make their premises accessible. For large businesses, the cost of adapting premises can be substantial. In both cases businesses have to abide by the new laws, regulations and so on, and so have to adjust their operations accordingly. When costs rise there are three main things that the business can do to cope.

1 Absorb the costs themselves.
2 Pass on the cost to the consumer in the form of higher prices.
3 Find a way of increasing productivity to help reduce the average costs and maintain margins.

The degree to which they can do one or a combination of these will be important in the way they are able to remain competitive and continue in business. Which option or combination of options they choose will have an impact on their profitability, but it may well be that some businesses will be prepared to sacrifice short-term profits for longer-term survival and strategies which can lead to greater market share in the future and thus the possibility of higher future profitability.

Coping with the impact on competitiveness

Changes in regulation, legislation and so on can be a burden to business but can also be used as a means of highlighting differences between businesses, especially in a highly-competitive environment. Some businesses are able, for example, to highlight the extent to which they take their legal responsibilities seriously and show that they go far beyond the minimum legal requirements to cater for the needs of their employees and customers.

Subsidies can help to give a business a competitive advantage, but it must be remembered that the subsidy may not always be there and so the business has to build in efficient operations and contingencies for the time when the subsidy is removed. The farming industry has been particularly hard hit by the move to scale down and remove subsidies. In relying on subsidies, some farmers have found that when they are removed they are no longer able to operate. Others have seen the changes coming and have looked at ways in which they can diversify their operations and/or make their core operations highly efficient as a means of coping with the changes.

Where taxes are imposed or where the business has to incorporate minimum wage legislation, the situation is likely to be the same for all businesses in that sector. For example, the hotel and catering industry tends to employ a large number of low-paid staff who receive the minimum wage. If the minimum wage is increased then they will all have to pay it. However, some may choose to make some staff redundant; others may adopt one or more of the three responses outlined above.

Firms hit by increases in taxes or duties on their products might have to think of other ways to market the products to maintain or increase sales. This might involve looking at the marketing mix carefully and analysing markets, both existing and new, to see whether there are opportunities for expansion elsewhere or modifying the mix to better meet customer needs.

For example, whisky producers in Scotland invariably complain about any increase in duty on their product. Many, though, have been able to expand their operations and have sought new markets abroad. The strength of these markets will determine whether they can remain competitive in response to the rise in price that will result – unless they absorb the duty and accept slimmed-down profit margins.

Coping with the need to change behaviour

Invariably the rulings of politicians and changes in the legal and regulatory framework will mean that a business has to change its behaviour. The extent of the effect of the change will depend on just how significantly it will be affected by the changes concerned. In some cases the change will require adjustments to its systems or operations, or adjustments to software and IT systems to manage the change. For example, the Data Protection Act 1998 has presented significant challenges to many businesses in the way in which they operate. Systems have had to be put in place to ensure data is secure; staff have had to be trained to understand the implications of the Act and what they can and cannot do with individuals' data. For example, if an individual hires a motor vehicle, the hire company will take details of the driving licence of the hirer. The company has a legal responsibility to destroy those details after a period of time. Staff have to be aware of this and have a system in place to regularly review files and destroy data.

In other cases, the change in behaviour might actually have implications for other legal requirements. Laws giving mothers greater rights during and after pregnancy in terms of maternity leave and maternity pay may sound perfectly reasonable and socially desirable. Large firms may be in a position to meet the legislation and be able to manage its human resources appropriately to minimise disruption to production and its operations. Small firms may face a very different situation.

Take the case of a small firm who employs just three people. If one of these is a female who becomes pregnant, then finding ways to cover for that worker and find the money to pay for maternity benefit may be prohibitive. In response some may avoid offering jobs to females aged between 20 and 35 because they may fear that there is a possibility they will get pregnant. This contravenes equal treatment directives and the Sex Discrimination Act, as well as age discrimination legislation, but it may be the only way the business sees as being able to cope with the legislation.

Laws passed to help a particular group in society may end up creating problems for them that were unintended because businesses begin to behave in a different way. Of course, no business could admit that they did not offer a job to a 25-year old newly-married woman because they feared they might start a family soon, but the business will try to find other reasons why that potential employee was not suitable to avoid the possibility of legal action being brought against them.

Responding through changes to product development and innovation

Many of the issues covered in this chapter will have an effect on competitiveness in some way. One of the ways of responding will be to look at developing new products and to innovate to cope with the changes and maintain and even increase competitiveness. Innovation refers to the process by which a new idea is put into practice, and can include bringing new products or services to the market and developing new ways of working within the organisation.

If taxes, for example, have been imposed on a product to deter its use, then there is an incentive for businesses to try and develop new and different products to meet customer needs but which might not be subject to the tax. For example, taxes on cigarettes have led to a number of initiatives by tobacco companies to reduce the amount of tar and even produce tobacco-free and smokeless cigarettes.

The tax on fuel and the increasing concerns over vehicle emissions has led to motor manufacturers investing large sums in finding more energy-efficient engines and into smaller cars, as well as hydrogen cells and electric cars. In the UK and elsewhere, the ban on smoking in public places means that pubs and clubs have had to try and think of ways to meet the needs of their smoking customers, whilst at the same time not breaching the law.

New product development and innovation can be on different levels; some large organisations may be able to invest large sums of money to research products that meet legislative and regulatory guidelines; smaller firms might not be in such a fortunate position, but it will depend to a large extent on the size of the impact on the business of the changes.

Summary and exam guidance

Summary

- Governments intervene to protect individuals and to implement policies outlined in its election manifesto.

- Governments will have both economic and non-economic objectives and both will affect how businesses operate.

- The main areas of government intervention include:
  - levying taxes
  - implementing subsidies
  - passing laws
  - economic policies to help direct the economy.

- Key government economic policies include:
  - monetary policy – controlling the price of money and the money supply
  - supply-side policy – used to try and improve the efficiency of the economy
  - fiscal policy – using government income and expenditure to influence economic activity.

- Both at national and international level, political decisions relating to free trade and economic cooperation (such as the EU) present both threats and opportunities.

- There are wide-ranging laws covering almost every aspect of business operations.

- Key laws affecting businesses relate to consumers and employees, but also affect systems operations such as that generated by the Data Protection Act 1998.

- Businesses have to find ways around the challenges that political and legal changes present.

Exam practice

Read the article below and then answer the questions that follow.

Article A

A fiscal boost

The response to the slowdown in the economy in the United States (US) in 2008 saw two major initiatives. First there were several cuts in interest rate by the Federal Reserve. Then an announcement from the US government that Democrats and Republicans had reached an agreement to inject $150 billion worth of cash into the economy. This was done by sending US citizens cheques of up to $1,200 per household. US citizens earning at least $3,000 but less than $75,000 a year (around £38,000) will receive the cheques and children will get $300. The aim was to put money in the hands of 'those who will spend it immediately' and thus help to provide a boost to consumption and kick-start the economy.

This package is being seen as a highly unusual step but then again, commentators view the situation as being highly unusual. There are many people who have never experienced a recession and those who have been touched by such an economic slowdown might see such a move by the US government as being a useful step to help soften the economic landing.

Commentators were asking whether the fiscal boost was targeted at the right people. Primarily the money needs to be given to those who have a high marginal propensity to consume – those for whom the proportion of any extra $1 in income spent on consumption is high rather than being saved. Should such money, therefore be targeted at low income earners or middle income earners?

Other questions that were asked included whether $150 billion would be enough? There were incentives for business but some US politicians, whilst agreeing with some sort of fiscal boost, suggested that the money could be better spent in different ways. Would a temporary rise in unemployment benefits have a bigger effect on the economy, for example?

Source: Biz/ed 'In the News':
http://www.bized.co.uk/cgi-bin/chron/chron.pl?id=3014

(a) Analyse the way in which the joint monetary and fiscal boost was designed to 'kick-start' the economy in the US. (16 marks)

(b) Assess the likely impact on businesses of the measures adopted by the US authorities. (34 marks)

Total: 50 marks

Breakdown of assessment objectives

AO1 – Knowledge and understanding – 10/50
AO2 – Apply knowledge and understanding – 5/50
AO3 – Analyse problems, issues and situations – 15/50
AO4 – Evaluate, distinguish between fact and opinion, assess and judge information from a variety of sources – 20/50

Suggested structure

For part (a) you will need to:

- Give a clear definition of both fiscal and monetary policy in the context of the United States.
- Provide a breakdown of the way in which reductions in interest rates by the Federal Reserve will feed into the economy and promote economic activity.
- Provide a breakdown of the way in which the fiscal injection will feed through to increased economic activity by demonstrating how consumption is expected to be affected.

For part (b) you will need to:

- Demonstrate how a range of different businesses might expect to be affected by the fiscal stimulus.
- Include reference to the way businesses might expect to be affected by both the cut in interest rates and the spending by the US government.
- Your analysis should include businesses of different sizes that produce different products.
- Utilise key concepts such as income elasticity of demand.
- Take account of the point in the evidence of the effect that the amount people choose to spend might have on businesses.
- Consider the implications to businesses on stock levels, short-term effects, the longer-term impact after the initial spending has worked its way through, the effect on suppliers, and so on.
- Make judgements throughout about the extent to which businesses will benefit and be affected by the measures. Will the reduction in interest rates affect businesses more, or will the fiscal stimulus have more of an effect?
- Relate your judgements to the different effects on large and small businesses – those that are likely to benefit to a large extent and those that might hardly notice any change at all.
- Arrive at a conclusion in direct response to the question about the extent of the impact – will it really make the difference that was hoped or might there be other factors that will reduce the impact of the policies?

Chapter 23   The relationship between businesses and the social environment

The social environment looks at the interaction of business with society – the way people act in groups. Social change can be slow but can also be rapid. There are difficulties in predicting how people will respond to different issues that emerge, and this puts pressure on business to adapt in the right way to meet the changing needs of customers which they might not be able to predict with any certainty!

There are some aspects of social behaviour that will be more predictable. For example, we know that the way the population is changing will have major effects on demand in the future and that this presents both threats and opportunities for businesses. The problem is that some of these changes present huge challenges and require structural and possibly legal changes to occur to enable them to happen. For example, it has been known for some time that the UK, like many other countries, has an ageing population. The proportion of people over 65 is set to rise in the next fifty years. This will have an effect on the type of housing required, on health provision, pensions, insurance, transport and many other areas. Meeting this changing demand is not going to be easy and will require a considerable degree of foresight and planning – not to mention investment – by businesses and by the government.

Key terms

Birth rate The number of live births per thousand of the population.

Corporate Social Responsibility (CSR) A measure of the impact that a business has on society and the environment as a result of its business actions, and the extent to which a business recognises and acts on this impact.

Death rate The number of deaths per thousand of the population.

Demography The study of the population.

Ethics The accepted rules governing the behaviour of individuals and organisations that are widely accepted in society.

Household People who live and eat together, or people who live alone.

Assessing the effects of changes in the social environment

This section will look at different aspects of the changing social environment which include changes in the population (demographic factors), flexible working, changes in the family, in lifestyles and crime.

Demographic factors

POPULATION SIZE

The size of the population is one of the determining factors affecting the demand for goods and services. In very simple terms, the larger the population, the greater the demand for goods and services will be. Of course, this is a very simplified relationship and the changing structure of the population – the number and proportion of people of different ages – is likely to be something that will have a significant effect on businesses of all types.

In 1971 the UK population was 55.9 million; this has risen to an estimated 60.6 million in 2006. The rate at which the population changes is determined by three key factors:

- **the birth rate** – the number of live births per thousand of the population
- **the death rate** – the number of deaths per thousand of the population
- **the net migration rate** – the difference between the number of immigrants coming into a country and the number of emigrants – the number of people leaving the country.

The relationship between the first two factors will determine the natural rate of growth of the population over time. If the death rate is higher than the birth rate, then the population will fall over time, and vice versa.

If the net migration rate is positive then more people will be coming into the country than leaving it, and vice versa. The migration rate in relation to the difference between the birth rate and death rate will influence the overall size of the population over time.

The changes in these factors have a major impact on businesses for a variety of reasons. In the UK, there has been much reported in the press regarding the number of immigrants coming to the country from the new member states of the EU since enlargement in 2004. There has been a large influx of workers from countries like Poland and the Baltic states of Latvia, Lithuania and Estonia. These workers have brought with them different cultures, but also a work ethic and a range of skills that has been widely praised in many circles.

In construction, businesses have found that workers from the new EU states are highly skilled and have helped ease labour shortages. In addition, many are willing to work for wages that are considerably less than their equivalent UK counterparts. The result for these firms is an increase in productivity and a reduction in cost pressures. Many other businesses, for example, in hotel and catering, have also benefited from this migrant labour.

THE STRUCTURE OF THE POPULATION

The pattern of population growth also affects the structure of the population. It is usual to classify the population in terms of age groups. These age groups are 0–15, 16–65, and 65 and older. These are important as they broadly categorise the population into the dependent groups (those who are not in full-time work, that is, children aged 0–15 and the over 65s) and the population of working age (those aged 16–65). Of course, not everyone in this age group will be working and equally there are many active people in the 65 and over age group who regularly work. However, it is useful for giving an indication of the extent to which those in the working age group have to generate the income to support those who do not work and are classed as dependent.

Classifying the population in this way also gives some guide to the different market segments that exist and who are likely to have different consumer behaviours. Within these age groups there are also a number of other important pieces of information that businesses can use to help them in their planning and in meeting customer needs more effectively. For example, if the birth rate is increasing then it implies that there will be more babies, and these babies will grow into children and then adults. As they grow, their needs change and businesses can use this data to plan ahead to manage these changes when they arise.

Ageing population

In the UK one of the most important demographic features is the fact that it is experiencing an ageing population. The Office for National Statistics (ONS) publishes a comprehensive

document describing society each year called 'Social Trends'. The 2007 edition reports that by 2021 the number of people in the 65+ age group will exceed that in the under-16 category for the first time. People in the UK are living longer, are wealthier and more active than ever before, but the increasing number of people in this age group presents enormous challenges to business and government alike. Those in this age group have different wants and needs; they are more likely to require additional health care, they tend to have different lifestyles and buying habits, they are more likely to live alone and have different requirements with regard to transport needs, amongst many other things. The different needs of these people has led to the 'grey pound' becoming an important target market for many businesses that are looking to take advantage of the possibilities provided by this demographic change.

An ageing population or the 'grey pound' is providing businesses with new challenges

Businesses have to be in a position where they are planning to meet those needs. For example, car manufacturers are looking at ways in which vehicles suited to those in this age group can be tailored to suit their needs. There may be a far greater demand for eye care and for devices to help with hearing. Housebuilders will have to think about the type of properties that they are building and the facilities that have to be included in these new buildings. There may be an increase in demand for smaller houses, for housing away from urban centres and for different types of facilities within the houses. For example, the design of taps on sinks has changed to make it easier to be able to turn them on and off which is a great help to the elderly who may start to suffer from arthritis.

Other key features

There are also a number of other features of the population that are of importance to businesses.

- Since 1922, there have been more males born than females. The ratio of male births to female in 2006 was 105:100, yet despite this there are more females than males in the population (30.9 million compared to 29.7 million). This has implications not only for the demand for goods and services, but also for the future of the labour market and the way that businesses might have to adapt their operations to cope with the different needs of women in the workforce. These different needs include the necessity of managing time out of work to raise a family, the training needs of women who may have been out of work and wish to return to work, the importance of offering flexible working arrangements to facilitate childcare arrangements, and so on.

Skills watch!

A01/A02/A03/A04

Take the following three businesses and explain how each might be affected by the changes in the population level and structure outlined above. Try and provide some judgement about the extent to which they will be affected.

1 A housebuilder such as Barrett Homes or Persimmon.
2 Car manufacturers.
3 Retailers of spectacles and hearing aids.

- The number and range of different ethnic groups living in the UK has changed considerably in the last 30 years. Some ethnic groups have a younger profile than that of the white British population. The fastest growing ethnic group in the UK population has been the Chinese, with a growth rate of 11% a year from 2001 to 2005.
- There has also been a rise in the number of people entering the UK to seek work from the EU following enlargement in 2004. Many of these workers are from the former communist countries like Poland, Latvia and Lithuania.

Internal migration

Internal migration highlights some interesting trends. The south west of England saw inflows of people moving to the area, whereas parts of London have seen increasing numbers of people leaving. London as a whole has seen an average of 60,000 people leaving every year for the last 30 years, whereas parts of Devon and Wales have seen increases in the number of people moving to these areas. These internal migration patterns also change the pattern of demand in the regions, for example, they affect house prices (which can affect those who were born and bred in the area who may not be able to afford to get on the housing ladder), they change the demand for local services and change the structure of the population.

The family

The family is one of the basic units of life in most countries and the UK is no different. However, what we understand by 'family' has and is changing and this has a significant effect on businesses and how they market products, as well as the type of products that they are producing for this changing market. The changes in the family structure also tend to be long term in nature and reflect changing social attitudes. For example, the passing into law of arrangements for civil partnerships led to a rise in the number of gay couples getting 'married' and this has led to a rise in the so-called 'pink pound', where market opportunities have opened up to satisfy the needs of gay couples who are now able to live together and enjoy far greater rights than was the case previously.

MAIN TRENDS IN CHANGING FAMILY STRUCTURE

The ONS highlights some of the main trends in households and families over the last 30 years or so. The term 'household' is defined by Social Trends as 'people who live and eat together, or people who live alone'.

The main trends include:

- A rise in the number of households from 5.8 million in 1971 to 24.4 million in 2007.
- 12% of people live alone – double that of 1971.
- A fall in the number of marriages – 284,000 in 2005, 27,000 fewer than the year before and 197,000 fewer than in 1972.
- There has been a rise in the number of unmarried men and women under 60 cohabiting; for men the rise is from 11% to 24%, and for women 13% up to 25%.
- Married women are having their first child much later – 30 on average for women in England and Wales compared to 24 in 1971.
- There were 16,000 civil partnerships in 2006, with London being the most popular area accounting for a quarter of all UK registrations. Males accounted for 60% of all civil partnerships.

Changing attitudes and laws have led to new segments of the market which businessmen target, such as the so-called 'pink pound'

Marriage and divorce

Marriage is still popular in the UK but there have been important changes in the success rates of marriage reflected in the number of people seeking divorces. In 1969 there were around 56,000 divorces, but this figure rose to 155,000 in 2005 and reached 167,000 in 2004. Divorce has a number of effects including invariably creating two separate households when once there was one; it has implications for those working in the legal profession and those in social and family units in the public sector.

A traditional view of a woman's role – at home looking after the family

The role of women

Perhaps one of the most important features of the family has been the changes in the role of women. More women now work than ever before; the types of jobs they do, their expectations, aspirations and career objectives are different, and the decisions they make with regard to their lives has led to major social changes. Family roles are changing with more men getting involved in aspects of family life that may have been attributed to women 30 years ago. This means that many businesses have had to change their systems and operations to be able to accommodate these social changes. This includes offering more flexible working arrangements, including part-time work, flexible shift patterns, working at home, and so on, in order to help women meet childcare responsibilities, responding to legal changes in terms of maternity allowances, holding jobs open when women leave to have a family to avoid losing the skills that the business may have invested in, and so on. There are now more women entrepreneurs than ever before and the future labour market is likely to depend more on female labour as the population structure changes and the working population becomes ever more pressured to generate sufficient income to support the dependent population.

Lifestyles

Lifestyle refers to the way we live our lives, what we buy, what we do with our time, how we buy, when we buy and where we buy it, and are all factors that will influence consumer behaviour. Changes in these factors are of obvious interest to businesses that are looking to develop an understanding of their market and the changes that are occurring in that market. Changing lifestyles help new markets to develop but can also lead to the market becoming saturated, with growth opportunities severely limited.

TRENDS IN CHANGING LIFESTYLES

Key changes in lifestyles include the following:

- The change from analogue to digital television and the growth of satellite and *Freeview* TV stations.
- 85% of homes had a digital TV in 2007 – a rise of 65% since 2000.
- 23 million people engaged in some form of gambling (not including the National Lottery) in 2007 – 1 million more than in 1999.
- In 2005–2006, nearly one third of all adults admitted to not participating in any sport in the previous 12 months.
- Charitable donations in the UK totalled £9.5 billion in 2006–2007. The average donation (measured over a four-week period in that year) was £16.
- The use of technology equipment such as mobile phones, PCs, laptops, home entertainment equipment, MP3 players, and so on, has risen dramatically.

- In 2007, 51% of all households in the UK had broadband Internet access and 61% had some kind of access to the Web.
- Watching TV is still the most popular form of use of free time, with over 80% of the population citing it as the main way they use their free time.
- The number of people buying goods and services online has increased significantly with 53% of adults having purchased goods and services online.
- In 2006, cinema admissions fell by 4.9% compared to 2005. The vast majority of those who go to the cinema are aged between 7 and 35.
- 57% of adults regularly buy tickets for the National Lottery.
- The number of holiday trips abroad reached a record 45.3 million in 2006 – a rise of 153% since 1986.
- Spending on health clubs has increased but there is also evidence of rising obesity levels, particularly in children.
- Spending on outdoor living such as barbeques and gardening has risen significantly.
- Both workers and employers are becoming more concerned with maintaining a healthy balance between work and leisure – the 'work–life balance' – in the face of a rising trend towards working longer hours. A healthy work–life balance can have an impact on productivity.

Spending on leisure activities has risen significantly

THE EFFECTS OF CHANGING LIFESTYLES ON BUSINESS

The past 30 years have seen significant changes in our lifestyle which have affected different businesses in different ways and present major challenges to business. For example, the monopoly position enjoyed by BT for many years has now changed as mobile phones and the Internet have changed the way we communicate with each other. This is not to say that BT is not still a major player, but it has had to adjust to the changes in the way we wish to communicate.

Many markets are now becoming saturated and this provides businesses with major challenges. The revolution in mobile phone technology has been rapid in the last 10 years, but whether the new developments will continue at the same pace they did over the last decade remains to be seen. Many people now have more than one mobile phone and the market is such that phone companies and service providers are attempting to find ever more sophisticated ways to attract use to their products as the growth in the market slows down.

Other lifestyle changes might be associated with more problematic effects. Smoking and drinking have both been the subject of considerable column inches in the press. The ban on smoking in public places is now a legal requirement in the whole of the UK and the move is increasingly being adopted throughout the world, with 33 countries at least at the time of writing either having smoking bans in place or considering introducing some kind of restriction. High taxes on tobacco have led to changes in the way that people buy such products, with a rise in the number of cigarettes being smuggled. Tobacco manufacturers face significant regulation, including the requirement to place health warnings on packets and bans on advertising tobacco products in certain areas, for example, through sport.

Alcohol consumption in the UK is another issue for concern. There has been a massive increase in the number of different types of drinks available, and attitudes amongst young people to drinking seem to have changed. The problem of binge drinking, for example, causes significant problems in society as a whole, as well as placing additional burdens on the emergency services, the health system and affecting businesses through absenteeism.

Crime

The way that crime is measured but possibly most importantly of all, perceived, has an influence over the way we live our lives along with the subsequent effects on businesses. Crime figures are based on the annual British Crime Survey which is carried out on behalf of the Home Office. There are those that criticise the statistics that are derived from the survey; however, it not only provides data about the number of crimes committed, but also the attitudes and perceptions people have of crime.

Fear of crime is more prevalent than the likelihood of being a victim of crime, but its effects should not be underestimated. Spending on products and services to protect us from crime are dependent to a large extent on our perceptions of how vulnerable we are to crime. For example, the number of parents who fear for the welfare of their children affects their attitudes to whether they are allowed to go out on their own, how they spend their leisure time, how they get to and from school, and so on. The school run is now a major topical issue given that it can contribute to increased congestion and has even been a factor in the changing demand for certain types of vehicle. For example, the number of parents who have bought a Sports Utility Vehicle (SUV) or 4x4 has risen, although changes in fuel prices and taxes on such cars may well reverse that trend.

The increasing prevalence of closed-circuit security cameras (CCTV) has increased the extent to which our behaviour and actions are monitored and recorded, and can influence our

Skills watch!

A02 / A03 / A04

Consider the following two scenarios:

1 A small corner newsagent on an estate relies on local custom for the majority of its business. The owner knows the majority of the locals and they know him well. Over the years he has regularly served people with alcohol and tobacco knowing that they are underage, but at the same time he knows that this is their lifestyle and it provides him with his income.

To what extent should he ignore the legal responsibilities he has and meet his customers' needs?

2 A small business with six employees is grappling with the need to meet orders which is placing increasing demands on the workforce. The workforce has been with the owner for many years and is fiercely loyal. Most are prepared to work long hours for the sake of the business. However, the owner is starting to get an increasing number of complaints related to mistakes being made, and the owner suspects that the work–life balance may be wrong and that productivity is being affected as a result of the number of hours the staff are putting in.

Discuss the issues facing the owner and make a justified recommendation of an appropriate course of action.

perspectives about how safe and comfortable we feel in particular areas. For retail stores and the leisure industry, the importance of making sure that customers feel safe and secure can make a difference to the number of people using their stores and facilities. As new shopping and entertainment centres are developed to help provide the 'right' sort of environment that consumers feel they need, the effect on other areas of the town or city might be quite dramatic, in that customers are diverted from these areas and the pattern of use changes.

The changing nature of the ethical environment

What is meant by 'ethics'?

Ethics refers to the rights and wrongs associated with behaviour; it relates to the moral judgements that businesses make about their behaviour, and the way they operate and interact with their stakeholders. The approach by businesses to their operations has increasingly come under the microscope, and developments in the use of the Internet and news organisations mean that business behaviour is scrutinised like never before.

What are the main ethical issues facing business?

Business operations impact on the environment and on the stakeholders that are involved with the business. The extent to which a business's actions affect the environment is a cause for increasing concern. Pollution, exploitation of workers, economic degradation and climate change are some of the key areas where businesses are seen to have some responsibility and obligation. Part of this recognition is that there is a responsibility to carry out their operations with differing and often conflicting stakeholder interests in mind, which was covered in Chapter 20.

Many businesses have responded to this interest and see the moral obligations that they have to their stakeholders. The growing concerns both about the environment and corporate behaviour have meant that many organisations see benefits not only for themselves, but also to their stakeholder groups, of exercising corporate social responsibility and behaving in a more ethical manner. Such benefits might bring with them some element of competitive advantage. There are critics who argue that moves by businesses to enhance their corporate social responsibility (CSR) are merely an attempt to enhance their image and reputation, and are a cynical ploy to increase sales and gain competitive advantage. The truth in the motives for a more ethical approach probably lie somewhere in between these two extremes.

What are the key responsibilities of businesses to stakeholders?

The key responsibilities of businesses to their stakeholders can be summarised as follows:

- **Employees:**
  - to implement employment law fully and clearly;
  - to ensure that Health and Safety legislation is applied appropriately across the organisation;
  - to promote health and financial wellbeing (promoting good health, staff pay and benefits);
  - employee training and development.
- **Customers:**
  - upholding consumer rights, providing goods and services at reasonable prices and of an appropriate quality;
  - treating customers with respect;
  - being honest and open as to price and consumer rights (heavily related to anti-competitive practices);
  - promoting health and responsible consumer behaviour.

- **Shareholders:**
  - providing accurate and timely details of the performance of the business;
  - maximising shareholder return.
- **Suppliers:**
  - complying with the terms of the contracts, e.g. payment, and treating suppliers fairly;
  - choosing suppliers that promote responsible practice, e.g. human rights, environmental concern relating to the impact of actions by suppliers and promoting ethical trading.
- **The wider community:**
  - complying with legal aspects of planning, transport, storage and safety of goods;
  - improving the local economy through choice of local suppliers;
  - supporting local projects;
  - encouraging education and training;
  - creating employment opportunities for socially-disadvantaged groups;
  - encouraging environmental good practice.
- **The environment:**
  - waste management;
  - recycling;
  - using sustainable resources;
  - reduction of carbon footprint;
  - avoiding unnecessary energy consumption.

In relation to these obligations, businesses have to balance out the way that different groups are treated. Ethical considerations may necessitate treating suppliers differently, in terms of making sure that there is no exploitation of workers and that prices paid to suppliers are fair, whilst at the same time the business has an obligation to make sure that shareholder value is maximised, and there can be conflicts between the two (see Chapter 20 for more on these stakeholder conflicts).

Businesses will also have to consider the need to have to maintain security as much as possible within all its operations, not only to protect its workers from injury or threat, but also to ensure that information is kept secure to protect customers and also shareholders. Corporate fraud is an increasing problem and the sophistication of systems used and the complexity of modern large corporate organisations mean that the scope for widespread fraud is greater. Reports to shareholders must be accurate if confidence in the business and the whole system is to be maintained.

Inclusion, equality and diversity in the workplace

In addition to these areas of concern, there are increasing pressures on businesses to assess their policies with regard to inclusion and diversity within the workplace. This may relate to making sure that access to equal opportunities for all is maintained and monitored, but also that accessibility in the workplace and in the way that the business communicates with its external and internal stakeholders adheres to accessibility rules.

Equality and diversity can be improved through training, but it is important that this is seen as being a serious commitment by the business rather than simply paying lip-service to the latest trends. This might be more difficult to achieve than is sometimes thought. Non-discriminatory policies with regard to pay and recruitment have to be set out and implemented. All these things will have an impact on costs but the benefits that can be gained must be weighed against these costs; many businesses will feel that the benefits do outweigh the costs and thus it is a worthwhile process in setting up policies and systems to ensure these issues are dealt with. Not withstanding the moral duties of a business to follow through these issues, there is also extensive legislation that covers many of these, which were outlined in Chapter 22.

The impact of business operations on the environment

THE NEGATIVE IMPACT

The concern over the impact on the environment of a business's activities can be highlighted by looking at the negative impact that business operations can have. These include:

There is conflict between meeting legal requirements and not overdoing packaging

- **Closure of other related businesses** – there can be a devastating effect on the local community as a result, in terms of the loss of jobs, the effects on businesses who supplied the affected firm, as well as the indirect effect on other businesses such as shops, restaurants, leisure firms, and so on, that are likely to see a reduction in their sales as incomes in the area fall.
- **Exploitation of market power** – incentives to collude or enter into other anti-competitive practices mean that consumers and suppliers are often affected in a negative way.
- **Energy use** – some businesses use large amounts of energy and there are issues as to whether this energy use is efficient and whether it could be generated in more environmentally-friendly ways.
- **Waste** – the large amounts of waste generated by business as well as the amount of packaging that is used has been criticised in recent years. There is a tension between meeting legal requirements and ensuring consumer safety and overdoing the packaging that is required. Whatever the issue, the packaging has to be disposed of and with less land available for landfill this is a serious concern.
- **Outsourcing** – is primarily used as a means of reducing costs but there has to be consideration of the customer experience as a result, as well as the way in which domestic employees are treated who are replaced by outsourced labour and production processes, and the way in which businesses treat their outsourced labour.
- **Supply chain impacts** – many businesses look to build close relationships with suppliers to reduce their vulnerability to external shock, but such relationships do break down and can impact on those in the chain significantly.
- **Congestion on roads and public transport** – there has been much concern over the extent to which large supermarkets in the UK contribute to congestion and damage to road use, as well as their carbon footprint with goods criss-crossing the globe. Questions have been asked whether the benefits to the consumer of having access to fruit, for example, strawberries and cherries, 12 months a year is outweighed by the costs in terms of the environmental impact of this trade. Balanced against this is the benefit that growers around the world gain from such trade.
- **Noise and air pollution and public health** – this is highlighted by the arguments over air travel. Cheap air travel has opened up massive opportunities for many people, but at the same time the pressure on airports, the problems suffered by those living under flight paths and the environmental effects of air travel have been aspects that have been widely criticised.

THE POSITIVE IMPACT

There are, however, many possible positive impacts of an organisation on the local community. These benefits have to be balanced against the costs in order to arrive at a reasoned judgement in relation to ethical behaviour and CSR. These benefits include:

- **Improved employment opportunities** – the fact that cherries are available 12 months of the year in UK supermarkets means that growers in countries like Chile who supply some of these fruits have a market for their products and this creates employment opportunities for thousands of people.

- **Provision of high-quality goods and services** – the globalisation of business has led to the greater availability of goods and services than ever before, giving people more choice and more quality at reasonable prices which leads to an increase in standards of living.
- **Sponsorship** – many businesses will involve themselves in sponsorship in a wide variety of ways in order to put something back into the communities they are part of. Sponsorship of sports clubs like Premier League football clubs, for example, is a clear commercial decision, but many businesses carry out far smaller sponsorship deals designed to help promote and fund individuals and local groups that often go unreported and unnoticed.
- **Business growth** – the opportunities that arise for employment, and improvements to standards of living for those involved in businesses that are growing, can be seen from the way in which many businesses provide bonuses and rewards to their staff for the work they have done in helping to generate that growth. Business growth also provides opportunities for other businesses to expand on the back of orders, as well as new business opportunities to service the growth that occurs – in banking, finance, insurance, and so on.
- **Potential for increased cultural diversity** – by attracting people locally from outside the community/country, many businesses, especially those that are multi-national, provide such opportunities. Members of the business will travel to different countries, experience different cultures and vice versa, which leads to an enriching of life experiences in general. In the UK the diversity of ethnic and cultural background has provided extensive opportunities that would otherwise not have been available – witness the huge range of different cuisines available!
- **Various schemes** – for example, encouraging employees to take paid time off work to act as volunteers, providing educational visits and work experience for those attending local schools and colleges, providing publicity for local groups and becoming involved in community regeneration projects.
- **Financial donations** – businesses often have sums of money set aside to provide grants for individuals, projects, schools or community groups, and for charitable causes, giving to local or national charities.

Tensions in business ethics

The costs and benefits highlighted above have to be set in the context of the balance that businesses have to strike between their main purpose – generating profit for shareholders in the case of large businesses – and meeting the pressure to behave ethically and responsibly. There will be inevitable tensions that arise between these different aims. These can be summarised as:

- profits versus higher wages
- expansion versus development
- production versus pollution
- supplier benefits versus consumer prices/lower costs
- survival of the business versus the needs of the stakeholders.

External organisations involved with CSR

FTSE4 GOOD INDEX SERIES

The FTSE is the Financial Times Stock Exchange Index. It has been responsible for developing the FTSE4Good Index. To be included in the Index, companies must meet certain corporate social responsibility standards. The criteria for inclusion include evidence of their environmental record, whether they develop positive relationships with their stakeholders and whether they are supporters of universal human rights.

There are four main areas where businesses can develop to enable them to become part of the Index:

- **Investment** – to monitor where businesses are putting their money and who shareholders and debenture holders are.
- **Research** – to identify socially-responsible companies.
- **Benchmarking** – to track the performance of socially-responsible companies.
- **Reference** – to provide a standard of how socially-responsible companies are behaving.

Companies that would find it extremely difficult to meet the criteria for inclusion would include tobacco companies, and arms and weapons manufacturers.

THE INSTITUTE OF SOCIAL AND ETHICAL ACCOUNTABILITY

AccountAbility is an international, non-profit-making, professional institute dedicated to the promotion of social, ethical and overall organisational accountability. The organisation aims to promote social and ethical accountability for sustainable development. It has a number of standards that businesses can use to benchmark themselves against the standards. These include:

- Developing standards that can be measured by accounting methods which are based on a sound framework.
- Enabling firms to gain certification against the standards and to provide professional development for members of the business.
- Pushing for a greater role for public policy in developing organisational accountability for CSR.
- Encouraging and promoting innovation and research into ways in which CSR can be improved.

AccountAbility is over 10 years old and is gaining in credibility. Part of this credibility lies in the fact that the organisation promotes not simply talk about CSR, but practical action to ensure that CSR is improved and practical. This means that AccountAbility looks at how companies take action with regard to their CSR and how it considers its wider stakeholders. The framework of the organisation is highlighted in Figure 23.1 which shows how an organisation is primarily accountable to its

Figure 23.1 The AccountAbility Matrix

Source: http://www.accountability21.net/

shareholders: the major stakeholders in any company. It also highlights the fact that managers are accountable for all the business's actions and the way this is reported to its shareholders and also its wider stakeholders who are embedded in the whole organisation.

Evaluating responses of businesses to a changing social environment including CSR

Responses to demographic change

Much of the response of a business to the changing social environment will depend on how long it takes the business to recognise the changes that are occurring and the extent to which it can change to meet the new environment. There is plenty of research and many publications into changing demographics, and given that these changes are relatively slow, businesses do have time to be able to organise their resources to be able to invest in meeting changing needs. However, that can also present other inherent problems. The effects of an ageing population creep up on businesses and it may be that other priorities appear to take precedence over the investment in providing for this eventuality.

The influx of Polish workers to the UK has opened up new market needs

In the UK in recent years the influx of Polish migrants has led to a number of businesses introducing products and services that meet the needs of this section of society. In areas where there are concentrations of Polish workers, some supermarkets have created dedicated sections where traditional Polish products and foods can be bought. The extent to which this phenomena will continue will depend on the degree to which Polish people become integrated into society and indeed, how long they choose to stay. There are already reports that many Polish workers are now returning home, partly disillusioned by the way they have been treated and partly through the fact that the Polish economy has picked up and the economic reasons for coming to the UK are not as strong any more. Businesses that have changed to meet the needs of Polish people will find that they will have to adapt in the future. The extent to which they are able to anticipate these changes is going to be crucial.

Responses to changes in lifestyle

For businesses that are able to plan ahead and make resources available – often the very large corporations – the chances of exploiting the benefits that arise as a result of changing social trends are likely to be greater. In many cases, meeting the needs of changing demographic trends will require substantial market research, new innovation, and research and development to anticipate customer needs and plan the business to enable these needs to be met.

For example, the changes in lifestyle have been shaped by the availability of products like mobile phones, but also by the response and expectations of consumers who come to use such devices and how businesses respond to the demands of consumers. When the first mobile phones came on the market they were bulky, limited in range and options, not totally reliable and expensive. Twenty years later they are very different beasts and have changed our lifestyles completely. In addition, in order to meet these changing lifestyles, businesses invested heavily in developing the technology so that we now have (at the time of writing) phones that can view TV programmes, send and receive text messages, images and video, play a range of multimedia activities, act as a music system and enable access to e-mail and to the Web. The way we work has now been changed by the availability of such technology, and businesses have been able to adapt their work practices to meet other social requirements like changes to the family and the role of women as a result.

The changes in mobile phone technology have changed our lives completely

Business and CSR

With regard to CSR and ethical behaviour, there are certainly no right or wrong answers about what should be done in terms of how a business should respond. In many cases it will depend on how the business responds to criticisms or reports of unethical behaviour. If the response is swift and decisive and matches the standards that they set themselves, then the business might be able to avoid long-term damage. The damage to Nike of reports that workers at subcontracted plants in Asia were being exploited took longer to deal with than the company might have hoped for and also dented its sales for a time. Primark, in a similar position in 2008, responded almost before the stories appeared in the press and the company lost no time in publicising the high standards it set itself and why its prices remained lower than its rivals and how this did not equate to exploitation. The aim was to reassure customers that the offering it was making was consistent with ethical standards and that they could continue to buy with a clear conscience. Its actions in cancelling the contracts of three Indian companies who had been using child labour immediately helped to dispel the fears that the company would seek to brush such an incident under the carpet.

Some may suggest that such a reaction is merely a response to criticism, but that the underlying philosophy of using cheap labour and production facilities in less-developed countries is essentially flawed. The problem is that a business might take many years to build up a reputation but this can be destroyed in a very short time. It often takes huge amounts of time and money to rebuild reputation and trust in the organisation. It is in the interests of many businesses, therefore, to ensure that they do manage their responsibilities appropriately – even if it is for essentially selfish reasons.

Having said this, the fact that more companies are producing CSR audits and making these available, is leaving them more open to criticism about their actions if they do not meet the standards they set for themselves.

Many businesses now produce CSR reports and audits to help stakeholders understand the measures being taken by the firm to reduce the impact of its actions on the environment

As accounting standards in CSR improve and become more consistent throughout the world, businesses will have fewer places to hide and more to lose. The existence of the Internet and the fact that information can now travel widely in a short space of time, and the growing role of blogs in so-called 'whistle-blowing cases' where employees reveal what might be going on in a business that the managers might not want the public to be aware of, is placing further pressure on businesses to behave. This is in addition to the existence of a wide range of pressure groups who lobby for particular causes and who put pressure on businesses to adjust their behaviour to meet particular standards and behaviours.

Many companies now prepare social accounting reports and audits as an integral part of their financial reporting cycle. These are serious documents and can be very expensive to produce. Corporate social accounting is a growing area in the accountancy industry, and standards to monitor and develop appropriate ways of measuring CSR are being improved all the time. There are currently no legal requirements in the UK relating to the preparation, publication or independent review of corporate environment and social reports.

CSR presents its own problems; its effects are manifested throughout the organisation. A business cannot simply express its CSR in relation to pollution; it has to run through all its activities – both internal and external – from the impact that it has on carbon emissions and energy use right down to the way it runs its staff welfare programmes. Governments are also keen to see the development of social reporting and accounting, as they are keen for organisations to include corporate social responsibility as part of their everyday decision-making routine. The UK Government has given its Department of Trade and Industry (DTI) the job of working with the business community with regard to social accounting.

Summary and exam guidance

Summary

- Changes in both the size and structure of the population affect businesses in the short and long term.

- The composition of the population – its ethnic make-up, the age distribution of the population, where people live and move to, and so on – are important to businesses in trying to anticipate and meet changing consumer needs.

- The size of the population is affected by the birth rate, death rate and net migration.

- The UK has an ageing population which will have a significant impact on changing consumer needs and markets in the future.

- There have been major changes to the make-up of the family unit in the last 30 years.

- Changes in lifestyles have an impact on businesses in terms of changes in market segments and what people buy and need.

- Crime, and importantly the perception of crime, provide both opportunities and threats for businesses.

- Businesses are increasingly aware of the effect of their operations on the environment and their wider stakeholders.

- Businesses are now taking more responsibility for the impact of their actions on society.

- More businesses are producing CSR accounts, and monitoring and communicating their actions and how they are changing their behaviour in the light of environmental and other concerns.

Exam practice

Read the articles below and then answer the questions that follow.

Article A

All you can eat!

Spectator numbers at major league baseball rose in 2007 to record levels. The 80-plus home games for each franchise every year present challenges to the marketing teams to look at ways in which revenues can be maximised. One idea that was extended in the 2008 season was the provision of 'all-you-can-eat seats'. These are seats that fans can buy and have almost unlimited access to food and drink during the average 3 hours of the game. The logic is fairly simple. The designated seats tend to be in areas of the ballpark where capacity tends not to be used up. The fact that nearly half of the franchises are offering these seats might suggest that it is financially worthwhile.

cont...

However, the idea has raised some concern in the US. The food available at ball games tends to be the less healthy variety (although some clubs are saying that they will offer all-you-can-eat salads and fruit cups). Hot dogs, nacho chips, peanuts and popcorn form a typical ball game diet and when washed down with liberal quantities of fizzy drink and in some cases beer, health watchdogs are labelling the idea as 'disgusting'. The reports of father–son hot dog eating contests and nacho eating contests will do little to allay the fears of health officials.

The clubs say that they are meeting the fans' needs and that for families the seats can represent a saving on the whole game cost. They also point out that they are not forcing anyone to eat to excess but merely providing a different option for fans to choose. There are some restrictions in place to limit the amount of times people can return to the concessions.

Source: Biz/ed In the News: http://www.bized.co.uk/cgi-bin/chron/chron.pl?id=3043

Article B

Right or wrong?

A new product launched in France attracted a market of 1.2 million people and after its launch in February 2008 in the UK built up an audience of 200,000 in the first month. Nicolas Jacquart is the 23-year-old web designer based in London who is the entrepreneur behind the product. There is a bit of a problem though: the product has generated a number of concerns and news media are falling over themselves to take the moral high ground. The product in question is a virtual game played through the web called Miss Bimbo. Like other virtual games, players enter a world where they are competing with others and can use money to help them win – in this case the money is bimbo dollars or 'mula'. The game is free to register but when the player runs out of 'mula' they can top up their accounts by text message priced at around £1.50 per text.

The idea of the game is to create the 'hottest, coolest, most famous bimbo in the whole world'. To do this players are encouraged to stop at nothing to get their bimbo clad in the latest fashions, be seen at the best clubs and to 'look the best'. Therein lies the problem. The thought of players buying breast implants, checking into a clinic for a facelift or going on diets to achieve their bimbo targets is concerning some.

Depending on which news media you read, the game has attracted girls from anything between 7 and 19. The attraction to young girls aged between 7 and 12 seems to be particularly upsetting if you believe the news reports. Parents' rights groups, nutritionists, child health specialists and organisations treating young girls with eating disorders argue that the game sends out the wrong messages to young impressionable girls. It promotes the image that the only way to be successful is to have the 'perfect figure'. Encouraging players to buy diet pills, hit target weights and have cosmetic surgery is clearly uncomfortable for these groups.

The entrepreneur behind the game sees it as just that – a game. He argues that there are warnings on the site about the dangers of using diet pills and is planning to review the site to ensure that it meets some of the concerns expressed. He goes on to argue that there are moral lessons to be learned from playing the game and that the game is not a bad influence on children; it reflects the real world, he adds.

Source: Biz/ed In the News: http://www.bized.co.uk/cgi-bin/chron/chron.pl?id=3055

(a) Discuss the ethical issues that arise for the businesses in both of the articles above. (16 marks)

(b) To what extent would a CSR audit help to alleviate the ethical concerns that exist in the two articles? (34 marks)

Total: 50 marks

Breakdown of assessment objectives

AO1 – Knowledge and understanding – 5/50
AO2 – Apply knowledge and understanding – 15/50
AO3 – Analyse problems, issues and situations – 10/50
AO4 – Evaluate, distinguish between fact and opinion, assess and judge information from a variety of sources – 20/50

Suggested structure

For part (a) you will need to:

- Identify the key ethical issue related to each article.
- Offer some explanation of the ethical dilemma facing the businesses in both articles and what stakeholder conflicts exist.
- Make some judgements about the extent of the ethical dilemmas highlighted – are they really very serious or are those who are offering criticism doing so unjustifiably?

For part (b) you will need to:

- Offer a clear explanation of the role of a CSR audit along with some examples of how it is used.
- Demonstrate how a CSR audit might take into consideration the issues highlighted in the two articles.
- Consider the value of a CSR report in the context of the two articles – would production of a CSR report help to allay fears expressed in either or both cases?
- Discuss at least one other way that the businesses concerned might use to help allay the concerns raised.
- Draw your argument together to arrive at a conclusion about the value of a CSR audit – would it help to alleviate the ethical concerns a great deal, to some extent or hardly at all?
- In the light of the above, draw a conclusion about the strengths or limitations of a CSR audit.

Chapter 24 The relationship between businesses and the technological environment

One of the things that will become apparent as you work through this chapter is that technology is not simply the use of computers in the workplace. Computers have had a considerable effect on the way that business is conducted in the last 30 years, but alongside the computer revolution has been a similar revolution in the way that technology in its widest sense has been utilised by businesses. In many respects, computers are merely the workhorse; the real drivers behind technological change are in the way that these machines are used – in other words, **innovation**. Innovation in this context is the dissemination of technology and its applications within organisations and society as a whole. Behind these innovations is software which helps to utilise the power of computers to help businesses operate more efficiently, to understand and reach their market more effectively and to create new markets that we could not have imagined even 20 years ago.

What is technology?

Technology is the use of knowledge applied to the environment to enable people to exercise greater control over that environment. Knowledge is applied in a wide variety of ways, but in business, knowledge is applied to finding practical ways of improving business operation, that is, of finding a product or service that enough people will buy at a price that will more than cover the costs of production.

Within this definition we can see that the development of robots, computer-aided design (CAD) and computer-aided manufacturing (CAM) systems, fuel-efficient engines, methods of collecting data about customers, the sharing of information between different parts of a business, improving communications and developing products that enable consumers to do new and interesting things, are all part of this process. All the things mentioned above enable a business to be able to either find a way of reducing the cost of production or increase the number of sales to consumers – or a combination of both. When either of these things happens, a business is in a better position to be able to be successful, although it has to be stressed that technology is not a guarantee of success by any means!

How is technology used in business?

The application of technology to business is extensive. The scope to apply knowledge to business operations is limitless, bounded only by the human imagination and ingenuity. The ways in which technology is currently used is way beyond anything that many could have imagined 30 years ago and what can be achieved in the future is equally difficult to comprehend.

The following are just some of the important roles of technology in modern business:

The ways in which technology is used in business could not have been imagined 30 years ago

- The use of telecommunications – e-mail, the web, telephone, mobile phones, teleconferencing, video-conferencing, podcasts, blogs, fax, and so on.
- The development and use of databases for storing information.
- The advances in science to develop new systems, processes, drugs, ways of finding energy, understanding of the human brain, and so on.
- The application of machinery to manufacturing processes to improve efficiency and productivity.
- The developments in nanotechnology to enable more things to be done by ever-smaller devices and machines.
- The understanding of chemical and physical properties that provide the opportunity to be able to develop and use new products.
- The use of technology to establish supply chains that are incredibly complex but which enable products to be produced at low cost and subsequently make more products available to more people at lower prices.
- Technology enables us to better understand what the impacts of our operations are on the environment and how pollution affects both the environment and human welfare.
- Technology enriches our lives by providing us with labour-saving devices, entertainment and leisure facilities – the question might be whether we get the time to be able to enjoy these benefits given the fact that many businesses have access to their staff 24 hours a day!
- The opportunities for businesses to operate in different ways that allow their employees to get a better quality of life, but which can also improve productivity and reduce cost.

The above are just some examples of broad uses and implications of technology in business. The depth and complexity of technology is effectively embedded into the very fabric of our lifestyles and we rely on businesses to provide us with so much. The extent to which we all specialise has reduced the degree of human independence, and increased dramatically interdependence. The trade-off for those in developed economies (and hopefully for all others in the future) is a quality of life and standard of living that has improved and is likely to continue to improve.

Assessing the effects of technological change

There are a number of overarching changes that we can consider. These include marketing opportunities, the culture of the business, and processes and systems used within a business. We will look at each in turn.

Marketing opportunities

The opportunities presented by technology for marketing mainly focus on the way in which businesses are able to gather data about customers and use this to target their markets more effectively. The basic elements of so-called customer relations management (CRM) were outlined in Chapter 8. However, we will consider further some of the possibilities in this section.

CRM is a process whereby the business focuses on specific customer groups as a means of maximising awareness, sales, revenue and profitability. CRM enables a business to understand its market more effectively and be able to use that understanding to be more efficient in its marketing approach.

There are three main ways that a business can capture customer information:

- **Web-based** – getting customers to register on a website and providing summary details such as e-mail address, age group, gender, occupation, key interests, and so on, to help to build a profile. The use of cookies also enables a business to collect information about the buying behaviour of customers and their browsing history.
- **Point-of-sale** – these can be in the form of information centres in stores where consumers can ask questions and get information about products – the customer volunteers information about themselves and the products they buy as a result, and this data is collected by businesses. Loyalty cards are also a way of collecting point-of-sale information. Such information is also collected through the required completion of guarantees.
- **Transactions** – the increased use of credit cards enables a business to use the data collected to build customer profiles. Every time a credit card is swiped the seller is able to collect data about buying habits linked to the bar codes on products they have bought.

At the heart of any successful CRM is the gathering and organisation of data. Technology allows this to occur far more effectively and efficiently than ever before. Not only can more information be gathered, it can also be organised and filtered to allow the business to group customers into recognisable market segments. CRM tracks spending patterns and identifies customer behaviours. The information gathered can be used to be able to group customers with similar characteristics, which the business can use to deliver messages and information about products or services that these people are interested in, as indicated by their buying preferences. In addition, it enables the business to be able to interact with the consumer on a one-to-one basis like never before. Consumers can be sent individual messages alerting them to products and services which they may be interested in. In so doing, the business is more likely to gain the customer's interest and turn that interest into sales (see the box on the next page).

CUSTOMER RELATIONSHIPS

Establishing some form of contact with customers through CRM is a key part of the process. The depth of the relationship that is developed is another. In some cases, the data collected can be used to send out occasional flyers or information, either online or through more traditional avenues such as the mail. Supermarkets, for example, will send customers leaflets highlighting special offers on particular products or offering discount vouchers. The products that are selected will not be the same for everyone. The included products will be dependent

For example...

Amazon.com

Consider the difference between direct marketing techniques and that used by a company like Amazon. Many householders will be familiar with the flood of mail that comes through the door every day relating to external treatment for their homes (for example, pebbledashing!), home insurance, vehicle insurance, and so on. The vast majority of this finds its way into the bin without ever being read. The very fact that it is referred to as 'junk mail' is indicative of the view of customers to this sort of marketing technique. Interestingly, few people regard the messages sent to them by firms like Amazon as being junk mail. Whenever an account holder logs onto Amazon they will be presented with a wide range of recommendations based on previous viewings and purchases. Many people regard these recommendations as very helpful. One reviewer commented that, had it not been for Amazon alerting them to the existence of a particular band, they would never have been able to enjoy the music they were reviewing!

on the buying habits of the individual customer as identified through the data gathered by the use of loyalty cards. However, it is likely that there will be broad groups of customers who will receive the same information because the cost of totally individualising the leaflets would be too great. The leaflets, therefore, will be designed based on age, gender, income category, ethnic background, the postcode where they live, and so on. It is remarkable how similar the buying habits of the average 45-year old female houseowner, earning between £30,000 and £50,000 joint-income a year with two children can be!

In other cases the relationship can be much deeper. The availability of technology to capture particular buying habits and patterns through the use of cookies means that some firms are able to target particular products and services at particular individuals on a regular basis. Amazon, again, is a good example of this approach. An individual who buys a CD, DVD or book from a particular genre, such as thrash metal, horror or romantic fiction, will be sent other products from those same genres linked to what other people buying those types of products have bought as well as within its own categorisations within the genre.

CRM also helps a business to identify its 'important customers'. It might be argued that every customer is important, but some are more important than others. Chapter 8 introduced the idea of the 80/20 rule. This is also referred to as the 'law of the few' and states that 80% of businesses' revenues are generated by 20% of its customers. In B2B businesses this is especially relevant. CRM can help a business to identify who this 20% is and enable it to develop closer relationships to help maximise revenue and focus on customer needs. The information gathered will also be able to find out which of its customers are the ones that are profitable and which are not. For example, the insurance company esure was set up specifically to exploit the Internet to 'give a better deal to responsible drivers and careful homeowners'*. The focus on customers who were less likely to make claims meant that the company could offer competitive premiums. Customers who are not careful and who make regular claims are not profitable for the insurance industry!

The culture of the business

Culture refers to the beliefs and values shared by people who work in an organisation. It covers how people are expected to behave with each other within the organisation, how people behave with customers/clients, how people view their relationship with stakeholders, employees' responses to energy use, community involvement, absence, work ethic, etc., and how the organisation behaves to its employees – training, professional development, and so on.

* Source: http://www.esure.com/about_esure/

The culture of an organisation may be driven by the firm's vision – where the organisation wants to go in the future – and its mission – where it stands at the moment. It may be reflected in the attitude and behaviour of the leadership, the attitude to the role of individuals in the workplace (whether there are open-plan offices, team-based working, and so on), the logo of the organisation, the image it presents to the outside world and its attitude to change.

It is this last point that is particularly relevant to technology. History tells us that new technology can create a climate of fear. New technology has replaced the work of human beings for centuries, and when new technology is developed, there will be a problem for the organisation in managing the implementation of this technology. On the one hand it might feel it needs the technology to maintain its competitive position against its rivals or even to gain a competitive advantage, but at the same time it will be conscious of the disruption that this will cause, and the possible negative effects both on the employees who may lose their jobs or have to retrain, and the possible damage to its reputation as a result of the changes it implements.

For example...

The print industry

In the 1980s, the News International Group, headed by Rupert Murdoch, sought to introduce new working practices and technology to its print division. It built a new plant in Wapping in East London, and when workers at the existing Fleet Street offices found out, a bitter dispute broke out. 6,000 workers voted to go on strike against the proposed changes; News International responded by effectively sacking all 6,000. During the dispute there were ugly scenes and repeated violent confrontation as striking print workers tried to prevent News International

from running operations from the new Wapping plant which it had staffed with workers from other unions. The dispute eventually ended with a loss for the print workers.

The Wapping dispute was a high-profile example of how new technology can create fear in workers, but also highlights how businesses need to be sympathetic in the way in which new technology is introduced. To help in the process, the right culture has to be developed and this can take a long period of time to develop. If a culture that embraces change can be created, then workers will feel challenged by new technology but not threatened by it. They can come to see it as offering new opportunities for both their own advancement and as a benefit to the business itself.

In order to achieve this, a business has to create a working atmosphere and culture that supports workers and builds trust between the different levels of management and employees. Part of this is a commitment by employers to employees to provide them with the training and skills to be flexible, but to acquire the means to be able to move on to other employment if necessary. The employee has to feel that they are comfortable handling the new technology and to feel that they will get the support of the business in providing them with the continuing professional development (CPD) that maintains their skill levels, makes them employable and enables them to progress within the business if that is possible.

The culture of an organisation can also have some impact on the extent of the effect of new technology on the success of the business. Technology can improve efficiency and productivity, but only if it is used appropriately, and it is something that is embraced by all in the organisation. Businesses will have to consider the value of the benefit of implementing new technology and the potential costs, and make judgements on whether it is worth introducing it in the first place, as well as reviewing its contributions when it has been introduced. This can be affected by the degree to which employees accept and utilise the new technology.

THE INTERNET AND E-MAIL – A GOOD THING OR NOT?

The increasing use of the Internet and e-mail in a business can have a powerful and highly beneficial effect on business operations. However, many businesses are increasingly finding that it also has its drawbacks. There have been reports that e-mail can be abused and that staff may spend significant proportions of the working day engaged in e-mail conversations that have nothing to do with the business. Equally, the time spent browsing the Web, for example, auction sites and social networking sites, is also something that is seen as being a distraction and which reduces productivity.

Businesses may introduce some form of monitoring and blocking system on e-mail and Web browsing, but such a policy does reflect on the business's culture. Any sort of blocking will send a message that the business does not trust its employees which may conflict with its mission and vision statements, but at the same time may have been identified as being necessary because of the abuse of these facilities. The use of e-mail might also reduce some of the more beneficial lines of communication within a business; there are numerous examples every day in workplaces up and down the country were workers send an e-mail to someone sitting on the opposite desk rather than simply talking to them!

Skills watch!

AO3 / AO4

How might a business evaluate the extent to which e-mail and the use of the Internet in the workplace brings benefits to them?

To what extent is restricting or banning the use of e-mail and the Internet the answer to the problems faced by many larger organisations?

These two questions are heavily weighted towards the higher order skills of analysis and evaluation. The key word in each case is 'extent'. This means that you have to make some judgement in your answer about the size of the benefits that the business will gain —will they be very large, quite large, relatively small or almost totally insignificant?

Processes and systems used within the business

Processes and systems relate to the whole range of business's operations. The process might be related to manufacturing; it could cover ordering, distribution and despatch; it might be the way in which the human resources (HR) function operates; the way that the supply chain is managed; it might provide information to machinery in the production process to change various settings, pull in stock from warehouses or distribution centres, manage information and customer details, trigger sell or buy options in financial trading, and get machines and databases to share information automatically. The application of technology to the way in which a business operates and carries out its daily activities is now almost completely embedded to the extent that few people ever notice or appreciate just how far processes and systems are governed by technology.

In the list above there are a number of major applications of technology that are worth pursuing further.

TECHNOLOGY IN PRODUCTION

The use of machines and robots in operations management was covered in some detail in the AS book (see Chapter 27). However, the benefits of technology in production can be further summarised in the way in which it can be used to improve productivity and efficiency. Many production processes are now highly complex and interchangeable. They rely on information being fed through the process to be able to amend production to create customised products that meet specific customer needs. The ability of these machines to be quickly programmed and reprogrammed enables them to be able to cope with large amounts of different production runs, components and ingredients.

This means that businesses are able to build in flexibility to their production runs. Particular customer requirements can be catered for, thus meeting their needs more appropriately. It also means that production can be carried in relation to firm orders rather than producing for stock. Such processes and systems help to reduce unnecessary cost and lower the unit cost of production. Of course, the cost benefits have to be balanced out against the investment costs associated with this sort of technology. This might mean that only businesses of a certain size and scale of operations can afford to be able to buy the sort of sophisticated technology and software systems that allow them to build in this sort of flexibility. This would be one of the technical economies of scale that would exist for larger businesses.

Skills watch!

A01 / A02

Describe how customised ordering processes might benefit:

(a) a car manufacturer and
(b) a book publisher (hint – how many people/ institutions buying textbooks want or need all the chapters in a textbook?).

SUPPLY CHAIN MANAGEMENT

The term 'supply chain' refers to the web of suppliers, manufacturers working under contract to another firm, manufacturers of component parts, distribution firms, logistics analysts and businesses, wholesalers, security firms and retailers that are involved in getting products from a business to its customers. No longer does a manufacturer produce everything themselves under one roof, ship it to a wholesaler who then distributes it to retailers for final sale. The complexity of the relationships between all these different businesses is mind-boggling. In Chapter 26 of the AS book, a diagram highlights the journey of an Intel processor. The manufacture of these processors involves four journeys across the Pacific Ocean and numerous other journeys across America, Japan, China, Taiwan, Malaysia, Brazil and Ireland. Even then the journey is not over because they have to be shipped to customers from Dell's production sites across the globe.

The number of businesses involved in this sort of operation is considerable; it will not just involve Intel and Dell, but a whole host of specialist businesses offering different products and services to ensure that the basic business transaction, the purchase by Dell of processors for its PCs and laptops from Intel, can take place. Some of these services will include legal, banking and insurance services and, increasingly importantly, security services.

At every stage in the process, technology has been applied to try and increase the profitability of both key businesses, reduce costs to a minimum, ensure safety of those involved in the operations, reduce the impact on the environment to a minimum and ensure that the vulnerability of the operation to problems such as fraud, theft, natural elements such as the weather, damage and terrorist attack are kept as low as possible.

Technology will be used to gather and share information between all these different firms and processes to ensure that the supply chain operates as smoothly as possible. The complexity is such that without technology it is unlikely that such an operation could be carried out, and the existence of supply chains in business is testament to the application of knowledge to solving problems and improving solutions to those problems, as well as the growing importance placed by businesses on the relationships it has with its suppliers.

JUST-IN-TIME (JIT)

The increasing importance of JIT systems in manufacturing as ways in which companies can reduce their reliance on holding stock is well documented. The aim of JIT is to design processes so that added value can be maximised and waste minimised. All those involved in the business have to maintain a degree of flexibility and willingness to change tasks as situations demand. In addition, the relationship between the business and its suppliers has to be extremely close. Part of that relationship will involve the sharing of information and excellent communication networks. Technology plays a vital role in making sure that the whole system operates efficiently and that it actually works! The sort of technology that might be used includes mechanical, which moves parts from one place to another, logistics planning to reduce waste and duplication in making sure parts and goods are where they need to be when they are needed, IT applications that help share information and databases, communications technologies to enable individuals and groups to coordinate activities, and financial packages that help to record and manage the payments systems that will be generated as a result of the flow of stock.

Evaluating the response of businesses to technological change

One of the problems facing most businesses in a world where technology is changing rapidly is keeping up with the pace of change and getting a deep understanding of what the changes can mean for their business. The change might affect sales, competitive advantage, and provide opportunities for cost savings and increases in productivity. However, it may be that there is a time lag between changes in technology occurring and when a firm can start to appreciate what opportunities and threats it provides.

The effects will also be dependent on where the change in technology has come from. If it has been generated from within the firm itself, then there is a good chance that this will lead to some degree of competitive advantage. If another firm has created the technology, the competitive landscape may be changed for the firms who have yet to understand and develop the technology.

We can identify a number of main characteristics related to the way in which businesses can respond to changes in the technological environment.

Research and Development (R&D)

R&D acts as an accelerator for technological change. R&D is defined as the systematic attempt to build and create new knowledge and to find ways of using this knowledge in society. The average spending on R&D in the EU is around 2% of GDP; in Japan and the United States it is nearer 3.0%. Many large firms place importance on R&D as a means of seeking and maintaining competitive advantage. From R&D come new ideas, new technologies and new ways of working that help to improve productivity and efficiency, develop new products, find different uses for and improve existing products. Some of the work carried out by R&D departments will be based on feedback from market research and some will be based on what some like to call 'blue skies' thinking. Blues skies thinking refers to a way of coming up with new ideas that are not influenced by any preconceptions – any idea is accepted and deemed worthy of possible further investigation.

For many large firms, their product portfolio will be an important aspect of their overall business strategy. Products will be at different stages of the product life cycle and in order to maintain their position in the market, it will be important that they have products in the pipeline at various stages of development. The pharmaceutical industry is a good example of this. Pfizer, for example, were responsible for developing the impotence drug, Viagra. Having spent millions developing the drug (they did not start out to develop a drug for impotence, by

For example...

Technology and the music industry

One of the most obvious examples of how business has responded to change is in the music industry in the first decade of the 21st century. The developments in technology meant that music lovers were interested in buying and using their music in different ways to that which the industry had traditionally supplied this product. The response of the mainstream industry to music downloading (mostly illegal in the early stages) was to look at enforcing copyright laws and attempting litigation against high-profile music downloaders. The emphasis seemed to be on trying to enforce the status quo.

The problem was that the market had changed and most of the main firms supplying music were reluctant to accept this or may have believed they had the power to prevent the changes – a sort of King Cnut approach to the industry! One firm who was not part of the traditional industry, but was very much at the forefront of technological change that had acted as a catalyst for the new music environment, was Apple. Apple saw the opportunities that existed and acted. It was the development of the *iPod* that had allowed music lovers to download music they wanted and listen to it wherever they wanted. The launch of the *iTunes* service provided music lovers with what they wanted at a price that was deemed reasonable and the business became hugely successful. Other firms sought to enter the market to take advantage of the demand that was clearly there, but *iTunes*, being the first, had gained a significant advantage. The mainstream music industry was slow to recognise the changes and even slower to react.

the way, it came out of other research!) they were able to establish patents that gave them monopoly power for a period of time. This is important for such firms to help them make a return on their investment. However, as time moves on the firm will be aware that the patent will run out and it will have to have other new drugs coming along to generate the income streams that drive the business. When the patent for Viagra ran out in 2000 there was a flood of rival drugs coming onto the market which drove down price and margins. New products coming on stream which will generate future income, therefore, are essential to the long-term health of the business.

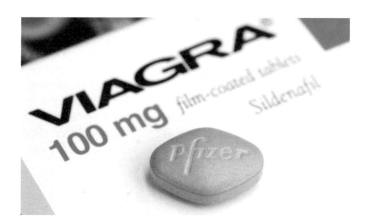

Once patents for products such as Viagra run out, firms face fierce competition from rival drugs, so it is essential to have new products in the pipeline

Speed of response – building competitive advantage or catching up?

Technology will change – of that there is little doubt. The speed with which it changes varies in different industries, but one common theme for most businesses will be the speed with which they recognise and/or are able to respond to the changes in the market. The example given above of the response of Apple to the changed circumstances in the music industry is typical of this situation.

Much research and development may be in areas where the commercial viability is unknown!

In judging the response to changes in technology, firms must use the so-called risk–reward ratio to assess the extent of the costs and benefits of investing in a particular project. The usual questions must be answered. Is there a market? How big is this market and what is the growth potential in the market? However, one of the problems of technology, especially cutting-edge technology, is that many firms do not know what the market is likely to be. Developments in genetic engineering and stem cell research, for example, promise a great deal, but whilst there are theories as to the possible uses of stem cell technology – for example, there is a potential that such research could help treat sufferers of Parkinson's Disease or those with injuries to the spinal cord – the reality is many years ahead and may not even be realised. For firms in this line of business there may be the temptation to watch from the sidelines as others do the research, but if they are not involved then a huge amount of knowledge and expertise that comes with the research is not gained and if the possibilities are realised then the firm on the outside is left at a significant disadvantage.

Building culture

The speed with which a business responds to changes in technology is dependent to some extent on the culture within the organisation. If the culture is one of risk-taking, empowerment, challenge, competition and dynamism, then many new ideas can be developed and used to good effect. However, if the culture is highly autocratic with decision-making concentrated in the hands of a relatively small number of people in the organisation, then it could be that excellent ideas and new products do not ever see the light of day. Some of the most famous products of recent times have been developed by 'accident' from within the organisation, for example, the *Post-it* note developed within the 3M organisation. In 1968, an adhesives analyst in 3M developed the glue but it was another employee, Art Fry, who several years later used it to create a bookmark and the *Post-it* note was born. The key is whether the organisation has the culture to recognise these ideas and to help the originator exploit them.

Evaluating the costs and benefits

The extent to which a business will adopt and try to exploit new technology will depend in part on the relative costs and benefits associated with it. Investing in technology brings with it many potential problems; processes might need to be changed, plant might need to be reorganised, whole new buildings or locations might be warranted, not to mention the potential costs of training employees to work with the technology. The costs associated with this have to be balanced out against the potential benefits that the technology can bring over a period of time. These benefits might relate to sales revenue and profits but they might also be associated with productivity and efficiency. Technology is not always 'good'. It has to be right for the organisation, its culture and its workflows, and ultimately it has to benefit the 'bottom line' – the net income of a business.

Size

A larger business will invariably be in a better position to exploit the benefits of technology than a smaller firm. This is simply because it has the funds to be able to invest in new technology if it can be proved to be of benefit to the business. This is one of the benefits of economies of scale; not only will larger firms have the financial backing, but they are also able to exploit the benefits of technology more effectively and so help reduce average or unit costs.

However, there are occasions when a small firm will be in a position to be able to outperform its large rival, especially if it is more flexible, able to make decisions more quickly and to see the possible benefits of technology before its larger, possibly lumbering, rivals. The more specialised technology is, the more likely it is that a small firm might be in a position to exploit that technology. For example, some firms supplying the medical industry develop highly-specialised tools and equipment to manufacture relatively small quantities of high value-added goods to a very specialised market. It would not be efficient or viable for a large firm to invest in such specialised services in many cases.

Human resources

The possible benefits a business gets from technology will depend not only on the culture as described above, but also in how a business utilises its human resources. There are a number of health and safety considerations that technology will bring. For example, in the office, businesses have to consider the working environment of those who spend their day using computer screens; chairs have to be provided that encourage appropriate posture, regular breaks have to be allowed and consideration has to be given to the possibility of injuries such as repetitive strain injury (RSI) and carpel tunnel syndrome. Such considerations will have an impact on the costs of implementing technology and the ease with which some firms are able to embrace technology.

Technology can also bring other benefits in terms of cost-saving beyond that of simply using machines, for example. The development of communications technology means that many businesses are now in a position of being able to change working practices so that more staff can work remotely and flexibly. This can have a very positive impact on motivation and job satisfaction, and also on productivity. In addition, some firms are finding that they can close down office blocks since they do not need to maintain high-cost work centres in high-priced city locations. Sun Microsystems, based in San Francisco, California, have done just this as part of a policy to encourage workers to be more flexible. They estimate that the cost savings in overheads amounts to $71 million and that is money they can better use on recruiting high-quality staff who will drive their business growth.

Skills watch!

AO3 / AO4

Decisions about implementing technology in a business will be made in relation to the costs and benefits associated with the investment in and the returns from the technology, and the impact on its human resources.

Sun Microsystems not only encouraged a greater degree of homeworking amongst its staff, but also set up flexible access sites called iWork Cafés, which enabled staff to work remotely but still have access to the business and its systems.

How might Sun Microsystems evaluate the net benefits to its business of introducing this type of technology and changed work practices?

Summary and exam guidance

Summary

- Technology is the use of knowledge applied to the environment to enable people to exercise greater control over that environment.

- Technology is used extensively in every business in one way or another.

- Technology affects businesses in three main ways:
  - marketing opportunities
  - the culture of the business
  - its processes and systems.

- Businesses respond to these changes in various ways. They can develop R&D functions, through the speed with which they respond to changes in technology, by evaluating the costs and benefits of adopting new technology, through their size and their HR functions.

Exam practice

Read the article below and then answer the questions that follow.

Article A

Product innovation

The drive to constantly innovate is ever present in the computer industry. However, could there be a limit to the innovation? Silicon Valley in California is the home to some of the most successful companies in the world including Intel, the manufacturer of microprocessors for a range of computer applications. In 1965, one of Intel's founders, Gordon Moore, made an observation on the future of computer power. He stated that the number of transistors per square inch on a chip would double every two years. Moore, who is now retired from Intel, has since suggested that this cannot continue indefinitely.

What this means in practical terms is that manufacturers are looking at ways in which they can fit more and more computing power onto their chips. This means getting the gap between the lines of circuits closer and closer together. Nanotechnology is helping this to occur but the standard format of chip design has largely remained unchanged – it is just more compact and getting more so as time goes by. These grids are capable of hundreds of millions of instructions per second. They are the most complex products to manufacture in the world and are produced in some of the cleanest environments on the planet.

The problem is that as the grids get closer and closer, problems start to occur. The silicon base on which the grid is etched has been used because it has particular qualities. It is a semi-conductor which means that it can either conduct electricity or act as an insulator. These properties are now being tested to their limits and as the

cont...

lines get closer and closer, leakages are starting to occur along with an increase in heat generated. Is Moore's Law, as it is known, about to reach its end?

There is still some way to go before silicon becomes redundant but businesses in Silicon Valley are still looking to the future. Some are looking at ways in which the traditional design of the lines on a chip can be changed. The traditional design of a chip is called the Manhattan design. It is based around connections that run in lines at ninety degrees (think of the road map of Manhattan Island to get the idea). However, designers are now looking at so-called X architecture where interconnections move not only in straight lines and at ninety degrees but also diagonally. This could reduce chip costs whilst continuing to increase power.

Intel is also looking into using a different material to silicon. The material they and others are looking at is called hafnium. Hafnium is a metal that is used in the nuclear industry. Intel and its rivals AMD are exploring the viability of using hafnium as the base on which chips are made. This material may allow the manufacturers to be able to reduce yet further the distance between the lines that are etched and so continue to increase computing power at the rate suggested by Moore back in 1965.

Source: Biz/ed In the News: http://www.bized.co.uk/cgi-bin/chron/chron.pl?id=2923

Discuss the view that the future success of business is largely dependent on the development of new technology.

Total: 50 marks

Breakdown of assessment objectives

AO1 – Knowledge and understanding – 5/50
AO2 – Apply knowledge and understanding – 5/50
AO3 – Analyse problems, issues and situations – 15/50
AO4 – Evaluate, distinguish between fact and opinion, assess and judge
       information from a variety of sources – 25/50

Suggested structure

You will need to:

- Make clear what definition of 'success' you are using as the basis for your answer.

- Provide a detailed consideration of the role of technology in business success.

- In your consideration, make sure that you structure your answer so that each point flows from the previous to the next.

- Make sure that you clearly show the link between the technology you are talking about and how it promotes success as defined earlier.

- It is likely that you will structure the above in relation to the key ways in which technology affects business success – communications, culture and processes and systems. (This is not the only way to do it though!)

- Provide some balance to the answer by referring to other factors that might also contribute to success (again as you have defined it).

- You should consider at least two other relevant factors to provide the appropriate balance to the answer. What these other factors are is not that important – the way you justify them later will be. There are no right and wrong factors to include but they do have to be appropriate to the context of the question – business success – and the way that you have defined it.

- Provide a commentary where you make some judgements about the importance of technology against the factors that you have chosen. You will have to have made your mind up before this point what the overall outcome of your answer is going to be; do you agree whole-heartedly with the statements, to a large extent, a reasonable amount or hardly at all?

- Having such an outcome in mind at the outset is important and is the reason why you should consider a brief outline plan of the structure and the subject of each paragraph before you begin writing.

- Draw your answer together in the final paragraph by summing up your argument in response to the question. Remember, you must make direct reference to the question at this point – that is why it was asked in the first place! Don't answer the question you wanted to answer; answer the one that has been given to you.

Chapter 25 The relationship between businesses and the competitive environment

Key terms

Barriers to entry Methods either natural or deliberate which make it harder for new entrants to enter a market.

Competition A situation where there are rivals who allow the customer a choice.

Concentration ratio The proportion of total sales accounted for by a specified number of firms in an industry.

Contestable market A development in the theory of market structures that suggests that a firm's behaviour will be affected by the cost of entry and exit to the industry or market.

Interchangeability A process whereby businesses develop processes that enable them to standardise parts, processes and production systems across the business to build flexibility and competitive advantage.

Monopsony A situation where there is only one buyer in a market.

Price elasticity of demand The responsiveness of demand to changes in prices.

Product differentiation Making a product offering either physically or technically different from rivals, or building the perception that it is different.

Businesses exist in a competitive environment. Rarely is any business immune from the effects of competition. Competition is defined as a situation where there are rivals who allow the customer a choice. The more competition there is in an industry, the more choice a consumer has, which can affect the way a business behaves. The following highlights some important factors about competition that needs to be borne in mind when looking at this section.

- Competition exists where there is more than one firm offering the same or a similar product or service.
- But, competition may also exist where businesses in other industries are offering a product that consumers could use instead. For example, a gas cooker could be used instead of an electric cooker. In other words, there are normally some substitutes that exist for any product. The key will be the ease with which one product can be substituted for another.
- The extent of the competition will depend on the degree of substitutability between the products – how easy it is for one product to be used instead of another.
- Competition will be affected by the extent to which consumers develop and maintain habits in buying, the quality of the product or service, as well as the price consumers have to pay.
- Competition may also be affected by factors other than the product itself: for example, the way people in the business respond to customers, how they deal with complaints and queries, after-sales service, and so on.

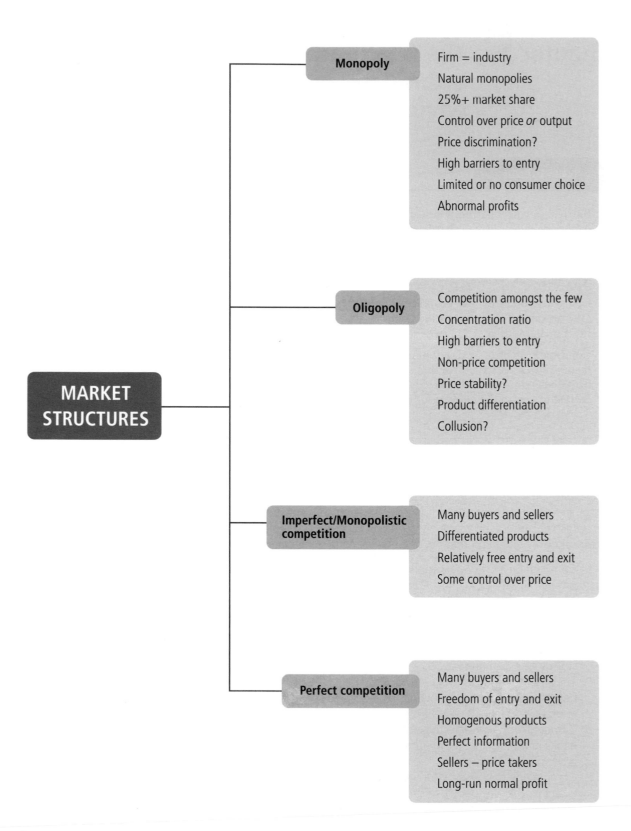

Figure 25.1   Summary of market structures

Synoptic search

In your AS studies you will have had an introduction in the marketing section on market structures. You should go back to this and ensure that you understand the basic principles of the different market structures and the characteristics of competitive behaviour in each.

The main characteristics of each market structure is summarised in Figure 25.1.

Porter's 'Five Forces'

Michael Porter is a respected academic at the Harvard Business School. He has researched and written extensively on the competitive environment. One of the key elements of Porter's analysis is that it is important to understand the market structure to be able to understand business behaviour in response to changes in the competitive environment. Porter suggested that there were five forces that affected a business's ability to be able to respond to changes in competition. These five forces are:

- Extent of rivalry between firms – how competitive is the existing market?
- Strength of barriers to entry – how easy is it for new rivals to enter the industry?
- Supplier power – the greater the power, the less control the organisation has on the supply of its inputs.
- Buyer power – how much power do customers in the industry have?
- Threat from substitutes – what alternative products and services are there and what is the extent of the threat they pose?

At the heart of the competitive environment is the rivalry between firms in an industry. The extent of this rivalry will be dependent on a variety of factors. As you work through the remainder of the rest of this section you should bear in mind the following factors:

- The market structure in which firms operate, the rate at which the market they are involved in is growing, the cost conditions that exist in the industry (for example, how important a role fixed costs play in total costs), which in turn can affect pricing strategies. For an airline, for example, a high proportion of the cost of operating a flight between (say) London and New York is in the form of fixed costs. This means that the airline has a number of pricing tactics it can use to fill seats.
- The degree of product differentiation can be related to physical and perceived differences in a good or service, with perceptions able to be altered by advertising and promotion.
- Entering an industry has costs but so does exiting. For example, in the chemical industry large amounts of plant are needed. Much of this plant does not have alternative uses in production and so it can be expensive to leave the industry.
- The threat of entry will be affected by the extent to which products are differentiated and the cost of entering the industry. Existing businesses may have considerable cost advantages which prohibit new entrants from easily trying to take advantage of any growth or profit that exists in the industry. Existing businesses may also benefit from being in the most appropriate locations, having access to raw materials, and from the experience they have gained in being in

British Airways have a considerable degree of market power at Heathrow but have to consider the threat of new entrants, the fact that they have to pay fees to BAA and that they operate in a highly-competitive global market

the industry for a long period of time – something called the experience curve, which leads to lower average costs over time through the benefits of specialisation.

- Legal barriers which include government licences, charters and patents.
- The access to distribution channels, for example, potential landline and broadband suppliers may be affected by the ease and cost of accessing existing networks that are owned by BT, or the way in which some businesses access cheaper branded items such as clothing and medicines which are subject to restrictions on distribution (also referred to as the grey market).
- The threat of retaliation – how will existing firms respond to the threat of entry by a competitor? If the perception is that existing firms would respond aggressively by engaging in price cutting or even some form of collusive activity, then it might affect the decision by a possible new competitor to enter the market.

Assessing the effects of changes in the competitive structure

There are four main areas that we will look at in this section which highlight the main changes in the competitive structure facing a business. These include the entry of new competitors, the effect of acquisitions on the competitive environment, the buying power of consumers and the power of suppliers.

The entry of new competitors

Every business faces the possibility of the entry of other firms to provide it with competition. It is important to understand what this process is and why it happens. Assume that a business happens to be the only firm producing a particular product at this point in time. The product is extremely successful and currently the business is making very healthy profits. The existence of healthy profits is a sign that there is a market for the product – people to sell to that are willing to buy – and that the product can be produced at a cost that is lower than revenues and hence can generate a profit.

There is an incentive for entrepreneurs and/or other firms to look to see whether they could also produce this product and offer it for sale in the market. The ease with which they can do this will be a factor in whether there will be a flood of new entrants or a very limited number. If new firms do enter the market, then the supply of the product available will rise and consumers will have more choice. Basic supply and demand analysis tells us that a rise in supply, other things being equal, will tend to have the effect of forcing down price and in so doing, profits will start to be squeezed – perhaps not by much at this stage, but the process will begin.

As more entrants come into the market, profits will eventually get to the stage where they are relatively small and the profits will start to be exhausted. At this time, as the product reaches the end of its life cycle, firms may well be looking round at other new products and markets to enter to gain better returns, and so the process continues.

We can see this happening in a number of markets. For example, in the 1970s, the development of the electronic calculator was seen as being a major breakthrough. The first firms in the market with these products were able to make good returns on their investment, but over time the technology became more accessible to new businesses and more and more entered the market. Today we almost take the calculator for granted and can easily buy one for just a few pounds.

Similar stories exist in markets such as that for mobile phones, personal computers, laptops and other technical products, but also in less obvious markets like animated movies. The success of computer-generated films, like *Toy Story* produced by Pixar, led to a number of other similar films that appealed to children but which had a clear appeal to adults through the humour in the films (which most children never understood and which provided adults with their own little reason for watching the film). Other films in the same genre came thick and fast, such as *Antz, Shrek, The Incredibles, Ice Age, Cars, A Bug's Life, Monsters Inc., Finding Nemo* and many others produced by studios such as Dreamworks, Sony Pictures Animation, DNA Productions (Paramount and Warner Bros) and 20th Century Fox. Each was trying to capitalise on the market for these types of films and take a slice of the profits that *Toy Story* clearly identified exists in the market.

Toy Story **was a huge financial success for Pixar but led to a number of similar types of films being produced by other film companies looking to take advantage of the profits that existed for computer-generated animation pictures**

THE EFFECT OF NEW ENTRANTS

The extent of the effect on existing businesses of new entrants depends on a variety of factors. These include:

- The nature of the product – how easy is it to replicate and copy?
- The existing market structure – is the market dominated by a small number of large firms or does the market consist of a dominant firm?
- The legislative and regulatory structure of the market – how easy is it for new entrants to gain the right documentation and permissions to compete?
- The degree of existing brand loyalty and the price elasticity of demand (ped) for the product concerned.

As outlined above, in any market if there are new entrants to the industry then in theory there is a greater degree of choice for consumers and thus more competition. In theory this would force existing firms to take a greater degree of concern over the prices they are charging, the quality of their product or service, the quality of the customer service they offer and looking at ways in which they can maintain or extend any competitive advantage they may already have.

For consumers the competition should mean lower prices, greater choice and better-quality products. Firms know that if they do not provide the right sort of products and the right sort of price and quality, then consumers can switch to their rivals and they will lose sales and market share.

The reality might be somewhat different, however. For the new entrant the task of breaking into a market, especially if it is already established, might be very difficult. Existing distribution outlets might be difficult to access and the new firm has to find a way of convincing the consumer that what they are offering represents a better all-round experience than what they are already using.

In such circumstances the price elasticity of demand (ped) is a factor. If existing firms have managed to develop brand loyalty and buyer habit, then the ped might be relatively low. Even if a new firm enters the market and offers a lower price than that of the existing firms, the proportionate change in demand is likely to be limited and as such, revenue will also be lower than might be expected. The new entrant will have to try to find ways in which they can increase the ped and make consumers more aware of the degree of substitutability of the product they are offering compared to existing rivals.

The effect of new entrants in the competitive environment will therefore depend on how many new entrants there are, how close a substitute for the existing products the new entrants are offering, and how easy it is for the new entrant to be able to bring their product to the market. If barriers to entry can be erected, then it will be much harder for new firms to provide the competition that consumers might desire, and as a result the benefits of increased competition may be limited.

For example...

Anti-competitive practices

In the UK the regulator of the energy industry, Ofgem, is keen to promote the installation of so-called 'smart meters' in homes to more accurately record domestic usage of gas and electricity. There are a number of firms who are in a position to manufacture and supply these meters but they face a problem in that to access the market they have to enter into an agreement with National Grid, which is responsible for the electricity transmission network and for the gas pipeline system in the UK. National Grid has a 40% market share in the replacement of these meters; around 1 million are replaced every year and the total number of meters in existence is around 18 million. If firms had access to the market, consumers would get cheaper meter installations and a better service from the new entrants. However, the dominant position of National Grid has made it more difficult for them to access the market. In February 2008, Ofgem fined National Grid £41.6 million pounds for abusing its monopoly position and restricting competition in the meter installation market.

A microbrewery may have some advantages over global brewers, but to what extent can they really make inroads into a market dominated by global brewers?

If a new microbrewery was set up in a large town, the effect on prices to the consumer might be minimal. Microbreweries are often started by enthusiasts but are characterised by the fact that they produce limited amounts of beer a year compared to the large breweries that dominate the industry. The microbrewery itself tends to be part of a building incorporating a restaurant and bar, and can be seen by pub-goers. Existing pubs might recognise that there is new competition, but the overall effect on their business is likely to be limited. The chance that the microbrewery could offer cheaper prices than established brewers is weak; they can compete on quality but many drinkers might already be very satisfied with the quality and range that they get from other brewers (and in reality, how many people can really distinguish between different beers). The microbrewery will also be competing against a considerable degree of brand loyalty that larger brewers will have been building and investing in for many years backed by multi-million dollar advertising and promotion campaigns.

The effect of acquisitions – mergers and takeovers

There has been a trend to greater concentration in many industries in recent years. The concentration ratio refers to the proportion of total sales accounted for by a specified number of businesses in the industry. The greater the concentration, the smaller the number of firms who account for the total sales. The concentration ratio is usually prefaced by a specified number of firms. A four-firm concentration ratio of 75% means that four firms together account for 75% of the total sales in the industry; a three-firm concentration ratio of 89% means that three firms account for 89% of total sales, and so on.

Whenever mergers or takeovers in an industry occur, there will be a change in the concentration ratio. Many of the more high-profile acquisitions in recent years have fundamentally changed the industry landscape. It must be remembered that many of these acquisitions relate to global business activity, even if the main headquarters of one or both companies is in the UK or any other individual country.

The effect on the competitive environment therefore tends to be rather different as a result. In the brewing industry there has been a move to a far greater degree of concentration. To the average customer visiting pubs and clubs, the acquisitions activity might have very little obvious direct impact. The acquisitions have tended to preserve many of the major brands that are popular and there may be the illusion of choice in the market. However, when it is realised that brands such as *Becks*, *Stella Artois*, *Jupiler*, *Hoegaarden*, *Staropramen* and *Leffe* are all owned by Belgian brewer InBev, whilst *Grolsch*, *Miller Light*, *Peroni* and *Castle* are all owned by SAB Miller, the extent of the choice that consumers really have might be less obvious. In July 2008, InBev announced that it had agreed to the acquisition of the major US brewer Anheuser-Busch in a deal worth $52 billion. This would make Anheuser-Busch InBev, the new name for the company, the world's largest brewer.

The market for alcoholic drinks, therefore, tends to appear to be highly competitive with a wide variety of choice of products. However, the extent of the concentration may mean that the price benefits that the consumer might hope to get from the appearance of competition may not materialise and prices will tend to be largely similar across the board. In addition, in this industry there has also been a move by the larger brewers towards vertical integration so that many own outlets which sell their products. Again, there may be the illusion that there is a wide range of choice of different beers but when they are all owned by the same brewer the choice may be more limited.

However, mergers do provide the opportunity for businesses to combine their respective talents and skills to raise their profile, and present a greater competitive challenge to their rivals as well as benefiting consumers. The acquisition of Anheuser-Busch by InBev means that *Budweiser* will be able to gain greater exposure in parts of Europe and elsewhere where it had limited sales, and in the US, *Stella Artois* can be made more widely available. This does lead to greater consumer choice.

In other cases, mergers have led to the opportunity for businesses to combine different skills and expertise to improve the quality of the research and development programmes. In the pharmaceutical industry, the sheer scale of R&D investment means that the groundbreaking research into important drugs and medicines can only be done by businesses with very large assets who are able to withstand the considerable risks involved.

GlaxoSmithKline (GSK), for example, spends £7.2 million every day on research into finding new medicines. Its total turnover in 2007 was £22,716,000,000* (£22.7 billion). The business is the result of a series of acquisitions over the last 50 years which have included firms such as Wellcome, Beechams, Glaxo and SmithKline. The business has interests in vaccines and consumer health care products, including over-the-counter and prescription medicines. The range of products that are produced by the business is extensive and include some of the best-known household brands such as *Gaviscon*, *Ribena*, *Panadol*, *Aquafresh* toothpaste, *NiQuitin*, *Lucozade*, *Horlicks*, *Macleans* toothpaste, *Sensodyne*, *Zantac* and *Zovirax*, amongst hundreds of others.

* Source: www.gsk.com

Without some sort of monopoly power, many large pharmaceutical companies would be reluctant to invest the millions needed to bring new medicines to the market

Skills watch!

AO3 / AO4

In 2006, the Walt Disney Corporation bought the computer-generated image company Pixar, who had produced a number of hit movies including *Toy Story*, *Finding Nemo* and *The Incredibles*.

To what extent does such a merger impact on competition in the market for this type of movie?

The cost of developing new medicines and health care products is very high. Economies of scale in such an industry are vitally important to enable the business to compete. Developing these types of products through small firms is simply not feasible in the modern world and so competition tends to be limited in terms of the number of companies in the market. For consumers, the choice of products still tends to be overwhelming but they might be paying a price that reflects the significant risks involved to a firm such as GSK in developing new products.

The competition in the industry comes between the different brands in many cases. A business like GSK will provide customers with a number of different brands and the competitive element will not simply be between the brands, but in the slightly different offerings and marketing mix that will be applied to each. This helps to differentiate the product and also helps to build strong customer loyalty. This not only boosts GSK's total sales, but also gives it some protection against competition from rivals. The heavily-concentrated pharmaceutical industry also has the effect of deterring new entrants and is a form of barrier to entry. The only way that the industry really changes is through some form of acquisition activity within the industry itself rather than from the threat of new entrants.

The buying power of consumers

When looking at the buying power of consumers we have to remember who the buyers are! In B2C industries the buying power of consumers is likely to be very limited; there are possibly millions of consumers and a relatively small number of firms. It would take a herculean effort on the part of consumers to organise themselves to be able to influence the behaviour of a business to any great extent. In years gone by, various pressure groups have tried to organise boycotts of certain businesses because of their links with a particular political regime or because of alleged effects on the environment. In the 1970s, for example, there were attempts to organise boycotts of Barclays because it had alleged dealings with the apartheid regime in South Africa. In the 1990s, the oil company Shell was similarly targeted because it allegedly caused environmental damage in Nigeria. In both cases the results were limited in terms of the effect on each, although the bad publicity did prompt some defensive tactics from both companies.

The alleged environmental damage caused by Shell's operation in Nigeria caused widespread concern and a call to boycott Shell's products

The lack of buyer power in such cases is why there are regulatory authorities like the Office of Fair Trading, the Competition Commission and the various regulatory authorities associated with the former nationalised industries. These bodies are supposed to represent the interest of consumers who individually have very little power. The advances in technology, however, have created a slight shift in the balance towards the consumer. The work of consumer authorities like the Consumers' Association, now known as Which?, and TV programmes like *Watchdog*, have made it more likely that poor service and quality and excessive prices will receive some publicity which is invariably unwelcome for most businesses. In addition, the work of trading standards offices also gives consumers a way in which inappropriate business behaviour can be highlighted and dealt with.

The existence of blogs and forums is also giving consumers more access to information to help them make better decisions when considering purchases. For example, if an individual is contemplating buying double glazing or a conservatory, they can get a considerable amount of information from the Web by simply typing the company name and 'customer reviews' into a search engine. The results provide the consumer with the chance to read about the experiences of other customers of the business which then enables them to be able to make a more informed decision. Companies ought to be aware of the existence of these types of reviews and that they are likely to have increasing currency as technology develops. Some businesses will respond to the comments on the reviews and attempt to change their behaviour to improve service, prices and quality.

Despite this, the power of consumers in high-volume markets is limited. The consumer always has the ultimate choice in where to spend their money, but in some cases there are precious few alternatives available to them if they are not happy with the service they receive and many businesses know that. In the privatised utilities, there is some degree of competition, but for many people the difficulties they face in searching out different price tariffs is not warranted in relation to the savings they will make. Water companies, energy companies and telecommunications companies know they have a considerable degree of market power and are able to exploit it, hence the need for regulation and legislation.

In B2B businesses the situation might be quite different. Here the number of consumers might be very small in relation to the number of businesses they deal with. A situation where there is only one buyer in an industry is called a **monopsony**. As with a monopoly, the extent of the monopsony power that the buyer has will depend on the number of buyers in the industry. The smaller the number of buyers, the greater the degree of monopsony power they can exert. An example where monopsony power may exist is in industries like the electricity-generating industry, where the power generator buys from a small number of coal or gas producers, or in the supermarket industry where some supermarkets have agreements with producers and are effectively the only buyer. In such cases, their power may be substantial because if they were to withdraw their business the supplier is likely to face serious consequences.

Electricity generation is a good example of where monopsony power rests with the buyer, who may be able to exert pressure on a small number of suppliers who are dependent on the buyer for their business

In some industries the power of buyers can influence the behaviour of firms. In the toy industry, a major buyer such as Toys R Us is able to get involved in design and planning decisions at an early stage in manufacturing and influence what will be in their stores; a small number of mobile phone manufacturers may buy specific items such as micro chips from companies; Nike and Adidas may be dominant buyers of footwear; and PC manufacturers like Dell might be a major buyer for a company like Intel.

Skills watch!

AO3 / AO4

In 2008, the Competition Commission delivered a report on its investigation into grocery retailing in the UK. There had been a number of concerns raised that the power of the big four supermarkets in the UK, Tesco, Asda, Sainsbury's and Morrisons, was detrimental to the welfare of small businesses, especially farmers. It was argued that farmers had been subject to low prices and aggressive pressure from the supermarkets.

The Commission reported that there was little evidence for such behaviour although it was decided that a new code of conduct covering relationships between farmers and retailers would be set up.

Activity

To what extent is the decision to set up a new code of conduct recognition that there is a problem in the relationship between buyers who have considerable powers, and suppliers who have little?

There are two main theories about how such a relationship might affect the firms concerned. The first is that the dominant buyer exerts a considerable degree of pressure on the other firm and squeezes its profit margins to the minimum, holding, as it can, a fear factor over the supplier. This aggressive and rather negative view could indeed happen and possibly does happen in certain markets, but the complexity of business in the 21st century has tended to bring about a different view.

Many businesses now see the relationship with their suppliers in a different way to that of being a dominant, superior partner. They recognise that the advantages of building relationships with their suppliers are vital to helping them sustain their business and in building not only competitive advantage, but also in protecting themselves against shocks. Resilience in the face of an uncertain business, and political and economic climate, are seen as being of increasing importance.

For example...

Recovering from shock

Businesses like Toyota rely on other smaller businesses for particular parts for their vehicles. One example is a company called Aisin, which made a part for the brake system on Toyota cars called a P-valve. Aisin supplied around 99% of all these parts to Toyota. In February 1997, the Aisin factory in Japan caught fire which destroyed its production capabilities. The knock-on effects to Toyota were substantial and were predicted to cut production by over 15,000 vehicles per day. Within nine days of the fire all Toyota's plants were operational. Both Toyota and Aisin lost large sums as a result of the disruption but it could have been much worse. The reason it was not much worse was because of the extent of the relationship between Toyota and Aisin where both worked together to find solutions to the problem and get other sources of supply for the P-valves.

A buyer who has monopsony power, therefore, may find that it is in its own long-term interest to nurture the relationship between itself and its supplier to ensure that there are benefits to both businesses.

Supplier–producer relationships in the motor industry have become closer in recent years

The power of suppliers

In many respects the analysis of the power of suppliers is the exact opposite to that of the power of buyers. Firms will enter into agreements with suppliers to provide component parts, raw materials, goods for final sale and to provide various services. In other words, suppliers provide the inputs for production. These agreements are often established through contracts and there are various rules and terms within the contract that define the relationship between the two parties.

These terms can be influenced by the degree of power that the supplier has. In general, as with the case of buyers, if there are few suppliers then their power is greater. This power can be strengthened further if the item being supplied has few substitutes or where the item is of great importance in the production process to the buyer. In the case of Toyota in the example above, the P-valves were relatively low cost but important items in the production process representing a high-volume item, but in other cases the supplier may be providing a good that represents a significant proportion of the total cost and in this scenario the supplier power might also be significant.

If supplier power is significant it can have an effect on prices. If the buyer cannot source supplies easily elsewhere, then in theory the price they will have to pay to secure inputs will be higher and, other things being equal, this will reduce profit margins. The buyer will not be in a position to be able to switch to an alternative supplier very easily if the characteristics of the market are as described above. Where the supplier is providing a component that is highly specialised, the buyer may not be in a position to produce the item themselves nor will it be able to easily source supplies from elsewhere.

However, having outlined the possible effects of this power, the proviso mentioned in the section on buyer power is also increasingly becoming a feature of business. This is especially so where just-in-time (JIT) systems have been developed. One of the key features of these systems is the development of close relationships between buyer and supplier. In such a relationship it may not be appropriate or in the interests of the supplier to exercise any market power that they might have.

For example...

BUILDING relationships

The symbiotic relationship between buyer and seller is illustrated in the case of PC manufacture. A company like Dell relies on another company, Intel, for chips that power the processors in their PCs and laptops. At the same time, Intel relies on Dell to provide a major source of demand for its chips. For Dell, the opportunity to substitute processors exists – they could use Intel's rivals, AMD. However, the two have developed a relationship that seems to suit both parties. In theory each has a considerable degree of power over the other, but it is this very power that each recognises that moderates the behaviour of the two firms and leads to them both establishing and building a working relationship that benefits both.

Evaluating responses of businesses to a changing competitive environment

There are a number of ways that a business might respond to a change in its competitive environment.

Organisational learning

An important development in organisational behaviour is in the concept of a learning organisation. The concept has been written about in detail by Peter Senge, a lecturer at the Massachusetts Institute of Technology (MIT). Senge defines learning organisations as:

'…organizations where people continually expand their capacity to create the results they truly desire, where new and expansive patterns of thinking are nurtured, where collective aspiration is set free, and where people are continually learning to see the whole together.'*

* Source: *The Fifth Discipline. The art and practice of the learning organization*, P M Senge, Random House, London, 1990

Organisational learning means that firms can benefit from the experience they have in a particular industry and can also adapt and see new possibilities and opportunities. Changes in the competitive environment provide such opportunities, but these can only be taken if the organisation is willing to embrace the change and find ways of working with it to their advantage. The development of relationships between buyers and suppliers outlined above is one aspect where businesses have had to 'unlearn' one reality and replace it with something completely different. For some organisations, adapting to such a changed competitive landscape can be too daunting and they tend to be the ones that try and rely on past success as the source of future prosperity. In many cases these types of firms are the ones that do not survive. For example, Rover cars and Polaroid cameras both accepted too late that the competitive landscape had changed. Others like Apple, for example, with its *iTunes* service, saw that consumer needs were different and that the traditional way of buying music was changing. They learned quickly and were able to take advantage of the changed environment to a remarkable degree.

Barriers to entry

The very act of merger and takeover tends to have the effect of building barriers to entry. The trend to greater concentration in many large industries increases the economies of scale and provides even fewer opportunities for new entrants. In addition to this, businesses will often look to erect barriers to entry to protect their competitive position. Some of these barriers will be erected deliberately. Ways in which this could be done include:

- Investing in R&D (note that GSK spend £7.2 million every day on R&D whilst Astra Zeneca spends £2.5 billion a year and Pfizer invests around $4 billion a year).

The firm behind many of the major detergent brands is unlikely to be a household name, but their brands will be – a good example of brand proliferation

- Through extensive advertising which has the effect of reinforcing brand loyalty and reducing the price elasticity of demand (for example, Nike, Coca Cola and McDonald's spend heavily on advertising and Nike sees one of its key tasks as marketing its brand).
- Legal action – for example, Asda was taken to court by McVities for releasing a biscuit product called *Puffin* which they argued was too similar to their long-standing brand *Penguin*. The courts agreed and Asda had to withdraw its product. Legal barriers can also be obtained through patents, licences and charters.
- Illegal means – tactics such as predatory pricing, price fixing, collusion and market-sharing agreements.
- Brand proliferation strategies – the aim here is to flood the market with many brands which are each differentiated but in the same market. Proctor and Gamble and Unilever are good examples of firms who have many different brands in their portfolio which compete against each other but which make it much harder for new entrants to compete.

In addition to deliberate barriers, firms can also benefit from so-called 'innocent barriers'. These occur where the size of the business gives it significant cost advantages through economies of scale and through the so-called 'learning curve'. In heavily concentrated industries these cost advantages make it very difficult for any new entrant to be able to compete. In the airline industry, the competitive landscape has been changed by the entry of the low-cost airlines, but a number have tried to enter and found it difficult to survive. For example, Oasis hoped to be able to provide a long-haul, low-cost airline service, and business class operators Silverjet and Eos both had to withdraw from the low-cost airline market.

Many firms who have been in an industry for some time will be able to benefit from the experience they have built up in that industry and learn from that experience. The advantages of specialisation, which new entrants cannot replicate, lead to reductions in unit costs which further compliment the economies of scale they have.

New product development and innovation

The investment in R&D is likely to generate new products that a business can use to secure its competitive position. In addition, product innovation – bringing new product ideas to the marketplace – can also make it much harder for new entrants to compete. Product innovation may involve utilising existing products to meet market needs. For example, detergent manufacturers have found different ways of repackaging what is basically the same product – washing powder – and making it into tablets, liquid, gels, and so on. Fruit juice producers make their product available in a variety of ways each suitable for a different market: large cartons, lunchbox size, drinks to go, and so on.

These methods can be used to maintain a competitive advantage and also to make it harder for new entrants to compete. The extent to which they can be used depends on the size of the business and the overall market. In highly-concentrated markets they are generally effective methods of preventing competition, but in markets that have the characteristics of monopolistic or imperfect competition, they are likely to be less effective because of the number of firms in the market.

Differentiation

Finding ways of differentiating the product helps to reduce the price elasticity of demand and also give the product a different identity which helps to build brand loyalty. It does this by reducing the actual or perceived substitutability of the product with others in the market. Firms may differentiate their product by actually changing the physical or technical characteristics of it or by extensive advertising to build the perception that it is different.

Contestable markets

This is a theory developed by William Baumol in the early 1980s. It has come to be seen as a valuable addition to the theory on market structures. A **contestable market** has the following characteristics:

- Firms' behaviour influenced by the threat of new entrants to the industry.
- No barriers to entry or exit.
- No 'sunk costs'. Sunk costs are the costs of entering a market which cannot be recovered in the event the business leaves the market. Eurotunnel, for example, incurred extraordinary sunk costs in building the channel tunnel. If it had to exit the market then those costs could not be recovered.
- Firms may deliberately limit profits made to discourage new entrants – entry limit pricing.

Sunk costs: the Channel Tunnel has only one use – as a tunnel. Once constructed the costs could not be recovered by changing the use of the tunnel or trying to sell it off as something different!

- Firms may attempt to erect artificial barriers to entry, for example:
  - overcapacity – providing the opportunity for a business to flood the market and drive down price in the event of a threat of entry;
  - aggressive marketing and branding strategies to 'tighten' up the market;
  - the potential for predatory or destroyer pricing;
  - finding ways of reducing costs and increasing efficiency to gain competitive advantage.
- 'Hit and run' tactics – enter the industry, take the profit and get out quickly (possibly because of the freedom of entry and exit).
- Cream-skimming – identifying parts of the market that are high in value added, for example, Rolex watches, and exploiting those markets.

Examples of perfectly contestable markets are rare (there are always likely to be some sunk costs) but there are some examples where there are some of the characteristics described above. In the airline industry, for example, an airline such as Ryanair can expand its existing operations at an airport to launch new services to new destinations relatively easily because it is already established at that airport. Supermarkets have the facilities and shelf space to devote to its own brand products which means that the entry costs are very low and can be recovered when they exit the market.

Interchangeability

Many large firms are building flexibility into their production processes through **interchangeability**. This means that they use a large number of common parts over a variety of production processes for different products. If problems develop they can easily switch to other production lines to maintain output. This makes it more difficult for other firms to enter such a market because it is difficult to compete with this level of flexibility.

Intel, the computer chip maker, has a number of plants around the world but each plant is an exact copy of the others, even down to the orientation of the plant to the sun! The exacting nature of chip production and the necessity of having extremely high specification levels at all stages have led the company to develop a so-called 'Copy Exact!' policy. Some car manufacturers also use a similar principle; there are a number of Audi, VW and Skoda cars that are fundamentally the same vehicle. The addition of certain embellishments enables the company to be able to sell in different markets and at different prices. The Skoda *Superb* is essentially the same car as the Audi *A4* but retails at a fraction of the price.

Building this sort of interchangeability helps businesses maintain a presence in multiple markets, reduces unit costs and makes it more difficult for new entrants to compete. This is further exacerbated by the tendency to greater concentration in such markets.

An Audi and a Skoda – same car or different? One is certainly a higher price than the other.

Summary and exam guidance

Summary

- Businesses have to accept they operate in a competitive environment.

- The degree of competition they face affects their behaviour.

- The market structure they operate in is a major determinant of this behaviour.

- Porter's 'Five Forces' provides a useful structure with which to analyse competitive behaviour.

- The rivalry between firms in an industry is a key element of the competitive environment.

- Changes in the competitive structure is determined by:
  - the entry of new competitors
  - the effect of acquisitions
  - the power of buyers
  - the power of sellers.

- Businesses respond to the changing competitive environment by learning, erecting barriers to entry, developing new products and finding ways of utilising existing products for new markets, differentiation, operating in a way that is characteristic of firms in a contestable market, and developing interchangeability.

Exam practice

Read the article below and then answer the questions that follow.

Article A

Royal Mail

In January 2006, the monopoly of the Royal Mail came to an end. From that point on competitors were able to enter the market and provide mail services to customers. In 2008 a report commissioned by the government and carried out by an independent panel published interim findings on the effects of competition on the industry.

Competition comes in the form of other firms carrying out services that was the preserve of the Royal Mail; this might include the collection of bulk mail for sorting and transportation before handing it over to the Royal Mail for final delivery – the so-called 'final-mile delivery'. The report said that large corporations had seemed to benefit from the growth in competition in this sector and that as a result they experienced the benefits of competition, lower prices, greater choice and quality of service.

However, for the ordinary customer and for small businesses, the report concluded that there had been little or no benefit of the liberalisation of the market. For ordinary households, the options for accessing different postal services is limited and for smaller firms the cost of accessing

cont...

competing mail services might be too high for the small volumes of mail they generate. For households, the attachment and convenience of the Royal Mail means that it is likely to take many years to break the brand loyalty that has been generated – there had been a monopoly in mail services for over 350 years prior to the new Act in 2000!

Source: Biz/ed 'In the News': http://www.bized.co.uk/cgi-bin/chron/chron.pl?id=3085

(a) Analyse the competitive environment of the UK postal service. (16 marks)

(b) To what extent will the removal of Royal Mail's monopoly benefit consumers in the long term? (34 marks)

Total: 50 marks

Breakdown of assessment objectives

AO1 – Knowledge and understanding – 10/50

AO2 – Apply knowledge and understanding – 10/50

AO3 – Analyse problems, issues and situations – 10/50

AO4 – Evaluate, distinguish between fact and opinion, assess and judge information from a variety of sources – 20/50

Suggested structure

For part (a) you will need to:

- Provide a breakdown of the market for mail in the UK – who uses it, how do they use it and how does mail get processed and delivered?
- Ensure that your analysis refers to ordinary domestic users, small businesses and large businesses.
- Consider the competition issues that arise in the case study – the nature of the barriers to entry, the extent of the brand loyalty that the Royal Mail holds, the distribution networks it has, and so on. Use the points raised in this chapter to help you apply your knowledge in this respect.

For part (b) you will need to:

- Use the information provided in part (a) on which to base your answer.
- Be clear about who the customers are – individual users, small businesses and large businesses.
- Look at how each might benefit (or not) from increased competition in the industry. Make sure you make reference to the time period – how long is the long term in your view?
- Make some judgements about the extent to which these different customers will be affected by competition – a great deal, quite a lot or hardly at all – and support your judgement with reasons.
- Draw the answer together by arriving at an overall judgement about the effect of removing the monopoly.

The Business Environment and Managing Change

Section C
MANAGING CHANGE

Any business organisation will operate in an ever-changing environment. These changes can present significant threats to the long-term survival of the business, but can also open up new opportunities that can be exploited to the benefit of the business and its stakeholders. Major causes of change that businesses have to cope with include: technology, which can either open up opportunities or make existing products/processes redundant; changes in economic conditions; changing social trends; terrorism and conflict; and natural disasters such as earthquake, flood and even climate change. Change can be something that happens over a period of time or could be something very sudden. For example, social trends may change over a period of many years, whereas businesses have to adapt to natural disasters when they occur, immediately. This section will look at the issue of change in business and how businesses respond to and manage change.

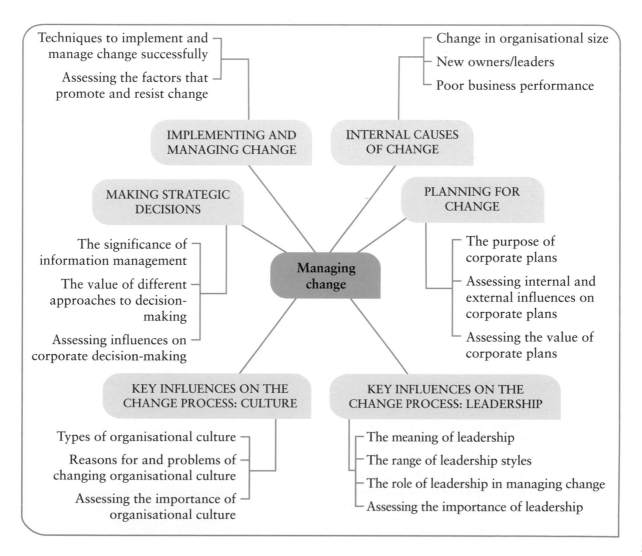

Chapter 26 Internal causes of change

Key terms

Downsizing Reducing the size of the business by cutting costs most obviously through making large-scale redundancies of employees.

Economies of scale The advantages of large-scale production that result in lower average (unit) costs.

Retrenchment The process whereby a business reduces its size and finds ways of cutting costs.

Synergy The benefits that arise from the joining together of two firms such that the combined business is more efficient and effective than their individual parts.

Change can occur not just because of events that happen outside the business's control, such as natural disasters, terrorism or economic change, but through the decisions that the business itself makes. This is referred to as internal change. Internal change comes about as a result of a change in the size of the business, whether this is through internal growth or through external growth that results from acquisition. These changes invariably lead to the firm being bigger but it is also possible for a business to contract in size, maybe as a result of changed economic circumstances. If a business has grown or contracted there may well be new owners or leaders installed to run the business, and with them come different directions, philosophies, emphasis and priorities. All these can present both challenges and opportunities for a business.

Change in organisational size

Businesses change size through three main ways:

- acquisition – either a merger or a takeover
- organic growth
- retrenchment – primarily downsizing.

It is important to remember that businesses do not simply always get bigger; many businesses see the need and benefit of becoming smaller and may divest themselves of sections of their business that do not meet with the strategic direction which has been identified.

Changes in organisational size present many challenges to a business. We will look at some of the implications of these changes in relation to these three main causes of change.

For example...

Business restructuring

In 2007, the Thomson Corporation, which owned interests in business information, finance and education amongst other things, made the decision to sell off its educational publishing division, Thomson Learning. Thomson Learning did not fit with the direction that the Thomson Corporation had decided to take. Its future interests were going to be in news services and providing information systems and technology to the financial world. Thomson Learning was sold to a private equity firm and became Cengage Learning. The changes meant that Thomson was able to complete the merger with the Reuters organisation whilst Cengage Learning, now a smaller company than when it was part of the Thomson organisation but still a major business in its own right, followed a different strategic direction.

Change through acquisition

Businesses can change size through decisions to **merge** with another business or to launch a **takeover** of another business. The new business is very likely to be much larger as a result of the acquisition and this presents new challenges and opportunities. Acquisition can result in **synergies** that benefit both businesses. Synergies refer to the fact that the combined business is more efficient and effective than the sum of their individual parts.

The precise effect on the business and its stakeholders will depend to a large extent on the nature of the acquisition. If two firms agree to merge, it may well be that they believe they have complimentary but different products or services that would present a stronger competitive proposition in the market compared to remaining separate. For example, in 2008, British Airways (BA) and Spanish airline Iberia entered into talks about a merger. There was a great deal of logic in the proposal, especially given the problems facing the industry at that time through high fuel prices and falling demand due to economic slowdown.

Merging two airlines can give the resulting organisation greater competitive power

Both firms had slightly different markets and could make use of the coverage they have across the world to improve their competitive position. The extent to which their employees would be affected would depend on the extent of the duplication of resources between the two airlines. Some job losses may be inevitable but shareholders may believe that the resulting business would be better placed to compete in an increasingly challenging industry. The merger will retain the brand identities of both BA and Iberia.

In a takeover, one firm acquires control of the other. The firm taken over might lose its identity completely. The resulting business is also likely to be much bigger as is the case with merger. Whether the acquisition is through merger or takeover, the fact that the resulting organisation is larger tends to give it greater competitive power in the market. It will have greater combined market share, access to new markets, access to the expertise that exists within the two businesses and, of course, eliminates one competitor from the marketplace. The larger organisation can benefit extensively from economies of scale which lead to lower average costs per unit produced.

The effects of acquisition will depend on the extent to which there is overlap between the two businesses. If the two firms are very similar with operations that are duplicated, then there is likely to be a period where the new business has to rationalise and this may lead to a number of members of staff being made redundant. In addition to the trauma that this causes those involved (and those who have to manage the redundancy process), there are likely to be considerable changes in the way that the new organisation operates. Systems will have to be aligned, new ways of working learned and new priorities and aims taken into consideration and implemented.

Communication lines will also have to be implemented and in many cases strengthened. One of the most damaging aspects of change can be through poor communications. If employers and other stakeholders feel that they are not being informed about the changes and how it affects them, then dissatisfaction, poor morale and reduced motivation can soon set in, and this affects productivity and efficiency as well as generating rumours and gossip which can be destabilising.

Change through organic growth

As firms get established and develop they will experience **organic growth** – growth from within. This growth arises as a result of the rise in sales and consequently, the increase in production and output. Firms will use the profits generated to re-invest in the business which in turn allows them to grow. This growth can be over a long period of time, but there will come a point when the existing size of the firm is no longer suitable in relation to the demand for the product, or where the business believes that there are new markets that can be exploited and which will necessitate expansion. Many small business owners comment that the biggest change they ever experience is when the firm first looks to expand its scale of operation. Many will have worked with the business since its inception and will be familiar with the current working and operation of the business. However, when the firm grows in size, new problems, challenges and opportunities arise which the business owner may not be equipped to deal with.

Internal growth can help the business to access economies of scale which lead to a reduction in average costs. This can help the business to be more competitive against their rivals. However, some firms may start to experience diseconomies of scale, especially in relation to communications and decision-making. Larger organisations are more difficult to control and to monitor, and as a result, inefficiencies can arise that lead to a rise in average costs. This might be because a larger organisation also has wider spans of control for managers, a longer chain of command which increases the speed with which the business can respond to changes and make decisions, and may involve more levels of management which again can result in the business becoming less flexible in the face of change.

Some businesses, especially smaller businesses, may find themselves caught up in the pace of change. They may try to expand too quickly and find themselves in a position where they are overtrading. This means that they are unable to meet demand because they do not have access to the resources they need or are unable to pay for the resources they need because their cash flow is compromised in some way.

As a result, the owner may well have to make significant changes in the way the business is run and managed, and this represents a steep learning curve. For example, business owners may find that they can no longer maintain control over all aspects of the business and have to recruit other staff to deal with these different aspects. The opportunity will arise for specialists to be employed in marketing, accounts, sales, and so on, and the management of these new functions takes on a different set of priorities and directions. The larger organisation will present different communications challenges, there may be differences in the belief about direction and policy, and clashes of culture and personality, as well as facing a new competitive landscape.

Change through retrenchment

Retrenchment refers to a decision by a business to reassess its position, look at its costs and find ways of reducing those costs and stripping out unnecessary waste. One of the main ways in which a business will do this is through what has been called 'downsizing'. This refers to the reduction in the size of the business either by closing redundant plant, moving location to smaller premises or through large-scale redundancies of staff. Some of these redundancies will be realised through natural wastage, that is, staff not being replaced when they leave or retire, but others will be compulsory. This may involve extensive and difficult negotiations with the staff involved, the management who have to follow through the process, and trade unions where appropriate.

Such a policy is inevitably stressful for all involved and leaders will be acutely aware that such significant change can have a considerable impact on morale, loyalty, productivity and efficiency. The whole process can also be very expensive and is not something that is entered into lightly. Costs come through having to settle redundancy payments and through involving staff in the management of the process. The whole process can also take a long period of time, during which the business might anticipate disruptions to production and a dip in productivity as the change takes effect.

For example...

JJB

In April 2008, the sports clothing and equipment retailer, JJB, announced that its profits for the year to the end of January 2008 had fallen by 72% to £10.8 million. The challenging trading conditions that it was facing led to the firm reviewing its operations and reducing the number of stores that it had. This review led to the closure of 72 of its 410 stores. The closures would result in around 1,200 people losing their jobs, but 400 of these would be offered the opportunity to be re-employed in other stores.

New owners/leaders

New owners can come into a business as a result of acquisition, but not necessarily. One feature of private sector business is the rapidity with which people are moved into new positions in an organisation. People can be brought into an organisation from outside or promoted from within. However they arrive, the change can often be swift with one person leaving and another taking his/her place with immediate effect. In other cases the transition from one leadership team to another can be more managed. This might occur if a person in a senior position announced their retirement or has negotiated a structured move to another organisation or position.

Changes in leadership and management teams can come about for a variety of reasons. It might be because the business decides on a change of direction; it might be that a business has a particular job that needs to be done in relation to a strategic or marketing plan, and it needs an individual with particular skills and a proven track record in that line of work. Once they have completed their task, they move on somewhere else now seemingly not deemed as being useful to the organisation any longer. Leadership change can also come about because the business is not doing as well as its shareholders might expect. The pressure to get results, and to at least meet target numbers for revenue, net income and profit, is intense, and if it is felt that the leadership are not doing their job, change can occur quickly.

In the case of acquisition, mergers or takeovers can lead to new leadership teams being installed, which might be through negotiation or imposition depending on the nature of the acquisition. This is largely to be expected given the circumstances of an acquisition. Whether as a result of acquisition or internal restructuring, changes in leadership can bring with it changes in direction, culture, approach, ways of working and philosophy to a business. For those working with the business, this change can be significant or subtle but it will involve some form of change. The introduction of new leaders or owners can lead to significant changes within a firm. New leaders may be brought in specifically because they have different ideas and approaches which it is thought will benefit the business or move it in a different direction. New people may have a different approach to the business: their leadership may be more autocratic or democratic than existing; there might be a different emphasis – the new leadership might be more willing to look at riskier projects; priorities might be different and there might be effects on motivation and productivity as a result.

The top leadership position in many larger corporations is the chief executive officer (CEO). This person is often the public face of the organisation and is the head of the organisation. However, the CEO reports to the board of directors and ultimately the shareholders. The CEO invariably sets the underlying direction of the corporation. The other executive officers on the board will be tasked with carrying out their roles within this overall strategy. The marketing functions, sales, production, and so on, will all have their functions defined to a large extent by the overall direction established by the CEO.

Poor business performance

What constitutes poor business performance will depend on how the business defines 'success'. It could be that the targets or forecasts set by the managers of the business have failed to be reached, that profits have fallen, that the business has had to announce a series of profits warnings, that revenue has dropped, costs have risen too fast, the market has changed leaving the business behind or that growth has been far less than expected.

Whatever the definition used, the response is to try and do something to rectify the position, and get the business back on the track which it has either set itself, or which market analysts have deemed appropriate for the particular business given the market they are operating in. The strategy adopted will be dependent on the severity of the position. It could be that the poor performance makes the business a target for acquisition; new leaders may be brought in or the existing leadership team has to take a long hard look at the position the business finds itself in and come up with some new policies and strategies to reverse the situation.

For example...

Sir Stuart Rose and Marks and Spencer (M&S)

Sir Stuart Rose has a career that typifies many in senior positions in business. Part of his early career was with M&S, but he also worked at the àBurton Group, Argos, the Booker Group and Arcadia, the retail group which includes Dorothy Perkins, Miss Selfridge and others. In 2004, Rose became the CEO at M&S replacing Roger Holmes. Rose was brought in to fight moves by the head of the Arcadia Group, Philip Green, to takeover M&S. In the next four years Rose not only succeeded in fighting off the takeover, but turned round the fortunes of the business. His performance in changing the direction of the company and introducing new product lines, changing the focus of the business and its look was widely praised.

However, by mid-2008, the economic slowdown led to announcements from Sir Stuart that future performance looked weaker and the share price slid alarmingly. Some questioned whether Sir Stuart was the person to lead the

company in the next phase of its growth. One of the reasons there was some concern was a decision Rose made in 2007 to appoint Steven Esom as head of food from rivals Waitrose only to dismiss him a year later. Sir Stuart said that changes in the market meant that the food division had to increase the pace of change and that whilst Mr Esom had done some good work in the year he had been with the company, it was right to change and introduce a new person to the post.

The impact on the business and its stakeholders will depend on the strategies that are implemented to correct the business performance. We have already seen how new personnel brought in to the business might affect it, but there are other effects that can be noted. The reason for the poor performance will either be due to a lack of control on costs or poor revenue streams – or a combination of both. As a result, the changes that the business makes may either be targeted at reducing/controlling costs or boosting revenue.

If the focus is on controlling costs then there might be plant closures, redundancies and other aspects of retrenchment covered earlier in this chapter. Managers may have their budgets trimmed and have to work to more stringent targets. Efforts might be made to find ways of improving productivity and this might affect the working practices of employees. Longer shifts and changes in shift patterns might be two ways in which workers in some businesses might be affected. In other cases there might be a tightening of travel and expense budgets, a requirement by workers to learn new skills or to do different tasks so that they are more flexible and can be utilised in different ways by the business.

Many businesses have moved to reduce trade union membership, develop individual pay and conditions negotiations, and shift the balance between full-time workers and part-time or temporary contract workers. This helps the business to be more flexible in the way it responds to changing demand and market conditions, and does not mean that it has to be saddled with idle staff during times when business is slow.

These changes may benefit a business and ensure it is more equipped to deal with the changes that occur and improve the chances of long-term survival, but it also means a far greater degree of uncertainty for employees. Once again the business has to balance out the value of the benefits it gains through these changes with the costs associated – not least in terms of the effect on motivation and morale.

For example...

Justin King and Sainsbury's

Justin King took over as CEO of the supermarket retailer Sainsbury's in 2004. At that time the business had suffered a number of problems and had lost market share to its rivals for 14 years in succession, as well as posting the first loss in its history. A £3 billion investment plan in its distribution system had failed to deliver the promised benefits, and shoppers seemed to desert Sainsbury's when it appeared that shelves were not fully stocked and products not available.

King set about a £550 million restructuring package to turn round the fortunes of the company, and had to do so at a time when there were plenty of rumours that the business was facing the prospect of takeover bids. His strategy was relatively simple and unspectacular, but one that seemed important to the customers of Sainsbury's who, after all, are the ones that make the real difference. The emphasis was on making sure that shelves were fully stocked, that costs were cut and controlled,

that the key focus of the business was on food rather than other activities, and that customers were happy with the experience they gained when visiting stores.

Since he became CEO, Mr King has guided the business to over three years of like-for-like growth, increased sales by £2.7 billion and doubled profits to around £500 million. Mr King has also enabled Sainsbury's to regain market share and in terms of total revenue (including petrol sales), is the second largest supermarket in the UK.

Summary and exam guidance

Summary

- Every business has to be able to accept, confront and manage change.

- There are three main drivers of change to an organisation's size.
  These are:
  - acquisition – merger or takeover
  - organic growth
  - retrenchment.

- Other causes of change include the introduction of new leaders or owners to the business and the response to poor business performance.

Exam practice

Read the article below and then answer the questions that follow.

Article A

Bob the Builder – has he fixed it?

In 2005, Hit Entertainment, the company behind the children's TV programmes *Bob the Builder* and *Thomas the Tank Engine*, was the subject of a takeover bid by a private investment firm, Apax Partners, for £489.4 million. Private equity groups like Apax look to buy businesses which have the potential to be improved. Such groups tend to institute a number of changes to the business, improve its performance and then look to sell on the business after a relatively short period of time to recoup their investment.

Hit Entertainment also owned the rights to the popular US children's characters, Barney the Dinosaur and Pingu, the mischievous penguin. The new company formed by the takeover, called Sunshine Acquisition, hope to exploit the popularity of the brands owned by Hit to help boost fortunes on both sides of the Atlantic, but in particular to take advantage of the launch of the US Digital Pre-school Channel. The takeover will

cont...

enable Hit to secure funds for investment into developing brands like *Bob the Builder* and reach new market segments.

Brands like *Bob the Builder* have declined in popularity in recent years in relative terms due to the extent of the competition and the availability of other forms of entertainment for children. The funds made available by Apax as a result of the takeover were used to find new ways in which the name of *Bob the Builder* and others could develop new programmes and merchandise and introduce new characters to enliven the programmes.

The move by Apax suggested that there was a belief amongst them that the market was ripe for further growth and development despite the difficult trading conditions faced by Hit in the 18 months prior to the takeover.

Source: Biz/ed In the News: http://www.bized.co.uk/cgi-bin/chron/chron.pl?id=2318

(a) Analyse the possible changes that Hit Entertainment may have had to face following the takeover by Apax. (12 marks)

(b) To what extent will the fact that Apax is a private equity group rather than another business in the industry have on the way in which Hit might be run? (18 marks)

Total: 30 marks

Breakdown of assessment objectives

AO1 – Knowledge and understanding – 6/30
AO2 – Apply knowledge and understanding – 6/30
AO3 – Analyse problems, issues and situations – 8/30
AO4 – Evaluate, distinguish between fact and opinion, assess and judge information from a variety of sources – 10/30

Suggested structure

For part (a) you will need to:

- Select at least three key areas of the business that are likely to have been affected by the takeover.
- Offer a detailed explanation of the changes in each case above.
- Break down the factors into their constituent parts to highlight the key issues involved.

For part (b) you will need to:

- Make it clear at the outset what the difference is between an acquisition by a private equity company and another business in the same industry as Hit, or from outside but pursuing interests in a different market.
- Make it clear that the aims of a private equity group like Apax might mean that different aims and objectives might be emphasised compared to other forms of acquisition.
- Look at how some of these different aims and objectives might impact on some key stakeholders in the business – employees, customers and suppliers (for example). You should probably select no more than three stakeholders.
- Make some judgements about the extent of the effect of the changes – will these be a significant change in the way the company is run, a considerable change, a large change, or will it only have a minor impact on the business?
- Draw your answer together to arrive at an informed and supported conclusion in relation to the answer.

Chapter 27 **Planning for change**

The purpose of corporate plans

The aim of planning is to try and make some form of prediction about the future and about desired outcomes, putting in place strategies and tactics to cater for anticipated outcomes and events, which steer the organisation towards desired goals. The very nature of planning means that it has to be largely inexact simply because we are not capable of predicting the future. However, that is not to say that we cannot try and use historical data, information provided from expert analysts, secondary research and a host of other sources to try to anticipate future events.

At the heart of any corporate plan will be the corporate strategy. This, to remind you, is a statement of where the business wants to be at some point in the future. We have seen (see Chapters 1 and 20) that businesses can make broad statements about where they want to be in the future. The purpose of a corporate plan is to try to chart a path to enable that goal to be reached. It also enables a business to consider how it might gain competitive advantage from its rivals and how it might seek to retain that advantage.

At one time, a great deal of emphasis was placed on the production of a corporate plan. Senior managers would spend considerable amounts of time on producing thick documents that tried to detail every possible scenario and route to the goal that the business had set. It soon became clear that the plan produced had a high degree of relevance to those that produced it, but was inaccessible to many in the rest of the organisation and invariably was left on a shelf to gather dust.

The problem was that the documents were too detailed, and often by the time the finished document was made available, the market and the competitive environment had moved on and the plan was obsolete. The trend changed to producing much slimmer and less detailed corporate plans. However, the importance of planning was not totally jettisoned; it was simply that the nature of corporate plans had changed.

What is in a corporate plan?

A corporate plan is likely to have a number of common features (although every organisation may have a slightly different emphasis):

- An outline of the mission and value statement.
- An overview of the key strategy, outlining overall aims and goals.
- An analysis of the current state of the market and the position of the business in that market. This is likely to be informed by market analysis and techniques such as SWOT analysis.
- An outline of the growth potential of the market and the implications on the business.
- Possible hazards/vulnerabilities that the organisation might have to consider (informed by the SWOT analysis).
- The human resources implications that the plan identifies.
- Financial implications of strategic aims – this may include some outline budgets and an identification of possible sources of finance for any investments needed.

A corporate plan is likely to try and identify routes between three and five years ahead, but may be over a shorter period of time depending on the industry. In a fast-changing market like fashion clothing, the time frame for the planning process might be much shorter, but for a pharmaceutical or energy company the time frame may be much longer. Corporate plans have to adhere, as far as possible, to SMART criteria. Such a requirement means the business has to think carefully to avoid excessively optimistic or unrealistic goals and objectives being set.

One of the key areas of future planning relates to attempts to try and predict trends in the future. Historical and current trends do not always translate to what might happen in the next year, let alone three or five years! The content covered in Chapter 8 on methods of forecasting will be highly relevant here. However, there are also other factors that a business has to consider in relation to the future that are extremely difficult to predict, but the possibility of them happening and the way in which the business will cope has to be considered.

Business also has to consider in its planning the possibility of natural disasters like earthquake, flood, hurricane, and so on, as well as security breaches. These are all different events, of course, but do have some similarities in that they are likely to result in problems such as communications disruptions, loss of information and data, and so on. Plans can be put in place as a result to cope with such disruptions with the intention of minimising the effects to the business and to customers, and to reducing the cost of restoring operations.

For example...

Business resilience

The morning of September 11th 2001, dawned like any other working day for many individuals and businesses at the World Trade Center in New York. The events of 9/11 not only devastated lives and families, but also highlighted to many businesses that they were now operating in a very different world. Some of these businesses had considered how they would cope if all their databases, information and so on, were destroyed. They may not have imagined the precise circumstances under which operations would be disrupted so spectacularly, but many had some sort of operations up and running within a very short space of time. What happened that day, however, was anything but ordinary.

Cantor Fitzgerald is a major financial trading business which lost 658 of its 1,050 US workers in the attack on the Twin Towers. Some of these workers were the brightest and most experienced traders in the company. The attack left the company with no offices, few staff and extremely limited communications systems. The disaster recovery systems that it had in place, however, meant that within 48 hours of the attack, the business was ready to trade again. The business had used its planning process to take into account how it could recover from some form of catastrophic collapse of its systems.

Contingency planning

The vulnerability of a business to disruption means that many – even small businesses – can benefit from contingency planning. Contingency plans aim to try to consider potential disruption to the business and put in place procedures and processes to recover from the disruption as soon as possible. Contingency plans are also referred to as scenario plans. In this case, a business might consider different scenarios – some more serious than others, to think through how to respond and minimise disruption.

A scenario plan might take different potential outcomes or events and look to assess the likely impact on the business and how the business might react and respond. The basis for the planning might be market research, forecasting and other market analysis data. This data might show most likely outcomes, but there will also be a range of outcomes giving a 'confidence interval' with worst case outcomes at one extreme and best case at the other.

Within any contingency plans, there will be factors that the business will be able to identify that it can control and influence, and others which it can not. Contingency planning can increase awareness of possible future outcomes and events as a result of considering a range of future possibilities. Such an approach helps to inform decision-making and allows the business to react faster when changes (however they are caused) do occur.

The extent to which contingency planning can be successful depends upon the quality of the information the business has at its disposal and the accuracy of the data on which it has to base its plans and subsequent decisions. Given the long-term nature of the planning process, the accuracy of data cannot be guaranteed, which is why the planning process outlined above is so important. Changes in the nature of scenarios have to be factored in as and when they occur, or when new and more accurate information comes to light that can be fed into the plan.

For example...

British Airways and rising costs

British Airways will know that a major proportion of their costs are taken up by fuel. Between 2007 and 2008, fuel prices rose dramatically. Given their exposure to any rise in oil prices, BA are likely to have taken steps to plan ahead to take account of such a rise. If they used contingency planning they may have planned for the effect of different price rises. What if oil prices rose to $100 a barrel, $150 and $200? There are plenty of analysts who have predicted that oil prices will rise to $200 a barrel by 2010. If this scenario did happen then it is highly likely that BA will have to face the fact that fuel will account for over 50% of the cost of any flight.

To plan ahead, BA might need to think about ways that it can combat or cope with such a rise in costs. They might consider the extent to which the cost can be passed on to consumers, what their rivals are likely to do (especially the low-cost carriers), whether they can build in more efficiencies into their operations, for example, through rationalising some less-profitable routes or even cancelling some routes; they might look to consolidate by opening talks with other airlines to merge or enter into joint agreements. In the long term they might also be looking at replacing existing aircraft with more efficient planes – such an option would, by necessity, involve a long period of time and careful planning and negotiation with aircraft manufacturers.

Assessing internal and external influences on corporate plans

There are a number of factors, both internal and external, that will influence the ability of corporations to plan effectively. These include the availability of finance, the type of business – extent of predictability, and the state of the economy.

Internal influences

THE AVAILABILITY OF FINANCE

Planning relates to where a business wants to go, but this has to be linked to the capacity of the business to go where it wants to go – it has to be realistic. Part of this will be related to the availability of finance to meet its plans. The finance can come from retained profit or it can be raised externally to the business. If it is raised externally then the opportunity cost of raising the finance has to be taken into account. This will depend in part on where the finance has been raised from. If it is through an investment bank, then the cost of setting up the deal as well as servicing the debt has to be taken into consideration in relation to the value of the benefits outlined by the proposed plans. It will also depend on the prevailing financial conditions and the prospects for the near future or the period of time over which the debt has to be serviced.

For example, during the first part of the first decade of the 21st century, interest rates around the world were relatively low. The global economy was relatively stable and inflation low. The conditions for borrowing were very favourable and many corporations took advantage. However, around 2007–2008, global economic conditions changed; interest rates started to rise as a result of the rising inflationary pressures that existed around the world and the credit crunch meant that funds became much harder to acquire and more expensive to raise. As a result, the whole investment scenario changed and this might not have been taken into consideration in corporate plans. As a result, many corporations will have had to amend their plans to take into account the changed financial circumstances.

The financial position of the business might also dictate, to some extent, what goes in to the plan in the first instance. A business will have some idea of the extent to which it is able to access finance and this might impact on the scope of its future planning. The business might want to expand its operations overseas but might appreciate that the cost of doing so would be beyond it, given its financial position over the next five years. However, that does not mean that such an objective would be impossible, but simply not realistic at the moment. The longer-term planning might have this as an aim and the shorter-term plans geared to trying to get to the position where it can expand its operations in this way.

RESOURCE CONSTRAINTS

Access to appropriate resources might be a factor that a business has to consider in its planning. Global changes in the price and availability of commodities can have a significant effect on production schedules and plans. For example, between 2004 and 2008, the price of many metals rose significantly, as did commodities such as wheat. Oil prices, and the derivative products of oil, have also risen sharply, and firms who use such resources in their production will have to consider these in their planning.

It is not only physical resources that can be short in supply and thus costly. Human resources, especially those with specialist skills, can often limit proposed expansion. The firm might find that it does not have the expertise to expand in the way that it wants to, and this can prevent plans from being realised but might also have to be taken into consideration when the plan is being drawn up in the first place.

EXISTING STRENGTHS AND WEAKNESSES

As part of the market analysis, a business will have to think about its strengths and weaknesses, and this will have to be taken into account in the planning process. Strengths can enable the business to perhaps do far more than its rivals, and it might need to focus on exploiting these whilst planning to either reduce the impact of its weaknesses on the business, or putting in place plans to try and build capacity and strength in the areas where it is weak.

VIEW OF OWNERS AND MANAGERS

Some owners and managers have particular views about their business's role and this may be built into the plans of a business. Such views might include ethical considerations relating to the use of suppliers and outsourcing, the impact of the business on the environment, particular views about ethical trading, scientific testing procedures, and so on. Taking into account such views may manifest themselves in the objectives set in the first place, as well as the nature of the plans put into place.

External influences

THE TYPE OF BUSINESS – THE EXTENT OF PREDICTABILITY

The future is never wholly predictable but some businesses will operate in a climate that is more predictable than others. For example, supermarkets are less vulnerable to changes in demand than furniture and carpet retailers. The latter are highly dependent on the state of the economy and the housing market in particular. If the economy suffers a slowdown then furniture retailers tend to be affected significantly. The swings in demand that these types of business have to face can be considerable and it is difficult to predict and foresee exactly how the economy is going to change. There may be signs that demand is slowing or rising, but it is not always possible to detect a trend from short-term data that might be some months out of date before it is published. In such an environment, planning ahead is more difficult and it is more likely that there will be considerable variances in actual outcomes compared to planned outcomes. In such a situation the plan has to be flexible to cope with such unforeseen variances.

For grocery retailers, the extent of the effects is less likely to be as dramatic. Supermarkets will almost certainly be affected by changes in the economy, for example, but whilst they may see a change in the demand for certain types of goods, the overall effect on sales is less likely to be so significant. This is because food has a relatively low income elasticity of demand compared to items like furniture. Particular foods may be substituted by consumers looking to cut back expenditure, but it is unlikely that the total amount spent on food is going to change that much.

THE STATE OF THE ECONOMY

The section above alluded to the impact of changes in the economy on businesses. The state of the economy is subject to a number of influences, many of which are outside the control of a corporation and therefore likely to impact on future planning. The global economy is now heavily interdependent and changes in economic conditions in one part of the world can quickly affect most other parts. The UK, in particular, is heavily dependent on the state of the US economy as well as that of Europe.

The latter part of the first decade of the 21st century highlighted this very clearly. In 2007 it became clear that a number of banks in the US were being affected by an increasing number of customers who were unable to meet repayments on so-called 'sub-prime' mortgages. These were mortgages lent to customers who had high-risk and low credit ratings. The low interest rates had made it relatively easy for financial institutions to raise funds for this purpose, but as the number of those unable to meet repayment rose, the true extent of the problem started to unravel. Financial institutions around the world revealed the extent to which they were exposed to the problem, and the ensuing economic slowdown was not something that might have been predicted by many in 2005 or 2006.

Equally in times when the economy is growing, few might have any idea how long that the period of growth will continue. Businesses may need to be in a position where they have to plan ahead to meet potential demand, and without knowing the length of the growth period, there is the very real possibility that capacity will be increased and stocks built up only to find in a relatively short period of time that demand starts to slow and the business is left with stock and excess capacity which drains its cash flow.

COMPETITOR ACTIONS

Part of the planning process will involve the monitoring and evaluation of competitor action. This action may be in response to the plans being implemented by the business but also by the plans that competitors are putting in place themselves. The competitive environment is subject to constant change, and these dynamics have to be considered by businesses in their initial plans and in the ongoing planning process.

THE VIEWS OF WIDER STAKEHOLDERS

Many businesses are acutely aware of the range of views of wider stakeholders and may look to try and take these into account when formulating plans. It may feel that consideration of such views may provide a source of competitive advantage, but might also believe that these views are representative of the competitive environment in which they are operating. For example, Primark are very keen to make it clear that the low prices they are able to charge for their products is not the result of exploitation of suppliers and workers, but the fact that they choose to focus on low-profit margins but high-volume sales to generate profits. For a company like Primark, gaining the confidence of its customers and prospective shareholders might be an important part of its business.

Assessing the value of corporate plans

There has been much criticism of corporate plans. The main criticism has been around their value. The level of detail put into corporate plans, in terms of the steps to be taken by different parts of the organisation to achieve the goals outlined, was one of the main problems. The detail was simply too much and lacked the flexibility to be able to respond to the changes that inevitably occurred. Corporate plans might be appropriate for businesses where the future was more predictable and where there were a greater number of elements that the business could control. However, the start of the new century made it even clearer, if any doubt continued to exist, that change was inevitable and that unpredictability and shock were too great to allow for detailed planning. In addition, there were other theories that cast doubt upon the wisdom of too detailed a corporate plan.

Chaos theory

The movement away from detailed planning in recent years has been largely related to the recognition that the world is not subject to any degree of certainty that plans might imply exist. One explanation for this is **chaos theory**. The theory recognises the intricacy of the way in which order and disorder impact on our behaviour. We may believe that we behave in relatively predictable and regular ways, and to an extent this may be true, but these broad categories of behaviour contain an infinite variety and number of irregularities which make planning more difficult.

Planning implies that humans are able to exercise some element of control on the future – if not, then why do we plan? The planning process will outline a series of actions that the organisation is going to take at specified points in the future. Part of the planning process will involve reviewing these actions in relation to the planned outcomes. Chaos theory states that the long-term future is inherently unpredictable and unstable. Any long-term planning procedures, therefore, will not achieve outcomes unless by chance.

Mintzberg and strategic thinking

Henry Mintzberg wrote *The fall and rise of strategic planning* in 1994. The article in the Harvard Business Review cast doubt upon the wisdom of corporate planning, arguing that planning was preventing the important process of strategic thinking. Mintzberg argued that corporate planning was an attempt to formalise a process which by its very nature was not really capable of being formalised; the future was too turbulent for such formalised planning to take place.

Once a corporate plan had been made, its authors (who may have been planners rather than managers or leaders) were often reluctant to let it go and to deviate from the plans that they had laid out. This lead to a greater degree of inflexibility in the firm in the face of constant change and turbulence.

Instead, Mintzberg argued for a greater degree of **strategic thinking**. Strategic thinking was more about having a vision of where the organisation should be heading and ensuring that this vision was communicated with all in the organisation. Within that vision there ought to be the possibility for everyone in an organisation to contribute in some way. The corporate vision would be the thing that would guide people to where the organisation was going, but any sort of detailed plan would not be capable of adjusting quickly enough to change. Change did not have to deflect an organisation from its vision; it was simply that everyday operational events might have to change.

From this analysis a number of academics and management gurus developed the thinking around corporate strategic thinking as opposed to planning. It is important to bear in mind that planning was not totally rejected, but long-term detailed corporate plans were. Planning for short-term predictable outcomes was appropriate; it was just that detailed planning which had to be followed regardless of the changes in circumstances was not the way that business would be best positioned to cope with change in a turbulent world.

Strategic intent

In 1995, Max Boisot published a chapter in a book called *Developing strategic thought* in which he outlined a development of the notion of **strategic intent** that had been formulated by Gary Hamel and C.K. Prahalad in a Harvard Business Review article in 1989. The intention of any plan, he argued, was to attempt to gain control which, as we have seen, is difficult if not impossible in a turbulent chaotic environment. As a result, he argued for different responses to change.

Strategic planning could be effective if the level of turbulence was low, but the understanding of the firm and its market and of the change it is experiencing must be high. Boisot suggested this sort of situation was rare. What was more common was a case where understanding might be relatively high but turbulence also very high. In this situation strategic intent is an appropriate response. Strategic intent refers to the setting of a series of achievable but challenging goals that would improve the organisation in the future and which would allow the organisation to perform at a higher level.

Strategic intent is a far looser concept than a strategic plan; an example of a strategic intent might be to gain market leadership. Hamel and Prahalad had outlined the desire by Canon to take over market leadership from Kodak. How it would do this might once have been laid down in a detailed manner in a corporate plan. The idea of strategic intent is to inform decision-making in the organisation and accept that change will occur that will blow the organisation off course from time to time. If the thinking of decision-makers at Canon, for example, when proposing a new strategy is 'how does this help us beat Kodak?' then the corporate vision is preserved and serves to act as a means of making decisions in the organisation.

FUTURES THINKING

Part of the process associated with strategic intent is **futures thinking**. Futures thinking is not a wish list or an attempt to predict the future, but is an attempt to think through possible trends and directions in the future, and allows an organisation to put itself on the boundary between stability and instability. For many organisations this might mean trying to envisage what might happen in 10 to 20 years' time and where the business might be in relation to that changed position. It is a difficult thing to achieve but is something that businesses that are planning for long-term survival have to contemplate. The thinking may be totally inaccurate, but the process will mean that the business will have considered how it might respond to changes that could occur and this in itself will be a healthy process.

The case for planning

Despite the comments above, there is still a place for planning in an organisation. It is simply that detailed planning over anything other than the short term (which might be defined differently in different organisations) is now seen as being of limited value. In this respect we can distinguish between strategic and operational planning. **Strategic planning** refers to plans developed to meet long-term goals (which is now seen as being limited) as opposed to **operational planning** which deals with the day-to-day operations of the business. Operational planning is seen as being appropriate and valuable because the time horizon is short and the predictability of future events much higher.

Planning therefore can be useful in some circumstances, in particular, where the business is able to predict with a relatively high degree of certainty what the future might bring. It can help the business to be clear about what it is doing, increase awareness of the strengths and limitations of a particular procedure or process, and to prepare for possible opportunities and threats. In addition, planning can help a business to use its resources in a more effective and efficient manner.

Summary and exam guidance

Summary

- Corporate plans aim to look ahead to the future to consider what might happen and how a business might respond to such events and changes.

- Planning helps a business think ahead to how it will react to different situations such as natural disasters, terrorist attacks, and so on.

- Contingency planning helps businesses to think about required responses to different situations ranging from best-case to worst-case scenarios.

- Key influences on corporate plans include the availability of finance, the nature of the business and the state of the economy.

- Corporate plans have been heavily criticised because of their detail and the degree of inflexibility they can impose on a business.

- Planning still has a role, however, especially over short periods of time covering operational planning.

Exam practice

Read the article below and then answer the question that follow.

Article A

The 'Starship' Enterprise?

Sir Richard Branson is well known for being enterprising. The Virgin Group, which he founded, has interests in many business areas including transport, financial services, music and communications. His latest venture has been some time in the planning but is now set to gather pace before it literally launches! Virgin Galactic is a business venture designed to provide the opportunity for private individuals to experience space travel. The business will not only provide a service carrying private passengers but will also be used for scientific equipment and satellites amongst other things.

Virgin Galactic is a new business venture and one that is very risky. As such, even more meticulous planning may be needed to help consider the potential problems that might arise.

Sales for the flights are priced at $200,000 or customers can express interest by putting down a $20,000 deposit. Mr Branson has said that he plans to build a space hotel which can be used to provide excursions for passengers around the Moon which could be possible in 20 years' time. The initial part of the project however is closer to realisation.

The service which people are paying for involves taking off in a high-altitude jet which carries a spacecraft. At 50,000 feet, the space craft will be jettisoned from the jet and the six passengers and two crew blast their way to 360,000 feet where they will be able to experience weightlessness and see Earth. The space craft will then return to Earth, completing the final part of the journey through an unpowered glide. Virgin Galactic says that in addition to those who have paid, there are around 85,000 people who have registered an interest. Flights are due to start sometime in 2010.

Source: Biz /ed In the News: http://www.bized.co.uk /cgi-bin/chron/chron.pl?id=3144

To what extent would planning be important to a business like Virgin Galactic? (50 marks)

Total: 50 marks

Breakdown of assessment objectives

AO1 – Knowledge and understanding – 8/50
AO2 – Apply knowledge and understanding – 12/50
AO3 – Analyse problems, issues and situations – 15/50
AO4 – Evaluate, distinguish between fact and opinion, assess and judge information from a variety of sources – 15/50

Suggested structure

- You will notice that a relatively high proportion of the marks are for application. You will need to make sure, therefore, that you have some understanding and awareness of the business idea behind Virgin Galactic.

- The planning for this business has been going on for some years and the article makes it clear that Sir Richard has plans for what might be offered in 20 years' time.

- You will need to make a distinction between the type of planning that may have gone on in the development of the project – was it strategic or operational?

- What level of detail will have been necessary and what possible problems might have arisen that would have thrown plans off course?

- What benefits would Virgin Galactic have gained through planning?

- What possible costs might Virgin Galactic have experienced by the planning and what does this depend upon (hint – think about the level of detail)?

- Does the nature of this particular business mean that planning is more or less important than other types of business?

- Introduce the idea of strategic intent as opposed to that of a more detailed strategic plan and its relevance to this type of business.

- Try to draw your analysis together by making a judgement on the extent of the importance of planning to this type of business.

- You may consider, because this is such a new and unusual venture, that planning (and be careful to make it clear what sort of planning you are referring to) is going to be essential.

- Or you may conclude that it is the vision that is more important.

- You may conclude that some types of planning may be essential for this business because of its very nature, but other forms of planning less useful.

- Ensure you complete your answer by summarising the argument and the judgement you are making in relation to the question asked.

Chapter 28 Key influences on the change process: leadership

The role of leadership in bringing about change is now seen as being extremely important. The pace of change is such that the ability to see beyond the short term and have a vision for the organisation, as well as convincing and taking others along with that vision, requires particular qualities that are often difficult to quantify. Much research has been done on leaders and leadership styles, however, and there is a growing consensus that there are particular characteristics that make a good leader.

It is important to recognise that leadership qualities in an individual are not necessarily 'good' things by definition. An individual may have highly-developed leadership qualities, but it depends on how they use those qualities and what they are 'leading'. It is well documented that Adolf Hitler possessed leadership qualities, but few would suggest that they were used appropriately or that much good came from his leadership. Equally, Saddam Hussein exercised strong leadership over Iraq but, again, many would suggest that this leadership was damaging rather than positive. Having a vision is an important element of leadership, but that vision has to lead to a positive outcome for the majority for it to be seen as being appropriate.

The meaning of leadership

The act of leading and managing are often confused and intertwined, but it is important to have a clear definition of each and an understanding of the distinction between the two. Leaders may manage but managers may not always lead. The word 'management' derives from the French term '*ménagement*' which means to conduct or direct. Managers are tasked with getting things done, and doing so by directing or guiding other people and resources. What it is they have to get done is not necessarily their idea, and this is where we can see the distinction between a leader and a manager. A leader is the one who establishes the vision and the direction; the manager carries it out. The story at the top of the next page is a good example of the key difference between the two.

From the story we can begin to develop some ideas about the difference between leaders and managers, and thus establish what leadership is all about. In making the distinction between the two, it must be borne in mind that many leaders do manage but we can identify a number of characteristics that set leaders apart.

> ## Key terms
>
> **Leadership** The process of establishing a vision of where an organisation will be at some point in the future, and influencing resources to realise this vision.
>
> **Management** The act of directing and controlling resources to achieve specified ends.

Individuals with highly-developed leadership qualities do not always put these qualities to good use. Successful business leaders consider all their stakeholders.

A group of workers and their leaders are set a task of clearing a road through a dense jungle on a remote island to get to the coast where an estuary provides a perfect site for a port.

The managers organise the labour into efficient units and monitor the distribution and use of capital assets – progress is excellent. The managers continue to monitor and evaluate progress, making adjustments along the way to ensure the progress is maintained and efficiency increased wherever possible.

Then, one day amidst all the hustle and bustle and activity, one person climbs up a nearby tree. The person surveys the scene from the top of the tree and shouts down to the assembled group below… 'Wrong way!'

(Story adapted from *The Seven Habits of Highly Effective People* by Stephen Covey, Simon & Schuster, 2004.)

Vision

Perhaps the main difference is the possession of a vision. A vision implies having some clear idea of where the individual wants the organisation to be at some point in the future. This suggests that leaders have a longer-term view of the organisation and may be more concerned with making decisions and instituting changes that may have short-term disadvantages but long-term benefits. Managers may be concerned with the bottom line – the net income of the business – but leaders with a vision may be able to envisage a time in the future when changes now will realise far greater bottom line benefits.

Innovation and initiative

Many leaders are creative and willing to take risks that some managers may not. This may be partly because they are in a position where they feel they have the power to influence rather than control. A manager is invested with some power and responsibilities, but some may not be prepared to go beyond those defined powers and responsibilities. Leaders tend to do so. As a result, leaders may often be challenging the existing structures and beliefs of an organisation. They will ask the question 'why?' on a regular basis – why do we do that, why don't we do it differently, why does it have to be done this way? – and may not be happy with the answer especially if it is 'because we have always done it that way'! As a result, we can say that managers tend to imitate or copy the actions of others, whereas leaders develop their own way of doing things and generate new ideas, new ways of working and new processes as a means of moving the organisation forward and realising the vision.

People

The relationship between a leader and the people in an organisation, and that of a manager and people tends to be different. Managers are responsible for people and for making sure that these people in relation to the resources also at their disposal are organised in a way that gets things done. This implies that managers have to exert control and this may be done through different ways including fear and intimidation (although not exclusively, of course). The examples of Hitler and Saddam Hussein given earlier may provide a point of contradiction here. Saddam Hussein, in particular, ruled through fear, and certainly there are leaders who do that and who get results in that way. In business, the relationship between leaders and people may be very different, and different to that which exists between some managers and leaders. A leader is likely to value the people they have around them and see them as being vital to the realisation of the vision. This implies that it is necessary to get people in the organisation to 'buy into' the vision, to believe in it and to carry out their tasks with the aim of helping to realise that vision.

Establishing the right relationships where employees feel involved, part of the vision, where they have the responsibility and power to make decisions, and crucially, where they feel trusted and respected, may be a vital part of the work of a leader. Leaders understand that they cannot realise the vision on their own and that it takes a whole corporate will to make it happen. As a result, leaders will look to focus on the importance of people, inspire trust and look to avoid control but to empower workers. In so doing, the full potential of the organisation can be developed. Typical of such an approach is the willingness to delegate the responsibility to make decisions across the whole organisation and to encourage 'leadership throughout the organisation'.

The quote below perhaps summarises the key difference between leaders and managers:

'Management is doing things right, leadership is doing the right things.'*

Skills watch!

Happiness at work

Read the article below.

The City and Guilds organisation publishes a survey called the Happiness Index. The most important factor in workplace happiness and fulfilment, according to the survey, was having an interest in your job. If there is a personal connection with the job then it provides happiness and fulfilment regardless of the salary being paid. 57% of the survey said that they stayed with their current employer because they have a strong interest in what they are doing for a living. Close behind was the relationship and friendship with work colleagues at 56%. 48% of respondents rated a good work–life balance as being an important determinant of whether they stayed with an employer and 44% said that the pay they received was the reason they remained in their job.

AO2 / AO3 / AO4

The Index is important in giving a picture of how business leaders view the way in which they might motivate workers and improve happiness at work. The survey suggested that 43% of managers give bonuses whilst only 20% use other methods, such as flexible working practices, and only 10% use working from home as a means of empowering their workforce.

Activity

Study the results of the Happiness Index and the information about how business leaders look to motivate staff. Comment on the appropriateness of these motivation techniques in the light of the findings of the survey. What does this tell you about the qualities needed by a 'good' leader?

Theories of leadership

What makes a good leader is something that academics have studied for some time. There are a number of theories relating to what qualities make a good leader. If we can understand these qualities then we may be in a position to put in place training and education to try to encourage these qualities in people.

The main theories are discussed on the following pages.

* Warren Bennis and Peter Drucker.

TRAIT THEORIES

Trait theories ask if there is a set of characteristics that determine a good leader. Some of the characteristics that have been suggested include:

- personality
- dominance and personal presence
- charisma
- self-confidence
- achievement
- ability to formulate a clear vision.

Trait theories have been criticised as implying that such characteristics are inherently gender-biased and that they emphasise male characteristics more than female. Do such characteristics produce good leaders and is leadership more than just bringing about change? Trait theories may imply that leaders are born and not bred.

BEHAVIOURAL THEORIES

Behavioural theories are based on the idea that leaders can be trained, and focus on processes and strategies that leaders can learn and employ to get the best out of their workers, and to take the business to where they want it to be. Within these theories are **structure-based behavioural theories** which focus on the leader establishing structures to bring about change and which are essentially task-orientated. For example, a leader may believe that if the right management structure and lines of communication are put in place, this will lead to a more dynamic organisation which is responsive to change. Individuals are given tasks which are designed to achieve this aim and which help the leader to work towards the vision.

The second sub-section consists of **relationship-based behavioural theories**. These focus on the development and maintenance of relationships, and are primarily process-orientated. In this situation, leaders look to achieve their aims through building relationships with people, which in turn improves the willingness of workers to implement the vision. There may be a strong reliance placed on communicating the vision, and the very process of discussion and relationship-building plays a part in the realisation of the vision.

CONTINGENCY THEORIES

These theories stress the importance of leadership as being more flexible: different leadership styles will be used at different times depending on the circumstances. They suggest that leadership is not a fixed series of characteristics that can be transposed into different contexts. Instead it may depend on:

- The type of staff that the business has – the age balance, their approach, willingness to change, and so on.
- The history of the business – whether it has developed as a family firm, for example, or whether it has developed organically or through acquisition.
- The culture of the business – is it highly flexible, responsive to change, forward-looking, or one that is inward-looking and resistant to change?
- The quality of the relationships – in any business there can be different levels of relationship; some can be highly developed and based on a significant degree of trust, whereas others can be strained and difficult.
- The nature of the changes needed – if there are very significant changes needed in the organisation, for example, wholesale restructuring which necessitates a relocation or a large number of redundancies, then this will require a different leadership approach to one where a new product is being launched.

TRANSFORMATIONAL THEORIES

Some leaders have the ability to institute and oversee widespread changes to a business or organisation. Transformational leadership refers to situations such as where widespread change occurs. To bring about such change will require some or all of the following:

- long-term strategic planning (but not necessarily detailed plans!)
- clear objectives
- a clear vision
- leading by example – 'walk the walk'
- a high degree of efficiency in systems and processes.

A decision to relocate customer service operations to a new location will involve a significant change to an organisation and will need high-quality leadership skills to carry it out successfully

INVITATIONAL LEADERSHIP THEORIES

These are relatively new theories that focus on the messages that businesses send – both physical and non-physical. The intention is to improve the atmosphere and message sent out by the organisation. There will be a focus on reducing negative messages sent out through the everyday actions of the business both externally and, crucially, internally. Such messages may be very simple, for example, a bold 'No Entry' sign emphasises the negative and may be replaced with something that is not quite so blatant such as 'This is a restricted area. Please seek assistance before entering'.

Invitational leadership may require a review of internal processes to reduce the negative messages sent out by the organisation, and instead look to try to accentuate the positive. The aim of this style of leadership is to build relationships and a sense of belonging and identity with the organisation, which in turn gets communicated to the stakeholders of the business.

TRANSACTIONAL THEORIES

These theories place an emphasis on the management of the organisation, and on procedures and efficiency. In such organisations, there may be considerable importance placed on working to rules and contracts, and managing current issues and problems. By doing this, the leader is able to focus on using resources efficiently, identifying what works well in the organisation, establishing procedures and using training as a means of generating improvements in the business.

The range of leadership styles

Different styles of leadership have been identified. It is possible to associate a particular style with particular individuals or organisations, but it is also important to appreciate that there may be times when one sort of leadership style is necessary and in others a different style will be required. Good leaders are able to adopt different styles to suit different situations, so treat the information below as an overall guide only.

Autocratic

An autocratic leadership style is associated with one where an individual or a small number of designated individuals make decisions, with little or no reference to anyone else. In such

organisations there tends to be a high degree of dependency on the leader and few in the organisation feel comfortable about making decisions without reference to the leader. This can create demotivation and alienation of staff who may not feel they are trusted or have responsibility. However, some staff may feel more comfortable in such a role, especially where decision-making leads to potentially serious consequences.

An autocratic style may be valuable in some types of business where decisions need to be made quickly and decisively, or where decisions may have extreme consequences or rely on highly-specialised knowledge.

For example, in the chemical industry, the production of highly-volatile chemical compounds may require a level of knowledge and expertise that is highly specialised. Workers at such plants may have defined roles, but expecting them to exercise their own initiative in making decisions which could have catastrophic consequences might be highly inappropriate. Reference, in this situation, must be made to the appropriately-qualified and experienced leader in order to ensure the safety of the plant and the environment. In the military and in some aspects of the health service similar scenarios exist which may make an autocratic leadership style appropriate.

Paternalistic

Sir Alex Ferguson – acknowledged as a highly-successful leader. Is his style autocratic, democratic or paternalistic? The public image of his style might be quite different to the private one!

In a paternalistic leadership regime, the leader acts as a 'father figure' in the organisation. Paternalistic leaders make decisions but may consult, and there is a heavy reliance on the importance of support staff. Paternalistic styles look to generate a culture where the organisation has a feeling of belonging. Such styles can generate strong bonds of loyalty and this can be beneficial in reducing the incidence of labour turnover, but could also create an organisation that suffers from inertia, a lack of dynamism and unwillingness to change.

Democratic

A democratic leadership style is one where a wide range of people in the organisation are encouraged to be involved in decision-making. The benefits to the organisation are that there are many different perspectives that are brought to bear on decisions and it may be that the democratic leader encourages a focus on leadership throughout the organisation. These different perspectives may help to solve problems more quickly, bring about new ideas and new processes that can improve efficiency and lead to a more productive working environment.

Motivation theorists point to the role of responsibility and a feeling of belonging in motivating workers, and a democratic style of leadership can help to encourage that. More recent theories on motivation refer to employees' 'happiness', and a number of surveys in relation to this conclude that working environments where workers feel they have control over their lives and their work can significantly improve motivation and improve productivity as a result, as well as reducing labour turnover.

Within this style of leadership there are various sub-sections that have been identified. These are listed below.

CONSULTATIVE

Consultative leadership styles emphasise the importance of the process of consultation before decisions are taken. Views are requested from appropriate team members and considered before decisions are taken.

PERSUASIVE

In this situation, the leader may be in a position where they have made a decision, but before implementing that decision seeks to persuade others that the decision is correct. This may involve a number of meetings and discussions as the issue is thrashed out and it may well be that the leader will need to hear very strong arguments to the contrary to persuade them that the decision they wish to make is wrong.

One of the problems with a democratic leadership style is that decisions take longer to make and this could be significant, especially where time is of the essence. Many businesses need to react to changing competitive conditions and to changes in technology, and if there are lengthy periods of discussion and debate whilst all views are canvassed, it can lead to the business falling behind its competitors or its competitors gaining competitive advantage that is then very difficult to make up.

EMPOWERED WORKERS

This sub-set of a democratic leadership style is one where workers are invested with a degree of trust and empowerment to make decisions. These decisions might be about how they work and contribute to corporate decision-making. Examples of such power might include quality circles and works councils, where regular meetings of a range of members of the business are held to listen to views and find ways of improving efficiency, as well as getting ideas from those who are closest to the actual production. Often these people will have a far greater understanding of the practical problems that arise, and equally have a good insight into ways in which these problems can be solved and how work practices can be improved.

Another example is seen in cell production. Cell production breaks up production into self-contained units acting as teams. The teams are given wide-ranging powers to make decisions and manage budgets. The teams are often given the power to organise their own work schedule and in some cases there have been reports that productivity rises as a result. Efficiencies can be gained by removing waste, making the actual production runs more efficient, improving organisation and communication, as well as giving responsibility to a wider range of workers.

Laissez-faire

The term 'laissez faire' means 'let it be' and this leadership style is one where leadership responsibilities are shared by all in the organisation. It can be very useful in businesses where creativity and creative ideas are important, for example, in marketing and advertising. This style of leadership can be highly motivational as people have control over their working life. However, it can make coordination and decision-making time-consuming and there could be a lack of overall direction which may mean that the organisation can drift and lose its way. Such a leadership style relies on good teamwork and on highly-developed interpersonal relations.

Assessing internal and external factors influencing leadership style

It was mentioned earlier in this chapter that we must guard against the idea that there is one leadership style that will be adopted by an organisation and one only. In most large organisations there will be a number of people in leadership positions responsible for different aspects of the business, and each might adopt a slightly different style with their team. The overall direction and vision will be given by the chief executive officer who may surround him/herself with people who are of a similar disposition and who share similar approaches and beliefs to leadership.

It is important to understand, when considering factors affecting leadership style, what the key drivers of change are likely to be. The style adopted may depend on the type of change being experienced. The main drivers are discussed below.

INTERNAL DRIVERS

These include:

- New production methods – including decisions to outsource production or other aspects of the business, such as customer service or distribution.
- New working methods – flexi-working, job sharing, etc.
- Job redesigns – delayering, downsizing, etc.
- New methods of motivation or managing of human resources, for example, appraisal.
- New product development.
- Risk – decision-making and change initiatives will involve varying degrees of risk. The style of leadership may differ according to the level of risk with higher levels of risk associated (possibly) with more autocratic styles of leadership.
- The type of business – is it a creative business or supply-driven? If it is creative then it might imply that more democratic styles of leadership are appropriate.
- Organisational culture – may be embedded and difficult to change (see Chapter 29).
- The nature of the task – does it require cooperation, direction or structure? Different tasks might require a different leadership style.
- The nature of the change. If change is important to the future direction or survival of the firm, then it may be that the leadership style will need to be different to a situation where a new leader comes in and makes change for the sake of it – to establish their position in the organisation, for example.

EXTERNAL DRIVERS

These include:

- New markets – Eastern Europe, Asia, the Far East, Africa – not only new market opportunities but also how emerging markets impact on the business.
- New technology.
- Acquisition through mergers or takeover.
- External economic factors – economic growth, changes in interest rates, etc.
- Legislation – health and safety, Disability Discrimination Act, etc.
- Actions by competitors.
- Natural disasters.
- Terrorist activity.

Whatever the change that is occurring – and it is highly likely that there will be a number of changes all happening at the same time – the business might have to respond in a different way. Some changes will require decisive action to be taken. For example, the terrorist attacks in London on 7 July 2005 created substantial disruption for many businesses, not just in London, but in the UK as a whole and throughout their global business activities. The response necessitated strong leadership to ensure that disruption to customers and other stakeholders was minimised. Such a response may require a more autocratic style of leadership.

In the case of the development of a new product or when new technology needs to be incorporated into the business, the appropriate leadership style may be more democratic in nature. It may be necessary to think through a number of issues, and the input and expertise of a wide range of people in the organisation might be required. A democratic style of leadership may be the best way of ensuring that the business is able to maximise the potential from the new product or the technology.

Skills watch!

A03 / A04

What leadership style?

A marketing company, well known for the creativity of its designs, has been struggling with one account that it runs. The success rate of the marketing it has carried out has been below the client's expectations and there have been top-level meetings between executives on both sides. The client's business is high-quality hi-fi equipment with a reputation for technical innovation, style, design and high-quality sound with a high price tag.

As a result of the meeting, it has been made clear by the client that they are prepared to agree to one further marketing drive. If this fails to deliver the required results then the account will be closed, losing the marketing company over £1 million a year.

Activity

Select **two** internal and **two** external drivers from the list opposite which you think will be highly relevant in this case. Evaluate these drivers and discuss which will be the most likely to influence the leadership style adopted by the marketing company in its attempts to keep this important account.

Types of change: predictable and unpredictable

The appropriate leadership style to be adopted, therefore, will depend on the types of change that can confront a business. Given that these changes do not just come singly, the business has to be flexible enough to be able to cope with them when they arise. The appropriate leadership response will also be related to the characteristics that change possesses.

LINEAR CHANGE

In some cases change can be linear – this means it proceeds through a series of set changes. This might be the case when a business has made a decision to launch a new product. The development process is usually well established and will be clear. Of course, there could be any number of things that happen along the way which could disrupt the process.

In some respects, change can be predictable in that most businesses know that there will be changes in economic conditions over a period of time. They know that interest rates are going to change, that the economy will experience periods of slowdown and growth, but at the same time they do not know when these changes are going to occur. The leader is able to

Businesses can plan for unpredictable events like a terrorist attack but they will not know if and when they will ever be affected by such an event – in that sense it is unpredictable. Leaders have to take such possible events into account, however, to ensure disruption to the business is minimised.

put in place appropriate strategies to take into account the response to these changes when they do occur.

With many of the internal changes listed above, leaders have some degree of control over when and if they occur. That is not the case for the external factors. Many businesses will plan for the possibility of external change but may not know precisely when they are going to occur. With events such as terrorism or natural disasters, the actual event might be exceptional and relatively rare, but this does not mean that leaders can afford to ignore what the appropriate response might be if and when they do happen.

RANDOM CHANGE

In reality, it is likely that change is not going to be predictable. Change can happen anywhere, any time and come from any direction. It is certainly not linear or predictable. For example, a key worker in a small business could have an accident on the way to work meaning they will be off work for six months. This could have a significant effect on the business and is not something that any business could necessarily anticipate. However, leaders may have to consider such scenarios in their planning and put in place systems and processes for dealing with such an eventuality.

For larger businesses, political changes in international markets can cause sudden significant effects on a business. New technology or new information can have a significant impact on many businesses – largely unpredicted.

The role of leadership in managing change

For many established businesses, large and small, one of the most challenging aspects is leading and managing change. We have already seen how the business environment is subject to fast-paced economic and social change. Modern businesses must adapt and be flexible to survive.

Problems in leading change stem mainly from human resource management. Humans make up a key part of most businesses and change is likely to affect them directly and indirectly. Leaders need to be aware of how change impacts on workers and have appropriate strategies in place to drive through the change, but also to ensure that workers feel part of the change, informed, and that their fears are confronted and dealt with.

The three quotes in the boxes highlight some of the key issues here.

'There is nothing more difficult to take in hand, more perilous to conduct, or more uncertain in its success, than to take the lead in the introduction of a new order of things.' (Niccolo Machiavelli, 15th century philosopher)

'No organization can depend on genius; the supply is always scarce and unreliable. It is the test of an organization to make ordinary human beings perform better than they seem capable of, to bring out whatever strength there is in its members, and to use each one's strength to help all the others perform. The purpose of an organization is to enable common people to do uncommon things.' (Peter Drucker, management guru)

'You can only go halfway into the darkest forest; then you are coming out the other side.' (Chinese proverb)

The three quotes above highlight the importance of change in our lives. For business, change is something that is ever present. No business or business environment ever stands still. It follows from this that every business has to cope with change. At the frontline of most change in business will be humans. The workforce will be the ones who have to adapt to new situations and to the effects of changes inside and outside the business. Making sure that they are suitably trained to be able to cope with these changes is an important part of the leadership and management process.

In leading change there are likely to be a series of reactions and responses by people in the organisation to change. The length of time in each of these 'states' will be dependent on the nature of the change and the type of organisation and its culture. These states have been categorised as a series of so called 'self-esteem states' identified by Adams et al.*

1 **Immobilisation** As rumours of the change circulate, the individual feels some sense of shock and possible disbelief – so much so that they deem it worthy of doing nothing.

2 **Minimisation** As the change becomes clearer, people try to fit in the change with their own personal position and may try to believe that it will not affect them.

3 **Depression** As reality begins to dawn workers may feel alienated and angry; feelings of a lack of control of events overtake people and they feel depressed as they try to reconcile what is happening with their own personal situation.

4 **Acceptance/Letting go** The lowest point in self-esteem finally sees people starting to accept the inevitable. Fear of the future is a feature of this stage.

5 **Testing out** Individuals begin to interact with the change; they start to ask questions to see how they might work with the change.

6 **Search for meaning** Individuals begin to work with the change and see how they might be able to make the change work for them – self-esteem begins to rise.

7 **Internalisation** The change is understood and adopted within the individual's own understanding – they now know how to work with it and feel a renewed sense of confidence and self-esteem.*

* Source: *Transition. Understanding and managing change: personal change*, J. Adams, J. Hayes and B. Hopson (eds), Martin Robertson, 1976.

These feelings are not unusual, but leaders have to understand that these states are likely to occur. They need to help workers to come to terms with them, and to get to the state where they accept the change and are able to internalise it as quickly as possible.

At the early stages of the change process, the leader may find that there are a number of workers, some inevitably in senior management positions, who will be highly resistant to change. Such resistance can often make the whole process much harder for all concerned. Typical responses in an organisation to change are summarised as a series of statements below; most people who have worked in any organisation will be able to identify with such sentiments!

RESPONSES TO CHANGE THAT ARE ASSOCIATED WITH RESISTANCE

'Oh, we've tried that before and it failed then...'

'You might have done that elsewhere but this is a different place...'

'It's their fault!'

'We're too busy!'

'You can't teach an old dog new tricks!'

'We don't have enough time as it is...'

'Let's form a committee to investigate and report back...'

'But we have always done it this way...'

'If it ain't broke, don't fix it!'

'I can see where you are coming from but...'

'Let's think about this a bit more – sleep on it for a while...'

'The customers won't like that!'

'Great idea but totally impractical...'

'You're not living in the real world...'

'They are just incompetent!'

'Present it in the form of a report and we will see where it goes...'

'That's not really our problem...'

Synoptic search

In your AS studies you will have covered work on 'Managing a business'. The emphasis was on structures and how to develop an effective workforce.

How might your knowledge of this section of the AS course help you to understand the issues facing leaders in managing change?

The role of leadership is to find ways of not only helping workers through the effects on their self-esteem in the stages outlined above, but to find ways of circumventing the sort of resistance that is characterised by the comments above. One of the ways of doing this is for the leader to surround themselves with people in senior positions who are of a similar mind and approach, to make sure that the vision is not only communicated clearly to all in the organisation, but to help drive it through. There may be times when the leader has to be decisive and remove the potential barriers to change, either through redundancies or relocation to a different plant, or to a different role/post where the individual/s are not in a position to exercise the power to prevent the change from taking place.

Components of leadership for change

Michael Fullan, a leading writer on change leadership, has identified five components of leadership for change. Each of the five is important in their own right but becomes more powerful when they are used together. The five components give some insight into the leadership qualities required to drive through change. The five are:

- Moral purpose – acting with the intention of making a positive difference to the business and its stakeholders.
- A deep understanding of the change process and its effects on people and organisations.
- Relationship-building – at all levels of the organisation.
- Knowledge creation and sharing – which involves making sure that workers in the organisation are fully aware of what the changes are that are being made and what the implications are to them. Within any organisation there is a range of expertise and skills, and without knowledge-sharing, these can be ignored and important internal synergies lost. This is perhaps best summed up by a comment from Lew Platt, a former CEO of Hewlett Packard, who was reported to have said, 'If only we knew what we know at HP.'
- Coherence – the importance of the leader being able to guide events because they will have created an environment where innovation, creativity and change are accepted, valued and are in progress.

Assessing the importance of leadership

Leaders play a vital role in any business. They are the people who provide the vision, often the inspiration, the direction and challenge to a business to take it from one level to another. They are the ones that are credited with turning a business around and for steering a business through difficult times. They are criticised when things go wrong and also for earning large sums of money. Many, however, are also highly valued and their skills widely praised and coveted. There are plenty of people who are happy to justify the often considerable sums of money that they receive.

The value added to the business as a result of their leadership can be significant but often difficult to quantify. Sir Stuart Rose, the boss of Marks and Spencer (at the time of writing!), has been praised for turning around that company, but in 2008 when external economic pressures hit profits, his critics were quick to point to some decisions he had made as contributing to the weaker performance of the company.

The market value of a good business leader is extremely high. Many earn very high salaries and, with bonus payments and share options, can take their annual earnings to well in excess of a million pounds a year. However, their skills are very limited in supply. This chapter has given an outline of some of the theories of leadership and has asked the question whether leaders can be trained or whether their particular skills are 'natural'. It is likely that leadership competencies can be the subject of training, but the ability to carry out these competencies in a highly-competitive environment and to make the right decisions at the right time and have the vision to lead a business through a period of change is not something that anyone can do.

The limited supply of such talented individuals means that they are likely to be in very high demand and as a result it is no surprise that they can command very high salaries as a result. The very fact that businesses are prepared to pay these high salaries suggests that there is a premium on individuals with these skills, and in turn that they are seen as being vitally important to a business.

However, we must also put the role of an individual, often the public face of the company, into some sort of context. Many of these individuals are brought into established businesses where the reputation and fundamentals are sound. What is needed is

For example...

Terminal problems for BA?

In March 2008, British Airways (BA) looked forward to the opening of its new Terminal 5 at Heathrow. Most of BA's operations were supposed to have been transferred to the new terminal, but the first week was marred by problems and was branded shambolic. The chief executive, Willie Walsh, was quick to face the media and to accept the criticism that he knew would come his way. Whilst it may not have been his incompetence or lack of planning that contributed mostly to the fiasco that faced customers using the new terminal, he as the leader, accepted that the buck stopped with him. Later in the year, announcing increased revenue and profits for the previous financial year, Walsh also announced that he would not be taking his bonus entitlement following the performance surrounding the opening of Terminal 5.

Willie Walsh, CEO of BA, faces the press to explain the problems which beset the company during the first week of the opening of Terminal 5 at Heathrow

a fresh set of ideas, a different approach and a new direction, but often the new leaders will emphasise their commitment to 'getting back to basics' and to returning to the fundamental qualities and principles of the business.

This suggests that leaders might be able to do a great deal to improve the performance of a business, but that there can also be lots of other things in place that can contribute to the success of a business. Putting a value on the reputation that a business has built up over a long period of time, the brand loyalty of consumers and competitive advantages that a business possesses is very difficult, but it is highly likely that good leaders will recognise this value and attempt to exploit it within their own vision for the future development of the company. This is what makes them so valued.

In the case of business start-ups and small and medium-sized businesses, the role of the leader may be less spectacular than those we tend to hear about in the press with regard to very large corporations. However, the skills they possess are no less valuable, and without the benefit of a strong brand behind them and the disadvantages of trying to compete in often very strong markets, it could be argued that many of the leadership qualities demonstrated by these people is a testament to the entrepreneurial spirit that exists in the UK.

There are some occasions when an individual receives considerable press attention for starting a company from scratch and making it a success. The measure of the real success might not be in the fact that an individual has become a millionaire in two years, but in the extent to which they are able to sustain the success that they may experience in the initial stages of the business. One of the tests of leadership quality is the ability of the individual to be able to maintain and improve success over a period of time. The transition from one scale of business operation to another (in other words, when change really starts to impact on the business) is often the time when the individual's true leadership qualities are tested to the full!

Summary and exam guidance

Summary

- Leadership and management are interlinked but there are characteristics of leaders that set them apart from managers.

- There are a range of theories about leadership that attempt to identify key characteristics of what makes a good leader and to explain whether leaders can be trained or whether their talents are 'natural'.

- There are a range of leadership styles but in many businesses, leaders may adopt different styles depending on the circumstances they are facing and the nature of the change.

- The main influences on leadership style will come from internal factors which the business has some control over and external factors over which the business may have little control.

- There are two main types of change that leaders will have to cope with – predictable and unpredictable change. In both cases, however, leaders may plan to be prepared for both.

- Leaders have a key role to play in managing change, especially with regard to human resources.

- Leadership can and does play an important role in successful change management, but in some cases the leader would not be successful without the fundamental strengths of the business built up over many years behind them.

Exam practice

Read the article below and then answer the questions that follow.

Article A

The art of good leadership

At the end of the 2005/06 Premiership football season, Sunderland were relegated with the then, lowest points tally in the history of the Premiership. As they started life in the Championship, it became clear that the club might find life in the lower division no less easy. The club had been bought by a former player, Niall Quinn, who set about trying to get the club back on track. Quinn took over management of the team as well as trying to direct the financial affairs of the club. His stint as manager was not going well. As the end of August approached, the club was near the bottom of the Championship and things looked bleak.

cont...

Disagreements in football or business (or both) are not unusual, but the way they are handled is a testament to the leadership skills and personalities of those involved. Niall Quinn and Roy Keane both played for the Republic of Ireland and were at the centre of a famous argument in which Keane criticised the then Republic manager, Mick McCarthy, and much of the supporting organisation at the World Cup in 2002 for the poor organisation and facilities the

Niall Quinn and Roy Keane: their leadership skills have been highly praised

team faced. At the time, Keane was accused of petulance and of being spoilt by being at super-rich Manchester United.

The two former players, however, put aside their differences when Quinn approached Keane to take over the team in August 2006. Quinn happily sacked himself to install Keane and returned to the boardroom to run the business side of affairs.

Under Keane's management the club started slowly, but as the season progressed, they climbed the table and after a sensational run of form, Sunderland won the Championship and gained promotion to the Premier League. Keane and Quinn's leadership credentials were highly praised, especially given that both were new to their respective positions. 'Fail to prepare, prepare to fail' were Roy Keane's words in the fallout of his departure from the World Cup in 2002. Now Keane was in a position to apply that mantra. He put success down to preparation and treating players and staff with respect. Giving them time to settle, to make sure all the non-work things in life, like family welfare and support and the players' happiness, was taken care of off the field. Keane believed if this side of the club was right then the results would come on the field. Given the season that Sunderland had, who could argue with this common sense management and leadership philosophy. How many business leaders could also learn from this case study in person management and leadership?

Source: adapted from Biz/ed In the News: http://www.bized.co.uk/cgi-bin/chron/chron.pl?id=2825

(a) Analyse the appropriate leadership style for an individual in charge of a top flight football club. (16 marks)

(b) Evaluate the role of someone like Roy Keane in managing change in an organisation like a football club. Your answer should show some awareness of the need to ensure that success on the field is closely related to the success of the organisation as a business. (34 marks)

Total: 50 marks

Breakdown of assessment objectives

AO1 – Knowledge and understanding – 10/50
AO2 – Apply knowledge and understanding – 10/50
AO3 – Analyse problems, issues and situations – 15/50
AO4 – Evaluate, distinguish between fact and opinion, assess and judge
     information from a variety of sources – 15/50

Suggested structure

For part (a):

* An important part of the answer will be in your ability to be able to apply your knowledge of types of leadership to the specific context of this case study.
* You will need to consider the different leadership styles you have studied in this chapter and make a decision about which you think is the most appropriate for this context.
* You will need to think about the nature of this particular context – top flight football clubs contain employees that are invariably on very high salaries; it is a results-driven business, highly unstable and with a lot of egos to be managed. What type of leadership will get the best out of this type of business organisation?
* Offer an explanation of the leadership type you have chosen and ensure that you apply it directly to the context. It is not sufficient to simply trot out the characteristics of the type of leadership you have chosen; it must be applied to the context at this level.

For part (b):

* You will need to offer some explanation of what managing change in a football club might look like. Use the context of the turnaround in fortunes at Sunderland as the basis for your answer.
* The article gives a brief guide to some of the things that Keane did – use these to help you offer your explanation and analysis.
* You will need to be clear – and outline this – what the role of a leader of a football club is. Note the comments in the question relating to the need to link the on-field and off-field activities of the club as a business entity.
* You must offer an explanation and analysis of what role Keane played in Sunderland's success (this will be linked to the points in bullet point 3 above).
* You will then have to offer some balance to the answer by suggesting and explaining what other factors may have played a part in the change in fortunes that the club had – in other words, was the success all down to Keane or could there have been other factors that contributed?
* Make some judgements as to the relative importance of these factors and give some support to the points that you have made.
* Draw your answer together by arriving at a supported conclusion relating back to the question.

Chapter 29   Key influences on the change process: culture

What is culture?

In short, corporate culture refers to the way that things are done in an organisation. Behind this relatively simple definition, however, lies a far more complex set of relationships between leaders and the rest of the organisation that has been the subject of increasing research and discussion over the last 30 years. One of the key drivers for this research has been the pace of change that organisations have been subject to.

Business has to deal with social, economic, political and legal change as we saw in Chapters 21–24. In addition to this, there is an increased awareness by all stakeholders of the effect of corporate behaviour on the environment and the impact of globalisation. This in turn has coincided with the ability of people to be able to access and disseminate information as a result of information **and** communications technology, which means businesses are more likely to be under greater scrutiny. If we then add in the effect of other changes, such as the increased threat to security from criminal activity and terrorism, then the challenge of leadership becomes even more daunting. Researchers have been asking whether leaders can adapt the culture of an organisation to take account of these changes or whether organisations are subject to an evolving culture that is largely determined outside the organisation.

The nature of corporate culture means that it is difficult to measure. Corporate culture is about the way that humans react within the organisation and outside it, and about the degree to which there are shared values, beliefs and norms about what is important to the organisation. Norms are the rules and processes that are seen as being generally acceptable. The fact that corporate culture relates to human beings and how they interact and behave means that there are likely to be rules and acceptable ways of doing things, but the question that researchers have been asking is whether this can be imposed by a leader or whether it simply exists and is not a variable that can be manipulated.

Culture might be reflected in some of the following ways:

- The atmosphere of a business – is it welcoming, threatening, intimidating, friendly, relaxed, professional?
- The energy levels of staff, their willingness to respond to customers and the extent to which they are customer-focused.
- How things are done in the organisation – are there lots of procedures to go through, lots of paperwork, or do people respond quickly and use their initiative?
- How are workers treated – are they trusted and respected, or seen as being inherently lazy and in need of constant monitoring and control?
- The degree of individual freedom and the amount of space that people have.
- The personality and approach of the senior leadership team.
- Dress codes.
- Do staff in the organisation dwell on problems or look for solutions?
- How do people relate to each other – do people, including the senior team, refer to each other by Christian name or is there a more formal way of addressing people? Do staff call each other by their Christian names but are expected to refer to senior staff as Mrs, Ms or Mr?

- What is valued most – is it initiative and risk-taking, conforming to the rules or even breaking the rules?
- How authority is used and shared out – is it used constructively or unfairly? Is it centralised or are employees empowered to make their own decisions?

The role of culture

A corporate culture, whether it is imposed or exists, helps to define an organisation. It provides an identity for those most closely involved in the business and its wider stakeholders who interact with it. Culture helps workers to address key questions such as 'Who am I?', 'What is the purpose of my role in the organisation?' and 'What does my organisation do and

For example...

Dell Inc.

The two examples that follow are of Dell and Nokia. The statements that the two companies make are designed to try and make it clear what their values are and establish the type of corporate culture they wish to project to all their stakeholders.

The Soul of Dell

The Soul of Dell is our statement of corporate philosophy. It provides a common statement of our basic values and beliefs and serves as a guide for our company in the many cultures we call home. Our values and beliefs communicate the kind of company we are and aspire to be. This document is intended to assure that our actions – worldwide – are consistent and supportive of our values and beliefs.

The Dell Team

We believe our continued success lies in teamwork and the opportunity each team member has to learn, develop and grow.

We are committed to:

- Being a meritocracy.
- We value accountability and reward those teams and team members who continually improve their capability and contribution.
- Developing, retaining and attracting the best people, reflective of our worldwide marketplace.
- Hire and promote based on performance, capability and qualifications as key criteria. Look first to promote from within Dell.

- Providing training and learning opportunities to maximize team and individual performances.
- Investing in our People Leadership capabilities as a competitive advantage.
- Managing our talent as a key asset.
- Utilizing job assignments across and within regions to build global leadership capability.
- Promoting an environment that values individual differences, engages people in decision-making and encourages employees at all levels and across all parts of the company to work as a team.
- Maintaining base pay and benefit programs competitive with successful companies relevant to our marketplace.

Winning

We have a passion for winning in everything we do.

We are committed to:

- Building a culture of operational excellence.
- Delivering superior customer experience.
- Leading in the global markets we serve.
- Being known as a great company and a great place to work.
- Providing superior shareholder return over time.

Source: Dell Inc., http://www.strategy-business.com/press/16635507/04305

For example...

Nokia

Nokia values

The values of our company make us different. They provide a sense of direction for consistent behaviour as employees and citizens of the world, and in our quest to be a great internet company. Through extensive employee engagement, Nokia has now created new values that reflect our business and changing environment. They act as a foundation for our evolving culture and are the basis of our operational mode. Living them every day is our shared philosophy.

- **Engaging you** For us 'Engaging you' incorporates the customer satisfaction value and deals with engaging all our stakeholders, including employees, in what Nokia stands for in the world.

- **Achieving together** Achieving together is more than collaboration and partnership. As well as trust, it involves sharing, the right mind-set and working in formal and informal networks.

- **Passion for innovation** Passion for innovation is based on a desire we have to live our dreams, to find our courage and make the leap into the future through innovation in technology, ways of working and through understanding the world around us.

- **Very human** Being 'Very human' encompasses what we offer customers, how we do business and the impact of our actions and behaviour on people and the environment. It is about being very human in the world – making things simple, respecting and caring. In short, our desire is to be a very human company.

Source: http://www.nokia.com/A4254188

stand for?' In developing a culture, a business sends messages to its stakeholders about its shared commitments to particular ways of doing things and how the organisation treats its staff.

Business organisations that developed in the period up to the 1960s are more likely to have reflected a culture that was also dominant in society as a whole; one based on social class and a strict hierarchy. The difference between workers was made very clear with senior members of staff treated in quite different ways to that of 'ordinary' workers. Obvious examples of where this was manifested were in such things as separate canteen areas for senior staff, where metal cutlery and proper glasses were used whilst 'ordinary' staff had plastic tables and cutlery along with plastic glasses. Senior staff may even have had access to different toilet facilities; having access to the management toilet was, in some cases, a mark that you had started to make it in the organisation!

The 'us' and 'them' culture might be seen to be linked with McGregor's Theory X and Theory Y. Theory X emphasised the need to control workers because they were inherently lazy and did not enjoy work. However, there has been a growing recognition that for many people work is an important aspect of their lives, and as work roles have changed, many people do not look at work as a means to an end but as an integral part of their lives, and where the mix between 'work' and social interaction becomes progressively blurred. In addition, new production methods like just-in-time (JIT) required a greater degree of flexibility from the workforce and also necessitated that they be committed to the organisation and its goals and values. Businesses had to change to encourage this to happen.

The decline in an approach to leadership that was focused on management science, where staff can be controlled and managed through applying scientific and mathematical principles, has largely died out. It has been replaced with a view that staff are the lifeblood of an organisation and need to be treated as possibly the most important resource a business has. Part of this change has also come about because the nature of work has changed. The UK is now far more dependent on service industries than manufacturing, and service businesses are not as open to management science principles. In addition, the skills required for many jobs mean that workers do become valuable to a business and are not necessarily ones that can be replaced quickly or easily without considerable cost.

The level of trust between leaders and the workers in an organisation is such that the need to control is not as great as it might have seemed to have been prior to the 1960s, and this has led to changes in the approach by leaders to the development of organisational culture.

Types of organisational culture

Whilst many businesses might want to suggest that they do not have any one dominant culture, researchers have identified particular characteristics that can be associated with four main types of culture: **power**, **task**, **entrepreneurial** and **role**. The main characteristics of different organisational cultures were identified by Charles Handy, a management thinker with an expertise in organisational behaviour.

Power culture

The main elements of this type of culture are listed below:

- The organisation is dependent on a main power source which is usually the owner or founder of the organisation.
- The key to an effective power culture is the relationship that exists between the power source and the staff.
- The power source will tend to surround themselves with people with a similar outlook and set of beliefs.
- There are few rules and routines, with decisions tending to be made on the basis of the balance of power between the different groups in the organisation rather than any specified procedures.
- The organisation tends to be flexible but bound together in a strong cohesive structure.

- When the organisation expands, the power source becomes less important and weaker.
- Such an organisation can be highly competitive and this can lead to lower morale amongst workers and the risk of increased labour turnover.
- Replacing the power source when he/she leaves or retires can present a major challenge to the business and might lead to some form of disruption.
- Such a culture tends to be more common in small to medium-sized enterprises.
- Whilst the power source can be seen as being firm and fair to those who are loyal, there is also the danger that such a culture can harbour fear and resentment, with the power source seen as making decisions and running the business for personal gain.

Task culture

Task culture places the emphasis on individual projects and small teams. Teams consist of a number of individuals, probably bringing different but complimentary skills with them, to work towards the completion of a task which has been given to them or which they have identified needs doing. The teams might be pulled in from different parts of the organisation to deal with particular problems that arise, and may manifest themselves as working parties or study groups focusing on a particular issue.

Task culture has the following characteristics:

- There is a focus on getting the task completed and this means it is important to make sure that the right people are brought together at the right time and given the appropriate resources to carry out the task set.
- The teams place a great emphasis on expertise and teamwork.
- The allocation of resources allows the organisation to exert a degree of control.
- Such a culture is appropriate to markets where the product life cycle is short (such as the fashion industry) or where the market is highly volatile or relies on a greater degree of creativity. In such markets, speed of response and cooperation between team members is important.
- The creation of small teams makes decision-making faster and thus enables the organisation to respond to changing markets faster.
- One potential problem is that the constant switch between different projects means that some people may not build up expertise in one area and this can lead to a sense of frustration and possibly affect motivation.
- Such cultures are common in marketing companies and management consultancies.

Entrepreneurial culture

An entrepreneurial culture is one where the characteristics of enterprise are encouraged. These characteristics include using initiative, being creative, determined, innovative, taking the lead and taking risks. In organisations that develop an entrepreneurial culture, work becomes synonymous with lifestyle and there may be a team approach that borders on feeling like part of a family. Generating such a culture requires the leader to place a great deal of trust in the staff, which implies that there need to be excellent lines of communication established. Other key characteristics of an entrepreneurial culture are listed below:

- Providing the opportunities to let individuals grow and for teams to be able to evolve and grow. A delicate balance needs to be practised by the leader to ensure that they guide and participate without being seen to interfere, thus destroying the relationships and trust that have been built up.
- There is a great emphasis placed on attention to detail. This might involve seemingly minor things such as making sure that the leader knows who people in the organisation are and their family backgrounds, stopping to engage in conversation – not only about work but also about social and non-work issues – helping people

settle, remembering birthdays, and so on. All these little things are part of the development of the family atmosphere.

- Providing opportunities for staff to get to know each other outside of the working environment, but which allow ideas and new strategies to be discussed in an informal setting, thus encouraging greater participation.

Role culture

Larger corporations which have developed over a long period of time may be typical of organisations which have a role culture. Such organisations tend to be highly bureaucratic and highly structured with specialist departments who, whilst working for the whole organisation, have identities of their own. Each of these departments or functions will support the senior leadership team but may be competitive and often secretive between each other.

As its name suggests, role culture tends to place an emphasis on particular roles that each person in the organisation and in each function has. Operations are heavily controlled by the job description that each person has, and there may be particular views in the organisation about the appropriate person specification for these roles. The organisation will be heavily controlled by reference to various policy documents that exist including reporting and communication policies, disciplinary and grievance policies and recruitment and induction policies.

Some other characteristics are listed below:

- Power stems not from the charisma of an individual but from the role that s/he possesses in the organisation. As a result, respect may not necessarily have been earned (or even deserved) but flows from the role. There can be a significant number of conflicts that arise as a result.
- Staff have roles that they are expected to fulfil, but beyond this their roles are limited. This can result in individuals refusing to give more than they are expected to do which can lead to inflexibility and intransigence in the organisation.
- Such a culture can provide a degree of security for individuals in that there tends to be a very defined career ladder which they can climb and aspire to, as well as clearly defined rules within which everyone operates.
- The culture can lead to the organisation being slow to respond to change.

Reasons for and problems of changing organisational culture

Why seek to change a culture?

There are three main reasons why there might need to be a change in corporate culture: to improve performance or productivity, or to respond to changed conditions.

TO IMPROVE PERFORMANCE

A succession of poor results and possible dwindling profits may be a sign that the organisation needs to change. Since profits are generated through revenues being greater than costs, it would seem common sense that one or both has to be the focus for the change. A change in corporate culture can help all in the business to focus on the importance of reducing and controlling costs in the business. This can be supported by an equally improved focus on increasing revenues. A different corporate culture can try and direct the attention of staff on the need for greater customer focus, or the generation of new and creative ideas to improve their position in the market.

TO IMPROVE PRODUCTIVITY

As with the performance section above, a change in corporate culture might be carried out to try and improve productivity. This might include productivity improvements of all resources, not just labour. For example, a business might decide to invest into new technology and does this in conjunction with a more entrepreneurial culture. The expectation will be that staff will respond to the culture by being more creative and working more efficiently. This can be seen in some technology businesses, where the freedom staff have to work remotely not only reduces overheads but also increases empowerment of workers who respond by being more productive. Working remotely might mean they are spending less time commuting, for example, and feel fresher and more relaxed.

A RESPONSE TO CHANGED CONDITIONS

This third area can include a wide range of conditions, some of which are discussed below.

Changes in market conditions

The farming industry has changed considerably in recent years as subsidies have been removed and the Common Agricultural Policy (CAP) has been reformed. For many farmers this has necessitated a change in the way they have to operate and they have had to adjust to become more ruthless and competitive in the way they run their business. This has been and has required a culture change for many farmers.

Changes in the competitive environment

New entrants to a market will cause a change in the competitive landscape and the response to the changed competition might require a change in culture. For example, BT has had to respond to a very different competitive environment as a result of the growth of mobile phone and Internet technology which has challenged its position as the leading (and at one time) only telecommunications operator in the UK.

Changes in economic circumstances

If the economy moves into a different phase of the business cycle, it is likely that there might be tougher conditions in which to trade. Companies in businesses that tend to have a high income elasticity of demand, such as furniture and household goods retailers, might have to adopt a different approach to business to maintain sales compared to times when the economy is expanding rapidly.

Changes occurring because of acquisition

Businesses that are subject to takeover or merger are also likely to face a number of changes in approach. When takeovers occur, the new owners may have a different culture and might want to change the firm taken over to reflect their own culture. The number of acquisitions that have involved private equity firms in recent years is also likely to bring with it a change in culture, given that the private equity groups tend to buy with the intention of leveraging value out of the business before selling it on again a few years later.

Change because of a new leader

A change to the CEO of a business is also likely to mean that there will be a change in culture, as the new leader seeks to impose her/his beliefs and philosophy on the business in an attempt to create success. Sir Stuart Rose at Marks and Spencer, Justin King at Sainsbury's and Willie Walsh at British Airways are three examples of where new leaders have brought quite different cultures to the respective businesses.

Any or all of these could necessitate a change in approach from the business and its people.

New leader, new approach but back to basics

The supermarket, Sainsbury's, faced a combination of problems in the early part of the first decade of the new millennium. An investment into a new distribution system by the CEO, Sir Peter Davis, had led to problems with empty shelves; its rivals Tesco and Asda had ramped up the competition, the latter posing a different threat after it was taken over by US giant Wal-Mart. The nature of supermarket retailing was changing with smaller stores being opened in towns and cities to complement larger stores which were now selling a wider range of goods than just food and groceries. Sainsbury's looked as though it was relying on past glories. It lost market share and announced its first ever loss in 2004.

John Davison, an analyst at research and consultancy firm, Gartner, said of Sainsbury's that it had failed to tackle the problems that had been looming, believing that the strength of its brand would be enough to compete. 'It's not arrogance, it's just a belief that everything will come right in the end and customers will keep on coming through the door. Sainsbury's has been in [a] downward spiral for a long time but no one thought to tackle the problem. There were people before [Peter Davis] that should have made the change,' he said.*

A new chief executive, Justin King, was brought in and gave himself three years to turn the business round. Davison said that Justin King had to 'challenge and transform the corporate culture at Sainsbury's if he is to stand a chance of reversing the retailer's declining fortunes'. It seems that the culture of the business has changed along with other physical manifestations including the distribution system. The business has returned to profit and its market share has been steadily increasing. King's approach has been widely praised.

* Source of quote: http://www.talkingretail.com (see http://www.talkingretail.com/news/62/Corporate-culture-the-root-of-.ehtml)

Activity

From the article, identify **three** possible factors that led to the change in culture at Sainsbury's after the arrival of Justin King.

Problems in changing corporate culture

One of the main issues that have interested academics and management theorists has been the extent to which corporate culture can be changed. Whatever the theory, attempts to change a culture are not easy. The main argument in relation to this is whether culture is a variable that can be changed by a leader, or whether it is something that the organisation is and which is not subject to internal change.

CAN CULTURE BE IMPOSED?

Much has been written on what contributes to organisational success, and there are any number of supposed management and leadership gurus who have written handbooks on creating the winning business formula. Such a view implies that a culture can be imposed onto a business; that a new leader can be drafted in to make changes which will lead to an improvement in performance and productivity. There are plenty of published articles that give broad outlines as to key facets that have to be in place to create this sort of winning formula. One of the first to try and list such characteristics was an article by Peters and Waterman in 1982, who wrote a paper entitled *In Search of Excellence: Lessons from America's Best-Run Companies*. The key features they identified were:

- A preference for action over words – a 'let's do it' approach.
- Strong customer focus.
- Employees are empowered, are encouraged to innovate, are creative, and risk-taking is encouraged.
- Employees are valued and seen as an important resource in the business.
- Leaders adopt a hands-on approach and lead by example.
- There is a focus on the core competencies of the business and diversification is regarded with caution.
- There is a flat and lean structure.
- Businesses have 'loose-tight' properties: employees have discretion or 'loose properties' but are bounded by a strong set of centralised values or 'tight properties'.

Leaders seeking to implement cultural change could, therefore, look at the extent to which their business has some or all of these features, try to develop and incorporate them and in so doing, would begin to change the culture of the organisation.

CULTURE FROM OUTSIDE

However, there are those that believe that culture is not something that can be imposed and that everyone participates (not necessarily as equals) in the creation of organisational culture. Businesses start to take on a reflection of the prevailing culture that exists in society and which in turn is shaped by social, political, legal and economic changes.

The growth of youth cultures like hippies and mods and rockers and the rise in the women's lib movement made people question the accepted norms of society at the time

The 1960s began to see a number of major changes in attitude in society; rebellion, challenges to authority – both violent and peaceful – and a greater degree of questioning of the prevailing establishment began to surface. Youth cultures like mods and rockers, hippies and later skinheads, all were symptomatic of wider changes in society. Greater economic prosperity and a more secure world may have also contributed to such changes, but as time progressed the questioning of the status quo led to even greater changes.

The role of women in society and the arrival of large numbers of immigrants from former Commonwealth countries led to changes in legislation that affected businesses. Why should women and people of different ethnic backgrounds be discriminated against in the workplace? Businesses had to rethink the way they did things and the relationships that they had taken for granted in the light of these changes. As a result, members of an organisation come to reflect societal changes; they reproduce in the workplace the values, beliefs and norms that are emerging in a dynamic society.

In the 1980s, society changed once more. The accepted economic policies for solving problems came to be questioned as inflation and unemployment rose sharply in the 1970s. The recession of the early 1980s and the election of the Thatcher government gave rise to a new approach. Many businesses and traditional industries disappeared and slowly, in their place, arose new businesses that were more independent, entrepreneurial and which were not reliant on the traditional relationships between workers (and their trade union) and management. Some argued that the new entrepreneurial culture was selfish and greedy. The 1990s saw further changes to the way business operated and the focus on culture as a means of coping with and confronting change really took hold.

As we move into the 'noughties', and into the new decade, the emphasis will no doubt change further. The concerns over the environment and the global nature of business will mean that business has to operate still differently. Business culture – suggest proponents of this view – cannot be imposed therefore, but the business has to accept that in a dynamic environment the business must also be dynamic, and that culture will largely be determined outside the business as a reflection of the society in which it operates.

> **Skills watch!**
>
> **AO3 / AO4**
>
> Look back at the two value statements by Dell and Nokia on pages 423 and 424. Evaluate whether an organisation is capable of imposing such a culture or whether their culture is a reflection of current society.

ONE SIZE FITS ALL?

The amount of research into leadership and successful businesses has not revealed any sort of magic formula that can be applied in one business and transferred to another. The work of Peters and Waterman cited above reveals some key factors that might be appropriate in building cultures that improve performance, but it is by no means certain that simply introducing these factors will automatically guarantee success. Companies that were involved in Peters and Waterman's research included General Electric, McDonald's, Disney and Hewlett Packard. Since their research, a number of the firms they studied and selected because they were 'successful' have experienced difficulties, including Disney, who have suffered from leadership changes which have in turn changed the culture. What this shows is that no firm is the same and whilst general principles can be applied, there are lots of other factors that have to be in place to create a culture that leads to increased performance.

Some of these factors might include the charisma of the leader – workers have to believe that the leader is a role model and sets the example about behaviour and approach. An existing culture can be difficult to change, especially if it is highly bureaucratic and established, and wholesale change might be necessary to bring about change, with key personnel moved on.

It has also been noted that many change initiatives focus on operational and technical issues but do not pay sufficient attention to the human side of change. We have seen above the process by which humans react to change; for some these responses can be deeper and longer-lasting than others, and resistance to change because of the emotional turmoil that it creates can be stubborn and difficult to bring about. When change occurs, people feel threatened and in most cases they have a cause to feel this way. Their jobs, their routines, their comfort zones will all be challenged and this can create barriers to change.

THE SIGMOID CURVE

The idea that a business's culture can be changed might have some truth, but how does the leader (or the business for that matter) know when it *has* changed and what does it then do? Is there a time when the leader can sit back and survey the business and be satisfied that they have succeeded in changing the culture?

Even if things are looking as though they are improving, good leaders might need to think about the next phase of change. Complacency can set in when changes are made, and improvements in terms of profits and productivity are realised. There might be a temptation to rest on laurels which may lead to problems further down the line. Such a view might have been exemplified by the example of Sainsbury's in the late 90s given on page 429.

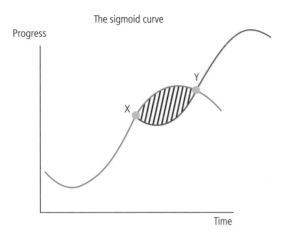

The sigmoid curve

Progress

Time

Figure 29.1   The sigmoid curve

Charles Handy suggested that change might result in improvement and progress but that progress will plateau and eventually decline. To avoid such decline, decisions have to be made about further improvement at the point where success is growing and before the business starts to experience this plateau. The idea is captured by the sigmoid curve as illustrated in Figure 29.1.

If we follow the green line we can see that initial change is likely to result in a dip in progress as the business comes to grips with the changes, but eventually, progress will be made. Without further change, the business will eventually witness a decline in progress around point Y. For many businesses in a rapidly-changing global market this may be too late. However, if the business looks at its position at point X, it can look back to see how far it has come and could sit back and reflect on its success. If it looks ahead, it can try to forecast the likely dip in progress and begin to implement changes that will take it onto a new sigmoid curve (the blue line). This period (indicated by the shaded area) is a very difficult time for leading change; there may well be anxiety, confusion and cultural change required before the successful transition to the new curve.

For many in business, this is a difficult thing to get staff to do; many may have just been through testing and anxious times, and just when it appears that there might be time to relax and bask in success, the leadership are asking for further sacrifices and effort to be made. The leadership skills required here could make or break the change process and it is this skill that many corporations are willing to pay big money to acquire!

Skills watch!

AO2 / AO3 / AO4

Your school/college is an organisation; it will have a culture. Carry out some research on the type of organisational culture that exists in your institution. You might gather information from interviewing some of the staff to find out what change initiatives have been made and what the response was. It might also be useful to arrange a meeting/ interview/presentation with/by the head or principal to get his/her view on what sort of culture they wish to lead and what problems they have had in initiating change.

Conclude your research by producing a 500-word report titled: 'Organisational culture and change in [my institution]: a case study.'

Assessing the importance of organisational culture

Any organisation is a complex mix of resources but at the heart of this are people. The relationships between people with different roles and the message that this relationship gives to all stakeholders in the business will be an important part of the business. It has been said by some researchers that change initiatives can fail because of the culture of the organisation.

We have seen that change can come in many forms: acquisitions, attempts to introduce new IT systems, new production schedules, changes to working practices, changes in location, restructuring of the business, and so on, but to make these changes work, humans have to understand and accept the change and be willing to work to realise it. On the face of it, many changes will be imposed and staff may need to be convinced that the changes being proposed are going to be of benefit to them – many may not automatically think of the benefit to the organisation as a whole!

Change may appear to be being made, but in some cases it can be cosmetic and at some point it grinds to a halt. One of the main reasons cited is the failure of the culture of the organisation to change and to fully embrace the new routines and schedules. To really bring about change, leaders also have to work on changing the culture to reflect the new initiatives being introduced. Without this change in culture, without getting the staff to buy into it, change is going to stall and this can impact on the performance and profitability of the business.

We have seen in this chapter something of the debate between academics about whether culture is a variable that can be imposed and changed by leaders, or whether culture in a business is a reflection of the prevailing social culture. If it is the former, then it is capable of being manipulated although we have seen that this is not always easy. If it is the latter, then leaders are fighting a losing battle. The truth may lie somewhere in between the two. Leaders can bring about changes in attitude and mindset, and can bring in and surround themselves with others who share the beliefs and outlook of the leader. Cultural change may be slow, but it can be changed although the changes that are being made may well be reflective of wider changes in societal culture. For example, the number of businesses that are now concerned to demonstrate their green credentials may be reflective of the wider concern in society about climate change and the impact of business on the environment. Would businesses produce CSR reports if there was not this wider concern?

It is important to remember, as with the section on types of leadership covered earlier in this book, that there is not one type of culture that is 'good' or better than another. Charles Handy observed that any culture can work and be successful, but the danger was that leaders could be culturally blinkered and ignore changes in culture that could benefit the business, and in some cases may simply believe that what works in one place will work in another. Handy suggested this was not the case and was something that leaders needed to avoid.

Leaders also need to understand the importance they have in setting the right tone for the type of culture that they want in the business. There is a feeling that some leaders have covered change leadership and business culture in some masters degree course or their MBA, and simply try and transfer the knowledge to the organisation they are working with. Having an understanding of the deeper nature of change leadership and culture, especially the human element, is essential.

Leaders have to be aware of so-called cultural transmission mechanisms. Are they trying to change, maintain or build a culture? Whatever it is, they have to accept that they have to lead by example and be the role model for the sort of culture they want to instil. Workers will very quickly see through a leader who does not lead by example; in business jargon it is referred to as 'walking the walk' and 'talking the talk'. Management by example (MBE) is thus vital in leadership and in bringing about cultural change.

Leaders also have to have an understanding of the range of sub-cultures that exist in a business if they are to change culture. In any organisation there will be a range of formal structures reflecting the culture of the organisation. For example, in many financial companies such as dealers and brokers in stock and bond markets, there will be a formal culture that espouses values such as equality of opportunity, inclusivity and diversity. There might, however, exist an underlying sub-culture that pays lip service to these values but where the dominant culture is one that is highly male-oriented and sexist. Female staff may work for these organisations but they might feel pressured to behave in a way that reflects a male-oriented culture. There might not be as much equality of opportunity as the formal culture would like to reflect.

There have been a number of cases in these types of businesses where women have sought to take legal action against employers for discrimination. The pressure on women in these cases has been immense, and in many cases they have not been successful in proving that their treatment was due to sex discrimination or victimisation. If leaders do not understand these sub-cultures, any change becomes cosmetic and is not embedded throughout the organisation.

For example...

Cultural change at British Airways

In the 1990s, the chief executive officer of British Airways, Bob Ayling, attempted to bring about a major culture change at the company. A number of strategies were put in place including a drive to improve customer service, new livery for the aircraft and various employee initiatives that aimed to improve the relationship between the company and its staff. However, Mr Ayling's plans seemed to fail. The new designs were famously 'dissed' by Mrs Thatcher, customer service improvements did not appear to have materialised in the way that Ayling had expected despite heavy investment, and the staff did not buy into the employee initiatives. A survey conducted by the company in 1999 of its staff revealed a considerable degree of disenfranchisement with the organisation and its aims. The workers simply did not believe in the culture that was being imposed on them. Instead, the company's fortunes took a downward turn and in 2000 it had to announce a loss for the first time since it had been privatised in the 1980s. The CEO earned the nickname 'Bob Failing' and many of the initiatives were reversed including the livery on the aircraft when he was replaced by Rod Eddington.

Bob Ayling may have enjoyed the initial launch of the new tail fin designs for BA, but this idea along with many others were not popular with staff, customers and, famously, Mrs Thatcher, the then Prime Minister

Summary

Changing culture in an organisation is a difficult and challenging task, and any leader will suggest that this is probably the most difficult thing they have to do. This is because there are numerous barriers to change in an organisation. We have already seen the debate about whether organisational culture can be changed from within, or whether culture change is something that evolves with society. In spite of this debate, there is no doubt that many leaders will try and change the culture of an organisation. If they try they will face a number of barriers to change as we have outlined in more detail above.

In summary these barriers are:

- **Employee resistance to change** – the need for employers to have to move out of their routine and comfort zone, and the various stages of self-esteem that this is associated with as change progresses. In addition, leaders will have to be aware of a 'tribe' mentality that can exist within organisations – groups of people with common but often conflicting interests who may be particularly resistant to change.

- **Organisation structures** – the existing type of organisational culture can make it more difficult to create change, especially if the culture to be changed has been embedded for many years and there is a high proportion of the staff who have been at the organisation for a long time and have thus been used to this culture.
- **Leadership type** – as with the organisational structure above, there is likely to be a close link between the organisational structure and the leadership type that is associated with it.
- **Legal issues** – business will have to be aware of the legal requirements that must be complied with and which arise from change, for example, if employee's contracts are to be changed or if there are redundancies that have to be made.

Summary and exam guidance

Summary

- Culture relates to a complex set of relationships that reflect how a business does things.

- Corporate culture defines the organisation and gives it an identity.

- Cultural changes in society are reflected in the way in which businesses operate and how they want to be seen.

- There are four main types of organisational culture: power, task, entrepreneurial and role.

- Reasons to change culture include the need to improve performance, productivity and to respond to changing market conditions.

- There is a debate about whether businesses can have a corporate culture imposed or changed by a leader, or whether business culture is more a reflection of the prevailing culture in society as a whole.

- Successful cultures cannot simply be transferred from one organisation to another.

- The sigmoid curve suggests that businesses have to think about constant change rather than once-and-for-all cultural change.

Exam practice

Read the article below and then answer the questions that follow.

Article A

Dissent at Disney?

Two of the biggest companies in the movie world joined forces in 2006. Walt Disney agreed to buy Pixar, the company behind the computer-generated hit films *Toy Story, Finding Nemo* and *The Incredibles,* for $7.4 billion.

Pixar was bought by Steve Jobs, the founder of Apple, for $10 million in 1986. Pixar was a small firm working on developing animation systems. Some of its staff had formerly worked for Disney, in particular, the creative director John A. Lasseter. The company was able to secure a significant competitive advantage by not only creating visually stunning and extremely accurate computer graphics, but also combining this with a storyline that appealed to adults as well as children.

Such a combination is not something that can be done easily but Pixar seemed to be able to capture this perfectly. *A Bug's Life,* for example, broke box office records in the late 1990s with a story of one ant's quest for recognition and thirst for adventure, tinged with the right amount of the dark and sinister (in Hopper the grasshopper), romance, hero worship and friendship.

Part of the reason for this success has been the management approach of Pixar. It was recognised as having a culture that was hands-off and which encouraged creativity. Such a style was not what Disney was necessarily noted for. Its involvement with Pixar was in the form of a distribution deal. Disney, of course, has had its own share of the animation market but it had been accused of falling way short of the high standards that Pixar had set.

The distribution deal was due to run out and there were no plans to renegotiate any such deal. Part of the reason for this was the relationship between Jobs and the former head of Disney, Michael Eisner. Eisner not only upset Jobs, but also seemed to create considerable boardroom tension at Disney. Eisner, however, left Disney in 2005 and the new boss, Robert Iger, tried to mend some of the broken bridges with Jobs and the deal is the result of this new understanding. Disney has had to accept and embrace the philosophy behind Pixar – its creative freedoms have been what have enabled it to become so successful.

Source: adapted from Biz/ed In the News: http://www.bized.co.uk/cgi-bin/chron/chron.pl?id=2524

(a) Contrast the types of organisational culture that appeared to exist in Disney and Pixar. (18 marks)

(b) To what extent can an organisation like Disney change its culture to one that might be quite different? (32 marks)

Total: 50 marks

Breakdown of assessment objectives

AO1 – Knowledge and understanding – 10/50
AO2 – Apply knowledge and understanding – 10/50
AO3 – Analyse problems, issues and situations – 15/50
AO4 – Evaluate, distinguish between fact and opinion, assess and judge information from a variety of sources – 15/50

Suggested structure

For part (a):

- Make a judgement about the possible types of culture that existed at Disney and Pixar given the information in the article. Note that there is not any one right answer here but you will get some credit for justifying your choice.
- Provide an explanation of the two types of culture that you have chosen.
- Ensure that you attempt to apply the culture type to the specific context of the article.
- What is it about a business like Pixar that makes the culture you have chosen appropriate and successful?
- What sort of culture seemed to exist at Disney?
- The command word is 'contrast' so make sure that in this section you clearly state the differences between the two culture types you have chosen but equally make sure that you refer to the context of the two.

For part (b) you will need to:

- Outline the main argument about the extent to which a culture is subject to change from within.
- Explain what an organisation like Disney might need to do to bring about cultural change.
- Outline some of the potential problems and difficulties that it might face in trying to change its culture – would it be dependent on one person? Would the fact that Eisner left make it any more likely that Disney would change?
- Consider factors such as the length of time that Disney has been in operation in comparison to Pixar and the deep-rooted cultural characteristics that may be present.
- Provide some judgements relating back to the question about whether a company like Disney can really change its culture and the extent to which it could become something different. You will need to use the arguments and analysis you have provided to help support your judgements.

Chapter 30   **Making strategic decisions**

The significance of information management

Information management refers to the way in which information is collected by a business and how that information is then circulated to appropriate people/functions within the business to aid in decision-making. The last 30 years have seen a proliferation in the amount of information that a business can gather and which it has access to. The development of technology has made collection, storing and analysis of this information more efficient, more sophisticated, but also more demanding than ever before.

We have seen in Chapters 8 and 24 how technology is used in analysing markets and the effects that technological change has on business. This chapter will look at the way in which businesses use the information they have at their disposal to make strategic decisions.

Information management should not be confused with the provision and management of information technology, such as computers, mobile phones, BlackBerry devices, and so on. The technology is the means by which the information that is so important to a business is shared between users. There is likely to be an IT department in most businesses that manage the IT provision, monitor software use, security, and so on. However, the management of the information which these various devices store and which is used by those in the organisation is the real value to the business.

Technology will be used to manage information which relates to organisation-wide systems that affect everyone. For example, the payroll will be largely automated, there will need to be systems that can handle expense accounts, and many businesses will have systems to manage human resources. Such systems might include information to staff about the organisation and its market, details about pay slips (which may be available online rather than in paper form), training courses, sales conference details and agendas, appraisal information such as agreed goals and targets, professional development plans, and records of appraisal meetings that have been held.

In the AS book, we saw how technology is used in operations management with robots, CAD/CAM systems, communications, and so on. In other areas of the business there will be marketing information collected through CRM systems (see Chapter 8 in this book) which can provide the organisation with a great deal of valuable information about the types of customers the business has, who they are, what their lifestyles are like, what they buy and when, and so on. In the finance and accounting departments, information management systems will be used to support budgetary control, accounts and payment and credit systems.

The aim of all these systems will be to collect, store and manage information that can be used to further the strategic goals of the organisation. Such information can help the business to analyse its current position, plan for the future and assess the progress it is making in relation to its stated aims and goals. Sales staff, for example, will have targets at the start of the financial year, and both individual and group progress towards these targets can be made available on a regular basis. Sales staff can amend their schedules and act on the information that they are given – in conjunction with that for the marketing department – to ensure that they target the customers that are most likely to buy and thus meet the organisation's (and their own) targets.

The information that a business has access to can be of two main types: quantitative and qualitative.

QUANTITATIVE INFORMATION

Quantitative information relates to data that can be verified by some reference to statistical or measurable devices. As such it tends to relate to numbers, frequencies or values, such as sales volumes, revenues, costs, the number of enquiries made, the number of complaints received, the number of page accesses on a website, and so on. This type of information is subject to various types of statistical manipulation to help identify trends and patterns, and to derive measures of tendency such as averages.

QUALITATIVE INFORMATION

Qualitative information does not allow measurement; instead it describes. It may describe behaviour, what staff think about the organisation, how working practices could be improved, the results of discussions in quality circles, why people buy the products they do, what they think about them, what they like and dislike about products, their feelings about products, store layouts or adverts, and so on. Qualitative data may provide more in-depth information for a business, but is often more difficult to organise because it is harder to categorise and code.

Few businesses will simply rely on quantitative information in making decisions because this ignores many of the other factors that must be considered – the potential for future development, qualitative market research information and not least, the impact on human resource management of decision-making amongst others.

The balance between quantitative and qualitative information is important to get right if a decision is to be made which will realise the business's strategic aims most appropriately. The skill for many business leaders is in judging what decision to make, what weight to place on

For example...

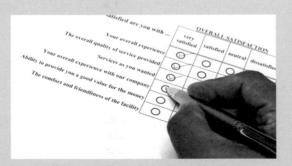

A business might carry out some market research which provides it with lots of data. Some of this data may be very easy to interpret, for example, a business might ask how many times a year an individual buys a particular product. It can collect that data from all the respondents to the survey and present it in a statistical format which is easy to understand. For example, 20% of respondents might buy the product up to five times a year, 35% up to 10 times a year, 23% between 11 and 15 times and 16% might buy the product more than 15 times a year, and so on. However, if there was also a question which asked why they bought the product, the range of responses might be very wide and not capable of being neatly classified. Some respondents might offer a one-word response, others may write several sentences and some might even write an essay! The difficulty is in finding a way to summarise all this type of information to enable the business to make sense of it.

the qualitative factors, as well as looking at the long-term success of the business. Having access to a greater degree of information means a business is in a better position to be able to make decisions that are more accurate and which are more likely to lead to the desired results that the business is seeking from its strategy. To understand the importance of the value of information in decision-making, consider the following example.

For example...

You need to attend an interview for a job. The interview requires that you have to travel and you start to look at your options. You can either go by train or by coach. You manage to find out that the train is more expensive, but is likely to be more convenient in that it is more direct and quicker. You try to check the train timetable and refer to a small booklet you picked up at the train station last year. You settle on getting the 08.00 train. You set off in good time to get to the station, and arrive at 07.50 only to find that the train timetable has changed in the meantime and that the 08.00 train now leaves at 07.45. The next one is not until 08.45. This makes you late for your interview and you do not get the job. If you had access to accurate information you would have been able to change your schedule and ensure you get to the interview on time.

The simple example above shows how accurate information is essential for appropriate decision-making. Given the amount of information that a business has available to it, the task of sifting through it, analysing it, drawing conclusions and using these as the basis for decision-making becomes a significant task and one which demands a high level of skill and considerable cost to do properly. If a business is basing decisions on inaccurate or poor-quality information, then its decisions will in turn be less likely to bring about the desired strategic aims.

The value of different approaches to decision-making

Given the importance of high-quality information management, businesses use two main approaches to decision-making. On the one hand, a great deal of information available to the business is capable of being collected and analysed using mathematical, statistical and scientific methods. Indeed, for some businesses, there can be opportunities to generate competitive advantage through such analysis. In the City, for example, a high premium is placed on those who have high-level skills in maths, statistics and computing because these people are the ones that can identify trends and patterns which may provide the opportunity of developing new products and finding new ways of generating revenue for dealers.

The other main method used to make decisions is called 'intuition'. Intuition is less easy to define and to quantify. Some leaders appear to act on intuition that seems to work. Intuition is the act of knowing or sensing something which is not reliant on any form of rational process or analysis. It is the gut feeling that some people have and which makes them behave in a particular way. For example, a doctor may be looking at a patient who is wired up to various machines monitoring aspects of their vital signs after a serious heart operation. The machines are telling him that everything is stable but somehow the doctor senses there is something wrong. Should s/he act on the basis of what the machinery is telling her/him or act on their intuition? In such cases, rational analysis might lead to a loss of life – the machines might not be conveying the whole picture.

In business, many highly successful entrepreneurs might use a combination of intuition and scientific analysis in deciding on a new business venture. In some cases, most cannot explain how they got their ideas in the first place, but that they simply had a hunch that the product or service that they had thought of would be successful.

At this level of study, there are a number of traditional methods of scientific analysis to help decision-making that we will consider. Businesses will look at data – sales figures, sales forecasts, and so on, information from market research, cost estimates, SWOT analysis, investment appraisal techniques and decision trees. Most of these can be described as quantitative methods – they have some sort of quantifiable data at their heart.

Scientific approaches to decision-making

Scientific approaches seek to use a quantifiable and measurable way to justify decisions. In using rational analysis, decisions are reduced to placing a monetary value on different choices. For example, a decision to restructure a business might weigh up the estimated cost of redundancies which will have to be made in the first two years of the restructuring against the longer-term financial benefits to the firm of this process which may be calculated over a five-year period.

The planning process can be highlighted in the diagram below (see Figure 30.1). This process is likely to be ongoing but the nature of the objectives may change. An objective might be to increase revenue in a particular market. The research and analysis will help decision-makers to gain a greater awareness of the market that they are operating in and thus be in a position to understand the opportunities and also the problems they face in achieving their objectives. This in turn helps to inform the various options that are available to them. If increasing revenue is the objective, then a pricing strategy may be appropriate, but similar results could also be achieved through targeted promotion.

Discussion of the various options available in the light of the analysis of the market will enable the business to select an appropriate option they feel will be the most likely to deliver the objective. Once this option is put into place it will need to be monitored against the expected results to ensure that it is indeed meeting the objective set. If not, then this may serve to inform a new set of objectives, and so on. If the objectives are met then equally, this will lead to a further set of objectives being established, and so the process continues.

Some of the methods used to quantify the value are discussed on the next page.

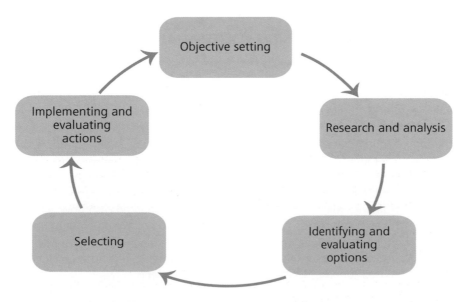

Figure 30.1 The planning process

DECISION TREES

Decision trees are used as a means of attempting to quantify different outcomes of different decision routes based on estimates of the probability of outcomes. They are very useful when outcomes are uncertain or where there are different ways in which a particular outcome could be reached or where there are different options open to a business. Decision trees allow a comparison of different possible decisions to be made.

The benefit of decision trees is that they enable a business to make use of existing historical data that it possesses and to use this as the basis for its estimates. It encourages a greater degree of objectivity in decision-making as it forces those involved to think clearly, plan ahead and be realistic in their analysis of the likely outcomes. The process involved in creating decision trees involves the following steps:

1 The initial strategic aim is established.

2 Potential routes and options for achieving the desired outcome are considered.

3 Estimates of financial costs and benefits are researched and applied to the different options.

4 An estimate of the probability of outcomes is made and applied to the different routes.

5 Squares are drawn where decisions have to be made, and circles identify the possibility of different outcomes.

6 A calculation is made of an expected financial outcome based on the probability.

7 A comparison of the expected financial outcomes of the different options gives the basis for decision-making.

An example of the use of decision trees is shown opposite. The limitations associated with the use of decision trees, therefore, relate to the accuracy of the data that is used to construct the decision tree and the reliability of the estimates of the expected financial outcomes and, crucially, the probabilities assigned. It may be that some of the data used to base the estimates of outcome are historical and this information may not be accurate. As we shall see later, such decision-making methods need to be made in conjunction with qualitative factors, such as human resources, motivation, reaction, relations with suppliers and other stakeholders, and so on.

OTHER METHODS UTILISING SCIENTIFIC APPROACHES

Any major strategic initiative is likely to involve investment of some kind. Remember that investment is the purchase of capital equipment that is designed to improve productive capacity. The investment will be expected to generate a return in the form of income streams which may arise at different times over a period of time – sometimes very long periods of time. The cost of such investments means that they are not undertaken lightly, and help in the form of quantifiable evidence to support the decision is usually considered very important.

Investment appraisal, therefore, is a means of assessing whether an investment project is worthwhile or not. There is a range of different types of investment appraisal and each may be used at different times. Much larger projects that involve long periods of time and large amounts of finance might use net present value or discounted cash flow, whilst smaller projects in smaller businesses might use payback period or average rate of return.

In Chapter 6 of this book you will have read about a number of methods of investment appraisal. You should ensure that you revisit this chapter to remind yourself of the techniques that can be used to make decisions on investment projects.

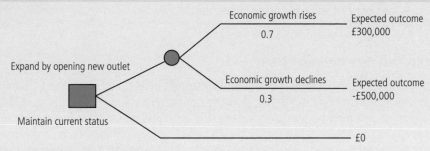

Figure 30.2   The decision tree

Assume that a business is considering a decision to open a new outlet. It has identified that one of the key uncertainties is the state of the economy which might grow at different rates (see Figure 30.2 above).

If economic growth continues to rise at a healthy rate, then the expected outcome for the business is estimated at £300,000 over the year. However, if economic growth is slower, then the new outlet could result in a financial loss of £500,000. There is also the option of not doing anything and maintaining its current position which would cost it nothing.

If it chooses to expand then there are two possible outcomes as outlined above. The circle denotes the point where these different outcomes could occur. The firm uses various data to make an estimate of the probability of each outcome. They estimate that the probability of economic growth rising at a level that will generate the expected financial return is 0.7 (or 70%), whilst its estimates of the probability that economic growth will slow down is given as 0.3 or 30%. The estimates of the probability and the knowledge of the expected outcome

allow the firm to make a calculation of the likely return. In this example it is:

- Economic growth rises:
  0.7 × £300,000 = £210,000
- Economic growth declines:
  0.3 × £500,000 = −£150,000

Given the calculation, the net 'benefit' figure (the difference between the two outcomes) of +£60,000 would suggest it is wise to go ahead with the decision. Crucial to the success of decision trees is an accurate estimate of the probabilities. If we use the same scenario as above but change the probabilities slightly, we get a quite different outcome (see Figure 30.3 below).

If the firm is unsure of the potential for growth, it might estimate it at 50:50. In this case the outcomes will be:

- Economic growth rises:
  0.5 × £300,000 = £150,000
- Economic growth declines:
  0.5 × −£500,000 = −£250,000

In this instance, the net benefit is −£100,000 – the decision looks less favourable!

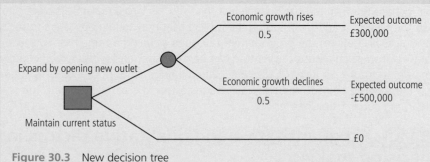

Figure 30.3   New decision tree

The main methods you should review are:

- the payback period
- the average rate of return (ARR)
- net present value and discounted cash flows.

In addition, the following can also be used.

Internal rate of return (IRR)

IRR allows the risk associated with an investment project to be assessed. The IRR is the rate of interest (or discount rate) that makes the net present value equal to zero. It helps measure the worth of an investment and allows the firm to assess whether an investment in a machine, for example, would yield a better return based on internal standards of return. IRR allows comparison of projects with different initial outlays and sets the cash flows to different discount rates. Most firms will use software or simple graphing techniques to allow the IRR to be found.

Profitability index

This allows a comparison of the costs and benefits of different projects to be assessed and thus allows decision-making to be carried out. The formula is:

$$\text{Profitability index} = \frac{\text{Net present value}}{\text{Initial capital cost}}$$

Scientific versus intuitive approaches

Given that investment assumes a yield of future income streams, investment appraisal is all about assessing these income streams against the cost of the investment. Whilst it tries to apply rationality and logic to decision-making, investment appraisal is not a precise science. In considering which type of investment appraisal technique to use, a firm will also consider the ease of use/degree of simplicity, the degree of accuracy required, the extent to which future cash flows can be measured accurately, the extent to which future interest rate movements can be accounted for and predicted, and the necessity of factoring in the effects of inflation.

A scientific approach to such decision-making will be based on facts and evidence. The facts and evidence will be gathered from historical data and from other market research and information flows that the business has access to. This will allow the business to make decisions based on clearly-identified and quantifiable costs and benefits. In general, if the benefits are greater than the costs, then it is likely that there will be a case for going ahead with the investment. Such methods are also useful for comparing different investment decisions.

Despite the existence of very sophisticated methods of approaching decision-making outlined above, there is also room for intuition. There will be times when there appears to be little logic for the development of a project or investment, yet the leader may believe that there is a risk worth taking to gain the benefits of stealing a competitive advantage on rivals. Sir Richard Branson may have done just this with his Virgin Galactic project (see Chapter 27). On the face of it an investment in the project that may take many years to realise a profit (if it ever actually gets off the ground) might be seen as being a huge risk. However, the potential returns from such a business venture can be extensive, and whilst others may well enter the market in future, Sir Richard will have gained a huge amount of expertise in developing the business which helps to reduce the average costs and is associated with the so-called 'learning curve' (see Chapter 25).

Balancing quantitative and qualitative factors in decision-making

In considering the use of a more scientific approach to decision-making which is based around finding quantifiable evidence, it is important to realise that this approach can only tell a business part of the picture. Quantifiable methods may tell the business that a decision to invest is likely to generate the sort of returns it is looking for, but such data provides only part of the story, and when other, qualitative factors are taken into account, the returns may not be as healthy as a scientific approach might suggest.

The other factors that need to be taken into account invariably involve the effect of the decision on the wider stakeholders. Qualitative factors look to take account of these other

For example...

Wind power in Scotland

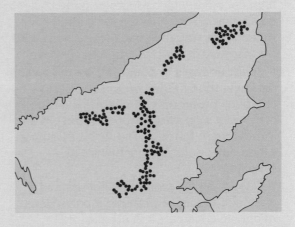

A company called Lewis Wind Power, a part of the AMEC group, applied to the Scottish Executive to construct a wind farm on the Island of Lewis off the west coast of Scotland. The farm would consist of 181 wind turbines, a number of electrical sub-stations, overhead lines and underground cables, and new access roads. The project would be the largest onshore wind farm in Europe, create hundreds of jobs and provide energy to around 450,000 homes. The company carried out extensive environmental and economic studies to justify their case, which

included involving the local people in ownership of the site to generate income. However, despite the weight of the evidence they produced, the project was eventually rejected by the Scottish Executive after more than six years of discussion and planning by the company, the government and local people.

Despite the extensive scientific evidence, the company simply could not convince the local people that the benefits would be greater than the costs. Many of the local people and representatives of Scottish environmental and heritage groups lodged objections and ultimately their objections held sway.

A visual representation of the effect on the wind farm at Barvas Moor

Outsourcing

During the late 1990s and the early part of the new millennium, a number of companies made announcements that they were outsourcing aspects of their business overseas. The three main functional areas where this was most obvious were in IT, finance and human resources, particularly call centres. The main reason quoted in most cases was the cost savings that could be made by moving operations overseas.

Labour costs in countries like India were far lower than in the UK and companies like banking group HSBC and insurance firm Aviva closed operations in the UK and moved them to India. The whole operation made considerable financial sense – on paper.

However, the reality has not been as clear cut as the initial financial projections might have indicated. A number of firms, including Aviva, have now taken the decision to reverse some of the moves to outsource and bring some functions back in to the UK. In 2006, Aviva announced that it was bringing back over 5,000 outsourced jobs to the UK. There have been a number of reasons put forward for the move, including the fact that many people using call centres found the help they received less than satisfactory.

Some credit card companies, such as Capital One, found that customers had been given misleading information by its Indian call centre operation; other companies received complaints from customers that call centre operatives did not have the local knowledge and awareness of UK culture to be able to offer the right sort of help and advice, which led to customers expressing dissatisfaction with their experience. In addition, a survey carried out by accountants Deloitte in 2005 suggested that 75% of companies that had outsourced had experienced 'significant problems' and around 44% had not generated the cost savings that they expected.

issues that may influence the outcome of a decision. A decision, for example, over the investment in a new production plant could be considered not only in financial terms, but also by applying other techniques of decision-making to look at wider issues: a SWOT or PEST (Political, Economic, Social and Technology) analysis might be part of this process.

Decisions, therefore, may rest on the balance between the perceived effects of quantitative and qualitative. If the long-term effect on the workforce, for example, was to reduce productivity or increase absence because of the impact on motivation and morale, the fact that a decision makes financial sense may be better off shelved. Qualitative data, by its nature, is very subjective, and the effect on decision-making difficult to quantify by definition. It is here that the use of scientific means of decision-making might be tempered by intuition.

Intuition is difficult to pinpoint; we have seen examples earlier how intuition can end up making more sense than scientific data. Intuition relies on a great deal of experience, skill, risk-taking, judgement and probably large slices of luck. It could be argued that many new businesses and new products are the result of intuition, the feeling that the product or business idea is worth gambling on. The very fact that only something like one in six new products actually make it is testament to the fragility of using intuition as the basis for making decisions.

The conclusion to this discussion, therefore, is that ideas that spring from intuition are likely to have to be supported by some scientific data to provide a more sound and secure business case as the basis for decision-making. Market research, sales forecasts, cost projections, return on investment data, and so on, can be generated to provide some measurable data that can help the business to make a more informed decision. The scientific data may have its weaknesses, but together the two provide a stronger case than either of them on their own.

For example...

Business flops

The examples below come from ideas of an entrepreneur in the United States called Jeremy Schoemaker who runs a search engine optimisation (SEO) business called Shoemoney.com. SEO is the process of finding ways to maximise traffic flows to a website from search engines like Google. The more traffic a site gets, the higher the advertising revenue can be because advertisers are willing to pay for a site that generates large traffic!

Schoemaker is a risk-taker and many of his ideas spring from gut feeling. By his own admission only a small number of his ideas ever make money but this does not stop him acting on intuition. However, these are some of the ideas that did not make it! (His business overall is successful, however!)

Jeremy Schoemaker presenting at a conference in Chicago in 2006

- **Firefox Forum (firefoxforum.com)** On hearing some news that the browser firm Firefox was going to enter into a joint venture with Google, Jeremy purchased the site on digitalpoint for $800. Jeremy hoped to make money on the number of people visiting the site and even though the joint venture went ahead, the site flopped and he only made $50 in the first year.

- **BabyCalc.com** This was a site giving prospective parents information about how their baby was growing. Parents could input data and receive e-mails about information relating to the pregnancy. For example, it could tell the parent when they would be able to find out the sex of their baby, when the heart would start to function, and so on. Jeremy paid $1,500 to develop the backend for the site but then something

happened. A close friend of the family had a miscarriage about 15 weeks into her pregnancy. However, the friend had signed up for a similar site but was now receiving large numbers of e-mails which she did not want and which were causing her great upset. Jeremy decided he did not want to pursue the idea!

- **Pimp My Blog** On the back of the popular TV series, *Pimp my Ride,* and the associated 'pimping' activity, Jeremy thought this idea would be a sure-fire winner. He purchased the domain *pimpmyblog.org* but wanted to also own *pimpmyblog.com* which was owned by someone else. He negotiated with the owner to buy the .com domain for $2,000 and set about developing tools to enable users to pimp their blog. The idea ran out of steam and never saw the light of day.

- **Omaha-Used-Cars.com** Jeremy thought this would be an easy way to make money. The idea was to create a website for used cars in the Omaha area and charge dealers 25 cents for each listing. It turned out that no one was interested.

Assessing influences on corporate decision-making

Whilst decision-making will be based on a mixture of science and intuition in many cases, there are also other influences that a business will have to take into consideration when making decisions.

Ethical position

The increased emphasis on business ethics means that many businesses want to be seen to be behaving in an ethical manner and will go to great lengths to justify their decisions on ethical grounds. Some would argue that some companies will claim to make decisions based on an ethical standpoint but that this standpoint may not be as transparent and as ethical as the business might want people to believe.

The big four supermarkets in the UK, for example, have all received publicity about behaviour that appears to question their ethical standpoint.

For example...

When is a price cut a price cut?

In March 2007, Trading Standards officials launched an investigation into Tesco after it was alleged that the company misled customers about price cuts in its stores. The Department for Trade and Industry (DTI) has a rule whereby if there is a price reduction offered to consumers on a good, the good must have been offered for sale at the highest price for a period of 28 consecutive days before the advertising of the price reduction. Perishable goods such as fruit and vegetables are not covered by this rule and it was alleged that Tesco used this to mislead customers. It was an allegation that Tesco denied emphatically.

Tesco was accused of advertising some of its fruit and vegetables as having prices cut by half. To the consumer, this might sound like an impressive offer. However, it was claimed that Tesco had increased the prices of some of the products concerned before offering the discounted prices. If it were true, this would not be in the spirit of the 28-day rule and was, according to Tesco's accusers, an example of Tesco exploiting loopholes in the rule.

The Times newspaper reported that the price of peaches stood at £1.99 for 500g in early December 2006 but rose to £2.99 just after Christmas before being 'reduced' to £1.48 at the start of January. Similarly, the price of Gala apples per kilo was £1.19 in early December, rose to £1.99 in the middle of December and was reduced to 99p on January 1st; 500g of nectarines were priced at £1.49 on December 11th, were £2.99 on December 28th and £1.48 on January 1st 2007. The effect was that the extent of the price cuts Tesco had been claiming were not as dramatic as first appeared. The price cut of plums, for example, from 28th December when they were priced at £2.99 to early January, when they were on sale at £1.48, might be 50%. However, compared to the 11th December, when they were also £1.48, this represents no price reduction at all.

Tesco admitted that the prices of some of its fruit had risen prior to the price cuts but claimed that this was due to seasonal effects on the availability of fruit rather than any cynical attempt to exploit the rules and mislead consumers.

The example on page 448 highlights the issue very clearly. Tesco's claims may be perfectly legitimate but the publicity it gained shows how ethical behaviour can have very blurred edges and is not clear cut. The following example further highlights the problem facing businesses in making decisions that respect their ethical standpoints compared to the perspectives that customers and critics might have.

For example...

Primark

The BBC carried out an investigation into factories in southern India in which it found children employed making garments for companies sub-contracted to Primark. The BBC informed Primark who immediately announced that they had broken its relationship with three suppliers in southern India. The company said that only a tiny fraction (0.04%) of the goods affected were sourced from these factories and that the actions by the suppliers in instituting home working and employing child labour were not sanctioned or condoned by Primark. The company also announced that it would set up meetings with its suppliers to 'reinforce the stringent trading standards it expects and to emphasise that it will not tolerate this type of sub-contracting'. It also said that it was appointing a non-governmental organisation (NGO) to 'act as its eyes and ears on the ground' and to report any unauthorised sub-contracting by its suppliers.

The company justified its low prices by stating: 'Primark's prices are low because we don't overcharge our customers. Most of our clothes are bought from the same factories as other fashion retailers and people producing them are paid exactly the same whatever the label and whatever the price in the shop. We are able to offer good value and good quality because of low mark-ups and big volumes. We use simple designs, our overhead costs are extremely low and we don't run expensive advertising campaigns.'*

* Source of quote: www.ethicalprimark.co.uk

Most businesses, especially those that have a high profile, will have to consider the ethical standpoint they claim to have in the light of the decisions that they choose to make. If the decision seems to go against that ethical standpoint, then the company stands to gain adverse publicity which can cause lasting damage in terms of sales and reputation, and which cost it a great deal to put right and overcome. Reputations can take many years and a great deal of money to build up, but only a short time to destroy. Consideration of the ethical issues relating to a decision, therefore, is increasingly important.

The availability of resources

As with many of the issues discussed in this book, decisions on implementing strategic plans will be influenced by the availability of resources and the funding that will be required. Very large firms may have relatively easy access to raising finance to fund investments, but this does not mean that the investment can go ahead. Funding is one thing, but getting access to resources is another.

In the period 2003–2008, the price of oil, metals and other commodities like wheat rose dramatically. One of the main reasons in each case was a shortage of supply in relation to demand. Various factors may have caused the shortage, but the fact remained that for some companies, sourcing raw materials became more difficult. This would have to be a factor in the consideration of decisions about what materials to use, whether there were other materials that were easier to source and possibly cheaper that would also do the same job.

Another key consideration that firms have to consider in decision-making is the availability of human resources. Investment decisions may require highly-skilled labour to enable the project to be completed successfully and this labour may not be readily available. People with high-level skills in computer programming, for example, may be short in supply and with little prospect of any sharp increase in the availability of such labour coming on stream in the medium term. Such skills and experience tend to take a long time to develop!

Firms have to consider whether they are willing to pay premium salaries to attract the right sort of workers and to 'head hunt' them from rivals. In some cases, this approach can force up the cost of a project considerably, but the business might also face the prospect of not being able to carry out the task without the right people in place. If they do opt to pay what is necessary to acquire the right people, they could face the prospect of having to pass on the cost to the consumer and this might then change the viability and dynamics of the project.

The relative power of stakeholders

Public limited companies exist for the benefit of their shareholders. Decisions have to be taken on the basis of the benefit to the shareholders who are the owners of the business. However, the board of directors, which carries out the day-to-day operations of the business, will be very aware of the extent to which other stakeholders influence business decision-making. They will be in a position to make judgements about the short-term benefits to the shareholders of a decision compared to the longer-term benefits that might accrue. It will be their responsibility to justify to shareholders why possible short-term profit should be sacrificed for longer-term gains. They may do this based on judgements about the effect of decision-making on other stakeholders.

Businesses involved in high-profile and often controversial activities have to take account of the strength of feeling of these wider stakeholder groups. Businesses such as BP and Shell, for example, are very aware of the need to consider the environmental impact of their operations and to take additional, and often costly, steps to ensure that they are satisfying environmental groups and local communities in their activities.

Pharmaceutical companies have to take account of the interest of employees and the wider community, as well as satisfying pressure groups that what they are doing is safe and appropriate. Decision-making can be heavily influenced by the need to satisfy legal and safety requirements. For example, procedures will have to be built into any investment plan to minimise the risk of catastrophic failure in systems and processes that might cause loss of life to people in the local community and to employees. The amount of testing and trials that have to be carried out before a product is deemed safe for commercial release is extensive, and all this will increase the cost and also make the decision-making process more complex.

In the example opposite, external stakeholders are able to wield considerable power over the activities of the business which, in some cases, borders on the illegal. Government and the local community through representatives can also have a significant impact on the decision-making process of businesses. Laws and regulations introduced by government are designed to protect the public and those stakeholders of a business who may not have as much power, such as employees. Many of these laws will have been passed in response to the changes in cultural attitudes that were outlined in Chapter 29. For many businesses, their activities and decisions will need to reflect these changing attitudes and most will feel that they can find ways of gaining benefits out of so doing.

Huntingdon Life Sciences

Huntingdon Life Sciences is a company based in Huntingdon, Cambridgeshire. It does research for companies in the pharmaceutical, biochemical and agricultural industries. This research involves the use of animals for experiments. Huntingdon Life Sciences has been subject to a concerted campaign by pressure groups that object to its work and its treatment of animals. Pressure groups opposed to the work of Huntingdon have been taking ever more extreme measures to make their point, prompting the government to pass new legislation.

One example that prompted new legislation to prevent excesses of protest was the case of Gladys Hammond, the mother-in-law of a guinea pig breeder on a farm in Staffordshire, whose grave was desecrated and her body removed allegedly by animal rights activists complaining about the work of the farm.

The activities of pressure groups in raising attention of the work of companies like HLS, have prompted a response to such pressure. Many animal rights campaigners would still like to see HLS closed down but the company itself insists that the work it does is important and that it takes its responsibilities to animal welfare seriously as the quote which follows highlights:

'It is our job to ensure that these tests are performed to strict scientific criteria, provide reliable results that can be reproduced, and with leading standards of animal care and welfare. This places an important burden of responsibility upon us, one which we do not take lightly. We have to respect the needs of the animals and be fully aware of the welfare issues involved. We are committed to providing the highest levels of animal husbandry and welfare. In May 2003 Huntingdon Life Sciences was awarded an Achievement of Accreditation by the Association For Assessment and Accreditation of Laboratory Animal Care, AAALAC (aaalac.org). We are one of only a few Contract Research Organisations in the world to be accredited.'

Source: http://www.huntingdon.com/index.php?current Number=3&currentIsExpanded=0

The publication of corporate social responsibility reports by many larger businesses is an example where the businesses believe that a decision to improve the transparency with regard to their operations not only satisfies the need of their wider stakeholders, but can also be a source of competitive advantage and is good for business.

Summary and exam guidance

Summary

- Business has access to far greater amounts of information than ever before.

- Information management refers to the ways in which information is collected, stored and managed.

- Businesses use both quantitative and qualitative information on which to base decisions.

- Two main approaches to decision-making are scientific and intuition.

- Examples of scientific analysis include decision trees and investment appraisal techniques.

- Decisions have to be made by balancing out the qualitative factors with the quantitative.

- Intuition has to be supported by more scientific evidence to help reduce risk.

- Decisions will also be affected by ethical considerations, the availability of resources and the relative strength of stakeholders.

Exam practice

Read the article below and then answer the questions that follow.

Article A

Solving the bag problem?

In 2006, supermarket retailer Sainsbury's, announced that it was intending to pack some of its own brand products in packaging that could be composted. That measure was designed to save an estimated 3,500 tonnes of plastic each year. Now Sainsbury's have gone a step further and made another announcement regarding the use of its plastic carrier bags.

Shoppers will now use an orange bag which replaced the existing white ones – 1.7 billion of which are used by the 16 million shoppers at its stores every year. The new bags are made up of 57% plastic, 10% chalk and 33% recycled material. The company estimates that this will save a further 6,500 tonnes of plastic and, as a result, 53,500 barrels of oil each year. Sainsbury's are also going to encourage customers to recycle their bags and have promised to use these to make new bags. The move will cut the use of raw plastic in the bags by 43%. Recycling existing bags has led to around 100 million being collected by the store; it hopes this new initiative will help to double that figure.

As with the announcement about its compostable packaging, this needs to be put into some perspective. 53,500 barrels of oil might sound a lot but the average output of barrels of oil **per day** by the Organisation of Petroleum Exporting Countries (OPEC) alone is in excess of 31 million.

Source: adapted from Biz/ed, In the News: http://www.bized.co.uk/cgi-bin/chron/chron.pl?id=2685

(a) Analyse the quantitative and qualitative factors that Sainsbury's might have considered in making the decision to change the type of shopping bags it offered its customers. (18 marks)

(b) Evaluate the likely effect that ethical considerations and the power of stakeholders would have had on Sainsbury's decision to introduce the new bags. (32 marks)

Total: 50 marks

Breakdown of assessment objectives

AO1 – Knowledge and understanding – 8/50
AO2 – Apply knowledge and understanding – 12/50
AO3 – Analyse problems, issues and situations – 15/50
AO4 – Evaluate, distinguish between fact and opinion, assess and judge information from a variety of sources – 15/50

Suggested structure

For part (a) you will need to:

- Identify at least two quantitative and two qualitative factors that it might have considered in arriving at its decision.
- Offer an explanation of each of the factors that you have identified – remember that the command term 'analyse' expects you to break down the issue into manageable chunks to help explain the issue/problem.
- Show how the factors it might have had to consider would have related to a business case, that is, that there would be some cost savings and possible benefits in terms of competitive advantage to the business which drove them to make the decision.

For part (b):

- Provide an analysis/explanation of the ethical issues related to the introduction of new bags.
- Show how these ethical considerations might have led to its decision.
- Provide an analysis/explanation of the views of different stakeholders to the decision.
- Make some judgement about the extent of the importance of ethical considerations to its decision – would they have been extremely important or only of minor importance?
- Would the ethical considerations have been a marketing ploy or can you present an argument that the decision was made with the highest ethical considerations in mind (use the entire article to help you with this!).
- Explain how Sainsbury's might have been able to justify the decision to its key stakeholders (that is, its shareholders) but also to other groups such as customers.
- Offer some judgement about how important the views of its stakeholders might have been in relation to its decision – very important, quite important or of no importance at all?
- Make some judgements about the relative importance of the two influences on the decision – would one have been a more important influence than the other and if so, why? This will serve to draw your argument to a conclusion which should relate back to the question.

Chapter 31   Implementing and managing change

Key terms

Emotional intelligence The ability to be able to show awareness, understanding and appreciation of the emotions of the self and other people around the self.

Project champion An individual who is identified as being someone who can support and promote change throughout the organisation.

Project group A team of people brought together with the aim of driving through a change project in an organisation.

Techniques to implement and manage change successfully

We have seen in the preceding chapters the complex nature of change. In any organisation, the leader will be the one who sets the vision and has to find a way of taking the others in the organisation with her/him to help realise that vision. Along the way they are likely to face considerable difficulties and no little resistance to the change initiatives they are trying to introduce. To combat this and lead the change there are various techniques that can be employed to increase the chances of success. Two such examples are project champions and project groups.

Project champions

Once a change initiative has been established, it will need someone or a small group of people who believe in the change to drive it through the organisation, and to make sure that the change is successfully explained and disseminated throughout the organisation. This is the primary role of a project champion. A project champion has to be someone who firmly believes in the change initiative and is prepared to support it, promote it within the organisation and outside in order to get across the benefits of the change.

Any change is likely to involve significant investment and there may be some in the organisation who will question that investment. The project champion will be someone who is able to articulate the benefits, explain how the benefits outweigh the costs and bring advantages to all in the organisation, and help it to achieve its strategic goals. In doing so, they help to justify the investment being put into the change.

A project champion does not have to have any formal title and may not even know they are a project champion, but any leader will recognise the importance of having key people in their team who share their vision and goals, and are able to communicate both successfully. As a result, it is likely that most project champions will be drawn from middle to senior management ranks and many will have potential leadership qualities. These qualities might include a firm belief in the project, a determination to see things through and the ability to 'get the job done'. Project champions, therefore, are likely to be 'finishers' – they will be able to see a project through to completion. Project champions are also likely to be drawn from those who are respected within an organisation and who have good connections and communication skills with a wide range of people in the organisation and outside it.

The main characteristics of a project champion can be summarised as:

- **Respect** Project champions have to have some influence in the organisation; they have to be people that others in the organisation will respect and look up to, and whose opinions and views can be trusted. Given the potentially disrupting nature of change, this will be important. They are likely to be people in the organisation who may have been earmarked for leadership positions and who are ambitious to advance their career.

- **Positive** A project champion is likely to be someone who has a track record of having a positive outlook, is responsive to change and enjoys the challenge of seeing things through to completion. As a result, they are likely to be people who are proactive, use their initiative and are determined to see things through.
- **Good communicators** Given the nature of change and the likelihood that it will affect a wide range of people, it will be important to make sure that the project champion is a good communicator. They will need to give both good and bad news as the change process is likely to create some division in an organisation. Consequently, they will need to be capable of being able to bring opposing views together and to heal divisions caused by change.

Having identified the appropriate person/people, the project champion will have two key roles in driving change.

THEY WILL ACT AS ADVOCATES

An advocate is a supporter who, in the process of actively promoting the project, will be looking to gain the support of other members of the organisation to drive the project through. It is also a person who the leader is able to take into their confidence and who will not simply act as a 'yes person', but who will be capable of posing questions to the leader to help clarify thinking about the project. Such support is invaluable, especially when the project is aiming to carry out significant and possibly controversial change. The leader may well have a particular view in mind, but a so-called 'critical friend' acts as a counterpoint to the enthusiasm of the leader and may help to identify potential problems and pitfalls that could be accounted for and make the project run more smoothly.

REDUCING BARRIERS TO CHANGE

Barriers to change are very likely to be human but there will also be a number of other barriers, including securing appropriate funding and finding the right resources. Project champions can act as a conduit to help remove or reduce the effect of these barriers, and thus enable the project to make progress. In fulfilling this role, the project champion will have to utilise many of the skills that have been identified above.

The discussion so far would imply that a project champion is someone who is closely involved in the project. That may be the case in some respects, but it is also important to note that the project champion is not likely to be the project leader. That is a different role associated with the planning, organisation and execution of the project. The project champion may not be part of the project team, but will be actively involved in making sure that the project is promoted and moves through to completion. Project champions need to be identified and 'recruited' early on in the project's development. Appropriate people may be those who stand to benefit most from such a project, or who can see how the project will improve the strategic goals of the business.

Potential problems with project champions

Whilst a project champion can have a number of advantages in helping to manage change, leaders have to be aware of the potential problems that can arise. By their very nature, there is a danger that project champions can simply be seen as being 'yes people' who tend to be seeking personal benefit and career advancement from championing projects that have been proposed by the leadership of the business. This is why the characteristics of project champions as outlined above are so important to the successful deployment of such a position.

Business leaders will need to be aware of the potential for bias in the selection and development of projects. A project champion, by definition, is likely to be very supportive of the leadership's plans, and if there is more than one project on the table, then it could be that a project champion assigns a lower risk but higher level of benefit than other members of the decision-making team. If this is the case, then the project might not be in the best interests of the organisation. Leaders will have to be aware of this and use other techniques to try and reduce the possibility of this happening. An example of such a technique would be something called Financial Appraisal Profile (FAP) which looks at a project on the basis of three criteria: finance, the risk associated with the project and the strategic benefits that might arise.

There has also been some research into trying to assess the extent of the effect of project champions on the successful implementation of projects. This research has not been able to identify conclusive evidence that project champions work, but none have found evidence that they do not! As a result, the decision by leaders as to whether to identify project champions remains one which individual leaders will have to decide for themselves. If they have appeared to have worked for the organisation in the past then they are likely to be used again!

For example…

Project champions at The Cotswold School

The Cotswold School in Gloucestershire is one of England's most successful comprehensive schools. In 2007, the School Leadership Team recognised that the way students learned – in the classroom and at home – could potentially be transformed by the introduction of the school's own Virtual Learning Environment (VLE). A VLE would enable students to access multimedia learning resources 24 hours a day, 365 days a year. Homework tasks would be completed, submitted, marked and returned online. Student online forums would enable students to ask questions, swap ideas and share views on what they were learning.

The challenge facing the school was that introducing a VLE would require a massive change in how teachers taught and students learned. Teachers in particular would need to be trained to use the VLE effectively and any concerns about the impact of the change would need to be addressed.

To enable the change to be introduced successfully, the Leadership Team identified and approached a small number of 'project champions'. These were neither senior managers, nor staff with responsibility for leading ICT in the school. Rather they were teaching staff who had a genuine enthusiasm for using technology in their teaching and a personal expertise in using ICT to improve learning. They were all well-respected staff who would be able to communicate the benefits of the VLE effectively to other staff. The project champions led staff training sessions in which they explained how the VLE could change teaching and learning. They followed this up with one-to-one support for teachers to help them develop their own online resources. The project champions pioneered the use of the VLE with their own students and shared their successes with others to show what could be done. Their enthusiasm, patience and persistence were key qualities in the successful introduction and development of the VLE.

Skills watch!

AO3 / AO4

To what extent do you think that project champions are appropriate for all types of strategic change in a business? Try to illustrate your answer with appropriate examples.

Project groups

Many businesses recognise the benefits that can arise from people working in teams. Project groups are essentially groups of people brought together to direct and guide a project through to completion. The way that groups are put together and allowed to operate provides the members with a considerable degree of autonomy and empowerment, and this can act as a motivating factor as well as helping to make sure that the project gets completed successfully.

Project groups are seen as being effective, as they can lead to problems being solved more rapidly and effectively than by individuals or larger departments. Groups can be flexible and adjust to changing circumstances, and comprise people who have a common purpose and often drawn from different parts of the organisation. Because they have a specific purpose they are likely to be disbanded once the project has been completed, and this can help to maintain dynamism and enthusiasm, although can also lead to some frustration and uncertainty for group members.

Effective groups bring together a range of different but complementary roles. Some people in the team need to be creative, others need to be able to attend to details and procedures, others need to be more extroverted and good communicators, whilst others need to be the ones who ensure that ideas are developed and also completed. Putting together the right group to ensure that a project is developed and carried out is not an easy task, and leaders have to be skilled at creating the right sort of groups to see through different types of project.

If groups are not put together properly then they can create problems. There can be tension within the group with different people having different views or feeling that they are pressured to conform to the majority view, even if they have cause to believe that this is incorrect or inappropriate. Some individuals may see a group as a means of imposing their view or of being able to score points against colleagues, and some people are simply not team players and prefer to work as individuals. In other cases, being in a team means that responsibility can sometimes be passed on to others in the team and this can lead to poor decision-making and puts the project at risk.

Despite the disadvantages outlined above, teams can be very successful and there are a number of characteristics that can be identified and associated with successful teams. Some of these are listed below.

- A team must have a collective sense of purpose and urgency – a desire to get the project completed successfully.
- There must be a clear identification at the outset of what the project is about, why it needs to be implemented and what the various roles of the team members are going to be. This sets the right atmosphere for the group and helps to clear away possible obstacles to progress.
- Team members need to be selected on the basis of the expertise that they bring to the project and their skills in being able to solve the problems that are likely to arise during the project.
- Those selected have to be fully committed to the project and its aims and outcomes.
- Clear lines of communication need to be established at the outset and the importance of both listening and contributing have to be made clear to all group members.
- Appropriate reward mechanisms, feedback and recognition need to be given to the group to ensure that motivation is maintained and that the project does not start to falter.

- The group needs to be working to a clear set of guidelines and goals that all understand.
- Training and support will be important to enable group members to have the necessary skills and expertise to be able to manage and lead the project through to completion. Certain gaps in skills or techniques may come to light as the project progresses, and any deficiencies need to be filled quickly to ensure the project does not go off track.

It follows that the reverse of some of these are the reasons why project groups may not be as effective as they can be. If there is not a clear sense of direction and set of goals, gaps in skills, lack of trust and cooperation between the members of the group, and so on, then it is likely that it will not be as effective in getting the project completed and the change will not be as successful.

For example...

New location

Cengage Learning is a major publishing firm with an extensive presence in higher education publishing and the provision of high-quality digital products for libraries in universities and elsewhere. Its main headquarters were in central London, but it also had an extensive warehouse and administration facility in Andover, Hampshire.

The lease on its offices in central London came to an end in 2009 and the company decided not to renew the lease. Instead it intended to move all its operations and staff under one roof in Andover. For the staff working in London this was a major change. Many lived on the outskirts of London and would have to consider whether they wanted to commute to Andover.

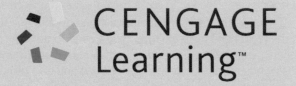

The company set up a project group from the human resources department to coordinate the move with staff, and to ensure that all the staff were consulted and given the appropriate advice and support for the move. The project group knew that some people would not want to make the move and so there would be some staff turnover. It was their job to ensure that the staff were supported, but at the same time the disruption to the business was minimised.

Synoptic search

In your AS studies, you will have learned about organisational structures. In a matrix structure there is often a project-based approach to work. You should note how different organisational structures, such as this, link to the techniques being described here.

Assessing the factors that promote and resist change

Earlier in this section we saw how there were various stages that have been identified that people go through when faced with change. The necessity of moving away from a comfort zone, and from routine and predictability that is created by change, means that there are very likely to be different degrees of resistance to change at any one time in an organisation. The leader has to be in a position to understand and recognise these stages, and be mindful of particular strategies to promote the change they wish to make and to reduce the resistance to that change.

Emotional intelligence

Given the fact that much of the resistance to change will stem from humans, the necessity of understanding the emotional responses of people to change is vital. The concept of emotional intelligence has been developed by Daniel Goleman and has gained a great deal of support in recent years. Goleman's work focuses on how a greater degree of understanding about relationships and emotional responses can lead to increased productivity and performance, and break down the resistance to change.

Goleman identified such things as the way in which criticism is given and received, how comments can make people feel that they have been treated unfairly and how those in senior positions may be seen as dodging their responsibility. Leaders have to be aware of the feelings that comments, criticism, and so on will have on motivation, confidence and energy and as such need to be considered as a part of promoting change.

This implies that leaders must not only have emotional intelligence but have emotional intelligence about those around them. This implies that they must know their staff and the organisation intimately to be able to reduce resistance and promote change. Taking the time to get to know colleagues – knowing their names, their basic family circumstances, and so on – was mentioned in Chapter 28 as a key leadership quality. If change is to be promoted and resistance reduced, this quality may take on added significance.

Clear objectives

As outlined above, any change initiative has to be clear in its intentions and in many respects in its goals. These have to be communicated and disseminated across the whole organisation to ensure that members of the organisation understand the change and be in a position to begin to internalise it. Where stakeholders receive different and often conflicting messages about the nature of change and the purpose of it, there is likely to be an increase in anxiety, and resistance to change.

Making sure that objectives are clear means that everyone in the organisation is under no illusion about what the direction of change is and where change will lead; it means that everyone is clear about their role in the change process. However, it may be important that the leader takes time to ensure that the objectives are restated from time to time. This serves as a reminder to all stakeholders that the objectives are still present, that they are still relevant and being actively pursued.

Resources

The pace of change can start to decline or even come to a grinding halt if those charged with implementing the change do not feel they have the appropriate resources to be able to carry out their work. These resources might include the appropriate technology, the time, space and also the human resources that are required. This latter point relates to making sure that there are people in key positions in the change process that have the skills – both technical and emotional – to be able to manage the project and see the change through to completion.

In the early period of the change process, the leader will have to ensure that there are people in place who are able to identify what resources might be needed and to be able to source those resources. This might involve identifying the types of skills and qualities required of individuals, but might also be identifying component parts, suppliers, sources of raw materials, and so on. Such identification is important in making sure that the costs of the change process are kept to a minimum to ensure that the anticipated benefits from the change are merited in relation to the investment that is going into it.

Training

In the discussion above, if it appears that there is likely to be a shortfall in some of the skills or abilities required for a change programme, the leader will wish to arrange for appropriate training to be identified and provided. This training might be something that is needed at the start of a change programme but might also be something that is identified as the programme progresses and gaps become obvious.

Some of the training may be given to staff in relation to coping with the change, helping to provide the support and the information necessary to internalise the change. If, for example, staff are going to be expected to work with new technology as a result of the change, then they will need to have the necessary training to be able to cope with the technology. If this is not provided, the change process may not be successful and staff can be left feeling further alienated from the organisation. The provision of suitable and appropriate training will also help staff to feel more comfortable about the change and that their role in it is being taken seriously and catered for.

Provision of training will have to be balanced against the potential costs of such provision, and whether it is possible to do the training in house or whether external suppliers, possibly from specialist software companies who have developed the technology, will have to be brought in to do the training. In some cases, it may be appropriate for the training to be carried out outside the work environment with a specialist facility hired for the purpose. This can be turned into a combined training and social event and can be very effective in helping to alleviate anxieties and make the change process more transparent and acceptable to those who will be most affected.

Key determinants of successful change

Throughout this section we have been looking at change, the causes of change, planning for change, the influences on the change process, decision-making and implementing change. As we conclude this chapter we can summarise the main characteristics that are likely to lead to successful change. These are listed below.

PLANNING

We have seen that there are different views about the effectiveness of planning but we have also seen that the mantra 'fail to plan, plan to fail' has some bearing on bringing about successful change. The key is to make sure that what can be planned for is planned but that the planning process builds in sufficient flexibility to be able to cope with changing circumstances as they arise.

PEOPLE

Having the right people with the right skills, in the right place at the right time, is vitally important. Most businesses rely on their people to carry change through, and the work of project champions and project groups in implementing change is important, but the attitude and cooperation of all workers in bringing about successful change cannot be overestimated. It is sometimes said that people are the most important asset to a business, but it might be more accurate to say that the *right* people are the most important asset. There is a difference.

BEING REALISTIC

The change programme has to be one that conforms to SMART criteria and in the first place, the leader and the staff have to be realistic about what the organisation can achieve in the time available and with the resources at its disposal. Targets can be set, change programmes outlined, but if these merely act to raise hopes that cannot be fulfilled, then very quickly disillusionment sets in and motivation will be affected. In addition, those who financed the change may be inclined to cut off the finance or be reluctant to come up with any further funding which they might simply see as being a waste. Many change programmes are successful when small incremental steps are targeted and reached. Over a period of time these incremental steps can lead to quite significant change which might have been part of the vision of the leader in the first place. For example, the football clubs Wigan Athletic and Hull City set themselves small targets to improve their position in the football leagues and eventually made it to the Premier League.

HOW THE CHANGE IS CARRIED OUT

There are different ways of implementing change. Sometimes the position of the organisation is such that there has to be a brutal approach to change which might cause a great deal of short-term damage and emotional turmoil, but in the medium to long term is going to be beneficial to the organisation and its stakeholders. Along the way many people will be affected in a bad way but leaders have to keep their eye on the ultimate goal and have an unshakable belief that this goal is for the benefit of the majority. The changes made at EMI (see Chapter 16) might seem very harsh, but if the organisation emerges leaner, stronger and in a better position to be able to meet the competitive challenges of the next 20 years, then those workers and other stakeholders that stay with the company will be in a better position than if the company was forced into insolvency through a failure to change.

Of course, change can also be carried out in a far less brutal fashion, but it has to be realised that any change has negative impacts on some people. Sometimes change can be carried out over longer periods of time so that the impact on people is minimised. For example, redundancies may be necessary, but can be carried out through natural wastage – not replacing people when they leave or when they retire. Whatever the method, the leader and the key people driving the change will have to have high levels of determination and discipline, an attention to detail and an understanding of the change process amongst many other qualities.

CULTURE

We have seen how different types of culture can affect the change process. Whatever that culture, one of the key tasks of a leader is to ensure that workers are ready to accept and confront change and not be frightened of it. They have to be aware that change is an integral part of business and that if the business does not change, then it is likely to cease to exist. The post-war period up to the early 1970s was one of almost continual growth but also a great deal of stability. The economic shocks of the 1970s and '80s led many businesses, and those involved with them, to adopt a different view about business and their role and place in business. No longer do people have jobs for life and this realisation has gradually made people aware of the need for skills and qualities other than paper academic qualifications. Instead, flexibility, a willingness to adapt and work with change, and skills that are transferable across different industries are now seen as highly complementary to academic qualifications. Businesses have a responsibility to instil such a culture in their organisations, to help people to become more aware of the changed world we now live in and their role in that world.

Summary and exam guidance

Summary

- Project champions and project groups are two ways of implementing and managing change.

- Project champions take on the role of supporting and promoting the change throughout the organisation.

- Project champions should be those who have the respect of people in the organisation; they should be positive and proactive, and be good communicators.

- Project champions have a dual role as advocates and in reducing barriers to change.

- Leaders have to be aware of bias from project champions and whether champions actually work in effecting change.

- Project groups are teams of people brought together for the specific purpose of implementing and seeing a project through to completion.

- Factors that promote and resist change might include emotional intelligence, the setting of clear objectives, adequate provision of resources and appropriate training.

Exam practice

Read the article below and then answer the questions that follow.

Article A

All change at Cadbury

Cadbury is a highly-complex organisation which employs 50,000 people worldwide. It has its headquarters in London, a main factory in Bournville, near Birmingham, a cocoa processing plant in North Wales, a milk-processing plant in Herefordshire, a sugar factory in Sheffield, a medicinal confectionary business in Devon and a chocolate-making factory just outside Bristol.

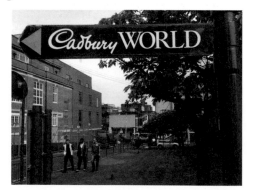

cont...

In 1969, Cadbury merged with drinks manufacturer Schweppes, which makes drinks such *as Dr Pepper and 7-Up* as well as mixer drinks like tonic water and bitter lemon. This is another aspect to its business.

From time to time, companies have to look at their business and make changes. In June 2007, Cadbury announced that it was going to carry out a significant reorganisation of its business over the next four years. It planned to reduce staff levels by 15% which equated to around 7,500 jobs. The cost savings as well as the efficiencies that resulted will have helped to boost its margins; Cadbury reported that it expected margins to rise from 10.1% to 'the mid-teens' as a result of the reorganisation. Cutting staff and reorganising the business is not a costless exercise; Cadbury said that the staff cuts will cost around £450 million but that this would be recorded as a one-off cost in its accounts.

Cadbury has also said that it intends to sell off the drinks manufacturing business. As seems to be the case with many corporate deals these days, it is private equity groups that seem to be favourite to buy the Schweppes business, with a price tag of around £7 billion.

Source: adapted from Biz/ed In the News: http://www.bized.co.uk/cgi-bin/chron/chron.pl?id=2873

(a) Analyse **three** possible problems that the leadership at Cadbury might face in seeing through the change that they had planned. (18 marks)

(b) Evaluate the possible techniques for reducing the problems in implementing that change that you have identified in part (a) above. (32 marks)

Total: 50 marks

Breakdown of assessment objectives

AO1 – Knowledge and understanding – 8/50
AO2 – Apply knowledge and understanding – 8/50
AO3 – Analyse problems, issues and situations – 18/50
AO4 – Evaluate, distinguish between fact and opinion, assess and judge information from a variety of sources – 16/50

Suggested structure

For part (a) you will need to:

- Identify three problems that Cadbury might face as a result of the changes outlined in the article.
- Note the emphasis given in the article about the size of the organisation – this might help you to identify some of the problems it might face.
- Offer a detailed and balanced analysis of all three. These should be around the same length in terms of the explanation you give them.
- Make sure that you relate your answer to Cadbury specifically!

For part (b) you will need to:

- Identify and briefly explain some possible techniques to help implement the changes.
- Take each of the problems you have identified in part (a) and provide an explanation of how the techniques you have identified might help to reduce the problems.
- In each case, make sure that you offer some sort of balance to your answer by highlighting some of the benefits of the techniques and also some of the disadvantages associated with them. Try to ensure that you keep your answer related to Cadbury as opposed to just any business to improve the marks awarded for application.
- Make a judgement about the value of the techniques that you have identified and explained. Is one better than the other; if so, why? If not, why not?
- Do Cadbury need to apply one technique or a combination of more than one?
- Make a judgement in relation to the bullet point above.
- Draw your answer together by presenting a final judgement in relation to the question set.